W9-AGY-892

WORLD ERAS

VOLUME 5

ANCIENT EGYPT
2615 - 332 B.C.E.

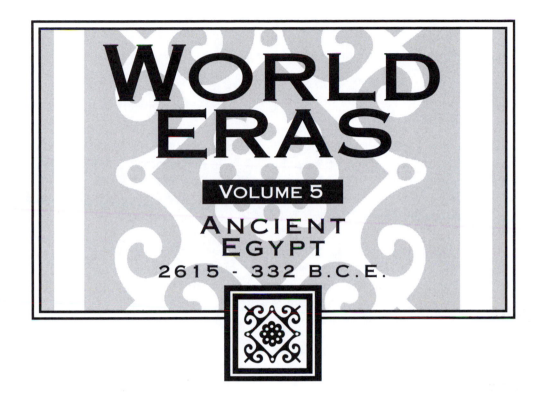

WORLD ERAS

VOLUME 5

ANCIENT EGYPT

2615 - 332 B.C.E.

EDWARD I. BLEIBERG

A MANLY, INC. BOOK

GALE GROUP

THOMSON LEARNING

Detroit • New York • San Diego • San Francisco
Boston • New Haven, Conn. • Waterville, Maine
London • Munich

WORLD ERAS VOL. 5
ANCIENT EGYPT
2615-332 B.C.E.

Matthew J. Bruccoli and Richard Layman, *Editorial Directors*

Anthony J. Scotti Jr., *Series Editor*

Library Of Congress Cataloging-in-Publication Data
World Eras vol. 5: Ancient Egypt, 2615-332 B.C.E./
    edited by Edward Bleiberg.
        p. cm.— (World eras; v. 5)
"A Manly, Inc. book."
Includes bibliographical references and index.
ISBN 0-7876-4505-2 (alk. paper)
1. Egypt—Civilization—To 332 B.C. I. Bleiberg, Edward, 1951–   .
II. Series.

DT61.A55 2000
932—dc21   2001040387

10 9 8 7 6 5 4 3 2 1

Advisory Board

CONTENTS

CHAPTER 4: COMMUNICATION, TRANSPORTATION, AND EXPLORATION

CHAPTER 5: SOCIAL CLASS SYSTEM AND THE ECONOMY

CHAPTER 8: THE FAMILY AND SOCIAL TRENDS

Chapter 9: RELIGION AND PHILOSOPHY

Chapter 10: SCIENCE, TECHNOLOGY, AND HEALTH

ABOUT THE SERIES

PROJECT DESCRIPTION

Patterned after the well-received *American Decades* and *American Eras* series, *World Eras* is a cross-disciplinary reference series. It comprises volumes examining major civilizations that have flourished from antiquity to modern times, with a global perspective and a strong emphasis on daily life and social history. Each volume provides in-depth coverage of one era, focusing on a specific cultural group and its interaction with other peoples of the world. The *World Eras* series is geared toward the needs of high-school students studying subjects in the humanities. Its purpose is to provide students—and general reference users as well—a reliable, engaging reference resource that stimulates their interest, encourages research, and prompts comparison of the lives people led in different parts of the world, in different cultures, and at different times.

The goal of *World Eras* volumes is to enrich the traditional historical study of "kings and battles" with a resource that promotes understanding of daily life and the cultural institutions that affect people's beliefs and behavior.

What kind of work did people in a certain culture perform?

What did they eat?

How did they fight their battles?

What laws did they have and how did they punish criminals?

What were their religious practices?

What did they know of science and medicine?

What kind of art, music, and literature did they enjoy?

These are the types of questions *World Eras* volumes seek to answer.

VOLUME DESIGN

World Eras is designed to facilitate comparative study. Thus volumes employ a consistent ten-chapter structure so that teachers and students can readily access standard topics in various volumes. The chapters in each *World Eras* volume are:

1. World Events
2. Geography
3. The Arts
4. Communication, Transportation, and Exploration
5. Social Class System and the Economy
6. Politics, Law, and the Military
7. Leisure, Recreation, and Daily Life
8. The Family and Social Trends
9. Religion and Philosophy
10. Science, Technology, and Health

World Eras volumes begin with two chapters designed to provide a broad view of the world against which a specific culture can be measured. Chapter 1 provides students today with a means to understand where a certain people stood within our concept of world history. Chapter 2 describes the world from the perspective of the people being studied—what did they know of geography and how did geography and climate affect their lives? The following eight chapters address major aspects of people's lives to provide a sense of what defined their culture. The ten chapters in *World Eras* will remain constant in each volume. Teachers and students seeking to compare religious beliefs in Roman and Greek cultures, for example, can easily locate the information they require by consulting chapter 9 in the appropriate volumes, tapping a rich source for class assignments and research topics. Volume-specific glossaries and a checklist of general references provide students assistance in studying unfamiliar cultures.

CHAPTER CONTENTS

Each chapter in *World Eras* volumes also follows a uniform structure designed to provide users quick access to the information they need. Chapters are arranged into five types of material:

- **Chronology** provides an historical outline of significant events in the subject of the chapter in timeline form.

- **Overview** provides a narrative overview of the chapter topic during the period and discusses the material of the chapter in a global context.

- **Topical Entries** provide focused information in easy-to-read articles about people, places, events, institutions, and matters of general concern to the people of the time. A references rubric includes sources for further study.

- **Biographical Entries** profiles people of enduring significance regarding the subject of the chapter.
- **Documentary Sources** is an annotated checklist of documentary sources from the historical period that are the basis for the information presented in the chapter.

Chapters are supplemented throughout with primary-text sidebars that include interesting short documentary excerpts or anecdotes chosen to illuminate the subject of the chapter: recipes, letters, daily-life accounts, and excerpts from important documents. Each *World Eras* volume includes about 150 illustrations, maps, diagrams, and line drawings linked directly to material discussed in the text. Illustrations are chosen with particular emphasis on daily life.

INDEXING

A general two-level subject index for each volume includes significant terms, subjects, theories, practices, people, organizations, publications, and so forth, mentioned in the text. Index citations with many page references are broken down by subtopic. Illustrations are indicated both in the general index, by use of italicized page numbers, and in a separate illustrations index, which provides a description of each item.

EDITORS AND CONTRIBUTORS

An advisory board of history teachers and librarians has provided valuable advice about the rationale for this series. They have reviewed both series plans and individual volume plans. Each *World Eras* volume is edited by a distinguished specialist in the subject of his or her volume. The editor is responsible for enlisting other scholar-specialists to write each of the chapters in the volume and of assuring the quality of their work. The editorial staff at Manly, Inc., rigorously checks factual information, line edits the manuscript, works with the editor to select illustrations, and produces the books in the series, in cooperation with Gale Group editors.

The *World Eras* series is for students of all ages who seek to enrich their study of world history by examining the many aspects of people's lives in different places during different eras. This series continues Gale's tradition of publishing comprehensive, accurate, and stimulating historical reference works that promote the study of history and culture.

The following timeline, included in every volume of *World Eras*, is provided as a convenience to users seeking a ready chronological context.

TIMELINE

This timeline, compiled by editors at Manly, Inc., is provided as a convenience for students seeking a broad global and historical context for the materials in this volume of World Eras. *It is not intended as a self-contained resource. Students who require a comprehensive chronology of world history should consult sources such as William L. Langer, comp. and ed.,* The New Illustrated Encyclopedia of World History, *2 volumes (New York: Harry N. Abrams, 1975).*

CIRCA 4 MILLION TO 1 MILLION B.C.E.
Era of *Australopithecus,* the first hominid

CIRCA 1.5 MILLION TO 200,000 B.C.E.
Era of *Homo erectus,* "upright-walking human"

CIRCA 1,000,000-10,000 B.C.E.
Paleolithic Age: hunters and gatherers make use of stone tools in Eurasia

CIRCA 250,000 B.C.E.
Early evolution of *Homo sapiens,* "consciously thinking humans"

CIRCA 40,000 B.C.E.
Migrations from Siberia to Alaska lead to the first human inhabitation of North and South America

CIRCA 8000 B.C.E.
Neolithic Age: settled agrarian culture begins to develop in Eurasia

5000 B.C.E.
The world population is between 5 million and 20 million

CIRCA 4000-3500 B.C.E.
Earliest Sumerian cities: artificial irrigation leads to increased food supplies and populations in Mesopotamia

CIRCA 3000 B.C.E.
Bronze Age begins in Mesopotamia and Egypt, where bronze is primarily used for making weapons; invention of writing

CIRCA 2900-1150 B.C.E.
Minoan society on Crete: lavish palaces and commercial activity

CIRCA 2700-2200 B.C.E.
Egypt: Old Kingdom and the building of the pyramids

CIRCA 2080-1640 B.C.E.
Egypt: Middle Kingdom plagued by internal strife and invasion by the Hyksos

CIRCA 2000-1200 B.C.E.
Hittites build a powerful empire based in Anatolia (present-day Turkey) by using horse-drawn war chariots

CIRCA 1792-1760 B.C.E.
Old Babylonian Kingdom; one of the oldest extant legal codes is compiled

CIRCA 1766-1122 B.C.E.
Shang Dynasty in China: military expansion, large cities, written language, and introduction of bronze metallurgy

CIRCA 1570-1075 B.C.E.
Egypt: New Kingdom and territorial expansion into Palestine, Lebanon, and Syria

CIRCA 1500 B.C.E.
The Aryans, an Indo-European people from the steppes of present-day Ukraine and southern Russia, expand into northern India

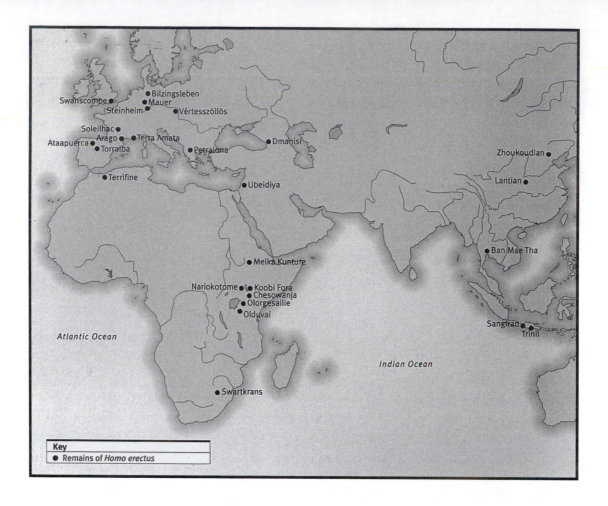

Key
● Remains of *Homo erectus*

CIRCA 1500 B.C.E.
Phoenicians create the first alphabet

CIRCA 1400-1200 B.C.E.
Hittites develop the technology of iron-smelting, improving weaponry and agricultural implements, as well as stimulating trade

CIRCA 1200-800 B.C.E.
Phoenicians establish colonies throughout the Mediterranean

CIRCA 1122-221 B.C.E.
Zhou Dynasty in China: military conquests, nomadic invasions, and introduction of iron metallurgy

CIRCA 1100-750 B.C.E.
Greek Dark Ages: foreign invasions, civil disturbances, decrease in agricultural production, and population decline

1020-587 B.C.E.
Israelite monarchies consolidate their power in Palestine

CIRCA 1000-612 B.C.E.
Assyrians create an empire encompassing Mesopotamia, Syria, Palestine, and most of Anatolia and Egypt; they deport populations to various regions of the realm

1000 B.C.E.
The world population is approximately 50 million

CIRCA 814-146 B.C.E.
The city-state of Carthage is a powerful commercial and military power in the western Mediterranean

753 B.C.E.
Traditional date of the founding of Rome

CIRCA 750-700 B.C.E.
Rise of the polis, or city-state, in Greece

558-330 B.C.E.
Achaemenid Dynasty establishes the Persian Empire (present-day Iran, Turkey, Afghanistan, and Iraq); satraps rule the various provinces

509 B.C.E.
Roman Republic is established

500 B.C.E.
The world population is approximately 100 million

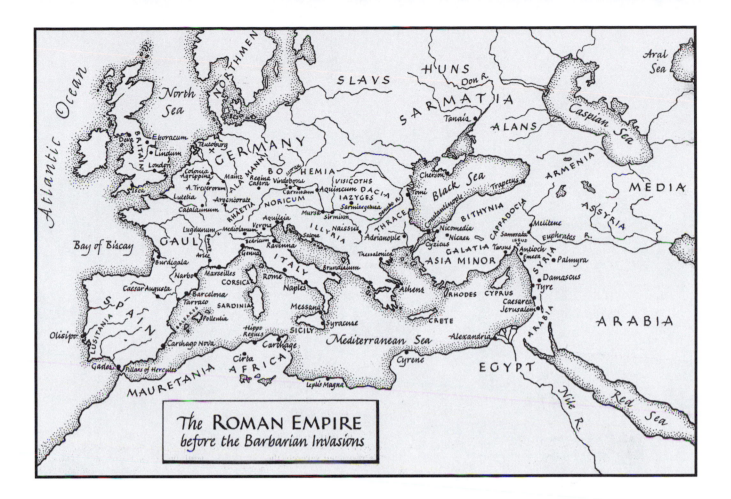

The ROMAN EMPIRE
before the Barbarian Invasions

CIRCA 400 B.C.E.
Spread of Buddhism in India

338-323 B.C.E.
Macedon, a kingdom in the central Balkan peninsula, conquers the Persian Empire

323-301 B.C.E.
Ptolemaic Kingdom (Egypt), Seleucid Kingdom (Syria), and Antigonid Dynasty (Macedon) are founded

247 B.C.E.-224 C.E.
Parthian Empire (Parthia, Persia, and Babylonia): clan leaders build independent power bases in their satrapies, or provinces

215-168 B.C.E.
Rome establishes hegemony over the Hellenistic world

206 B.C.E. TO 220 C.E.
Han Dynasty in China: imperial expansion into central Asia, centralized government, economic prosperity, and population growth

CIRCA 100 B.C.E.
Tribesmen on the Asian steppes develop the stirrup, which eventually revolutionizes warfare

1 C.E.
The world population is approximately 200 million

CIRCA 100 C.E.
Invention of paper in China

224-651 C.E.
Sasanid Empire (Parthia, Persia, and Babylonia): improved government system, founding of new cities, increased trade, and the introduction of rice and cotton cultivation

CIRCA 320-550 C.E.
Gupta Dynasty in India: Golden Age of Hindu civilization marked by stability and prosperity throughout the subcontinent

340 C.E.
Constantinople becomes the capital of the Eastern Roman, or Byzantine, Empire

395 C.E.
Christianity becomes the official religion of the Roman Empire

CIRCA 400 C.E.
The first unified Japanese state arises and is centered at Yamato on the island of Honshu; Buddhism arrives in Japan by way of Korea

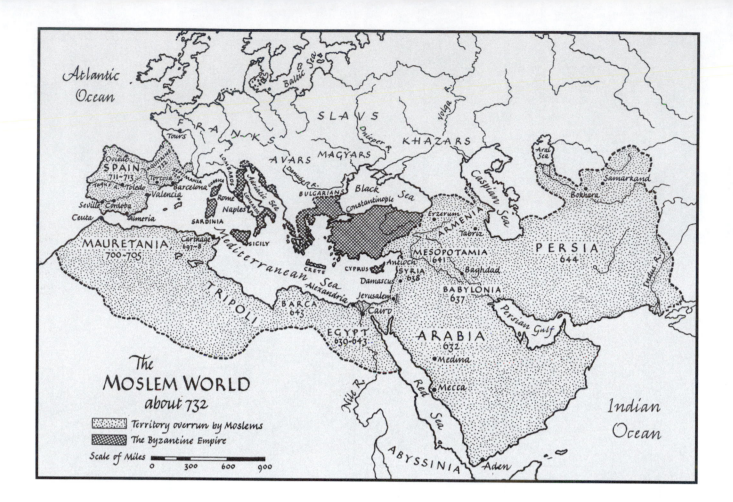

The
MOSLEM WORLD
about 732

Territory overrun by Moslems
The Byzantine Empire

Scale of Miles
0   300   600   900

CIRCA 400 C.E.
The nomadic Huns begin a westward migration from central Asia, causing disruption in the Roman Empire

CIRCA 400 C.E.
The Mayan Empire in Mesoamerica evolves into city-states

476 C.E.
Rome falls to barbarian hordes and the Western Roman Empire collapses

CIRCA 500-1500 C.E.
Middle Ages, or medieval period, in Europe: gradual recovery from political disruption and increase in agricultural productivity and population

618-907 C.E.
Tang Dynasty in China: territorial expansion, government bureaucracy, agricultural improvements, and transportation and communication networks

632-733 C.E.
Muslim expansion and conquests in Arabia, Syria, Palestine, Mesopotamia, Egypt, North Africa, Persia, northwestern India, and Iberia

CIRCA 700 C.E.
Origins of feudalism, a political and social organization that dominates Europe until the fifteenth century; based on the relationship between lords and vassals

CIRCA 900 C.E.
Introduction of the horseshoe in Europe and black powder in China

960-1279 C.E.
Song Dynasty in China: civil administration, industry, education, and the arts

962-1806 C.E.
Holy Roman Empire of western and central Europe, created in an attempt to revive the old Roman Empire

1000 C.E.
The world population is approximately 300 million

1096-1291 C.E.
Western Christians undertake the Crusades, a series of religiously inspired military campaigns, to recapture the Holy Land from the Muslims

1200 to 1400 c.e.
The Mali empire in Africa dominates the trans-Saharan trade network of camel caravans

1220-1335 c.e.
The Mongols, nomadic horsemen from the high steppes of eastern central Asia, build an empire that includes China, Persia, and Russia

Circa 1250 c.e.
Inca Empire develops in Peru: civil administration, road networks, and sun worshiping

1299-1919 c.e.
Ottoman Empire, created by nomadic Turks and Christian converts to Islam, encompasses Asia Minor, the Balkans, Greece, Egypt, North Africa, and the Middle East

1300 c.e.
The world population is approximately 396 million

1337-1453 c.e.
Hundred Years' War, a series of intermittent military campaigns between England and France over control of continental lands claimed by both countries

1347-1350 c.e.
Black Death, or the bubonic plague, kills one-quarter of the European population

1368-1644 c.e.
Ming Dynasty in China: political, economic, and cultural revival; the Great Wall is built

1375-1527 c.e.
The Renaissance in Western Europe, a revival in the arts and learning

1428-1519 c.e.
The Aztecs expand in central Mexico, developing trade routes and a system of tribute payments

1450 c.e.
Invention of the printing press

1453 c.e.
Constantinople falls to the Ottoman Turks, ending the Byzantine Empire

1464-1591 c.e.
Songhay Empire in Africa: military expansion, prosperous cities, control of the trans-Saharan trade

1492 c.e.
Discovery of America; European exploration and colonization of the Western Hemisphere begins

LATIN AMERICAN STATES after the REVOLUTIONS

Circa 1500-1867 c.e.
Transatlantic slave trade results in the forced migration of between 12 million and 16 million Africans to the Western Hemisphere

1500 c.e.
The world population is approximately 480 million

1517 c.e.
Beginning of the Protestant Reformation, a religious movement that ends the spiritual unity of western Christendom

1523-1763 c.e.
Mughal Empire in India: military conquests, productive agricultural economy, and population growth

1600-1867 c.e.
Tokugawa Shogunate in Japan: shoguns (military governors) turn Edo, or Tokyo, into the political, economic, and cultural center of the nation

1618-1648 c.e.
Thirty Years' War in Europe between Catholic and Protestant states

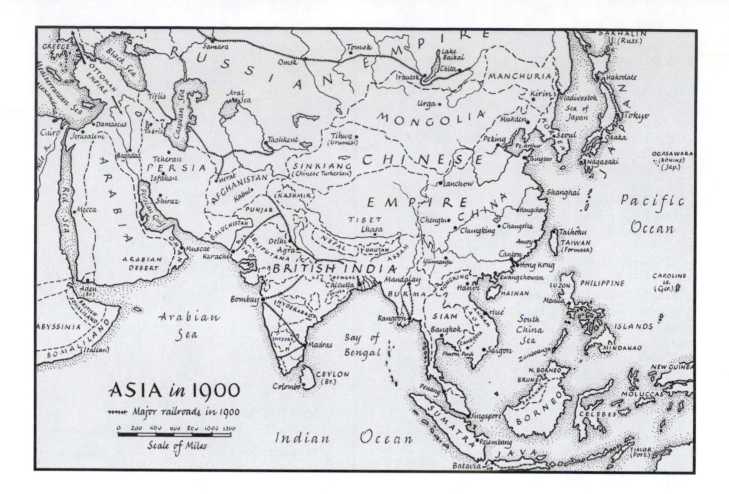

ASIA in 1900

Major railroads in 1900

Scale of Miles

1644-1911 c.e.
Qing Dynasty in China: military expansion and scholar-bureaucrats

1700 c.e.
The world population is approximately 640 million

Circa 1750 c.e.
Beginning of the Enlightenment, a philosophical movement marked by an emphasis on rationalism and scientific inquiry

1756-1763 c.e.
Seven Years' War: England and Prussia versus Austria, France, Russia, Saxony, Spain, and Sweden

Circa 1760-1850 c.e.
Industrial Revolution in Britain is marked by mass production through the division of labor, mechanization, a great increase in the supply of iron, and the use of the steam engine

1775-1783 c.e.
American War of Independence; the United States becomes an independent republic

1789 c.e.
French Revolution topples the monarchy and leads to a period of political unrest followed by a dictatorship

1793-1815 c.e.
Napoleonic Wars: Austria, England, Prussia, and Russia versus France and its satellite states

1794-1824 c.e.
Latin American states conduct wars of independence against Spain

1900 c.e.
The world population is approximately 1.65 billion

1914-1918 c.e.
World War I, or the Great War: the Allies (England, France, Russia, and the United States) versus Central Powers (Austria-Hungary, Germany, and the Ottoman Empire)

1917-1921 c.e.
Russian Revolution: a group of Communists known as the Bolsheviks seize control of the country following a civil war

1939-1945 C.E.

World War II: the Allies (China, England, France, the Soviet Union, and the United States) versus the Axis (Germany, Italy, and Japan)

1945 C.E.

Successful test of the first atomic weapon; beginning of the Cold War, a period of rivalry, mistrust, and, occasionally, open hostility between the capitalist West and communist East

1947-1975 C.E.

Decolonization occurs in Africa and Asia as European powers relinquish control of colonies in those regions

1948 C.E.

Israel becomes the first independent Jewish state in nearly two thousand years

1949 C.E.

Communists seize control of China

1950-1951 C.E.

Korean War: the United States attempts to stop Communist expansion in the Korean peninsula

1957 C.E.

The Soviet Union launches *Sputnik* ("fellow traveler of earth"), the first man-made satellite; the Space Age begins

1965-1973 C.E.

Vietnam War: the United States attempts to thwart the spread of Communism in Vietnam

1989 C.E.

East European Communist regimes begin to falter and multiparty elections are held

1991 C.E.

Soviet Union is dissolved and replaced by the Commonwealth of Independent States

2000 C.E.

The world population is 6 billion

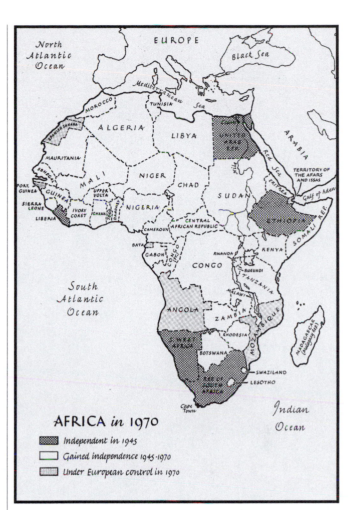

AFRICA *in* 1970

- Independent in 1945
- Gained independence 1945-1970
- Under European control in 1970

INTRODUCTION

Legacy. Today, a study of almost any historical subject can begin with the phrase, "Ever since the Egyptians." In fact, claims for Egyptian civilization have been used to place a special seal of approval on everything from cosmetics, to wine, to engineering feats, and even theories of slavery and prison construction in nineteenth-century America. Only by looking at the actual evidence the Egyptians left behind can these claims be evaluated.

Accomplishments. The Egyptians did develop an amazing society. At the root of this accomplishment was their invention of writing more than five thousand years ago. This tremendous innovation, the ability to represent language graphically, allowed for accurate communications across space and time and led to a revolution in intellectual history. For the first time, it was possible to send words and thoughts formulated in one place hundreds or thousands of miles away. It was also possible to build on an intellectual heritage and accurately remember words the ancestors uttered generations ago. The Egyptians themselves recognized the importance of this accomplishment. As with anything truly important, they attributed the invention of writing to the gods. Hieroglyphs were to the Egyptians the "words of the gods." Thoth, the ibis-headed scribe of the gods, was patron for all human scribes. The Egyptians also recognized that writing had shifted the balance of power in their society. Though physical force still had great importance in Egyptian life, a new expression of intellectual power emerged with writing and the existence of the scribal class. Scribes, as the Egyptians were fond of saying, were really the people in control of everything.

Parallels. This revolution in communications was not so different from the revolution twenty-first-century Americans are experiencing. Just as writing changed and shaped Egyptian communications and then the nature of society, Americans are experiencing fundamental changes in their attitudes toward communications with the use of the computer. Though it is not possible to draw direct lines between Egyptian and American experience, the lessons the Egyptians learned during the nearly four thousand years that their society existed still have much to teach modern people.

Complete Society. Ancient Egyptian civilization has something to tell modern scholars and students whether they are attracted to the practical or the mystical. The Egyptians built a complete society that was internally consistent. Many students

of Egyptology are awed by the breadth and antiquity of Egyptian objects. The ancient Egyptians left evidence about nearly every aspect of life. They were able to solve the engineering problems involved in building the pyramids by simple and practical means. They also developed an elaborate set of beliefs about the next world that occupied generations of ancient priests in composing the proper magical spells.

Dates. *World Eras* is a reference series intended for high-school students and general library patrons. The series must maintain a consistency of style from entry to entry and volume to volume. The need for consistency has meant that this volume relies heavily on absolute dates rather than merely names of periods or king's reigns to place an event in time. Egyptologists do not always agree on the exact dates of kings' reigns or the length of certain periods of history. The disagreements that used to separate interpretations by more than one thousand years have now narrowed to ten- to twenty-five-year differences in dates assigned to key kings such as Ahmose, Amenhotep III, and Ramesses II. Even so, many Egyptologists refer to events as occurring in "the reign of King X" rather than an absolute year. This approach allows scholars to ignore small differences in absolute dates when discussing some other historical problem. When such phrases are used in this book, the reader should refer to chapter 6, where the dates of dynasties and periods are summarized.

Consensus. The absolute dates used in this volume were refined by the Egyptologist William J. Murnane. They were published in *Civilizations of the Ancient Near East* (1995), and they have been adopted by many scholars. Readers might notice that a different set of dates is used in *The Oxford Encyclopedia of Ancient Egypt* (2001). Conflicting sets of dates stem from different ways of interpreting the available data. Egyptologists generally accept that there will be minor differences of opinion on the absolute dates of ancient Egyptian history.

Periods of History. Egyptologists today use a scheme of time periods that can be traced to the historian Manetho who lived in Egypt in the second century B.C.E. He worked from Egyptian texts to develop thirty dynasties of Egyptian kings, and his work remains the framework for all current chronologies of ancient Egypt. In modern times Egyptologists have grouped the dynasties into larger periods. Recent discoveries in Abydos in central Egypt have established the existence of a royal dynasty predating Dynasty 1. It has been called Dynasty 0 for convenience.

Otherwise, the period before Dynasty 1 has been called the Predynastic Period. Dynasties 1 and 2 are called the Archaic or Early Dynastic Period. Dynasties 3 to 6 form the Old Kingdom. Dynasties 9 to 11, a period of decentralization, are called the First Intermediate Period. It is followed by the Middle Kingdom, Dynasties 11 to 14. Dynasties 15 to 17, when the West Semitic people called the Hyksos ruled Lower Egypt, are known as the Hyksos Period and/or the Second Intermediate Period. From Dynasty 18 to Dynasty 20, when Egypt was an international power, the period is called the New Kingdom. Subperiods of the New Kingdom are the Amarna Period, when the religious radical Akhenaten ruled, and the Ramesside Period—Dynasties 19 and 20—when kings who claimed descent from Ramesses I ruled. The Third Intermediate Period includes Dynasties 21 to 25. It is followed by the Late Period, Dynasties 26 to 30. Within the Late Period are the Saite Period (Dynasty 26) and the First Persian Period (Dynasty 27). Finally, the Ptolemaic Period follows Alexander the Great's conquest of Egypt after 332 B.C.E. when kings and queens were descended from Alexander's general named Ptolemy. The Roman Period follows Cleopatra VII's defeat at Actium (31 B.C.E.) by the future Roman emperor Octavian.

Spelling. The spelling of kings' names and of places in ancient Egypt also presents a problem for modern writers. Again, this volume has followed the spellings established in *Civilizations of the Ancient Near East.* The Egyptians wrote only the consonants in their language. Modern scholars have pursued different theories of how to add the vowels to names. In addition, many scholars have followed the spellings of ancient Greek historians in reproducing the names of Egyptian kings. Thus Khufu, the Dynasty 4 king who built the Great Pyramid, is known as Cheops, following the Greek pronunciation, in some books. This book uses spellings based on ancient Egyptian rather than ancient Greek.

Egyptology and Egyptosophy. This volume is a work of Egyptology, a modern academic discipline that grew directly from Jean-François Champollion's work on the Rosetta Stone. In 1822 Champollion published *A Letter to M. Dacier.* This letter was actually a scholarly article that explained that ancient Egyptian hieroglyphs formed a writing system that was basically phonetic and represented an ancient, but perfectly ordinary, human language. Reading this language would allow scholars to study ancient Egyptians' own words and to gain knowledge of this ancient culture using ordinary historical methods. Champollion's discovery was judged at the time and in the following 180 years against a nearly 2,000-year tradition that the Egyptologist Erik Hornung has called "Egyptosophy." This discipline regards ancient Egypt as the source of all wisdom and arcane knowledge. Egyptosophists are not a unified group, but rather among them are people who hold a variety of views about ancient Egypt. These views include the belief that the Egyptians invented usable astrology, alchemy, and magic. Among them are also individuals who believe that they have access to "hidden" Egyptian knowledge. This alternative tradition also includes the work of Rosicrucians, Masons, the late-eighteenth-century German Romantics, nineteenth-century Theosophists, Anthroposophists, and a wide variety of internet site content providers. None of these groups and individuals rely on knowledge of the ancient Egyptian language—the Egyptians' own words—for their insights into Egyptian culture. For that reason they represent a different kind of interest in ancient Egypt from Egyptology's concerns and they are thus not included in this volume.

Subdisciplines. Egyptologists work both from the ancient language and from actual objects that the Egyptians left behind. Though all Egyptologists study the Egyptian language, philologists specialize in this field. In general, Egyptian philologists are familiar with the five historical dialects of Egyptian and the four ways of writing those dialects. The dialects are Old Egyptian, Middle Egyptian, Late Egyptian, Demotic, and Coptic; they roughly represent the spoken language of the Old Kingdom, Middle Kingdom, New Kingdom, Late Period, and Greco-Roman Period. The earliest four dialects were written with hieroglyphic signs and hieratic signs, a simplified, cursive writing system. Demotic had its own writing system based on hieratic, while Coptic was written with the Greek alphabet. Philologists study the grammatical systems of the dialects and are generally less interested in the writing system itself. They often specialize in one or more of the dialects. Paleographers and epigraphers, on the other hand, specialize in the writing itself. Paleographers study handwriting such as is generally found on papyrus and on limestone ostraca. Epigraphers, in contrast, are generally interested in the carved and painted hieroglyphs found on temple and tomb walls. Paleographers and epigraphers make texts available through publication for philologists to study. Historians of ancient Egypt are trained primarily as philologists.

Archaeologists. Though most philologists have spent some time studying objects, archaeologists specialize in this field. Many subdisciplines among archaeologists have developed in the years since World War II in Egyptian archaeology. Traditionally archaeologists studied only art and architecture. These fields remain vital and continue to progress as new methods of analysis emerge. Other scholars concentrate on less glamorous objects such as ceramics, tools, and human, animal, and plant remains. These objects are important for understanding daily life and the lives of those ancient people who could not write. As is true in history generally, post–World War II scholars have tried to learn about all classes in the ancient world rather than concentrating only on the elite. Generally, some archaeologists prefer to work in the field, excavating new objects for study. Others research the existing collections of Egyptian artifacts found in museums and other private and public collections. Most are involved in studying a combination of the two, both newly excavated objects and those already in collections.

Afrocentrism. According to Ann M. Roth's analysis in *The Oxford Encyclopedia of Ancient Egypt,* Nile Valley Afrocentrism is an approach to ancient Egypt emphasizing that Egypt is an African country. Afrocentrism aims to counteract negative stereotypes of Africans in cultures dominated by people of European heritage by focusing on Egyptian achievements as African achievements. The positive outcome of this view for Egyptology has been to focus attention on the relationship between Egypt and the rest of the African continent. New research on the Egyptian language family and its relationship with other African languages, for example, has to some extent been stimulated by Afrocentrism. This research has revolutionized Egyptologists' understanding of the history and prehistory of the language and its place in the family of languages.

Kemetology. Many Afrocentric writers prefer to call Egypt "Kemet," believing that its translation, "The Black Land," refers to the people rather than the soil. This approach faces two obstacles. First, "Black Land" is usually contrasted in ancient Egyptian with "Red Land" (*Desheret*), the desert, a clear reference to the color of the soil rather than its inhabitants. Second, if Kemet meant "Land of Black People," the grammatical form and the writing would be different from what is found in hieroglyphs. Undoubtedly, the final sign in such a hieroglyphic word would be *people* rather than *land*, as is always found. Egyptologists disagree with many of the ideas that have been propounded by Kemetology, and this volume thus prefers to use "Egypt" as the best way to refer to the Nile Valley in English.

Unsubstantiated Claims. Some Afrocentrists believe that the Egyptians were more technologically and mentally advanced than the evidence can support. They have suggested that the Egyptians used gliders to fly and that they used electricity. Others have suggested that the Egyptian's mental powers allowed them to use levitation, telepathy, and prophecy. Again, the evidence available from ancient Egypt does not support such claims.

Egypt and Greece. The relationship between Egypt and Greece also interests Afrocentrists. Many argue that Egypt was the original source of all Greek philosophy. These assertions were made by George James in his 1954 book *Stolen Legacy* even before Martin Bernal popularized such ideas in his *Black Athena* (1987–1991). James and Bernal have charged that racist European and American scholars concealed the cultural debt Greece owed to Egypt. Mary Lefkowitz and Guy Rodgers in *Black Athena Revisited* (1996) have answered the many unsubstantiated claims made against scholars.

Cultural Arrogance. Some Afrocentrists have maintained that all African civilizations originated in Egypt. This argument actually stems from racist European beliefs that among Africans, only the Egyptians were capable of cultural innovation.

Vandalism. Other Afrocentrists believe that Egyptologists have vandalized Egyptian statues in order to disguise their African appearance. The often-repeated but false charge that Napoleon Bonaparte's French soldiers shot the nose off the Great Sphinx at Giza stems from this belief. The Sphinx's nose was already missing in Fredrick Norden's drawing of it made in 1755, more than forty years before Napoleon arrived in Egypt. In fact, the nose was damaged by a Muslim fanatic in the fourteenth century C.E. The equally false claim is also made that European Egyptologists purposely have mutilated the noses of other statues. Clearly, the nose is the most prominent section of any statue and most liable to break in a fall.

Racism. Egyptology was born in Europe in the early nineteenth century. It was certainly a product of its time and the men and women who studied Egypt shared the prejudices common to their time and place. Thus, many histories of Egypt from the earlier period are condescending or denigrate Egyptian

achievements. Furthermore, earlier Egyptologists' interest in the Bible and the classical world of Greece and Rome led them to isolate Egypt from Africa and incorporate it into the East Mediterranean world exclusively. Clearly one contribution that Afrocentrism has made to Egyptology is to highlight these problems. The new interest that Egyptologists currently show in Egypt's African context can certainly be traced to Afrocentrism's influence.

Primary Texts. This volume's contributors have based their interpretations on primary texts, the ancient Egyptians' own words. The chapters contain many extracts from Egyptian texts to allow readers to form their own judgments of the interpretations offered here. These texts more than adequately demonstrate the accomplishments of Egyptian culture from earliest times.

Citations of Papyri and Ostraca. Papyri and ostraca are cited by their names, sometimes followed by a series of numbers. The naming of papyri and ostraca has always been arbitrary. *Papyrus Westcar*, for example, is named after its first European owner in modern times. The Berlin Egyptian Museum purchased it in the mid nineteenth century, but it remains known by this name. Other papyri and ostraca are named after the museum that owns them. For example, *Papyrus Berlin 3022*, the earliest text of the epic poem *Story of Sinuhe*, is named after the Berlin Egyptian Museum and is numbered 3022 in its collection. Other numbers following the name and number of a papyrus or ostracon refer to column and/or line numbers. These numbers, much like the numbers used to quote the Bible, are an aide for scholars and students to find citations. Other names for texts, such as *The Wisdom of Any*, were given by the modern translator. In general, ancient Egyptians used the first line of a text as its name.

Current Thinking. The editor of this book also has tried to reflect current thinking on a wide variety of issues in Egyptology. The authors have tried to synthesize the major arguments in the field but to offer the most widely accepted views for the reader. As is true in most fields of history, the range of questions asked of the data is much broader than would have been true fifty years ago. Great advances have been made in our understanding of the lives of ancient Egyptians outside of the elite since World War II. Thus, much attention is paid to daily life and concerns as well as to the lives and concerns of the rich and powerful. This approach has led to a fuller and more sophisticated understanding of ancient Egypt.

Debt of Gratitude. This volume has benefited from the work of many people. I thank its two other contributors, Stephen Thompson and Steve Vinson, for their hard work and willingness to adapt to a short schedule and an unfamiliar format. Anthony Scotti has labored long and hard to bring the manuscript into conformity with the series' requirements. I thank him for his work and his patience. Finally, many thanks to the editorial directors of Manly, Inc. for entrusting this volume to me.

Edward Bleiberg

Brooklyn, New York

ACKNOWLEDGMENTS

This book was produced by Manly, Inc. Karen L. Rood is senior editor and Anthony J. Scotti Jr. is series editor. James F. Tidd Jr. was the assistant in-house editor.

Production manager is Philip B. Dematteis.

Administrative support was provided by Ann M. Cheschi, Amber L. Coker, and Angi Pleasant.

Accountant is Ann-Marie Holland.

Copyediting supervisor is Sally R. Evans. The copyediting staff includes Phyllis A. Avant, Brenda Carol Blanton, Worthy B. Evans, Melissa D. Hinton, William Tobias Mathes, Rebecca Mayo, Nancy E. Smith, and Elizabeth Jo Ann Sumner.

Editorial associates are Jennifer S. Reid and Michael S. Martin.

Database manager is José A. Juarez.

Layout and graphics supervisor is Janet E. Hill. The graphics staff includes Karla Corley Brown and Zoe R. Cook.

Office manager is Kathy Lawler Merlette.

Photography supervisor is Paul Talbot. Photography editor is Scott Nemzek.

Permissions editors are Ann-Marie Holland and Kathy Lawler Merlette.

Digital photographic copy work was performed by Joseph M. Bruccoli.

The SGML staff includes Frank Graham, Linda Dalton Mullinax, Jason Paddock, and Alex Snead.

Systems manager is Marie L. Parker.

Typesetting supervisor is Kathleen M. Flanagan. The typesetting staff includes Jaime All, Patricia Marie Flanagan, Mark J. McEwan, and Pamela D. Norton.

Walter W. Ross supervised library research. He was assisted by Steven Gross and the following librarians at the Thomas Cooper Library of the University of South Carolina: circulation department head Tucker Taylor; reference department head Virginia W. Weathers; Brette Barclay, Marilee Birchfield, Paul Cammarata, Gary Geer, Michael Macan, Tom Marcil, Rose Marshall, and Sharon Verba; interlibrary loan department head John Brunswick; and interlibrary loan staff Robert Arndt, Hayden Battle, Barry Bull, Jo Cottingham, Marna Hostetler, Marieum McClary, Erika Peake, and Nelson Rivera.

Anthony Scotti wrote the biographies in the Geography chapter and the sidebars on Herakleion and the Valley of the Kings. James Tidd wrote the biographies in the Arts and Science chapters and the sidebar on papyrus.

WORLD ERAS

VOLUME 5

ANCIENT EGYPT

2615 - 332 B.C.E.

WORLD EVENTS:
SELECTED OCCURRENCES OUTSIDE EGYPT

by EDWARD BLEIBERG

2600-2350* **B.C.E.**	• A fully developed writing system and literature in the Sumerian language emerge in Mesopotamia. It includes the first law codes and anonymous poetry. Political organization is by city-states. The *Ram and Tree* offering stand and *Bull's Head from a Harp* are created in Ur.
2500* **B.C.E.**	• Ebla is established in Syria-Palestine, becoming the earliest known city with a literate population. • Native peoples populate permanent settlements on the Pacific coast of South America along the Andes mountain range.
2500-2350* **B.C.E.**	• The First Dynasty of Lagash, a leading city-state in Mesopotamia, flourishes.
2500-2200* **B.C.E.**	• Early Helladic II culture flourishes on the Greek mainland.
2500-2000* **B.C.E.**	• Early Kerma culture (Kingdom of Yeram)—characterized by black and brown pottery with incised decorations found in oval-shaped burials with stone superstructures—flourishes in Nubia.
2500-1800* **B.C.E.**	• Early Minoan II culture—characterized by the earliest stone vessels, jewelry, copper daggers, imported obsidian, and textile manufacture—flourishes along areas by the Aegean and Mediterranean seas.
2350-2193* **B.C.E.** *****DENOTES CIRCA DATE**	• The empire of Akkad is founded by Sargon, who organizes the military. He conquers much of the Euphrates River region and establishes trade with areas such as the Indus Valley, Crete, and the Persian Gulf.

2350-2193*
B.C.E.
(CONT'D)

- The first known published poet, Enkheduanna, daughter of Sargon, writes "Hymn to Inanna." Inanna was the Akkadian goddess of love and war.

- The bronze sculpture *Head of an Akkadian Ruler,* possibly a representation of Sargon, is created in Niniveh. The *Victory Stele of Naram-Sin,* an iconographic sandstone monument commemorating the victory of Sargon's son over a local mountain tribe, is carved in Mesopotamia.

2350-2150*
B.C.E.

- The Awan Dynasty of the Old Elamite Period flourishes on the Iranian Plateau.

2200 B.C.E.

- People identified as "Greeks" arrive on the Greek mainland during the Bronze Age, establishing the Early Helladic III Period.

2193-2100*
B.C.E.

- The Gutians, tribesmen from the northeastern mountains, invade and settle in North Mesopotamia, ending the Akkadian empire.

2150* B.C.E.

- Gudea becomes governor of Lagash, a leading Sumerian city-state in Mesopotamia. A series of statues of Gudea are created.

2112-2004*
B.C.E.

- The Third Dynasty of Ur flourishes. Ur becomes the leading Sumerian city-state. The earliest version of the Gilgamesh epic known in the Sumerian language is written, and the Ziggarat of Ur, a three-storied stepped brick pyramid-like structure, is built.

2100-1900*
B.C.E.

- The Shimaskhi Dynasty of the Old Elamite Period flourishes on the Iranian Plateau.

2004* B.C.E.

- Amorites, a Caananite people from the mountainous northern Jordan River region, invade Mesopotamia and end the Sumerian city-states.

2000* B.C.E.

- The Amorites sack Ebla, establishing their temple and a palace in the city.

2000-1550*
B.C.E.

- Palaces and cities are established on Crete during what is known as the Middle Minoan Period. The earliest Greek writing, called Linear A and B, is developed in the Aegean area and on islands in the region.

2000-1500*
B.C.E.

- An Indo-European people known as the Hittites arrive in Anatolia. They establish a Middle Bronze Age city-state culture known as the Hittite Old Kingdom.

*DENOTES CIRCA DATE

1980-1630* B.C.E.
- The earliest alphabetic writing of Semitic languages occurs.
- Nubia is occupied by Egyptian forces.

1950-1750* B.C.E.
- Independent city-states are established in Anatolia.

1900* B.C.E.
- The Assyrian trading colony of Kanesh (present-day Kültepe in Turkey) is active in Anatolia.
- Middle Helladic Period flourishes on the mainland of Greece. It is characterized by pottery with a soapy texture.

1900-1650* B.C.E.
- A new culture (designated C group IIA), characterized by rectangular burials with super-structures and clay figurines, flourishes in Nubia.

1900-1500* B.C.E.
- The Sukkalmakh Dynasty (Ebartids) of the Old Elamite Period flourishes on the Iranian Plateau.

1894* B.C.E.
- The Old Babylonian Period, a time in which several city-states vied for power, begins in Mesopotamia.
- The earliest known flood narrative appears in the poem *The Atrakhasis* which is composed in the Akkadian language.

1813* B.C.E.
- Shamshi-Adad I, an Amorite king, conquers Ashur (Assyria).

1792-1750* B.C.E.
- The Babylonian king Hammurabi issues a written law code in Mesopotamia and orders the carving of a stele with the law code.

1700-1550* B.C.E
- A new group of people (designated as Classic C II B)—characterized by massive tumuli with chapels over graves and the use of pottery, figurines, and cattle skulls as grave offerings—flourishes in Nubia.

1595* B.C.E.
- The Hittite king Murshili I conquers parts of Syria and captures Babylon, ending the Old Babylonian Period.

*DENOTES CIRCA DATE

1595-1158* B.C.E.

- The Kassite Dynasty takes control of Mesopotamia, ending the city-state period and establishing its capital in Babylon. The kingdom is a center of architectural and artistic achievement, and becomes known for trade and science.

1550* B.C.E.

- The Indo-Iranian Mitanni empire emerges in northern Mesopotamia and competes with Egypt for control of Syria.

- A Late Bronze Age Minoan artist creates the *Octopus Vase,* an example of dark-on-light pottery painting in the Marine Style. The Minoans also construct the *Palace of Minos* on the island of Crete.

1539-1075* B.C.E.

- The Late Helladic (or Mycenean) Period flourishes on the Greek mainland. Several fortified population centers emerge, burial circles are constructed, and graves are filled with luxury items such as gold and art.

- The Egyptians dominate in Nubia.

1530* B.C.E.

- Ugarit flourishes as a city-state in Syria-Palestine. Its merchants trade with Cyprus and Greece, and its artists develop literature and ornamentation.

1456* B.C.E.

- Thutmose III defeats a coalition of city-states at Megiddo.

1450* B.C.E.

- Hittite king Tudkahliya I defeats the Assuwa (people from Asia Minor).

1400* B.C.E.

- Minoan civilization declines in the Aegean.

1400-1200* B.C.E.

- The Lion Gate is built in Hattusas (modern Bogazkale) in Anatolia, a Hittite religious center that was known as the City of Temples.

1322* B.C.E.

- Tutankhamun's widow asks the Hittite king to send her a husband; her prospective groom is murdered on the way to Egypt.

1274* B.C.E.

- Troops of Ramesses II fight those of the Hittite king Muwattalli II at Qadesh in Syria.

1250* B.C.E.

- An Elamite ziggurat is built in honor of the bull-god Inshushinak at Dur Untash on the Iranian Plateau.

- The *Lion Gate,* a tomb portal of limestone and masonry in a Mycenae citadel, and the *Treasury of Atreus,* a fifty-foot domed masonry tomb, are built at Mycenae.

*DENOTES CIRCA DATE

1245* B.C.E.

- Ramesses II signs a treaty with the Hittite king Khattushili III. The two kingdoms agree to divide disputed lands, and the Egyptian king takes a Hittite princess as a wife.

1200* B.C.E.

- The Sea Peoples, ancestors of the Philistines, destroy the Hittite Empire in Anatolia and initiate a Dark Age in the region. Ugarit experiences a decline of power, as do the city-states in Syria-Palestine. Another group, the Aramaeans, migrates out of the Arabian peninsula and arrives in Syria-Palestine, where they establish many centers, including the city of Damascus.

1200-1000* B.C.E.

- Early Iron archaeological culture emerges in Syria-Palestine.

1200-759* B.C.E.

- A Dark Age descends in the regions around the Aegean and Mediterranean Seas. Linear B writing disappears and there are few surviving records.

1183* B.C.E.

- Troy, a city-state in northwest Asia Minor situated not far from the Dardanelles, is destroyed by the Greeks.

1158-1027* B.C.E.

- The Second Dynasty of Isin, an ancient city located in southern Mesopotamia, is established by Marduk-kabit-ahheshu.

1150* B.C.E.

- The Olmec of southern Mexico, living along the coast of the Gulf of Mexico, begin carving large stone heads, some as tall as nine feet, that appear to wear helmets. The Olmec also produce beautiful pottery and jewelry. Their culture spreads throughout Central America. The oldest known center for the Olmecs is at San Lorenzo.

1115-1077* B.C.E.

- Assyrian king Tiglath-pileser I defeats the Mushki from southern Armenia and the small Hurrian states of southern Armenia. He spreads Assyrian power into the lands around the Mediterranean Sea and fights against Babylonia, eventually plundering the capital.

1074-1057* B.C.E.

- King Ashur-bel-kala of Assyria, the son of Tiglath-pileser I, continues Assyrian warfare against the Aramaeans and Babylonians, although his empire is unstable.

1050-1032* B.C.E.

- Ashurnasirpal I, the brother of Ashur-bel-kala and new king, fights defensive actions against the enemies of Assyria.

* DENOTES CIRCA DATE

1025-900*
B.C.E.

- The Geometric Period of art, especially in the painting of vases, is active on the Greek mainland, particularly in Athens.

1000 B.C.E.

- Saul, the first king of the United Monarchy of Israel and Judah, defends his lands against the Philistines. He is killed at the battle of Mount Gilboa.

1000-960
B.C.E.

- David, who succeeds Saul as king of the Israelites, conquers Jerusalem.

1000-612*
B.C.E.

- The Neo-Assyrian Empire develops in Mesopotamia.

960-932
B.C.E.

- Solomon, the son of Bathsheba—the second wife of David—becomes king of the United Monarchy of Israel and Judah. He makes Palestine a trading center, as well as constructs many major temples and buildings.

932-911
B.C.E.

- Jeroboam I of Israel, who had plotted against Solomon and Rehoboam, returns from exile and becomes king of the northern tribes. He makes his capital in Shechem in northern Israel.

931-915
B.C.E.

- Rehoboam, the son of Solomon, becomes king of Judah, only to see Jeroboam withdraw the northern tribes. He then faces an invasion by the Egyptians.

915-913
B.C.E.

- Abijah, the son of Rehoboam, becomes the second king of Judah.

913-873
B.C.E.

- Asa, the son of Abijah, becomes king of Judah and purges his country of opposing religious cults.

911-910
B.C.E.

- Nadab, the son of Jeroboam I, becomes king of Israel.

910-887
B.C.E.

- Upon the death of Nadab, Baasha becomes king of Israel and attacks Judah.

900-331*
B.C.E.

- Syria-Palestine is dominated by Assyria, Babylon, and Persia.
- The Napatan kings, named for the city in the Sudan where the Egyptian governors ruled, control Nubia.

***DENOTES CIRCA DATE**

887-886 B.C.E.	• Elah, the son of Baasha, rules over Israel until he is assassinated in a palace coup d'état.
886 B.C.E.	• Zimri, one of the generals who killed Elah, takes over the leadership of Israel.
886-875 B.C.E.	• After defeating a rival claimant to the throne, Omri becomes the king of Israel. The Moabites, a people living around the Dead Sea, are subjugated.
883-859 B.C.E.	• The Assyrian king Ashurnasirpal II rules Mesopotamia with an iron hand, reestablishing the former supremacy of the empire. He makes his capital at Nimrud on the east bank of the Tigris River. Assyrian artists create the *Lion Hunt* relief, which depicts archers in a horse-drawn chariot.
875-854 B.C.E.	• King Ahab of Israel, the son of Omri, restores alliances with Judah and other local rivals. His forces defeat an Assyrian incursion at Karkar (853 B.C.E.), but he dies the following year fighting the Damascans.
873-849 B.C.E.	• Jehoshaphat succeeds his father, Asa, as king of Judah. Allied with Israel, his troops fight against Syrian incursions.
858-824 B.C.E.	• King Shalmaneser III of Assyria rules Mesopotamia. His troops conquer the Hittites and the Damascans, fight against the forces of Israel at Karkar (853 B.C.E.), and defeat the opposition on Tyre and Sidon.
854-853 B.C.E.	• Ahab's son, Ahaziah, serves as king of Israel. His troops were unable to defeat a revolt in Moab.
853-842 B.C.E.	• Jehoram (or Jeram), another of Ahab's sons, succeeds Ahaziah as king of Israel. With Judean aid his troops defeat the Moab opposition.
842* B.C.E.	• Ahaziah, the son of Jeram, becomes king of Judah. • Jehu, an army commander, kills Jehoram and takes the throne of Israel. He also kills Ahaziah and destroys the royal family, making Athaliah the queen of Judah. Jehu wages war against the Damascans but is subservient to the Assyrians and tries to eliminate all followers of the god Baal. He rules until 815 B.C.E.

*Denotes Circa Date

836-797 B.C.E.

- Joash (or Jehoash) leads a revolt against Athaliah; he takes the throne after her assassination.

823-811 B.C.E.

- Assyrian king Shamshi-Adad V rules in Mesopotamia. He wages war against Urartu, an emerging Armenian civilization.

815-799 B.C.E.

- Joahz (or Jehoahas) succeeds his father, Jehu, as king of Israel.

810-783 B.C.E.

- Adad-Nirari III of Assyria serves as king of Mesopotamia. His troops will fight against peoples to the west of his empire.

800* B.C.E.

- The Urartu in Anatolia are defeated by the Assyrians.
- The Olmec city of La Venta is established, becoming the most important center of Mesoamerican culture in Central America for almost four hundred years.

799-784 B.C.E.

- Jehoash (or Joash) succeeds his father, Jehoahas, as king of Israel.

797-769 B.C.E.

- Joash's son, Amaziah, serves as king of Judah. He defeats the Edomites, who occupy the hilly lands south of the Dead Sea (in modern Jordan) in 798 B.C.E. The Israelites capture and assassinate him.

784-744 B.C.E.

- Jeroboam II succeeds Joash as the king of Israel. He restores the traditional borders of Israel and captures Damascus.

776 B.C.E.

- The earliest-known recorded observation of a solar eclipse is documented by the Chinese.

769-741 B.C.E.

- Uzziah (or Azariah), the son of Amaziah, enjoys a prosperous reign as king of Judah. His troops defeat the Philistines. Despite his military successes, the Hebrew prophets Amos and Hosea warn of an eventual downfall because of rampant corruption.

760* B.C.E.

- Greek colonizers begin to expand into Italy and Sicily.

760-747 B.C.E.

- King Kashta of Kush, one in a line of hereditary Egyptianized Nubian rulers, conquers and rules Upper Egypt.

*DENOTES CIRCA DATE

753 B.C.E.

- Rome is allegedly founded by Romulus, leading to the development of a period of monarchical rule in Italy. The first king and religious leader, traditionally, is considered to be Numa Pompilius, who takes the throne in 715 B.C.E.

750* B.C.E.

- Neo-Hittite states emerge in Anatolia.

750–550* B.C.E.

- The Archaic Period flourishes on the Greek mainland. Greeks colonize Sicily, Italy, and the Ionian coast.

747–716 B.C.E.

- King Piye of Kush controls both Nubia and Egypt.

744 B.C.E.

- Zechariah succeeds Jeroboam as king of Israel. He is assassinated by Shallum, who in turn is killed by Menachem, who takes the throne. Menachem rules until 735 B.C.E.

744–727 B.C.E.

- Tiglath-pileser III of Assyria rules in Mesopotamia. In 743 B.C.E. he attacks the Urarteans at Arpad. He then turns his attention in 739 B.C.E. To the west, forcing Judah and Israel, as well as smaller states, to submit to his authority.

743–642* B.C.E.

- The Neo-Elamite Period, in which the Elamites meddle in Babylonian affairs, flourishes on the Iranian Plateau.

741–726 B.C.E.

- King Jotham and King Ahaz of Judah serve as co-regents in Syria-Palestine.

735 B.C.E.

- Tiglath-pileser III sends his forces against Urartu.

735–734 B.C.E.

- Pekahiah, the son of King Menachem, serves as king of Israel.

734 B.C.E.

- Ahaz rejects an alliance with Israel and seeks support of the Assyrians.

734–731 B.C.E.

- Pekah reigns as king of Israel. He invades Judah in an attempt to force it into an alliance against Assyria. He dies in a conspiracy and is replaced by Hosea, whom the Assyrians claim to have put on the throne.

* Denotes Circa Date

731 B.C.E.

* Tiglath-pileser III is forced to return home to put down a revolt in Babylon, which he accomplishes by 728 B.C.E.

726-697 B.C.E.

* King Hezekiah of Judah in Syria-Palestine rules. Twice he rebels against Assyrian domination but is forced to pay tribute.

725 B.C.E.

* King Hosea of Israel rebels against Assyria, whose king, Shalmaneser V, orders an invasion of Samaria.

722 B.C.E.

* Samaria is defeated, and the son and successor of Shalmaneser V, Sargon II, removes thousands of Israelites to captivity in Mesopotamia. During the next sixteen years Sargon captures most of the region and defeats Tyre after a long siege.

721 B.C.E.

* Elamite king Humbanigash, along with Merodach-baladan of Babylon, attack Sargon's forces at the indecisive battle of Der.

721-705 B.C.E.

* Sargon II builds the Gate of the Citadel at Khorsabad (Dur Sharrukin) in Mesopotamia. The giant carvings depict two winged bulls with male faces.

720 B.C.E.

* The Chinese build a canal connecting the Huai and Yellow Rivers.

716-702 B.C.E.

* King Shabako of Kush rules in Nubia and in Egypt.

714 B.C.E.

* Sargon II's troops defeat Urartu. His forces next break the alliance of the southern Palestinian states with Egypt in 712 B.C.E.

710 B.C.E.

* Merodach-baladan of Babylon revolts against Sargon II but is defeated and forced into exile. He returns in 703 B.C.E. to reclaim the throne but is again defeated by the Assyrians.

704-681 B.C.E.

* King Sennacherib of Assyria reigns in Mesopotamia.

702-690 B.C.E.

* King Shibitqu of Kush rules both Nubia and Egypt.

*DENOTES CIRCA DATE

700* B.C.E.

- Celtic peoples begin settling in the Iberian Peninsula.

697-642* B.C.E.

- King Manasseh, the son of Hezekiah, rules over Judah.

690* B.C.E.

- Phrygia, a Thracian city-state in Asia Minor along the Black Sea, is attacked by the Cimmerians, a people who occupy most of the Crimea.

690-664 B.C.E.

- King Taharqo of Kush rules in Nubia and in Egypt.

680-669 B.C.E.

- Sennacherib's son, Esarhaddon, becomes king of Assyria. He conquers Babylon, razes the Phoenician city of Sidon, and incorporates Egypt into his empire after capturing Memphis.

675* B.C.E.

- Lydia, a city-state in western Anatolia, rises in power. The Lydians are credited with being the first people to employ coined money.

668-627 B.C.E.

- Ashurbanipal succeeds Esarhaddon as king of Assyria. He attacks and defeats the Elamites, destroying the city of Susa in 639 B.C.E.

664-653 B.C.E.

- King Tanwetamani of Kush rules in Nubia and in Egypt. The Assyrians are expelled from Egypt by the Saite kings of Dynasty 26.

660 B.C.E.

- The Persian prophet Zoroaster, the founder of Zoroastrianism, is born.
- Jimmu becomes the first emperor of Japan, according to tradition.

658 B.C.E.

- Lydian, Ionian, and Carian mercenaries join the Egyptians in their fight against the Assyrians.

653 B.C.E.

- The Median king Phraortes, who conquered many of the peoples in the region, is killed in battle against the Assyrians.

653-643 B.C.E.

- King Atlanersa of Kush rules over Nubia.

*Denotes Circa Date

650 B.C.E.

- The carved limestone relief *Dying Lioness,* depicting the feline being pierced by three arrows, is created in Ninevah.

650-590* B.C.E.

- A series of leaders known as "lawgivers" rule in Greece.

643-623 B.C.E.

- King Senkamanisken of Kush reigns in Nubia.

642 B.C.E.

- Ancus Martius becomes the king of Rome. A bridge is built across the Tiber River during his reign.

640 B.C.E.

- King Amon has a short reign in Judah; he is assassinated after two years by his own officials.

640-609 B.C.E.

- King Josiah serves as king of Judah. By 627 B.C.E. he reclaims the provinces of Samaria, Gilead, and Galilee from the Assyrians, who are experiencing domestic upheaval because of the death of Ashurbanipal.

626 B.C.E.

- Scythians, nomadic warriors from northern Europe (around the regions of modern Ukraine and Russia), invade Syria and Palestine.

625 B.C.E.

- The Chaldean Dynasty is established in Mesopotamia by Nabopolassar, who consolidates power in the empire. The dynasty lasts until 539 B.C.E.

623-593 B.C.E.

- King Anlamani of Kush reigns for thirty years in Nubia.

612 B.C.E.

- The Scythians, Medes, and Babylonians—led by the partnership of Nabopolassar and Cyaxares, the king of Media—capture and destroy the Assyrian city of Ninevah. Urartu is also invaded and conquered. The Assyrians put up a spirited resistance at Harran, but are defeated, and then they look to Egypt for assistance in recapturing the city.

609 B.C.E.

- King Jehoahaz of Judah fights off Syrian and Israelite attacks on Jerusalem by turning to Assyria for help.

609-598 B.C.E.

- Josiah's son, Jehoiakim, serves as the king of Judah after Jehoahaz is deposed by the Assyrians.

*DENOTES CIRCA DATE

605 B.C.E.
- Nebuchadrezzar, who was the crown prince, becomes king of Babylon after defeating an Egyptian army led by Neko II at Carchemish. He remains in power until 562 B.C.E.

600* B.C.E.
- A Phoenician fleet sails around the continent of Africa.

598 B.C.E.
- Jehoiachin becomes king of Judah and faces an invasion launched by Nebuchadrezzar. The Babylonians capture Jerusalem and remove thousands of Israelites as captives.

598-587 B.C.E.
- Nebuchadrezzar places Zedekiah on the throne of Judah. Zedekiah is taken to Babylon as a captive after a failed revolt.

593-568 B.C.E.
- Aspalta is made the ruler of Kush, becoming the first Meroitic king in Nubia.

590 B.C.E.
- The Greek tyrant Cleisthenes of Sicyon founds the Pythian Games in honor of the god Apollo. By 582 B.C.E. the competitions are held every four years.

587-586 B.C.E.
- Jerusalem is again captured by Nebuchadrezzar and the city is razed. Judah is destroyed as a nation and the Babylonian Exile begins.

578 B.C.E.
- Rome joins the Latin League.

575 B.C.E.
- The fifteen-meter-high masonry (glazed brick) Ishtar Gate, one of eight portals into the city, is built in Babylon and dedicated by Nebuchadrezzar.

573 B.C.E.
- The port city of Tyre, which resisted a thirteen-year siege, is captured by Nebuchadrezzar.

568-555 B.C.E.
- King Aramatelqo of Meroe reigns over Nubia.

563 B.C.E.
- Siddhartha Gautama, the founder of Buddhism, is born in Kapilavastu (in present-day Nepal).

560 B.C.E.
- Croesus becomes king of Lydia and consolidates Lydian control in Asia Minor.
- The Athenian statesman and lawgiver Solon dies.

* DENOTES CIRCA DATE

559-530 B.C.E.

- Cyrus (the Great) becomes king of Persia, establishing the Achaemenid (Persian) Empire, which lasts until 330 B.C.E.

556 B.C.E.

- Nabonidus becomes the new Babylonian king and allies with Cyrus of Anshan, a small Persian kingdom north of Babylon, against the Medes.

555-542 B.C.E.

- King Malonqen of Meroe rules in Nubia.

551 B.C.E.

- The Chinese philosopher Confucius (K'ung Fu-tzu) is born.

550* B.C.E.

- Persia expands into Anatolia under the direction of Cyrus the Great. Within five years most of the Greek cities in Asia Minor provide tribute to the Persians.
- Celts expand their settlements into the British Isles and Ireland.

547 B.C.E.

- Lydia is conquered by Cyrus the Great.

542-538 B.C.E.

- King Analmaaye of Meroe rules over Nubia.

540 B.C.E.

- The Indian religious leader and founder of Jainism, Mahavira (Vardhamana), is born.

539 B.C.E.

- The Babylonian Exile ends after Cyrus the Great captures Babylon and releases the captured Jews. Persia rules over Israel and Judah and dominates Mesopotamia.

538 B.C.E.

- Cyrus the Great issues an edict to rebuild the Temple in Jerusalem.

538-519 B.C.E.

- King Amani-natake-lebte of Meroe rules over Nubia.

534 B.C.E.

- The Romans build the Temple of Juno.

533 B.C.E.

- The Indus River Valley is conquered by Cyrus the Great, who creates another Persian satrapy.

*DENOTES CIRCA DATE

529 B.C.E.
- Cambyses II becomes the king of Persia after the death of his father, Cyrus the Great, who was killed in 530 B.C.E. near the Sea of Aral in a battle against the Asiatic people known as the Massagetae.

522 B.C.E.
- Upon ascending to the throne of Persian, Darius I is forced to quell revolts against his leadership. The empire is broken up into twenty satrapies. Darius completes a canal linking the Red Sea and the Nile River. Thrace and Macedonia are forced during his reign, which lasts until 486 B.C.E., to pay tribute to the Persians.

519–510 B.C.E.
- King Karkamani of Meroe rules over Nubia. He is followed by King Amaniastabarqo (510–487 B.C.E.).

509 B.C.E.
- The Roman Republic is founded, with Lucius Junius Brutus and Lucius Tarquinius Collatinus serving as the first consuls. The Temple of Jupiter Optimus Maximus (the "best and the greatest"), the supreme god in the Roman pantheon, is built on the Capitoline Hill.

506 B.C.E.
- Rome and Carthage sign a noninterference treaty.

500* B.C.E.
- Ionian city-states revolt against Persian rule.
- Bantu peoples of Africa begin migrating throughout the continent. Also in Africa, the Nok civilization of West Africa (Nigeria) flourishes.

500–323 B.C.E.
- The Greek Classical Period flourishes on the Greek mainland.

496 B.C.E.
- The Romans become the leading power in Italy after defeating the Latins at the Battle of Lake Regillus.

494 B.C.E.
- Roman plebeians wrest political reform and addition rights from the ruling patrician class.

491 B.C.E.
- Indian ruler Bimbisara dies. He had been a protector of Siddhartha Gautama.

490 B.C.E.
- Darius II reasserts control of Macedonia, but the Persian Empire is defeated by Athens and other mainland Greeks at the Battle of Marathon, blocking further expansion in the region.

*Denotes Circa Date

487 B.C.E.	• Siaspiqa of Meroe becomes the king of Nubia and reigns until 468 B.C.E..
486 B.C.E.	• Roman consul Spurius Cassius Vecellinius, who had brokered a peace between the Romans and the Latin League in 493 B.C.E., is accused of trying to make himself the king of Rome after he tries to change agrarian laws to favor the plebian class. He is condemned and executed.
	• Xerxes I (the Great) becomes king of Persia following the death of his father, Darius I. He maintains Persian control over Egypt and Babylonia. He sends troops against the Greeks, defeating a heroic rearguard stand by the Spartans and other Greeks, under the generalship of the Spartan king Leonidas, at the Battle of Thermopylae (480 B.C.E.). Persian troops burn Athens, but Xerxes' fleet is destroyed at Salamis, forcing his withdrawal to Asia Minor. He rules until 464 B.C.E., when he is killed by the captain of his personal guard.
484 B.C.E.	• The Greek dramatist Aeschylus wins his first prize in the competition for tragedy at Athens.
	• Herodotus is born. His great work on the Greco-Persian wars garners him the title "the Father of History."
470 B.C.E.	• The teachings of Confucius, which were known as the Analects, are collected by his disciples.
468-463 B.C.E.	• King Nasakhma of Meroe serves a five-year reign in Nubia.
465-423 B.C.E.	• The son of Xerxes the Great, Artaxerxes I, becomes king of Persia after killing his father's assassin.
463-435 B.C.E.	• King Maloiebamani of Meroe takes the throne and rules over Nubia for nearly thirty years.
458 B.C.E.	• Lucius Quinctius Cincinnatus, a Roman consul and farmer, is made dictator by his people in order to lead an army against the Aequi, who have besieged a force led by Lucius Minucius Esquilinus Augurinus. Quinctius triumphs, then steps down from the position to return to his farm.
457-445 B.C.E.	• Ezra serves as governor of Judah.
451 B.C.E. *Denotes Circa Date	• The Twelve Tables, the basis of Roman law, are codified.

449 B.C.E.
- The Peace of Callias is negotiated between Athens and Persia. A more-permanent treaty of peace is agreed upon four years later.

447 B.C.E.
- The Parthenon, a temple to Athena, is built on the Acropolis in Athens. Construction of this prime example of Doric architecture is completed in 432 B.C.E.

445 B.C.E.
- Nehemiah begins a twenty-year term as governor of Judah. He rebuilds the walls of Jerusalem.

435 B.C.E.
- Talakhamani of Meroe takes the throne in Nubia and rules until 431 B.C.E., when he is replaced by Irike-Amanote, who leads the country until 405 B.C.E.

431–404 B.C.E.
- The Great Peloponnesian War between Athens and Sparta is fought on the Greek mainland.

425 B.C.E.
- The Romans conclude a peace with the Veii, with whom they have fought for thirteen years.

423 B.C.E.
- Xerxes II becomes king of Persia and serves until 405 B.C.E.

423–404 B.C.E.
- The Greek general and historian Thucydides writes *History of the Peloponnesian War.*

410 B.C.E.
- The Gauls, Celtic tribes living in the German regions of Europe, begin migrations across the Alps into Italy.

409 B.C.E.
- Troops from the North African city-state of Carthage capture Sicily from its Greek colonizers. The Carthaginians are forced out in 406 because of the plague and make peace in 405 B.C.E.

405–404 B.C.E.
- Baskakeren of Meroe has a short one-year reign in Nubia, to be followed by the three-decade reign (404–369 B.C.E.) of Harsiyotef.

404 B.C.E.
- Artaxerxes II, the son of Darius II, succeeds his father as the king of Persia. The Persians are driven out of Egypt in 404 B.C.E. Artaxerxes ends a rebellion, led by his brother Cyrus, in Anatolia.

*Denotes Circa Date

390 B.C.E.
- After its legions are defeated at the Battle of Allia, Rome is besieged by Gallic invaders, who take the city but are unable to take the capitol.

381 B.C.E.
- Cyprus, under King Evagoras, submits to the Persians.

371 B.C.E.
- Chinese philosopher Mencius (Meng-tzu), the son of a student of Confucius, is born.
- The Spartan king Cleombrotus I is killed by the Thebians at the Battle of Leuctra.

367 B.C.E.
- The Romans begin eighteen years of warfare against tribes from Gaul. In all, four separate wars are fought.

359 B.C.E.
- Philip II becomes the king of Macedon and rules until 336 B.C.E. He oversees an expansion of Macedonian power over the Greek mainland, conquering Peloponnesus by 338 B.C.E.

358 B.C.E.
- Artaxerxes III Ochus becomes the king of Persia. He faces and quells severe revolts throughout the kingdom during his twenty-year reign.

356 B.C.E.
- The first parts of defensive fortifications, which will become the Great Wall, are constructed by the Chinese in an attempt to block invasions by the Huns.

353-340 B.C.E.
- The Noba occupy Kush and replace the kingdom of Meroe. King Akhratan rules in Nubia 328 B.C.E.

343-341 B.C.E.
- Rome becomes embroiled in the First Samnite War, gaining for the Romans control of northern Campania, a fertile and mountainous region.

340 B.C.E.
- Roman consul Titus Manlius Imperiosus Torquatus defeats the Latins at Campania and then again at Trifanum. The Latin League is disbanded and the former allies are made dependent partners in the expanding Roman empire.

340-335 B.C.E.
- King Nastasen of Meroe rules over Nubia.

336 B.C.E.
- Philip of Macedon is assassinated, and his son, Alexander (the Great), takes the throne.

*DENOTES CIRCA DATE

335 B.C.E.	• Darius III becomes king of Persia.
334 B.C.E.	• Alexander the Great defeats the Persians at the Granicus River and conquers Anatolia. His armies then capture the Phoenician cities, with the exception of Tyre, on their way toward Egypt.
332 B.C.E.	• Alexander the Great conquers Egypt as the Persians withdraw. The Greeks besiege Tyre for seven months. The city of Alexandria in Egypt is founded the following year.

*DENOTES CIRCA DATE

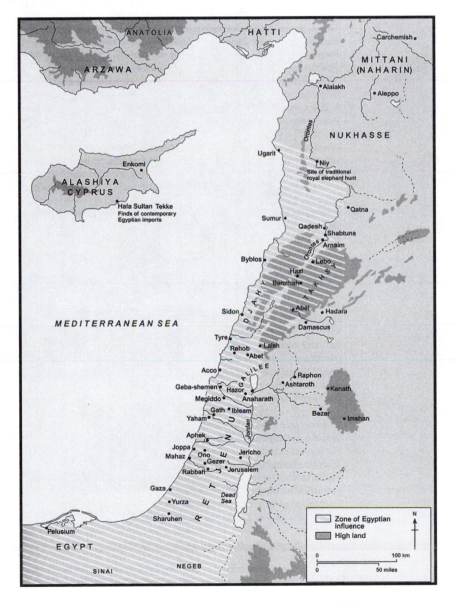

Map of Syria-Palestine, early New Kingdom, circa 1539–1075 B.C.E.
(from Ian Shaw, ed., *The Oxford History of Ancient Egypt*, 2000)

Stone relief of the gods Horus (Lower Egypt) and Seth (Upper Egypt) knotting the plants of the North and South around the symbol of union that supports the cartouche of Senwosret I, circa 1919–1875 B.C.E. (Egyptian Museum, Cairo)

GEOGRAPHY

by EDWARD BLEIBERG

CONTENTS

Sidebars and tables are listed in italics.

2615* B.C.E.

- With a steady increase in the Nile River flood, agricultural development of the delta region occurs. Farming institutions known as Mansions of the Gods are established, where laborers tend fruit orchards, vineyards, and cattle herds.

2585* B.C.E.

- By the end of his rule, King Sneferu has led military expeditions into Nubia (present-day Sudan and southern Egypt), Libya, and the Sinai Peninsula.

2500–2350* B.C.E.

- There are thirty-eight *sepawt* or nomes (administrative provinces), in Egypt.

2460–1880* B.C.E.

- Rainfall levels rise, causing a settlement at the Dakhla Oasis to flourish.

2455–2425* B.C.E.

- Relief sculptures from the reign of King Nyuserre depict abundant fauna and flora in the deserts.

2200* B.C.E.

- An abrupt decrease in the Nile flood contributes in part to the eventual collapse of the Old Kingdom in 2130 B.C.E.
- Neferkare Pepy II orders an expedition to be made to the land of Punt (present-day Ethiopia and Djibouti).

1980–1630* B.C.E.

- Commercial activity with Anatolia (present-day Turkey), the Aegean Islands, and Greece begins.

1938–1759* B.C.E.

- New settlements, palaces, and temples are built in the area known as the Faiyum Depression.

1840* B.C.E.

- A rise in Nile flood levels lasts until 1770 B.C.E., corresponding to the height of the Middle Kingdom.

1479–1425* B.C.E.

- During the reign of Thutmose III, the first geographical lists of foreign place-names are carved at a temple.
- Trade expeditions to Punt are recorded on the walls of Queen Hatshepsut's temple at Deir al Bahri.

* DENOTES CIRCA DATE

1300* B.C.E.

- A major decrease in the Nile flood begins and some areas of Lower Nubia are abandoned.

1210* B.C.E.

- An increase in desert rains lasts to about 1110 B.C.E. and causes settlements to thrive in some parts of the Sahara.

1190-1075 B.C.E.

- Amenemope's *The Onomasticon*, a list of the names of Egyptian towns, is compiled.

1170 B.C.E.

- Another decrease in the Nile flood causes food shortages for about seventy years.

950 B.C.E.

- A new series of reliable Nile floods lasts about 250 years, corresponding to Dynasties 21–24 (circa 1075–712 B.C.E.).

945-924 B.C.E.

- During the reign of Shoshenq I, an older list of towns in Syria-Palestine is updated.

664-332 B.C.E.

- There are forty-two nomes in Egypt.

380 B.C.E.

- Nectanebo I places a giant stone at Herakleion, declaring the port city to be the Nile's exit into the Mediterranean Sea.

*DENOTES CIRCA DATE

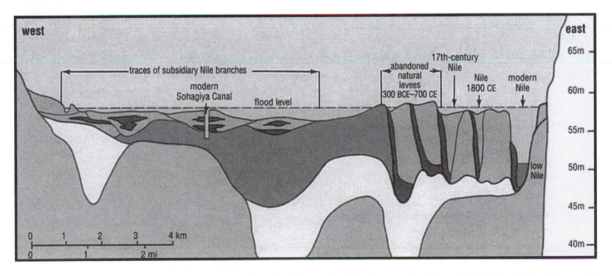

Cross-section diagram of the Nile Valley between Sohad and Asyut showing flood and sediment levels (from John Baines and Jaromir Malek, *Cultural Atlas of Ancient Egypt,* 2000)

OVERVIEW

Natural Divisions. Egypt comprises two inhabitable zones—the valley and the delta of the Nile River. The valley divides into the east and west banks of the river, each with a desert beyond the area of cultivation. The delta also divides into two zones, east and west. Some scholars have argued that these divisions suggested to the Egyptians that the world could be conceived as a series of dualities. Certainly the Egyptians described their country in complementary pairs. The Egyptians commonly called their country "The Two Lands" (*tawy*), referring to Narmer's unification of Upper and Lower Egypt around 3000 B.C.E. The desert, called the Red Land (*desheret*), and the inhabitable zone, called the Black Land (*kemet*), were another duality in Egyptian thought. The Egyptians also contrasted the inhospitable mountains in view of the valley as the *Haset*, while the fertile valley was called the *Ta*.

The Nile. The two branches of the river begin in Ethiopia and eastern equatorial Africa. They are called the White Nile and the Blue Nile. The united river travels through Sudan, passing over four granite outcrops called cataracts. The Aswan High Dam, dedicated in 1971 C.E., created Lake Nasser. The lake covers the area of ancient Lower Nubia, about 2,316 square miles. The river then flows through Egypt, about 725 miles to the Mediterranean Sea. In Egypt the river averages one-half mile wide with a flood plain of about 6.2 miles. The total arable land in the valley is thus approximately 3,861 square miles.

Delta. About thirteen miles north of Cairo the river divides into two branches, forming the delta. In ancient times the river divided into seven different branches. Many of these ancient riverbeds have been traced and lead to ancient towns. At the northern end of the delta are lagoons, lakes, and marshes bordering the Mediterranean Sea. The delta occupies about twenty-two-thousand square kilometers of fertile land.

Political Divisions. The division into "The Two Lands" was true in ancient and modern times. Lower Egypt (the delta) was called *ta-mehew* while Upper Egypt (the valley) was called *ta-shemayet*. Each part had separate administrations. The Hebrew Bible also recognized that Egypt was divided into two parts. The Hebrew word for Egypt, *Mizraim*, contains a grammatical ending called "the dual" to indicate something with two parts. Modern Egyptians divide their country into the areas called the *Wagh Bahari*, or Northern Egypt, and the *Wagh Gibli*, or Southern Egypt. Today even the people of each region are called in Arabic the *Baharawiya* (Northern Egyptians) and the *Sayidi* (Southern Egyptians).

Nomes. Ancient Egypt was further subdivided into administrative provinces each called a *sepat* (nome). Each nome had a local governor called a *nomarch* (*haty-a*). In periods of strong central government, the king established the borders of each nome at the beginning of his reign. Each nome had a capital town. The number of nomes varied over Egyptian history. In Dynasty 5 (circa 2500–2350 B.C.E.) there were thirty-eight nomes, while in the Late Period (664–332 B.C.E.) there were forty-two.

Nubia. In all periods both ancient and modern, the Egyptians distinguished their country from Nubia (ancient name *Ta-Sety*), present-day Sudan. The Nubians were grouped with Libyans, Semites, and Mediterranean islanders as foreigners.

Cultural Differences. The Egyptians also recognized cultural differences between Upper and Lower Egypt. Ancient Egyptian literature commented on the differences in language between Aswan in the far south and Memphis in the north. One text says that people from each place had difficulty speaking to each other. Dialectical differences in the Arabic of Upper and Lower Egypt still exist today.

Conclusion. The earliest historian of ancient Egypt, Herodotus, who lived in the fifth century B.C.E., called Egypt "the Nile's gift." More than two thousand years of research on Egypt only confirms the vital connection between the Nile River and the possibility of life and prosperity in Egypt.

TOPICS IN GEOGRAPHY

CLIMATE

Irrigation Agriculture. Egypt's prosperity was founded upon irrigation agriculture. The surplus food that farmers produced supported the bureaucracy, priesthood, artists, and royal family. When the Nile flood brought new topsoil to the river valley and enough water to fill the irrigation canals, Egypt was stable and prosperous. When the Nile flood failed for long periods, the central government and all the activities that government supported collapsed.

Desert and River Valley. The Egyptian desert and river valley have two distinct climates. The desert's climate depends on local rainfall, while the moisture level in the valley depends entirely on the water that the river brings from its source, the monsoon rains in Ethiopia.

Rainfall Levels. Local rainfall levels in the desert fluctuated within a narrow range during ancient Egyptian history. Yet, even small increases in rainfall made life possible in the oases of the Sahara. Bundles of leaves excavated in the oases indicate a slight increase in rainfall during the Old and Middle Kingdoms (circa 2675–1630 B.C.E.). These leaves have been radiocarbon dated to the Old Kingdom. Settlements in the Dakhla Oasis also flourished in the Old Kingdom. Relief sculpture from the reign of Nyuserre (Dynasty 5, circa 2455–2425 B.C.E.) depicted antelopes, ibex, gazelles, and ostriches

Modern view from the eastern cliffs at Amarna showing the desert and cultivated plains of the Nile Valley

in the desert in a landscape of grass, shrubs, and small trees. A second period of wetter weather occurred circa 1210–1110 B.C.E. during Dynasties 19 and 20. Again there is some evidence of Ramesside settlement in the Sahara during this period. A tree root excavated in a desert wadi radiocarbon dated to 1150 B.C.E. Another increase in rainfall occurred in the period 65 B.C.E.–560 C.E. with a new flourishing of settlement in the oases.

Flood Levels. The Nile River brings water from its source in Ethiopia to the valley in Egypt. Thus, the amount of water in Egypt itself was unrelated to the amount of local rainfall. Local records for Nile flood levels are available beginning about 3000 B.C.E. The earliest records from the Nilometer on Roda Island in modern Cairo indicate that the flood decreased abruptly for nearly two hundred years until circa 2800 B.C.E. Karl W. Butzer has calculated a 30-percent decrease in the volume of water from the earlier period. Beginning in Dynasty 3 and lasting until Dynasty 5, there was an increase in Nile levels (circa 2675–2400 B.C.E.) that corresponds to the prosperity otherwise in evidence in Egypt during this period. About 2200 until 2000 B.C.E. the Nile flood failed, perhaps contributing to the collapse of the Old Kingdom. Both literary evidence and relief sculptures recorded social disorder and famine during this time period. Between 1840 and 1770 B.C.E. the Nile floods were high. This time period again corresponded with the prosperity enjoyed by Egypt during Dynasty 12. About 1300 B.C.E. the flood was high but began to fall after a period of good floods that correspond with Dynasty 18. Some areas in Lower Nubia received no floodwaters and were abandoned. By the twelfth century B.C.E. (circa 1170–1100 B.C.E.), low floods caused food shortages. Food prices rose sharply during this time period, according to records from Deir el Medina. Real instability in food sources probably led to the end of the New Kingdom. Stronger floods again occurred in the period from 950 to 700 B.C.E., guaranteeing the relative stability of Dynasties 21–24. Other periods of good floods during the first millennium B.C.E. were the fifth century and the first century, both periods of relative prosperity. Clearly, the evidence of good Nile floods correlates directly with evidence of prosperity and political stability in Egypt.

Sources:
Karl W. Butzer, *Early Hydraulic Civilization* (Chicago: University of Chicago Press, 1976).

Barry J. Kemp, *Ancient Egypt: Anatomy of a Civilization* (London & New York: Routledge, 1991).

William J. Murnane, *The Penguin Guide to Ancient Egypt* (Harmondsworth, U.K.: Penguin, 1983).

KNOWLEDGE OF GEOGRAPHY

Limited Worldview. The Egyptians' knowledge of geography was restricted to Egypt itself and the eastern Mediterranean. The primary sources preserving Egyptian knowledge of geography are lists of place-names and relief sculptures that depicted foreign countries.

Lists of Place-Names. Egyptian student scribes learned the names of Egyptian towns and foreign locations by

---

LIST OF AMENEMOPE SON OF AMENEMOPE

The introduction to Amenemope's list of names described the purpose and the content of the list. Amenemope's list is the best-preserved example of a widespread practice in ancient Egypt.

Beginning of the teaching for clearing the mind, for instruction of the ignorant and for learning all things that exist: what Ptah created, what Thoth copied down, heaven with its affairs, earth and what is in it, what the mountains belch forth, what is watered by the flood, all things upon which Re has shone, all that is grown on the back of earth, excogitated by the scribe of the sacred books in the House of Life, Amenemope son of Amenemope . . .

Source: Alan H. Gardiner, *Ancient Egyptian Onomastica* (London: Oxford University Press, 1947).

---

memorizing lists. The best-known example of such a list was prepared on papyrus by a scribe named Amenemope during Dynasty 20 (circa 1190–1075 B.C.E.). The geographical list is included along with lists of names of things in the sky, earth, and water; names of persons, offices, and occupations; names of classes, tribes, and types of humans; names of buildings; and names of foodstuff, beverages, and types of meat. There is a logical order to the list. The towns of Upper Egypt are arranged in the list from south to north. The towns of Lower Egypt, however, have no order that modern scholars have recognized. This list was used by students to learn how to spell place-names and to learn where towns were located in relation to each other.

Inscriptions. The lists of foreign countries and towns were carved on temple walls and on statues. They first appeared at the beginning of Dynasty 18 in the reign of Thutmose III (1479–1425 B.C.E.), though they might have been based on lists first made in the Middle Kingdom (circa 1980–1630 B.C.E.). Typically, the purpose of the lists was to allow the king or a god to magically protect Egypt from foreigners.

Accuracy. The lists were organized in sections that recorded the names of towns, regions, or ethnic groups. The sections grouped peoples in Africa, the Near East, or the Aegean Islands. Though some lists seem traditional, depending on earlier lists, King Shoshenq I (circa 945–924 B.C.E.) updated the older list of towns in Syria-Palestine used in the New Kingdom (circa 1539–1075 B.C.E.) to make a modern list of towns. As far as they can be verified, the lists appear to be accurate.

Translating the Text. The great difficulty with the lists of foreign names is to understand what the scribe was trying to convey. The names of foreign places, of course, were not in the Egyptian language. The hieroglyphic signs were used to try to convey syllables that represented a non-Egyptian language. It has sometimes proved difficult to understand their meanings unless they can be compared

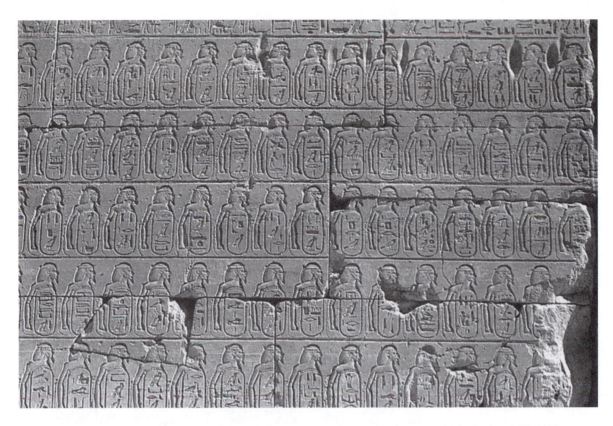

A "geographical list" of localities in Syria-Palestine on a pylon in the temple of Amun at Karnak, circa 1479–1425 B.C.E.

to local texts. Thus, the Near Eastern names can sometimes be verified from the Bible or from texts written in Babylonia and Assyria. The Aegean and African place-names are more difficult to understand because the ancient languages of those places are less understood today.

Logical Arrangements. Even with this difficulty, it seems safe to assume that the lists were arranged in geographical order along roads or routes. The Near Eastern lists, for example, follow known routes from Egypt to Syria. The same organizing principle probably applied to lists of African place-names, perhaps following the Nile River southward.

Expeditions. Exploration in ancient Egypt was related to military and commercial expeditions. There is no recorded instance of exploration in search of knowledge, though some information on foreign lands and cultures was gained from these trips. In the late Old Kingdom (circa 2675–2130 B.C.E.) Harkhuf and Weni traded with Nubia and also made claims that they had explored new roads to the south. Trade expeditions to the land of Punt in Ethiopia were recorded in Hatshepsut's reign (circa 1478/1472–1458 B.C.E.). The relief sculptures carved on the walls of her Mortuary Temple are keenly observed. They show the typical thatched huts on stilts of the area and the local flora and fauna. Military expeditions to Syria-Palestine led Thutmose III's artists to record the unusual plants that they observed there, though the degree of fantasy in these representations is still debated. Herodotus's claim that Necho II (circa 610–595 B.C.E.) sent an expedition around Africa is not accepted by scholars.

Sources:

Hermann Kees, *Ancient Egypt, A Cultural Topography* (Chicago: University of Chicago Press, 1961).

William J. Murnane, *The Penguin Guide to Ancient Egypt* (Harmondsworth, U.K.: Penguin, 1983).

Ian Shaw, ed., *The Oxford History of Ancient Egypt* (Oxford: Oxford University Press, 2000).

Map of the Nile Valley and surrounding areas in circa 1630 B.C.E. (from Ian Shaw, ed.,
The Oxford History of Ancient Egypt, 2000)

The Giza necropolis with the Sphynx and the pyramids of Menkaure (left) and Khafre (right)

THE PEOPLE

Debate. The people of ancient Egypt were typical North Africans. Their direct descendants are the current population of Egypt. A history of racist interpretation of ancient data by scholars in Europe and America claimed the Egyptians as Near Eastern or Indo-Aryan, disregarding the African component in Egyptian culture. In reaction to this racism that denied African achievements, a group of Afrocentric scholars has developed an equally misguided view of the Egyptians as racially "black." As Stuart Tyson Smith has observed, both groups mistakenly equate cultural achievement with race.

Misconception. Early white scholars did not believe that Africans could have achieved the sophistication of Egyptian culture. Afrocentric scholars equate the value of their own humanity with ancient cultural achievement. Neither group is quite right. Egyptian culture certainly had some characteristics in common with other African cultures including divine kingship, use of headrests, body art, circumcision, and male coming-of-age rituals. Egyptian culture also shared characteristics with the ancient cultures of the Near East.

Close Relations. One new area of research shows the widespread connections of ancient Egyptian culture. The ancient Egyptian language shares vocabulary and grammatical structures with modern languages spoken in Ghana, Chad, Morocco, Libya, Sudan, and Ethiopia. It also shares vocabulary and grammatical structures with ancient Semitic languages such as Akkadian used in

Mesopotamia, Hebrew used in ancient Israel, Ugaritic used in ancient Lebanon, and Aramaic, the Near Eastern diplomatic language of the first millennium B.C.E. These connections form the clearest evidence of Egyptian culture's many close relatives.

View of Race. The Egyptians called themselves "people" (*remetch*). They divided the rest of the people they met into four groups including Libyans, Nubians, Near Easterners, and Aegean islanders. "People" were culturally Egyptian. Skin color was unimportant to being an Egyptian. Many Libyans, Nubians, and Near Easterners became Egyptian by adopting the culture. Nubians were members of the royal family as early as Dynasty 4 (circa 2625–2500 B.C.E.). A statue head found in a mastaba tomb in Giza clearly represented an individual with African facial features. The family of Nebhepetre Mentuhotep II (2008–1957 B.C.E.), one of Egypt's three greatest political heroes, was most likely originally Nubian. The kings following the New Kingdom (after 1075 B.C.E.) were almost entirely of Nubian or Libyan origin until the arrival of the Macedonian Greeks with Alexander the Great (332 B.C.E.). Near Easterners also achieved political power rising as high as vizier (prime minister) during the New Kingdom. A late Dynasty 18 (circa 1539–1295/1292) vizier had the name Aper-el, a name that certainly contains the name of the Semitic god El.

Acceptance. Religious doctrine, however, defined foreigners in the abstract as a threat to Egypt. Thus, Near Easterners and Nubians were usually depicted as

Limestone statuette of a woman, a man, and a boy,
from the reign of Akhenaten, circa 1353–1336 B.C.E.
(Metropolitan Museum of Art, New York)

the god Amun. Punt was clearly near the end of the Egyptian's known world since they emphasized the difficulty of reaching this place in their inscriptions.

Western Asia. The Egyptians became aware of the Near East at an early time. Trade with Syria-Palestine (present-day Israel, Jordan, Lebanon, and Syria) began before Dynasty 1 (circa 3000–2800 B.C.E.). There was also contact with Mesopotamia (Iraq, eastern Syria, and western Iran) from the Old Kingdom (circa 2675–2130 B.C.E.). Egyptians traveled there and in the New Kingdom (circa 1539–1075 B.C.E.) conducted an extensive diplomatic correspondence with rulers there.

Europe. Anatolia (present-day Turkey), the Aegean Islands, and the Greek mainland were known to the Egyptians at least since the Middle Kingdom (circa 1980–1630 B.C.E.). Minoan products have been discovered in Egypt from the Middle Kingdom. The Hittites conducted a foreign policy in competition with the Egyptians during the New Kingdom. Ultimately, Europeans in the form of Macedonian Greeks ruled Egypt after the conquest by Alexander the Great in 332 B.C.E.

Sources:

John Baines and Jaromir Malek, *Atlas of Ancient Egypt* (Oxford: Phaidon, 1980).

William J. Murnane, *The Penguin Guide to Ancient Egypt* (Harmondsworth, U.K.: Penguin, 1983).

Jack M. Sasson, ed., *Civilizations of the Ancient Near East,* 4 volumes (New York: Scribners, 1995).

defeated enemies. Relief sculptures carved on temple entrances often showed the king smiting the peoples surrounding Egypt and offering them to the god. Oddly, this religious belief did not prevent foreigners from assimilating to Egyptian culture and full acceptance by other Egyptians.

Sources:

William J. Murnane, *The Penguin Guide to Ancient Egypt* (Harmondsworth, U.K.: Penguin, 1983).

Jack M. Sasson, ed., *Civilizations of the Ancient Near East,* 4 volumes (New York: Scribners, 1995).

Ian Shaw, ed., *The Oxford History of Ancient Egypt* (Oxford: Oxford University Press, 2000).

Stuart Tyson Smith, "People," in *Oxford Encyclopedia of Ancient Egypt,* edited by Donald B. Redford, volume 3 (New York: Oxford University Press, 2001), pp. 27–32.

THE SURROUNDING WORLD

Knowledge. The Egyptian world was the eastern Mediterranean. The Egyptians knew of areas currently in Africa, Western Asia, and Europe. There is no convincing and scientific evidence that the Egyptians were aware of North or Central America or that the "lost continent" of Atlantis ever existed.

Africa. Egypt itself is an African country. The Egyptians were aware of their neighbors in modern Libya, Sudan, and Ethiopia. There is abundant evidence that the Egyptians explored, traded with, and sometimes conquered Sudan (Nubia). The Egyptians also traded with Ethiopia and Djibouti, which they called Punt. This area was the source of incense used in the cult of

THE WORLD OF THE EGYPTIANS

Political divisions in the ancient Egyptian world differed from those of the present day, changing many times during the 2,283 years that this volume covers. Ancient historians often use the names of geographical areas to refer to certain regions. The following list gives the names of those regions and of the nations located there today.

GEOGRAPHIC REGION	MODERN NATION(S)
Anatolia	Turkey
Aegean and Mediterranean	Greece, Cypress, and Turkey
Iranian Plateau	Iran and western Afghanistan
Mesopotamia	Iraq and parts of eastern Syria and western Iran
Nubia	Sudan and the southern area of Egypt
Punt	Ethiopia and Djibouti
Syria-Palestine	Israel, Jordan, Lebanon, and Syria

Source: Ian Shaw, ed., *The Oxford History of Ancient Egypt* (Oxford: Oxford University Press, 2000).

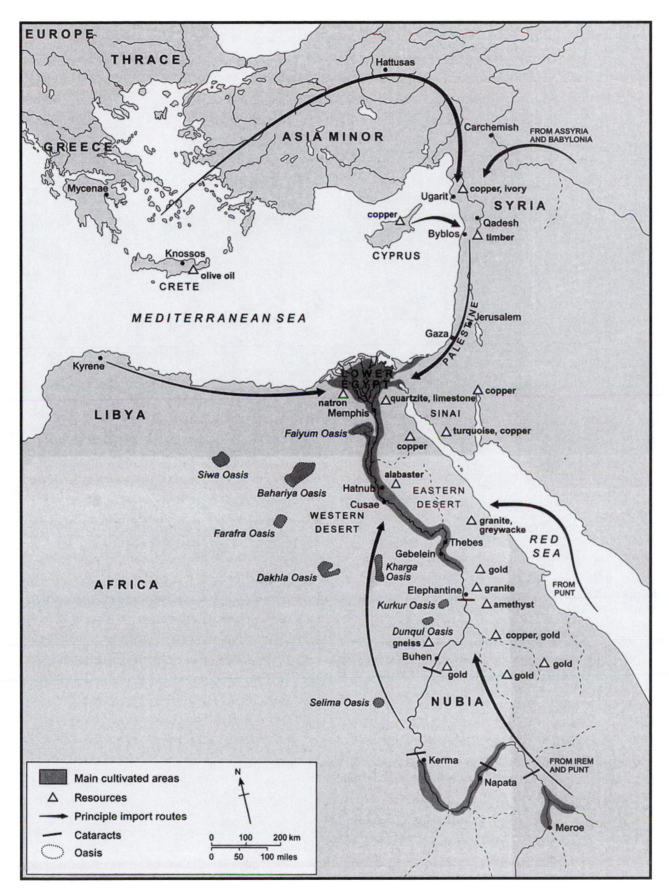

Map of trade routes between Egypt and the ancient Near East (from Ian Shaw, ed., *The Oxford History of Ancient Egypt*, 2000)

Modern view of the Nile River at Thebes

TOPOGRAPHY

Features. Egypt naturally divides into the river valley, the delta, the Faiyum depression, the mountains running parallel to the river, and the deserts both east and west of the river. The valley is a broad floodplain of black clay alluvium that runs from the first cataract near Aswan to the tip of the delta just north of Cairo. The delta consists of land bordered and crossed in ancient times by seven branches of the Nile. The land is moist and becomes marshy as it nears the coast of the Mediterranean Sea. The Faiyum depression was a lake in ancient times that collected excess water from the Nile. It was connected to the river by a channel now called the Bahr Yousef. The mountain ranges on either side of the river are limestone cliffs in the north, sandstone south of Esna and granite in the Aswan area.

River Valley. The river valley is a convex floodplain. This configuration causes the silt carried by the river to be deposited faster in the middle of the river channel than it is on the plains. These deposits formed high natural levees made of silt and sand. The levees reached heights of five to ten feet and provided protection from the flood during most of the year. Basins formed behind the levees allowing the water to collect when the river did overflow its banks. These basins collected water to a depth of about seven feet. They served as collection centers for water. Irrigation canals could then channel the water to the fields.

THE SUNKEN CITY OF HERAKLEION

Until the founding of Alexandria by Alexander the Great in 331 B.C.E., Herakleion was the largest harbor in ancient Egypt. Hercules supposedly changed the course of the Nile River at this site. Located at the mouth of the Canopus branch of the Nile, the port city steadily declined in importance until about 800 C.E. when a massive earthquake sent Herakleion and the nearby cities of Canopus and Menouthis sliding into the sea. Until recently what little information archaeologists had on the three cities was derived from Greek tragedies and legends. However, in 2000 C.E. an underwater search approximately four miles off the coast of Egypt revealed the site of the ancient harbor. Archaeologists have discovered temples, foundations, and ten sunken ships in waters roughly twenty to thirty feet deep. Among the artifacts recovered thus far are statues of Hapi, the god of the Nile flood, and an unidentified pharaoh and his queen. Hieroglyphic text on a small stela, or stone tablet, gives the city's name. Other tablets announce the tariff rates on Greek trade items.

Source: Donald B. Redford, ed., *Oxford Encyclopedia of Ancient Egypt*, 3 volumes (New York: Oxford University Press, 2001).

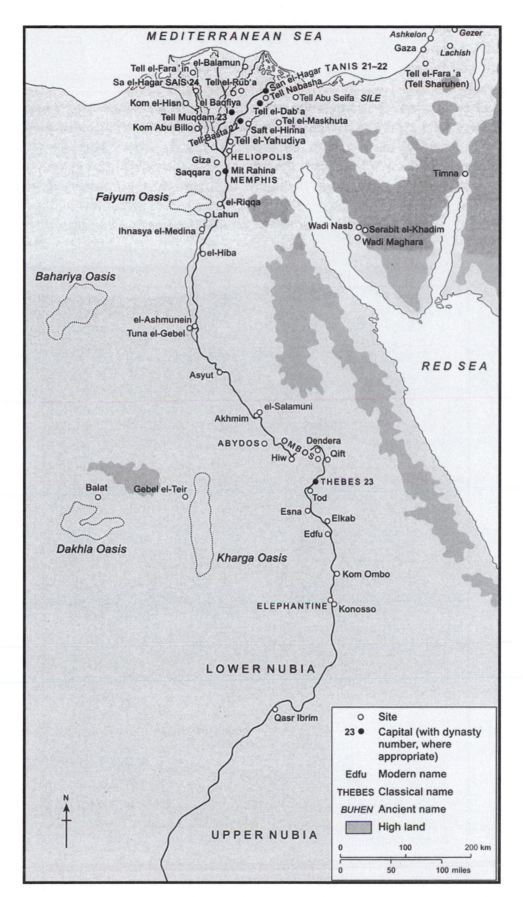

Map of Egypt in circa 1069 B.C.E. (from Ian Shaw, ed., *The Oxford History of Ancient Egypt,* 2000)

Shattered Myth. Irrigation was controlled locally in ancient times. There was no need to control the entire valley in order to practice local irrigation. Farmers could breach the levee to fill the irrigation basin and close the levee again without significantly depleting the stock of water downstream. Thus, early theories that civilization came to the Nile Valley stimulated by the need to control irrigation are likely untrue.

The Delta. During Dynasties 4 and 5 (circa 2700–2400 B.C.E.) the government established new farming institutions in the delta. These institutions, called Mansions of the Gods, managed fruit orchards and vineyards and raised cattle. This activity suggests that the delta was less densely populated than the valley in the earliest dynasties. Cattle remained important to the delta throughout Egyptian history, suggesting that pastureland was its major feature.

The Faiyum. This area experienced considerable development during Dynasty 12 (circa 1938–1759 B.C.E.). In this period the channel connecting the Nile with the lake was open and kept the lake full. New settlements, palaces, and temples were built in this area at the height of the higher floods occurring in the Middle Kingdom (circa 1980–1630 B.C.E.).

Sources:

Karl W. Butzer, *Early Hydraulic Civilization* (Chicago: University of Chicago Press, 1976).

Barry J. Kemp, *Ancient Egypt: Anatomy of a Civilization* (London & New York: Routledge, 1991).

William J. Murnane, *The Penguin Guide to Ancient Egypt* (Harmondsworth, U.K.: Penguin, 1983).

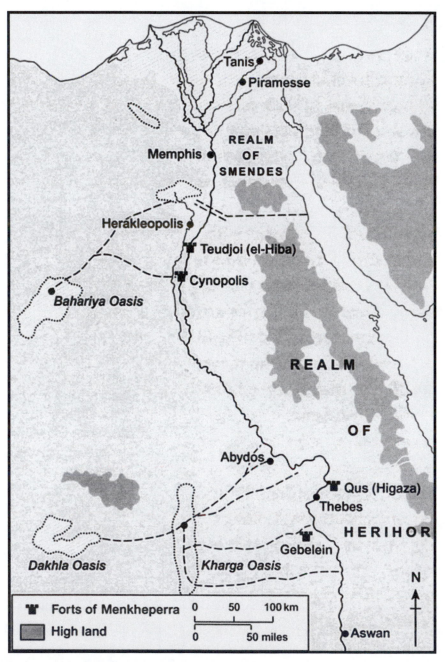

Map of principal cities and fortified sites, circa 730 B.C.E. (from Ian Shaw, ed., *The Oxford History of Ancient Egypt*, 2000)

SIGNIFICANT PEOPLE

NECTANEBO I

FLOURISHED FOURTH CENTURY B.C.E.
KING, DYNASTY 30

External Threat. Nectanebo I ruled Egypt from 381 to 362 B.C.E. In 373 the Persians attempted to reimpose their rule on the area, but Nectanebo I outmaneuvered the 220,000-man enemy army near Mendes in the Nile delta, forcing it to retreat. The external threat to Egypt diminished significantly thereafter as rebellions throughout their empire preoccupied the Persian kings.

Domestic Achievements. A patron of the arts, Nectanebo I also undertook a massive building program, especially at Philae, Edfu, and Hermopolis Magna. In 380 the pharaoh dedicated a large stone marker at the prosperous harbor of Herakleion, officially declaring it to be the Nile's exit to the Mediterranean Sea.

Sources:
Lionel Casson, *The Pharaohs* (Chicago: Stonehenge, 1981).

Peter A. Clayton, *Chronicle of the Pharaohs: The Reign-by-Reign Record of the Rulers and Dynasties of Ancient Egypt* (New York: Thames & Hudson, 1994).

Barry J. Kemp, *Ancient Egypt: Anatomy of a Civilization* (London & New York: Routledge, 1991).

NEFERKARE PEPY II

FLOURISHED CIRCA 2288 B.C.E.
KING, DYNASTY 6

Extensive Reign. Tradition claims that Neferkare Pepy II acceded to the Egyptian throne at age six and that he ruled for ninety-four years. His rule (circa 2288–2224/2194) was marked by not only internal turmoil but also by external pressure. Excessive expenditures on funerary endowments drained national resources, while nomarchs (provincial governors) gradually acquired more autonomy. Meanwhile, military and commercial expeditions to Nubia (the Sudan and southern Egypt) and Punt (Ethiopia and Djibouti) met with resistance. The successors of Neferkare Pepy II failed to deal effectively with the political and economic crises fostered by their father.

Sources:
Lionel Casson, *The Pharaohs* (Chicago: Stonehenge, 1981).

Peter A. Clayton, *Chronicle of the Pharaohs: The Reign-by-Reign Record of the Rulers and Dynasties of Ancient Egypt* (New York: Thames & Hudson, 1994).

Barry J. Kemp, *Ancient Egypt: Anatomy of a Civilization* (London & New York: Routledge, 1991).

SNEFERU

FLOURISHED CIRCA 2625-2500 B.C.E.
KING, DYNASTY 4

Military Raids. Sneferu was the first king of Dynasty 4 (circa 2625–2500 B.C.E.). His highly centralized administration marked a high point of the Old Kingdom (circa 2675–2130 B.C.E.). Records of his reign (circa 2625–2585 B.C.E.) are limited, but apparently he came to power by marrying his predecessor's daughter. He led several military expeditions against Nubia, Lybia, and Sinai, capturing much booty. Stone carvings of the king in the turquoise mines of the last region attest to his military prowess. Sneferu ordered the construction of two large pyramids at Dahshur, both of which still stand today. During the Middle Kingdom (circa 1980–1630 B.C.E.) his rule came to be viewed as a golden age and the king was pictured as a benevolent ruler.

Sources:
Lionel Casson, *The Pharaohs* (Chicago: Stonehenge, 1981).

Peter A. Clayton, *Chronicle of the Pharaohs: The Reign-by-Reign Record of the Rulers and Dynasties of Ancient Egypt* (New York: Thames & Hudson, 1994).

Barry J. Kemp, *Ancient Egypt: Anatomy of a Civilization* (London & New York: Routledge, 1991).

DOCUMENTARY SOURCES

Amenemope, *The Onomasticon*, Dynasty 20 (circa 1190–1075 B.C.E.)—A compilation of the names of towns in Egypt and Western Asia.

Anonymous, *Geographical Lists of Thutmose III* (circa 1479–1425 B.C.E.)—Lists of foreign nations that this king conquered. These regions include Nubia, Syria-Palestine, and Mesopotamia.

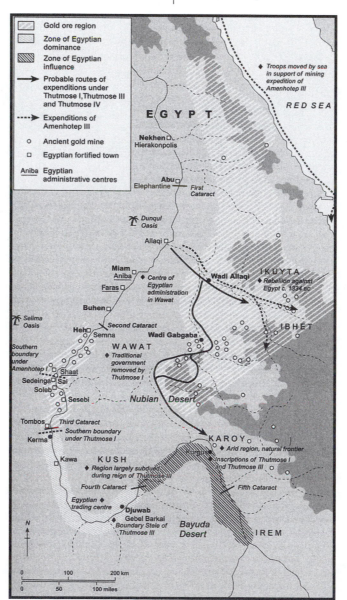

Map of Egypt and Nubia in circa 1550–1352 B.C.E. (from Ian Shaw, ed., *The Oxford History of Ancient Egypt*, 2000)

THE ARTS

by EDWARD BLEIBERG

CONTENTS

Sidebars and tables are listed in italics.

2615-2500 B.C.E.*

- The conventions of Egyptian visual art are firmly established. For instance, the first guidelines are founded that will develop into the grid system.

- The extensive building of mastaba (bench-shaped) tombs is commonplace.

- Music and dance are performed. Visual evidence from paintings and reliefs indicates that musicians played a wide range of instruments, including pipes, flutes, and harps.

2560 B.C.E.*

- Two schools of sculpture in the royal workshops appear, with a new group producing more detailed pieces. One famous example of this new movement is the limestone bust of Ankh-haf.

2555-2510 B.C.E. *

- The use of alabaster and gneiss for carving is common during the reigns of Khafre and Menkaure.

2542-2532 B.C.E. *

- The Great Sphinx, which guards the northern entrance to Khafre's pyramid complex, is constructed.

2532-2510 B.C.E.*

- The Standing Statue of King Menkaure and Queen Kha-merer-nebu II is carved. This statue was among several fine works discovered in Menkaure's valley temple, which is near the smallest of the pyramids at Giza. The two figures are for the first time less idealized than actual portraiture. He is also represented as standing, along with two female deities, in thirteen slab sculptures.

2525 B.C.E.*

- Artists use red quartzite to carve statuary of Redjedef.

2510 B.C.E.*

- A scene depicting dancers and musicians is painted in the tomb of Khuenra, a son of Menkaure.

2420 B.C.E.*

- A limestone carving, which has paint applied to its surface, is made depicting a potter at work. The detailed piece shows an emaciated figure working at his potter's wheel.

2400 B.C.E.*

- The twenty-one inch *Seated Scribe* is carved of limestone, painted, and inlaid with copper, quartz, and ebony.

*DENOTES CIRCA DATE

2338-2298 B.C.E.*

- The first preserved temple of a god in Lower Egypt is completed during the reign of Meryre Pepy I at Bubastis.

- The first rock-cut tombs are carved at Qubbet el Hawa opposite Aswan.

2081 B.C.E.

- Faience, a glazed ceramic, is a popular medium for earthenware artists. These items are often covered in a blue-green tint. Good examples are the representations of a hedgehog and hippopotamus that are later discovered during excavations in Thebes.

2055 B.C.E.

- A giant relief of Nebhepetre Mentuhotep II is carved on the cliffs of Wadi Shatt el-Rigal.

1980-1630 B.C.E.*

- Early autobiographies are written for publication in tombs, including one of the court official Tjetji.

- The first grids with the height of a standing figure established at eighteen units are preserved from relief sculpture.

1957-1945 B.C.E.

- Carvers achieve some of their best work for the Middle Kingdom, producing reliefs with extremely fine details and subtle spatial depth.

1938-1759 B.C.E.

- The golden age of Egyptian literature begins.

- The extensive use of rock-cut tombs in Middle Egypt begins.

1919-1875 B.C.E.*

- The *Story of Sinuhe*, the great epic poem of Egypt, is composed during the reign of Senwosret (or Sesostris) I.

1539-1292 B.C.E.*

- Extensive building of rock-cut tombs appears in Western Thebes, as well as temples for the gods and deceased kings.

- A small wooden representation of the singer Mi is carved, showing her wearing a tight dress, fake wig, and large earrings.

*DENOTES CIRCA DATE

1493-1479 B.C.E.*

- Grids with eighteen units are still used, but the proportions of figures become more graceful.

1426-1400 B.C.E.*

- A painted relief of four female oboe players and two dancing women is placed on the walls of a tomb for Nebamun and Ipuki, two sculptors who worked during the reign of Amenhotep II.

1390-1353 B.C.E.*

- The six-centimeter votive offering *Seated Scribe* is carved, an example of the fine and delicate basalt carving undertaken during the reign of Amenhotep III.

1353-1336 B.C.E.*

- Amenhotep IV (Akhenaten) instructs artists to capture everyday scenes in their work. A group of artists, including Bek (chief sculptor), Parennefer (chief overseer), Iuwty (sculptor and painter), and Tuthmose (sculptor), help develop a new style.

1322 B.C.E.

- Artisans construct a gold funerary mask for Tutankhamun. The mask and mummy were also covered in three coffins, one of which was made of more than one hundred kilograms of solid gold.

- Although discovered much earlier, glassmaking is conducted in Egypt, probably as a result of contact with Near Eastern kingdoms.

1292-1190 B.C.E.*

- The golden age of popular tales and stories begins.

1075-712 B.C.E.*

- Fine metalwork and inlaid bronze statuary are forged in Tanis in the east Nile delta region.

760-656 B.C.E.*

- Grids of twenty-one squares are used to create relief sculpture, perhaps changed from eighteen to simplify calculations and revise proportions of figures.

*DENOTES CIRCA DATE

OVERVIEW

Visual Art and Architecture. After an initial period of experimentation the conventions of Egyptian visual art were firmly established by the end of Dynasty 4 (circa 2500 B.C.E.). In fact, the most basic conceptual framework for Egyptian art was already established in the time of Narmer (circa 3000 B.C.E.). In two-dimensional relief sculpture and painting, the Egyptians created a distinctive style. They used a combination of perspectives, hieratic scale, baselines, and registers to organize composition, hieroglyphic labels, and fantastic figures combining animal and human bodies in one creature. The combination of perspectives meant that the human body was depicted with the head and legs in profile, while the upper torso and eye were presented frontally. Hieratic scale allowed the artist to represent the most important figure, usually the king or a god, on a larger scale than other figures. The size of a figure was based on its importance rather than visual reality. Compositions were laid out using baselines that divided the picture into separate registers with different scenes. A series of scenes could then depict a sequence of events. Labels were used to convey meaning quickly. For example, the identity of a king in a scene was obvious because his name was written next to the figure. Finally, gods and fantastic animals were depicted with combinations of animal and human characteristics to convey information about the individual being depicted.

Human Subjects. Sculpture in three dimensions also followed fixed conventions. The human form was the most common subject for the Egyptian sculptor, who developed poses that included seated and standing figures. Negative space, the blank area between the limbs, was avoided for both poses. Sometimes the space between the arm and torso was painted black, but the stone or wood was not removed. Seated figures commonly sat on blocklike chairs, facing front. Their arms rested on their laps, though this pose was perhaps understood as reaching forward to grasp offerings. Standing men advanced the left foot while both arms hung loosely at the side. They also faced forward. Women were portrayed standing with both feet together, in contrast to men. In both seated and standing poses a woman portrayed with a man had one arm around the man and one arm hanging loosely at her side. If a woman was represented alone, both arms were at her side. In the Middle Kingdom, so-called cube statues portrayed men squatting on the backs of their heels. The sculptor used the cube form to reduce the amount of carving necessary to complete the sculp-

ture. The cube form also created space for inscriptions. The rigidity of these poses resulted from the purpose for these statues, which were all ritual objects that had to be created in the proper form in order for them to function properly.

Architectural Categories. The basic categories of architecture were also established in the first dynasties. The Egyptians built only tombs and temples, which were considered permanent, from stone. Most habitations, including the royal palace, were built of mud brick. Wealthier individuals, such as the king, might have doorways and other elements such as window frames and roof supports built in stone. But mud brick was inexpensive to make, easy to use, and an ideal insulation against both heat and cold. Houses were often plastered and painted on the inside. Elaborate decorations in palaces mostly consisted of scenes from the natural world.

Literature. The Egyptians produced both poetry and prose throughout their history. They invented and developed many literary types and composed many types of verse. Religious works included hymns and prayers. Poems extolling the king's might and virtue were also popular forms, especially in the Middle Kingdom. The *Story of Sinuhe* was the most important epic poem. It was first written in Dynasty 12 (circa 1938–1759 B.C.E.), but was recopied and studied up until Dynasty 20 (circa 1190–1075 B.C.E.), a period of more than nine hundred years. Another poetic genre was biography. Nobles and other literate people composed poems about themselves for carving in their tombs from the Old Kingdom through the New Kingdom or on statues in the Late Period. Though these poems contained many stereotyped phrases, there was art in combining them in new and interesting ways. The instruction was another verse form. These poems contained advice for proper conduct in the world. These works have known authors, an unusual situation for Egypt. Ptahhotep, Imhotep, Kaires, and others remained famous for hundreds of years because of their writings. Love poetry was written during the New Kingdom. These poems contained ideas as familiar as pop-song lyrics about secret meetings between lovers and parental disapproval of the couple. The Egyptians also wrote short stories in prose. Ancient authors wrote about folk motives, fantastic tales, and accounts of war.

Music and Dance. A complex musical culture thrived in ancient Egypt; musicians used percussion, wind, and stringed instruments in ensembles and in solo performances. Singers were also known. Though the majority of surviving lyrics are religious, painted and sculpted scenes in tombs depict musicians and singers at parties and in other private settings, such as in bedrooms. Some texts indicate that some music was antiphonal—one group sang a question and a second group sang the answer. Repetition in texts also suggests that a musical form with a recurring chorus also existed. Yet, there is no evidence for musical notation and nothing that allows scholars to reconstruct the sounds of ancient Egyptian music. Dance also was highly developed in Egypt. Many Egyptian words were used to describe different dances that are depicted in tombs, though current understanding of their meaning is imprecise. Both men and women danced; however, representations always showed them dancing

separately. Most dances were part of the funeral ritual, perhaps to scare away demons. But the Egyptians incorporated dance into other religious ceremonies, including festivals of gods and of the king. Dance in general was associated with renewal and rebirth.

Theater. The existence of drama in ancient Egypt remains controversial. Some evidence suggests that the reenactment of mythological stories was part of the ritual for Osiris in the Ptolemaic period. Some scholars have also interpreted an illustrated text on the wall of the Temple of Horus at Edfu as the script for a drama. This text also was composed in the Ptolemaic period. No evidence exists for drama or theater examining individual characters such as existed contemporaneously in Greece. No concrete evidence exists for drama in Egypt before Alexander the Great conquered it.

TOPICS IN THE ARTS

ARCHITECTURE: PRIVATE TOMBS

Parts of the Tomb. Tombs helped ensure rebirth into the next world through design and decoration. Egyptian tombs were divided between a chapel in a superstructure and the actual burial place in a substructure. These two parts were constant, though there were many changes and developments in tomb plans over the course of three thousand years.

Superstructure Types. The Egyptians used three different structures for tomb chapels throughout their history. The mastaba was a freestanding structure built of stone; the rock-cut tomb was cut into the side of a mountain; and the temple-tomb was similar in plan to a temple. Mastabas and rock-cut tombs were used in all periods. Yet, the mastaba is considered characteristic of the Early Dynastic Period and Old Kingdom. Rock-cut tombs became most common in the Middle and New Kingdoms. Temple-tombs were most popular in the Late Period, but examples are known from the New Kingdom.

Bench Tombs. Mastaba tombs derived their name from the Arabic word meaning "bench." These tombs resemble a series of benches arranged in rows around the pyramids of Giza. They are built of stone with some niches in the facade that act as offering places. The interiors of mastabas included both a chapel and storage chambers. The chapel had an offering place carved in stone to resemble a door. Since they are only models of doors that

False door and doorjambs from the tomb chapel of Ka(i)pura, Saqqara, late Dynasty 5 (circa 2500–2350 B.C.E.)–early Dynasty 6 (circa 2350–2170 B.C.E.)

Tomb of Nefertari, queen of Ramesses II, Valley of the Queens, Western Thebes, circa 1250 B.C.E.

cannot be opened, Egyptologists call them "false doors." The chapel also included an area that Egyptologists call the *serdab*, from the Arabic word meaning "basement." The *serdab* was an enclosed area that contained a statue of the deceased. The enclosure had one wall in front of the statue that contained two holes allowing the statue "to see" the offering presented to the deceased. The walls of the mastaba chapel were decorated in painted relief sculpture, which portrayed life on earth as a way of magically re-creating it in the next world. The scenes often depicted food production, including agriculture, herding, and hunting. The walls also included scenes of the manufacture of various objects found in the tomb, such as coffins and statues. All of these scenes are related to further decoration depicting the transport of food and objects into the tomb. Other relief sculptures showed the deceased and spouse receiving the food offerings, sometimes at the hands of an oldest son acting as a priest. Some scenes of the tomb owner and spouse shown together sitting on a bed are interpreted as having erotic content as a means of "rebirth" into the next world. Mastabas varied greatly in size depending on the status of the deceased. Most officials built chapels consisting of one or two rooms. The vizier Mereruka, who was married to the king's daughter, had thirty rooms in his mastaba.

Rock-Cut Tomb Chapels. Rock-cut tomb chapels were already built at the end of the Old Kingdom in Upper Egypt. They became popular among the local rulers in Middle Egypt during the First Intermediate Period and Middle Kingdom. They were also the commonest tomb chapel form in the Theban area during the New Kingdom and were carved directly into the mountains on the western side of the Nile. Originally, they had facades carved from the living rock. Typically in Dynasty 18, open courtyards fronted the tomb chapel. In Dynasty 19 they often had courtyards surrounded by a portico. Above the entrance to the chapel on the mountain was a small pyramid with a niche, which held a stela with a prayer to the sun god carved on it. The entrance corridor led to a wide rectangular room. In the middle of the far wall of this room began a hallway forming a long room. Together the interior rooms of the chapel took the form of an inverted *T*. A staircase that led down to the actual burial chamber could be located inside the chapel at various places or in the courtyard outside the entrance. In any case, it was hidden from view.

Decorative Zones. New Kingdom tombs comprised three decorative zones, each dedicated to a separate deity or aspect of the deceased's life. The upper level was dedicated to sun worship. It took the form of a small chapel, pyramid, or a statue of the deceased holding a stela with a prayer to the sun god Re inscribed on it. It was located just above the entrance to the tomb chapel. The middle zone was the long room of the tomb chapel itself, decorated to show the deceased's position in life. Paintings in this area depicted the deceased supervising work in his fields or in workshops that he owned. The lower level was located beneath the tomb chapel. It was decorated to represent the next world and sometimes included representations of the deity Osiris.

Sources:

Kathryn A. Bard, *From Farmers to Pharaohs: Mortuary Evidence for the Rise of Complex Society in Egypt* (Sheffield, U.K.: Sheffield Academic Press, 1994).

Aidan Dodson, *Egyptian Rock-Cut Tombs* (Princes Risborough, U.K.: Shire, 1991).

Sigrid Hodel-Hoenes, *Life and Death in Ancient Egypt: Scenes from Private Tombs in New Kingdom Thebes,* translated by David Warburton (Ithaca, N.Y.: Cornell University Press, 2000).

Frederike Kampp-Seyfried, "Overcoming Death—The Private Tombs of Thebes," in Regine Schulz and Matthias Seidel, *Egypt, The World of the Pharaohs* (Cologne: Könemann, 1998), pp. 249–263.

Philip J. Watson, *Egyptian Pyramids and Mastaba Tombs of the Old and Middle Kingdoms* (Princes Risborough, U.K.: Shire, 1987).

GRID SYSTEMS IN VISUAL ART

Evidence for Grids. Egyptian artists drew on a grid that allowed them to control the proportions of figures in two-dimensional relief sculpture and to line up the sides, back, and front of sculpture in the round. Grids are often preserved in unfinished relief sculpture or in paintings where a finished layer of paint has fallen off to reveal the underlying markings. These remains of grids have provided the data to study how Egyptian artists worked.

Guidelines and Grids. In the earliest examples from the Old Kingdom, Egyptian artists used a system of eight horizontal guidelines and one vertical line bisecting the figure through the ear rather than a complete grid. Grids marked eighteen horizontal units for each figure and also fourteen vertical lines spaced at the same distance as the horizontal ones. Thus, the grid formed a series of squares. Grids are first preserved from Dynasty 11 and continue for nearly two thousand years, into the Roman period.

Old Kingdom Guidelines. Old Kingdom guidelines allowed the artist to divide the figure in half and/or in thirds. A line at the lower border of the buttocks divided the figure in half. Lines at the elbow and knee divided the figure into thirds. Artists drew additional lines at the top of the head, at the junction of the hairline and forehead, at the point where the neck and shoulders meet, at the armpit, and at the calf. The baseline of the register marked the bottom of the figure's foot. The proportions that were maintained made the distance from the bottom of the foot to the neck and shoulder line equal to eight-ninths of the figure's height. The distance from the bottom of the foot to the armpit was four-fifths of the figure's total height. This series of proportions gave figures their uniformity and most likely aided artists in drawing a figure on a large scale.

Grids in the Middle Kingdom. Grids of squares probably developed from guidelines and were certainly in use by the

The Narmer Palette, an elaborate ceremonial tablet decorated with relief carvings, circa 3000 B.C.E. (Egyptian Museum, Cairo)

The first known example of relief sculpture in the Egyptian style (circa 3000 B.C.E.) was the Narmer Palette, commemorating this king's victory over ten enemies of Egypt. Though scholars disagree on the precise details, the narrative would have been clear to viewers contemporary with Narmer. The palette, which in Egypt was used to grind mineral pigments, also represented a turning point in artists' experiments with carving in relief on stone. It is the earliest known example of mature Egyptian style that is preserved. It exhibits all of the major characteristics of the Egyptian relief style that artists used for the remainder of Egyptian history, for more than three thousand years.

The composition of the Narmer Palette, the manner that different figures and objects are arranged in the picture, utilized baselines and registers. Baselines are horizontal lines at set intervals across the entire area that is decorated. The baselines create a frame for the action in each register. They give each figure a place to stand. The sequence of actions in a narrative is also clear and logical. The obverse (front) of the palette shows Narmer defeating his enemy in the central register. His sandal bearer accompanies him as he strikes the enemy on the head with a mace. The god Horus, depicted as a falcon, symbolically restrains the enemy as the god perches on the flowers that represented Lower Egypt. In the bottom register, defeated enemies either fled Narmer or lied prone. On the reverse, a bull representing Narmer attacks a city in the bottom register. In the center, two registers servants restrain an animal that is part leopard and part snake. A third register depicts Narmer inspecting the enemy dead, who lie with their severed heads between their legs.

The figures of Narmer and the other individuals were carved in the typical Egyptian style. The way a person or object is portrayed in a work of art was distinctive in ancient Egypt. The Egyptian style integrated more than one perspective into one representation of a figure. The viewer "sees" a figure from more than one angle, all at the same time. The head was carved in profile, as if the viewer saw it from the side. Yet, the eye was carved frontally, as if the figure and viewer were face to face. The shoulders were also carved frontally, but the torso, legs, and feet were shown in profile. It is physically impossible to see this combination of body parts in reality. However, the artist's aim was not to present visual reality but rather an idea of what a person is. Thus, Egyptian style is described as conceptual rather than visual.

The Narmer Palette also used a canon of proportions for the figures. The proportions of each figure were standardized so that every figure could be plotted on an imaginary grid. Actual grids are only known from Dynasty 11 and later. Yet, this figure has similar proportions. In a standing figure, such as Narmer found on the obverse, the grid would have contained eighteen equal units from the top of the head to the bottom of the foot. Particular body parts were then plotted on the grid in a regular way. Counting from the bottom of the representation, the knee fell on grid-line six, the lower buttocks on line nine, the small of the back on line eleven, the elbow on line twelve, and the junction of the neck and shoulders on line sixteen. The hairline was on line eighteen. The same ratio of body parts would have applied to Narmer's standard bearer. The individual units would have been smaller in this case, since the overall figure is about one-quarter the size of Narmer. This standardized ratio of body parts gave uniformity to Egyptian representations of people. Seated representations used a grid of fourteen squares.

Though individual bodies all had similar proportions, the scale of figures varied widely even within one register. On the reverse of the palette, in the second register, Narmer was portrayed double the size of his sandal bearer and prime minister. The standard bearers are half the size of the sandal bearer and prime minister. The scale of any one person was based on their importance in society rather than their actual size. This method of depicting figures is called hieratic scale.

The Narmer Palette uses standard iconography for the king for the first time. On the obverse the king wears the cone-shaped White Crown of Upper Egypt. He also wears a bull's tail and a false beard that were associated only with the king. On the reverse the king wears a similar costume, but this time with the Red Crown of Lower Egypt. Many commentators have associated the wearing of each crown on the palette with the unification of Egypt about 3000 B.C.E.

Narmer's name appears in hieroglyphic writing at the top of both sides of the palette. It is also written in front of his face on the reverse. Hieroglyphic labels also identify the sandal bearer and the prime minister. These labels personalize these images, which otherwise could represent any king, prime minister, or sandal bearer. Hieroglyphic labels were a standard feature of Egyptian art.

The Narmer Palette was a turning point in Egyptian art. It marks not only the culmination of the tradition of carving stone palettes, but also the beginning of the typical Egyptian style in two-dimensional art.

Source: Cyril Aldred, *Egyptian Art* (New York: Oxford University Press, 1985), pp. 33–36.

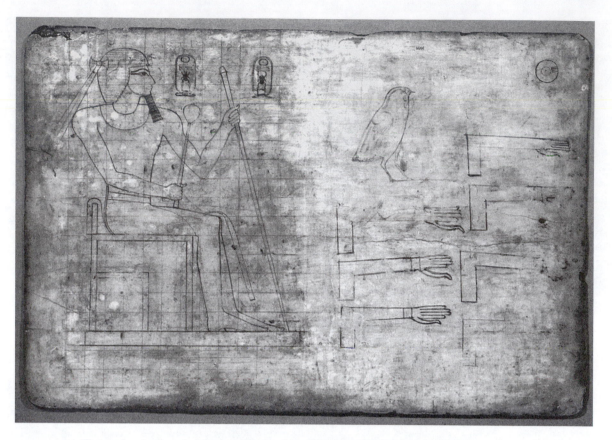

Theban drawing board with an artist's sketches of Thutmose III; pigment and plaster on wood, New Kingdom, circa 1539–1075 B.C.E. (British Museum, London)

Middle Kingdom. Eighteen squares separated the hairline from the bottom of the foot in the Middle Kingdom grid. Various body parts also fell on regular grid lines. For example, the meeting point of the neck and shoulders was at horizontal sixteen, the elbow at horizontal nine, the knee at horizontal six, and the calf line at horizontal three. The shoulders of males were roughly six squares wide, similar in proportion to Old Kingdom figures. Females were more slender, with shoulders between four and five squares wide.

Grids in the New Kingdom. The proportions of figures changed in mid Dynasty 18, becoming more elongated. The small of the back rose from grid-line eleven to grid-line twelve, making the leg longer in proportion to the body. At the same time, the width of the shoulders was reduced from six squares to five squares. This reduction also made the figure more elongated and graceful in the New Kingdom than it was previously.

Late Period Grid. Egyptian artists of the first millennium B.C.E. used a grid with twenty-one horizontal lines rather than the eighteen used previously. Though the exact time when the transition to twenty-one squares was made is not known, artists of Dynasty 25 were surely using this square grid to lay out relief sculpture. The new grid squares were thus five-sixths of the old grid squares. In the new system the following correspondences were made.

Line twenty-one passed through the root of the nose and upper eyelid.

Line twenty passed through the mouth.

Line nineteen passed through the junction of the neck and shoulders.

Line thirteen passed through the small of the back.

Line eleven passed near the lower buttocks.

Line seven passed through the top of the knee.

Line zero (baseline) passed through the sole of the foot.

The result of these changes was a slight alteration in the proportions of the figure. The knees, small of the back, and buttocks are all lower in figures drawn on Late Period grids than in Middle and New Kingdom grids. Thus, the torso and upper leg appear longer in proportion to the body as a whole.

Why the Change? The meaning of this change is not clear. Erik Iverson has suggested that the grid changed to accommodate a new measuring system that used a shorter unit of measurement. Gay Robins has convincingly argued that the Late Period system used the same measuring system but regularized the grid to make calculations easier. In the early system the arm length was five grid squares. This distance was the hypothetical value of one cubit, which was divided into six palms. A five-square arm thus equaled grid squares of one and one-fifth palms wide and long. The new Late Period grid square used an arm length that was six squares long. In the Late Period grid system each square was equal in measurement to one palm. All calculations would be simpler using grid squares equivalent to one palm rather than equivalent to one and one-fifth palms. The grid was an ingenious and simple way to maintain proper proportions for figures, no matter how large or small they were reproduced.

Sources:

Erik Iverson, "The Canonical Tradition," in *The Legacy of Egypt,* edited by J. R. Harris (Oxford: Clarendon Press, 1971), pp. 55–82.

Jaromir Malek, *Egyptian Art* (London: Phaidon Press, 1999).

Gay Robins, *Proportion and Style in Ancient Egyptian Art* (Austin: University of Texas Press, 1994).

LOVE POEMS

Sources. Egyptian love poems provide a rare view of human feelings in the ancient world. Four collections of love poems survive from ancient Egypt. They are known as Papyrus Chester Beatty I and Papyrus Harris 500 in the British Museum in London, Papyrus Turin 1966 in the Egyptian Museum in Turin, Italy, and Cairo Ostracon 2518 in the Egyptian Museum in Cairo, Egypt. They all date to Dynasty 19 (1292–1190 B.C.E.) but might have been composed somewhat earlier.

Poetic Structure. Egyptian poetry did not have end rhyme or meter as does most English poetry written before the twentieth century. Instead, Egyptian poets organized verses into structures called couplets, triplets, and quatrains. A couplet has two related phrases, a triplet has three related phrases, and quatrains have four related phrases. The relationship between and among these phrases is a single thought expressed in variations either two, three, or four times. For example, a poem in Papyrus Chester Beatty I begins, "My love is one and only, without peer, / lovely above all Egypt's lovely girls." Here the poet expresses the same thought in two ways. The relationship might also use parallel grammatical structures in a poetic fashion. Presumably there was a definite pause after each couplet, triplet, or quatrain when the poem was recited.

Themes. The themes of Egyptian love poetry would be familiar to lovers of all time periods. They describe the beloved's beauty, tricks used by both sexes to gain the attention of a desired lover, a plea to Hathor—goddess of love—to return a lost love, and the opposition of parents to a desired match.

Sources:

John L. Foster, ed., *Echoes of Egyptian Voices: An Anthology of Ancient Egyptian Poetry* (Norman: University of Oklahoma Press, 1992).

Foster, ed., *Love Songs of the New Kingdom* (New York: Scribners, 1974).

Barbara Hughes Fowler, *Love Lyrics of Ancient Egypt* (Chapel Hill: University of North Carolina Press, 1994).

Raymond A. McCoy, *The Golden Goddess: Ancient Egyptian Love Lyrics,* translated by McCoy (Menomonie, Wis.: Enchiridion Publications, 1972).

MUSICAL INSTRUMENTS

Variety of Instruments. The Egyptians used percussion, wind, and stringed instruments. Some of these instruments were imported from the Near East, while others were indigenous to Egypt. The simplest percussion instrument was two hands clapping. The Egyptians depicted singers clapping in Old Kingdom (circa 2675–2130 B.C.E.) tomb scenes, but the sound could be amplified by use of instruments they called "Two Hands," which were made from two pieces of curving ivory or bone with the image of Hathor or of hands carved at their ends. A smaller version of these instruments resembles castanets. A related instrument is the *menat,* which was also associated with the goddess Hathor. This instrument was worn around the neck like jewelry. All these instruments were in use during the Old Kingdom and later.

Percussion. Drums resembled a variety of shapes including barrels, goblets, and circles. From the Middle Kingdom (circa 1980–1630 B.C.E.) through the New Kingdom (circa 1539–1075 B.C.E.), drums were small enough to be held with one hand and beaten with the other. These smaller drums were played by women. The Egyptians did not use drumsticks. In the Late Period (664–332 B.C.E.) a larger barrel drum was worn with a strap around the neck and was played by a man. The drummer beat on both ends with his hands. These drums were all made by stretching skin across a wooden frame. The circular drum was probably introduced from Syria-Palestine during Dynasty 13 (circa 1759–after 1630 B.C.E.).

Sistra. The sistrum (plural "sistra") is an instrument resembling a rattle. Egyptian sistra include metal disks, pierced in the middle, which are strung on a metal bar that is suspended on another loop of metal. The loop is mounted on a wooden handle often decorated with Hathor's face. Other sistra used a rectangular frame shaped like a shrine in a temple. Sistra were commonly used in religious ceremonies and were played by women.

Wind Instruments. Egyptians played a variety of wind instruments, including flutes, parallel double pipes, and divergent double pipes. The flute was held to the side of the body, while the two kinds of pipes were held in front of the body. The parallel double pipes seem to have been bound together with string, while the divergent double pipes form a V-shape with the point at the mouth. Each half was played with one hand. These wind instruments all had a slightly different mouthpiece. The parallel pipes had a single vibrating element, so it is sometimes called a clarinet. The divergent pipes had a double vibrating element, similar to an oboe. Metal trumpets were used by the military.

Stringed Instruments. Stringed instruments included harps, lyres, and lutes. The shape of the harp was uniquely Egyptian, but lyres and lutes probably were based on Near Eastern types. In the arched harp the sound box and neck form a continuous curve. The arched harp was most popular during the Old and Middle Kingdoms. It had fewer than ten strings and thus had a limited range of sounds. In the angular harp the sound box and neck are at right angles to one another. Angular harps were known in Mesopotamia by 1900 B.C.E. but did not become common in Egypt until almost four hundred years later. Angular harps had more strings than arched harps. They introduced a much broader range of sound than the older arched harp. Thin, thick, and giant lyres were known throughout the Near East. Egyptian lyres are part of a broader, international

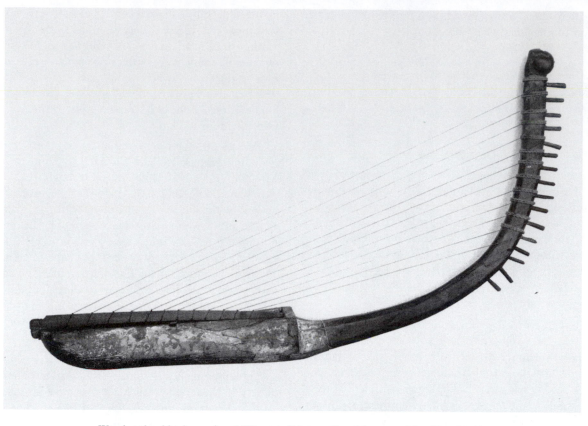

Wooden shoulder harp, circa 1400 B.C.E. (Metropolitan Museum of Art, New York)

musical culture. In the New Kingdom, the same name was used for the thick lyre both in the Near East and in Egypt (*kinnarum*). Giant lyre players, depicted in Egyptian scenes of the Amarna period, wore typical Canaanite dress. Lutes were invented in Mesopotamia in circa 1900 B.C.E. and quickly spread to Egypt. They were played both by men and women in ensembles or alone.

Sources:

Bo Lawergren, "Music," in *Oxford Encyclopedia of Ancient Egypt*, edited by Donald B. Redford (New York & Oxford: Oxford University Press, 2001), pp. 450–454.

Lise Manniche, *Music and Musicians in Ancient Egypt* (London: British Museum Press, 1991).

STANDING SCULPTURE: KING MENKAURE AND QUEEN KHA-MERER-NEBU II

Masterpiece. Carved circa 2532–2510 B.C.E., the Standing Sculpture of King Menkaure and Queen Kha-merer-nebu II is both a masterpiece of Egyptian sculpture and an illustration of the Egyptian conventions for representing a king and queen. The sculpture is just under life-size, 54¾ inches tall. The sculptor used graywacke, a hard gray stone that the Egyptians prized. Archaeologist George Reisner discovered the statue in 1910 in the valley temple of this king's pyramid at Giza.

Conventions. This sculpture clearly illustrates the main conventions of Egyptian royal sculpture. The sculptor placed Menkaure on the viewer's left and the queen on the right. The ancient viewer would have recognized immediately that Menkaure was the more important fig-

ure of this pair. The viewer's left is always the place of honor in Egyptian representations. The king and queen were also conventionally dressed to communicate their rank in Egyptian society.

Standard Royal Dress. Menkaure wears the *nemes*, a headdress worn only by the king. This headdress was made from cloth, folded to form triangular shapes framing the king's face. Two lappets hung from the triangles over the king's chest. The back of the cloth was twisted around a braid of hair. Though the headdress covered most of the king's hair and head, his sideburns and ears were visible. In examples where the artist used color, the *nemes* is striped blue and gold. The king also wears a rectangular false beard, which was made of leather and was attached by straps that would have tied under the *nemes*. This beard, worn only by the king, contrasts with the longer beard that ended in an upward twist and was worn only by the god Osiris. The king's chest is bare. He wears a distinctive kilt called the *shendjet*, worn only by kings. The kilt features a belt and a flap that was placed centrally between his legs. The king holds a cylinder in each hand, usually identified as a document case, which held the deed to Egypt thought to be in the king's possession. This statue also shows some conventions of representing the male figure used for both nobles and kings. The king strides forward on his left leg, a pose typical for all standing, male Egyptian statues. Traces of red paint on the king's ears, face, and neck show that the skin was originally painted red ocher. This coloration was the conven-

Cairo Ostracon 2518

A man speaks of his love:

If I could just be the washerman

doing her laundry for one month only,

I would be faithful to pick up the bundles,

Sturdy to beat clean the heavy linens,

But gentle to touch those finespun things

Lying closest the body I love.

I would rinse with pure water the perfumes

That linger still in her tunics,

And I'd dry my own flesh with the towels

She yesterday held to her face.

The touch of her clothes, their textures,

Her softness in them . . .

Thank god for the body,

Its youthful vigor!

Papyrus Chester Beatty I

A woman speaks of her intended boyfriend:

I just chanced to be happening by

in the neighborhood where he lives;

His door, as I hoped, was open—

And I spied on my secret love.

How tall he stood by his mother,

Brothers and sisters little about him;

Love steals the heart of a poor thing like me

Pointing her toes down his street.

And how gentle my young love looked

(there's none like him),

Character spotless they say . . .

Out of the edge of my eye

I caught him look at me as I passed.

Alone by myself at last,

I could almost cry with delight!

Now just a word with you, love,

That's what I've wanted since I first saw you.

If only Mother knew of my longing

(and let it occur to her soon)—

O Golden Lady, descend for me,

Plant him square in her heart!

Then I'd run to my love, kiss him hard

Right in front of his crew.

I'd drip no tears of shame or shyness

Just because people were there,

But proud I'd be at their taking it in

(Let them drown their eyes in my loving you)

If you only acknowledge you know me.

(Oh, tell all Egypt you love me!)

Then I'd make solemn announcement:

Every day holy to Hathor!

And we two, love, would worship together,

Kneel, a matched pair, to the Goddess.

Oh, how my heart pounds (try to be circumspect!)

Eager to get myself out!

Let me drink in the shape of my love

Tall in the shuddering night!

Sources: "Cairo Ostracon 2518," in *Love Songs of the New Kingdom*, translated by John L. Foster (New York: Scribners, 1974), p. 30.

"Papyrus Chester Beatty I," in *Love Songs of the New Kingdom*, translated by Foster (New York: Scribners, 1974), pp. 56–57.

tional male skin color in statuary, probably associating the deceased king or nobleman with the sun god Re.

Conventions for Female Sculpture. The statue of Queen Kha-merer-nebu II also exhibits the conventions for presenting women in Egyptian sculpture. Unlike kings, queens did not have their own conventions separate from other noblewomen. The queen's wig is divided into three hanks, two draped over her shoulders and one flowing down her back. There is a central part. The queen's natural hair is visible on her forehead and at the sideburns, another common convention. The queen wears a long, formfitting dress. The fabric is stretched so tightly that it reveals her breasts, navel, pubic triangle, and knees. Yet, the length is quite modest, with a hem visible just above the ankles. The queen's arms are arranged conventionally, with one arm passing across the back of the king and the hand appearing at his waist. The queen's other hand passes across her own abdomen and rests on his arm. This pose indicated the queen's dependence on the king for her position in society. In pair statues that show men who were dependent upon their wives for their status, the men embrace the women.

Style in Sculpture. The conventions of Egyptian art make it easy to stress the similarity of sculptures to each other. Yet, details of the style of this sculpture make it possible to identify Menkaure. All of his sculptures show distinctive facial features. His face has full cheeks and his eyes

Graywacke statue of King Menkaure and Queen Kha-merer-nebu II, Dynasty 4, circa 2625–2500 B.C.E.
(Museum of Fine Arts Expedition, Harvard University)

comes him back to Egypt with full honors. On Sinuhe's return, Senwosret I arranges for Sinuhe's burial in Egypt. The final verses describe Sinuhe's tomb and his last contented days in Egypt as he waits for death.

Themes. John L. Foster has analyzed Sinuhe's development from his loss of status when he fled from Egypt to his eventual restoration to his rightful place in Egyptian society. Foster has demonstrated that the real interest of the story for modern readers is in Sinuhe's personal development. When Sinuhe heard that Amenemhet was dead and that Senwosret had returned to the capital to claim the throne, Sinuhe panicked. He had reason to believe that there would be political turmoil and that his close relationship to Queen Neferu would doom him if Senwosret were not proclaimed legitimate king. He was so ill prepared for the trip to Syria-Palestine that he nearly starved and died of thirst while traveling through the desert. A bedouin chief, a man whom Sinuhe would never have recognized as an equal in his earlier life, saved him. Sinuhe then wandered northward to Byblos (in modern Lebanon) and finally settled in Upper Retenu (modern Syria). Here

---

NATIONAL EPIC

The *Story of Sinuhe* is the great epic poem of ancient Egypt. Here the author describes Sinuhe's panic attack and escape from Egypt after Amenemhet I's assassination.

The hereditary noble, mayor,

Seal-bearer of the goddess of Lower Egypt, Sole Friend,

Provincial governor,

Viceroy in the lands of the Asiatics,

Trusted adviser to the king, whom he esteems,

The courtier, Sinuhe, who speaks:

I was a follower who followed his lord,

A servant in the royal harem

[Of] the hereditary noblewoman, greatly esteemed,

The royal wife of Senwosret

In union with the Throne,

Royal daughter of Amenemhet

In the city of Qa-nefer, Neferu,

Possessor of blessedness.

Regnal Year Thirty,

Third month of the inundation, day seven:

The god mounts up toward his horizon,

King of Upper and Lower Egypt, Sehetepibre,

That he might fly up to heaven, one joined with the sun-disk,

The divine flesh mingling with the One who made him.

The royal city is silent, hearts are mourning,

The great double gates are sealed,

Attendants [sitting] with head on knee,

The nobles in grief.

Now then, his Majesty had passed on,

With the army over in the land of the Libyans,

His eldest son in command thereof,

The good god, Senwosret.

Now, he was sent to strike the foreign regions

In order to destroy those among the Tchehenu-Libyans.

Now, he was returning with what he had taken—

Those captured alive of the Tchehenu

And all sorts of cattle without end.

The Friends of the Palace,

They sent word to the western border

In order to cause that the king's son know

The events which had occurred in the audience chamber.

The messengers discovered him upon the road

Once they had reached him at time of darkness.

Not a moment at all did he wait;

The Falcon, he flew with his followers

Without causing that his army know it.

Not, [there was] sent word to the royal princes,

Who were accompanying him on this expedition

And someone summoned one of the—

While I, indeed, I was standing there!

I heard his voice as he spoke evil,

While I was on a distant rise [of ground].

Distraught was my heart, paralyzed my arms,

A shuddering fell upon each of my limbs.

I removed myself by leaping away

In order to search out for myself a place of hiding;

. . . I made a travelling upstream—

I did not intend to approach this Residence—

I expected that turmoil would occur,

Nor did I think to live on after this one—

This splendid god.

Source: John L. Foster, *Thought Couplets in the Tale of Sinuhe* (Frankfurt, Germany & New York: Peter Lang, 1993), pp. 39–41.

bulge slightly. The chin is knobby, while the nose is bulbous. His wife resembles him, probably because the king's face in any reign became the ideal of beauty. In almost every period everyone seems to resemble the reigning king.

Lack of Motion. Egyptian sculptors purposely avoided portraying motion. Unlike ancient Greek sculptors, Egyptian artists aimed for a timelessness that excluded the transience of motion. Thus, even though Menkaure and Kha-merer-nebu II were portrayed walking, the sculptor did not attempt to depict the weight shift in the hips and the stretch of the muscles that would create the illusion that the statue could move. This attitude toward depicting motion is a fundamental difference between ancient Egyptian and Greek art.

Structural Supports. Egyptian sculptors relied on back pillars and the avoidance of negative space to support their sculptures. The back pillar in this case forms a slab that reaches to the shoulders of the figures. In statues of individuals, enough of the block of the stone was removed so that the back pillar would cover only the spine of the figure. Here the entire back of the figures disappears into the remaining block. The negative space, the area between the arms and torso or between the legs, was not carved.

Inscription. This sculpture lacks the inscription that is usually found on the base and on the back pillar. In this case, Menkaure can be identified from his facial features and the fact that the statue was found in a temple built by Menkaure. The absence of an inscription indicates that the statue was not completed. Finished sculpture almost always included a hieroglyphic inscription that identified the subject.

Sources:

Kazimierz Michalowski, *Great Sculpture of Ancient Egypt,* translated by Enid Kirchberger (New York: Reynal, 1978).

Edna R. Russmann, *Egyptian Sculpture: Cairo and Luxor* (Austin: University of Texas Press, 1989), pp. 7–8.

Christiane Ziegler, "King Menkaure and a Queen," in *Egyptian Art in the Age of the Pyramids* (New York: Metropolitan Museum of Art, 1999), pp. 269–271.

STORY OF SINUHE

Epic Tale. The *Story of Sinuhe,* an epic poem that was popular for more than eight hundred years (Dynasties 12 to 20, circa 1909–1074 B.C.E.), was composed between circa 1909 and 1875 B.C.E. It narrates the adventures of a nobleman who served Queen Neferu, daughter of Amenemhet I (1938–1909 B.C.E.) and wife of Senwosret I (1919–1875 B.C.E.). When the story opens, Sinuhe is on a military campaign in Libya with Senwosret I. News of Amenemhet I's assassination reaches the army and Sinuhe panicks. He fears that Egypt will fall into turmoil and that his own life will be threatened. Thus, he leaves the army camp and travels across Egypt to the eastern border. After crossing into Syria-Palestine, Sinuhe travels to different countries and then settles with a bedouin named Amunenshi, who gives Sinuhe his daughter in marriage and land in a place called Yaa. Sinuhe prospers and has children, as well as more adventures, and reaches the end of life. He determines then that he wants to return to Egypt for burial. Sinuhe sends a letter to the king, and the benevolent Senwosret I wel-

Concluding stanzas of *The Tale of Sinuhe,* on limestone ostracon, Dynasty 19, circa 1292–1190 B.C.E. (British Museum, London)

he met a local ruler, Amunenshi, who recognized Sinuhe as an Egyptian nobleman. When asked why he had traveled away from Egypt, Sinuhe claimed ignorance of his own reasons. He told Amunenshi that it was the act of a god. Amunenshi then offered him land and his eldest daughter as a wife. From this point onward Sinuhe prospered. He raised a family and successfully led Amunenshi's army against other tribes. The real turning point in Sinuhe's life came when an unnamed "hero" challenged him to single combat. Though Sinuhe was smaller, he successfully overcame the hero through physical courage. This scene witnessed Sinuhe's transformation from the coward who abandoned Senwosret to an effective agent himself. Sinuhe recognized the change himself in the poem he recited after his victory over the hero.

A fugitive flees from his neighborhood;

But my fame will be in the Residence.

One who should guard creeps off in hunger;

But I, I give bread to my neighbor.

A man leaves his own land in nakedness;

I am one bright in fine linen.

A man runs (himself) for lack of his messenger;

I am one rich in servants.

Good is my home, and wide my domain,

But what I remember is in the palace.

(Lines 321–330, translated by John L. Foster, p. 116)

Here Sinuhe remembered the story of his life and contrasted his cowardly escape from Egypt with his current situation as a conqueror. Sinuhe now attempted to return to Egypt. He wrote to the king asking for forgiveness and for permission to return to Egypt and reestablish his relationship with the king, queen, and royal children. Most of all, he hoped to be buried in Egypt in a nobleman's tomb. The king's reply asked Sinuhe to return and be restored to his rightful place. Most commentators have seen the moment of the king forgiving Sinuhe as the central purpose of the story. As propaganda, the story established Senwosret's goodness and loyalty to those who remained loyal to him. But Foster's analysis, which stresses Sinuhe's development, demonstrates that this epic was also a close look at individual psychology. The *Story of Sinuhe* is political propaganda raised to the level of art and depicts Sinuhe's development starting with his removal from his own society to full restoration as a nobleman. Sinuhe moved from disgrace, to renewal, to forgiveness. In the course of this development he also passed from ignorance of his own motives to self-awareness and acknowledgment of his own responsibilities. Not only did he learn to take responsibility for his actions but he also pondered man's proper relationship to the temporal powers of the world.

Sources:
John L. Foster, "The Tale of Sinuhe as Literature," in *Thought Couplets in the Tale of Sinuhe* (Frankfurt, Germany & New York: Peter Lang, 1993), pp. 112–129.

William Kelly Simpson, *The Literature of Ancient Egypt: An Anthology of Stories, Instructions, and Poetry*, translations by R. O. Faulkner, Edward F. Wente Jr., and William Kelly Simpson (New Haven: Yale University Press, 1972).

STORIES AND TALES

Sources. From the Middle Kingdom through the New Kingdom the Egyptians wrote prose stories and tales. There are approximately eleven stories and tales in prose preserved from ancient Egyptian literature. Nearly all of these works survived in only one manuscript copy. These copies seem to have been privately owned rather than part of an institutional library. Thus, it is difficult to determine how widely these texts were read. However, some manuscripts dating to the New Kingdom clearly represent stories composed in the Middle Kingdom. This fact suggests a history of transmission over a long time period.

Anonymous Authors. The authors of these texts are never named. Though often stories are told in the first person, in some cases the "I" of the story is never given a name. For example, the first-person narrator of the story known as *The Shipwrecked Sailor* (Papyrus Hermitage 1115, St. Petersburg, Russia) has no name. In most cases even the person who copied the manuscript is unknown. Only *The Shipwrecked Sailor* has a concluding note, called a colophon, which claims that the scribe Amenyaa, son of Ameny, copied the story exactly from an original manuscript.

Differences. There is a marked difference between the stories told in the Middle and New Kingdoms. Middle Kingdom stories resemble tomb autobiographies. They are narrated in the first person and tend toward complexity. Sometimes they alternate prose and verse. The stories dating to the New Kingdom use more-casual and popular language and are usually narrated in the third person. There is more obvious humor in New Kingdom stories, at least humor seems to a modern reader to be intended. Many third-person stories from the New Kingdom are thought to derive from folktales and/or oral tradition.

Sources:
R. B. Parkinson, *Voices from Ancient Egypt: An Anthology of Middle Kingdom Writings* (Norman: University of Oklahoma Press, 1991), pp. 8–30.

William Kelly Simpson, *The Literature of Ancient Egypt: An Anthology of Stories, Instructions, and Poetry*, translations by R. O. Faulkner, Edward F. Wente Jr., and William Kelly Simpson (New Haven: Yale University Press, 1972).

TEMPLE PLAN: NEW KINGDOM

Temples. Although the primary Egyptian architectural form was the temple, no two Egyptian temples are exactly alike. The long history of building temples in Egypt stretches from the earliest days of Dynasty 0 (circa 3100–3000 B.C.E.) until Roman rule in Egypt nearly four thousand years later. Yet, most temples had common elements.

Function of Temples. Temples were important in the social, economic, and political structure of ancient Egypt. Yet, the primary religious purpose of temples was to delineate a sacred space where humans could contact the powers of the "other" world. These powers included the gods and humans who had become gods by dying and moving to the unseen world. Humans could most easily access these divine powers through statues. The main purpose of the temple, then, was to provide a home

Aerial view of the ruins of the New Kingdom temple complex at Karnak (circa 1539–1075 B.C.E.)

for a statue of the god, a deceased king, or even a deceased nobleman, which required a home that resembled those of living noblemen and kings. These homes are called temples.

Temenos. Temples were located inside surrounding walls called *temenos,* which was the first barrier between the sacred and the profane. It was built of brick arranged in courses that resembled the hieroglyphic sign for water. The wall stood both for and against the watery chaos that the Egyptians believed existed at the beginning of creation. Inside the wall, creation was perfected in the form of the temple.

Names of Parts. Inside the *temenos* the main temple building usually included five parts: the *pylon,* courtyard, hypostyle hall, *pronaos,* and *naos.* Only one entrance allowed access to the building. Thus, the visitor's route was controlled by the architecture, passing from light to darkness and toward increasingly sacred space as he or she came closer to the statue of the god.

Pylon. The entrance consisted of two tall towers called *pylons,* which were decorated on the exterior with images of the king destroying the enemies of Egypt. This decoration continued the overall decorative theme first stated in the *temenos.* The temple was a place where order triumphed over chaos, just as Egypt itself was a place where order reigned. The *pylons* each had two niches for flagpoles. The god had his or her own banner that would have flown from these flagpoles.

Courtyard. After the visitor entered between the pylons he or she would arrive in a central courtyard sur-

rounded by a colonnade. The central court was open to the bright Egyptian sun, while the colonnade would provide shelter during processions made by the god's statue. Often there were stations or chapels in the courtyard where parts of ceremonies were performed. This area was most likely open to some members of the public. It probably was the place where the distribution of rations was sometimes made. Nobles also placed statues of themselves here, which would allow the nobles to continue to participate in ceremonies after their deaths.

Hypostyle Hall. Directly opposite the *pylons* was the entrance to the third element in the temple, the hypostyle hall. Entering this structure, the visitor was now in a dark and shadowy room filled with columns, which were decorated to resemble papyrus and lotus plants. The bases of the columns stood on a floor that represented the waters of the marsh. The walls of this room also were decorated with marsh scenes. Above these scenes were representations of ritual offerings to the god of the temple. Decoration of the room made reference to the creation of the world when the water was transformed to a marsh. The sacrifices that kings made helped the gods maintain order against the forces of the water. This room was the beginning of the areas accessible only to the priesthood. Statues of gods and kings were also located in the hypostyle hall where they participated in the ritual.

Sacred Space. The *pronaos* and *naos* were the most sacred and darkest parts of the temple. The *pronaos* served as an antechamber to the *naos.* Here, priests gath-

Propylon gateway of the Khonsu temple, opening to the Avenue of Rams; construction begun by Ramesses III, circa 1187–1156 B.C.E.

ered to perform rituals that would take place in the *naos*, where the statue of the god was located. The statue was ritually awakened, washed, dressed, and fed before being taken out for processions. The decorative scheme in these rooms concerned the rituals that took place here.

Sources:
Dieter Arnold, *Temples of the Last Pharaohs* (New York: Oxford University Press, 1999).

Byron E. Shafer, ed., *Temples of Ancient Egypt* (Ithaca, N.Y.: Cornell University Press, 1997).

Richard H. Wilkinson, *The Complete Temples of Ancient Egypt* (New York: Thames & Hudson, 2000).

TJETJI AND AUTOBIOGRAPHY

Art and Life. Tjetji's autobiography provides a good example of this literary form in the First Intermediate Period (circa 2130–1980 B.C.E.) and the integration of words and pictures in Egyptian art. It reflects traditions of the late Old Kingdom and anticipates the best of Dynasty 11. It is carved on a stela that is divided into three unequal fields. At the top is a fourteen-line, horizontal, autobiographical inscription reading right to left. The lower left portion depicts Tjetji facing right, in high raised relief, with two members of his staff; a small figure presents offerings before him. The lower right field is an elaborate, five-line, vertical offering-prayer listing wishes for the afterlife.

Revived Tradition. Tjetji's autobiography revives an Old Kingdom literary tradition nearly two hundred years after its disappearance. In Tjetji's era, autobiographies typically praised nomarchs' efforts on behalf of their nomes. But Tjetji, a court official, returns to an Old Kingdom theme: the ideal of service to the king. He makes constant reference to his success at carrying out the king's wishes. This ideal would continue to dominate subsequent autobiographies written during the Middle Kingdom. Tjetji recounts his service as Overseer of the Seal Bearers of the King to Wahankh Intef II (2102–2063 B.C.E.) and Nakht-neb-tep-nefer Intef III (2063–2055 B.C.E.), establishing for historians the order of these kings. Tjetji also describes the borders of the Theban kingdom just before the reunification of Egypt under Nebhepetre Mentuhotep II (2008–1957 B.C.E.). These borders stretch from Elephantine Island in the south to Abydos in the north. The text is limited in length by the size of the stela, unlike later, extended autobiographies that were carved on tomb walls. Yet, Tjetji's use of the Egyptian language is striking and eloquent. Ronald J. Leprohon, in a conference paper, has recently suggested that this elaborate language, structured in tight grammatical patterns, derives from the deceased's own efforts to attain the ancient Egyptian ideal of "perfect speech."

Unusual Hieroglyphs. Many commentators have noted the unusual shapes of some common hieroglyphs in this inscription. The *ms*-sign in line one used to write the word "to give birth, to create," for example, could be read as an elaborate *ankh*-sign used to write the word "to live." The scribe has created a visual pun that the ancient reader would surely have noticed.

Details. The relief, like the text above it, relates to the end of the Old Kingdom and anticipates the mature Theban style of Dynasty 11. The large figure of Tjetji and the subsidiary figures of his Seal Bearer, Magegi, and his Follower, Tjeru, exhibit the features of this style. Cyril Aldred has identified the sharp ridge defining the edge of the lips, the accentuation of the muscles at the base of the nose, and the long ear lobes as typical of both late Dynasty 6 and mature Dynasty 11 relief styles. Edna R. Russmann has identified these same characteristics as elements of the Old Kingdom "second style," ancestor of the Theban style that is recognizable here. The Theban style also included high raised relief, deep sunk relief, and incised details. Gay Robins has pointed out the typically narrow shoulders, high small of the back, and lack of musculature in the male figures. Details of Tjetji's face are also typical of the Theban style. The eye is large, outlined by a flat band representing eye paint, and extended to form a cosmetic line that widens at its outer end; the inner corner of the eye dips sharply downward; and its eyebrow appears flat rather than following the curve of the eye. The nose is broad, while the lips are thick and protruding. The lines of the lips end at a vertical line, rep-

Limestone inscription containing the biographical text of Tjetji, Dynasty 11, circa 2081–1938 B.C.E. (British Museum, London)

resenting the cheek, rather than meeting in a point. The layout and contents of the offerings spread before Tjetji are also typical of this period.

Other Differences. The vertical columns of the offering prayer and afterlife wishes, written from right to left, lead the eye toward the main figure. Previously the offering prayer was included in the introduction to the autobiography. Tjetji's stela illustrates the changed position of the prayer that will continue into the Middle Kingdom.

High Standards and Unification. Tjetji's stela clearly demonstrates the high standards of language and relief carving that had been established in Thebes before politi-cal unification with Lower Egypt. These standards and their connection to the previous period of political unity perhaps point toward conscious political plans for reunifying the country during early Dynasty 11.

Sources:

Cyril Aldred, "Some Royal Portraits of the Middle Kingdom in Ancient Egypt," *Ancient Egypt in the Metropolitan Museum Journal*, volumes I–II (New York: Metropolitan Museum of Art, 1977), p. 5.

Miriam Lichtheim, *Ancient Egyptian Autobiographies Chiefly of the Middle Kingdom: A Study and an Anthology* (Freiburg & Göttingen: Vandenhoeck & Ruprecht, 1988), pp. 39.

Edna R. Russmann, "A Second Style in Egyptian Art of the Old Kingdom," *Mitteilungen des Deutschen Archäologischen Instituts Abteilung Kairo*, 51 (1995): 278.

SIGNIFICANT PEOPLE

BEK

FLOURISHED CIRCA 1353-1336 B.C.E.
SCULPTOR

Rock Carvers. Much of the art in ancient Egypt was executed by men who were considered simple artisans, and therefore their names often disappear from the historical records. A few, however, achieved high favor and are known largely from inscriptions in their tombs–such as the sculptors Ipuki and Nebamen (both flourishing circa 1425 B.C.E.), who worked on royal projects and were buried together at Thebes near Deir el Bahri. One sculptor for whom more information is known is Bek, the Chief Sculptor for Amenhotep IV (Akhenaten) (circa 1353–1336 B.C.E.), who helped transform Egyptian art to what has been called a more "realistic" style.

Artistic Heritage. Bek was the son of Men, a carver for Amenhotep III (circa 1390–1353 B.C.E.), and Roy of Heliopolis. Men had created a series of statues of his king from the granite quarries of Red Mountain. In his father's honor, Bek later carved a graffito (cliff relief) near Aswan, called the *Equipose of Two Masters of Works and Chief Sculptors*. In one of two panels Men is seen paying homage to Amenhotep III. Bek was probably apprenticed to learn his craft from his father, although he later gave credit for his artistic achievements to his employer. On Bek's own quartzite funerary stela he notes that he was only an "apprentice whom His Majesty taught." This inscription probably was Bek's way of saying that he followed well the instructions of his king, not that the king personally taught him how to carve. Bek was married to Taheret, appears to have adopted the religion of Akhenaten, and may have carved the small statue located in his tomb that depicts the couple.

Royal Supervisor. Bek served during a period of religious and social unrest. Once he became king, Akhenaten broke from past religious practice, promoting the worship of a new deity, Ra-Horus, a god of the sun whose name would later be shortened to Aten (sun-disk). As the master carver, Bek was responsible for supervising the construction of statues for the Aten cult temples, of which there were at least four at Karnak, as well as pieces featuring the king and his family. He created several large statues for these temples, which were later destroyed. One sandstone statue (called the *Colossal Statue of Amenhotep with Nemes and Double Crown*) shows the king with an elongated face and hooded eyes on a six-feet-high head and is the only one that survived from a colonnade of statues. (It now resides in a museum in Cairo.) Bek supervised the cutting of granite monuments for the Mansion of Ben-ben, a temple in East Karnak that was for the private use of Nefertiti, the wife of Akhenaten, who performed religious rites usually reserved for the king. He most likely also produced works for the new capital after Akhenaten moved the royal city from Thebes to Akhetaten (Amarna).

Realist Style. Bek and other carvers of the Akhenaten reign, under the personal direction of the king, loosened the artistic style and modified the subjects included in their works. Rather than adopting the old style that idealized the figure, the king was portrayed, according to historian Jacobus Van Dijk, with a "thin, drawn-out face with a pointed chin and thick lips, an elongated neck, almost feminine breasts, a round protruding belly, wide hips, fat thighs, and thin, spindly legs." These physical representations were also used to show other members of the royal house. Some scholars have surmised that the king suffered from a disfiguring disease, possibly a pituitary disorder. In another departure from the traditional way of sculpting human figures, Amarna artists often assembled the pieces rather than carving them out of single blocks of material. The subject matter in which the royals were represented also changed from statues and reliefs that featured only the king to ones that showed the monarch with his wife and children in intimate relationships. This "realistic" form was far different from the rigid constructions popular with earlier royal art.

Legacy. Bek appears to have died during Akhenaten's reign, as he was replaced by Tuthmose, whose carving style was even more realistic than his predecessor's. Much valuable information has been discovered in a workshop dug up from Amarna, which may have belonged to both Bek and Tuthmose, including plaster-cast heads and unfinished sculpture. Although traditional forms returned with the end of the Amarna period, some aspects of the contributions of these sculptors continued on.

Sources:

Cyril Aldred, *Akhenaten: King of Egypt* (London: Thames & Hudson, 1988).

Ian Bolton, "Bek: Master of the Works," *Egypt: Land of Eternity*, Internet website, http://members.tripod.com/ib205/bek.html.

Sergio Pernigotti, "The Mansur Collection," translated by Fred Stoss, ARCHEO (April 1994), Internet website, http://www.amarna.com/docs/archeo.htm.

Jacobus Van Dijk, "The Amarna Period and the Later New Kingdom (c. 1352–1069 BC)," in *The Oxford History of Ancient Egypt*, edited by Ian Shaw (Oxford & New York: Oxford University Press, 2000), pp. 272–313.

INENI

CIRCA 1514-1458 B.C.E.
ARCHITECT

Aristocratic Service. A famous royal architect and builder, Ineni, a member of the aristocracy, served Thutmose (or Thuthmosis) I and Hatshepsut, as well as two other kings. He may have begun his architectural work under Amenhotep I, and he seems to have been an honest and loyal government official. In addition to his construction duties he was also in charge of the granaries during his period of service.

Builder. Ineni supervised the construction of some of the impressive structures at the temple city of Karnak, including two giant quartzite obelisks for Thutmose. He built two pylons, the entrances to the temple, and possibly the great hall as well. He also designed and had a protective wall built around Amon's shrine at Thebes.

A Hidden Grave. Ineni is credited with camouflaging the location of the king's rock-cut tomb under a pyramid-shaped mountain by locating the upper structure in a different location, as he did for Thutmose I on the opposite (west) bank of the Nile from Karnak, south of Thebes, in an area that became known as the Valley of the Kings. He was well rewarded for his ingenuity in trying to keep the tomb away from potential robbers. After Ineni died and was buried, his tomb at Thebes boasted of his achievement in hiding his pharaoh's burial chamber. Paintings in his tomb also indicate that he was an avid hunter and gardener.

Sources:

Zahi Hawass, "Development of the Royal Mortuary Complex," *The Plateau*, Internet website, http://www.guardians.net/hawass/mortuary1.htm.

"Ineni," *Who's Who of Ancient Egypt*, Internet website, http://tour-egypt.net/who/ineni.htm.

W. Stevenson Smith, *The Art and Architecture of Ancient Egypt*, third edition (New Haven & London: Yale University Press, 1998).

KHAFRE (CHEPHREN)

CIRCA 2555-2532 B.C.E.
KING, DYNASTY 4

Pyramid Builder. The image that first comes to mind when most people think of ancient Egypt is the giant pyramids at Giza. The largest of these structures, the Great Pyramid, was built by Khufu; but his son, Khafre, contributed a matching pyramid that rivals his father's tomb. Khafre also built the Great Sphinx to guard his complex, which was built by a combination of professional artisans and drafted common laborers. Inside his temple were twenty-three statues of the pharaoh, among which is "one of the greatest works of Egyptian art" in the opinion of Richard H. Wilkinson. On Khafre's shoulders stands the falcon-god Horus, his wings spread downward as if to protect the neck of the pharaoh. Some estimates claim that there may have been nearly sixty statues of Khafre in the whole complex. The inside of his temple was lined with red granite and calcite; ceremonies and rituals in honor of the pharaoh cult were performed here.

Great Sphinx. At the northern entrance to his temple, alongside the causeway and in a former quarry, a two-hundred-feet-long, human-headed sandstone lion was placed, which became known as the Great Sphinx. The monument was carved from an existing outcrop of stone, as opposed to being put together as had the pyramids. Another temple was built to the front of the lion's body, and a chapel and an obelisk were later placed between his paws. Portions of the face and beard were later chiseled off. The giant sculpture suffered severely from the elements and is crumbling in modern times despite extensive restoration efforts.

Sources:

Zahi Hawass, *The Plateau*, Internet website, http://guardians.net/hawass/sphinx-pyramid-main.htm.

Jaromir Malek, "The Old Kingdom (c. 2686–2125)," in *The Oxford History of Ancient Egypt*, edited by Ian Shaw (Oxford & New York: Oxford University Press, 2000), pp. 89–117.

Richard H. Wilkinson, *The Complete Temples of Ancient Egypt* (New York: Thames & Hudson, 2000), pp. 116–118.

SENMUT (SENENMUT)

FLOURISHED CIRCA 1450
ARCHITECT

Court Favorite. Few artists and architects left behind clear indications of their work in the form of inscriptions or other evidence, not to mention drawings or statues featuring their faces. One, however, the architect Senmut, attempted to do so by carving small representations of himself and placing them in niches and recesses of the Hathor Chapel, which he built for his queen. Several of the carvings survive. A favorite of the female pharaoh Hatshepsut, Senmut was the primary architect of her temple at Deir el Bahari. Senmut had other important duties in her administration, such as royal steward and overseeing the construction of temples, and he also may have been her lover.

Beautiful Temple. The tri-terraced structure of pillars, with grand reliefs and statues inside, was placed against a towering concave cliff and was approached by a lane that had rows of sphinxes (featuring Hatshepsut's face) and trees lining each side. Visitors reached the two highest terraces via two grand centrally located ramps, and the structure was more than eight hundred feet wide. Interior reliefs celebrated Hatshepsut's alleged divine birth, her foreign expeditions, and other events of her reign. Senmut completed the design, originally started by Thutmose II (and possibly the architect Ineni), which was originally more boxlike. The temple took more than fifteen years to build. Although original plans called for her tomb to be placed under the structure, she was actually entombed in the Valley of the Kings. Most of the statues and other artworks were destroyed or covered up by her successor, Thutmose III. Senmut lost favor after his queen's death, and many of his statues were destroyed—even his carefully planned tomb was filled in and closed.

Sources:

Betsy M. Bryan, "The Eighteenth Dynasty Before the Amarna Period (c. 1550–1352 B.C.E.)," in *The Oxford History of Ancient Egypt*, edited by Ian Shaw (Oxford & New York: Oxford University Press, 2000), pp. 218–271.

W. Stevenson Smith, *The Art and Architecture of Ancient Egypt*, third edition (New Haven & London: Yale University Press, 1998), pp. 126–143.

Richard H. Wilkinson, *The Complete Temples of Ancient Egypt* (New York: Thames & Hudson, 2000), pp. 175–178.

DOCUMENTARY SOURCES

Anonymous, *Apophis and Seqenenre* (circa 1292–1190 B.C.E.)—One papyrus contains the story of the Hyksos king Apophis and his quarrel with the Theban king Seqenenre. Apophis complained that Seqenenre's hippopotamus disturbed his sleep. This odd complaint becomes the cause of a war. The story probably refers to the Theban expulsion of the Hyksos from Egypt during Dynasty 17.

Anonymous, *Astarte and the Sea* (circa 1539–1292 B.C.E.)—One fragmentary papyrus retells a Canaanite story in Egyptian guise. The god Seth battles the Sea with the help of the goddess Astarte. The god Baal usually takes this hero's role.

Anonymous, *The Doomed Prince* (circa 1292–1190 B.C.E.)—A young prince is fated to die by a snake, dog, or crocodile bite. He leaves Egypt to escape his fate and marries a princess in a foreign land. Before the papyrus breaks off, he avoids the dog bite. It is unclear how the story ends.

Anonymous, *Horus and Seth* (circa 1292–1190 B.C.E.)—One papyrus describes the civil trial that the gods hold to determine whether Horus or Seth should follow Osiris as king of Egypt. There are eighteen episodes, including magical transformations and trials by combat. The ending of the papyrus is unclear, though it is certain that Horus eventually became king.

Anonymous, *Neferkare and General Sisene* (circa 1980–1630 B.C.E.)—Preserved in a fragmentary papyrus and one ostracon, the story concerns secret, nighttime visits that King Pepi II made to General Sisene. The purpose of these visits is obscure.

Anonymous, *Papyrus Westcar* (circa 1980–1630 B.C.E.; preserved in the Hyksos Period, 1630–1523 B.C.E.)—The papyrus, now in the Egyptian Museum, Berlin, is named for its former English owner. It tells the story of three of Khufu's sons, who tell the king stories. They begin with stories of magicians and end with the miraculous birth of the kings of Dynasty 5.

Anonymous, *The Report of Wenamun* (circa 1075–945 B.C.E.)—One papyrus tells of the troubles that Wenamun experienced on a trade expedition to Lebanon to buy wood for a boat. The papyrus breaks off before the story ends.

Anonymous, *The Shipwrecked Sailor* (circa 1980–1630 B.C.E.)—A sailor tells a story of his own failed mission in order to comfort his commander, who is returning from another failed mission. He describes a shipwreck, a meeting with a gigantic talking snake, the snake's bad fortune, and the sailor's eventual return to Egypt. The commander dismisses the sailor's story as no use. One manuscript survives.

Anonymous, *Story of Sinuhe* (soon after 1875 B.C.E.)—The text exists in two manuscripts written close to the time of composition and more than twenty copies of excerpts written in the New Kingdom and afterward. Sinuhe was the closest thing to a national epic poem for the ancient Egyptians. The story illustrates Egyptian political values as well as tells an exciting adventure story.

Anonymous, *The Taking of Joppa* (circa 1292–1190 B.C.E.)—Preserved on one papyrus, the story concerns the capture of the city of Joppa, in modern Israel, in the reign of Thutmose III. General Djeheuty hides soldiers in the saddlebags of a donkey caravan and wins the day.

Anonymous, *Tale of Two Brothers* (circa 1292–1190 B.C.E.)—One papyrus tells how the wife of an older brother attempts to seduce her husband's younger brother. When the younger brother refuses her advances, the wife falsely accuses the younger brother of rape. When the older brother confronts his younger brother, the younger brother castrates himself to prove his sincerity. The story is related to the cult of a castrated bull.

Anonymous, *Truth and Falsehood* (circa 1292–1190 B.C.E.)—Falsehood accuses his brother, Truth, of stealing his knife. Truth is condemned and blinded. He becomes the doorkeeper of an evil woman, whose son eventually vindicates Truth by accusing Falsehood of stealing a prize bull.

Funerary images from a Theban tomb, Dynasty 18, circa 1539–1295/1292 B.C.E.

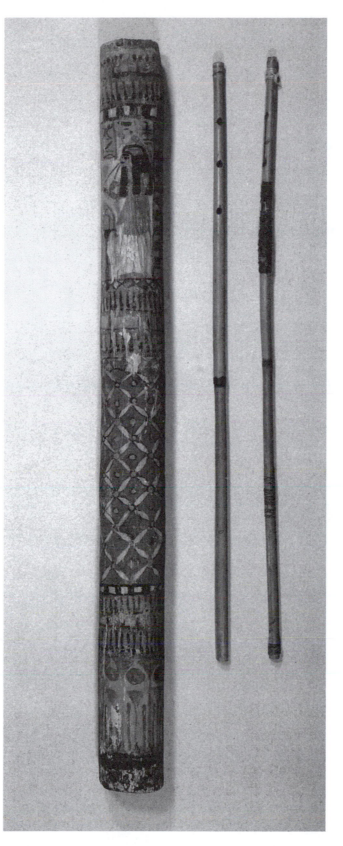

Painted oboe case with a reed and a double oboe, circa 1292–1075 B.C.E. (Musee du Louvre, Paris)

Aerial view of the terraced-style cult temple for Hatshepsut at Deir el Bahri, Dynasty 18, circa 1539–1295/1292 B.C.E.

COMMUNICATION, TRANSPORTATION, AND EXPLORATION

by STEVE VINSON

CONTENTS

Sidebars and tables are listed in italics.

2566* B.C.E.

- Two dismantled boats, probably intended to aid the deceased king in his travels with the gods, are buried near the pyramid of Khufu.

2555-2532* B.C.E.

- Diplomatic and trade contacts are established by Khafre with Byblos (Lebanon) and Syria.

2500* B.C.E.

- The cursive hieroglyphic script, called hieratic, is fully established for official documents.

2485-2472 B.C.E.

- Expeditions are sent out by Sahure to gather copper, turquoise, and gneiss from the Sinai and more-exotic materials (gold, malachite, and myrrh) from Punt (East Africa) and other areas of southern Africa.

2350* B.C.E.

- General Weni is active in leading military expeditions against the peoples of the desert. He serves under Teti, Meryre Pepy I, and Merenre, the first three pharaohs of Dynasty 6.
- Harkhuf, a contemporary of Weni, who serves under Merenre and Neferkare Pepy II, travels to Sinai and Nubia.

2170* B.C.E.

- The first depiction of a wheel is included in an Egyptian tomb painting.

2081-2075* B.C.E.

- Expeditions are sent out by Mentuhotep I to Sinai and Lebanon to gather materials such as cedar.

1980-1630* B.C.E.

- Letter writing is more common, as scribes are often employed to write for illiterate citizens desiring to send messages. Scribes were usually men, although there is some evidence that there were a few female scribes.

1957* B.C.E.

- Sankhkare Mentuhotep III sends Henenu, one of his officials, on an expedition to Punt to obtain incense.

1920* B.C.E.

- Trading caravans are active between Egypt and Syria, and frequent expeditions in search of precious materials are sent southward.

*Denotes Circa Date

1900* B.C.E.

- An alphabetic script is used for the first time, in an Upper Egyptian rock inscription.

1550* B.C.E.

- Minoan artists are at work in Egypt.
- Egyptian craftsmen adopt the chariot from Mesopotamia but make a lighter, faster version with the driver placed over the axle to reduce the workload on the horse.

1478* B.C.E.

- Hatshepsut is on the throne. She resumes sea connections to Punt, sending a five-ship fleet, each ship manned by thirty rowers.

1400–1390* B.C.E.

- Military expeditions are sent into Nubia, not for conquest but to keep open transportation routes through the desert. During this period, as well, royal scribes gain in influence and power, even over that of military officers.

1353* B.C.E.

- Amenhotep IV (Akhenaten) begins his reign. Aegean city names begin to appear in the hieroglyphs on his tomb, indicating greater contact between the two regions.
- Scribes begin using "Late Egyptian" as the common written language.
- "Sea Peoples" are first mentioned in the Amarna Letters, the diplomatic correspondence of Amenhotep III, Akhenaten, and Tutankhamun. This archive reveals an active level of communications with foreign powers in the region.

1104 B.C.E.

- Ramesses XI begins his reign on the throne, which lasts until circa 1075 B.C.E.
- Dhutmose, Scribe of the Necropolis, is active.

716–702* B.C.E.

- Shabaka orders the copying of ancient monumental texts to maintain a record of and the integrity of ancient writing.

650 B.C.E.

- The earliest use of Demotic script, a more cursive style of hieroglyphic script, appears in Egypt.

610 B.C.E.

- Necho II, according to Herodotus, sends Phoenician sailors on a voyage of exploration down the African coast, and they allegedly circumnavigate the African continent.

*Denotes Circa Date

525 B.C.E.	• The Persians conquer Egypt and promote the use of Aramaic.
521 B.C.E.	• Persian king Darius I completes the digging of a canal linking the Mediterranean Sea and the Red Sea, a project begun by Necho II.
332 B.C.E.	• Alexander the Great conquers Egypt. Greek begins to displace Demotic as the principal administrative language.
	• Egyptian traders travel by sea to India.

*DENOTES CIRCA DATE

Palermo Stone, a fragment of a basalt slab with the largest extant section of a Dynasty 5 (circa 2500-2350 B.C.E.) kings-list (Museo Archeologico, Palermo)

OVERVIEW

Good Communications. In ancient Egypt, communication was unusually easy. Of course, the Egyptians lacked most of the things twenty-first-century citizens think of as necessary for simple and effective communication: there was no organized postal system, no news media, and, obviously, no telephone service or World Wide Web. But of all the civilizations of the ancient Mediterranean world, the Egyptians probably enjoyed the most advantageous circumstances from the point of view of communication, and these favorable conditions probably explain in no small part the cohesion and long life of Egyptian Pharaonic civilization.

Egypt and the Nile. What were the advantages that Egypt enjoyed? First and foremost was the Nile River, a natural highway that made it possible to move people, goods, and ideas easily from one end of Egypt to another, a distance of about 650 miles. Egypt is mostly desert, and so the great majority of ancient Egyptians, like their modern descendants, lived close to this river or to canals leading to the river. This tendency meant that most villages and towns of any size at all were connected to each other by water. Even more convenient for the Egyptians, the Nile flows from south to north, but the prevailing wind in Egypt is from north to south. For this reason it was easy for boats to travel in either direction: heading north, they were helped by the current; heading south, they could hoist sail and use the wind.

Earliest Boats. What were the earliest boats in Egypt like? From both prehistoric drawings of watercraft and from later Egyptian mythology, it seems likely that the first boats on the Nile were made of bundles of papyrus. Early rock drawings on cliffs in Egypt show in-curving watercraft that look much like the papyrus raft built in the mid twentieth century for Thor Heyerdahl, the Norwegian explorer who sailed his reed vessel from Egypt to the Caribbean. Egyptian myth also suggests that the earliest boats were made of reed—late Egyptian stories and tales recall that the gods sailed on papyrus vessels, and illustrations in religious manuscripts also show the gods on boats that, in all likelihood, were thought of as being papyrus.

Early Wooden Boats and the Invention of Sails. However, it is thought that some time after 3500 B.C.E. the Egyptians learned to use copper tools to manufacture wooden planks. It seems most probable that it was about this time, known as the Gerzean, or Naqada II, Period, that the Egyptians probably made the transition from reed rafts to true wooden boats. By the end of the Gerzean Period, or around 3150 B.C.E., the first pictorial evidence reveals that the Egyptians had learned how to make sails and use them to propel their boats. No ancient peoples, as far as is now known, had the sail before the Egyptians. It is probably no coincidence that it was precisely at the time when the sail first appeared that Egypt was politically unified under Narmer, the first king of Dynasty 1 (circa 3000–2800 B.C.E.). While many factors were involved in the unification of Egypt, a powerful, new transportation technology made it possible for men, equipment, trade goods, and information to move throughout Egypt more quickly than ever before. This new capability, in turn, could only accelerate the growing cultural unity of Egypt and help an ambitious king in his attempts to create the first unified national kingdom.

Boats as a Key Technology. Once the sail was invented, Egypt began to depend on boats and ships for all sorts of purposes: to haul people, animals, and agricultural products; to travel on the Red Sea and on the Mediterranean Sea in search of exotic products; and to transport soldiers and assist in the conquest of foreign lands. Boats also played a key role in Egyptian mythology. Every god was supposed to travel in his or her own boat. The most important of these vessels were the two barks of the sun god Ra, which were called the "Day Bark" and the "Night Bark." These two vessels were thought to carry the sun around the world during the day and the night. The barks were crewed by gods who protected Ra from the forces of evil that were constantly trying to interrupt his voyage. Should they ever succeed, Egyptians believed, the universe would implode and return to the watery chaos from which creation first emerged.

Land Transportation. Boats were not the only means by which the Egyptians traveled. Land transportation played an important, if comparatively limited, role in the Egyptian economy. Unlike the Sumerians, who had wheeled vehicles at an early date, Egypt relied on animals or human porters for land transportation until the end of the Old Kingdom (circa 2130 B.C.E.). Large stone blocks or statues were usually dragged on wooden sledges. Expeditions set out across the deserts either to the Red Sea or into the Western Desert toward a chain of oases that is west of the Nile. A complex network of roads was developed, shortcutting the Nile at the so-called Qena Bend, the large curve in the course of the Nile near Luxor; from here travelers could head out toward the oases in the Western Desert, or even turn south by caravan to Nubia. Travelers and traders went by donkey caravan into Nubia at an early date and also across the northern parts of the Sinai Peninsula into southern Palestine. This route was especially heavily traveled, both by Palestinian nomads and merchants coming into Egypt and by Egyptian soldiers, traders, and diplomats heading north into Palestine. From Palestine, these traders could go even further, either north to Syria or east to Mesopotamia. This route was arduous; travelers were often beset by harsh climatic conditions and bands of marauders. Some letters from a Babylonian king to the Egyptian pharaoh Tutankhamun (King Tut), written sometime after 1330 B.C.E., complain about bandits and demand that the pharaoh compensate him for the losses of merchants who were robbed in Palestine, then a part of the Egyptian empire.

Egyptian Language as a Means of Communication. The other great advantage that Egypt enjoyed was its single language. Ancient Mesopotamia (modern Iraq), Syria-Palestine (modern Palestine, Israel, Lebanon, Jordan and Syria), and Anatolia (modern Turkey) were linguistically fragmented, with people living side by side but speaking many different languages and dialects. In contrast, the great majority of Egyptians spoke a single language, which is simply called "Ancient Egyptian" and which the Egyptians themselves called the *Ra en Kemet,* the "Speech of Egypt." It is true that in everyday speech the Egyptian language was divided into several regional dialects, and it may well be that people who lived far from one another might have had difficulty understanding each other if they happened to meet—one Egyptian writer tells that it was difficult for a man from the southernmost part of Egypt, around the modern city of Aswan, to speak with a man from the north of Egypt. Despite these dialectical differences, it seems that in writing, regional differences in speech were ignored in favor of a single standard Egyptian, normally the variety of language spoken by most elite governmental officials and religious leaders. Similar to a modern "Queen's English," an Egyptian undoubtedly would have spoken of the "Pharaoh's Egyptian"! Officials could easily communicate with each other by means of written dispatches that all could read. Religious texts and inscriptions throughout the land were also written in this standard style. Any educated Egyptian priest or royal official could read the inscriptions on any temple or palace in the country. This linguistic uniformity went a long way toward promoting and maintaining cultural unity in Egypt, even when political unity broke down.

Egyptian Language. It is helpful to know a little about the history of the Egyptian language and of the various scripts used to write it. The language of Egypt is a mem-

ber of a great group of languages most commonly called the "Afro-Asiatic" family which was spoken in western Asia and Africa and includes the Semitic languages (Hebrew, Arabic, and many of the languages of ancient Mesopotamia and Syria-Palestine), as well as North African languages such as Berber. Egyptian also has connections to languages currently spoken in Sudan and Ethiopia. It is important to keep in mind that Egyptian was spoken and written for an unusually long time—more than four thousand years. In fact, ancient Egyptian has a longer documented history than any other language, although this language changed a great deal through time. Egyptologists usually divide written ancient Egyptian into the following large chronological stages:

Old Egyptian (written from approximately 3000 to 2000 B.C.E.)

Middle Egyptian (written from approximately 2000 to 1300 B.C.E.)

Late Egyptian (written from approximately 1300 to 650 B.C.E.)

Demotic (written from approximately 650 B.C.E. to 450 C.E.)

Coptic (written from approximately 450 C.E. to 1500 C.E.)

At different times, the Egyptians used four different scripts:

Hieroglyphic: the pictorial script most familiar to non-Egyptians, ancient and modern (in use from approximately 3000 B.C.E. to 450 C.E.).

Hieratic: a cursive script that is closely based on hieroglyphic writing (in use during the same period as hieroglyphic writing).

Demotic: a script that developed out of hieratic around 650 B.C.E., but even more cursive than hieratic.

Coptic: an alphabetic script based on the Greek alphabet but supplementing it with a few letters that represent sounds that did not exist in Greek. Those additional letters are derived from Demotic signs and ultimately go back to hieroglyphs.

The names "Demotic" and "Coptic" are used for both specific phases of the development of the Egyptian language and for the scripts that were in common use during these periods.

How the System Works. The hieroglyphic system uses fewer signs than modern Chinese or Japanese, for example, and is essentially phonetic. Most individual signs represent either a single consonant, two consonants, or three consonants; a few may represent four or five consonants. Hieroglyphic signs did not ordinarily represent vowels, but there are special cases in which vowels might be indicated. (Exactly how this system worked is still not completely understood.) Signs took their phonetic values from the consonants that made up part or all of the name of the object depicted. For example, in English, a picture of a car might be used to write any word or part of a word with the sequence of consonants *c* and *r*. Thus, words such as *care, core, acre,* and *car* could all be written with the *car* sign.

Determinative Signs. The lack of any signs to indicate vowels presented a problem: how could one differentiate between the various possible words that have the consonants *c* and *r* in them? The Egyptians solved this problem with another type of sign, called determinative, that give the reader some idea as to the class of words to which a writing belongs. In this case, the word *care* might be spelled with a *car* plus a *heart,* to indicate a *c* and *r* word that indicates emotion; *acre* might be written with a *car* sign plus a symbol to indicate a word having to do with the measurement of land. To write the word *car,* one might well do exactly what the ancient Egyptians did: write the *car* sign and add a simple stroke to indicate that it was to be read literally.

Representative Language. Of course, context was also an important guide to which word was intended, as one can see from the following sentence: "Cn y rd ths?" Few people would hesitate long before coming up with "Can you read this," despite the absence of any vowels; an alternative reading such as "Coney arid teahouse" would probably not occur to someone who knows English. The Egyptian writing system was completely effective in representing the language, and the Egyptians held fast to it for centuries, even after they had become acquainted with the alphabetic scripts of their neighbors. (There is good evidence that these alphabetic scripts were ultimately based on the Egyptian hieroglyphic script itself.) The complexity of the script was probably not, in and of itself, a barrier to widespread literacy in ancient Egypt; after all, modern nations such as Japan and China have achieved nearly universal literacy with writing systems that are far more complicated. The most important factors were likely practical and social. Literacy was not considered either appropriate or necessary for most people, who could manage perfectly well without learning to read or to write.

Classical Egyptian. The phase of Egyptian that is called "Middle Egyptian" was considered to be the "classical" language of ancient Egypt by the Egyptians themselves. Long after Middle Egyptian ceased to be the most common spoken form, scholars returned to Middle Egyptian vocabulary and grammar. Using Middle Egyptian gave new compositions a classical, or archaic, feeling, much as one might today write "thou knowest" instead of "you know" if one wants something that sounds old-fashioned or poetic. For Egyptians, the "oldness" of Middle Egyptian was a good thing in itself since it suggested permanence, stability, and the long history of their culture. But there were also times when new language was appreciated, and the use of up-to-date language was stressed. The most important of these times was during the reign of the heretic king Amenhotep IV (Akhenaten, circa 1353–1336 B.C.E.), a pharaoh who rejected the traditional religion of Egypt, with its many gods, and instead insisted on the worship of a single god–the sun–for which he used the Egyptian name "Aten."

At the same time Akhenaten reformed Egyptian religion, he also urged scribes to stop writing in the old Middle Egyptian. Instead of using the language in a form that was more than six hundred years old, he urged scribes to write more like everyday speech—at least, the everyday speech of the royal court.

Success and Failure. Akhenaten's religious reforms failed miserably, but the linguistic changes that his reign ushered in were more durable, and the age of Akhenaten marks a fundamental break in Egyptian linguistic history. Even Akhenaten's enemies, who suppressed every vestige of his religious ideas, did not try to completely reverse the tide of linguistic reform. Instead, the old-fashioned Middle Egyptian remained in use, more or less, in official and especially religious inscriptions, while Late Egyptian was used for everyday purposes: business documents, personal letters, and so forth. But the two idioms tended to get mixed up, and so elements of Late Egyptian often turn up in texts that are quite formal, and Middle Egyptian can turn up unexpectedly in a letter or tax register. There was even a mixed style used for stories and tales, which used a combination of forms. This style must have sounded archaic to the Egyptians, but probably also appeared artificial, much like modern attempts to imitate the style of William Shakespeare or the King James Bible.

Development of Demotic. However, by circa 650 B.C.E., "Late Egyptian" was more than six hundred years old and even then it was probably beginning to sound old-fashioned. For reasons modern scholars cannot entirely explain, the language once again broke loose from the conservative moorings that worked to keep written Egyptian language as stable as possible and began to change rapidly. This time the change was not merely in grammar and vocabulary but also in the script. A new, highly cursive script called "Demotic" was developed to express what was, once again, probably something close to the everyday speech of the educated class. Hieroglyphic and hieratic writing did not disappear; although Demotic became the official administrative script, the former styles were still used to write religious texts or to inscribe public monuments. But Demotic expanded its range, and soon secular and religious literature was appearing in Demotic as well.

The Coming of Greek. In the middle of the first millennium B.C.E. there were two great divides among the Egyptians: one between the great majority of the population who could not read and the minority who could; the other between those literate persons who could read and write only Demotic and those who could still read and write hieroglyphics. But in 332 B.C.E. there was a radical shift in political and cultural fortunes: Alexander the Great and his army of Greeks and Macedonians conquered Egypt and brought it into the new Greek-speaking civilization called the "Hellenistic World." This subjugation had enormous consequences for language as an instrument of communication. Suddenly, the language of the ruling elite was Greek, not Egyptian, and linguistic competence in a completely alien language was the key to influence and power.

Almost none of the new kings of Egypt, descendants of Alexander the Great's general Ptolemy, could even speak Egyptian; only the last of the line, Cleopatra VII, ever learned to speak the language of the country she ruled. On the level of the middle and lower administration, Demotic continued for a while to be used alongside Greek. But increasingly, any Egyptian who wanted to advance in society had to learn to speak and write Greek.

Decline of Hieroglyphic, Hieratic, and Demotic. After the Roman takeover of Egypt in 30 B.C.E., Demotic quickly disappeared as an administrative language; its use was soon confined to the production of literary and religious texts by a learned elite. At the same time, and for the same reasons, the number of people who could actually read and write hieroglyphics and hieratic began to fall precipitously. The two older scripts soon became something like a secret code that could be understood by only the most highly educated members of the priestly class. At this point, non-Egyptians were not even sure that Egyptian hieroglyphs were used to write language in the usual sense. Many Greek and Roman travelers and intellectuals seemed to think that the strange jumble of images on Egyptian temple walls had to be understood purely symbolically. They thought hieroglyphic inscriptions embodied deep and esoteric knowledge that ordinary people could not understand and must not be allowed access to. Once knowledge of the hieroglyphic system disappeared completely, it was easy for medieval and renaissance European scholars to believe that all sorts of mystical and occult knowledge was embodied in the writings of the ancient Egyptians. This belief was not challenged until Jean-François Champollion deciphered the hieroglyphic script in 1822. Even today, modern groups such as the Freemasons and Rosicrucians, as well as many neopagans and believers in paranormal phenomena, still believe that the ancient Egyptians possessed a secret wisdom that surpassed the knowledge of the ancient Greeks and Hebrews.

TOPICS IN COMMUNICATION, TRANSPORTATION, AND EXPLORATION

CONTACT: AEGEAN

Greeks. The Aegean world can be defined as Greece, western Asia Minor, and the islands of the Aegean Sea, including Crete. It is still not clear how early the ancient Egyptians became aware of these areas. At a late date in Egyptian history, a peculiar term, *Hau-nebu,* is used for the islands of the Aegean. It is not completely clear how this term is to be explained; its literal meaning seems to be something such as, "Those who are behind the baskets," and the most common explanation holds that "basket" in this context refers to the Aegean islands. The term *Hau-nebu* occurs quite early in Egyptian history, as early as the Old Kingdom (circa 2675–2130 B.C.E.), but whether it refers to the Aegean at this early date is less clear and has been doubted by many. An early knowledge of the Aegean world has also been suggested by the finds of Predynastic Egyptian stone bowls on Crete; but it seems highly possible that these extremely fine bowls had been discovered by later grave robbers and found their way to Crete much later in the dynastic period of Egypt.

The Middle Kingdom. While the extent of Old Kingdom (and earlier) Egyptian knowledge of, and contact with, the Aegean remains problematic, it seems clear that by the Middle Kingdom (circa 1980–1630 B.C.E.), Egypt was certainly tied into trading networks that included the Aegean, and the Egyptians might have been acquiring more specific information about the north side of the Mediterranean. Minoan (referring to the ancient civilization of Crete, named by modern scholars after the legendary king Minos) seals were found in the "Treasure of Tod," a horde of imported objects discovered buried under a temple of the Egyptian god Montu at a town near Thebes with the modern name of Tod. Egyptian objects from the Middle Kingdom have been found on Crete itself, and Minoan ceramics have been found in Egyptian tombs of Dynasty 12 (circa 1938–1759 B.C.E.).

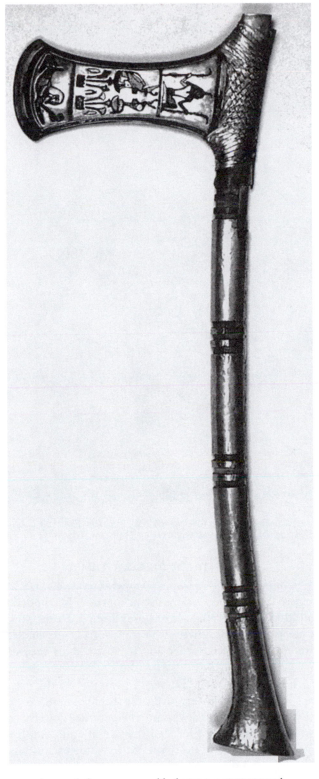

Axe made from copper, gold, electrum, gemstones, and wood, showing the influence of Eastern Mediterranean designs and styles; from the tomb of Queen Ahhotep at Dra Abu el-Naga in Thebes, circa 1539–1514 B.C.E. (from Ian Shaw, ed., *The Oxford History of Ancient Egypt*, 2000)

B.C.E.), 19 (circa 1292–1190 B.C.E.), and 20 (circa 1190–1075 B.C.E.). This time period is known to archaeologists and historians of the Mediterranean world as the Late Bronze Age. It is now known that as the kings of Dynasty 18 took over the old Hyksos capital at Avaris in the East Delta around 1539 B.C.E., the Egyptians imported Minoan artists to paint distinctive frescoes to decorate the new palace walls. These paintings include scenes of youths jumping over the horns of bulls, a non-Egyptian theme otherwise found only at the great royal palace at Knossos on Crete. As Dynasty 18 wore on, Egyptian tomb paintings showed Minoans in their distinctive garb bringing identifiably Aegean artifacts to Egypt as trade goods. Mainland Greeks were also in contact with Egypt during the Egyptian New Kingdom. At this time (between 1539 B.C.E. and around 1200 B.C.E.) the culture of mainland Greece is called "Mycenaean," after the city of Mycenae, known in Greek legend and through archaeology as the most important Late Bronze Age city in Greece. Finely decorated Mycenaean pottery is known from tombs in Egypt. A fairly detailed Egyptian knowledge of Aegean geography is indicated by place-name lists from the time of Amenhotep III, which include names plausibly identified with Mycenae, Knossos, and even Troy.

Pirates, Mercenaries, and Raiders. As the Late Bronze Age/New Kingdom continued, trade with the Aegean became less peaceful than earlier royal contacts would suggest. Egyptian records detail encounters, often not peaceful, with certain groups of peoples who are associated with the Mediterranean Sea and who seem to have been raiders, pirates, and mercenaries. These people, known collectively as "Sea Peoples," seem to have included Mycenaean Greeks as well as other groups, some of Mycenaean or Aegean culture but probably speaking non-Greek languages, from elsewhere in the Eastern Mediterranean. The most important of these peoples were known to the Egyptians as the "Peleset" and are known from the Hebrew Bible as the Philistines.

After the Late Bronze Age. While communication with the Aegean world seems to have been at least temporarily disrupted after the end of the Egyptian New Kingdom, revival of shipping by the Phoenicians and Greeks in the Iron Age brought a renewal of contact between Egypt and the Aegean world. Greek legends have it that many Greek philosophers and scientists traveled to Egypt to learn the "wisdom of the Egyptians." While no single example of this contact can be proved beyond doubt, cultural borrowing from Egypt by the Greeks is strongly indicated by, among other things, the development of large-scale Greek stone sculpture after the eighth century B.C.E., which is clearly based on Egyptian techniques and prototypes. The development of Greek military power led Egyptian pharaohs of Dynasty 26 (664–525 B.C.E.) to import Greek and Carian (non-Greeks from Asia Minor who used Greek military tactics) mercenaries to shore up their armies, and Greek traders were permitted to establish a trading colony called Naucratis in the western Delta. This colony, and the pres-

New Kingdom and Later. The great heyday of ancient Egyptian contact with the Aegean world, however, was during the New Kingdom Dynasties 18 (circa 1539–1295/1292

Fragmented wall painting from the tomb of Sobekhotep depicting Asiatics making offerings to Thutmose IV, circa 1400–1390 B.C.E. Included in the tribute is an eagle-headed rhyton on a dish (lower right), an object of Minoan origin (British Museum, London).

ence of Greek and Carian mercenaries in military posts around Egypt, increased Egyptian knowledge of foreigners and increased the Aegean peoples' understanding of Egypt. From the seventh century B.C.E. onward, commercial and cultural contacts between the two regions increased dramatically. Interest in things Egyptian on the part of the Greeks was greatly stimulated by Herodotus, who visited Egypt during the fifth century B.C.E. A large portion of his *History of the Persian Wars* is devoted to the history and anthropology of Egypt. All of this contact was instrumental in paving the way for the conquest of Egypt by Alexander the Great, the subsequent importation of many Greek settlers, and the imposition of Greek as the ruling language of Egypt; ultimately, this triumph contributed to the absorption of Egypt into the Roman Empire (30 B.C.E.).

Sources:

Trude Dothan and Moshe Dothan, *People of the Sea: The Search for the Philistines* (New York: Macmillan, 1992).

Alan Henderson Gardiner, *Egypt of the Pharaohs: An Introduction* (Oxford: Clarendon Press, 1961), p. 132.

Alan B. Lloyd, *Herodotus, Book II* (Leiden: E. J. Brill, 1975), pp. 1–77.

N. K. Sandars, *The Sea Peoples: Warriors of the Ancient Mediterranean, 1250–1150 B.C.* (London: Thames & Hudson, 1978).

Shelley Wachsmann, *Aegeans in the Theban Tombs* (Leuven: Peeters, 1987).

CONTACT: MESOPOTAMIA

Controversy. The earliest-known literate civilizations in the ancient Near East arose in southern Mesopotamia and in the Nile valley. It has long been a matter of dispute as to whether these two centers of advanced culture were aware of each other and to what extent they may have been in contact.

Early Theories of "Eastern Invaders." At the end of the nineteenth century C.E., Egyptologists discovered the first remains of Egyptian "Predynastic" culture, that which immediately preceded the rise of a unified, literate, Pharaonic state in Egypt. At first, the early archaeologists who discovered this stage were more impressed by the differences between Predynastic and Dynastic civilizations than by their similarities and did not see how the latter culture could have developed out of the earlier one. This conclusion convinced them that the Dynastic culture must have been suddenly imposed on Predynastic peoples by invaders, whom scholars termed the "dynastic race." Since the only other center of advanced culture in existence was in Mesopotamia, it was thought that these people must have come from the east. The origins of this group were thought to be either

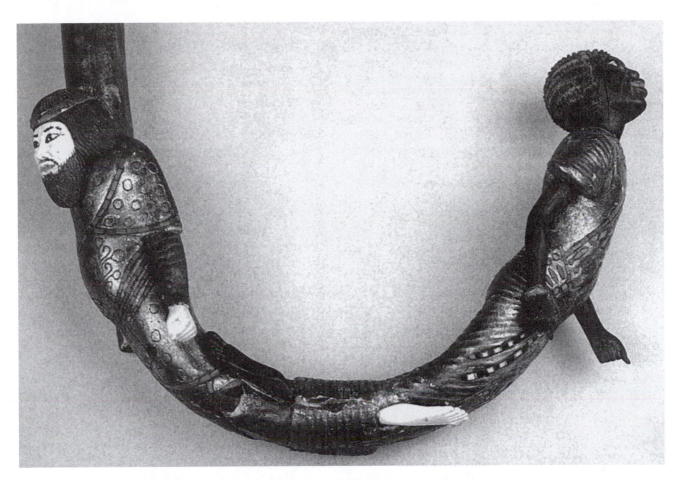

Handle of a ceremonial wood cane with carved and painted images of an Asiatic and Nubian; found in the tomb of Tutankhamun, circa 1332–1322 B.C.E. (from Ian Shaw, ed., *The Oxford History of Ancient Egypt,* 2000)

Sumeria (southern Mesopotamia, modern southern Iraq) or the areas immediately to its east (Elam, in what is now eastern Iraq and western Iran). This theory was bolstered by finds of individual objects that had come from Mesopotamia during the Predynastic Period, as well as certain artistic motifs that were found in Predynastic Egypt but that seemed more like Mesopotamian art than anything otherwise known in Egypt. This theory held that ancient Sumerians or Elamites must have sailed from southern Mesopotamia, around the Arabian Peninsula, and then north up the Red Sea to the vicinity of Mersa Gawasis, the port the later Egyptians used for launching their own Red Sea voyages. After hiking through the Wadi Hammamat, these eastern invaders would have reached the Nile, where they brought advanced civilization to the primitive Predynastic Egyptians.

A More Balanced View. This view, however, has fallen out of favor, in no small part because of the immense distances involved. It has been estimated that it might have taken primitive Sumerian seafarers up to two years to sail round-trip from Sumeria to Egypt. While it seems almost certain that there was some cultural contact between Egypt and Sumeria in the Predynastic Period, it is far more likely that this contact was indirect. Scholars know that Sumerian culture spread far to the north from its original heartland in southern Iraq

and that there were Sumerian colonies in the areas now comprising northern Iraq and eastern Syria. At the same time, Predynastic Egyptian traders were already in contact with peoples in southern Palestine (modern Israel). Sumerian colonists in Syria and Egyptian traders in Palestine were so close to each other that it seems almost certain that it was through this route that Egyptians became aware of Mesopotamian culture.

A Question of Influence. What was the result of this contact? The most intriguing question is whether Egyptian writing was somehow influenced by the development of writing in Sumeria. Until quite recently it was generally believed that Sumerian writing appeared at least a century or two before Egyptian hieroglyphic writing. While the two systems are quite different, it has often been thought possible that the idea of writing might have been brought to Egypt and that some individual Egyptian or small group of Egyptians might have been inspired to try to create a system of their own. In recent years, however, the Egyptologist Gunther Dreyer has found what he believes are genuine hieroglyphic inscriptions—very simple, to be sure—that may be as old or older than the earliest known Sumerian writing. If that conclusion is true, then it is probably more likely that the Egyptians themselves created their hieroglyphic writing system independently, without any knowledge of the achievements of their neighbors to the east.

Caravans, Heat, and Bandits. The theory that early Sumerians might have sailed to Egypt is also weakened by the fact that in later times contact between Egypt and Mesopotamia was always by land. Several of the "Amarna Letters" (the diplomatic correspondence of Amenhotep III, Akhenaten, and Tutankhamun) refer to this trade, and some highlight the great distances and dangers involved in this long, arduous journey.

Sources:

William S. Arnett, *The Predynastic Origin of Egyptian Hieroglyphs: Evidence for the Development of Rudimentary Forms of Hieroglyphs in Upper Egypt in the Fourth Millennium B.C.* (Washington, D.C.: University Press of America, 1982).

Raymond Cohen and Raymond Westbrook, eds., *Amarna Diplomacy: The Beginnings of International Relations* (Baltimore: Johns Hopkins University Press, 2000).

William L. Moran, ed., *The Amarna Letters* (Baltimore: Johns Hopkins University Press, 1992).

CONTACT: SYRIA-PALESTINE

Closest Contact. Probably the area of the ancient Near East to which the Egyptians traveled most often was Syria-Palestine, their neighbor to the immediate northeast. Inhabitants of this region were constantly coming into Egypt as well. Many of these people were nomads who were attracted to Egypt during times when climatic or political conditions in Syria-Palestine made life there difficult.

Earliest Contacts. It seems clear that contacts with Syria-Palestine began before the pharaoh Narmer created a united Egyptian state. The lower Egyptian site of Maadi (named for a nearby suburb of modern Cairo) showed that between 3600 and 3000 B.C.E., Lower Egyptians were heavily involved in trade with both Sinai and southern Palestine. Remains of houses at Maadi suggest that the buildings were similar to houses built in southern Palestine and point to the possibility that foreign traders lived there. Ceramics from Palestine have been found at Maadi, as well as some of the earliest remains of domesticated donkeys. This practice suggests the possibility of overland transportation between Maadi and southern Palestine. These traders may have come to purchase copper, which was being refined at Maadi.

Egyptians in Palestine. Traces of Egyptian interest in Palestine appear quite early, as far back as the Palestinian Neolithic period (sixth or fifth millenniums B.C.E.), when the first possibly Egyptian artifacts are found. Strong evidence for an identifiable Egyptian presence in Palestine, however, really begins around 3000 B.C.E. at the time of the transition to the Egyptian Dynasty 1 (the period called Early Bronze Age I by archaeologists of Syria-Palestine). Large numbers of Egyptian pottery vessels are seen in Early Bronze Age I Palestine, many bearing the name in Egyptian hieroglyphs of Narmer. Small ivory carvings from Egypt may well record these trade contacts between Egypt and Palestine—they show men with pointed beards, probably Palestinians, carrying pottery vessels that appear to represent imports from Palestine. It is difficult to say precisely how transportation between Egypt and Palestine was conducted in the early Dynasty 1/Early Bronze Age period. Most of the sites containing definite Egyptian artifacts have been discovered inland. Thus, it seems more likely that much of the trade between the two regions was conducted overland.

Syria-Palestine and Egypt after the First Dynasty. The nature of Egyptian relations with Syria-Palestine in the earliest phases of its dynastic history is not easy to reconstruct. It is not certain, for example, whether the Egyptians who brought jars inscribed with the name of Narmer were traders or conquerors. There is more definite evidence that Egypt, at least occasionally during the Old Kingdom, sent armies to Palestine. The most famous example of this activity is the autobiography of a Dynasty 6 official named Weni, an older contemporary of Harkhuf. Among Weni's achievements was his generalship of an army that was sent out five times against the "Sand Dwellers," who were either desert nomads or who lived on the desert fringes. The reference to a place called "Antelope Nose" as a target of Weni's activities has led some to propose that his forces actually went far up the Palestinian coast to Mt. Carmel. This area is a projection into the Mediterranean that is about as far north as the Sea of Galilee, or about one hundred miles from the modern Egyptian frontier with Israel and the Gaza Strip.

Faience tiles with foreign captives—a Libyan, a Nubian, two Syrians, and a Hittite (l.-r.)—from the temple of Ramesses III at Medinet Habu, circa 1187–1156 B.C.E. They were placed on the steps of a royal throne so that the king could purposely walk on them (Egyptian Museum, Cairo).

Contacts by Sea. Weni's army traveled north partly by land, partly by sea. The best evidence suggests that most contact between Egypt and southern Palestine was over land during Dynasty 1. But there was seagoing trade between Egypt and Palestine from an early date. The Sahure relief sculptures show ships that are probably "Byblos," the type of vessels that were used in trade between Egypt and the city of Byblos in modern Lebanon. One of the most important commodities that the Egyptians wanted from Byblos was good Lebanese timber of pine and cedar. In fact, Lebanese cedar was being imported into Egypt as early as Dynasty 1. The easiest way to transport large logs from Lebanon to Egypt would have been by sea—was there, then, a regular seaborne trade in Lebanese timber from the earliest days of the unified Egyptian state? So far there is no proof, but it does not seem to be impossible.

The Middle Kingdom and Later. In the Middle Kingdom there was special concern on the part of the Egyptians to prevent too much infiltration of nomads from Syria-Palestine, and a series of border fortresses called the "Walls of the Ruler" was constructed to control the frontier. These fortresses were, however, unsuccessful in stopping Palestinian immigration, and ultimately these immigrants set up an independent dynasty (the "Hyksos" dynasty, or Dynasty 15) in the Egyptian Delta and exercised control over large areas of northern Egypt. During the Egyptian New King-

dom, the "Ways of Horus," the road from Egypt into Palestine, carried many Egyptian traders, soldiers, and diplomats into Palestine. But sea trade flourished as well—several fine New Kingdom relief sculptures showing Syrian ships at port in Egypt have been found, and Egyptian texts refer to a lively trade being carried on between Egypt and its Palestinian vassal states. This trade continued until at least the end of the Egyptian New Kingdom, around 1050 B.C.E. From this time comes an amusing tale about an Egyptian envoy who booked passage on a ship to Lebanon in order to purchase wood for renovations to the sacred river barge of the god Amun.

Sources:

Amnon Ben-Tor, "The Early Bronze Age," in *The Archaeology of Ancient Israel*, edited by Ben-Tor, translated by R. Greenberg (New Haven: Yale University Press, 1992; Tel Aviv: Open University of Israel, 1992), pp. 81–125.

Michael A. Hoffmann, *Egypt Before the Pharaohs: The Prehistoric Foundations of Egyptian Civilization* (New York: Knopf, 1979), pp. 201–209.

Amélie Kuhrt, *The Ancient Near East, c. 3000-330 BC*, volume I (London & New York: Routledge, 1995), pp. 161–182, 317–331.

Samuel Mark, *From Egypt to Mesopotamia: A Study of Predynastic Trade Routes* (College Station: Texas A&M University Press, 1998; London: Chatham, 1998).

COPTIC

New Writing. As native Egyptian scripts slowly died out, the Egyptians still needed, occasionally, to have some way of putting their own language into writing. Many Egyptians had learned Greek and understood the advantages of the simple alphabetic script the Greeks used. There are examples of Egyptian words written in Greek letters from soon after Alexander the Great's conquest of Egypt (332 B.C.E.). This trend only accelerated in the Roman period as Egyptian scripts fell out of use. One early use of "Old Coptic"—a name given to the first systematic attempts to write extended Egyptian texts in Greek letters—was to make interlinear notations in Demotic magical texts, especially over magical names. Greek spellings, unlike Demotic orthography, included vowels, which helped ensure that the magician could pronounce the word properly and so be more likely to obtain the desired effect. Another Old Coptic document is an extended astrological text.

Coptic as a "Christian" Script. While Coptic may have been nurtured by Egyptian priests, magicians, and astrologers, the eventual triumph of Coptic and the final loss of native Egyptian scripts probably owed much to the decline of the native religion and its replacement with Christianity. Native Egyptian temples had always been the main centers for instruction in hieroglyphic, hieratic, and Demotic literature—as well as for the preservation of texts—and so their closure hastened the day when the old scripts were forgotten. It is also possible that, for Christians, the ancient scripts had uncomfortable, pagan associations. In the meantime, the priests of the new religion needed a way to bring the Christian message to the Egyptian people in their own language. Not many Egyptians could read, but there was a need to translate the Bible and other religious literature into Egyptian so that they could be read aloud to the faithful; sermons had to be written for reading in church services as well. The alphabetic script of the Greeks was the obvious choice, and Coptic finally emerged as the only way to write the Egyptian language some time in the fifth century C.E. The native language of Egypt was soon put under pressure by Arabic after the Islamic conquest of Egypt in 642 C.E., but Coptic survived as a spoken language at least down to the fourteenth century C.E., and is still used in religious rituals by Egyptian Christians.

Sources:

Roger S. Bagnall, *Egypt in Late Antiquity* (Princeton, N.J.: Princeton University Press, 1993), pp. 235–240; 251–255.

Leo Depuydt, *Conjunction, Contiguity, Contingency: On Relationships Between Events in the Egyptian and Coptic Verbal Systems* (New York: Oxford University Press, 1993).

Leslie S. B. MacCoull, *Coptic Perspectives on Late Antiquity* (Brookfield, Vt.: Variorum, 1993).

DIALECTS OF EGYPTIAN

Linguistic Differences. Even though scribal training worked to keep the written language of Egypt as stable and "correct" as possible, there were clear differences of speech among people who lived in various regions of the Nile Valley. When people are conscious of speaking a common language, but there are nevertheless noticeable differences in speech patterns among subgroups, then these people are said to speak dialects of the common language. Speakers of varying dialects of the same language can usually understand one another; if two dialects are so different that one cannot understand the speakers of another dialect, then it is often more accurate to consider them two different languages. Nevertheless, it is sometimes the case—as in the modern Arabic- and German-speaking worlds—that for cultural reasons, speakers of dialects that are virtually or completely incomprehensible to each other consider themselves to speak the same language. When this situation happens, there is often a standard "literary" language that all educated persons speak and write in formal situations, regardless of the dialect that they learned as their mother tongue and that they continue to use in day-to-day life.

A Problem of Mutual Misunderstanding. The Egyptians themselves occasionally mention the existence of dialects in ancient Egypt, and it is at least implied that some dialects were so far apart in their pronunciation, or perhaps their basic grammar, as to make comprehension difficult. This situation is expressed in a letter from the Egyptian Dynasty 19, in which the letter writer complains that in a previous communication his correspondent has been talking such nonsense that he might as well be speaking in some foreign language, or at least in some barely under-

THE DIALECTS OF COPTIC

The Coptic language shows several dialects being spoken in Egypt after about 450 C.E., dialects that, in all probability, were mutually comprehensible, at least for persons with some education. However, there is a problem: it is still not completely possible for scholars to tell what parts of Egypt were the homes to specific dialects. To take a few examples: the "Sahidic" dialect of Coptic has a name that suggests that it originated in southern Egypt, but many linguists believe it actually originated in the north. In contrast, Fayyumic is fairly easy to spot: like Demotic texts from the Fayyum, the consonant "l" (written with the Greek letter *lamda*) often appears where other Coptic dialects use the consonant "r" (written with the Greek letter *rho*). The variety of Coptic used most often by modern Egyptian Christians is Bohairic, a dialect that appears in written sources only after the ninth century C.E., and is traditionally believed to come from the western Delta region, including Alexandria. The fourth major dialect was called Akhmimic, usually associated with the city of Akhmim in central Egypt. Aside from these four major dialects, Coptic scholars have identified others, and undoubtedly there were many others, lost forever because none of their native speakers ever wrote them down in text. These Coptic dialects give us some hint of the richness of the Egyptian language that must have existed from the earliest times.

Source: Antonio Loprieno, *Ancient Egyptian: A Linguistic Introduction* (Cambridge & New York: Cambridge University Press, 1995).

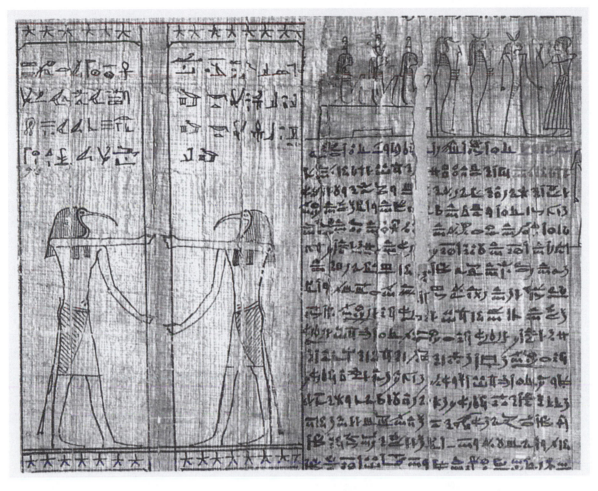

Book of the Dead of Kahapa with hieroglyphs, circa 1075–656 B.C.E. (Private Collection)

standable dialect. "There is no interpreter who can translate what you say," says the letter writer. "Your words are like the speech of a Delta man (from the far north of Egypt) with a man from Elephantine (an island at Egypt's extreme southern boundary)."

No Vowels. Aside from the inherent conservatism of Egyptian scribes, the other principal force working to disguise local dialects in documents is the fact that Egyptian writing did not ordinarily represent vowels, and often differences in pronunciation are primarily a result of how vowels are pronounced. Nevertheless, dialectical differences are occasionally visible in written Egyptian. In some cases, texts that earlier generations of Egyptologists could not understand and had pronounced to be either corrupt or the product of inept scribes have been shown to be written in local dialects that had grammatical rules different from the standard language. In other cases, spellings that were so different that they were thought to reflect entirely distinct words that have been shown to be merely regional variations.

Dialects in Coptic. Once native, consonantal Egyptian scripts fell out of use, however, and the fully alphabetic Coptic script became the main medium of writing the Egyptian language, at least some regional dialects became fully visible. Several major and minor dialects have been

identified for Coptic; the differences are more apparent in how vowels are supplied for words than they are in matters of grammar or vocabulary. There is little to suggest that educated speakers of any Coptic dialect would have had much difficulty in understanding speakers from other parts of the country. So one might surmise that the writer of the Dynasty 19 letter quoted above was deliberately exaggerating the differences in regional speech patterns.

Sources:
James P. Allen, *Middle Egyptian: An Introduction to the Language and Culture of Hieroglyphs* (New York: Cambridge University Press, 2000).

W. Vivian Davies and Louise Schofield, eds., *Egypt, the Aegean and the Levant: Interconnections in the Second Millenium B.C.* (London: British Museum Press for the Trustees of the British Museum, 1995).

Antonio Loprieno, *Ancient Egyptian: A Linguistic Introduction* (Cambridge & New York: Cambridge University Press, 1995).

FOREIGN LANGUAGES IN EGYPT

Diverse Languages. While the great majority of inhabitants of Egypt spoke a single language, there were always foreigners in Egypt who spoke other languages. Egyptians had a word for "interpreter" as early as the Old Kingdom (circa 2675–2130 B.C.E.), so there must have been a noticeable presence of speakers of foreign languages in Egypt by that time. The conservatism of the Egyptian language did not prevent it from taking up words from their neighbors. It is not always possible to identify the exact origin of words that are suspected to be foreign, especially when it seems likely that the donor language was unwritten, as was the case with many African tongues. (An exception to this general rule is Meroitic, the language of a kingdom that took root in the Sudan in the late ninth century B.C.E. It developed its own alphabetic script, which was based on Egyptian Demotic signs, in the early second century B.C.E. Several Meroitic loan words are attested in late phases of Egyptian). However, the Semitic languages of Syria-Palestine and Mesopotamia are much better known, and Semitic words were constantly being taken into the Egyptian language, a trend that is especially noticeable during the New Kingdom (circa 1539–1075 B.C.E.), when Egypt had an empire in Syria-Palestine. Semitic speakers had, of course, been in Egypt from quite early in Egyptian history, and a Semitic-speaking dynasty of Canaanite invaders (the Hyksos) had even conquered the Egyptian Delta and ruled it from 1630–1523 B.C.E.

Inspiration for the Alphabet. Probably the most important Semitic speakers to leave their linguistic mark in Egypt were an anonymous group of traders or mercenaries who, some time around 1900 to 1800 B.C.E., began to write their own language in a system of simplified Egyptian hieroglyphs. The discovery of the earliest examples of this script, written on a cliff face in the desert near ancient Thebes, was announced in 1999 C.E. The inscriptions cannot yet be read with much confidence, but it seems quite clear that they are written in a script that is ancestral to the alphabetic script called "Proto-Sinaitic," which was used several centuries later, during the Egyptian New Kingdom. Proto-Sinaitic gets its name from the fact that it is an early (proto) alphabetic script that was found for the first time in the Sinai Peninsula, the desert region between the continent of Africa and the modern territories of Israel, Palestine, and Jordan. Like the newly discovered Theban script, Proto-Sinaitic was an alphabetic system with a limited number of signs, all clearly derived from Egyptian hieroglyphs. It seems relatively clear that Proto-Sinaitic, or a close relative, must have been the ancestor of the alphabetic scripts that developed in Canaan and Phoenicia in the Iron Age (after 1200 B.C.E.). Phoenician script, of course, was adopted by the Greeks to write their language and became the ancestor of most alphabetic scripts in use in the modern world.

Later Influence. In later years other foreign words entered the Egyptian language, following a series of foreign conquerors. In Demotic script, words of Persian, Greek, and Latin origin, while not exactly abundant, are nevertheless not hard to find. The most influential of these languages was undoubtedly Greek. It is hard to know how long it took Greek to make inroads into spoken Egyptian in the years after Alexander the Great's

Early Demotic loan agreement from Thebes, circa 589–570 B.C.E. (British Museum, London)

Cuneiform document from Abi-Milki, king of Tyre, to Akhenaten, circa 1353–1336 B.C.E. Egyptian scribes learned to read and write Akkadian, the international language of the day (British Museum, London).

late Dynasty 18. These letters were found at the site of el-Amarna, the modern name of a town near Akhenaten's political capital, which he established as part of his religious reforms. The letters are written in Akkadian, the Semitic language of ancient Mesopotamia, which was the international diplomatic language of the time. They show the extent to which mastering foreign languages was necessary even for the proud Egyptians. Some of the Amarna texts are actually bilingual word lists to help Egyptian scribes master Akkadian and/or to help Akkadian-speaking scribes learn Egyptian.

Archive at Elephantine. A second great non-Egyptian archive comes from the much later Persian Period (525–404 B.C.E.) when Egypt was under the domination of the Persian Empire. One might think that this find means that large numbers of Persian (Iranian)-language texts have been discovered in Egypt, but this is not the case. Rather, non-Egyptian documents from the Persian Period are mainly in Aramaic, a Semitic language closely related to Hebrew and common to large areas of the ancient Near East in the last several centuries B.C.E. and first centuries C.E. Many Aramaic texts have been found on Elephantine, an island in the Nile opposite the town of Aswan, which was the historic southern border of Egypt. The Persians had established a military colony there to act as a border garrison, and it so happened that many soldiers stationed at Elephantine were Jews, whose vernacular language was Aramaic. The Elephantine Aramaic documents are an invaluable source for reconstructing the social, religious, and economic life of these soldiers and their families, as well as some of the political events of the day.

Sources:

Alan K. Bowman, *Egypt After the Pharaohs 332 BC–AD 642: From Alexander to the Arab Conquest* (Berkeley: University of California Press, 1986).

William L. Moran, ed., *The Amarna Letters* (Baltimore: Johns Hopkins University Press, 1992).

Bezalel Porten, *Archives from Elephantine: The Life of an Ancient Jewish Military Colony* (Berkeley: University of California Press, 1968).

J. N. Wilford, "Finds in Egypt Date Alphabet in Earlier Era," *New York Times*, CXLIX (14 November 1999): pp. 1, 16.

INTERPRETERS AND AMBASSADORS

Barbarians. The Egyptians had several related words that appear to have referred to speakers of foreign languages and, by extension, to interpreters. The precise significance of these words is not clear, in part because they appear ultimately to be nonsense syllables used in imitation of foreigners' incomprehensible speech, much like the Greek term "barbarian" is ultimately related to the Greeks' perception of foreigners as saying nothing but "bar, bar, bar." Speakers of foreign languages were used in Egyptian expeditions into and beyond border areas, such as into the Sinai or to the Red Sea. In other contexts, interpreters were needed when foreigners visited the court of Pharaoh or conducted other official business. Presumably, Egyptian envoys to foreign lands could either speak the language of

conquest. Aside from personal names, relatively few certain Greek words appear in Demotic and even fewer in hieroglyphic inscriptions. But once the Coptic script became the principal medium used to write Egyptian in the fifth century C.E., there was an explosion of Greek vocabulary that is conspicuous in any Coptic text. It seems likely that the conservatism of Egyptian scribes in the Ptolemaic and Roman periods may have worked to keep Greek words out of written Egyptian, even as Greek loan words were coming into spoken Egyptian in large numbers.

Foreign Archives. Documents written in non-Egyptian languages other than Greek are less common than Greek and Egyptian texts. Generally they come from official archives or from graffiti. One of the most important archives containing non-Egyptian texts is the corpus of "Amarna letters," an archive of official diplomatic correspondence carried on under Amenhotep III, Amenhotep IV (Akhenaten), and Tutankhamun, three pharaohs of

A relief of a group of emissaries from Libya and Asia in the presence of the king's deputy, circa 1319–1292 B.C.E. (Rijksmuseum van Oudheden, Leiden)

the country to which they were sent or had access to interpreters of their own.

Training? One question that remains unanswerable is how interpreters were trained. Could, and did, people learn foreign languages late in life, or were most bilingual people in the ancient world capable of speaking multiple languages from an early age? Unfortunately, little or no information is available on how the teaching of foreign languages was carried out in ancient Egypt.

Sources:

W. Vivian Davies and Louise Schofield, eds., *Egypt, the Aegean and the Levant: Interconnections in the Second Millenium B.C.* (London: British Museum Press for the Trustees of the British Museum, 1995).

William A. Ward, *Egypt and the East Mediterranean World, 2200–1900 B.C.: Studies in Egyptian Foreign Relations during the First Intermediate Period* (Beirut: American University of Beirut, 1971).

LITERACY

Divergent Skills. Exactly how many people in ancient Egypt could read and write is still largely a matter of conjecture. The first problem to face is precisely what is meant by "literacy." Undoubtedly, there were many levels of literacy. Some people could barely manage to read or write their own names. Others might be able to read a personal letter or simple list. At the highest level were skilled scribes who could read and write the most complex documents and had a thorough knowledge of secular and religious literature in Egypt. Finally, there were periods when even well-educated persons could read and write in one Egyptian script, but

Statue of a scribe, circa 1478–1458 B.C.E. (University of Pennsylvania Museum of Archaeology and Anthropology)

Writing board with hieratic text, from Abydos, late Ramesside Period, circa 1295–1069 B.C.E.
(Musees Royaux d'Art et d'Histoire, Brussels)

not in others. Many persons who could read and write Demotic for everyday purposes (such as the composition of personal letters, business accounts, or tax receipts), for example, probably had little or no knowledge of hieroglyphic and hieratic.

Literacy Estimates—or "Guesstimates." Some Egyptologists have made attempts to estimate the relative size of the literate population of Egypt. It seems likely that the bulk of the literate population consisted of middle-to-high-level officials in the government and/or in the major temples. These were the persons who would have had the most need of literacy because the royal house and temples were major economic enterprises with interests throughout the country. This role meant that scribes who could write for administrative purposes had to be on hand. And both the government and religious establishment—it would be a mistake to try and rigidly separate the two—were also in need of scribes who could produce monumental inscriptions and religious literature. The most typical estimate for literacy in Egypt, based on the size of the "elite" population, is about 1 percent during the Old Kingdom, a figure that is considered more or less plausible for the rest of Pharaonic history in Egypt.

Working-Class Literacy? However, estimates based on the number of the elite in Egypt overlook the fact that persons in the middle class—working as artisans or merchants—may, in many cases, have had need of at least some literacy skills. In the much later Greco-Roman Period there is at least some evidence that boat captains were often literate or semiliterate. This case may well have been true of other working class occupations as well, and it may turn out that literacy was more widespread in Egypt than many scholars have been willing to concede. The evidence, however, will probably never be sufficient for scholars to draw any firm conclusions.

Sources:

J. Baines and C. J. Eyre, "Four Notes on Literacy," *Göttinger Miszellen*, 61 (1983), pp. 65–96.

Raffaella Cribiore, *Writing, Teachers, and Students in Graeco-Roman Egypt* (Atlanta: Scholars Press, 1996).

Steve Vinson, *The Nile Boatman at Work* (Mainz: von Zabern, 1998), pp. 91–96.

For the ancient Egyptians one of the most important plants was the papyrus (*Cyperus papyrus*), a flowering reed that grew on the banks of the Nile River and in its marshy delta. It could grow up to ten feet tall and attain widths of around six to seven inces. The plant was used to make many products, from baskets and rope to footwear and bedding, and it could even be eaten. Papyrus was combined with plaster to make cartonnage, which was used to construct body-fitting coffins that were then painted. Hunters and fishermen plied Egyptian waters in small papyrus boats. The plant was so valuable that it was eventually cultivated and controlled by state monopoly. Products from the plant were exported throughout the region. By far the most notable use of the plant was as a "paper." Egyptians may have begun making papyrus as early as 4000 B.C.E. So good was this parchment that ancient Mediterranearn civilizations, including the Greeks and Romans, adopted its use for official government and religious documents, as well as for literary works.

Time-consuming and expensive to manufacture, papyrus was made from the triangle-shaped reeds, which were split; the pulp was then removed and pounded into thin strips. This material was soaked for several days to eliminate excess sugars and then was laid side-by-side with other strips in two-layered sheets (each layer was laid in the opposite direction) that were then beaten again or pressed. Individual sheets, or sometimes twenty or more attached pieces, were dried in the sun and then rolled. Reed pens were used to place inks, usually made form lampblack, onto the papyrus; painters could also apply pigments.

Sources: "Ancient Egyptian Papyrus," *Emuseum*, Minnesota State University, Internet website, http://emuseum.mnsu.edu/prehistory/egypt/dailylife/papyrus.html.

Rosalie David, *Handbook to Life in Ancient Egypt* (New York: Facts on File, 1998).

PILGRIMAGES

Religious Motivation. As in the modern Middle East, the desire to visit places of religious significance was an important motivation for travel. Egyptians often traveled to religious sites to perform rites, to participate in festivals, or just to view famous landmarks. Many of these trips are described in Egyptian art and literature. Others are commemorated by graffiti left behind by the pilgrims themselves. These graffiti can range from a simple name scrawled on a temple wall to an elaborate inscription. They include prayers to the god being visited, descriptions of good deeds performed by the authors, and requests to future readers of the inscription to pray for the authors. Most especially they ask that no one erase the graffiti.

Pilgrimage to Abydos. Perhaps the most famous of Egyptian pilgrimage destinations was Abydos, a holy city of great antiquity. It included the reputed grave of Osiris (actually the tomb of Djer, the third king of Dynasty 1) as well as another underground shrine of Osiris connected with the funerary temple of Dynasty 19 pharaoh Sety I. From the Middle Kingdom onward, Egyptian tombs often show representations of a voyage to Abydos that was to be undertaken by the deceased (in the form of a mummy or statue). Visitors to the cemeteries at Abydos left behind many private statues and steles (inscribed stones).

Temple of Isis at Philae. Late in Egyptian history, the temple of Isis at Philae, a beautiful, small island south of Aswan, became a popular destination for pilgrims, many of whom left graffiti behind to tell of their visits. This structure was actually the last of the pagan temples of Egypt to be closed by the Christian emperors of the late Roman Empire, and the graffiti at the Isis temple include both the last known Demotic and hieroglyphic inscriptions. Visitors at Philae recorded votive acts performed by one pilgrim, including payment to have the sacred river barge of Isis smeared with pitch, a means of waterproofing the hull and extending its lifetime.

Sources:
F. L. Griffith, *Catalogue of the Demotic Graffiti of the Dodecaschoenus*, volume 1 (Oxford: Oxford University Press, 1937), pp. 1–7.

Ian Rutherford, "Island of the Extremity: Space, Language and Power in the Pilgrimage Traditions of Philae," in *Pilgrimage and Holy Space in Late Antique Egypt*, edited by David Frankfurter (Leiden & Boston: E. J. Brill, 1998).

Eleni Vassilika, *Ptolemaic Philae* (Leuven: Uitgeverij Peeters, 1989).

Pilgrim flask, from Abydos, Dynasty 18, circa 1539–1295/1292 B.C.E. (University of Pennsylvania Museum of Archaeology and Anthropology)

MARDI GRAS ON THE NILE

The Greek historian Herodotus wrote much about Egypt and devoted all of Book II of his History to Egyptian history and anthropology. As part of his account of Egyptian religion, Herodotus left a vivid description of pilgrims on their way to the Delta city of Bubastis to take part in ceremonies honoring the goddess Bastet.

When they travel to Bubastis, this is what they do. They sail thither, men and women together, and a great number of each in each boat. Some of the women have rattles and rattle them, others play the flute through the entire trip, and the remainder of the women and men sing and clap their hands. As they travel on toward Bubastis and come near some other city, they edge the boat near the bank, and some of the women do as I have described (that is, sing and play flutes or shake rattles). But others of them scream obscenities in derision of the women who live in that city, and others of them set to dancing, and others still, standing up, throw their clothes open to show their nakedness. This they do at every city along the riverbank. When they come to Bubastis, they celebrate the festival with great sacrifices, and more wine is drunk at that single festival than in all the rest of the year besides.

Source: *The History: Herodotus*, translated by David Grene (Chicago: University of Chicago Press, 1988), p. 157.

An Unknown Destination. Of all the places to which the Egyptians traveled, probably the one that was for them most evocative of remote and distant locales was Punt. This area has never been located with absolute certainty but was probably a coastal region of southern Sudan or, perhaps, Somalia, and may also have included areas of southern Arabia, just across the Red Sea from Somalia itself.

Early Contacts. Punt was known as early as the Old Kingdom (circa 2675–2130 B.C.E.). The earliest reference is from the reign of Sahure, who sent an expedition there for myrrh and electrum (a mixture of silver and gold). Two pharaohs, Djedkare Isesi of Dynasty 5 (circa 2500–2350 B.C.E.) and Neferkare Pepy II of Dynasty 6 (circa 2350–2170 B.C.E.), reportedly received pygmies from Punt, although in all likelihood they had been captured further south and brought to Punt by middlemen.

During the Middle Kingdom. In the Middle Kingdom, inscriptions such as that of the Egyptian official Henenu (circa 2008–1957 B.C.E.) from the Wadi Hammamat attest to expeditions to Punt. These inscriptions show that for the Egyptians the route to Punt included an overland trek from Coptos (modern Qift) to the vicinity of a Red Sea coastal village called Mersa Gawasis, where ships were assembled and the sea voyage began. Few contacts are certain after early Dynasty 12 (circa 1938–1759 B.C.E.), but Punt nevertheless remained a legendary destination for foreign travel and adventure: an Egyptian prose work called the "Tale of

Detail from Queen Hatshepsut's funerary temple at Deir el Bahri depicting laborers carrying olive branches and herbs while on an expedition to Punt, circa 1478/1472–1458 B.C.E.

the Shipwrecked Sailor" recounts the experiences of a sailor who is marooned on a distant island during a voyage to Punt.

Renewed Contact. Under the Dynasty 18 woman pharaoh Hatshepsut a major expedition to Punt was launched, commemorated with splendid, detailed relief sculptures at her funerary temple at Deir el Bahri. Here one sees the ships that were dispatched, illustrations of the products of Punt, as well as some of the Puntites themselves, including the famous "Queen of Punt," a diminutive and wrinkled woman with an immense backside. Among the various products brought back from Punt were myrrh, electrum, gold, tropical woods, incense, baboons and monkeys, minerals for eye makeup, dogs, and panther, or leopard, skins. Several later New Kingdom pharaohs, including Ramesses III, mention other expeditions to Punt. It seems possible that the location of Punt was still known in Dynasty 26 (664–525 B.C.E.). But by the Greco-Roman Period, the name "Punt" was no longer connected with any specific place and was not, so it seems, known to real traders and merchants who traveled to the coast of eastern Africa.

Sources:

K. Kitchen, "The Land of Punt," in Thurston Shaw and others, *The Archaeology of Africa: Food, Metals, and Towns* (London & New York: Routledge, 1993), pp. 587–606.

Kitchen, "Punt and How to Get There," *Orientalia*, 40 (1971): 184–207.

Alessandra Nibbi, *Ancient Egypt and Some Eastern Neighbors* (Park Ridge, N.J.: Noyes Press, 1981).

SHIP CONSTRUCTION

Maritime Technology. Boats and ships were always a crucial technology in ancient Egypt because the Nile River tied Egypt together and the empire had long coastlines on the Mediterranean Sea and the Red Sea. Watercraft were an important theme in Egyptian art. In the Predynastic and Pharaonic Periods extraordinarily detailed paintings and models make scholars better informed about the actual construction of Egyptian ships than they are about any other ancient nautical tradition before the Greco-Roman Period. Even better than this artistic documentation, however, are the actual remains of Egyptian boats, which are known from Dynasties 1, 4, and 12, as well as from the Persian Period. Unlike most ancient boats or ships, Egyptian boat remains have all been discovered on land, not in underwater excavations. The Egyptian boats or boat fragments that are known are mostly funerary, designed to accompany a dead person into the next world. As such, they probably differ in many details from working boats of the time, but there is good reason to think that they also duplicate much of the basic technology that would have gone into any large wooden vessel.

The Royal Ship of Khufu (Cheops). The largest and best-preserved ship from antiquity is the funerary ship of Khufu (Cheops), the builder of the Great Pyramid at Giza. This ship, which is about 150 feet long and built mainly of imported Lebanese cedar, was found in the

1950s C.E. disassembled in a sealed pit next to the pyramid. It was in remarkably good condition and was reconstructed and put on display in a special museum near the pyramid, where it can be seen today. The remarkable thing about the Khufu ship, which it shares with most ancient Egyptian watercraft, is that it was not nailed together like a modern wooden ship would be, nor was it put together with wooden pegs, as the Greeks and Romans had built their ships. Rather, the Khufu ship was literally sewn together by means of heavy ropes that were threaded through channels cut in the inner surfaces of the planks. This type of construction was extremely long-lived in Egypt—there is evidence that it survived down to the Greco-Roman Period, possibly even into the early Middle Ages. Egyptian "sewn" vessel-construction technique was quite practical on many grounds. Maintenance was simplified: damaged pieces could be more easily removed than on a ship that was nailed or pegged together. A "sewn" ship could be taken apart and put back together again with a minimum of special tools, which was an advantage in the overland transportation of ships. Remember that to get their ships from the Nile River to the Red Sea, the Egyptians,

---

HERODOTUS DESCRIBES THE CONSTRUCTION OF AN EGYPTIAN BOAT

In the fifth century B.C.E., the Greek historian Herodotus, in the course of researching his great history of the wars between Greece and Persia, visited Egypt, then a province of the Persian Empire. Herodotus was fascinated with all aspects of Egyptian history and with the ways of life of the people of Egypt, and many of his descriptions of things he saw are among the most valuable sources for the history of Egypt. In one fascinating passage, Herodotus describes the construction of a particular kind of Egyptian freight boat, called a "baris."

The boats with which they carry cargo are made of acacia. Cutting two-cubit (approximately three feet) planks from this acacia, they build the hull like a brick-layer in the following way: they pound the two-cubit-long planks onto closely-spaced, large tenons (that is, flat pegs of wood), and when they have built up the hull in this way, they lay deck-beams above (at deck-level). They do not use frames (that is, ribs); and they lash the hulls together from the inside with papyrus (cords). There is one steering oar, which passes through the bottom-plank. They use acacia masts and papyrus sails. These boats are unable to sail upriver if the wind is not strong, so they are towed from the land. There are a great many of these boats, and some carry many tons.

Source: *The History: Herodotus,* translated by David Grene (Chicago: University of Chicago Press, 1988), p. 170.

Model of boat, from the tomb of Tutankhamun, circa 1332–1322 B.C.E. (Egyptian Museum, Cairo)

such as Henenu, would disassemble a vessel, carry it in pieces through the desert, and then put it back together again on the Red Sea coast.

Other Egyptian Vessels. Scholars know other Egyptian boats from Dynasty 1. These boats, which were buried in a royal cemetery, were also intended to accompany a pharaoh into the next world. Excavation of these vessels has only just begun, but it appears that, much like the Khufu boat, these vessels were lashed together. An unusual feature of the boats is that they seem to have had reed bundles fastened between the planks to act as caulking. Aside from these complete vessels, wooden fragments have been discovered in a nonroyal cemetery that were worked in ways that strongly recall the techniques that went into the construction of the Khufu vessel. While it is unsure whether these particular planks come from ships, they

do show that the techniques that went into the Khufu vessel were in use as early as Dynasty 1, and may well be far older. Four other intact boats are known from Dynasty 12, all excavated at the Egyptian site of Dahshur. These vessels, like the Khufu ship, were sewn together, although the technique was somewhat different. Finally, a boat that dates to the Persian Period, discovered near Cairo, shows an interesting mix of native Egyptian and Greek-style hull construction.

Sources:
Björn Landström, *Ships of the Pharaohs: 4000 Years of Egyptian Shipbuilding* (Garden City, N.Y.: Doubleday, 1970; London: Allen & Unwin, 1970).

Paul Lipke, *The Royal Ship of Cheops* (Oxford: B.A.R., 1984).

Steve Vinson, *Egyptian Boats and Ships* (Princes Risborough, Buckinghamshire, U.K.: Shire Publications, 1994).

Cheryl A. Ward, *Sacred and Secular: Ancient Egyptian Ships and Boats* (Boston: University Museum for the Archaeological Institute of America, 1999).

Funerary boat of Khufu, found in a pit at the south side of his pyramid at Giza, circa 2585–2560 B.C.E. (from Ian Shaw, ed., *The Oxford History of Ancient Egypt*, 2000)

THEBAN DESERT: ROAD SURVEY

A Discovered Road. The recent discovery of a very old alphabetic script in the desert near Thebes is only one of the fascinating results of a survey of desert transportation routes in the Theban area that has been undertaken by Egyptologists John and Deborah Darnell since 1992. The principal focus of the Darnells' work has been on the road that runs from Luxor to the village of Farshut—in other words, a route through the desert that shortcuts the great eastward bend of the Nile, called the Qena Bend.

A Very Old Route. The Luxor-Farshut road is only the central artery in a complex network of desert tracks on the west side of the Nile in the Qena Bend area. Stone huts and piles called cairns are abundant in the area and give evidence of travelers and dwellers all the way back to the Paleolithic period and extending up to modern times. Many fragments of more-permanent constructions, including small chapels with hieroglyphic inscriptions, have been found. An unusual feature of the area is the presence of chapels built high on mountains overlooking Thebes. Unlike ancient Syria-Palestine, for example, where "high places" were common, mountaintop shrines

were not the norm in Egypt. But in the area around ancient Thebes, the small temples perched high on cliffs provided orientation points for travelers out in the desert—they are visible for miles and would help people navigate toward their destination.

The Travelers. Who were the travelers that frequented these desert trails and what brought them out into the desert? Scholars can answer that question in considerable detail because ancient Egyptian travelers were often in the habit of leaving behind graffiti to mark their passage. Some of the graffiti on the cliffs along the Luxor-Farshut road are fairly elaborate, well-executed hieroglyphic inscriptions; others are the barely legible scrawls of semi-literate wayfarers. But in both cases, they provide tantalizing clues to moments in the lives of real people. One graffito is by a soldier named Wenkhu, who probably passed through in the late Old Kingdom (circa 2675–2130 B.C.E.); he drew a picture of himself and wrote his name on his shield. Other graffiti suggest that the route was used by "interpreters of Yam," Nubian speakers who used the track for overland travel southward to trade in Nubia for exotic products.

Soldiers and Policemen. The travelers left behind other clues as well: broken pottery attests to water jars and cooking pots used thousands of years ago. Huts and small walls of stone or mud brick point to more-permanent installations where soldiers or police would watch the desert to try to protect travelers from bandits or the settlements in the valley from incursions by unwelcome and possibly hostile nomads. One crude graffito actually shows a policeman grasping a prisoner, whose hands are raised in a gesture of surrender! The roads were also used by Egyptian troops during times of civil disorder or political turmoil. Several of the inscriptions appear to refer to military campaigns during the First Intermediate Period, the time after the end of the Old Kingdom when central authority had broken down. One inscription refers to the "strike force" of a local ruler named Antef, who happened to be an ancestor of the eventual founder of a reunified Egyptian state and inaugurator of the period called the "Middle Kingdom." Another refers to improving the road, possibly in connection with military activity.

Sources:

John C. Darnell and Deborah Darnell, "New Inscriptions of the Late First Intermediate Period from the Theban Western Desert and the Beginnings of the Northern Expansion of the Eleventh Dynasty," *Journal of Near Eastern Studies*, 56 (October 1997): 241–258.

Darnell and Darnell, *Oriental Institute 1992-1993 Annual Report* (Chicago: University of Chicago), pp. 48–55.

Darnell and Darnell, *Oriental Institute 1993–1994 Annual Report* (Chicago: University of Chicago), pp. 40–48.

Darnell and Darnell, *Oriental Institute 1994–1995 Annual Report* (Chicago: University of Chicago), pp. 44–53.

Darnell and Darnell, *Oriental Institute 1995–1996 Annual Report* (Chicago: University of Chicago), pp. 62–69.

Darnell and Darnell, *Oriental Institute 1996-1997 Annual Report* (Chicago: University of Chicago), pp. 66–76.

Darnell and Darnell, *Oriental Institute 1997–1998 Annual Report* (Chicago: University of Chicago), pp. 77–92.

WHEELED VEHICLES

Late Development. Wheeled vehicles appear relatively late in Egypt—surprisingly enough, there is no evidence that any sort of wheeled transport was available to the builders of the great Dynasty 4 pyramids at Giza, for example. Instead, wheels are pictured for the first time in the late Old Kingdom (circa 2675–2130 B.C.E.). From Dynasty 6, a tomb painting shows wheels used to help move a ladder in a scene of soldiers attempting to storm an enemy town. Wheeled sledges are pictured in tombs from the Dynasties 5, 11, and 13. All of these early examples are solid wheels, made without spokes.

Earliest Spoked Wheels. The use of spoked wheels appears to have been introduced into Egypt around the time of the transition from the Second Intermediate Period to the New Kingdom. The first known spoked wheels in Egypt are from a small wheeled cart with a model boat set on it from the tomb of Ahhotep, mother of Ahmose (Amosis), the first pharaoh of Dynasty 18. But the most important use of spoked wheels was as part of the basic construction of battle chariots, mentioned for the first time in an inscription of the very end of Dynasty 17. In all likelihood, chariots were not developed in Egypt but were, along with horses, introduced into Egypt from Syria-Palestine. Their actual original home is a matter of conjecture. The earliest examples of Egyptian chariots have wheels with only four spokes, but relatively soon afterward up to ten spokes were utilized. The construction of spoked wheels is illustrated in several tomb scenes.

King Tut's Chariots. Of course the best evidence of how wheeled vehicles in Egypt were constructed comes from actual examples, most of which come from the tomb of Tutankhamun. Six chariots were discovered in his tomb. All of their wheels have six spokes and are quite complex in their construction, involving artificially bent wood, glue, and rawhide as binding materials. A lining of leather, and probably a lubricant of animal fat, was used to make the revolution of the wheel on its axle smoother and quieter. Chariots had wheels set well apart so that they would remain stable during fast, tight turns; they were completely open in back so that the two passengers, a driver and an archer, could quickly enter and exit the car. Some illustrations show that a skilled driver could tie the chariot reigns around his waist and steer with his body movements, leaving his hands free to fire arrows.

A Royal Prerogative. Chariots were always associated with royalty in Egypt, and throughout Dynasties 18, 19, and early 20, images of the pharaoh in a chariot—hunting or battling his enemies—are a major piece of royal iconography. Aside from the chariots from the tomb of Tutankhamun, fragmentary remains of chariots have come from the tombs of Amenhotep II, Thutmose IV, Amenhotep III, and Ay. At least some high-ranking nonroyals could also take chariots into the next

Detail from an ostrich-feather fan handle of Tutankhamun showing him hunting in a chariot, circa 1332–1322 B.C.E. (Ashmolean Museum, Oxford)

world with them, such as Yuya and Tuya, the father- and mother-in-law of Amenhotep III. Another intact Egyptian chariot, now in a museum in Florence, Italy, may well have come from a nonroyal tomb, but its exact origin is unknown.

Sources:

M.A. Littauer and J. H. Crouwel, *Chariots and Related Equipment from the Tomb of Tut'ankhamun* (Oxford: Griffith Institute, 1985).

Robert Partridge, *Transport in Ancient Egypt* (London: Rubicon Press, 1996).

B. G. Trigger and others, *Ancient Egypt: A Social History* (Cambridge & New York: Cambridge University Press, 1983).

WOMEN IN TRANSPORTATION

Female Opportunities. Egypt was a land in which women were better off than in most parts of the ancient world. Few occupations were completely closed off to women, including occupations having to do with trade and transportation.

Old Kingdom Evidence. Several Old Kingdom relief sculptures show women aboard transport boats; in at least one case, a woman is actually steering the boat. Children aboard the same vessels suggest that in these cases one may be seeing an image of a boat that was owned by a family and that all family members—women, men, and children—worked together on what was essentially a small, mobile family business.

Women Skippers. Most interesting is the fact that several female skippers are known by name to scholars. These women all lived during the Ptolemaic period between 323 and 30 B.C.E. They are known because their names figure in real estate contracts. (Contracts and other legal documents are an invaluable source of insight into the Egyptian "middle class"—artisans and merchants who may not have been literate themselves, but who had to have dealings with the government and with the legal system.) One of the women is named Tawepyt, and she is described as a "woman skipper." Another woman, named Tameneh, is called the "fisherwoman"—the title does not guarantee that she was the operator of a boat, but the title "fisherman" often has this connotation. In light of the illustrations from the Egyptian Old Kingdom of women working aboard boats, one might guess that these Ptolemaic women also were probably part owners with husbands or other family members in small boats that were operated as family enterprises. Unfortunately, there is not much specific evidence for women involved in other facets of transportation or communication. Some women were referred to as "merchants," and this occupation may have involved them in arranging for the transportation of goods. A special case is the fact that in the Ptolemaic period, women of royal rank often owned large transport ships. Needless to say, these women never were involved in the actual running of their vessels. Probably they were simply investors who turned the operation of the ships over to their captains or special shipping agents called *naukleroi* (a Greek term meaning literally "man in charge of a ship").

Sources:

Zahi Hawass, *Silent Images: Women in Pharaonic Egypt* (New York: Abrams, 2000).

Gay Robins, *Women in Ancient Egypt* (Cambridge, Mass.: Harvard University Press, 1993).

Steve Vinson, *The Nile Boatman at Work* (Mainz: von Zabern, 1998), pp. 90–91.

WRITING

Letters. Epistolography simply means "letter writing." The Egyptians began to send one another letters almost as soon as they learned to write. Like modern letters, Egyptian ones had certain well-defined, regular features that anyone sitting down to write would employ automatically. A large number of letters from ancient Egypt are extant—some personal, some for business, and some even written to gods or to the dead! Scholars also have several "model letters," examples that may have been based on real letters that had at one time been exchanged between real people but were preserved and given to scribal trainees as models on which to base their own letters. It should be remembered that few people, even those who could read and write, would have written their own letters. Rather, it was normal to go to a scribe, a professional writer, who would compose letters for pay.

Structure of Egyptian Letters. Egyptian epistolography became more complex through history. Early Egyptian letters simply begin with a date and a statement of the letter writer's name and then go straight into the matter at hand. By the Middle Kingdom, letters are prefaced with various greetings, both to the recipient and to mutual friends. In the New Kingdom, this style becomes more elaborate still, with more-flowery greetings and lists of gods whose blessings the writer wishes to invoke on his behalf and that of the

Section of the *Pyramid Texts* in the tomb of Unas at Saqqara, circa 2371–2350 B.C.E.

There were times when a person was so outraged at the stupidity of another that he could not prevent himself from writing a hostile, abusive, or sarcastic letter. At least two such letters exist. One of them appears to have been a real letter written by a senior bureaucrat to an inept subordinate, a man who had bungled his duties in organizing shipping for an Egyptian temple. The other is a purely literary composition, written in the form of a letter. Here one scribe lambastes a colleague for his pretensions to the special knowledge required of an Egyptian envoy and attempts to show that his colleague could never survive one day outside of Egypt on a real diplomatic mission. The letter is extremely sarcastic and employs all sorts of rare words and expressions, many based on Semitic languages that an Egyptian envoy would be expected to know if he were to undertake a mission in Palestine. Here are two excerpts from these letters, first the real letter (P. Anastasi VIII), and then the fictional letter (P. Anastasi I). In the excerpt from P. Anastasi VIII, the writer is outraged that his subordinate has been so irresponsible as to let a ship travel from one port to another with a full crew but no cargo. The result was the shipowner was forced to pay for the operation of the ship without obtaining any benefit. The author uses a picturesque metaphor that appears to be an obscenity or vulgarity. The expression is unclear but it may imply that in making this mistake, the foolish scribe has smeared offal—the putrid remains of a dismembered, rotting carcass—all over himself. The meaning is probably something like the English expression "you've stepped in it."

Something else—you have smeared offal (?) (on yourself); you have smeared yourself well! Is it true that what you did was to send the cattle-transport boat that used to carry wool with the boat-captain Sety to Heliopolis empty, with a crew of six men? Really, these people are now your responsibility!

In Papyrus Anastasi I, the scribe Hori sends a sarcastic and elaborate letter to a colleague. This text was popular as a school text. There are at least eighty ostraca with portions of the text known. Hori upbraids the recipient of his letter for his lack of the multitudes of types of knowledge that an expert scribe was supposed to possess, including, in this extract, knowledge of the geography of remote areas of Syria-Palestine. The recipient had earlier written to Hori claiming to have just such knowledge; Hori demanded that he prove it.

I will mention to you another difficulty: "The Pass of Hornets" (a route to Tyre in Lebanon). You will say that it burns more than a hornet's sting. How miserable he is, a warrior! Come and put me on the road heading south to the region of Acco. Where does the route to Achshaph originate? Next to which city? Please inform me about the mountain of User. What is its summit like? Where does the mountain of Shechem rise? Who can conquer it? How does the warrior march to get to Hazor? What is its river like? Put me on the highway to Hamath, Dagel, and Dagal-El, the promenade of every warrior. Please instruct me about the soldier's route and let me visit Yan. If someone is traveling to Adumim, in which direction should he head? Do not falter in your teaching—guide us to know these places!

Source: Edward F. Wente, ed., *Letters From Ancient Egypt*, edited by Edmund S. Meltzer (Atlanta: Scholars Press, 1990), pp. 98–110.

Final section of the *Book of the Dead of Hunefer* showing the Great Cat killing a serpent, Dynasty 19, circa 1292–1190 B.C.E. (British Museum, London)

Jean-François Champollion, a decipherer of ancient Egyptian hieroglyphic writing, was born in 1790 and died in 1832. Champollion was a child prodigy as a linguist and believed from an early age that he was destined to solve the riddle of the hieroglyphs. As a boy of nine, he hoped to accompany Napoleon during the French invasion of Egypt, and at the age of sixteen he addressed a scientific meeting at the Academy of Grenoble, his hometown, in which he argued, correctly, that the ancient Egyptian language must be related to Coptic, the language of medieval Christian Egypt.

Champollion is best known for his decipherment of the hieroglyphic text of the Rosetta Stone, a large inscription with the text of a resolution by a college of priests conferring honors on the king Ptolemy V in 196 B.C.E. The inscription was discovered by French troops in 1799 C.E. but fell into the hands of the British after they drove the French invasion force from Egypt. Because the text of the Rosetta Stone was written in three scripts—Greek, hieroglyphic, and Demotic—it was recognized almost immediately that this inscription might provide the key to unlocking the mysteries of the system. After Napoleon's army evacuated Egypt, copies of the Rosetta Stone began circulating throughout Europe, and many scholars, including the young Champollion, began working on deciphering the hieroglyphic system.

Up until Champollion made his breakthrough, many scholars, including Champollion himself, labored under the misconception that hieroglyphic inscriptions did not embody language in the normal sense, but rather encoded ideas purely symbolically, much as mathematical equations can be understood by anyone who speaks any language. But Champollion's strategy was to concentrate on the personal names in the Rosetta Stone inscription, which earlier scholars had correctly guessed were enclosed in rings called cartouches. In this way, Champollion was quickly able to build up an inventory of signs that were clearly phonetic in character. Soon he was able to apply these signs to other words and, with his knowledge of Coptic grammar and vocabulary, he was able to unravel the gist of the text.

Champollion announced his breakthrough in 1822 C.E. in his *Lettre à M. Dacier* ("Letter to Monsieur Dacier," a public tract addressed to the permanent secretary of the French Academy of Inscriptions and Belles-Lettres) and followed up this message in 1824 with a more extensive *Précis du systèm hiéroglyphique des anciens Égyptiens* (Summary of the Ancient Egyptian Hieroglyphic System). Following these breakthroughs, he spent the rest of his short life continuing to decipher and collect hieroglyphic inscriptions. He became the curator of the Egyptian collection in the Louvre in 1826, and in 1828 and 1829 he visited Egypt with the intention of collecting and copying inscriptions. After his death, his elder brother, Jacques-Joseph Champollion, edited and published two other works, a grammar of the ancient Egyptian language and a hieroglyphic dictionary.

Sources: Carol Andrews, *The Rosetta Stone* (London: British Museum Publications, 1981).

R. Bianchi, "Champollion, Jean-François," *The Oxford Encyclopedia of Ancient Egypt*, volume 1, edited by D. B. Redford (Oxford & New York: Oxford University Press, 2001), pp. 260–261.

Alan Henderson Gardiner, *Egyptian Grammar*, third edition (London: Oxford University Press, 1957), pp. 12–13.

recipient. As a general rule, the proper style for writing letters was one of the most important elements of a young scribe's training, and many model letters have been discovered that were products of the educational process. Some of these letters are near-verbatim copies of real letters that the teacher may have composed or received himself, but others are elaborate exercises in rhetorical skill that teach not only basic letter-writing form but also obscure words and grammatical constructions that an advanced scribe was expected to be familiar with.

Sources:
Abd el-Mohsen Bakir, *Egyptian Epistolography from the Eighteenth to the Twenty-First Dynasty* (Cairo: Institut français d'archeologie orientale, 1970).

Edward F. Wente, *Late Ramesside Letters* (Chicago: University of Chicago Press, 1967).

Wente, ed., *Letters From Ancient Egypt*, edited by Edmund S. Meltzer (Atlanta: Scholars Press, 1990).

SIGNIFICANT PEOPLE

DHUTMOSE

FLOURISHED CIRCA 1190-1075 B.C.E.
SCRIBE OF THE NECROPOLIS

Troubled Times. Around 1090 B.C.E., Egypt was still an international power, but it was beset by internal and external crises and the New Kingdom was about to collapse. Ironically, it is from precisely this period that scholars have some of the best economic and social documentation from ancient Egypt, including a large number of personal letters and economic texts that concern the activities of a scribe named Dhutmose. His main title was "Scribe of the Necropolis," meaning that he was the business manager for the crew that was in charge of constructing the tomb of the reigning pharaoh. In the course of his job, he was responsible for dispatching boats and ships to collect grain taxes for the city of Thebes, and sometimes he personally went on these journeys. Men such as Dhutmose were also often called "controllers," a catch-all title for anyone with the responsibility for overseeing an economic enterprise.

Early Accounting or Fraud? Dhutmose's responsibilities included carefully accounting for grain that he had collected and dispersed. He arranged for the transportation of the grain and for the transportation that subordinate scribes needed. One well-documented case described the arrangements he made for his son, Butehamun, also a scribe. (The Egyptians had little or no problem with nepotism!) Most importantly, the scribe of the necropolis kept records of these transactions so that other scribes could audit all of these activities and make sure that grain or other valuable commodities were not being skimmed. Egyptian accounts are sometimes difficult to understand, and the records can sometimes seem haphazard. This problem led an eminent Egyptologist in the 1940s to conclude that Dhutmose had been skimming grain during one of his tax-collection voyages and had in fact tried to hide his embezzlements through extra-confusing accounting. A more careful analysis of the papyrus later proved that Dhutmose was innocent. There are other confirmed cases, however, of Egyptian scribes and boat captains embezzling their cargoes. But even in these cases—at least ones known about—Egyptian auditors were able to use the records at their disposal to discover who was responsible for the thefts and to calculate how much grain

had been diverted. Thus, the Egyptian system of fiscal controls was quite effective for its time and allowed officials of the New Kingdom to maintain a highly sophisticated economic system that was largely based on Nile River transportation.

Sources:
A. Gardiner, "Ramesside Texts Relating to the Taxation and Transport of Corn," *Journal of Egyptian Archaeology*, 27 (1941): 19ff.

Steve Vinson, "In Defense of an Ancient Reputation," *Göttinger Miszellen*, 146 (1995): 93ff.

Edward F. Wente, *Late Ramesside Letters* (Chicago: University of Chicago Press, 1967).

HENENU

FLOURISHED CIRCA 2008-1957 B.C.E.
TRAVELER TO PUNT

Route to Punt. For the ancient Egyptians, both land and sea travel might be required for a single expedition. This mode of travel was especially the case when the Egyptians wanted to go to Punt. The Nile River is not connected to the Red Sea, so it was necessary for the Egyptians to march overland through the Eastern Desert to reach the coast. The usual route was through a large natural passageway called the Wadi Hammamat (Hammamat Valley), which leaves the Nile valley at a town on the Qena Bend called Coptos and then proceeds eastward to reach the Red Sea coast. Because ancient Egyptian ships were sewn or lashed together, rather than nailed, it was possible for them to be built on the Nile River, taken apart into individual pieces, and carried overland to the Red Sea, where they could be lashed back together.

The Voyage of Henenu. One of the best documented of these expeditions was under the direction of a man named Henenu, an official of Dynasty 11 kings Mentuhotep II and III. How expeditions such as these proceeded can be best understood by simply letting Henenu speak for himself:

"My lord (may he live, be prosperous, and healthy!) sent me to dispatch a fleet to Punt to bring for him fresh myrrh from the chieftains of the desert. . . . Then I went forth from Coptos upon the road which his majesty commanded me. There was with me an army of the South . . . ; the army cleared the way, overthrowing those who were hostile towards the king; the hunters and the highlanders were posted as the protection of my limbs. . . . I went forth with an army of 3,000 men; I gave a leather bottle, a carrying pole, 2 jars of water and 20 loaves to each one among them every day. The donkeys were laden with sandals. . . . Now, I made 12 wells in the desert. . . . Then I reached the Sea, and I constructed the fleet, and I dispatched it with everything."

Thousands of Sandals. There were many logistical problems connected with such a large expedition. An army was necessary because the Egyptians did not have complete control over the dwellers of the desert. All of the food and drink of the expedition had to be carried, as well as the pieces of the fleet that Henenu was intending to build. Most interesting is the fact that the donkeys had to carry, so it would seem, thousands of extra sandals! Egyptian sandals were generally woven out of papyrus fibers and evidently did not stand up well to heavy marching through the stony desert tracks of the Wadi Hammamat.

Sources:

James Henry Breasted, ed., *Ancient Records of Egypt*, volume 1, *The First to the Seventeenth Dynasties* (Chicago: University of Chicago Press, 1906), pp. 208–210.

Gae Callender, "The Middle Kingdom Renaissance (c. 2055–1650)," in *The Oxford History of Ancient Egypt*, edited by Ian Shaw (Oxford & New York: Oxford University Press, 2000), pp. 148–183.

Aidan Dodson, *Monarchs of the Nile* (London: Rubicon, 1995).

SAHURE

FLOURISHED CIRCA 2485-2472 B.C.E.
KING, DYNASTY 5

Trade Promoter. Sahure, the second king of Dynasty 5 (2500–2350 B.C.E.), commissioned the earliest known oceangoing ships. Sahure's reign is credited with the earliest detailed representations of the types of seagoing vessels that were in use on the Mediterranean during the years of the Egyptian Old Kingdom. Early Egyptian annals mention that Sahure promoted trade all over the Egyptian world. He sent expeditions to the Sinai Peninsula and to the fabled East African land of Punt (probably in the vicinity of modern Somalia). Inscriptions also show that he sent miners for special hard stone far to the south of ancient Egypt, to the vicinity of the modern Egyptian-Sudanese border.

"Byblos" ships? What was the Egyptian name for the ships seen on Sahure's relief sculptures? It is often assumed that these vessels are the type called "Byblos" ships, named after the Lebanese city of Byblos with which the Egyptians had close trade relations. Inscriptions over the ships do not identify them by type—the main reason they are identified as "Byblos" ships is that there are men aboard them with pointed beards, a non-Egyptian style of wearing facial hair that in Egyptian art is usually associated with men from Syria-Palestine. But there are still a few questions that scholars would like to answer. They really have no idea why certain ships were called "Byblos." Was it because they were built in or near Byblos? Or was it because they were the type of ship that customarily traded with Byblos, much like in nineteenth-century America, when ships that sailed from the United States to east Asia were called "China Clippers"? One thing that can be said about Byblos ships in the Old Kingdom is that they were not confined to the Egypt-Byblos route. In fact, the earliest reference places them on the Red Sea, heading toward the East African land of Punt.

Anatomy of a Ship. What were these seagoing ships like? A plausible estimate suggests that they were fifty feet long, if the human figures aboard are drawn approximately to scale—if they are too big, then the ships might have ranged up to one hundred feet in length. The ships probably did not have any keel, or backbone, to make the hull rigid and keep it from bending and sagging as it traveled over the moving surface of the water. (This flexing of a wooden hull as it passes over waves and troughs is called hogging.) Instead, the Egyptians held the ends of their ship up with a heavy rope cable (called a "hogging truss"), tied to each end of the vessel, which they could twist to maintain proper tension. Another unusual aspect of these ships, from the point of view of modern sailing-vessel construction, is that they had "bi-pod" masts. The masts had two legs, unlike the single-pole masts that were more common in Egypt and are in almost universal use today for sailing craft. The bi-pod mast had the advantage of not putting all the weight of the rigging onto a single point in the bottom of the hull. Finally, although this detail is not completely visible in the Sahure relief sculptures, scholars know that Egyptian wooden boats and ships were literally sewn together, rather than nailed like modern wooden vessels. Channels were cut into the interior surfaces of planks, and heavy ropes were threaded through them to tie planks to each other—a practice that is rare but was actually still in use in the twentieth century C.E. for the construction of local freighters on the Indian Ocean.

Sources:

Björn Landström, *Ships of the Pharaohs: 4000 Years of Egyptian Shipbuilding* (Garden City, N.Y.: Doubleday, 1970; London: Allen & Unwin, 1970), pp. 63–69.

Steve Vinson, *Egyptian Boats and Ships* (Princes Risborough, Buckinghamshire, U.K.: Shire Publications, 1994), pp. 23–24.

Cheryl A. Ward, *Sacred and Secular: Ancient Egyptian Ships and Boats* (Boston: University Museum for the Archaeological Institute of America, 1999).

DOCUMENTARY SOURCES

Anonymous, *Story of a Shipwrecked Sailor* (circa 2200 B.C.E.)—A Middle Egyptian text written in Hieratic on papyrus that recounts the adventures of an unfortunate traveler.

Hatshepsut's temple reliefs (circa 1458 B.C.E.)—Inscribed reliefs found at Deir el Bahri, Egypt, which show the boats used for an expedition to Punt.

Herodotus, *History of the Persian Wars* (circa late fifth century B.C.E.)—Book 2 of this first work of history by the Greek historian covers Egypt after the invasion of the Persians.

Part of a wall painting from the tomb chapel of Sobekhotep depicting Nubians presenting gold rings, jasper, ebony logs, giraffe tails, a leopard skin, and live baboons, circa 1400 B.C.E. (British Museum, London)

Stone fragment of Amenhotep III as a conqueror returning to Egypt with African and Asiatic captives, circa 1390–1353 B.C.E. (Egyptian Museum, Cairo)

CHAPTER FIVE

SOCIAL CLASS SYSTEM AND THE ECONOMY

by EDWARD BLEIBERG

CONTENTS

Sidebars and tables are listed in italics.

2615 B.C.E.*

- The Egyptian population is approximately two million people.

- An elaborate system of titles for noblemen and noblewomen, and a central bureaucracy, are fully established. All officials below the king are referred to as the *pat;* commoners are known as *remetj.*

- A man named Metjen transfers his private property to heirs by a testamentary will in writing.

2585 B.C.E.*

- The corvée system (labor exacted in lieu of taxes by public authorities) is established. Work gangs are divided into groups called "phyles" and they build pyramid complexes for the first time.

2500-2485 B.C.E.*

- During the reign of King Userkaf the bureaucracy is opened to a wider group of people beyond the immediate royal family.

2485-2472 B.C.E.*

- Pictorial evidence from the Sun Temple of Sahure indicates that expeditions are sent to present-day Lebanon to obtain cedarwood. Inscriptions on other public edifices tell of trade expeditions to the land of Punt (Ethiopia and Djibouti).

2415-2371 B.C.E.*

- Royal bureaucrats begin to keep detailed papyrus records.

- Changes in bureaucratic titles reveal an attempt to bring officials under stricter royal control.

2298-2288 B.C.E.*

- The bureaucrat Weni leads expeditions to the stone quarries of Nubia (southern Egypt and the Sudan) and Hatnub (Middle Egypt). Another government official, Harkhuf, leads trade expeditions to Nubia.

2288-2224/ 2191 B.C.E.*

- Pepi-nakht heads an expedition to the Sinai Peninsula to punish Bedouin tribesmen who interfered with the building of ships destined for Punt.

- Harkhuf returns from Nubia with a dancing dwarf for the young king, Merenre. He also brings back ebony, elephant tusks, incense, oils, panther skins, and spears. He is rewarded with an official commendation and provisions of beer, bread, cakes, and wine.

*Denotes Circa Date

2130-1980 B.C.E.*

- Wealth increases among the lower classes as the central government collapses and there are no taxes to pay.

2008-1957 B.C.E.*

- The envoy Akhtoy leads a resumption of expeditions to Punt.

1980-1630 B.C.E.*

- *The Satire on the Trades* is composed by an anonymous scribe who describes professions practiced in ancient Egyptian society.
- The basic daily wage for a laborer is ten loaves of bread and one-third to two full jugs of beer. An expedition leader receives on average five hundred loaves a day.
- The slave class is composed mostly of criminals and foreign political prisoners.

1938-1759 B.C.E.*

- Trade occurs with the Minoan civilization on the island of Crete.
- Permanent Egyptian installations are built at Serabit el-Khadim in Sinai for mining turquoise. Meanwhile, forts are erected in Nubia to protect the gold trade.

1844-1837 B.C.E.*

- Another series of trade expeditions is sent to Punt.
- The village of Lahun has a manager's house that is at least ten times as large as any laborer's residence.

1539-1075 B.C.E.*

- Prisoners of war make up the vast majority of slaves in ancient Egypt.

1493-1479 B.C.E.*

- Deir el Medina, a village of artists and craftsmen who decorated and excavated tombs in the Valley of the Kings, is established. Each work gang is made up of a foreman, two deputies, scribes, and simple laborers.

1479-1425 B.C.E.*

- Thutmose III becomes the first Egyptian king to use the title *Pharaoh*, which means "The Great House."
- Trade flourishes with the Minoans, as indicated in tomb possessions and pottery remains.

*DENOTES CIRCA DATE

1478/1472-1458 B.C.E.*

- More trade expeditions are sent to Punt.

1390-1353 B.C.E.*

- Diplomatic gift giving becomes a form of trade between Egypt and various foreign kingdoms.

1353-1336 B.C.E.*

- The Deir el Medina village is closed, and the population is moved to Akhetaton (Amarna).

1292-1190 B.C.E.*

- Deir el Medina flourishes again after the population returns.
- At its height, the village has 70 houses and is the home of 120 workmen and their families. The estimated total population of the site is 1,200 people.
- The standard unit of weight for copper (and to a lesser extent gold and silver) is the *deben*. One *deben* equals ten *kite* while five *deben* equal one *senyu*. Prices of commodities include one *deben* for a razor; one *deben* for a *hin* (0.48 liters) of sesame oil; two *deben* for a *khar*, or sack (76.88 liters) of grain; twenty-five *deben* for a coffin; and seven *senyu* for a donkey.

1279-1213 B.C.E.*

- During the reign of Ramesses II, one *deben* of silver is valued at one hundred copper *deben*. With inflation, this ratio changes to 1:60 by the time of Ramesses IX (circa 1126–1108 B.C.E.).

1190-1075 B.C.E.*

- Inflation in the price of grain causes social unrest throughout Egypt. Strikes occur at Deir el Medina.

1075-1049 B.C.E.*

- The envoy Wenamun travels to Byblos (a coastal village in Lebanon) to buy cedarwood for the Barque of Amun, a sacred river barge. Wenamun provides the Prince of Byblos with gold, silver, linen, mats, ox hides, rope, lentils, and fish.

570 B.C.E.*

- All Greek imports are required by law to be unloaded at the port of Naukratis on the Canopic branch of the Nile near the capital of Sais.
- Egyptian agriculture has reached its highest levels of production and supports twenty thousand inhabitable cities and villages throughout the kingdom.

332 B.C.E.

*Denotes Circa Date

- The estimated population of Egypt is three million people.

OVERVIEW

Social Hierarchy. Ancient Egyptian society was highly stratified. There were six major divisions in society throughout roughly three thousand years of history. These divisions are reflected in honorary titles and occupational titles people used to describe themselves in their tombs. The groups included the royal family and nobles, the bureaucracy, the military, the priesthood, artisans, and agricultural workers. As early as the Predynastic Period (circa 3100–3000 B.C.E.) some graves contained more and better quality goods than others, suggesting that social stratification began early. The trend toward specialization and stratification accelerated as society became more complex in the historical periods.

Top to Bottom. Stratification began with the gods at the top of society. The king was the only point of intersection between gods and men. Beneath the king were the officials of all types, sometimes known in the Egyptian language as the *pat*, and the vast majority of people, the *remetj*, mostly farmers.

Old Kingdom. By the beginning of the Old Kingdom (2675–2130 B.C.E.) the royal family commanded the majority of wealth in the country. The king and his immediate family depended on a bureaucracy of family members, a class of artisans and laborers who created the monuments, and farmers who worked the land. In Dynasties 5 (circa 2500–2350 B.C.E.) and 6 (circa 2350–2170 B.C.E.) some kings reformed the structure of the bureaucracy to keep offices attached to the direct descendants of the royal family rather than becoming hereditary in families descended from an earlier king's younger sons. These nuclear families were now more distantly related to the direct line of the royal family. However, in general, the tradition of inheriting an office was so strong that it became impossible to keep offices from passing from father to son. King Userkaf of Dynasty 5 introduced new titles that perhaps reflect one reform of the bureaucracy. He created a new path to promotion with a series of new titles. King Djedkare Isesi, also of Dynasty 5, revised titles at funerary temples, perhaps reflecting an attempt to bring officials under centralized control. The continued stability of the central government in Dynasties 5 and 6 suggests that these reforms were successful. However, by the end of Dynasty 6 the system collapsed.

Labor Organization. Government labor was conscripted by a method that may have originated in prehistory. The system was surely in use for building the pyramids at Giza in the reigns of Khufu, Khafre, and Menkaure or Mycerinus during Dynasty 4 (circa 2625–2500 B.C.E.). This system provided labor for construction projects, maintenance of the irrigation system, agricultural work on crown-administered lands, and expeditions outside of Egypt for raw materials.

Phyles. During the Old Kingdom at least some Egyptians were members of labor groups called phyles. Each of the five phyles had a name: The Great Phyle, The Eastern Phyle, The Green Phyle, The Little Phyle, and The Perfection Phyle. Each phyle name probably made reference to its protective deity. The phyles served in rotation, each working for part of the year. The names of the phyles are preserved on the blocks of the Great Pyramid, telling us which phyle moved that block into place.

Reorganization. In the Middle Kingdom (circa 1980–1630 B.C.E.) the administration reduced the five phyles to four, each known by a number. The numbers might refer to the season of the year when the phyle served. By the New Kingdom (circa 1539–1075 B.C.E.) phyles disappeared. A different system of permanent work gangs present at Deir el Medina may indicate a reorganization of the labor force at this time. Foreign slaves also became a more important factor in the labor force than previously.

First Intermediate Period. In the First Intermediate Period (circa 2130–1980 B.C.E.) power was diffused to many centers throughout the country and thus the social hierarchy that had been centralized was now replaced. The Old Kingdom hierarchy, however, tended to be reproduced on a smaller scale in the nomes (provincial districts). Leaders of the nomes, called nomarchs, took many of the king's prerogatives but ruled over a much smaller territory.

Middle Kingdom. In the Middle Kingdom when the princes of Thebes reestablished central power, new opportunities arose for artisans and laborers to rise in the social hierarchy. The bureaucracy was reestablished on a national basis and heredity was no longer the main means of legitimating a claim to an office. Instead, a group of texts suggests that literacy was the key to a man's success. These texts were distributed widely and were apparently known beyond the limited circle of the existing bureaucracy. One such text, *The Instructions of a Man for His Son,* described a commoner taking his young son to the city to enter school with the hope that he would become a scribe and rise in the bureaucracy. A related group of texts written by successful "new men" emphasized loyalty to the king with literacy. This additional trait would lead to a place in the bureaucracy and thus a middle-class life. At least for a brief time, heredity was less important than ability and loyalty to the crown in achieving higher social status.

New Kingdom. The New Kingdom was born out of the war against the Hyksos. It is not surprising, then, that the new social hierarchy included a permanent army for the first time. Foreign slaves who were prisoners of war also became prominent for the first time in the social organization of Egypt.

The lives of artisans and laborers are better known in the New Kingdom because of excavations at Deir el Medina. The people of Deir el Medina village were literate and left behind written records that can be used to reconstruct their lives. In this village it is clear that all heads of families were assigned to one of two teams or work gangs, called "sides" in Egyptian. These gangs worked on the excavation and decoration of the king's tomb in the Valley of the Kings. Each team had four ranks including a foreman, two deputies, scribes who were both administrators and artists, and simple workmen. Women generally held the title *Lady of the House* which perhaps conceals in translation the more important meaning, "owner" of the house. Some women also held the title *Chantress of Amun.* A chantress was responsible for the music used in the rituals at the major temples in the area. Women with this title were earning salaries independent of husbands or fathers. Social mobility was possible in this community and was dependent both on education and personal connections.

Third Intermediate Period and Late Period. In the last stage of Egyptian history (circa 1075–332 B.C.E.), the priestly class took over the functions of the old bureaucracy. Wenamun, who led the expedition to obtain wood from Lebanon, was a "Gatekeeper of (the god) Amun." In the earlier periods, the officials responsible for foreign trading missions were representatives of the king's house. This shift represents a larger shift toward theocracy in the first millennium B.C.E.

Slaves. The absolute bottom rung of society consisted of slaves. In the earliest period they were unknown. In the Middle Kingdom there were political slaves who were either criminals or foreigners. They were responsible for many of the building projects in this period. New Kingdom slaves were generally foreign prisoners of war. In the first millennium it was increasingly common for impoverished Egyptians to sell themselves into slavery to pay their debts. In the Late Period (circa 664–332 B.C.E.), slavery was a legally recognized status where the individual was subject to control over his/her services, but the slave retained legal rights. An enslaved person retained control over his/her

property, could have a profession, and was entitled to compensation. A slave could marry a free person but a slave's children remained part of the master's household. Slaves were usually bound for life, but manumission was sometimes made.

Labor and Occupations. The majority of ancient Egyptians were farmers in all of the ancient period. Yet, the land was so rich that a surplus was created which supported the royal family, high officials, religious specialists, bureaucrats, the military, and craftsmen. Other professionals who helped feed the population in addition to farmers were fishermen and herdsmen. Lists and descriptions of occupations were prepared in the Middle Kingdom by Egyptian scribes. The written documents are prejudiced in favor of the scribal professions as the highest possible status for someone born outside the nobility. Yet, the range of occupations described in the Middle Kingdom, New Kingdom, and Late Period are similar. Herodotus, the Greek historian who visited Egypt in circa 450 B.C.E., compiled a list of occupations in Egypt. He lists priests, warriors, cowherds, swineherds, tradesmen, interpreters, and river pilots. He omits farmers, who must have existed. Notably absent from all the lists of the earlier period are merchants or traders, groups that are hard to locate in the historical record.

Wages. The Egyptians did not use money. The ancient Egyptians expressed payment in units of bread and beer, the two staples of an ancient Egyptian diet. It seems likely that the lower salaries, which were close to subsistence level, were actually paid by giving bread and beer to employees or conscripts. Just as all coins in the modern system must be guaranteed to contain equal amounts of metal, there was a way of ensuring that each loaf of bread was baked from a standard recipe, using equal amounts of ingredients, and that each loaf had a standard nutritional value.

Centralized Economy. The ancient Egyptian economy was structured so that the residents of the Nile Valley provided support for the king and government institutions by conveying crops to a central authority. At the same time, the king redistributed essential commodities to each class on the basis of rank and status in the society. Anthropologists call this type of centralized economy "redistributive." These deliveries to the government are called "taxes" in English. However, there is no single word in ancient Egyptian for "tax." Instead, there are specific names of levies based on modes of delivery. Typical names of taxes include: "That which is carried" (*fay*), "That which is brought" (*yenu*), "That which is given" (*redy*), and "That which is taken" (*shedy*). Taxation and also conscription were thus an essential element of a redistributive economy in which, as the Egyptians said, the king owned "everything, which the sun disk encircles." The redistribution of goods and services that had been collected by the central government was the glue holding society together. When, periodically, the central government lost the strength to maintain this system, there was a tendency to re-create it on a smaller scale in the nomes.

Barter Trade. The Egyptians had no independent vocabulary for buying, selling, and money. For this reason they did not clearly understand these ideas. Instead, they used common words such as "to bring, acquire" and "to give" to describe exchanges modern people would call buying and selling. For example, a passage in *Papyrus British Museum 10052 8:6-7* says, "I gave some barley to the workman Pnufer and he gave me 2 *kite* of silver." Here, no distinction is made between buying and selling because these exchanges of commodities are understood as barter. The psychological difference between buying and selling is not recognized if the actions of both parties in a transaction are described with the same verb. A true profit-making exchange would have to recognize this essential difference between buying and selling. These exchanges seem to be limited to food, livestock, and manufactured goods such as textiles, ceramic and metal containers, beds, and coffins. Women are often in charge of bartering food in scenes of markets carved on tomb walls.

Land Ownership. The question of who owned the land remains controversial among Egyptologists because the ancient sources conflict. On the ideological level, the king often expressed the idea that he owned "everything that the sun-disk encircles." Yet, on a practical day-to-day level, examples of individuals buying, selling, renting, and inheriting land are known. The two most detailed government documents describing landownership also conflict. The *Great Harris Papyrus,* written circa 1151 B.C.E. in the reign of Ramesses IV, describes the land owned by the temples of Re, Ptah, and Amun. The vast number of people and arable land accounted for in this papyrus has led many scholars to the conclusion that there was little land left to be privately owned. On the other hand, the *Wilbour Papyrus,* dating to circa 1141 B.C.E. in the reign of Ramesses V, suggests that the temples owned only 2 percent of the land. Even this land was divided into normal land worked by temple employees and rented land occupied by tenant farmers. These tenants owed only 15 percent of their crops to the temple. Furthermore, it is not clear whether the temples themselves were under strict royal control or if they were independent power centers. Further research is needed to answer these questions.

International Trade. Documents from the Old Kingdom through the Late Period suggest that institutions controlled international trade from the Egyptian side. These institutions were either the royal government in the earlier period or the temples in the first millennium. Royal help was needed to organize, support, and protect trading expeditions varying in size from one hundred to seventeen thousand individuals. These expeditions included brewers, millers, bakers, sandal makers, cooks, physicians, and in some cases, embalmers. Expeditions traveled up to four months outside the Nile Valley. Security was also important; the army protected trade expeditions. In fact, the Egyptian word for trade expedition was the same word used for military operation (*mesha*).

Imports. Good evidence exists for trade with neighbors to the south, east, and north of Egypt. Generally the Egyptians imported gold and other raw materials from Nubia and Punt and wine, oils, wood, and some finished goods from Syria-Palestine, Mesopotamia, Anatolia, and Greece.

TOPICS IN SOCIAL CLASS SYSTEM AND THE ECONOMY

FARMERS AND PEASANTS

Hard Life. Peasants and farmers were illiterate. They left no records of their own. Thus, all that scholars know of them depends on descriptions written by professional scribes and paintings and sculpture created by professional craftsmen. Archaeologists have discovered baskets, plows, sickles, and sieves used by farmers and peasants. All the sources agree that the farmer's life was extremely hard. He suffered from a high rate of disease and probably was not the recipient of the best medical care available.

The Masses. Most people in ancient Egypt were farmers and peasants. In all periods these individuals were tied to the

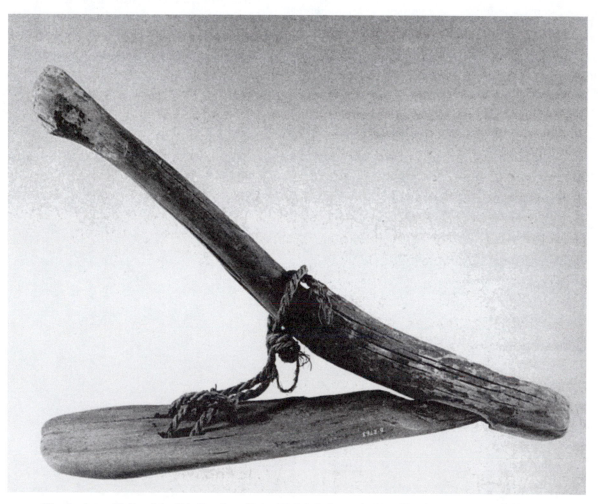

Wooden hoe, with its original binding, from Deir el Bahri, dating to the New Kingdom, circa 1539–1075 B.C.E.
(Royal Ontario Museum, Toronto)

Detail from a Dynasty 18 Theban tomb painting (circa 1539–1295/1292 B.C.E.) of laborers branding cattle while a scribe records the brands for tax purposes. The owner of the cattle, Nebamen, views the procedure (Metropolitan Museum of Art, New York).

land. It did not matter if the land was owned by the king, the temple, or entrusted to a nobleman. The farmer's life varied little.

Constant Labor. *Papyrus Anastasi II* provides a description of the farmer's life from a scribe's point of view. This text emphasizes the unending activity in a farmer's life. If he was not checking and repairing the irrigation canals, he was making tools for his own use. Even while eating, the farmer was forced to work. There were also potential problems with the farm animals. Teams of oxen could escape, forcing the farmer to spend valuable time searching for them.

Paying the Landowner. When all the backbreaking work of farming was completed, a scribe arrived to claim the landowner's share. Bodyguards and policemen accompanied the scribe. If the farmer could not produce the required amount of grain, he was subject to beatings. The papyrus also describes the farmer's family being taken away in chains when taxes were not paid promptly.

Supervision. Another papyrus, *Sallier I,* suggests that the overseers took pride in pushing the farmers to their limit. In a letter to the landowner, one overseer claimed to be treating the farmers "with the hardness of copper." Yet, he also claimed to be fair in that the farmers received their daily rations fully and promptly.

Sources:

Barry J. Kemp, *Ancient Egypt: Anatomy of a Civilization* (London & New York: Routledge, 1991).

Alfred Lucas, *Ancient Egyptian Materials and Industries,* fourth revised edition (London: E. Arnold, 1962).

William J. Murnane, *The Penguin Guide to Ancient Egypt* (Harmondsworth, U.K.: Penguin, 1983).

PRICES OF COMMODITIES

Lack of Money. The best information about prices of commodities is preserved from the village of Deir el Medina. The Egyptians did not have money; instead, prices were expressed by metal weights. The weights themselves were not exchanged. In a barter arrangement, the two parties calculated the values in units of the weights of the objects that they wished to exchange. Then each party grouped several objects together until each group was worth an equal amount of weights.

Problems in Interpretation. Prices are recorded on a few papyri and many ostraca—broken pieces of pottery and limestone basically used as "scratch paper" by the Egyptians. These prices all date to Dynasties 19 (circa 1292–1190 B.C.E.) and 20 (circa 1190–1075 B.C.E.), a period of about 150 years. Problems in interpreting this data include poor handwriting, faded ink, broken texts, and omitted information. The ostraca were written in the cursive hieratic script rather than hieroglyphic. Because professional scribes did not write them the handwriting is poor and difficult to read. The ostraca were often broken in antiquity, and ink is faded from storage in museums. Moreover, the texts were never intended for strangers to read, but were personal notes. Thus, many details that would have been known to the original reader were not recorded. The date is among the most important of these omitted details. Lack of dates often makes it difficult to compare prices with each other over time. Yet, scholars have overcome this problem by comparing the people named in these texts. This process entails other difficulties because the limited number of families living in the village drew on a limited stock of personal names. For example, it is sometimes difficult to pinpoint the identity of a particular "Pentaweret" because there was at least one in every generation for 150 years. Another difficulty in comparing prices is the lack of description of the goods that are priced. Some variation in the price of two chairs must have been in the quality of the workmanship. This variation in quality is almost never described in the ostraca. Finally, the precise meanings of words used to describe the commodities is often not understood. Often only the general category of the good can be determined from the writing. In spite of these difficulties, scholars have isolated four different units of value, which were used to price commodities. They include two units of weight—the *deben* and the *senyu* (originally called *shaty*)—and two units of volume (the *hin* and the *khar*).

Measures of Weight. The *deben* was a measure of weight used for gold, silver, and most commonly, copper. One *deben* of copper weighed 91 grams. It was divided into ten *kite*. It is rare to find a copper weight less than one-half *deben* (five *kite*) in the records. Only precious metals were usually available in amounts smaller than one-half *deben*.

As recorded in the *Papyrus Cairo 65739*, a woman named Erenofre described her purchase of a slave girl to the court of magistrates in the following words.

The merchant Reia approached me with the Syrian slave (named) Gemnihiamente who was still a girl and he said to me: "I will bring this girl and you will give to me in exchange for her"... and I gave for her:

1 shroud of Upper Egyptian cloth, makes 5 *kite* of silver,

1 blanket of Upper Egyptian cloth, makes 3 1/3 *kite* of silver,

1 garment of Upper Egyptian cloth makes 4 *kite* of silver

1 garment of fine Upper Egyptian cloth makes 5 *kite* of silver,

1 dress of fine Upper Egyptian cloth makes 5 *kite* of silver ...

1 vessel of bronze makes 18 *deben* which makes 1 2/3 *kite* of silver ...

10 *deben* of beaten copper makes 1 *kite* of silver ...

1 vessel of bronze makes 16 *deben*, makes 1 1/2 *kite* of silver,

1 vessel of honey, makes 1 *hekat*, makes 5 *kite* of silver, ...

1 cauldron of bronze, makes 20 *deben*, makes 2 *kite of silver*,

1 vessel of bronze, makes 20 *deben*, makes 2 *kite* of silver,

10 shirts of fine Upper Egyptian cloth makes 4 *kite* of silver.

TOTAL: 4 *deben* of silver and 1 *kite* of silver ... And I gave it to the merchant Reia and he gave me this girl, and I gave her the name Gemnihiamente.

Translation by Edward Bleiberg

Source: Alan H. Gardiner, "A Lawsuit Arising from the Purchase of Two Slaves," *Journal of Egyptian Archaeology*, 21 (1935): 140–146.

---

hold true. The *senyu* was used as a weight or value only in Dynasty 19 and early Dynasty 20 up to the first half of the reign of Ramesses III. The *senyu* could be used to express a value in the same column of figures with *deben*. *Ostracon Berlin 1268* states the value of objects in *senyu* but the total of the column is in *deben* of copper. *Ostracon Varille 25* totals a razor valued at one *deben* with a donkey valued at seven *senyu*.

Measures of Volume. The *hin* is a measure of volume equal to 0.48 liters. Its value is one-sixteenth *senyu*, but other calculations show that it was also equal to one copper *deben*. The value of the *hin* is probably based on the value of one *hin* of sesame oil, said to be equal to one copper *deben*. *Merhet*-oil and *adj*-fat, two commodity names that are not understood, were also measured in *hin*, but their values seem to vary in relation to *deben*, both more and less than one *deben*. Thus the economic historian J. J. Janssen believes that the value one *hin* is equal to one *deben* is based on one *hin* of sesame oil.

Grain. The *khar* is a measure of the volume of grain, either emmer wheat or barley, equal to 76.88 liters. It is divided into four *oipe*. The *khar* is translated as "sack" and was valued at two *deben* of copper. *Deben, senyu,* and *khar* are all found together in documents ranging from the time of Ramesses II through Ramesses V. The *khar* is most commonly found as a unit of value for baskets both because the volume of a basket was equal to its value and because baskets were relatively inexpensive. The same principle is at work in *Ostracon Cairo 25242* where a bed is valued in copper *deben* while its legs are valued in *oipe* of grain. Another text also differentiates between expensive items in *deben* and cheaper items in *oipe*.

Calculating Equivalents. The rough equivalent values among *deben, senyu, hin,* and *khar* given above reveal the difficulty of calculating precise values for commodities as well as

When applied to metal it is sometimes difficult to determine whether the actual weight or the value of the metal was being described. Perhaps the Egyptians made no such distinction. In *Ostracon Cairo 25242* verso, for example, twenty *deben* of copper is added to four *deben* as the value of a basket, demonstrating that the actual weight was difficult to separate from the idea of its value. *Deben* of copper were not distinguished from bronze *deben* in Egyptian. Both were valued as one *kite* of silver (9.1 grams). Silver *deben* are rarely mentioned in the ostraca, but are more common in the papyri. The Egyptians used papyrus to record official and thus more expensive transactions while villagers used ostraca to record private, smaller transactions. Thus, gold *deben* are never found in the ostraca but appear occasionally in the papyri. It must be assumed, then, that when the word *deben* is used alone on ostraca, copper *deben* are understood.

Senyu. The *senyu* was the second unit of weight used by the Egyptians. The word might mean "piece." It was a weight in silver equal to one-twelfth *deben* or 7.6 grams. Its value was equal to five copper *deben*, but this calculation does not always

Bull's-head weight from the reign of Akhenaten, circa 1353–1336 B.C.E. (Ashmolean Museum, Oxford)

Weight equal to 5 *deben*, standard measure for metals, from the reign of Userkaf, circa 2500–2485 B.C.E. (Metropolitan Museum of Art, New York)

Multiples of Five. Because the prices were set by barter, prices tended to cluster in amounts that were multiples of five, especially for amounts over ten *deben*. Numbers were usually rounded to the nearest five. Janssen illustrates this principle by the following example. *Ostracon Deir el Medina 73* verso describes the purchase of a coffin in the following way:

> Given to him in exchange for the coffin: 8½ *deben* of copper; again 5 *deben* of copper; 1 pig made 5 *deben*; 1 goat made 3 *deben*; 1 goat made 2 *deben*; 2 logs of sycamore wood made 2 *deben*. Total: 25½ *deben*.

Here the agreed value of the coffin was twenty-five *deben*. Then values were established for the individual items brought to the exchange. The coffin maker would decide how much use he could make of the two lots of copper, the animals, and the wood before determining the value he would assign to them. It is unlikely that these goods were accepted for resale at a profit since this concept seems to be unknown to the Egyptians. Thus, the actual desire to own these items becomes much more important than the abstract value assigned to them in *deben*.

Inflation and Price Fluctuation. There is some evidence for inflation and price fluctuation during the course of the Ramesside Period (circa 1292–1075 B.C.E.). During the reign of Ramesses II one *deben* of silver was valued as one hundred *deben* of copper. By the reign of Ramesses IX one *deben* of silver was valued as sixty *deben* of copper. Janssen believes this change occurred by the reign of Ramesses III when a typical *meses*-garment was valued at five *deben* or one *senyu*. Thus the silver to copper ratio would already be 1:60. It seems unlikely that the government would have intervened in setting prices of this sort, though not impossible. It is certainly clear that the Egyptian state regulated the standard measures of length

fixed ratios among the four different measures used. One document valued a basket at one-quarter *senyu* for a volume of one-half *khar*. Since one *khar* was equal in value to two *deben*, the logical conclusion would be that one *senyu* equaled four copper *deben* in value. Yet, another example shows that one *senyu* of *meses*-garments was equal to five copper *deben*. Finally, another document valued one *hin* of oil at one-sixth *senyu*. Since one *hin* was equal to one *deben*, the logical conclusion here is that one *senyu* was equal to six *deben*. Clearly, modern ideas about money and prices were not at work here. Modern conceptions of money would not allow one *senyu* to be equal to either four, five, or six *deben*. Yet, this was the actual state of affairs in Deir el Medina.

Case-by-Case Basis. Perhaps the real difficulty is that modern scholars are attempting to systematize a procedure that was actually determined on a case-by-case basis. All of these prices are derived from specific barter agreements. Barter prices are much more fluid than the fixed prices in modern, Western markets. Barter prices are set by the strength of each individual's desire to conclude an exchange and each individual's skill at arriving at a good price in addition to some abstract idea of value based on weight or volume. Use value was probably more important than any abstract value. All of the commodities exchanged at Deir el Medina were valued according to actual use. Grain was for eating and silver was a raw material for making some object. The value grew according to the need.

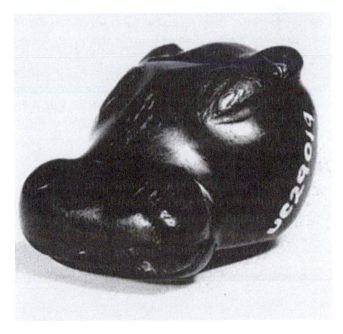

Weight in the form of a hippopotamus head, from the Set temple at Ombos, black hematite, Dynasty 18, circa 1539–1295/1292 B.C.E. (University College, London, Petrie Collection)

and volume. Thus the basic ratio of one sack of grain to one *deben* of copper seems not to have varied.

Loans and Credit. The best source of evidence for loans is also Deir el Medina. There are two kinds of loans attested from the village. One type is made with a fixed date for repayment and a penalty if that date is missed. A second type appears not to have a repayment date and is more likely to reflect an obligation for reciprocity between the lender and debtor. There is limited evidence that loans with fixed repayment dates were made from people of higher social status to those of lower social status while reciprocal loans were made between people of more equal status.

Sources:

Edward Bleiberg, "Prices and Payments," in *Oxford Encyclopedia of Ancient Egypt*, volume III, edited by Donald B. Redford (Oxford: Oxford University Press, 2001), pp. 65–68.

Jaroslav Cerný, *A Community of Workmen at Thebes in the Ramesside Period* (Cairo: Institut Français d'Archéologie Orientale, 1973).

Jac Janssen, *Commodity Prices from the Ramessid Period: An Economic Study of the Village of Necropolis Workmen at Thebes* (Leiden: E. J. Brill, 1975).

Barry J. Kemp, *Ancient Egypt: Anatomy of a Civilization* (London & New York: Routledge, 1991).

Alfred Lucas, *Ancient Egyptian Materials and Industries*, fourth revised edition (London: E. Arnold, 1962).

PRIESTS

Status. Priests in ancient Egypt were members of the larger society. They were religious specialists, but many priests also held civil positions simultaneously or before and after serving in the temple. They cannot be conceived to be like modern priests.

Dual Positions. From the Old Kingdom (circa 2675–2130 B.C.E.) through the New Kingdom (circa 1539–1075 B.C.E.) few details of the lives of individual priests are preserved. Individuals had their priestly titles carved on statues and in tombs, but without further details. These lists, however, demonstrate that men who held priestly titles often also held civil titles. Moreover, the highest priestly posts seem to have been held by men who also held the highest civil ones. For example, Hapuseneb was both First Prophet of Amun and vizier (prime minister) in the reign of Hatshepsut. Montuemhet, who lived in Dynasty 26 (circa 664–525 B.C.E.), was both Overseer of All the Priests of All the Gods of Upper Egypt and vizier.

Inherited Post. There was a tension between the priests' desire to have their sons follow them in office and the king's right to appoint and confirm high officials of the priesthood. Most priests assumed that their sons would follow them. In one case, a priest sold his right to be priest to another man, and the son of the priest claimed the rights to the proceeds of the sale.

Temple Autonomy. Each temple priesthood was autonomous, as was each deity. A First Prophet, the highest priestly title at a temple, was responsible only to the king. There was no other hierarchy outside the temple itself. As a result, it is important not to imagine that the ancient Egyptian priesthood was similar to the Catholic Church or that the priesthood was separate from the civil/secular hierarchy. Thus, modern people should not view internal conflict within Egyptian society as a contest between civil and religious authorities as is sometimes the case in European history. The two kinds of authority were too closely entwined. Further, each priesthood served the local god only. No formal hierarchy existed among gods except that Amun was King of the Gods. The only national god was the king himself and there was no real national priesthood even of the king. Thus there was no national priesthood to serve as an alternative to royal power.

Responsibilities. The priests were responsible for religious ritual and the administration of the temple and its property. Each temple was rich, had a large staff, and owned land, which it farmed. Therefore, priests' duties ran a wide spectrum of functions that were both religious and secular.

Hierarchy. The hierarchy of the priests started with the First Prophet. He reported directly to the king. He was assisted by the Second, Third, and Fourth Prophet. The next level of priest was called Servant of the God. These priests were divided into four groups; each group served the god for three months per year in rotation. These men had other jobs in the civil administration the other nine months of the year.

Block statue of Sitepehu, Overseer of Priests, from Abydos, circa 1478/1472–1458 B.C.E. (Museum of Archaeology and Anthropology, University of Pennsylvania)

Vignette from Paynedjem's *Book of the Dead*, with the High Priest of Amun, Paynedjem II, making an offering to Osiris, Dynasty 21, circa 1075–945 B.C.E. (British Museum, London)

God's Fathers were the next lower rank. The Pure Ones, who also served in groups for three-month periods, followed them. The exact functions of Servants of the God, God's Fathers, and Pure Ones are not understood. Lector Priests, however, were specialists who read the ritual aloud, while Hourly Priests computed the exact moment when particular rituals were enacted.

Women. Priestesses served the deities, and they, too, were arranged in a hierarchy. The God's Wife was often the wife or daughter of the king, making her a high-ranking official. Parallel to the king's harem, there were also Concubines of the God. As with the priests, it is difficult to determine the exact function served by these priestesses. The major function of lower-level priestesses was to serve as musicians. There were a large number of singers, instrumentalists, and dancers who served the god in an official capacity.

Sources:
Henri Frankfort, *Ancient Egyptian Religion: An Interpretation* (New York: Harper, 1961).

Sergio Pernigotti, "Priests," in *The Egyptians*, edited by Sergio Donadoni (Chicago: University of Chicago Press, 1997), pp. 121–150.

Gay Robins, *Women in Ancient Egypt* (Cambridge, Mass.: Harvard University Press, 1993).

Serge Sauneron, *The Priests of Ancient Egypt*, translated by Ann Morissett (New York: Grove, 1960).

PUNT EXPEDITIONS

Sahure. The Egyptians traded with an area of Africa called Punt as early as Dynasty 5 (circa 2500–2350 B.C.E.) and maintained contact with it until the end of the New Kingdom (circa 1539–1075 B.C.E.). Punt was located on the east coast of Africa in present-day Ethiopia and Sudan. The earliest reference to trade expeditions to the region is found in the reign of Sahure (circa 2485–2472 B.C.E.). In this reign the Egyptian king received eighty thousand units of incense as well as electrum (a natural compound of gold and silver) and two other (untranslatable) commodities. An inscription from the reign of Djedkare Isesi (circa 2415–2371 B.C.E.) records the arrival at the royal court of a dancing dwarf imported from Punt. The same reign records that bedouins had destroyed Egyptian boats built for the Punt trade.

Imports. Contacts were maintained with Punt in the Middle Kingdom (circa 1980–1630 B.C.E.), though no details of an expedition are known. The best documentation for this trading partner comes from the New Kingdom. In the reign of Hatshepsut (circa 1478/1472–1458 B.C.E.) a trading expedition to Punt was recorded both in words and in relief. In addition to incense, the Egyptians imported ebony, herd animals, ivory, gold, and panther and cheetah skins. The reliefs depict Puntites living in beehive-shaped houses on stilts. The men wore long hair in the earlier depictions and short hair in depictions during the reign of Amenhotep III. The men also wore goatees and long kilts.

JOURNEY TO NUBIA

Harkhuf, an expedition leader to Nubia (southern Egypt and the Sudan) in Dynasty 6 (circa 2350–2170 B.C.E.), described his travels in his autobiography:

His Majesty Merenre, my lord, sent me together with my father, the Sole Companion, Yeri, to Yam [a part of Nubia] in order to explore the way to this foreign country. I did it in seven months. I brought every product from there. I was greatly praised for it.

His Majesty sent me a second time, alone. I went forth upon the Elephantine Road [road south from Aswan]. I returned through Yertjet, Makher, Tereres, (all in) Yertjetj, [names of places]—an affair of eight months. When I returned, I brought the products from this country in great quantity. Never before was anything like this brought to this land [to Egypt]. I returned from the house of the ruler of Yertjet after I had explored these lands. Never before had any Companion [title of a person at the royal court held by Harkhuf] or Chief of Expedition Leaders [another title held by Harkhuf] who had gone forth to Yam done it earlier.

Translation by Edward Bleiberg

Source: *Autobiography of Harkhuf*, in *Urkunden des ägyptischen Altertums*, Part I, *Urkunden des alten Reichs*, edited by Kurt Sethe (Leipzig: J. C. Hinrichs, 1903), pp. 124–125.

Sources:

Barry J. Kemp, "Old Kingdom, Middle Kingdom and Second Intermediate Period, c.2686–1552 BC," in *Ancient Egypt: A Social History*, edited by Bruce Trigger and others (Cambridge: Cambridge University Press, 1983), pp. 71–182.

Kenneth Kitchen, "The Land of Punt," in *The Archaeology of Africa: Food, Metals, and Towns*, edited by Thurstan Shaw and others (London & New York: Routledge, 1993), pp. 587–608.

William Stevenson Smith, "The Land of Punt," *Journal of the American Research Center in Egypt*, 1 (1962): 59–60.

SCRIBES

Important Role. Scribes played a vital role in the government bureaucracy, religion, and intellectual life of ancient Egypt. There was a clear development over time from scribes who were recorders of the word to intellectuals who created the text they wrote. The Egyptologist Alessandro Rocatti has speculated that the scribe's importance during the Old Kingdom (circa 2675–2130 B.C.E.) was his ability to read words accurately. This capability was more greatly valued than the skill to write itself. Reading accuracy would have been especially important in religious rituals where priests recited spells exactly as the gods had ordained. During the same period, other scribes were charged with keeping administrative records, but they would have had a lower social status.

Growing Need. Literature beyond administrative lists and religious texts developed during the Middle Kingdom (circa 1980–1630 B.C.E.). It included narratives; manuals of medicine, mathematics, and astronomy; and maps. Government during the Middle Kingdom increased its dependence on the written word too. This dependence led to a need for more scribes, a source of social mobility in this period. At least some administrative scribes were descended from farmers who had somehow recognized their sons' abilities.

Intellectual Class. In the New Kingdom (circa 1539–1075 B.C.E.) an intellectual class of scribes developed. They admired the famous authors of the Old and Middle Kingdom—Hardjedef, Imhotep, Khety, and Neferti. These four men were high-ranking officials of the past whose memory was maintained through their writings. The new intellectual class called themselves scribes and produced in their own time manuals of behavior. This group includes Ani and Amenemope. The New Kingdom also produced scribes who could translate foreign languages such as Akkadian, used in Mesopotamia, and Hittite, used in Anatolia. By the Late Period (circa 664–332 B.C.E.) scribes emphasized their ability to find and interpret older texts.

Sources:

Pierre Montet, *Everyday Life in Egypt in the Days of Ramesses the Great*, translated and by A. R. Maxwell-Hyslop and Margaret S. Drower (London: E. Arnold, 1958).

Alessandro Roccati, "Scribes," in *The Egyptians*, edited by Sergio Donadoni (Chicago: University of Chicago Press, 1997), pp. 61–86.

John A. Wilson, *The Culture of Ancient Egypt* (Chicago: University of Chicago Press, 1956).

Early Dynasty 5 statue (circa 2500–2350 B.C.E.) of a seated scribe from his tomb at Saqqara (Musee du Louvre, Paris)

SERFS AND SLAVES

Restricted Freedom. Many words were used in ancient Egyptian for groups of people whose freedom was restricted. None of these words corresponds directly to either the Greek and Roman or the American legal concepts of slavery. More accurate translations of Egyptian would include "dependent" (*meryet*); "personnel" (*djet*); "forced laborer "(*heseb*); "worker" (*bak*); "servant" (*hem*); "royal servant" (*hem-nesu*); "prisoner of war" (*seker-ankh*); and "Asiatic" (*a-amu*). In the Old Kingdom (circa 2675–2130 B.C.E.) and Middle Kingdom (circa 1980–1630 B.C.E.), all people who lived within these classifications were restricted somewhat in their movements. Yet, there is no general term meaning "slave." Furthermore, there was no real consciousness during the Old Kingdom or Middle Kingdom of a class of people classified as slaves. *The Satire on the Trades,* the catalogue of occupations composed in the Middle Kingdom, does not mention slaves. Yet, by the New Kingdom (circa 1539–1075 B.C.E.) the term *servant* approached something like the legal status of slave. In the Late Period (circa 664–332 B.C.E.), the word *worker* was the word used to indicate a person who was a type of chattel.

Property. The difference between a slave and others was that a slave could be bought and sold. A slave was property but not exactly the same as other property. In the New Kingdom, slaves were generally foreigners captured in war. However, even foreigners were permitted to practice a variety of professions and could own property. Slaves could function as herdsmen, barbers, builders, sandal makers, and even administrators of cloth.

Legal Parameters. A slave was the opposite of a *nemhu*, a person who paid dues directly to the state. A *nemhu* also lived independently of state support, outside of the system of government rations. A slave, on the other hand, had the right of support from the master. By the Late Period, many individuals were willing to sell themselves into slavery in order to obtain regular support. Slaves could be sold to another master, but that master had to guarantee support. In return, the slave's labor benefited the master. Even so, slaves

Scene from the Dynasty 18 tomb of the priest Khamuas at Western Thebes (circa 1539–1295/1292 B.C.E.). He and his wife oversee the activities of servants (British Museum, London).

Servant girls and a guest at a banquet, from the tomb of Nebamun, Western Thebes; painting on plaster, circa 1360 B.C.E. (British Museum, London)

retained rights over property. A slave could also testify in court, marry a free person, and be responsible for restitution. In this sense a slave was a legal person and could establish contracts with third parties. Perhaps most important of such contracts were marriages. Some slave contracts were limited in time. Both parties would have to agree to extend the contract. Children of slaves, however, belonged to the master unless separately freed.

Assessment. In sum, a slave occupied a legally recognized status where the individual was subject to control over his services but still retained legal rights. A slave could have a profession and was entitled to compensation. A slave could be a native Egyptian or a foreigner and could marry a free person. Slaves were usually bound for life but could be freed and acquire complete control over the legal disposition of their property. While slaves the children were part of the master's household and received support.

Sources:

William O. Blake, *The History of Slavery and the Slave Trade, Ancient and Modern* (Miami: Mnemosyne, 1969).

Eugene Cruz-Urine, "Slavery in Egypt during the Saite and Persian Periods," *Revue International des Droits de l'Antiquité*, 29 (1982): 47-71.

Alan B. Lloyd, "The Late Period, c. 664–323 BC," in *Ancient Egypt: A Social History*, edited by Bruce Trigger and others (Cambridge: Cambridge University Press, 1983), pp. 279–348.

Robin W. Winks, ed., *Slavery: A Comparative Perspective. Readings on Slavery from Ancient Times to the Present* (New York: New York University Press, 1972).

SINAI DESERT EXPEDITIONS

Raw Materials. The Egyptians exploited the Sinai Desert for raw materials, mining lead, tin, galena, some gold, and most important, turquoise. The first known turquoise jewelry was discovered in the tomb of Djer, second king of Dynasty 1 (circa 3000–2800 B.C.E.). Thus, Djer's reign probably marks the beginning of Egyptian Sinai expeditions.

Permanent Settlements. The bedouin native to this region impeded Egyptian exploitation of Sinai. Beginning with King Den (fourth king of Dynasty 1), royal inscriptions mentioned pacification of the Sinai Bedouin. In Dynasty 3 (circa 2675–2625 B.C.E.), inscriptions continued at the mines in Sinai but it was only in Dynasty 4 (circa 2625–2500 B.C.E.) that the Egyptians established a permanent settlement there. King Sneferu received much of the credit for inaugurating a long period of peace in the region and establishing permanent installations at the copper, turquoise, and malachite mines of Wadi Nasb and Wadi Maghara. Later, in the Middle Kingdom (circa 1980–1630 B.C.E.), a Cult of Sneferu was established there, attesting to his importance for the Egyptians who worked and lived in Sinai. Four kings of Dynasty 5 (circa 2500–2350 B.C.E.)—Sahure, Nyuserre, Menkauhor, and Djedkare Isesi—left inscriptions at the Sinai mines. These inscriptions demonstrate that the Egyptians of this period made regular expeditions to the area.

Maintaining Control. The lack of Egyptian inscriptions in the Sinai during the First Intermediate Period (circa 2130–1980 B.C.E.) shows that the Egyptians only exploited the Sinai when there was a strong central government. Neb-

hepetre Mentuhotep II reasserted Egyptian claims to Sinai when he established the Middle Kingdom. He had to resubdue the Bedouin in order to make the trade routes in Sinai safe for the Egyptians to use. Amenemhet or Ammenemes I also reported expeditions to subdue the Bedouin, a sign that

THE REPORT OF WENAMUN

When the New Kingdom was on the point of collapse around 1050 B.C.E., a story was written about an Egyptian envoy who had been sent to Lebanon to purchase timber for some restoration work on the great sacred river barge of the god Amun, Egypt's national god during this period. Opinions have differed through the years as to whether the account of Wenamun's voyage is a work of fiction or a genuine report produced by Wenamun himself; the balance of opinion today is that the tale is a literary work, not an administrative document. What is perhaps most surprising about the tale is that it contains unmistakable elements of satire directed at Egypt itself and its loss of influence in Syria-Palestine, an area which for the previous five hundred years had normally been under Egypt's political and military thumb. The following passage provides unusual insight into the true nature of trade in the Late Bronze Age. Egyptian royal propaganda held that, because all the world outside of Egypt was under perpetual Egyptian domination, foreign products brought into Egypt were tribute, surrendered up by over-awed barbarians through fear of Pharaoh and the gods of Egypt. Yet, in the tale of Wenamun, the reader sees that the mundane reality was far different: even when Egypt was militarily and politically strong, Egyptians normally paid for their imports, and Wenamun was going to have to do the same. In this extract, Wenamun speaks in the first person, reporting his conversation with the prince of the Lebanese city of Byblos:

He spoke to me, saying: "On what business have you come?" I said to him: "I have come in quest of the timber for the great noble barge of Amun-Re, King of the Gods. What your father did, what the father of your father did, you too will do it." So I said to him. He said to me: "True, they did it. If you pay me for doing it, I will do it too. My relations carried out this business after Pharaoh had sent six ships laden with the goods of Egypt, and they had been unloaded into their storehouses. You, what have you brought to me?" He had the account books of his forefathers brought and had it read before me. They found entered in his book a thousand *deben* and all sorts of things. He said to me: "If the ruler of Egypt were the lord of what is mine and I were his servant, he would not have sent silver and gold. It was not a royal gift that was given to my father! I, too, am not your servant, nor am I the servant of him who sent you!"

Source: Miriam Lichtheim, *Ancient Egyptian Literature*, volume II (Berkeley: University of California Press, 1976), pp. 224–230.

Egyptian control was not yet complete at the beginning of Dynasty 12 (circa 1938–1759 B.C.E.). However, by the reign of Amenemhet III, there was a permanent settlement at Serabit el Khadim including houses, fortifications, wells, cemeteries, and a temple for Hathor. Amenemhet IV constructed additional buildings there.

New Kingdom Rulers. Again in the Second Intermediate Period (circa 1630–1539/1523 B.C.E.) the absence of a strong central government in Egypt corresponded with the absence of contemporary Egyptian inscriptions in Sinai. As soon as King Ahmose established the New Kingdom (circa 1539–1075 B.C.E.), his wife Ahmose-Nefertari's name was inscribed at Serabit el Khadim. She also had turquoise jewelry, showing that the mines were reopened at the beginning of the New Kingdom. Other New Kingdom rulers were attested at the Sinai mines. They include Hatshepsut, Ramesses I, Sety I, Queen Twosre (wife of Siptah), Ramesses III, and Ramesses V. Egyptian exploitation of the mines ended in the New Kingdom.

Sources:

Nicolas Grimal, *A History of Ancient Egypt* (New York: Barnes & Noble, 1997).

Barry J. Kemp, *Ancient Egypt: Anatomy of a Civilization* (London & New York: Routledge, 1991).

David O'Connor, "New Kingdom and Third Intermediate Period, 1552–664 BC," in *Ancient Egypt: A Social History*, edited by Bruce G. Trigger and others (Cambridge: Cambridge University Press, 1983.)

SKILLED WORKERS AT DEIR EL MEDINA

The Village. The ancient village located at Deir el Medina provides the best documentation for the social organization of a group of skilled workers during the New Kingdom (circa 1539–1075 B.C.E.). Deir el Medina is the modern name of a village on the west bank of the Nile at Thebes (present-day Luxor). In ancient Egyptian it was called "The Place of Truth" (*Set-Maat*) and was the home of the artists who decorated the tombs in the Valley of the Kings during the New Kingdom. Because the artists could read and write, they left behind personal records that allow Egyptologists to reconstruct their lives. For almost three hundred years, one can follow many families who worked directly for the pharaoh's building and decorated his tomb.

The Residents. The village at its greatest extent had seventy houses located inside a protective wall. Fifty additional structures were located just outside the walls. The adjacent hillside was the site of family tombs for the artists and workers. Approximately 120 workmen and their families lived at Deir el Medina. Estimates place the total population at about 1,200 people during Dynasties 19 (circa 1292–1190 B.C.E.) and 20 (circa 1190–1075 B.C.E.). Of these people, nearly all the adults had titles. More than twenty different titles are preserved at Deir el Medina. These titles provide the best evidence for understanding the high degree of stratification in ancient Egyptian society.

Carpenter tools, circa 1300 B.C.E. (British Museum, London)

Aerial view of the ruins of the village of Deir el Medina

Direct Governance by Pharaoh. The village was under the jurisdiction of the vizier, the pharaoh's prime minister. The Overseer of the Treasury of Pharaoh (finance minister) was responsible for the economic support for the village. The administrators of the village dealt directly with the highest levels of the government. The fact that the central government took a direct interest in the village shows that Deir el Medina was not a typical place. The people living here were probably more privileged than the average ancient Egyptian.

The Tomb. Overall in the documents, the governing structure of the village was called "The Tomb," naming it after its final product. Progress on the building and decorating of the pharaoh's tomb would have been one of his major concerns and the only official business of the village.

The Gang. The men who carried out the work were called the *yesu*, translated as "the Gang" in this context. The same name was used to describe a ship's crew. Just as was true of a ship's crew where oarsmen were assigned to the right or left side of the boat, the gang was divided into right and left sides both for administrative and labor purposes. Not all members of the gang were paid equal amounts. It is possible that bachelors were paid less than married men received. However, it might be that beginners were paid less than experienced workers. The vocabulary used to describe this situation is not clear.

Workload. The numbers of the gang varied between 16 and 120 during the time of its existence. The variation usually reflected the stage of work on the tomb. At the beginning when the tomb was excavated, more workers were needed. During the final stages of decoration, only the highly skilled carvers and painters were needed. After the pharaoh had died and work on a new tomb began for the new pharaoh, the number of gang members increased again.

Hiring Practices. The workers had many children, and it is clear that there was intense competition to have sons accepted into the gang. Members of the gang kept lists of gifts made to the administrators in charge of hiring in order to influence the hiring of their sons. Yet, not all children born in the village found employment there when they grew up. Scholars report some children became scribes both in the army and in temples.

Chief Workmen. Each of the two sides of the gang had a chief workman called the foreman. The two foremen were appointed by the pharaoh, probably on the recommendation of the vizier. Often, the foreman was a son of the previous foreman. When for some reason the son of a foreman was not available to fill the position, the new foreman was chosen from the gang.

Responsibilities. The foremen supervised the work in all its stages. They were present on the work site and encouraged the men. On site the foremen were responsible for inventories of metal tools issued to the workmen of the gang. They had to be certain that a blunted chisel or hoe was returned before a new sharpened one was issued. The foreman also represented the gang to the vizier. He wrote letters to report on the gang's progress with the tomb and even passed on complaints of late payments to the gang. The foreman also decided disputes among the members of the gang that were not sent to a court of magistrates.

Scribes of the Tomb. Scribes were an important part of the administration of the Tomb. They kept the records of wages and wrote the correspondence with other branches of government. There were at least two scribes at any one time, attached to the two sides of the gang. In some periods there were also two Scribes of the Serfs of the Tomb. Together with the foremen, the scribes formed the administrators of the Tomb.

Deputy. There were two deputies, one for each side of the gang. The foreman appointed the deputy, and usually the foreman chose one of his own sons for the post. This favoritism meant that the son of a deputy was often not chosen to follow his father and could only hope to be a member of the gang if he was to stay in the village. As a result some tension must have been caused in extended families where a new foreman would hire his son to be deputy and fire a near relative or return him to the gang.

Member of the Gang. The deputy acted in the foreman's place when the foreman was absent. When the foreman was present, the deputy worked like any other member of the gang. Yet, the deputy also was a member of the court of magistrates and was a witness to oaths. The deputy distributed less valuable supplies to the gang such as wicks for lamps and also food. The deputy, however, was not paid more than other members of the gang.

Guardians of the Tomb. The Guardians of the Tomb were not members of the gang, but they were closely enough associated with it that they received payment at the same time. There were two guardians at any one time. They often were hired from the gang and some seem to have been promoted from door keepers. The guardians were responsible for the storehouse. The most important objects kept there were the copper tools used in construction. The guardians protected the storehouse where the tools were kept. They also took blunt tools to be reconditioned by the coppersmiths. They thus worked closely with the foremen who made the lists of tools and who had ultimate responsibility for them. In addition, the guardians kept watch over the lamp wicks used for work in the tomb, pigments for painting, leather sacks used by the workmen, and sometimes the clothes that were part of the gang's wages. The guardian had high enough status in the village that he was a member of the court of magistrates and could witness oaths as well as barter transactions, oracles from the god, and other transactions.

Door Keepers. Two Door Keepers of the Tomb were also regular members of the Tomb, each one assigned to a side of the gang. They were not, however, members of the gang. They have no tombs in Deir el Medina and seem to have lived outside the village. They have the lowest status of the men in the wage lists, coming only before the slave women. The door keepers guarded the tomb itself but also were responsible for guarding other officials such as the scribes. They carried messages and acted as bailiffs of the court of magistrates. In this capacity they seized property of debtors. They also received deliveries of food rations for the gang. The door keepers were considered trustworthy enough to witness barter transactions, oaths, and oracles but were not members of the court of magistrates.

Slave Women. Slave women were assigned to both sides of the gang. As many as fifteen worked in the village at any one time. They were responsible for grinding the grain that the workmen received as wages. Their own wages were as little as a quarter of a workman's wages. The slave women belonged to the administration of the Tomb but were assigned to assist the families of the gang members.

Serfs of the Tomb. The serfs' main duty was to supply commodities to the gang. They were responsible for bringing water, vegetables, fish, wood, pottery, laundry, and gypsum to the members of the gang. They did not live in the village, though in some periods they seem to be former members of the gang.

Sources:

Morris Bierbrier, *The Tomb Builders of the Pharaohs* (London: British Museum, 1982).

Jaroslav Cerný, *A Community of Workmen at Thebes in the Ramesside Period* (Cairo: Institut Français d'Archéologie Orientale, 1973).

Alfred Lucas, *Ancient Egyptian Materials and Industries,* fourth revised edition (London: E. Arnold, 1962).

Gay Robins, *Women in Ancient Egypt* (Cambridge, Mass.: Harvard University Press, 1993).

SOLDIERS

Late Development. The class of professional soldiers developed late in Egyptian history. They did not exist until the Middle Kingdom (circa 1980–1630 B.C.E.). In both earlier and later periods the Egyptians depended on foreign mercenaries, especially from Nubia. This dependence led to the absorption of Nubians into the general Egyptian population. The professionalization of the military during the New Kingdom (circa 1539–1075 B.C.E.) led to a middle class of retired, landholding, military men.

Mercenaries. Though Egyptians served in military expeditions as part of the required government service called the corvée, many soldiers serving Egypt were foreigners. Artistic representations of soldiers often showed them in distinctive ethnic dress. The first inscription describing the army was written in Dynasty 6 (circa 2350–2170 B.C.E.) and explicitly names groups of Nubians as mercenaries. First Intermediate Period (circa 2130–1980 B.C.E.) figurines from Assyut depicted Egyptian soldiers carrying lances and shields while the Nubian soldiers carried bows and arrows. By the Middle Kingdom (circa 1980–1630 B.C.E.), a specific group of Nubians called the Medjoi were within Egypt as military police. This group was fully Egyptianized to the point where the word *medjoi* came to mean "policeman" rather than a separate ethnic group.

Terms of Address. In the earlier period there were few words for ranks of soldiers. Later, as the military became a professional group, terms for soldiers became more precise. Earlier texts referred to "warriors" and "young troops." By the Middle Kingdom the term "citizen of the town" referred to a soldier while "Follower," originally from the court rank "Follower of the King," came to mean military officer. The professional army of the New Kingdom had terms for a common soldier (*wa'u*), an officer commanding a unit of 50 men, an officer commanding 250 men, a superior of a fort, a general,

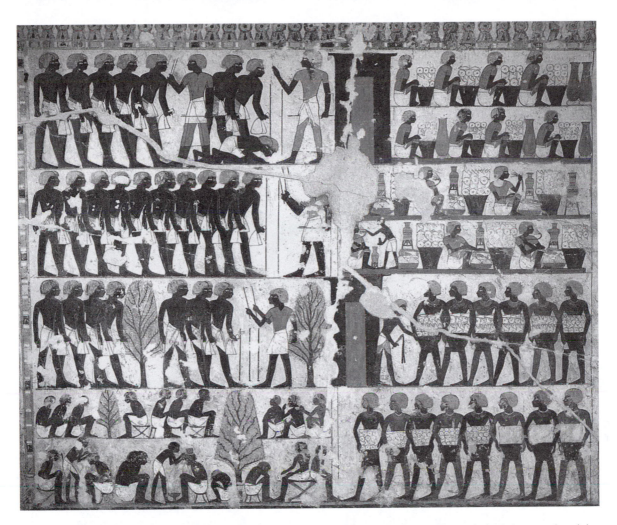

Wall relief from the tomb of Userhet, an army officer of the New Kingdom (circa 1539–1075 B.C.E.), depicting recruit training (upper left), grooming (lower left), officers drinking beer and wine (upper right), and soldiers carrying provisions (lower right) (from Denise Dersin, ed., *What Life Was Like: On the Banks of the Nile*, 1996)

and a chief general. There were also scribes of the army and scribes of the recruits among official titles.

Rewards of Land. Rewards of land to soldiers had a profound impact on the social/economic organization of ancient Egypt. This custom led to the creation of a class of small landholders in settlements throughout Egypt. This class could well have been the origin of the last king of Dynasty 18 (circa 1539–1295/1292 B.C.E.), Horemheb. He was a general without other connections to the royal family. He was followed by Ramesses I, another general and the founder of Dynasty 19 (circa 1292–1190 B.C.E.). His sons Sety I and Ramesses II (the Great) reestablished the hereditary principle but were also closely associated with the military.

Sources:

Nicolas Grimal, *A History of Ancient Egypt*, translated by Ian Shaw (Oxford & Cambridge, Mass.: Blackwell, 1993).

Sheikh Ibada el-Nubi, "Soldiers," in *The Egyptians*, edited by Sergio Donadoni (Chicago: University of Chicago Press, 1997), pp. 151–184.

Barry J. Kemp, *Ancient Egypt: Anatomy of a Civilization* (London & New York: Routledge, 1991).

WAGES

Rations. Wage payments in the Old Kingdom (circa 2675–2130 B.C.E.) are known from the Abu Sir Papyri written during that period. In the Middle Kingdom (circa 1980–1630 B.C.E.) there are temple documents, biographies, and archaeological data that include information about wages. New Kingdom (circa 1539–1075 B.C.E.) wages are known from Deir el Medina and from documents pertaining to shipping. All of these sources show that wage payments were made in rations of bread, beer, grain, meat, and cloth that were the necessities of life.

Bread and Beer. Most often rations were expressed in units of bread and beer, the two staples of an Egyptian diet. It seems likely that the lower salaries, which were close to subsistence level, were actually paid in bread and beer. Just as modern coins are guaranteed to contain standard amounts of metal, each loaf of bread was baked from a standard recipe, using equal amounts of ingredients, and had a standard nutritional value.

Baking Value. Standardization was assured through a system called *pefsu*, translated as "baking value." The employer could use *pefsu* to ensure that a predictable number of loaves would result from a known amount of grain. The baking value was based on the number of loaves or beer jars produced from a set measure of grain. The higher the value, the smaller the loaves, or the weaker the beer, the

Bread ration tokens made of painted wood from the Middle Kingdom, circa 1980–1630 B.C.E.
(Museum of Fine Arts Expedition, Harvard University)

smaller the jars. Most wage lists seem to assume that a standard *pefsu* has been used in baking and brewing.

Tokens or Tallies. Standardization could also be assured through the use of tokens or tallies. During the Middle Kingdom at Fort Uronarti in Nubia, ceramic tallies have been discovered in the shape of a standard loaf of bread. Presumably this tally could be used to check that a worker's wages in bread loaves were all the proper size. Beer jars were also presumably a roughly standard size.

Basic Wage. The standard basic wage was ten loaves of bread and one-third to two full jugs of beer per day. Egyptian beer was much less alcoholic than modern brews and higher in caloric content. This ration was for the lowest-paid staff members. Others were paid in multiples of this standard wage, varying from two to fifty times the standard wage for very highly paid people. Various methods could be used for apportioning wages. For example, documentation exists for a particular ship's crew where the captain and other officials received twice the ration of the ordinary sailors. There is another case where the highest-paid official received 38 1/3 loaves while the lowest-paid worker received 1 1/3 loaves.

Temple Day. In another example from the Middle Kingdom, it appears that the staff of a temple received a commission on all the goods that came to the temple. One inscription describes this occurrence as a "temple day."

As for a temple day, it is 1/360th part of a year. Now, you shall divide everything that enters this temple–bread, beer, and meat–by way of the daily rate. That is, it is going to be 1/360th of the bread, the beer, and of everything that enters this temple for (any) one of these temple days that I have given you.

In this temple the regular staff received 2/360ths of the total revenue of the temple while the chief priest received 4/360ths.

Keeping Accounts. In another case from the Middle Kingdom an expedition leader received five hundred loaves a day as his "ration." Clearly, large sums like this were not paid out in actual loaves of bread or jars of beer. It seems highly unlikely that an expedition leader could actually take his ever-increasing number of loaves of bread— fifteen thousand loaves after a month—with him on an extended trip into the desert. It also seems impossible that he could eat this much, even with a large family and servants to support. Thus, it seems possible that five hundred loaves of bread is actually a unit for measuring out commodities, approximating the modern idea of a unit of money. It must also have been possible to save and to draw against an account of bread and beer.

Deir el Medina. The New Kingdom craftsmen at Deir el Medina received all the necessities of life from their employer. Their houses were owned by the state. Food and clothing rations were given to them as well as most of the other necessities including water, fuel for their ovens, and the tools they needed to perform their duties. Yet, the robust trade among the workers demonstrates that they required additional goods and services that the state did not provide.

Sources:
Gae Callender, "The Middle Kingdom Renaissance (c.2055–1650 BC)," in *The Oxford History of Ancient Egypt*, edited by Ian Shaw (Oxford: Oxford University Press, 2000), pp. 148–183.

Barry J. Kemp, *Ancient Egypt: Anatomy of a Civilization* (London & New York: Routledge, 1991).

Alan B. Lloyd, "The Late Period, 664–323 BC," in *Ancient Egypt: A Social History*, edited by Bruce Trigger and others (Cambridge: Cambridge University Press, 1983), pp. 279–348.

SIGNIFICANT PEOPLE

HARKHUF

FLOURISHED CIRCA 2298–2194 B.C.E.
BUREAUCRAT

Trade or War. Harkhuf served as Governor of Upper Egypt after Weni. Harkhuf's career is not spelled out in his autobiography in as much detail as Weni gave in his text. Though Harkhuf achieved the rank of Count and Sole Companion, he also functioned as a Lector Priest, Chamberlain, Warden of Nekhen, Mayor of Nekheb, Royal Seal Bearer, and, most importantly, as a Chief of Scouts who led four trading expeditions to Nubia. His autobiography is most informative about the nature of trade relations between Nubia (southern Egypt and the Sudan) and Egypt at the end of Dynasty 6 (circa 2350–2170 B.C.E.). His autobiography also highlights the ambiguity surrounding these expeditions and the difficulty of classifying them as trade expeditions or military maneuvers.

Yertjet. King Merenre sent Harkhuf on his first trip to Nubia. Harkhuf's father, Yeri, accompanied him on this trip. Harkhuf opened new trade routes into the south to a place called Yertjet. This region was probably south of Yam, the area of Nubia explored in trips made before Harkhuf's time and closest to Egypt. The first trip lasted seven months. Harkhuf led a second expedition to Yertjet, this time exploring three settlements not mentioned in earlier explorations. This time he led the expeditions alone and traveled for eight months.

Local Strife. On his third trip to Nubia, visiting Yam this time, Harkhuf helped the local ruler in his war against Tjemeh-land. Though Harkhuf planned for a trading expedition and discovered the need for military action only after he had arrived in Yam, he was thoroughly prepared for it. Trade expeditions were heavily armed and could hardly be distinguished from military maneuvers. The same word in ancient Egyptian, *mesha*, was used to describe both trade expeditions and military actions.

Rewards. Harkhuf returned from Nubia with incense, ebony, exotic oils, panther skins, elephant tusks, throw sticks (used for hunting), and other products including a dancing pygmy for the king's entertainment. The king rewarded Harkhuf with luxurious provisions for his own use including wine, cakes, bread, and beer and a thank-you letter considered so important that it was carved on the walls of Harkhuf's tomb.

Sources:

Lionel Casson, *The Pharaohs* (Chicago: Stonehenge, 1981).

Peter A. Clayton, *Chronicle of the Pharaohs: The Reign-by-Reign Record of the Rulers and Dynasties of Ancient Egypt* (New York: Thames & Hudson, 1994).

Jaromir Malek, "The Old Kingdom (c.2686–2125 BC)," in *The Oxford History of Ancient Egypt*, edited by Ian Shaw (Oxford: Oxford University Press, 2000), pp. 89–117.

WENAMUN

FLOURISHED CIRCA 1104–1075 B.C.E.
EXPEDITION LEADER

Man of Mystery. Wenamun may have been a literary creation or a real person. He appears in the Papyrus Moscow 120, a report of his trading mission to Lebanon. Little is known of his personal life except that he was an Elder of the Portal of the Temple of Amun in Karnak. Herihor, High Priest of Amun, and effective ruler of Upper Egypt by 1075 B.C.E., sent Wenamun to Byblos to obtain cedarwood for a new barque of Amun–the ceremonial boat that the statue of the god used in traveling.

Robbery. Wenamun's journey reflected the declining fortunes of the New Kingdom (circa 1539–1075 B.C.E.) state at the end of Dynasty 20 (circa 1190–1075 B.C.E.). He traveled to Byblos in a boat crewed by Syrians rather than Egyptians. Unlike the bureaucrat Harkhuf in the Old Kingdom (circa 2675–2130 B.C.E.), Wenamun had no military escort. In fact, one of the Syrian sailors robbed him early in his journey while the boat was docked on the Levantine coast. Wenamun demanded justice from the Prince of Tjeker, who controlled the port where the robbery took place. Wenamun received no satisfaction and left. En route to Byblos, Wenamun robbed a Tjeker ship of the amount he believed the Prince of Tjeker's inaction had cost him.

Closing the Deal. Arriving in Byblos, Wenamun encountered many obstacles to concluding his dealings for the cedar. At last, a courtier of the Prince of Byblos fell into a trance, interpreted by all as a sign that the Prince should deal with Wenamun. Lengthy negotiations followed that resulted in Wenamun requesting further trade goods from Egypt to close the deal. The list of goods included four jars and one vessel of gold; five jars of silver; ten garments of royal linen; ten garments of fine linen; five hundred smooth linen mats; five hundred ox hides; five hundred ropes; twenty sacks of lentils; and thirty baskets of fish. This list provides some of the best evidence for Egyptian exports to the Levant preserved. The cedarwood was then provided.

Fate Unknown. Wenamun's troubles were not over, however. Ships dispatched by the Prince of Tjeker arrived at Byblos to arrest him for the robbery. Wenamun escaped but was blown off course to Cyprus. Unfortunately, what exactly happened to Wenamun after this point is unknown because the remainder of the papyrus is lost. Whether this story is fact or fiction, it presents a colorful account of the dangers of long-distance trade at the end of the New Kingdom.

Sources:

Lionel Casson, *The Pharaohs* (Chicago: Stonehenge, 1981).

Peter A. Clayton, *Chronicle of the Pharaohs: The Reign-by-Reign Record of the Rulers and Dynasties of Ancient Egypt* (New York: Thames & Hudson, 1994).

"The Report of Wenamun," in *Ancient Egyptian Literature,* volume II: *The New Kingdom,* edited by Miriam Lichtheim (Berkeley: University of California Press, 1976), pp. 224–230.

WENI

FLOURISHED CIRCA 2350-2288 B.C.E.
BUREAUCRAT

Three Kings. Weni served as a governor of Upper Egypt during Dynasty 6 (circa 2350–2170 B.C.E.). His autobiography traces his government service from his youth under King Teti to his maturity under both King Pepy I and King Merenre. Weni's career illustrates the life of a bureaucrat in the Old Kingdom (circa 2675–2130 B.C.E.).

Faithful Servant. Weni served the monarchy in civil, religious, and military functions. He began his career as custodian of the storehouse in the reign of Teti. In Pepy I's reign Weni was promoted to Overseer of the Robing Room, a position which must have brought him into direct contact with the king. This position led to increased rank as a Companion and the prestigious position of Inspector of Priests of the pyramid town. He was also entrusted with investigating a crime committed in the royal harem, but kept so secret that Weni's autobiography alludes to it in vague terms. Weni was so successful in these offices that Pepy I rewarded him with a limestone sarcophagus, doorposts and lintels for his tomb, and an offering table from Tura, the best quarry in Egypt.

Governorship. Weni's military career included five campaigns against the Sinai Bedouin and an additional campaign against Gazelle's-Head, an unidentified country. In the reign of Merenre, Weni was appointed Governor of Upper Egypt. In this position he was responsible for a census, expeditions to quarries, canal construction, and shipbuilding.

Significance. Weni's varied career demonstrates the ideal for a bureaucrat in ancient Egypt. He was primarily an organizer and expediter whom the king entrusted with a multitude of tasks. His remaining great asset was loyalty to the king.

Sources:

Lionel Casson, *The Pharaohs* (Chicago: Stonehenge, 1981).

Peter A. Clayton, *Chronicle of the Pharaohs: The Reign-by-Reign Record of the Rulers and Dynasties of Ancient Egypt* (New York: Thames & Hudson, 1994).

Jaromir Malek, "The Old Kingdom (c.2686–2125 BC)," in *The Oxford History of Ancient Egypt,* edited by Ian Shaw (Oxford: Oxford University Press, 2000), pp. 89–117.

DOCUMENTARY SOURCES

Anonymous, *Abu Sir Papyri* (circa 2675–2130 B.C.E.)—A list of wage payments in the Old Kingdom.

Anonymous, *Commemorating a Mining Expedition* (circa 1980–1630 B.C.E.)—A Middle Kingdom report.

Anonymous, *The Instructions of a Man for His Son* (circa 1980–1630 B.C.E.)—An account of a commoner's son enrolled in a school to become a scribe.

Anonymous, *A Lawsuit Arising from the Purchase of Two Slaves* (circa 1539–1075 B.C.E.)—A serviceable translation of a description of barter during the New Kingdom.

Anonymous, *The Monthly Report* (circa 1980–1630 B.C.E.)—An example of a report made by a phyle of wab-priests.

Anonymous, *The Satire on the Trades* (circa 1980–1630 B.C.E.)—Gives a scribe's view of other professions practiced in ancient Egypt. It does not mention slaves.

Anonymous, *Wilbour Papyrus* (circa 1141 B.C.E.)—Details the amount of land owned by various temples.

Harkhuf, *The Autobiography of Harkhuf* (circa 2298–2194 B.C.E.)—Recounts the life of a government official and expedition leader in Dynasty 6 (circa 2350–2170 B.C.E.).

Herodotus, *The Histories* (circa late fifth century B.C.E.)—Book II contains a list of occupations, compiled by the famous Greek historian after his visit to Egypt circa 450 B.C.E.

Ipuwer, *The Admonitions of Ipuwer* (circa 1980–1630 B.C.E.)—Describes the changing social structure of the early Middle Kingdom.

Wenamun, *The Report of Wenamun* (circa 1104–1075 B.C.E.)—An account of a trade expedition to present-day Lebanon in late Dynasty 20 (circa 1190–1075 B.C.E.).

Copy of a wall painting, circa 1400 B.C.E., from the tomb chapel of Nakht at Thebes, showing Nakht watching agricultural workers preparing land and sowing seed (Ashmolean Museum, Oxford)

Painting of a carpenter from a tomb at Deir el Medina, Dynasty 18, circa 1539–1295/1292 B.C.E. (Staatliche Museen zu Berlin)

Limestone relief of a metalworker and a scribe, from the tomb of Mereruka at Saqqara, circa 2300 B.C.E.

CHAPTER SIX

POLITICS, LAW, AND THE MILITARY

by EDWARD BLEIBERG

CONTENTS

Sidebars and tables are listed in italics.

2615* B.C.E.

- The Old Kingdom has been in existence for approximately sixty years (it ends in circa 2130 B.C.E.). During this period, the kings of Dynasties 3–11 establish the government departments of the Treasury, Agriculture, and Labor; there is no standing army.

2585-2560* B.C.E.

- Khufu or Cheops (Dynasty 4) associates himself with the sun god Re. As a result, his son Redjedef establishes himself as the first *Son of Re* in his royal titles. The three Great Pyramids of Giza are constructed as part of the new program associating kings with the sun god.

2500-2350* B.C.E.

- The first "Overseer of Upper Egypt" is established during Dynasty 5. This official is responsible for delivering the taxes of Upper Egypt to the court at Memphis. A second vizier for Lower Egypt is perhaps also created. The first provincial governors called "nomarchs" rule in the nomes (provincial territorial divisions).

2338-2298* B.C.E.

- In the reign of Meryre Pepy I (Dynasty 6), the general Weni organizes an army to fight the Bedouins in the Sinai.

2130-1980* B.C.E.

- The First Intermediate Period (Dynasties 9–11) occurs, and provincial governors rule the nomes as local kingdoms.

1980* B.C.E.

- Nebhepetre Mentuhotep II (Dynasty 11) unites Upper and Lower Egypt again to create the Middle Kingdom, twenty-eight years after ascending the throne of Thebes. The Middle Kingdom ends in 1630 and consists of Dynasties 11–14.

1945-1938* B.C.E.

- Nebtawyre Mentuhotep IV (Dynasty 11) builds the first forts in Nubia to protect Egyptian garrisons.

1938-1759* B.C.E.

- During Dynasty 12, the first extant laws concerning forced labor are compiled in papyrus records of the Great Enclosure, a prison.

1919-1875* B.C.E.

- Senwosret or Sesostris I (Dynasty 12) begins a second phase of fort building in Nubia. These structures have massive walls, towers, and complex moat defenses.

*Denotes Circa Date

1836-1818*
B.C.E.

- During the reign of Senwosret or Sesostris III (Dynasty 12), provincial governors are absorbed into the central government either through suppression or cooptation into the royal court. The Office of the Provider of the People replaces the Department of Labor. Local administrative councils answer directly to the central government. New forts are built in Nubia.

1630—1523*
B.C.E.

- The Second Intermediate Period or Hyksos Period (Dynasties 15–17) occurs. The Hyksos, a foreign people now identified as the Amorites, control Lower Egypt while the Theban royal house rules Upper Egypt.

1543-1539*
B.C.E.

- The Theban King Kamose initiates a war against King Apophis in the Delta to expel the Hyksos.

1539-1514*
B.C.E.

- Ahmose or Amosis defeats the Hyksos, reunites Egypt, and founds the New Kingdom. This period ends in 1075 B.C.E. and consists of Dynasties 18–20.

1539-1292*
B.C.E.

- The Dynasty 18 kings create three new offices for administering Nubia: King's Son of Kush (viceroy) and Overseer of Southern Lands; Deputy of Wawat; and Deputy of Kush. They also establish the Office of Overseer of Northern Lands for administration of the Levantine possessions. The Office of Vizier divides into two separate offices for Upper and Lower Egypt. The title *God's Wife of Amun* is bestowed upon the kings' daughters and wives. A standing army of charioteers and infantry is established.

1479-1425*
B.C.E.

- Thutmose III (Dynasty 18) is king of Egypt. In circa 1468 he defeats a coalition of Syrian city-states at Megiddo, thus establishing Egyptian dominance in Syria-Palestine. Marriage alliances are made with Mitanni, a state along the Euphrates River.

1478-1458*
B.C.E.

- Hatshepsut, regent for Thutmose II, reigns during Dynasty 18.

1390-1353*
B.C.E.

- Amenhotep III (Dynasty 18) makes the first attempt since the Old Kingdom to present the king as a god, perhaps as part of a political response to increased economic power of the temples. Marriage alliances with Mitanni are continued.

1353-1336*
B.C.E.

- Amenhotep IV or Akhenaten (Dynasty 18) counters increasing political power of the temples by creating a new religion based at a new capital city, Amarna.

*Denotes Circa Date

1332-1322*
B.C.E.

- Tutankhamun (Dynasty 18) reverses Akhenaten's policies and restores the cult of Amun.

1279-1213
B.C.E.

- Ramesses II (Dynasty 19) rules Egypt. At the Battle of Qadesh in 1274 B.C.E., he fights the Hittites to a stalemate. Ramesses II is forced to withdraw and later signs a peace treaty with the invaders from Anatolia.

1187-1156*
B.C.E.

- Ramesses III (Dynasty 20), the last significant king of the New Kingdom, reigns. He prevents an invasion from the Sea Peoples (ancestors of the Philistines). An assassination attempt against him is thwarted.

1075-656*
B.C.E.

- The Third Intermediate Period occurs during which nominal kings control only parts of the country.

760-656*
B.C.E.

- Except for brief periods, Dynasty 25 marks the beginning of continuous foreign rule in Egypt until 1952 C.E.

525-522
B.C.E.

- King Cambyses conquers Egypt and it becomes part of the Persian Empire. The First Persian Period (Dynasty 27) lasts until 404 B.C.E.

381-343
B.C.E.

- The kings of Dynasty 30 rule from Sebennytos, a city on the west bank of the Damietta mouth of the Nile River.

362-343
B.C.E.

- Nectanebo II (Dynasty 30) is the last Egyptian pharaoh of Egypt.

332 B.C.E.

- Alexander the Great conquers Egypt and absorbs it into the Hellenistic world.

*Denotes Circa Date

OVERVIEW

Dynasties. Modern scholars divide the history of Egypt into thirty dynasties, following the practice of a third century B.C.E. historian named Manetho. He was an Egyptian who wrote in Greek for the Ptolemaic kings. His *History of Egypt* was meant to impress these Greek kings with the long and significant history of the country they now ruled. Manetho's book has not survived to modern times, but it was widely quoted by ancient authors. These quotes are the source for present-day knowledge of Manetho's writings. Manetho probably could read hieroglyphs and did research on the ancient king lists. His criteria for beginning and ending a dynasty, however, are not always clear to modern scholars. Sometimes a dynasty represents a change in family. The royal family of Dynasty 18 (circa 1539–1295/1292 B.C.E.), descendants of Ahmose, was not related to the family of Dynasty 19 (circa 1292–1190 B.C.E.), descendants of Ramesses I. The transition between Dynasty 5 (circa 2500–2350 B.C.E.) and Dynasty 6 (circa 2350–2170 B.C.E.), however, does not seem to represent a change in families. In fact, to modern readers, there is no clear reason for a break between King Unas (circa 2371–2350 B.C.E.), last king of Dynasty 5, and King Teti (circa 2350–2338 B.C.E.), first king of Dynasty 6. This break, though, made sense to Manetho and is still reflected in modern histories. The groupings of "kingdoms" and "intermediate periods" is modern. They were originally developed by Karl Richard Lepsius in his *Chronology of Ancient Egypt* (1849). These divisions are still useful since they establish continuity between certain dynasties.

Old Kingdom. During the Old Kingdom (Dynasties 3 to 6, circa 2675–2130 B.C.E.) there was a highly centralized government. The monumental architecture of the era, especially the Sphinx and pyramids at Giza, has led scholars to characterize it as a time when kings were most distant from the people and were considered most god-like.

First Intermediate Period. Following the death of Neferkare Pepy II at the end of Dynasty 6, the central government of Egypt collapsed. Local rulers called nomarchs established courts that mimicked the former royal court at Memphis. A stylistic change in the art of the First Intermediate Period (Dynasties 9 to 11, circa 2130–1980 B.C.E.) has led earlier scholars to think of this era as one of decline. Decentralization, however, made possible some creativity and change that would not have occurred under the tighter rule of the Old Kingdom.

Middle Kingdom. The rulers of the Middle Kingdom (Dynasties 11 to 14, circa 1980–1630 B.C.E.) reestablished central control in Egypt. The kings only gradually took full control over the provinces during Dynasty 12 (circa 1938–1759 B.C.E.). The central government exercised most thorough control under King Senwosret (Sesostris) III (circa 1836–1818 B.C.E.) when the local courts of provincial rulers seem to disappear. Most likely they had moved to Memphis, where all real political power was now located. (They were no longer buried in their provinces but were given tombs near the king's tomb. Egyptologists understand this change in burial customs as a sign of a changing balance of power, now favoring central authority.)

Second Intermediate Period. During the Second Intermediate Period (Dynasties 15 to 17, circa 1630–1539/1523 B.C.E.), the last kings of Dynasty 13 (circa 1759–after 1630 B.C.E.) and Dynasty 14 (dates uncertain) ruled in Thebes, while the kings of Dynasty 15 (circa 1630–1523 B.C.E.) and Dynasty 16 (circa 1630–1523 B.C.E.) ruled the North. These northern kings were the Hyksos, Amorites from Syria-Palestine who controlled an area east of Egypt as well as the Egyptian Delta.

New Kingdom. Ahmose, founder of Dynasty 18, drove the Hyksos from the Delta and pursued them into Syria-Palestine. The next four kings, culminating in the reign of Thutmose III (circa 1479–1425 B.C.E.) built an empire in Syria-Palestine and to the south in Nubia. The New Kingdom (Dynasties 18 to 20, circa 1539–1075 B.C.E.) kings ruled over Egypt at its greatest extent in its history.

Third Intermediate Period. Egypt split into two parts during the Third Intermediate Period (Dynasties 21 to 25, circa 1075–656 B.C.E.). The South was ruled from Thebes by the High Priests of Amun. The North was ruled by kings in Tanis and then kings in Bubastis, two cities in the Delta. Dynasty 25 (circa 760–656 B.C.E.) Nubian kings restored central government and ruled both the North and the South. They are grouped with the Third Intermediate Period because they are foreigners.

Late Period. The Late Period (Dynasties 26 to 30, 664–332 B.C.E.) is an era when foreign rulers tried to respect Egyptian traditions. The kings worshiped Egyptian gods and often revived customs originating in the Old Kingdom. The kings included Libyans (Dynasty 26, 664–525 B.C.E.), Persians (Dynasty 27, 525–404 B.C.E.), a few Egyptian rulers (Dynasties 28 to 30, 404–343 B.C.E.), and then Persians again (Dynasty 31, 343–332 B.C.E.). This last group of Persians in Egypt fell to the Macedonians under Alexander the Great in 332 B.C.E. Foreigners then continued to rule Egypt until the modern period with the 1952 C.E. revolution led by Gamal Abdel Nasser.

King at the Center. The king played the central role in government and politics in ancient Egypt. His office was the most stable element in the country's long history. In all periods there was some tension between the ideology of the semidivine king and a human attempting the multiple roles of infallible chief executive, judge, priest, and military general. The hieroglyphic sources, however, portrayed the king successfully fulfilling all his duties. Thus, true politics, which would include dissent and power struggles, remains hidden from modern observers. The one fact that becomes clear is that the king had to delegate his duties in spite of his supposed divine being.

Limitations on Power. The theoretically all-powerful king faced some limitations. He had to appoint advisers who could carry out his plans. He also abided by *maat*, the Egyptian concept of right conduct approved by the gods. In New Kingdom accounts of royal decision making, advisers regularly objected to the king's plans. Though the advisors were always overruled with good results, their objections must have had some basis in reality. In a time when communication over long distances was relatively slow, officials outside the capital must have made decisions without immediate royal approval if the administration was to remain effective.

Royal Titles. Even more important, the king was bound to *maat* and to the gods who were the king's senior partners in ruling the country. Though the king was divine, Egyptian descriptions of kings demonstrate that he was not as divine as the gods themselves. For example, the *Turin King List* described the first kings as true gods. Demigods called the "Followers of Horus" succeeded them. Only then, in Dynasty 1 (circa 3000–2800 B.C.E.), came historical kings. These kings were called "Horus, son of Osiris" at first. Additionally, the king was called Son of Re, the sun god, beginning in Dynasty 4 (circa 2625–2500 B.C.E.). These limitations would have provided some means for other humans to effect the king's power.

King's Divinity. The meaning of statements that the king was a god or that he was the son of a god is difficult to determine. These statements perhaps meant that the king was "like" a god or that the king was acting on behalf of the god. Present-day difficulties in understanding these statements come from the modern understanding that these kings were human. It may be that the Egyptians also regarded the king as human and actually believed that the king was a god's junior partner in government. This concept was expressed when the king was called a *netjer nefer*. These words literally mean "Good God" but might mean that the king was a "perfect" or "young" god. As a "young" god, the king was subject to his "father," the senior god. As a son he was also dependent on his father god or mother god. A king received the gifts of life, stability, and dominion from the god while he offered in return food, incense, and other gifts. A standard scene representing this event was often carved on temple walls in prominent places such as doorways.

Tasks of Government. The major goals of the government were to maintain a good relationship with the gods and to protect the country from outsiders. These goals were attained through tax collection, building projects, and expeditions that mined or quarried raw materials or obtained exotic finished goods from outside Egypt. In addition, the government maintained law and order within Egypt. All of these tasks were performed to fulfill the basic goals.

Government Departments. The Egyptians had established the basic government departments by the Old Kingdom. These departments aided the king in the tasks of governing the country. Departments of the treasury, agriculture, and labor were established in Dynasty 5. These divisions and even the names of the departments changed little over the millennia.

Officials. After the king, the most senior official was the prime minister, often translated by Egyptologists with the Turkish word *vizier*. Below this office was the Overseer of Royal Works, who was the equivalent of a present-day U.S. secretary of labor. The Overseer of the Treasury, whose position was sometimes merged with the Overseer of the Granary, was the other high official who greatly influenced the success of a king's reign. Provincial administrators did not emerge until Dynasty 5, when the office of Overseer of Upper Egypt was attested. In Dynasty 6 a nomarch headed each of the administrative districts.

Structural Changes. The early Dynasty 12 government resembled the Old Kingdom government. The departments of the vizier, treasury, agriculture, and labor remained in place. Yet, the recently independent nomarchs maintained their local courts, modeled on the central government at least until the reorganization implemented by Senwosret (Sesostris) III. He created a new labor office called the Office of the Provider of the People. The vizier and treasury remained, however, the two major departments of the government. The provinces were then grouped into three administrative sectors with local councils. These councils owed their loyalty to the king and the central government rather than the local noble families. Finally, a foreign office was established for the first time to administer Egypt's new Nubian possessions (the Sudan and southern Egypt). This office reflected every branch of government in Egypt. Nubia only differed from Egypt by the presence of soldiers in forts who represented an occupying military force.

Refinement. The land acquisitions of the New Kingdom caused a need for further bureaucratic refinement. A viceroy called the King's Son of Kush and the Overseer of Southern Lands collected taxes and oversaw construction projects. There were also two junior officials called *yedenu*, one for Wawat (Northern Nubia from the First to Second Cataract) and one for Kush (South from the Second Cataract to the Fourth Cataract near Napata). A police force and local mayors kept the peace. The northern possessions were governed through the Overseer of Northern Lands, but the Egyptians also maintained native rulers as vassals.

Geographic Divisions. Internal government was also divided geographically in the New Kingdom. Two viziers, one for Upper Egypt, the other for Lower Egypt, were established. The Old Kingdom title *Overseer of Royal Works* was reestablished, and the Middle Kingdom Office of Provider of the People was dismantled. Perhaps because foreign slaves were now a larger percentage of the workforce than formerly, there were reforms in managing labor.

Priesthood of Amun. Another New Kingdom innovation was the political rise of the priesthood of Amun. The priests administered temple land, herds, and labor. Eventually the growth of the priesthood would affect the power of the central government.

Divine Adoratrice of Amun. The Nubian kings of Dynasty 25 introduced the office of Divine Adoratrice of Amun, held by the king's daughter. The Divine Adoratice controlled large tracts of land, herds, and human resources. Her assistants became the new aristocracy of the Theban area.

Saite Revival. In Dynasty 26 a Libyan family with long associations with Sais in the Delta controlled the whole country. They restored much of the government of the New Kingdom and added the Office of Religious Affairs under the direction of the Divine Adoratrice of Amun. The Saites also utilized regional governors of Upper and Lower Egypt and divided the country into forty nomes (provincial territorial divisions) with local rulers. The individual towns had mayors.

Law and Justice. There were neither lawyers nor professional judges in ancient Egypt. People represented themselves in disputes of all sorts. Local courts prosecuted minor criminal infractions. Members of the administration heard only issues that directly involved the central government.

National Law. Standard national laws concerned inheritance and labor. The method of inheriting land was standard throughout the country because one wealthy person could hold land parcels in different parts of the country. The central government depended on state labor, so national laws were required. Otherwise, many crimes were handled by local custom.

Local Court of Magistrates. The most extensive evidence for local customs comes from the *kenbet* (court of magistrates) at Deir el Medina during the Ramesside Period (circa 1292–1075 B.C.E.). In this specialized village the foreman of the work gang had charge of the court. In other villages, the mayor would have charge of the court. Ordinary citizens also participated in decision making. The vizier served as the court of appeals. In serious cases, especially in cases of treason, the king appointed the tribunal himself.

Investigating Crime. The court heard the case, but individuals had to investigate thefts of personal property for themselves. The usual procedure was to ask fellow villagers to take oaths until the responsible party was found, and then a man or woman brought charges to the court. False oaths or charges were punished with one hundred blows with a stick.

Torture. The state made use of the police to find perpetrators of crimes against the central government or the temple. Administrators formed tribunals that heard evidence. Those charged with a crime were interrogated and tortured. The goal of the torture was to induce the accused to confess, to name accomplices, and to describe the methods used in a crime. This last point was important for improving security in the future. Some of the accused survived such treatment and were acquitted. It is difficult to determine the conviction rate given the limited documentary sources.

Appeals Process. Appeals were made to the vizier. The king sometimes heard civil cases, but he was never involved in criminal cases. Even when Ramesses III (reigned circa 1187–1156 B.C.E.) survived an assassination attempt, he named a court of inquiry rather than involving himself in the court case.

Punishment. The same court that heard the case set punishments. The death penalty was not, however, decreed without confirmation from the vizier's office. Other crimes were punished with beatings, mutilation, and/or a term of forced labor for the criminal and his family.

Family Law. The law did not regulate marriage and divorce. Adultery was condemned socially but entailed no legal penalties. The only family law concerned inheritance.

The Military. The ideology of the semidivine Egyptian king prevented the military from assuming heroic proportions. The king was often portrayed in official accounts as winning battles single-handedly with the help of the gods. Since there was no foreign threat against Egypt until the Second Intermediate Period, the Egyptians saw no need for a standing army until the New Kingdom, when independence allowed the Egyptians to establish one. Though army generals such as Horemheb, Ramesses I, and Sety I provided stability for the government in the transition from Dynasty 18 to Dynasty 19, the military never achieved the importance of the bureaucracy or the priesthood for governing Egypt.

Army of Local Retainers. In the Old and Middle Kingdoms there was no professional standing army. The autobiography of Weni, from the reign of Meryre Pepy I (circa 2338–2298 B.C.E.) in the Old Kingdom, described raising an army from local retainers of noblemen to fight the Sinai Bedouin. There are few military titles in this period and even fewer terms to describe units and subunits of men. The Egyptian word *mesha*, also used for the personnel of trade, mining, and quarrying expeditions, referred to the men in a military expedition.

Shift to Professionalism. The situation was much different in the New Kingdom. The two major combat arms were the infantry and the charioteers. There does not seem to have been a navy that was separated from the army. Foreigners also began to play a role in the Egyptian army as early as the New Kingdom. By the time of Ramesses II (circa 1279–1213 B.C.E.) soldiers received grants of land as a reward for service. In the *Wilbour Papyrus*, a land register of Dynasty 20 (circa 1190–1075 B.C.E.) and dating to circa 1146 B.C.E., soldiers were also well represented among landholders.

Late Period Army. The army was more prominent in the first millennium B.C.E. In this period a warrior class was established, descended from Libyans who had infiltrated the Delta from at least Dynasty 21 (circa 1075–945 B.C.E.). This class survived through political changes including the restoration of the central government by the Saites in Dynasty 26 and the First Persian Period (circa 525–404 B.C.E.). Even with the establishment of this class, the army remained a militia living on land granted by the king. The king called them to action when they were needed.

TOPICS IN POLITICS, LAW, AND THE MILITARY

BATTLE OF QADESH

Ancient Descriptions. In the fifth year of his reign, circa 1274 B.C.E., Ramesses II fought the Hittite king Muwatallis at Qadesh, a city on the Orontes River in modern Syria. The ancient Egyptian description of the battle survived in eight different copies. These copies include long inscriptions at the Temples of Abydos, Karnak, Luxor, the Ramesseum, and Abu Simbel. The temple inscriptions also included elaborate relief with labels, depicting highlights of the battle. Three copies of the inscription on papyrus have also survived. This plentiful documentation is a unique situation in ancient Egyptian history. Yet, the interpretation of these documents is still debated.

Equipping the Army. Ancient descriptions of the battle started with the events of April 1274 in Memphis. The army first received weapons and other supplies for their march eastward. The narration continued with the journey across the Sinai Desert, through present-day Israel and into Syria. Another division of the army traveled by sea. One month after their departure from Memphis, the king, along with the Division of Amun, arrived within a one-day march of Qadesh and set up a camp. The next day the army traveled north through an area called the Wood of Labwi, where two Shosu tribesmen approached the Egyptians.

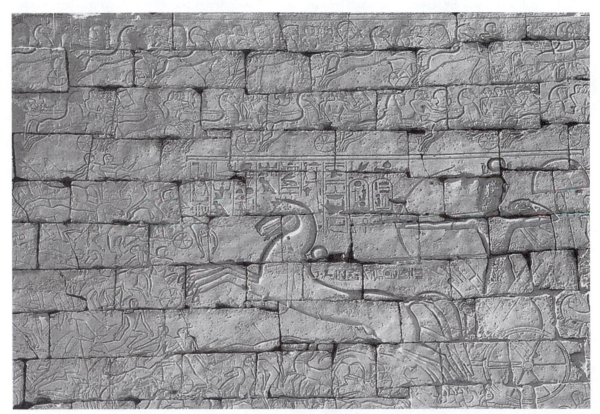

A relief, circa 1274 B.C.E., from the monumental gateway of the temple at Luxor depicting Ramesses II countercharging the Hittite chariots at the Battle of Qadesh

Before engaging the Hittites in battle in 1274 B.C.E., Ramesses II received military intelligence first from the Shosu, then from captured Hittite spies. According to an ancient inscription:

Ramesses II and the Shosu speak. Ramesses asked the Shosu where their chief was. The Shosu answered, "They are where the Ruler of the Hittites is, for the Hittite foe is in the land of Aleppo to the north of Tunip. He is too afraid of Pharaoh to come south since he heard that Pharaoh was coming north!" Dialogue of Ramesses II and the Hittite Spies, several hours later. "Then said His Majesty, 'What are you?' They replied, 'We belong to the Ruler of the Hittites! He sent us out to see where Your Majesty was.' Said His Majesty to them, 'Where is *he*, the Ruler of the Hittites? See, I heard it said that he was in the land of Aleppo, north of Tunip.' They replied, 'Behold, the Ruler of the Hittites has (already) come, together with the many foreign lands that he brought as allies. . . . See, they are poised armed and ready to fight behind Old-Qadesh.'"

Source: Kenneth A. Kitchen, *Pharaoh Triumphant: The Life and Times of Ramesses II, King of Egypt* (Warminster, U.K.: Aris & Phillips, 1982), pp. 55–56.

Deception. The Shosu offered their allegiance to the Egyptian king, claiming their willingness to betray their former pledge to the Hittite king. They also declared that the Hittite king had taken such fright at Ramesses II's approach that he had remained in the district of Aleppo north of Tunip, nearly 120 miles to the north. Ramesses II proceeded toward Qadesh assuming that the town was undefended and could easily be conquered. The king gave little thought to the absence of the remaining three divisions of the Egyptian army named after the gods Re, Ptah, and Seth. They were a half-day's march south of Qadesh, too far from Ramesses II if he needed help. The Shosu trick had worked.

Arrival at Qadesh. The town of Qadesh had strong natural defenses. The Orontes River, a tributary stream, and a canal that cut between the river and the stream protected it in a triangle of water. The king camped on the open plain nearby on the northwest side of the town. The Egyptians gave little thought to their own defense since they believed the Hittite king and his army were 120 miles away. As they set their camp, Egyptian reconnaissance scouts captured two Hittite spies. As the temple relief showed, a thorough beating led these two spies to admit the Shosu had deliberately misled Ramesses II. The Hittite king Muwatallis was actually only two miles away, behind the town.

Attack. Ramesses II must have been startled to receive this news. He immediately alerted the Division of Amun, which was with him, and sent a message to the nearest army division, the Division of Re. This division was at that moment crossing the river. Ramesses also sent a message to the royal family to leave the area. Certainly the royal family escaped, but the Division of Re was not so lucky.

Division of Re. The Hittites attacked the Division of Re, probably before they had received the king's message. The Hittites had been watching the Egyptians' movements from behind the woods at least since the two Shosu had been sent to trick Ramesses II. The Hittites now appeared on chariots just as the Division of Re was crossing the river. Several Hittite princes took the lead, cutting the Division of Re in two groups. According to the official account, the Division of Amun, which was with the king, panicked. Only Ramesses II remained coolheaded.

King's Bravery. Ramesses II strapped on his armor and jumped into his chariot. Accompanied only by his shield-bearer, Ramesses II charged the Hittite forces all alone six times. Though he could not have slaughtered all of the Hittites himself, he must have created some confusion among them.

Nearin. Just at this moment, a group of Egyptian soldiers called Nearin appeared west of the battlefield. These troops were not mentioned earlier in the inscription. Perhaps they were the Egyptian troops who had come by sea. Their name meant "young men." They now arrived in formation and joined the attack from the west. The Hittites, who surely had thought they would win the battle up until this point, now found themselves caught between the Nearin on their west and Ramesses II on their east. The Hittites wisely retreated to the south, covered by their reserve formations. In the Egyptian account they had to swim the river and some soldiers accompanying the Hittite prince nearly drowned.

Counting the Dead. Finally, Ramesses II was left on the west side of the river and the Division of Ptah appeared under the leadership of the vizier. These soldiers helped take prisoners who were left on the Egyptian-held west side of the river. They computed the number of enemy dead by the traditional method of cutting one hand from each corpse. They also collected military material that the Hittites had abandoned when they escaped across the river.

King's Anger. Ramesses II then addressed the regrouped Divisions of Amun and Re. The text emphasized the king's anger at these two divisions because they had fallen into disarray in the heat of battle. Ramesses II accused them of deserting him at his greatest moment of need. He told them that he was left with only his horses and his shield-bearer, Menna, to help him fight against millions of hostile soldiers. This speech is quite consistent with Egyptian ideology that only the king's efforts in battle are effective. However, the speech surprises modern readers because the king implied that he would have preferred some human help.

Egyptian Attack. At sunset of the same day, the final Egyptian unit, the Division of Seth, arrived in Qadesh. The whole Egyptian army was now assembled and camped for the night. The next day the Egyptians attacked. The Hittites had lost substantial chariots on the first day, but their infantry was still intact. The Egyptians, on the other hand, had preserved their chariots. Yet, the Egyptians were probably outnumbered two to one. The two armies fought to a stalemate.

Offer of Peace. The Hittites followed their own traditions in such a case, and offered a treaty to establish the status quo ante. They would permit Ramesses II to withdraw but would retain control of Qadesh. Ramesses II refused to agree with the Hittite terms, but he did withdraw from Qadesh. Thus, the Hittites were able to follow Ramesses southward and capture the Egyptian province of Upe in modern Syria and its capital city at Damascus.

Other Complications. Subsequent developments in the area prevented the Hittites from taking further advantage of this situation. The Assyrian king Adadnirari I moved to threaten Muwatallis on the east by taking the Hurrian state of Hanigalbat. Muwatallis was effectively prevented from expanding either eastward or southward.

Significance. Thus, in the end neither the Egyptians nor the Hittites could benefit militarily from the Battle of Qadesh. Egypt never again advanced so far north. Yet, twenty-seven years later Ramesses II signed a treaty with the Hittites that set the border where it had always been.

Propaganda. The enormous amount of wall space devoted to this battle in Egyptian temples that Ramesses II decorated suggests that the real importance of the battle for the king was in propaganda. Even though the foregoing description of the battle is drawn from the Egyptian texts, Ramesses II must have considered his exploits a success and expected those who viewed and read the relief and texts to understand that he had triumphed at Qadesh.

Sources:
Trevor Bryce, *The Kingdom of the Hittites* (Oxford: Clarendon Press / New York: Oxford University Press, 1998).

Adrian Gilbert, *The Encyclopedia of Warfare from Earliest Times to the Present Day* (Chicago & London: Fitzroy Dearborn, 2000).

Kenneth A. Kitchen, *Pharaoh Triumphant: The Life and Times of Ramesses II, King of Egypt* (Warminster, U.K.: Aris & Phillips, 1982).

THE BUREAUCRACY

Vizier. The *tjaty* (vizier or prime minister) was the second most important political figure after the king. According to a text called *The Duties of the Vizier,* dating to either Dynasty 13 (circa 1759–1630 B.C.E.) or to the reign of Thutmose III (circa 1479–1425 B.C.E.), the vizier met daily with the king to report on affairs of state. He coordinated and supervised the king's business. He probably also served as mayor of the capital city. The office of mayor was perhaps the original source of his power. Beginning in Dynasty 5 (circa 2500–2350 B.C.E.) there may have been two viziers, one for Lower Egypt and another for Upper Egypt.

Overseer of Royal Works. The Overseer of Royal Works was similar to a present-day U.S. Secretary of Labor. He was responsible for organizing labor for agriculture on the land that the king controlled directly and for royal building projects. In order to complete these tasks he had control over the work crew and the vast resources used to pay the workers, such as foodstuffs and clothing. This office existed in the Old Kingdom (circa 2675–2130 B.C.E.) and New Kingdom (circa 1539–1075 B.C.E.). In the Middle Kingdom (circa 1980–1630 B.C.E.) Senwosret (Sesostris) III (circa 1836–1818 B.C.E.) replaced it with the Office of the Provisions of the People.

Overseer of the Treasury. The Overseer of the Treasury collected, stored, counted, and disbursed commodities paid as taxes to the king. Many different products were included such as grains, vegetable oils, wood, metal, manufactured food, cloth, equipment, and weapons.

Overseer of the Granary. The Overseer of the Granary was closely linked with the treasury and was responsible for managing grain revenues. In some periods the Granary and the Treasury were combined in one department. This office must have been important because Egypt was an agrarian country.

Sources:
Ronald J. Leprohon, "Royal Ideology and State Administration in Ancient Egypt," in *Civilizations of the Ancient Near East,* volume I, edited by Jack M. Sasson (New York: Scribners, 1995), pp. 273 – 287.

Jaromir Malek, "The Old Kingdom (c. 2686–2125 BC)," in *The Oxford History of Ancient Egypt,* edited by Ian Shaw (Oxford: Oxford University Press, 2000), pp. 89–117.

William J. Murnane, *The Penguin Guide to Ancient Egypt* (Harmondsworth, U.K.: Penguin, 1983).

David O'Connor, "New Kingdom and Third Intermediate Period, 1552–664 BC," in *Ancient Egypt: A Social History,* edited by Bruce G. Trigger, and others (Cambridge, U.K.: Cambridge University Press, 1983), pp. 183–278.

Tomb model of the official Meketra counting and recording livestock for the royal tax to be calculated, circa 1938–1909 B.C.E. (Egyptian Museum, Cairo)

CRIME AND PUNISHMENT

Evading Conscription. Transgressions against the state were severely punished in ancient Egypt, with evading conscription being the most serious crime that peasants could commit. Papyrus Brooklyn 35.1446, Middle Kingdom (circa 1980–1630 B.C.E.) records from the Great Prison of Thebes, listed the specific crimes and punishments of those who evaded their work for the state. The Egyptians differentiated between failure to arrive at work and flight from a place of work. Two different crimes were recognized; four different laws were made regarding them. The four separate laws included "the law concerning deserters," "the law concerning deliberate desertion for six months, "the law concerning deliberate desertion from work," and "the law concerning the man who runs away without doing his duties." These crimes were so serious that they were investigated through the Office of the Vizier (prime minister). Whether the vizier himself gave judgments is not known. But a scribe of the vizier's office confirmed the sentence that was given to the guilty.

Ramifications. The punishments for these crimes were severe. The family of the offender was forced to fulfill his duties as a conscript for an indefinite period of time while the criminal performed state labor in the Great Prison. Each prisoner's case was reviewed after ten years of servitude. In seventy-eight of eighty cases known from the Brooklyn papyrus, the prisoner was then released. The other two prisoners were condemned to life in prison.

Tomb Robbery. There is reason to believe that tomb robbery was a problem in all periods of Egyptian history. Certainly all Egyptians knew that the tombs of the nobles were filled with valuable objects. The only documentation of an investigation and trial for tomb robbery comes from Dynasty 20 (circa 1190–1075 B.C.E.) in Years 16 to 18 of Ramesses IX. A group of documents in the British Museum in London and the Egyptian Museum in Turin preserved trial transcripts for a series of tomb robberies committed in western Thebes by workers from Deir el Medina. High officials assisted in the commission of these crimes and benefited from the sale of the stolen goods.

Targeted Items. The tomb robbers of Dynasty 20 were active in royal tombs of Dynasty 17 (circa 1630–1539 B.C.E.), in mortuary temples, and in the Valley of the Queens. The papyri describe how the robbers located tombs and the way that they unwrapped mummies and

Painting from the Theban tomb of Menna, Sheikh Abd el-Qurna, showing a delinquent farmer being shaken by a tax collector while another farmer is being beaten with a stick, circa 1539–1295/1292 B.C.E.

This short extract from Papyrus Abbott describes the inspection of a tomb belonging to Sobekemsaef II, a little-known king of Dynasty 17 (circa 1630–1539 B.C.E.). The extract conveys the tone of these texts and the difficulty of locating the tombs described.

The officials of the Great and Noble Necropolis and the Scribe of the Vizier, and the Scribe of the treasury of Pharaoh were sent in order to examine the tombs of the kings of former times and the tombs and resting places of the Blessed . . . by the Mayor of the City and Vizier, Khaemwaset and the Royal Butler Nesyamun, and the Scribe of Pharaoh. . . . The Pyramid of King Sehemshedtawy, the Son of Re Sobekemsaef (II) was found and thieves had violated it. It was the work of stone masons in the back of the pyramid, in the courtyard, outside of the tomb of the Overseer of the Granary Neb-Amun of King Menkheperre (Thutmose III). The burial place was found to be empty, and also the burial place of his queen. The robbers had stretched out their hands against the king and queen.

Source: Thomas Eric Peet, *The Great Tomb-Robberies of the Twentieth Egyptian Dynasty* (Oxford: Clarendon Press, 1930).

removed amulets made of precious metals and removed other valuable objects from tombs.

Preventive Measures. The extant papyri do not specifically discuss problems in the Valley of the Kings. However, shortly after the incidents discussed in these papyri, the priests of the necropolis relocated the mummies of the New Kingdom (circa 1539–1075 B.C.E.) kings to a common tomb. They remained protected there until the late nineteenth century, when they were removed to the Egyptian Museum in Cairo.

Assassination. The evidence for assassination in Egypt remains vague. The possibility that a person could murder the king would contradict the official ideology that he was at least semidivine. Thus, the hints of assassination plots found in Egyptian texts are veiled and difficult to interpret. The *Instructions of Amenemhet I*, a Dynasty 12 (circa 1938–1759 B.C.E.) wisdom text, warned in this king's voice that the price of trust for a king was death. It also seems to describe an attempt against the king's life.

Ramesses III. More detailed information on assassination dates to the reign of Ramesses III (circa 1187–1156 B.C.E.). A series of badly preserved papyri provide details on a plot against this king that originated among his wives and sons. Whether the plot involved murder or was an attempt to influence the succession in the favor of Prince Pentaweret rather than Prince Ramesses, the designated successor, is unclear. The price paid by the approximately forty plotters was death. Some of the higher-ranking plotters were given permission to commit suicide while others were killed. The reasoning behind this distinction is not clear from the evidence.

Name Changes. One culturally specific punishment for the plotters was changing their names so that their identity would be obliterated. One conspirator, for example, was called "Re hates him" in the trial transcript, probably a change from the more common Egyptian name *Meryre* ("Re loves (him)"). This punishment would have been serious for an Egyptian who hoped to live forever.

Judicial Oracles. Judicial oracles included the gods in a verdict. At Deir el Medina, the magistrates carried a statue of the Divine Amenhotep I before the assembled litigants. They then posed a yes or no question to the statue, asking if "x" were right and if "y" were wrong. The men carrying the statue then moved either forward or backward. This movement demonstrated that the god concurred with the verdict the court had reached. Judicial oracles were included in questions of real estate and tomb occupancy. These disputes included the interests of the government since houses and tombs at Deir el Medina were state property. Thus, the court asked the state god of the village to confirm a verdict rather than decide it independently. These oracles were not "fixed" but were instead a religious ceremony to confirm the verdict.

Harsh Penalties. Punishment for crimes committed against the state was harsh. Common punishments included one hundred to two hundred blows with a stick, one to five open wounds, mutilation of the nose or ears, and terms of forced labor. The death penalty, however, was rare. It was reserved for assassination of the king, tomb robbery, and official corruption. Loss of office was a common punishment for a variety of administrative misdeeds. This sentence was a double punishment since it also meant loss of the office to the criminal's son. Forced labor also meant that the whole family of a convicted criminal was put to work for periods of either ten or twenty years.

Means to an End. Torture was used to gain confessions to crimes. Torture victims also were forced to name accomplices in crimes, to reveal the hiding place of stolen goods, and to describe the methods used in a crime. Information on methods allowed the authorities to strengthen security measures. The most common torture was the *bastinato*, beating the bottom of the foot with a stick.

Sources:

David Lorton, "Legal and Social Institutions of Pharaonic Egypt," in *Civilizations of the Ancient Near East*, volume I, edited by Jack M. Sasson (New York: Scribners, 1995), pp. 355–362.

A. G. McDowell, *Jurisdiction in the Workmen's Community at Deir el Medina Egyptologische Uitgaven*, 5 (Leiden, Netherlands: 1991).

John A. Wilson, *The Culture of Ancient Egypt* (Chicago: University of Chicago Press, 1956).

FORTS

Knowledge from Images. The Egyptians built forts in all periods of their history. Abundant evidence for fortifications remains, giving a broad picture of the changes in fort building and location throughout the period under consideration. Because Egyptian hieroglyphic writing used pictures, some idea of the appearance of early forts was preserved in writing. The words for "mansion," "wall," and

"fortified building" are found on seals and sealings from the beginnings of Egyptian history. These writings show large buildings with thick, crenellated walls, towers, and monumental gates. The Narmer Palette, carved in the time of the first king of Dynasty 1 (circa 3000–2800 B.C.E.), depicted a bull destroying the walls of a fortified city or a fort. This scene represented the king's symbolic uniting of various Egyptian towns into one country.

Archaeological Evidence. Archaeological evidence for forts is rare in the first three dynasties. Yet, archaeologists have identified buildings at Elephantine, Abydos, and Hierakonpolis as forts. A fortified building containing Egyptian artifacts in En Basor (Syria-Palestine) might be a fort or a trading station. In general, the forts of this period were built of mud brick. Curved towers stood along the wall. At each corner a square tower defended the fort. The gate was also fortified.

Old Kingdom. In the Old Kingdom (circa 2675–2130 B.C.E.) a text mentioned a Fortress of the Bitter Lakes, which was located in the eastern delta. The only archaeological evidence for a fort from this period comes from the other end of the country. The Dakhla Oasis contains remains of a mud-brick fort with massive walls and a circular bastion at the corner and semicircular bastions along the walls. Piers flanked the gate and protected it.

First Intermediate Period and Middle Kingdom. In the First Intermediate Period (circa 2130–1980 B.C.E.) and the Middle Kingdom (circa 1980–1630 B.C.E.) literary and historical texts often mentioned forts. *The Instructions of Merykare for his Son, The Complaints of Neferty, The Story of the Shipwrecked Sailor,* and the epic poem *Sinuhe* all mentioned forts. Biographical texts written by Ankhtyfy of Moalla and King Wahankh Antef I of Thebes also discussed capturing forts.

Nubian Forts Phase I. However, archaeology provides the most plentiful information about forts built in the Middle Kingdom. The Egyptians constructed a system of forts in Nubia to guard their southern frontier, exploit natural resources, and administer trade. The forts were built during three distinct phases between the First and Second Cataracts. The earliest forts, built at the end of Dynasty 11 (circa 2081–1938 B.C.E.), are the least well understood. Archaeologists discovered their remains at Aniba, Ikkur, Kubban, and Wadi el Hudi. Yet, the second phase of forts, built by Senwosret I, is better preserved.

Nubian Forts Phase II. Senwosret I began a second series of forts, first improving on the design of the Dynasty 11 forts at the same sites. He also added one at Buhen. In general, these structures were built with massive mud-brick walls. External rectangular towers stood along the walls and at the corners. Buttresses on the exterior face of the walls supported wooden platforms. These platforms, called battlements, provided a place for soldiers to stand and fight. One wall of the fort stood parallel to the Nile River, and a gate gave access to the riverside quay. A dry moat surrounded the fort on the other three sides.

Buhen. The fortress at Buhen had additional defensive features. The dry moat was lined with bricks. The sharply inclined inner side of the moat (scarp) met a slope of earth (glacis) on the inside of the moat and would have further impeded an attacking soldier's progress. A low wall stood on a built-up area of earth between the glacis and the fort's

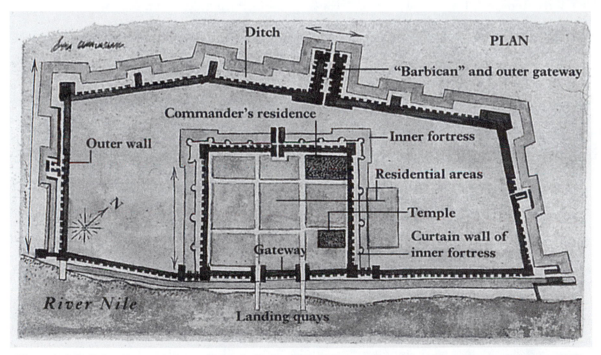

Diagram of the Buhen Fortress in Lower Nubia, built circa 1938–1759 B.C.E. (from David Silverman, *Ancient Egypt,* 1997)

Fortifications built on Egypt's southern border in the area of the Second Nile Cataract, circa 1980–1860 B.C.E.

walls. Behind this defense stood semicircular bastions. Small windows pierced these bastions. The opening of the windows pointed downward, giving the archer inside a good shot at attackers trapped in the moat. Other openings in the bastion allowed archers a straight shot across the moat. A main gate extended over the ditch. It had double wooden doors and a retractable wooden bridge that could be removed on rollers. These forts demonstrate a new sophistication in designing defensive structures.

Nubian Forts Phase III. Senwosret III built a third phase of Middle King forts in Nubia at the Second cataract. These forts, found at Askut, Shalfak, Uronarti Semna, Kumma and Semna South, represent a different construction type from Buhen. They were built following the hilly terrain, and thus they required no moats. Soldiers could access the Nile through a stairway. These forts lacked the mud-brick towers that had been so basic to the design of earlier forts. Now the Egyptians constructed spur walls that followed the contours of the land. These spur walls provided platforms for the soldiers defending the fort.

Interior Design. All the forts' interiors followed a regular plan. The Egyptians constructed streets that met at right angles in the center of the fort. Other streets followed the interior of the massive walls. Streets also divided the interior into units. These units included administrative buildings, soldiers' barracks, and officers' houses. Storerooms and granaries were in another section. Other areas were utilized for food production, including bakeries and a garden. One fort contained clear evidence of an armory.

Delta. In the Middle Kingdom the northern border is less well known. Texts refer to a frontier station called The Walls of the Ruler. Yet, scholars have not yet tied this name to an archaeological site. The Walls of the Ruler was either one fort or a series of forts in the delta and on the border. Some scholars have suggested it was a canal with a

dike on one or both sides. The poem *Sinuhe* clearly placed The Walls of the Ruler on the frontier near the Sinai. Since Egypt had trade interests with Syria-Palestine in this period as it did with Nubia, it is likely that part of the purpose of this installation was to control and monitor trade.

Second Intermediate Period and New Kingdom. The Nubian forts developed into towns during the Second Intermediate Period (circa 1630–1539/1523 B.C.E.). They must have been dominated by the Kerma culture of Nubia in this period. By the New Kingdom (circa 1539–1075 B.C.E.) the Egyptians had reoccupied the forts and added an Egyptian temple to these towns. The towns had thick walls with square towers at the gate, corners, and along the walls. The towns within the walls were planned with streets crossing at ninety-degree angles. The temples and storage areas were built of stone, while the houses were mud-brick. Some settlements remained outside the walls of the town. Middle Kingdom sites such as Aniba and Buhen were modified to fit this pattern. Newly built towns included Aksha, Amara West, Sai, Sesebi, and Soleb. These towns were administrative centers responsible for sending taxes north to Egypt proper, protecting trade and preserving the frontier.

Evidence of the Hyksos. In the north the earthen embankments at Heliopolis and Tell el Yehudyyah, once thought to be forts, are now recognized as foundations for temples. True forts have been identified at Tell el Daba and Deir el Ballas. The use of the site of Tell el Daba can be identified with the town fortress of Avaris described in the Kamose Stela. Remains of earthwork platforms and a thick-walled superstructure have been excavated. This town is associated with the Hyksos occupation.

Syria-Palestine. In the New Kingdom, Thutmose III established garrisons in Syria-Palestine to supervise trade, tribute, and communication with Egypt. The garrisons

also maintained the peace among city-states in Syria-Palestine and provided a buffer between Egypt and the empires of the Hittites, Babylonians, and Hurrians. Ancient lists of forts by place-names were composed in Thutmose III's reign. They are arranged from north to south and from east to west. But the sites on the ground have not been identified.

Residence-Forts. In Dynasty 19 (circa 1292–1190 B.C.E.) archaeologists can trace a development in Egyptian forts found in Syria-Palestine. The first common type was a small square tower known as a *migdol*. Later forts resembling Egyptian houses replaced the *migdol*. Archaeologists believe that these forts were the Residence of the Egyptian governor. They were built with a central courtyard and rooms were arranged around it. The plan resembled a large Egyptian house. Residence-forts were excavated at Tell Farah, Tell esh-Sharia, Aphek, Tell Jemmeh, Tell Masos, and Tell Hesi.

Beth Shan. Archaeologists have discovered the complete sequence from Dynasties 19 and 20 (circa 1190–1075 B.C.E.) of Egyptian forts at Beth Shan in modern Israel. In Dynasty 19 the site contained a residence, Egyptian temple, granary, and *migdol*. The large house and *migdol* were unoccupied in Dynasty 20, but there was still an Egyptian residence.

Karnak Temple. A relief at the Karnak Temple carved in the reign of Sety I preserved depictions of a series of small fortresses. These fortresses were located on the Ways of Horus, the main ancient road from the eastern delta and across the northern Sinai to modern Israel. Many of these buildings were discovered archaeologically in the late twentieth century C.E., but exact identifications between the relief representations and the sites have not been made.

Northwest Border. The northwest Egyptian border was first fortified in Ramesside times (circa 1292–1075 B.C.E.). Ramesses II, Merneptah, and Ramesses III built forts against the Sea Peoples in this area.

Third Intermediate Period. During the Third Intermediate Period (circa 1075–656 B.C.E.) Egyptian towns became fortified as the central government broke down. Notable fortified towns included Medinet Habu, El Kab, and Herakleopolis. In Dynasty 26 (circa 664–525 B.C.E.) there were forts at Tell Kedwa in northern Sinai and at Dorginarti, an island near the Second Cataract.

Frontier Relations. By studying the location of forts in various periods Egyptologists determine Egypt's ancient borders and the degree of hostility it experienced with its neighbors. The extent that the buildings were fortified suggests to historians the nature of Egypt's foreign relations. Clearly, Nubia and Syria-Palestine must have been safer places for the Egyptian garrisons in the New Kingdom than in the Middle Kingdom. The open towns found in Nubia and the residence-forts found in Syria-Palestine dating to the New Kingdom are nearly undefended in comparison to the Middle Kingdom forts. Further research on

forts should yield even more information on Egyptian foreign relations.

Sources:
John Carman and Anthony Harding, eds., *Ancient Warfare: Archaeological Perspectives* (Stroud, U.K.: Sutton, 1999).

Adrian Gilbert, *The Encyclopedia of Warfare from Earliest Times to the Present Day* (Chicago & London: Fitzroy Dearborn, 2000).

A. W. Lawrence, "Ancient Egyptian Fortresses," *Journal of Egyptian Archaeology*, 51 (1965): 155–179.

THE HYKSOS

Divided Rule. During the Second Intermediate Period (circa 1630–1539/1523 B.C.E.) Egypt was divided into two spheres of influence. While native Egyptian princes ruled Upper Egypt from Thebes, foreign kings called the Hyksos (Egyptian *Heka-Hasut*, "Rulers of Foreign Lands") controlled the Delta from Avaris (modern Tell el Daba). The near absence of contemporary written documents and the conflict between the rulers inferred from archaeological evidence combined with subsequent Egyptian descriptions of the Hyksos have hindered modern understanding of this period. Though scholars have now established who the Hyksos were, debate continues over how they gained power.

Origins. The Egyptian expression *Heka-Hasut* was used as early as the Old Kingdom (circa 2675–2130 B.C.E.) to describe rulers of foreign lands from both Nubia and the Levant. The term in Egyptian carried no racial or national designation. In the Second Intermediate Period, however, the specific foreign rulers were Semites from Syria-Palestine. Their personal names, such as Yaqob-har (compare Hebrew *Yaqub* = Jacob) certainly represented a

Stela of the ruler Kamose in the temple of Amun at Karnak commemorating his campaign against the Hyksos, circa 1543–1539 B.C.E.

Semitic dialect and were sometimes compounded with the Semitic deities Baal or Anat. The non-Egyptian artifacts found in their settlements include typically Levantine and Canaanite jugs, juglets, weapons, and toggle pins. The plans of their god's temples followed a Canaanite model while their characteristic burials with donkeys were paralleled in Canaan, the Levant, and Mesopotamia but not found in Egypt outside Hyksos-controlled areas. They made Egyptian-style scarabs but their typical spiral design was more commonly found in Canaan than in Egypt. Earlier scholars attempted to equate the Hyksos with Hebrews, Arabs, Aryans, and Hurrians. Most scholars now believe that the Semitic names, deities, and archaeological assemblage indicate a west Semitic group known as Amorites were most likely the foreign kings who ruled in Egypt.

War or Infiltration? Though most historians agree today that the Hyksos were Amorites, they remain divided on the question of how these foreigners came to power in Egypt. Some argue—based on texts written after King Ahmose of Dynasty 18 (circa 1539–1295/1292 B.C.E.) expelled the Hyksos—that a military invasion resulted in Hyksos conquest. In an inscription describing the reconstruction of a temple, Hatshepsut (circa 1478/1472–1458 B.C.E.) remarked:

> I have raised up what was dismembered from the first time when the Asiatics [i.e. Hyksos] were in Avaris of the North Land (with) roving hordes in the midst of them overthrowing what had been made; they ruled without Re and he acted not by divine command. . . . I have raised up what was.

Other scholars reconstruct from the archaeological evidence a peaceful infiltration of foreigners who gradually became the majority in the eastern delta and filled a power vacuum left by the decline of the kings of Dynasty 13 (circa 1759–1630 B.C.E.). Austrian archaeologists working at Avaris since the 1960s have revealed evidence for Canaanites in increasing numbers starting in Dynasty 12 (circa 1938–1759 B.C.E.). A papyrus in The Brooklyn Museum attests large numbers of Semites in Egypt during Dynasty 13. The Hyksos rulers who emerged from this group formed Dynasty 15 (circa 1630–1523 B.C.E.), concurrent with the last twenty-seven kings of Dynasty 13. The roles played by the Hyksos Dynasties 14 (dates uncertain) and 16 (circa 1630–1523 B.C.E.) remain disputed by scholars.

Upper Egypt. In Thebes, Dynasty 13 and its successor Dynasty 17 (circa 1630–1539 B.C.E.) continued the traditions of the Middle Kingdom (circa 1980–1630 B.C.E.). Though the known monuments are relatively modest in scale, the central administration, the army, and the priesthood continued to function efficiently in Upper Egypt.

Threat. Thebes benefited from trade between Kush and the Hyksos, but the last kings of Dynasty 17 felt militarily and economically threatened. Archaeological evidence seems to confirm a Nubian military threat to Thebes while it seems logical that Upper Egypt was marginalized economically. King Kamose, one of the leaders of the war that expelled the Hyksos must have believed that his enemy would unite with Kush against him. In fact, during the war Kamose intercepted a Hyksos messenger to the Kushite ruler carrying the message:

> Come North! Do not hold back! See he (Kamose) is here with me: There is none who will stand up to you in Egypt. See, I will not give him a way out until you arrive! Then we shall divide the towns of Egypt. . . .

Kamose's brother Ahmose finally succeeded in driving the Hyksos from Egypt, leading to the founding of Dynasty 18 (circa 1539–1295/1292 B.C.E.) and the reconquest of Nubia.

Sources:

Nicolas Grimal, *A History of Ancient Egypt,* translated by Ian Shaw (Oxford & Cambridge, Mass.: Blackwell, 1993).

Eliezer D. Oren, ed., *The Hyksos: New Historical and Archaeological Perspectives* (Philadelphia: University Museum, University of Pennsylvania, 1997).

John Van Seters, *The Hyksos: A New Investigation* (New Haven: Yale University Press, 1966).

THE KING

A Fine Line. The boundary between politics and religion is hard to draw in ancient Egypt. The vocabulary used to describe the king illustrates the interconnectedness of these two categories in Egypt. Five different Egyptian words were used to refer to the king. These words cannot be translated clearly because the English language has no vocabulary to describe a man who becomes semidivine when taking a political office. Translations sometimes also blur the distinctions among the king's roles. The following words (with their common translations) were used to describe the king:

A palace doorjamb relief of Merneptah receiving the insignia of royalty from the god Amun, circa 1213–1204 B.C.E. (University of Pennsylvania Museum of Archaeology and Anthropology)

Overlapping dates indicate coregencies and/or multiple claims to the throne.

Predynastic Period

Dynasty 0 (circa 3100–3000 B.C.E.)

Early Dynastic Period (circa 3000–2675 B.C.E.)

Dynasty 1 (circa 3000–2800 B.C.E.)

Dynasty 2 (circa 2800–2675 B.C.E.)

Old Kingdom (circa 2675–2130 B.C.E.)

Dynasty 3 (circa 2675–2625 B.C.E.)

Dynasty 4 (circa 2625–2500 B.C.E.)

Dynasty 5 (circa 2500–2350 B.C.E.)

Dynasty 6 (circa 2350–2170 B.C.E.)

Dynasties 7 and 8 (circa 2170–2130 B.C.E.)

First Intermediate Period (circa 2130–1980 B.C.E.)

Dynasties 9 and 10 (circa 2130–1980 B.C.E.) ruling from Herakleopolis

Dynasty 11 (circa 2081–1938 B.C.E.) ruling from Thebes

Middle Kingdom (circa 1980–1630 B.C.E.)

Dynasty 11 (after circa 1980 B.C.E.)

Dynasty 12 (circa 1938–1759 B.C.E.)

Dynasty 13 (circa 1759–after 1630 B.C.E.)

Dynasty 14 (dates uncertain)

Second Intermediate Period or Hyksos Period (circa 1630–1539/1523 B.C.E.)

Dynasty 15 (circa 1630–1523 B.C.E.)

Dynasty 16 (circa 1630–1523 B.C.E.)

Dynasty 17 (circa 1630–1539 B.C.E.)

New Kingdom (circa 1539–1075 B.C.E.)

Dynasty 18 (circa 1539–1295/1292 B.C.E.)

Dynasty 19 (circa 1292–1190 B.C.E.)

Dynasty 20 (circa 1190–1075 B.C.E.)

Third Intermediate Period (circa 1075–656 B.C.E.)

Dynasty 21 (circa 1075–945 B.C.E.) ruling from Tanis

Dynasty 22 (circa 945–712 B.C.E.) ruling from Bubastis

Dynasty 23 (circa 838–712 B.C.E.) ruling from Thebes

Dynasty 24 (circa 727–712 B.C.E.) ruling from Sais

Dynasty 25 (circa 760–656 B.C.E.)

Late Period (664–332 B.C.E.)

Dynasty 26 (664–525 B.C.E.) ruling from Sais

Dynasty 27 or First Persian Period (525–404 B.C.E.)

Dynasty 28 (404–399 B.C.E.)

Dynasty 29 (399–380 B.C.E.) ruling from Mendes

Dynasty 30 (381–343 B.C.E.) ruling from Sebennytos

Dynasty 31 or Second Persian Period (343–332 B.C.E.)

Source: Jack M. Sasson, ed., *Civilizations of the Ancient Near East*, 4 volumes (New York: Scribners, 1995).

1.) *Nisut:* A religious concept used to describe the king as the representative of justice and legal order (*maat*).

2.) *Nisut-biti:* "King of Upper and Lower Egypt"; this term described the king as the embodiment of power on earth.

3.) *Hemef* ("His Majesty") or *Hemei* ("My Majesty") described the human ruler who sees orders carried out.

4.) *Neb* ("Lord") and *Iti* ("Sovereign") were used parallel to *Nisut.*

5.) *Netjer* ("God") was never used alone of a living king except Amenhotep III (circa 1390–1353 B.C.E.) and Ramesses II (circa 1279–1213 B.C.E.). For deceased kings, *netjer* referred to the king becoming Osiris, the divine king of the dead. *Netjer nefer* ("Good God" or "Perfect, Youthful God") was used when the king was described as the junior partner in government with the Great God Amun.

Pharoah. The word *pharoah* was transmitted to English from Greek and Hebrew transcriptions of the Egyptian expression *pev-oa*, which literally meant "Great House." It was used to refer to the Egyptian king in the same way in the United States the expression "White House" is used to refer to the president. Pharoah is actually a more casual expression than terms such as *Nisut* and *Hemef.* The Egyptians did not begin to use the term until the reign of Thutmose III (circa 1479–1425 B.C.E.).

Co-regency. One means the Egyptians sometimes used to ensure a smooth succession from one king to the next was co-regency. A father could name his son "co-king" and rule jointly with him. Some kings of Dynasties 12 (circa 1938–1759 B.C.E.), 18 (circa 1539–1295/1292 B.C.E.), 19 (circa 1292–1190 B.C.E.), 22 (circa 945–712 B.C.E.) and 23 (circa 838–712 B.C.E.) appointed co-regents. Most often an older king would appoint his son so that the son could

Colossal carving of Ramesses II (the Great) from his temple at Abu Simbel

lead the army and travel around the country. The senior king could then concentrate his energy on administration.

Jubilee (Sed) Festival. The jubilee festival, called the *Sed* in Egyptian, was celebrated throughout history. Though there must have been changes in detail and even in meaning over the three thousand years it was celebrated, the basic outline of the festival remained stable. Preparations included building a festival hall specifically for this purpose, quarrying obelisks, preparing for feasts, and bringing the cult statues of the major gods to the site of the festival. The king and the gods participated in a variety of ceremonies together and exchanged gifts. The king either walked or ran in a ritual race, participated in a mock funeral, and reenacted the coronation. Though these rituals seem designed to reinforce the legitimacy of the king's rule, there is no evidence, as is so often claimed, that this ritual derives from a prehistoric tradition of murdering a king after thirty years of rule. It is also not clear how often the ritual occurred, though it is often stated that it was performed thirty years after the coronation.

Dynasty and the Royal Family. Egyptologists divide Egyptian history into thirty dynasties following a history of Egypt written by Manetho in the third century B.C.E. Recently, a dynasty preceding Manetho's Dynasty 1 (circa 3000–2800 B.C.E.) has been discovered and named Dynasty 0 (circa 3100–3000 B.C.E.). In general, the reasons for designating a change in dynasty are not clear. Sometimes, however, it is possible to deduce that a change in royal family led Manetho to designate a change in dynasty. For example, a Middle Kingdom (circa 1980–1630 B.C.E.) literary text described Khufu's efforts (Dynasty 4, circa 2585–2560 B.C.E.) in the Old Kingdom (circa 2675–2130 B.C.E.) to discover the birth of divine triplets whose names are those of three kings of Dynasty 5 (circa 2500–2350 B.C.E.). Such a change in family is also clear in the transition from Dynasty 11 to 12 (circa 1938 B.C.E.) and from Dynasty 18 to 19 (circa 1292 B.C.E.) when the childless Tutankhamun's throne was inherited by his generals, Ay, Horemheb, and Ramesses I in succession. If

indeed the importance of the royal family was so great that a change in family required a change in dynasty, it is odd that the royal family itself is so little known. Younger sons of the royal family in the Old Kingdom did not have tombs larger than other officials had. (Tomb size remains the best indicator of social status.) Names of royal sons are rarely preserved, as in the case of Ramesses II's forty-five-plus sons. Daughters are also little known unless they married the next king.

King Lists. The Egyptians made lists of the order of their kings for dating purposes. Rather than calculating the year from a fixed date and adding one at each new year, the years were named after the number of years a king ruled. For example, "Year 21 of King Thutmose III" came twenty-one years after he ascended the throne. In order to calculate when an event had occurred, it was necessary to know the order of the kings and the number of years that each one ruled. King lists were consulted, for example, to calculate that Year 12 of Sety I was eight years before Year 6 of Ramesses II. This date could be determined because the list would show that Sety ruled for fourteen years immediately before Ramesses II.

Sources:

Nicolas Grimal, *A History of Ancient Egypt,* translated by Ian Shaw (Oxford & Cambridge, Mass.: Blackwell, 1993).

Barry J. Kemp, *Ancient Egypt: Anatomy of a Civilization* (London & New York: Routledge, 1991).

Kemp, "Old Kingdom, Middle Kingdom, and Second Intermediate Period, c. 2686–1552 BC," in *Ancient Egypt: A Social History,* edited by Bruce G. Trigger, and others (Cambridge: Cambridge University Press, 1983), pp. 71–182.

Donald B. Redford, *Pharaonic King-Lists, Annals and Day-Books: A Contribution to the Egyptian Sense of History* (Mississauga, Canada: Benben, 1986).

WAR

A Royal Task. There was no word for war in ancient Egyptian. Defending the country from foreign invasion was always represented as a royal task. All wars against foreigners, whether defending the borders of Egypt or moving beyond the Nile Valley into the Levant, were described as directed against rebels. Theoretically, everyone was subservient to the Egyptian king

Wooden models of Egyptian spearmen and Nubian archers found in the tomb of Mesehti at Asyut, circa 2000 B.C.E. (Egyptian Museum, Cairo)

The following are extracts from the autobiography of Weni, an army leader in Dynasty 6 (circa 2350–2170 B.C.E.). He described raising an army, the administrative structure of it, and the measures he took against looting. He also wrote a poem about his victory against the Bedouin. This victory allowed the Egyptians free access to the Sinai mines.

Raising an Army

His Majesty took action against the Asiatics and the Bedouin. His Majesty created an army of tens of thousands from all of Upper Egypt, from Elephantine to Aphroditopolis in Lower Egypt, these being the two sides of the kingdom in their entirety of borders. [He created an army from among] the Nubians of Irtjet, of Djaw, of Yam, of Wawat, of Kaw and of Ta-sety.

Administrators of an Army

His Majesty sent me before this army while Mayors, Seal Bearers, Sole Companions of the Palace, Priests of the Temples of Upper and Lower Egypt, Translators, Chiefs of Priests of Upper and Lower Egypt, Chiefs of the borders, were (also) before the troops of Upper and Lower Egypt, of the administrative districts, towns, and Rulers of the Nubians of these foreign countries.

No Looting Permitted

I made a plan for it . . . so that no one set his hand against his companion, so that one did not rob another of bread or sandals from those on the road, so that no one seized the clothing of anyone in a town, so that no one seized any goat in another's possession.

Poem Describing Victory

This army returned in safety,

It destroyed the land of the Bedouin.

This army returned in safety,

It flattened the land of the Bedouin.

This army returned in safety,

It ripped up its town walls.

This army returned in safety,

It cut down its figs and its vines.

This army returned in safety,

It shot fire [into all its houses.]

This army returned in safety,

It slaughtered troops by tens of thousands.

This army returned in safety,

It brought many troops to be living prisoners with it.

His Majesty praised me about it more than anything.

Translations by Edward Bleiberg

Source: *Autobiography of Weni*, in *Urkunden des ägyptischen Altertums*, Part I, *Urkunden des alten Reiches*, edited by Kurt Sethe (Leipzig: J. C. Hinrichs, 1903), pp. 101–104.

Reconstruction from a relief of Ramesses II at the siege of Dharpur carved on the inner south wall of the Hypostyle Hall in the Ramesseum, circa 1279–1213 B.C.E. (from Peter A. Clayton, *Chronicles of the Pharaohs*, 1994)

and the king ruled the whole world. The army itself was included as a type of corvée labor. The troops protected mining expeditions and trade missions and also made war against the Bedouin in the desert, the Hyksos to the Northeast, and the Nubians to the South. However, sophisticated military techniques were known. Scenes from Old Kingdom (circa 2675–2130 B.C.E.) tombs depicted siege techniques and sappers undermining foundations of town walls. War machines such as ladders on wheels were used against fortified towns in the New Kingdom (circa 1539–1075 B.C.E.). Other weapons illustrated in Old Kingdom tombs were bows and arrows and axes in hand-to-hand combat. The chariot was added to the list of weapons in the New Kingdom.

Sources:

John Carman and Anthony Harding, eds., *Ancient Warfare: Archaeological Perspectives* (Stroud, U.K.: Sutton, 1999).

John Hackett, ed., *Warfare in the Ancient World* (New York: Facts on File, 1989).

Alan Schulman, "Military Organization in Pharaonic Egypt," in *Civilizations of the Ancient Near East*, volume I, edited by Jack M. Sasson (New York: Scribners, 1995), pp. 289–302.

Sheikh Ibada al-Nubi, "Soldiers," in *The Egyptians*, edited by Sergio Donadoni (Chicago: University of Chicago Press, 1997), pp. 151–184.

WOMEN: ROLE IN GOVERNMENT

Importance. Officially, women's main political roles were mother or wife of the king. Women, however, gained some political power through religious offices. The most important priestess from the New Kingdom (circa 1539–1075 B.C.E.) through the Late Period (664–332 B.C.E.) was the God's Wife of Amun, later called the Divine Adoratrice of Amun. This office varied in importance from the early New Kingdom through the Late Period.

Titles. The two most important titles for women identified their relationship with the king. A queen who was the mother of the reigning king held the Egyptian title that translates literally as "King's Mother." The second important title was "King's Wife" (Queen). Usually more than one woman was King's Wife at one time, but only one woman at a time could be King's Principal Wife. Sometimes the King's Wife was a biological sister to her husband, though half sisters and unrelated women were more common in this role. Even nonroyal women who became King's Wives or King's Mothers were from elite Egyptian families or foreign royal families.

Queens and Other Elite. Queens had no clear secular duties differing from the duties of other elite women. The difference between queens and other elite women was the scale of the wealth they helped administer. Queens managed their palaces and their estates. They also produced children who would later take over the bureaucracy, military, and priesthood. The king had many wives who lived together, probably raising their children together. The institutional setting where the

Relief from a granite obelisk at Karnak of Queen Hatshepsut in the dress of a Pharaoh having the "crown of victory" placed upon her head by the god Amun, circa 1478/1472–1458 B.C.E.

royal women lived is often translated as the *harem*, using a Turkish word for women's quarters. The King's Principal Wife had religious duties but was not necessarily the mother of the next king.

Religious Role and Real Power. One road to increased political power for women was through the queen's religious role. At the beginning of Dynasty 18 (circa 1539–1295/1292 B.C.E.), the office of God's Wife was filled first by the King's Mother Ahhotep and later by Queen Ahmose-Nefertary, wife of King Ahmose. The God's Wife controlled large tracts of land associated with her office. Hatshepsut held the title God's Wife when her husband, King Thutmose II, assumed the throne in circa 1493 B.C.E. After Thutmose II died in circa 1479 B.C.E., Hatshepsut acted as regent for her nine-year-old stepson, Thutmose III, using the title God's Wife rather than King's Wife or King's Mother. Two years later, Hatshepsut declared herself female king and appointed her own daughter God's Wife. When Thutmose III assumed sole rule after Hatshepsut's death in circa 1458 B.C.E., he downgraded the role of the God's Wife. Perhaps Thutmose III feared that the God's Wife could threaten his own power. The God's Wife was not prominent again until the reign of Amenhotep IV or Akhenaten (circa 1353–1336 B.C.E.), when it assumed a different importance.

Amarna Religion. Akhenaten rejected the god Amun, but his new religion of the god Aten stressed the correspondence between the gods and the royal family. His wife, Nefertiti, and their daughters played significant religious roles as the only legitimate priesthood in the new religion. When Tutankhamun (circa 1332–1322 B.C.E.) restored the cult of Amun, he retained this correspondence between the king, his wife, and child; and the deity, the deity's wife, and child. Thus, the role of God's Wife assumed somewhat greater importance. The succeeding kings of Dynasties 19 (circa 1292–1190 B.C.E.) and 20 (circa 1190–1075 B.C.E.) maintained the ritual role of the God's Wife of Amun without allowing her to gain political power. For example, Ramesses II established parallel cults for himself and his principal wife Nefertary. This situation changed again in the Late Period beginning with Dynasty 21 (circa 1075–945 B.C.E.).

Legitimate Power. The last kings of Dynasty 20 had lost political control of Upper Egypt. The General and High Priest of Amun, Herihor, assumed secular power in the south in the king's place. Though Herihor clearly had the military power to dominate Upper Egypt and Nubia, something restrained him from declaring himself legitimate king. He preferred to receive the god's endorsement of his political control through representatives of the royal family headed now by King Smendes. Smendes's daughter became the God's Wife of Amun who legitimated Herihor's secular power. Herihor thus successfully separated the military and religious power of the cult of Amun. He enhanced the religious role of the God's Wife of Amun and reserved secular power for himself. However, Herihor had also effectively established the principle that the God's Wife of Amun could bestow political legitimacy. All the high priests of Amun who followed him found they

Painted limestone sculpture of the head of Queen Nefertiti, Dynasty 18, circa 1539–1295/1292 B.C.E. (Ägyptisches Museum, Berlin)

were dependent on an increasingly wealthy and powerful God's Wife of Amun.

Kushite Kings. The Kushite kings of Dynasty 25 (circa 760–656 B.C.E.) also used the office of God's Wife of Amun to legitimate their rule over Egypt. They appointed their own daughters to this pivotal position, gaining control both of Amun's resources and the legitimacy that Amun's representative could bestow.

Conclusion. Women were not, in general, members of the bureaucracy or military. With a few exceptions, they could not be king. Elite women certainly had status over nonelite men, but overall women were subservient to men in ancient Egypt.

Sources:
Betsy M. Bryan, "'In Women Good and Bad Fortune Are on Earth': Status and Roles of Women in Egyptian Culture," in *Mistress of the House, Mistress of Heaven: Women in Ancient Egypt*, edited by Anne K. Capel and Glenn E. Markoe (New York: Hudson Hills, 1996), pp. 25–46.

Jacobus van Dijk, "The Amarna Period and the Later New Kingdom (c. 1352–1069 BC)," in *The Oxford History of Ancient Egypt*, edited by Ian Shaw (Oxford: Oxford University Press, 2000), pp. 272–313.

Marianne Eaton-Krauss, "Tutankhamun," in *Oxford Encyclopedia of Ancient Egypt*, volume III, edited by Donald B. Redford (New York: Oxford University Press, 2001), pp. 452–453.

David Lorton, "Legal and Social Institutions of Pharaonic Egypt," in *Civilizations of the Ancient Near East*, volume I, edited by Jack M. Sasson (New York: Scribners, 1995), pp. 355–362.

Gay Robins, "Women," in *Oxford Encyclopedia of Ancient Egypt*, volume III, edited by Redford (New York: Oxford University Press, 2001), pp. 511–516.

SIGNIFICANT PEOPLE

AMENHOTEP III

FLOURISHED CIRCA 1390-1353 B.C.E.
KING, DYNASTY 18

Historical Record. Amenhotep III ruled Egypt at the height of its prosperity and prestige. His nearly thirty-eight-year reign is well documented in comparison to that of most ancient Egyptian kings. Yet, outstanding problems in understanding the events of the reign, especially concerning his relationship with his son Amenhotep IV, cannot be solved because of the lack of data.

Family. Amenhotep III was the son of the preceding king, Thutmose IV, and a minor wife named Mutemwia. Amenhotep III was no older than twelve when he ascended the throne. Yet, by Year 2 he had married Tiye, his Great Royal Wife. Tiye was the daughter of Yuya and Tuya of Akhmim. Yuya was a high military official with responsibility for the chariots. The rich tomb given to Yuya and Tuya in the Valley of the Kings suggests their importance in this reign. Amenhotep III also married two Mitanni princesses named Giluhepa and Taduhepa, sealing the peace treaty with their country negotiated by his father. His children with Tiye included the next king, Amenhotep IV/Akhenaten, and perhaps Tutankhamun, whose parentage remains uncertain. His daughters who reached prominence were Sit-amun and Isis, who both bore the title of Royal Wife. Betsy M. Bryan has suggested that the king married his daughters in order to maintain control over the estates they owned.

Military Actions. Amenhotep III's reign was unusual because of its peaceful nature. In Year 5 three different stelae recorded a minor military action in the far south of Nubia, above the Fifth Cataract. Another text referred to a military action that might be the same one or another action near the Second Cataract. This record is the full extent of documentation for warlike activities during the reign. In contrast to his ancestors and his successors in Dynasty 19 (circa 1292–1190 B.C.E.) no major wars were fought in this reign.

Foreign Relations. Trade and gift exchange with rulers in the Near East dominated Amenhotep III's foreign relations. Archaeologists have discovered trade goods from Amenhotep III's reign in Mycenae (Greece), Yemen (Arabian Peninsula), and Assyria (modern Iraq). The Amarna letters, an archive of letters in the Akkadian language, document the petty competitions and demands for gifts that concerned Amenhotep III in Syria-Palestine. Egypt dominated these small city-states and had thoroughly Egyptianized the culture of Nubia. There was an effective peace treaty with Mitanni, and the Hittites had not yet asserted themselves. The coalition of Syro-Palestinian city-states led by Qadesh had been defeated by Thutmose III and would not reassert itself until prodded by the Hittites in the reign of Ramesses II (circa 1279–1213 B.C.E.).

Foreigners in Egypt. More and more foreigners resided in Egypt during this period. The prisoners of war who had entered the country in proceeding reigns were originally agricultural and construction workers. Over time some foreigners married Egyptians and rose in the bureaucracy and the army. Canaanites, Hurrians from Mitanni, and Nubians became fully integrated into Egyptian society. Not only are foreign names found in Egyptian genealogies in this period, but also foreign gods were worshiped in Egypt. The military use of foreign terms for equipment and ranks reflected this influence.

Administration. Growing wealth presented new problems in administration for the Egyptians. Many of the resources that entered Egypt from abroad came to the temples. Some scholars believe that an increasing amount of land passed from royal to temple control in this period. Though it was true that temples increased in wealth, it is not entirely clear that the temple's wealth grew proportionately more than the royal family's own wealth. Some scholars believe that a genuine power struggle arose between the royal family and the temples. This presumed power struggle would then explain some religious policies initiated by Amenhotep III and perhaps continued by his son Amenhotep IV/Akhenaten.

clearly demonstrated the lack of official hostility from one generation to the next.

Designing the Pyramids. When Khufu moved to Giza, it was uninhabited. Khufu's architect, his nephew Hemiunu, might have trained when his grandfather Sneferu built his pyramids at Dahshur. He designed the pyramid and two associated temples and a causeway that led from the Nile Valley up to the desert plateau. Some scholars associate the Great Sphinx at Giza with Khufu's pyramid, though traditionally the Sphinx has been interpreted as an image of Khafre, Khufu's son.

Mastaba Tombs. Hemiunu also designed rows of mastaba tombs for the bureaucrats who ran the government and the family members who were mostly priests of Khufu's cult. There were at least fifty tombs neatly arranged in rows on streets around the Great Pyramid. They were built of stone and contained delicate relief carving. In general these tombs lacked large-scale sculpture of the deceased. Only the king's direct descendents or the highest officials had three-dimensional sculptures representing them. Some scholars have interpreted the lack of sculpture as part of Khufu's religious program to associate himself with the sun god Re.

Politics and Religion. The restrictions on sculpture suggest part of Khufu's religious program. In addition, Khufu's son Djedefre was the first Egyptian king to call himself by the title *Son of Re*. This title implied that Khufu was more strongly associated with the god Re than previous kings had claimed. Children with royal blood, the blood of Re, were restricted from government positions outside the priesthood. In contrast, Sneferu's children in the previous reign had held government positions of real power.

Length of Reign. The length of Khufu's reign is unclear. The Turin Canon, a king list from the New Kingdom, listed Khufu with twenty-three years. The highest year date contemporary with his reign is Year 22. Yet, many scholars believe that twenty-three years would not have been sufficient time to build the Great Pyramid. Rainer Stadelmann has suggested that *23* is an inversion of *32*, an amount of time that would have permitted the completion of Khufu's building projects.

Memory of Khufu. The Egyptians remembered Khufu as a cruel man, though he was honored as a god as late as the first millennium. A papyrus from the Hyksos Period (circa 1630–1539 B.C.E.) that probably was originally composed in the Middle Kingdom (circa 1980–1630 B.C.E.) described Khufu's indifference to human life. Khufu ordered a magician to demonstrate his claim that he could sever and rejoin a head and its body with human prisoners. The magician was forced to warn the king that such tricks were only safe with animals. The Greeks also remembered Khufu as cruel and impious. This opinion was probably based on the size of the Great Pyramids. The Greeks could only see it as an example of overweening pride. In reality, little can be known of the king's personality. His success as an administrator who could organize and command large groups of people, however, cannot be denied.

Sources:

George Hart, *Pharaohs and Pyramids: A Guide through Old Kingdom Egypt* (London: Herbert, 1991).

Zahi Hawass, "Khufu," in *Oxford Encyclopedia of Ancient Egypt*, volume II, edited by Donald B. Redford (New York: Oxford University Press, 2001), p. 234.

Jaromir Malek, *In the Shadow of the Pyramids: Egypt During the Old Kingdom* (Norman: University of Oklahoma Press, 1986).

Peter Tompkins, *Secrets of the Great Pyramid* (New York: Harper & Row, 1971).

NEBHEPETRE MENTUHOTEP II

FLOURISHED CIRCA 2008-1957 B.C.E.
KING, DYNASTY 11

National Hero. Nebhepetre Mentuhotep II reunited Egypt after the First Intermediate Period (circa 2130–1980 B.C.E.) and is considered to be the founder of the Middle Kingdom (circa 1980–1630 B.C.E.). Egyptians remembered him with Menes, founder of Dynasty 1 (circa 3000–2800 B.C.E.), and Ahmose, founder of the New Kingdom (circa 1539–1075 B.C.E.), as great national heroes. Yet, his policy of frequent name changes, reflecting different phases of his career, has confused modern scholars so that they cannot agree on whether he should be numbered Mentuhotep I, II, or III. This volume follows the most recent scholarship, which argues that he was Mentuhotep II.

Family. Nebhepetre Mentuhotep II claimed descent from Inyotef III and Queen Iah. He depicted himself in a graffito at Wadi Shatt el-Rigal and at the temple of Montu in Tod with the Inyotef family, the princes of Thebes. Recently, Cae Callender has suggested that Nebhepetre Mentuhotep II's insistence on this connection casts doubt on its validity. Both Neferu and Tem bore the title *King's Wife* during this reign. Tem was also the mother of the following king, Sankhkare Mentuhotep. Six other female burials were included in Nebhepetre Mentuhotep II's funeral temple. All six were priestesses of Hathor, a cult that was important to Nebhepetre Mentuhotep. Four of them were named as King's Wife. All were young, ranging in age from five to twenty-two years old. Sankhkare Mentuhotep was Nebhepetre Mentuhotep II's son with Queen Tem. He ruled Egypt after his father's death.

Warrior. Nebhepetre Mentuhotep II came to the throne of Thebes in a period when Egypt was divided. The princes of Thebes ruled Upper Egypt from Aswan to the Tenth Nome on the border with Asyut. The princes of Asyut remained loyal to the kings in Herakleopolis in Lower Egypt. Asyut thus protected a militarized border between Upper and Lower Egypt. The two halves of Egypt seem to have existed in a state of armed peace.

Two Lands United. In Year 14 of Nebhepetre Mentuhotep II this situation changed. A text called *The Teachings* of *Merykare* from Herakleopolis referred to the capture of Abydos. A stela from Thebes dated to Year 14 of Nebhepetre Mentuhotep II described a rebellion in the Abydos Nome against Thebes. If these two events were in reality two descriptions of the same situation from different viewpoints, then it is likely that a war began at this point in the reign. The ruling family of Asyut disappeared at this time, suggesting that Theban forces had defeated them. Though no details of this war survive, at some point Herakleopolis was destroyed. A mass grave of sixty Theban soldiers from this period graphically demonstrates the human cost of this war. When the war ended, however, Nebhepetre Mentuhotep II added to his name Sematawy, "One Who United the Two Lands."

Nubia. Nebhepetre Mentuhotep II's success in defeating Herakleopolis allowed him to turn his attention to Nubia (southern Egypt and the Sudan). Northern Nubia had returned to local rule after the collapse of the Old Kingdom (circa 2675–2130 B.C.E.). Nebhepetre Mentuhotep II reestablished Egyptian claims in the area by building forts for Egyptian garrisons.

Continued Insecurity. Sporadic fighting might have continued within Egypt for many years after the defeat of Herakleopolis. In their autobiographies, some Egyptian nobles mentioned fighting, but it is difficult to identify the exact time when this fighting occurred. Many nobles included weapons in their burials during this period. Since Egyptians expected the next world to resemble this world, the need for weapons suggests that there was continued insecurity during the early years of the reunification.

Administrator. Nebhepetre Mentuhotep II rewarded his supporters with continued administrative positions. Those who had supported Herakleopolis, especially the princes of Asyut, disappeared from history. The local ruling families of Beni Hasan, Hermopolis, Nag ed-Deir, Akhmim, and Deir el Gebrawi—all in Middle Egypt—continued to rule. Some of these families established continuous lines until the time of Senwosret III, approximately 150 years later.

Benefits. Theban officials also gained from Nebhepetre Mentuhotep II's success. The officials Khety, Henenu, Dagi, Bebi, and Ipy all received tombs that recount their accomplishments in this period. The office of vizier (prime minister) was reestablished and a Theban now had primary responsibility for Lower Egypt. Theban officials traveled to Lebanon for cedar, to Sinai to subdue the Bedouin, and to Nubia.

Builder. Nebhepetre Mentuhotep II also initiated an extensive building program. Combined with a renewed effort to deify the reigning king, new temples in Dendera, Gebelein, Abydos, Tod, Armant, Elkab, Karnak, and Aswan in Upper Egypt and in Qantir in Lower Egypt would have clarified his intention to reestablish a united kingdom on the model of the Old Kingdom.

Deir el Bahri. The king's mortuary temple at Deir el Bahri was surely the most important building of the reign. Though today the king's temple is overshadowed by Hat-shepsut's nearby mortuary temple, Mentuhotep's temple must have been an inspiring symbol for those promoting the new state. The approach to the temple was lined with trees planted in specially prepared pits that had been lined with topsoil. The building itself consisted of a series of ramps and terraces surmounted by a structure that has been reconstructed as a cube or a pyramid. The decorative program of the building stressed the cult of Osiris rather than the cult of Re found in the Old Kingdom mortuary complexes. The Osiris cult that had now spread to a wider group throughout Egypt would have linked the king with his people. This building was surely the inspiration for Hatshepsut's more famous mortuary temple built five hundred years later.

Delicate Balance. Recent scholarship has stressed the vitality of the First Intermediate Period immediately preceding the reign of Nebhepetre Mentuhotep II. Archaeologists have also recognized that wealth was more widely spread before reunification. Yet, Nebhepetre Mentuhotep II must have provided greater security for Egyptians in a strong, centralized state. This balance between independence and stability was a constant theme in ancient Egyptian history.

Sources:

Cae Callender, "The Middle Kingdom Renaissance," in *Oxford History of Ancient Egypt*, edited by Ian Shaw (Oxford: Oxford University Press, 2000), pp. 148–183.

Peter A. Clayton, *Chronicle of the Pharaohs: The Reign-by-Reign Record of the Rulers and Dynasties of Ancient Egypt* (New York: Thames & Hudson, 1994).

Nicolas Grimal, *A History of Ancient Egypt*, translated by Shaw (Oxford & Cambridge, Mass.: Blackwell, 1993).

RAMESSES II

FLOURISHED CIRCA 1279-1213 B.C.E.
KING, DYNASTY 19

Progeny. Ramesses II (the Great) successfully ruled Egypt for sixty-six years in spite of military setbacks. He was the son of Sety I, the previous king, and his wife Queen Tuya. Evidently reacting to the lack of heirs at the end of the previous Dynasty 18 (circa 1539–1295/1292 B.C.E.), Ramesses II began his reign with two principal wives, Nefertary and Isetnefret. Two Hittite princesses also became his wives, one in Year 34 and one about Year 44. Four of Ramesses II's daughters also held this title. They were among approximately forty daughters and forty-five sons born by various royal women. Many of the sons were buried in the Valley of the Kings (Tomb number KV 5) in an unusual tomb designed for multiple burials. Four of the daughters—Henutmira, Bintanat, Merytamun, and Nebettawy—had decorated tombs in the Valley of the Queens. His thirteenth son, Merneptah, followed Ramesses II on the throne.

Foreign Relations. The earlier part of Ramesses II's reign included largely unsuccessful wars with the Hittites and more successful wars in Nubia. An initial campaign in Year 4 secured the Palestinian coast for Egypt, but the Battle of Qadesh in the following year (1274 B.C.E.) failed to win the town back for Egypt. The propaganda campaign that followed the battle, however, was a great success. By emphasizing Ramesses II's personal bravery, the king succeeded in presenting the battle in the best possible light. He reached a wide public through carving scenes of the battle at temples throughout Egypt. Minor campaigns in modern Jordan and Syria occurred in Years 7, 8, and 10. Ramesses II avoided another Qadesh in all of these battles.

Negotiated Peace. A further strain in Ramesses II's relations with the Hittites occurred in Year 18. Ramesses II gave sanctuary to the former Hittite king Mursili III (Urhi-Teshub), whose uncle Hattusili III had deposed him two years earlier. Though Hattusili III threatened to invade Egypt because Ramesses II helped Mursili III, the Hittite king was unable to execute his threats. The Assyrians attacked the Hittites' eastern border that same year, giving Hattusili III more important problems to solve. By Year 21, Hattusili III and Ramesses II negotiated a peace treaty that ended hostilities between Egypt and the Hittites.

Frontier Forts. Ramesses II turned his attention to the western border with Libya, the new trouble spot for Egyptian defense. A series of forts kept this frontier quiet through Ramesses II's reign, though Libyans would be ruling Egypt by Dynasty 21 (circa 1075–945 B.C.E.).

Internal Developments. Ramesses II carried out a vast building program, adding monumental rooms at Luxor and Karnak, a new temple at Abydos, and the now famous temple at Abu Simbel. He also built a new capital in the eastern Delta called Pi-Ramesses (the House of Ramesses.) In fact, almost every site in Egypt witnessed new building activity during Ramesses II's reign. Perhaps he was continuing the temple restoration needed after Akhenaten's closing of the old temples; or perhaps his long reign followed by a period of relative poverty in Egypt meant that Ramesses II was simply the last king to follow such a large-scale building program. Thus, his buildings remain the last on a site. Whatever the cause, the architecture of Ramesses II's reign remained the most plentiful from any period in Egyptian history.

Deification. Among the temples that Ramesses II built were chapels dedicated to the king himself as a god. Colossal statues of Ramesses II were erected in front of many temples with cults dedicated to the divine Ramesses II. Chapels in temples depicted Ramesses II making offerings to himself as a god. Ramesses II had deified himself to a much greater extent than previous kings of the New Kingdom (circa 1539–1075 B.C.E.).

Legacy. Ramesses II outlived the first twelve sons he designated as his successor. Merneptah, his fourth son by Isetnefret, followed him on the throne after his death in about 1213 B.C.E. Even though he had lost a major battle with the

Hittites at Qadesh, his reign was remembered as one of the greatest in Egyptian history.

Sources:

Kenneth A. Kitchen, *Pharaoh Triumphant: The Life and Times of Ramesses II, King of Egypt* (Warminster, U.K.: Aris & Phillips, 1982).

William MacQuitty, *Ramesses the Great: Master of the World* (New York: Crown, 1978).

Charles L. Nichols, *The Library of Rameses the Great* (Berkeley, Cal.: Peacock, 1964).

Kent R. Weeks, *The Lost Tomb* (New York: Morrow, 1998).

RAMESSES III

FLOURISHED CIRCA 1187–1156 B.C.E.
KING, DYNASTY 20

Attempted Assassination. Ramesses III was the last significant king of the New Kingdom (circa 1539–1075 B.C.E.). His parents, King Sethnakhte and Queen Tiye-Merenaset, were the founders of Dynasty 20 (circa 1190–1075 B.C.E.). Ramesses III had at least three wives. Queen Isis-Hemdjeret was the mother of Ramesses IV, the next king. An unknown queen or queens bore ten other sons. Among these sons were the future kings Ramesses VI and Ramesses VIII. (Ramesses V was perhaps Ramesses III's brother.) Another secondary queen named Tiye was the mother of Prince Pentaweret. Their plot to assassinate Ramesses III was discovered and led to their death by suicide.

Diplomacy. Ramesses III's early reign was dominated by war. The Meshwesh tribe, with origins in Libya, continued to infiltrate the delta from the west. Egypt had accepted the presence of these Libyans but the king expected to control the succession of their "kings." In Year 5 of his reign Ramesses III fought the Meshwesh to settle local disputes. Another campaign in Year 11 led to further pacification of the Meshwesh.

Sea Peoples. An even more important battle was fought against the Sea Peoples in Year 8. Scholars still debate the origins of this confederation of ethnic groups that the Egyptians called the Sea Peoples. Archaeological evidence demonstrates that they first destroyed the Hittite capital and brought the Hittite Empire to an end. They were then present in northern Syria, along the Levantine coast, and finally in Cyprus. They attacked the Egyptian delta in a huge battle commemorated at Ramesses III's mortuary temple in Medinet Habu. The Egyptians must have been well prepared for this battle. Scholars do not doubt that Ramesses III successfully repulsed the Sea Peoples and forced them to settle in Syria-Palestine. They were most likely the ancestors of the Philistines. The Sea Peoples never invaded Egypt successfully but they changed the politics of the Near East and northern Africa permanently by destroying the long-established power structure of the east Mediterranean.

Internal Policy. Ramesses III built a major mortuary temple at Medinet Habu during the first twelve years of his reign. The building imitated Ramesses II's Ramesseum in plan. In fact, Ramesses III used the reign of Ramesses II as a model. He constructed buildings at the same sites as his predecessor and named his sons after Ramesses II's sons.

Punt and Sinai. Ramesses III sent expeditions to Punt and to Sinai in Year 20. These expeditions were the first documented contact with Punt since the time of Hatshepsut more than three hundred years previously. The Sinai expeditions brought copper from Timna and turquoise from Serabit el-Khadim.

Papyrus Harris I. Scholars have offered differing interpretations of the meaning of Papyrus Harris I, the major source that described Ramesses III's relationship with the god's temples. According to the papyrus, in Year 15 Ramesses III ordered an inspection of the temples that revealed extensive internal corruption. Ramesses III both reformed the temple administration and enriched it by assigning large tracts of land to the temples of Thebes, Memphis, and Heliopolis. Some scholars link the temples' increased control of land with the inflation in grain prices that occurred about ten years later. Whatever the validity of this interpretation high grain prices led to food shortages at Deir el Medina, the workman's village. During the course of a strike in Year 29, the men refused to work until they received their wages from the temple. Perhaps in spite of these problems Ramesses III celebrated a Sed festival in Year 30 as was traditional. Some scholars have linked the lavish spending on the festival in the face of grain shortages to the assassination attempt against Ramesses III led by Tiye and Pentaweret. Jacobus van Dijk has suggested that at the least, Tiye and Pentaweret believed they could succeed because both officials and workers were so dissatisfied. Ramesses III died soon after this attempt on his life, though not all scholars believe the assassination attempt was the direct cause of his death.

Decline. Thus, Ramesses III's legacy was insubstantial probably because of economic problems beyond his control. With his death, the final phase of the New Kingdom began. This era ended about eighty years later after ineffective rule by eight kings named Ramesses.

Sources:

Lionel Casson, *The Pharaohs* (Chicago: Stonehenge, 1981).

Jacobus van Dijk, "The Amarna Period and the Later New Kingdom (c. 1352–1069 BC)," in *The Oxford History of Ancient Egypt*, edited by Ian Shaw (Oxford: Oxford University Press, 2000), pp. 272–313.

Pierre Grandet, "Ramesses III," in *Oxford Encyclopedia of Ancient Egypt*, volume III, edited by Donald B. Redford (New York: Oxford University Press, 2001), pp. 118–120.

THUTMOSE III

FLOURISHED CIRCA 1479–1425 B.C.E.
KING, DYNASTY 18

Model King. Thutmose III, a gifted warrior and administrator, consolidated his grandfather's conquests and continued to build important monuments throughout the country. He ruled from circa 1479–1425 B.C.E. during the New Kingdom (circa 1539–1075 B.C.E.), and he is the prototype of the ideal ancient Egyptian pharaoh.

Family. Thutmose III was the son of Thutmose II and his minor wife Queen Isis. He came to the throne as a child after the death of his father. The Great King's Wife Hatshepsut acted as regent while Thutmose III remained a minor. He had one half sister named Neferure. She was the daughter of Thutmose I and Hatshepsut. No other siblings are known. Though some scholars have argued that Thutmose III married Neferure, there is no concrete evidence to back this claim. Thutmose III did, however, marry Sit-iakh, who became the mother of his oldest son, Amenemhet, who died young. A second wife, Meryetre-Hatshepsut, was the mother of the next king, Amenhotep II. She was likely a commoner. A third wife, Nebtu, is only known by name. Four other royal children are known.

Early Training and Career. Thutmose III claimed his early life was spent in training as a priest of the god Amun. In this period he learned to read and write hieroglyphs, a skill not always mastered by kings. During a procession of the god, the priests carrying the god's statue stumbled in front of the young Thutmose III. This event was interpreted as a sign that Amun had chosen the child to follow Thutmose II on the throne. This inscription is interpreted to mean that Thutmose III was not the obvious heir to the throne, but needed the endorsement of the Amun priesthood before he could be recognized. This text also resembled in its details a description of the accession of Thutmose I to the throne, another king who was not the obvious heir.

Military Indoctrination. The remainder of Thutmose III's early years was spent with the army. Military training was the most common education for future kings. It is possible that Thutmose III led his first military expeditions later in this period, while Hatshepsut remained chief administrator of the country.

Sole Rule. Following Hatshepsut's death in 1458 B.C.E., the now adult Thutmose III assumed sole control of the throne in Year 22 of his reign. During the following seventeen years, Thutmose III undertook at least fourteen military campaigns, consolidating Egyptian control as far as the Euphrates River to the east and the Fourth Cataract of the Nile River in Nubia to the south. He thus completed the conquests that his grandfather, Thutmose I, had begun. Thutmose III became the New Kingdom prototype of the warrior-king, describing himself as "a king who fights by himself, to whom a multitude is no concern; for he is abler than a million men in a vast army. No equal to him has been found, a fighter aggressive on the battlefield."

Campaigns. Thutmose III's army fought during fourteen military campaigns between Year 22 and Year 42 of his reign. The three most significant campaigns were fought against Egypt's most important northern enemies. In Year 22 he defeated the coalition of Syrian city-states led by Qadesh at the town of Megiddo. In Year 33 he defeated the state of Mitanni located on the east side of the Euphrates River. In Year 42 he defeated the Syrian city-state of Tunip. In each of these campaigns, Thutmose III demonstrated superior military abilities.

Building Projects. Thutmose III also initiated many building projects within both Egypt and Nubia. Eight temples have been discovered in Nubia, while seven temples are known in Upper Egypt. Texts from the reign referred to nearly fifty separate building projects. In Thebes he constructed mortuary temples for his father and grandfather as well as his own. He also added important buildings to the Karnak complex, including the Hall of Annals and the Akh-menu, decorated with the unusual plant life that Thutmose observed on his foreign expeditions.

Death. Thutmose III died in Year 54 of his reign. He had appointed his son Amenhotep II co-regent in the previous year, ensuring a smooth transition to the new reign. He was buried in the tomb prepared for him in the Valley of the Kings. Thutmose III remained a model of the ideal king for many subsequent generations of Egyptians.

Sources:

Betsy M. Bryan, "The Eighteenth Dynasty Before the Amarna Period (c. 1550–1352 BC)," in *The Oxford History of Ancient Egypt*, edited by Ian Shaw (Oxford: Oxford University Press, 2001), pp. 218–271.

Peter A. Clayton, *Chronicle of the Pharaohs: The Reign-by-Reign Record of the Rulers and Dynasties of Ancient Egypt* (New York: Thames & Hudson, 1994).

Jadwiga Lipinska and G. B. Johnson, "Thutmose III at Deir el Bahri," *KMT: A Journal of Ancient Egypt*, 3 (1992): 13–25.

TUTANKHAMUN

FLOURISHED CIRCA 1332-1322 B.C.E.
KING, DYNASTY 18

Intact Tomb. Tutankhamun is famous today because English archaeologist Howard Carter discovered his intact tomb in 1922. His historical importance rested on the reversal of Akhenaten's policy that suppressed the traditional Egyptian religion as well as its administration and political structure.

Family. The identity of Tutankhamun's parents is uncertain. DNA studies have demonstrated that he was descended from members of the royal family of Dynasty 18 (circa 1539–1295/ 1292 B.C.E.). His parents could have been either Amenhotep III and Queen Tiye or Akhenaten and an unknown queen. Tutankhamun never claimed a king or queen as a parent and no previous royalty claimed him as a son. His birth name was Tutankhaten, which clearly indicates that he was born in Tell el Amarna during the time that the Aten was worshiped there as the sole god of Egypt. He married the third daughter of Akhenaten and Nefertiti, whose birth name was Ankhesenpaaten. She changed her name to Ankhesenamun when Tutankhamun changed his name to honor the restored god of Egypt, Amun. No children were born to this couple and the family of Dynasty 18 died out with them. Since Tutankhamun was a child of nine or ten when he came to the throne, two army generals, Ay and Horemheb, advised him on policy. First Ay, then Horemheb, followed Tutankhamun on the throne. There is no evidence that Tutankhamun was murdered, though much speculation surrounds his death at around age nineteen.

Politics. Tutankhamun followed Akhenaten's immediate successors who ruled perhaps four years on the throne. He returned the royal court to Memphis, the traditional residence for the royal family before the time of Amenhotep III. The *Restoration Stela*, a text found in the Karnak Temple of Amun, recounted the young king's policy to restore the cult of Amun throughout Egypt after a period of disorder. The stela used language familiar from many previous kings' inscriptions. The land was said to be in disorder; the gods' temples were in ruins. Even more specifically, the stela described a military defeat in Syria. Tutankhamun then claimed that he had restored order and rebuilt the temples. The gods now aided the army. In spite of the fact that the stela used many well-known formulae to describe the situation, the language probably matched the facts better than it ever had previously. The treasurer Maya depicted scenes of a trip he made to each of the temples to oversee their restoration. Horemheb also used similar language when he came to the throne. Scholars believe that Horemheb referred to policies he initiated along with Ay while acting as regent for Tutankhamun.

Death and Burial. Tutankhamun's death came while the army was fighting the newly active Hittites at Amqa near Qadesh. Queen Ankhesenamun sent a letter to the Hittite king Shupululiuma asking for a Hittite prince to assume the Egyptian throne. After several letters were exchanged, the suspicious Shupululiuma sent his son Zananza. Some scholars have blamed Horemheb for this prince's murder while on his way to Egypt. Ay and then Horemheb followed Tutankhamun on the throne.

Vast Riches. Tutankhamun's opulent burial revealed the riches Egypt buried with its dead kings. Unfortunately, few of the thousands of objects buried in the tomb have been studied in much detail.

Sources:

Howard Carter, *The Tomb of Tutankhamen* (London: Sphere, 1972).

Peter A. Clayton, *Chronicle of the Pharaohs: The Reign-by-Reign Record of the Rulers and Dynasties of Ancient Egypt* (New York: Thames & Hudson, 1994).

Christine El Mahdy, *Tutankhamen: The Life and Death of a Boy-King* (New York: St. Martin's Press, 1999).

Nicholas Reeves, *The Complete Tutankhamun: The King, the Tomb, and the Royal Treasure* (London & New York: Thames & Hudson, 1990).

DOCUMENTARY SOURCES

Anonymous, *Annals of Thutmose III* (circa 1458–1437 B.C.E.)—This year-by-year account of Thutmose's wars began in Year 21 and included Year 42. It also detailed the goods he collected from foreign countries. The author extracted information from a daily journal of the king's activities. The inscription was carved on the walls of the Temple of Amun at Karnak. Its original purpose was to inform the god Amun of the king's activities. The inscription included a detailed description of the Battle of Megiddo in circa 1468 B.C.E. The text supplies a picture of war and the role of the king in battle.

Anonymous, *The Duties of the Vizier* (circa 1759–1630 B.C.E. or circa 1539–1479 B.C.E.)—The best-preserved copy of *The Duties of the Vizier* belonged to Thutmose III's vizier, Rekhmire. Scholars disagree on whether this text was composed in Dynasty 13 or at the beginning of Dynasty 18. The primary responsibilities of the vizier are enumerated in this text. They include personnel management, internal security, and rendering justice. A clear picture of late Middle Kingdom and/or early New Kingdom administrative priorities is presented in the text.

Anonymous, *Papyrus Brooklyn 35.1446* (circa 1818–1772 B.C.E.)—The papyrus originated in the Great Enclosure, a forced labor camp or prison, in the reign of Amenemhet III. It contains case-by-case descriptions of individuals who violated the laws concerning forced labor. It gives the name of the criminal, place of birth, gender, a note on the crime committed, current location of the criminal, and status of the case. Careful study of the text provides information on crime and punishment.

Anonymous, *Papyrus Harris I* (circa 1156 B.C.E.)—Lists Ramesses III's contributions to the temples of Heliopolis, Memphis, and Thebes. These contributions included land, herds, and vessels. Either Ramesses III or Ramesses IV prepared it to illustrate the king's generosity to the temples at a time when political conflict between the king and the temple arose again. It illustrates the final attempt by a New Kingdom (circa 1539–1075 B.C.E.) ruler to accommodate the priesthood.

Anonymous, *Papyrus Westcar or Tales of Wonder* (circa 1938–1759 B.C.E.)—Known by the name of its first modern owner, this text survives in a copy made in the Hyksos Period (circa 1630–1523 B.C.E.). However, its language is purely Middle Kingdom (circa 1980–1630 B.C.E.). The text originally contained five stories, three of which are complete enough to understand and translate. The preserved stories described the courts of Dynasty 4 (circa 2625–2500 B.C.E.) kings and contrasted the good king Sneferu with his son and builder of the Great Pyramid, Khufu. The stories also speculate on the origins of Dynasty 5 (circa 2500–2350 B.C.E.).

Anonymous, *Qadesh Inscriptions of Ramesses II* (after circa 1274 B.C.E.)—These inscriptions include a connected account of Qadesh called the Poem, an extended caption to the relief sculptures of the battle called the Bulletin, and the relief sculpture itself that illustrates the first day of the engagement. These inscriptions constitute the fullest account of any ancient battle that the Egyptians fought. They also illustrate the difficulties inherent in interpreting the Egyptian view of history.

Anonymous, *The Story of Sinuhe* (after 1875 B.C.E.)—The text exists in two manuscripts written close to the time of composition and more than twenty copies of excerpts written in the New Kingdom and after. Sinuhe was the closest thing to a national epic poem for the ancient Egyptians. The story illustrates Egyptian political values as well as tells an exciting adventure story.

Neferty, *The Prophecies of Neferty* (circa 1938–1909 B.C.E.)—The prophecies attributed to Neferty claim to foretell the reign of Amenemhet I, founder of Dynasty 12 (circa 1938–1759 B.C.E.). The text is set in the Old Kingdom (circa 2675–2130 B.C.E.). The prophet described the chaotic events of the First Intermediate Period (circa 2130–1980 B.C.E.), and Egypt's salvation by the first king of Dynasty 12 for King Sneferu of Dynasty 4 (circa 2625–2500 B.C.E.). The language of the writing places its composition squarely at this same time. The oldest copy of the prophecy that survives was written in Amenhotep II's reign, circa 1426–1400 B.C.E. Two additional copies from mid Dynasty 18 exist along with nineteen Ramesside copies from Deir el Medina. The text describes the Egyptian view of the king's legitimate rule. The king who maintains the cosmic order (*maat*) is the proper king.

Ptahhotep, *Teaching of Ptahhotep* (circa 1938 B.C.E.)—The thirty-seven maxims included in Ptahhotep's teaching illustrate the ideal behavior of a government official. Maxims and illustrations touch on the virtues expected of those who serve the king, including honesty, judiciousness, respect for superiors, and moderation. The text claims its author was the vizier serving the Dynasty 5 King Djedkare Isesi (circa 2415–2371 B.C.E.). The language, however, belongs to the beginning of Dynasty 12 (circa 1938–1759 B.C.E.). Two Dynasty 12 manuscripts exist along with New Kingdom (circa 1539–1075 B.C.E.) copies, illustrating the continuity of Egyptian ideals for their bureaucrats.

Sehetepibre, *Stele of Sehetepibre* (circa 1818 B.C.E.)—Written between the reigns of Senwosret III and Amenemhet III. This long inscription was recorded on a stela found in Abydos. The author combines an autobiography with wisdom literature. The wisdom portion defines the proper attitude toward the king, pointing out the importance of praising him. The text is especially significant for understanding the Middle Kingdom (circa 1980–1630 B.C.E.) view of the king.

Sety I, *Nauri Decree, year of Sety I* (circa 1290 B.C.E.)—The decree is a copy of the charter Sety I dedicated to his temple at Abydos. Among the provisions for the temple, Sety gave detailed accounts of the crimes that might be committed against the temple and its staff. The appropriate punishment for each crime is also described. The crimes are various ways the temple goods could be misappropriated or the staff could be forced to do other work. Mutilation is the commonest form of punishment.

Weni, *Autobiography of Weni* (circa 2350–2288 B.C.E.)—This inscription was recorded on a limestone stele erected at Abydos. As a royal official he described his roles as investigator of a crime committed by a queen and as a general raising an army. The inscription reveals the way Egyptians discussed such matters. It gives information on secrecy in royal dealings and the details of raising an army.

Part of the *Abbot Papyrus* (circa 1110 B.C.E.) that records the official inspection of royal tombs undertaken in the sixteenth year of Ramesses IX's reign (British Museum, London)

LEISURE, RECREATION, AND DAILY LIFE

by EDWARD BLEIBERG

CONTENTS

Sidebars and tables are listed in italics.

2585-2560*
B.C.E.

- The tomb of Hetepheres I, the wife of Sneferu and mother of Khufu (or Cheops), is filled with elaborate wood and gold furniture.

- Imported cedar wood is used in making furniture, which is put together with mortise and tenon joints, a technique used since the Predynastic Period (circa 3000 B.C.E.)

2008-1957*
B.C.E.

- Nebhepetre Mentuhotep II's wife has a hairdressing scene painted on her sarcophagus showing professionals attaching hairpieces with pins.

1980-1630*
B.C.E.

- The Middle Kingdom mummy of Amunet, Priestess of Hathor, shows evidence of tattoos.

- Art within the tombs at Beni Hasan illustrates the process of perfume making.

- Utilitarian furniture, such as stools with tapered or animal legs, animal-legged chairs, and tables imitating architectural elements, are made. The first folding stools are made.

- Carpenters build furniture in assembly-line style, with each man performing one task.

- Middle Kingdom men wear long, straight wigs—but push the hair behind the ear. Though the mustache disappears, some men wear full beards.

- Women begin to wear the Hathoric wig, which is similar to the tripartite wig, but the hair is curled over the chest around ball-like ornaments.

1919-1875*
B.C.E.

- Senwosret I's officials include the Overseer of Swineherds, suggesting that the Egyptians ate pork.

1630-1523*
B.C.E.

- Medical papyri, recopied during the Hyksos Period, give recipes for soap and wrinkle removers.

1539-1075*
B.C.E.

- Female musicians wear tattoos of the demigod Bes on their thighs.

- New Kingdom furniture imitates Middle Kingdom styles but adds round-legged stools to the variety of types.

- Craftsmen make complete pieces of furniture alone rather than working assembly-line style.

1479-1425*
B.C.E.

- Thutmose III has representations of exotic plants from Syria-Palestine carved in the garden at the Temple of Amun at Karnak.

*DENOTES CIRCA DATE

1426–1400*
B.C.E.

- Amenhotep II emphasizes his athletic skills using political propaganda.

- The earliest known illustrations of the effects of drunkenness are painted in tombs of the scribes Djeserkareseneb and Neferhotep.

- Men begin to wear layered wigs.

1390–1353*
B.C.E.

- Amenhotep III offers pork to the gods.

1353–1336*
B.C.E.

- Modern excavations of houses at Amenhotep IV's (Akhenaten's) capital city at Amarna reveal pig bones with butcher marks.

- *Shaduf,* a pot attached to a swinging pole, simplifies irrigating gardens.

- Unisex hairstyles, including the Nubian wig and round wig, become popular.

- The *khat* and *afnet,* two kinds of cloth head coverings, are popular items of clothing.

1332–1322*
B.C.E.

- Furniture from the tomb of Tutankhamun displays a variety of decorative techniques, including marquetry veneer and scenes made from inlays of glass, silver, and stone.

1292–1075*
B.C.E.

- Wine prices are five times as much as beer.

- Longer hairstyles become popular for men and women. Nubian wigs and round wigs are abandoned.

1290–1279*
B.C.E.

- Sety I establishes swineherds at his temple in Abydos.

760–656*
B.C.E.

- Dynasty 25 men and women revive the Nubian wig.

684 B.C.E.

- Taharqa orders daily runs for the army and organizes a round-trip race from Memphis to the Faiyum, a distance of sixty-two miles.

*Denotes Circa Date

OVERVIEW

Housing. Egyptian houses were built of mud brick in ancient times, as are many modern village houses. The exterior was often whitewashed, which reflected the bright sun and made the building more attractive. Interior surfaces had less decoration than the exterior. The plan of houses changed from the Old Kingdom (circa 2675–2130 B.C.E.) to the later periods in Egyptian history, probably as a result of changes in the supports used for roofs. Builders during the Old Kingdom and Middle Kingdom (circa 1980–1630 B.C.E.) depended on barrel vaults to support the roofs, which required thick walls and narrow rooms. During the New Kingdom (circa 1539–1075 B.C.E.) columns were used, which allowed for wider rooms with thinner walls, and the walls no longer supported the full weight of the roof. Windows were generally placed high in the walls. Glass was not used to cover windows, but some elite houses had wooden grates.

Open Space. In general, there was little natural light inside a house—thus, many activities took place in the courtyard. The roof was also an important living space in many Egyptian houses. Fires for cooking were sometimes maintained on the roof. People often slept on the roof, where it was cooler than in the small, poorly ventilated rooms of the house. A staircase, either inside the house or on an outside wall, led to the roof.

Clothing. Painting, relief sculpture, and statues present a picture of clothing in ancient Egypt that conflicts with examples of clothing found in tombs. Artistic representations, however, were never intended to show clothing as it actually existed. In sculpture and paintings, clothing conveyed information about status. Because many representations of women were intended to convey their potential for fertility, clothing was often portrayed closer fitting than it was worn in reality. In addition, clothing in art was often inappropriate for the task portrayed. A man and woman, for example, are shown plowing in their best clothing in the tomb of Sennedjem. For men, clothing also indicated status. More-elaborate clothing indicated higher status. Scribes, for instance, were shown wearing complicated outfits. Boatmen, in contrast, wore only a belt or loincloth. Kings had special ceremonial clothes, while other members of the royal family dressed in clothing similar to upper-class individuals.

Family Clothing. Although children often wore smaller versions of adult clothing, as depicted in some tombs, nude children were a convention of art. Men wore wraparound skirts that modern scholars call kilts, which were wrapped in various ways in different periods. Men's clothing became more elaborate in the New Kingdom when pleated tunics were worn with the kilt. The most common women's clothing was the "sheath dress" for all periods and all classes. Goddesses were often portrayed wearing bright colors in paintings. Perhaps clothes were painted, embroidered, or woven with decorations. Though there were changes in women's styles during the three thousand years of Egyptian history, most changes were achieved through different ways of wrapping a large piece of cloth around the body.

Food. The fertility of Egypt allowed people to have a balanced and healthy diet. Bread and beer were basic foods. Wealthy Egyptians had access to meat more often than commoners. The most popular meats were from sheep and goats. Unexpectedly, archaeology has demonstrated that people also ate pigs, antelopes, mice, and hedgehogs. Cereal crops were the most important food for the majority of people. Wheat and barley were made into bread and beer. It is not clear when Egyptian bakers began to use yeast in bread. New Kingdom bread might have included yeast, but it was surely used by the first millennium B.C.E. Bread also was prepared in many shapes, including round, square, and triangular loaves. The major cooking methods included boiling, grilling, frying, and roasting; few recipes remain from ancient Egypt.

Drink. Wealthy people also drank wine made from grapes. Vineyards were located in the delta and in the oases. Pottery wine containers, called amphora, were inscribed with the vintage year, name of the vineyard, and the quality of the wine—much like modern wine labels. Wine was also manufactured from dates, figs, and perhaps pomegranates. Egyptian beer was like gruel, very thick and high in calories. It had a low alcohol content and was drunk by people of all ages and social levels.

Vegetables. Egyptian vegetables and herbs included onions, garlic, leeks, and lettuce. In the New Kingdom, celery, and perhaps cucumbers, were introduced as foods. The Egyptians also ate papyrus and tiger nuts (cyperus grass), which were used to make a dessert flavored with honey. They also consumed lentils, peas, fava beans, and chickpeas. These foods are still popular in Egypt. They are easy to grow and have high nutritional value.

Fruits and Nuts. Dates were the most common fruit that Egyptians ate. Figs and grapes were also common. In the New Kingdom some plants were introduced from the Near East, including pomegranates, apricots, and apples; melons may have been introduced as well. The Greeks brought pears, quince, plums, peaches, walnuts, and pine nuts to Egypt. Previously, the only nuts eaten in Egypt were almonds, which were probably imported and limited to wealthy people.

Sweets and Spices. Honey was the main sweetener used by wealthy people. The use of the carob, a nut from a Mediterranean evergreen tree, was probably more widespread. In fact, the hieroglyph for the word meaning "sweet" was the carob pod. Egyptians also had access to many native-grown spices, including dill, fenugreek, parsley, thyme, coriander, white and black cumin, fennel, marjoram, and mint. Cinnamon and peppercorns were imported from southeast Asia as early as the New Kingdom.

Sports and Recreation. The Egyptians enjoyed athletic events and board games as part of recreation. In athletics, running is the earliest documented sport. King Djoser (circa 2675–2625 B.C.E.) ran a ritual race during the Sed festival on a specially designed course in front of his Step Pyramid. The title "swift runner" was an honor accorded to some soldiers who followed the king while he rode in his chariot. In the reign of Taharqa (circa 690–664 B.C.E.) a stela was carved describing a footrace from Memphis to the Faiyum (an area of swampland west of the Nile River) that was run by a large number of soldiers. Archery was also an important sport. Stelae of Dynasty 18 (circa 1539–1295/1292 B.C.E.) describe both Thutmose III and Amenhotep II as expert archers. Combat sports were popular, though they might have had ritual significance. Wrestling was represented in art as early as Dynasty 1 (circa 3000–2800 B.C.E.) and is found in Old, Middle, and New Kingdom relief sculptures. Mock combat with sticks is widely represented in art, as are fights between men, armed with sticks, standing on small papyrus boats. A Dynasty 11 (circa 2081–1938 B.C.E.) autobiography also mentions swimming.

Games. Children's games included "Hitting the Ball," which is represented in art from Dynasty 18 to Dynasty 30 (381–343 B.C.E.). Other children's games included jumping contests, races on piggyback, tugs of war, whirling (to get dizzy), and hoops and sticks. All of these games are represented in relief sculptures of daily life dating as early as the Old Kingdom. Archaeological evidence demonstrates that a game similar to jacks was played as early as the Middle Kingdom. Jacks, shaped from broken pieces of pottery, are still used by children in modern Egyptian villages. Adults also played board games, but they seem to have had ritual significance. They included *senet* (passing), *men* (endurance), *mehen* (snake), and Twenty Squares, a game imported from the Near East. This game was also played in India, where it was the ancestor of Parcheesi.

TOPICS IN LEISURE, RECREATION, AND DAILY LIFE

BANQUETS

Sources for Banquets. Banquets were part of ritual and of daily life. Tomb paintings of the New Kingdom (circa 1539–1075 B.C.E.) are the major source for information about banquets in ancient Egypt. There is little information from texts except for advice from Egyptian wisdom literature on how a guest or a host should behave at a banquet. The Egyptian word for banquet is the same as the one used for "festival" or "holiday." This word choice suggests that banquets were a component of a larger festival. British archaeologist Walter B. Emery discovered the archaeological remains of a banquet in a tomb dating to Dynasty 2 (circa 2800–2675 B.C.E.).

Guests. Family members attended these banquets, as is illustrated in tombs from the Old Kingdom (circa 2675–2130 B.C.E.) to the New Kingdom. In the New Kingdom, family friends were also included at banquets. In some cases deceased relatives were depicted at the banquet as if they

Painted tomb relief of a banquet scene from West Thebes, Dynasty 18, circa 1539–1295/1292 B.C.E. (British Museum, London)

were alive. In the tomb of Ramose, a vizier who served during the reigns of Amenhotep III (circa 1390–1353 B.C.E.) and Amenhotep IV (Akhenaten, circa 1353–1336 B.C.E.), deceased ancestors wear "old-fashioned" clothing contemporary with their lifetimes. These peculiar guests raise the question of whether such events were held in life or whether the art in tomb scenes depicts banquets in the next world. The answer is probably that Egyptians thought banquets in the next world would imitate those held in this world. There is some evidence that banquets were held at birth, death, and marriage. There were also religious banquets held during the Festival of the Valley, when the living met to eat in the family tomb.

Royal Banquets. Royal banquets were held during the Sed festival, a celebration of a king's long rule. The king ate his meal on a balcony overlooking the guests in a courtyard below. Other royal festivals likely included banquets, since distribution of food to the population was an integral part of all Egyptian holidays.

Daytime Banquets. The typical banquet began in the afternoon. Egyptologists believe that depictions of the blue lotus bloom in banquet scenes indicate these were feasts were held in the daytime. The blue lotus opens during the day and closes at night. In Theban tombs 46, 96, 100, and 155 the blue lotus blooms worn by women are all open. Corroborating evidence comes from the biblical book of Genesis. In Genesis 43:16 Joseph invited his brothers for a feast at midday. Egyptian holidays are also known to have started during the day.

Seating. The host greeted his guests as they arrived at the door. In tomb scenes the host is the deceased. The guests were conducted to a place at the table with men and women seated separately. The extent of the separation is not clear from the tomb scenes. Men and women are always in different registers. It is not clear whether they ate in different rooms or on different sides of one room. Seating, however, was hierarchical—the most important guests sat on chairs nearest the host. Stools were available for the next-lower rank of guests. Least important guests sat on mats on the floor. In general, male servants served men, and female servants served women.

Preparations Before Eating. After guests reached the table, servants washed guests' hands in a basin. They gave the guests cones of fat containing either perfume or an insect repellant. These were worn on the head and melted during the course of the meal. Tomb scenes and actual wigs preserved in tombs display the remains of these cones. The servants also gave guests lotus flowers to sniff during the meal. Because lotus flowers could serve as a mild intoxicant, offering them was similar to offering guests a cocktail at the beginning of a meal. Guests also received flower wreaths to wear. When these arrangements were made the food was brought. Sometimes tomb scenes depict food piled on the table. Other scenes show servants handing food to the guests.

Menu. The food served at banquets was more elaborate than that prepared for ordinary meals. It was also the occasion for eating meat, such as ox. Fowl—such as ducks, geese, and pigeons—were also often on the menu. Sometimes stews were served, as well as bread, vegetables, fruit, and cakes.

Beverages. Wine, beer, and pomegranate wine were served at banquets. The tombs of the scribes Neferhotep and Djerkaraseneb (circa 1426–1400 B.C.E.) illustrate what happened when a guest drank too much. Guests are depicted in their tomb scenes as vomiting and passing out.

Entertainment. Entertainment was provided by professional musicians and dancers. Musicians played harps, lutes, drums, tambourines, and clappers. A singer was often included. Professional dancers also entertained the guests.

Sources:
Edda Bresciani, *Food and Drink: Life Resources in Ancient Egypt,* translated by Hayley Adkins (Lucca: M. Pacini Fazzi, 1997).

William J. Darby, Paul Ghalioungui, and Louis Grivetti, *Food: The Gift of Osiris,* two volumes (London & New York: Academic Press, 1977).

Norman de Garis Davies, *The Tomb of Rekhmire at Thebes* (New York: Metropolitan Museum of Art Press, 1973).

Walter B. Emery, *A Funerary Repast in an Egyptian Tomb of the Archaic Period* (Leiden: Nederlands Instituut voor het Nabije Oosten, 1962).

BEER AND WINE

Sources. Beer was a staple for all Egyptians, while wine was the drink of choice for the elite. Scholars have learned about the use of beer and wine from archaeological evidence and tomb art. There are both paintings and small wooden models that depict beer making. Tomb paintings also illustrate winemaking.

Origins of Beer. The Egyptians made beer in the Predynastic Period (circa 3100–3000 B.C.E.) and perhaps even earlier. Evidence comes from Hierakonpolis, where archaeologists have discovered large ceramic vats that contained a residue they believe was created during brewing. The residue contained wheat chaff fixed in a clear substance. Ash and charcoal surrounded the vat, and the vat's sides were reddened. Since beer processing includes heating grain until it ferments, this evidence suggested that the vat was part of a beer-making site.

Brewing. Beer results from the fermentation of grain, which contains starch. A microorganism, such as yeast, acts on the starch, changing it first to sugars and then to alcohol. This process is speeded by heating the ingredients. Brewing is the management of this process. Egyptologists have offered two hypotheses for the way Egyptians made beer. The older consensus view is that Egyptian beer started with bread that was leavened but not baked sufficiently, so that the yeast was killed. The

Tomb painting from West Thebes of servants treading on grapes, circa 1539–1295/1292 B.C.E.

Model from the tomb of Meketra at Deir el Bahri showing preparation of bread and beer from barley and emmer wheat, circa 1990 B.C.E. (Metropolitan Museum of Art, New York)

bread was then crumbled over a sieve, washed with water, and then fermented in a vat. Many scholars believe that either dates or malt (barley) was added to the vat at some time in the process.

New Theory. British archaeobotanist Delwen Samuel has studied ancient Egyptian beer residue through an electron microscope, which has allowed him to identify the ingredients and changes in the structure of the ingredients. These changes suggest the procedure that was followed. The Egyptians seem to have combined sprouted grain with grain cooked in water. The sprouted grain contained enzymes that attacked the starch dispersed in the water of the cooked batch. The enzymes created sugar in the water. Then the mixture was sieved, and yeast and perhaps lactic acid was added to the liquid. These two ingredients converted the sugars to alcohol. There is no evidence of dates or other additives. This method also resembles beer making in other parts of Africa.

Beer Consistency. Egyptian beer was not clear like modern commercial beer. It was cloudy and contained remains of the grain that was its major ingredient. Samuel points out that it was rich in complex carbohydrates, fatty acids, amino acids, minerals, and vitamins. It had a high caloric value and a relatively low alcohol content. It was a major source of calories in an Egyptian's daily diet.

Wine Originally Imported. Syrian jars that archaeologists have found in Predynastic sites suggest the origin of wine brought to Egypt. Grape wine was probably an import from Syria, dating to the Predynastic Period. The Egyptians must have imported grape vines soon after the introduction of Syrian wine and adopted their techniques of making it.

Winemaking. Tomb paintings from the Old Kingdom (circa 2675–2130 B.C.E.) through the New Kingdom (circa 1539–1075 B.C.E.) depicted winemaking in Egypt. Grapes were collected in large vats and crushed with bare feet. Vineyard workers then transferred the juice to a new container and let it ferment for a few days. Then workers strained the juice and transferred the slightly fermented liquid to large jars. They covered the opening of the jar with stoppers made of woven reeds covered with mud. A small hole in the stopper allowed carbon dioxide to escape. Once fermentation was complete, the winemakers sealed the jars, which were usually long and narrow at the bottom. Two handles were attached to the shoulder of each jar, and the container was placed in a stand. The narrow bottom allowed residue to collect. By tipping the jars in the stands, servants could more easily pour wine into cups. Inscriptions in ink identified the vineyard, year, and quality of the wine—ranked from good to best.

Red or White? Red wine includes the grape skin, while white wine does not. Egyptologist Mu-Chou Poo believes that the grape skin remained in the mixture long enough to color the wine red. Some references in texts, for example, refer to wine as being red. The Egyptians named wine according to the vineyard where it was made, as is common

in modern Europe. Popular wines were "Wine of the Eastern Delta," "Wine of Pelusium," and "Wine of Lower Egypt." As these names show, the delta, or northern Egypt, was home to most vineyards.

Prices and Consumers. In the Ramesside Period (circa 1292–1075 B.C.E.) wine cost five times more than beer. Thus, wine was the upper-class drink, while all Egyptians included beer as part of their diet. Priests also offered wine to the gods and to deceased wealthy Egyptians. Wine was also associated with the goddess Hathor, who was celebrated in a "Festival of Drunkenness."

Sources:

Mu-Chou Poo, "Wine," in *Oxford Encyclopedia of Ancient Egypt*, volume 3, edited by Donald B. Redford (Oxford & New York: Oxford University Press, 2001), pp. 502–503.

Poo, *Wine and Wine Offerings in the Religion of Ancient Egypt* (London & New York: Kegan Paul International, 1995).

Delwen Samuel, "Beer," in *Oxford Encyclopedia of Ancient Egypt*, volume 1, edited by Donald B. Redford (Oxford & New York: Oxford University Press, 2001), pp. 171–172.

Samuel, "Investigation of Ancient Egyptian Baking and Brewing Methods by Correlative Microscopy," *Science*, 273 (1996): 488–490.

CLOTHING AND JEWELRY: THE TOMBS OF KHA AND HATNOFRE

An Architect's Tomb. The tomb of Kha and Merit, discovered by the Italian Egyptologist Ernesto Schiaparelli in 1906, is one of the three intact burial chambers found in Deir el Medina. Kha was the chief architect of Amenhotep III (circa 1390–1353 B.C.E.); his official title was "Chief of the Works in the Place of Truth," which indicates that he was responsible for overseeing the construction of Amenhotep III's tomb in the Valley of the Kings. Merit was probably his second wife. All of Kha's and Merit's belongings removed from their tomb are currently in the Egyptian Museum in Turin, Italy.

Kha's Clothing. Kha was buried with fifty triangular loincloths, twenty-six knee-length kilts, seventeen sleeveless tunics, and four shawls. Seven of the loincloths and kilts were wrapped together. Surprisingly, some of the clothing in the tomb was dirty, although most was laundered. Almost all of the items showed characteristics of wear—they were torn, frayed, and mended, and all had laundry marks added in black ink.

Winter Clothing. Though sixteen of the seventeen linen tunics were all of the same weight, one of the tunics was heavier. Linen was produced from flax, which was beaten and spun and then woven on looms. The tunic was ornamented with woven bands at the hems on the side and neckline; it was wrapped in two cloaks, and kept in a linen sack. Worn with a shawl, this tunic would have kept Kha warm on a winter day.

Dressing Gown. Merit's most important item of clothing found in the tomb was a dressing gown. It was made from a wide, fringed linen sheet, which was spotted with the oils from cosmetic cones that contained either perfume or insect repellant and were worn at parties.

Tomb painting from Deir el Medina, West Thebes, of a foreman and his wife, circa 1292–1190 B.C.E. The man is dressed in a pleated kilt while his wife wears a pleated dress.

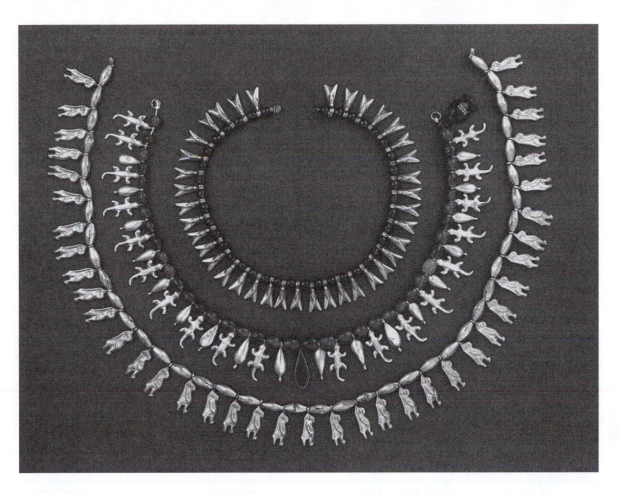

Necklaces with solid-cast flies and beads (inner), date-shaped pendants alternating with lizards (middle), and hollow beads and amulets (outer), circa 1539–1295/1292 B.C.E. (British Museum, London)

Hatnofre's Clothing. The tomb of Hatnofre, mother of Hatshepsut's vizier, Senenmut, was excavated in 1936 by archaeologists from the Metropolitan Museum of Art in New York. Her clothing is presently in that museum. Hatnofre was buried wearing eighteen shawls and sheets of fine linen. The different shapes of dresses, which are represented in tomb paintings, would have been created by wrapping and knotting these sheets in various manners. She was also wrapped in two shirts that were fashioned into a loincloth.

Sources:
Rosalie David, *Handbook to Life in Ancient Egypt* (New York: Facts on File, 1998), pp. 290–292.

Rosalind M. H. Janssen, "Costume in New Kingdom Egypt," in *Civilizations of the Ancient Near East*, volume 1, edited by Jack M. Saasson (New York: Scribners, 1995), pp. 383–394.

COSMETICS AND PERFUMES

Sources of Knowledge. Cosmetics and perfumes were included with the burials of both men and women in ancient Egypt. Additional knowledge of the use of cosmetics can be deduced from funerary paintings and relief sculpture.

Hygiene. Cleanliness was the most important component of ritual purity for Egyptians and was also considered significant in daily life. Upper-class homes were equipped with areas containing an early variant on the shower stall—a slab of stone with a drain provided a platform where people knelt as a servant poured water from a bucket.

Soap. The ancient Egyptian equivalent of soap was a body scrub made from salt, natron, and honey. In the Edwin Smith Surgical Papyrus (circa 1630–1539 B.C.E.), the author suggests that calcite granules also were added to the body scrub. A skin cleanser found in a tomb of a wife of Thutmose III (circa 1479–1425 B.C.E.) was made from vegetable oil and lime. Natron, the drying agent used to preserve mummies, contained calcium carbonate and calcium bicarbonate. These two compounds are the major ingredients in some modern bath salts. Thus, natron was likely also used by the Egyptians for cleansing.

Eye Makeup. Both men and women wore kohl, a makeup applied in an outline around the eyes. Egyptians believed that the preparation kept the eyes healthy as well as beautifying them. It is likely that kohl reduced the glare from the sun. Kohl could be made from galena, malachite, manganese oxide, brown ocher, iron oxide, copper oxide, or antimony. Any of these elements were mixed with fat. Kohl was stored in containers of various shapes.

Lip Color. Women colored their lips with a mixture of red ocher in a base of animal fat. Some scholars believe henna, a reddish-brown plant dye, was also used to color lips, cheeks, and fingernails. The Turin Erotic Papyrus (circa

Cosmetic set of Sit-hathor-yunet, one of the daughters of Senwosret II, from her tomb at el-Lahun in the Faiyum, circa 1844–1837 B.C.E. (Metropolitan Museum of Art, New York)

1190–1075 B.C.E.), for example, depicts a woman applying lipstick.

Wrinkle Remover. Several recipes in the Ebers Medical Papyrus (circa 1630–539 B.C.E.) are suggested for removing wrinkles. These recipes include fenugreek, an aromatic Asian herb that was boiled in oil, or frankincense combined with balsam.

Tattoos. Known examples of tattoos from ancient Egypt are limited to women. The Middle Kingdom (circa 1980–1630 B.C.E.) mummy of Amunet, a priestess of Hathor, shows a pattern of dots on the torso. Other figurines of women from this period also show patterns of dots that might represent tattoos on the hips and the pubic area. New Kingdom (circa 1539–1075 B.C.E.) female musicians sometimes had tattoos of the demigod Bes on their thighs. Cultic use of the tattoo is still found among modern Egyptian Christian women.

Pleasing Smells. Scents in Egypt were made from oils and fats impregnated with the scent of plants. True perfume (made with alcohol) was unknown in Egypt. The most common scent was made from the lotus flower and the henna plant. Other scented substances used for Egyptian scents were cedar wood, cinnamon, thyme, and coriander. Imported resins—such as myrrh, frankincense, laudanum, and galbanum—might also have been used to create scents.

Perfume Makers. Perfume makers, as depicted in tombs at Beni Hasan dating to the Middle Kingdom, gathered flowers and put them in large bags. Sticks attached to the mouths of the bags were twisted to squeeze the essence from the flowers. This liquid would then be combined with fats or oils to make scent.

Sources:
Joann Fletcher, *Oils and Perfumes in Ancient Egypt* (London: British Museum Press, 1998).

Lyn Green, "Toiletries and Cosmetics," in *The Oxford Encyclopedia of Ancient Egypt,* volume 3, edited by Donald B. Redford (Oxford & New York: Oxford University Press, 2001), pp. 412–417.

Lise Manniche, *Sacred Luxuries: Fragrance, Aromatherapy, and Cosmetics in Ancient Egypt* (Ithaca, N.Y.: Cornell University Press, 1999).

Edwin T. Morris, *The Scents of Time: Perfume from Ancient Egypt to the 21st Century* (Boston: Metropolitan Museum of Art / Bulfinch Press / Little, Brown, 1999).

FOOTWEAR

Bare Feet. The average ancient Egyptian did not wear shoes most of the time. Among workmen, quarrymen received sandals as part of their pay. Agricultural workers, even in modern times, went barefoot. Otherwise, footwear was restricted to the elite.

Materials and Form. Sandals were made from grass, reeds, rawhide, and leather. The typical sandal had a strap between the big and second toes, which attached to a crosspiece that went over the inner side of the ankle and attached to the sole on both sides of the ankle. The sole of the sandal was cut to the shape of the foot. Leather sandals found in the tomb of Tutankhamun (circa 1332–1322 B.C.E.) were decorated with gold. On the bottom of these soles were figures of the enemies of Egypt, so that the king could trample them each time he took a step. Two types of sandals were "worn" by mummies and would have been useless in life: ones made of cloth, impregnated with plaster, called *cartonnage,* and others made from thin sheets of gold.

Footwear Etiquette. Egyptians removed their sandals in the presence of their superiors. The most memorable example of this custom is found in the biblical book of Exodus, where Moses removed his sandals when he realized God was in the Burning Bush.

Sources:

Rosalie David, *Handbook to Life in Ancient Egypt* (New York: Facts on File, 1998), pp. 294–295.

Lyn Green, "Clothing and Personal Adornment," in *Oxford Encyclopedia of Ancient Egypt*, volume 1, edited by Donald B. Redford (Oxford & New York: Oxford University Press, 2001), p. 278.

Miriam Stead, *Egyptian Life* (Cambridge, Mass.: Harvard University Press, 1986).

FURNITURE

Tomb and Household Furniture. Egyptian craftsmen were famous for their chairs, stools, beds, and storage boxes, and they improved their techniques in the course of a long history. Almost all of the furniture preserved from ancient Egypt comes from tombs. Some furniture was specifically made for tombs and thus is less functional. Other furniture found in tombs shows signs of wear, demonstrating that it was originally used in households. This household furniture is generally of a higher quality and sturdier than furniture manufactured only for burial.

Early Dynastic Period. British archaeologist W. M. F. Petrie (1853–1942) discovered furniture dating to Dynasties 1 (circa 3000–2800 B.C.E.) and 2 (circa 2800–2675 B.C.E.) at Abydos, Saqqara, and Tarkhan. The legs of both beds and chairs were carved to resemble a bull's legs. Imitation of animal forms in furniture elements continued throughout Egyptian history. The earliest chairs and bed frames were made of wood, with some elite examples in hippopotamus ivory. The chair seats were made of rushes that were woven and plaited across the frame.

Old Kingdom Furniture. In the Dynasty 3 (circa 2675–2625 B.C.E.) tomb of Hesyre, a government official who served under Djoser, family furniture was illustrated. Some beds had bull-shaped legs, while others were made of bent wood. Stools and chairs had both bull-shaped and straight legs. Hesyre also owned boxes decorated with hieroglyphs. This type of decoration for wooden boxes and chests continued throughout Egyptian history. Furniture found in the tomb of Queen Hetepheres I, mother of Khufu, illustrates the high quality of Dynasty 4 (circa 2625–2500 B.C.E.) craftsmanship, at least among products made for the royalty. Hetepheres' bed was surrounded by a canopy frame, armchairs, and storage boxes that were made from wood covered with a thin sheet of gold. The canopy frame supported a curtain designed to keep out insects and the cold. The curtain was stored in a gilded box, inlaid with faience. The canopy frame had joints sheathed with copper coverings, which would have protected them during repeated assembly and dismantling. Armchairs had lion-shaped legs and solid panels on the back and seat. These panels were covered with goose-feather cushions. Decorative panels, placed between the armrests and seat frame, were carved with the hieroglyphic sign for Lower Egypt, which is three papyrus flowers entwined.

Middle Kingdom Furniture. By the Middle Kingdom (circa 1980–1630 B.C.E.) utilitarian furniture included simple stools with tapered legs, which can be found at the site of Beni Hasan. Stools were in widespread use, and many have animal-leg designs based on bulls, gazelles, and lions. There were also folding stools with two rectangular interlocking frames fastened by a bronze rivet. A stool made from latticework was popular, as was a simple three-legged stool used in the workshop. Tables were manufactured

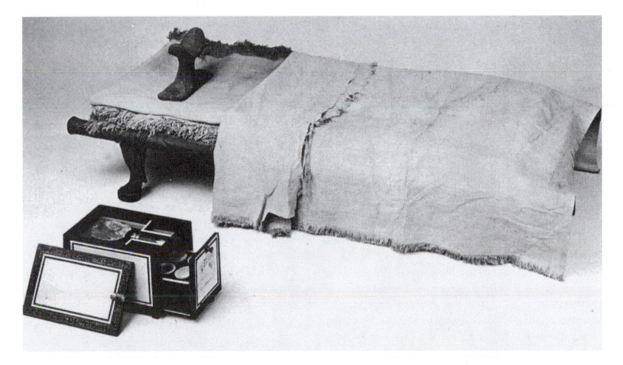

A royal butler's wooden bed (with leather slings for support and a mattress of folded linen sheets) and headrest, next to a cedar chest inlaid with ebony and ivory, circa 1800 B.C.E. (Metropolitan Museum of Art, New York)

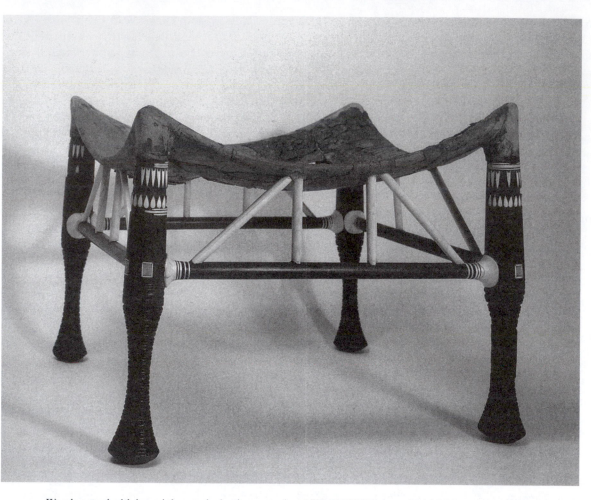

Wooden stool with ivory inlays and a leather seat, circa 1539–1295/1292 B.C.E. (British Museum, London)

with a cavetto cornice, a concave element at the top, and torus molding, a rounded side. These tables thus imitate architectural elements, which are also found on many boxes and are found on temple pylons.

New Kingdom Innovations. Most of the New Kingdom (circa 1539–1075 B.C.E.) designs follow Middle Kingdom prototypes. Yet, the majority of preserved furniture comes from the latter period. The new type made in the New Kingdom is a round-legged stool. Round legs were hand-carved with a spike at the top, with a pivot at the bottom that might have been turned on a lathe, though there is no other evidence for the turning lathe in Egypt before the arrival of Alexander the Great (332 B.C.E.).

Types of Wood. The earliest Egyptian furniture was made from acacia, sycamore fig, and tamarisk wood. All of these woods are indigenous to the Nile valley and continued to be used in all periods, but the better furniture was made from imported woods. The Egyptians began to import cedar from Lebanon in Dynasty 4. Ebony came from parts of Africa south of Egypt by Dynasty 6 (circa 2350–2170 B.C.E.). These two woods were used in elite-quality furniture. A coffin discovered at Saqqara was made from a kind of plywood that alternated layers of wood at right angles that were then pegged together.

Tools. Early stone tools used in the Predynastic Period (circa 3100–3000 B.C.E.) were not appropriate for making

fine wooden furniture. When copper tools began to be used in Dynasties 1 and 2, the quality of furniture improved dramatically. The tomb of Ti, carved in Dynasty 5 (circa 2500–2350 B.C.E.), depicts a carpenter's shop. In this shop artisans used adzes, saws, chisels, and a bow drill to make furniture. Sandstone was used like sandpaper to smooth the surface of boards. Geoffrey Killen, an authority on ancient furniture, believes that Middle Kingdom representations of carpenters' shops show an assembly line with a workman repeating one task and passing the furniture on to a colleague. New Kingdom illustrations of carpenter shops, in contrast, show one craftsman using all of the tools at his disposal, apparently making a complete object by himself.

Joints. Egyptian carpenters invented several methods of joining pieces of wood, many of which are still used by modern carpenters. The most important of these joints is the mortise and tenon, known since the Early Dynastic Period (circa 3000–2675 B.C.E.). The dovetail joint was already used on Hetepheres' furniture in Dynasty 4. Nails were nearly unknown.

Surface Finishes. Many furniture pieces were coated in white plaster. This coating allowed the carpenter to disguise the poor quality of wood. Other pieces were painted over a thin gesso foundation. Gesso was also used to set inlay, which could be made from faience, colored stone, or gold foil. Furniture from Tutankhamun's tomb was finished with marquetry and veneers. Tutankhamun's chairs were also decorated with scenes. Among the most famous is a chair back depicting the king, seated, while his wife rubs his shoulder with oil. The scene is created entirely from glass and silver inlay pressed into gold foil.

Sources:
Geoffrey Killen, *Ancient Egyptian Furniture*, volume 1, *4000–1300 B.C.* (Warminster, U.K.: Aris & Phillips, 1980.

Killen, *Egyptian Woodworking and Furniture* (Princes Risborough, U.K.: Shire, 1994).

GARDENS

Functions. Gardens were a common component of an ancient Egyptian house. They provided food, medicine, flowers, and a place to enjoy leisure time—especially for wealthy Egyptians. Gardens symbolized the well-ordered cosmos when they were represented in tomb paintings. Perhaps educated Egyptians were aware of this idea when they planned and enjoyed their gardens in life.

Plans. Gardens were formally arranged in ancient Egypt. They contained a pool with fish and lotus flowers. At the edge of the pool were papyrus plants, rushes, cornflowers, poppies, and mandrake. Shrubs and small bushes stood beyond the flowers. Trees often found in gardens were fig, sycamore fig, and willow. Acacia and date palm trees often alternated in a row around the shrubs and small trees. Grape arbors also were included, suggesting the possibility of locally produced wine for the wealthy.

Products. Garden products were both practical and religious. Gardens provided some kitchen staples. Recognizable plants from tomb paintings include lettuce, onion, garlic, and leeks. The herbs Egyptians used in medicine were also grown in their gardens, including coriander, caraway, dill, and cumin. Flowers served a religious purpose as well as being used as decoration. The god Amun was worshiped with bouquets of flowers tied into a vertical arrangement that resembles a decorated stick. Flowers were also used to adorn mummies.

Irrigation. Major crops were raised near the river, where irrigation canals could be used to water the plants. Houses were built nearer the desert edge so that crop land would not be wasted. Thus, house gardens were not close to the large-scale irrigation canals. Servants carried water in large pots to the gardens of wealthy people. The *shaduf,* a pot attached to a weighted, swinging pole on a base, was used from the time of Amenhotep IV (Akhenaten, circa 1353–1336 B.C.E.) until modernity to raise water from the pool to plants in the garden. Gardens were thus labor intensive.

Temple Gardens. Temples were houses for the gods and thus had gardens as did any other house. Temple gardens could be more elaborate because their owners were wealthy. The garden of the god Amun at Karnak, for

Relief painting from a Theban tomb depicting the watering of the garden of Ipuy, circa 1539–1075 B.C.E.
(Oriental Institute, University of Chicago)

example, had unique plants imported from Syria-Palestine by Thutmose III (circa 1479–1425 B.C.E.). Even the mortuary temples of the kings on the west bank at Thebes had gardens. Avenues of trees in the desert required deep planting holes filled with soil. Walls were built to retain the soil. The trees were watered constantly to keep them alive.

Sources:

Renate Germer, "Gardens," in *Oxford Encyclopedia of Ancient Egypt*, volume 2, edited by Donald B. Redford (Oxford & New York: Oxford University Press, 2001), pp. 3–5.

Lise Manniche, *An Ancient Egyptian Herbal* (Austin: University of Texas Press, 1989).

Alix Wilkinson, *The Garden in Ancient Egypt* (London: Rubicon Press, 1998).

HAIRSTYLES

Value of Study. Hairstyles help art historians determine the date of works of art because hairstyles change through time. They also reflect the age, status, and sex of the person represented. Egyptologists have studied hairstyles through works of art, wigs found in tombs, and mummies. In ancient Egypt fashions changed slowly during the Old Kingdom (circa 2675–2130 B.C.E.) and Middle Kingdom (circa 1980–1630 B.C.E.). During the New Kingdom (circa 1539–1075 B.C.E.) there was an acceleration in the rate of change in fashion.

Men's Styles. During the Old Kingdom men wore wigs that had thick, straight hair. Wigs reached shoulder length and were sometimes shown swept back over the shoulder. These wigs covered the ear. Other men wore their natural, short-cropped hair. This hairstyle included rows of curls arranged neatly around the head. Old Kingdom men were more likely to have facial hair than in other periods. Noblemen usually had a mustache during this period. Middle Kingdom men's wigs were similar to the long, straight wigs of the Old Kingdom. These wigs were somewhat longer but worn pushed behind the ears. Middle Kingdom males revealed their natural hair more rarely than men in the Old Kingdom. Fewer men wore facial hair in the Middle Kingdom. In both periods a low forehead was considered a mark of beauty, so wigs were pushed forward over the forehead.

Facial Hair. Fashions in facial hair changed over time also. Mustaches were popular in the Old Kingdom for noblemen. Some Middle Kingdom men wore beards. The majority of Egyptian men were clean-shaven. Kings and gods wore false beards made of braided leather. The king's beard ended in a square shape, while a god's beard curled at the end.

Women's Styles. Women's hairstyles changed slowly in the Old and Middle Kingdoms. Beginning in Dynasty 4 (circa 2625–2500 B.C.E.), thick, long hair styled with heavy ringlets was popular. Women wore their hair shoulder length and longer. Occasionally, short styles were worn. The most overwhelmingly popular hairstyle was the tripartite wig, in which the hair was divided into three sections. Two sections were arranged over the front of the shoulders and the third section was arranged over the back. This style was worn by all

PAPYRUS WESTCAR

This extract from the stories told to King Khufu (circa 2585–2560 B.C.E.) by his sons demonstrates the joys of the garden and the Egyptian's interest in hair and hair ornaments.

Bauefre [one of Khufu's sons] arose to speak that he might say: "May I cause that Your Majesty hear about a miracle which occurred in the time of your father, Sneferu, the justified, that which was done by the Chief Lector Priest, Djadjaemonkh. . . ." [Sneferu] wandered around every room of the palace to seek for himself some recreation, but he could not find it. Then he said: "Go! Bring to me the Chief Lector Priest, the Scribe of the Mat, Djadjaemonkh!" Then he was brought to him immediately. Then His Majesty said to him, "I have wandered about all the rooms of the palace, seeking for myself some recreation, but I could not find it." Then Djadjaemonkh said to him, "Would that Your Majesty proceed to the lake of the palace. Acquire for yourself a boat with all the beautiful women of the private rooms of your palace. The heart of Your Majesty will be refreshed at seeing their rowing, northward and southward. At the same time, you will be seeing the beautiful marshes of your lake and your fields, and its beautiful riverbanks. Your heart will be refreshed by it." Then His Majesty said, "I assuredly will act that I might be rowed. Cause that one might bring to me 20 oars of ebony worked in gold, the handles of sandalwood and worked with mixed gold and silver! Cause that one bring to me 20 women with beautiful bodies, with deep bosoms, and with braided locks, who have not born children! Also cause that one bring to me 20 nets and give the nets to these women when their clothes are laid aside!" All that His Majesty commanded was done. Then they rowed, heading north, then south. Then His Majesty's heart was happy at seeing the way that they rowed. Then one who was at the stroke-oar became entangled in her braided lock of hair. Then a fish shaped pendant of new turquoise fell in the water. Then she became silent, without rowing. Then her side of the rowers became silent, without rowing. Then His Majesty said, "Are you not able to row?" Then they said, "Our stroke-oar fell silent, without rowing." Then His Majesty said to her, "Why aren't you rowing?" Then she said, "My fish pendant of new turquoise has fallen in the water.". . . [In a broken passage she demands the original back rather than a replacement offered by the king. The king calls for his Chief Lector, Djadjaemonkh.] Then Djadjaemonkh said his sayings of magic. Then he placed a side of the water of the lake on one side. He found the fish shaped pendant resting on a potsherd. Then he brought it to give it to its owner.

Source: Translated by Edward Bleiberg, based on the hieroglyphic text in Kurt Sethe, "Aus den Wundererzählungen vom Hofe des Königs Cheops," *Aegyptischen Lesestücken* (Leipzig: J. C. Hindrichs, 1927), pp. 26–28. Published translation of the complete story in Miriam Lichtheim, *Ancient Egyptian Literature: A Book of Readings*, volume 1, *The Old and Middle Kingdoms* (Berkeley: University of California Press, 1973), pp. 215–221.

Wooden comb from Dynasty 18, circa 1539–1295/1292 B.C.E. (from Rita Freed, *Ramses II*, 1987)

upper-class women and goddesses in the Old Kingdom. It remained popular even in the New Kingdom for conservative dressers, such as goddesses. During the Middle Kingdom a short, curled wig was popular with many upper-class women. For those who preferred a tripartite wig, a new variation called the Hathoric wig was developed, which included the traditional division of the hair. The change came in the arrangement of the front sections, with the hair wrapped around a ball-like ornament. Sometimes the woman's natural hair can be seen on the back in art. This style was often worn by goddesses and a few queens of the Middle Kingdom and early Dynasty 18 (circa 1539–1295/1292 B.C.E.). In spite of the name, it was not limited to Hathor, and this goddess could also wear other styles. The tripartite wig continued to be worn in the New Kingdom by queens and goddesses. More-adventurous women adopted the enveloping wig, a massive, elaborately braided, curled, and frizzed style that arranged hair in one continuous mass over the chest and back. It was not pushed behind the ears, as was common with the Hathoric wig.

Unisex Styles. In late Dynasty 18 men and women adopted a hairstyle called the Nubian wig, which included tapering rows of tightly rolled ringlets arranged in layers. This style is still found in parts of modern Africa. Another Nubian style, the rounded wig, reached the nape of the neck and was set in ringlets. Men could alternatively wear shoulder-length wigs cut in two layers, with lappets of hair hanging over their chests. In the later part of Dynasty 18 it is striking that both royalty and nobles wore these new styles. Previously, kings were the most conservative in both their style of dress and hairstyles. But now, kings wore a variation of the Nubian wig that was even more elaborate than the wigs of noblemen. Notably, they had more curls. Older noblemen tended to wear long, straight styles that would have been more conservative.

Changes. In Dynasties 19 (circa 1292–1190 B.C.E.) and 20 (circa 1190–1075 B.C.E.) new long styles became fashionable for both men and women. Women wore their hair down to their waists. Men abandoned the Nubian wigs and layered wigs for longer, shoulder-length wigs. Artistic conventions from earlier periods were revived during Dynasty 25 (circa 760–656 B.C.E.) and also revived historical hairstyles. The Nubian round wig became especially popular again.

Shaving Heads. Many priests had shaved heads while on duty in the temple. Egyptologists believe that priests removed all the hair from their bodies because doing so was considered a sign of ritual purity. Certainly shaving the head helped priests avoid head lice, a common problem found in archaeological examples of wigs. Children's heads are also often shown shaved with only a remaining side lock. This style was associated with the god Khonsu, the son of Amun and Mut.

Nonelite Hairstyles. Lower-status males were the only men that artists represented with male pattern

Limestone tomb relief from Deir el Bahri, West Thebes, of servants attending Queen Kawit, wife of Nebhepetre Mentuhotep II, circa 2008–1957 B.C.E.; the servant on the right is adjusting the queen's wig.

baldness. Herdsman and other agricultural workers were often depicted with thinning hair and beard stubble. Servant girls wore the most-elaborate hairstyles among women—complicated styles that are completely unknown among the elite. Textual references to the erotic component of women's hair may well be reflected in tomb representations of female servants' hair.

Hairdressing Tools. Many archaeological examples of hairdressing tools survive from ancient Egypt. Hairpins made of bone, ivory, and metal are commonly known from all time periods. Combs were made of wood and resemble modern examples. A scissors-shaped implement made of metal was used for curling or braiding. Wigs made from human hair are also known.

Lotions and Dyes. Beeswax and resin were used as setting lotion for elaborate hairstyles. Representations in tombs and on statues are idealized, so no one is portrayed with gray hair. Natural hair was dyed with juniper berries and other plants. Cosmetic cones of tallow infused with myrrh were worn on the hair as a perfume and perhaps as an insect repellant.

Hair Ornaments. Women often added various ornaments to their hair. Pendants shaped like fish were worn, perhaps as charms to protect the wearer against drowning. Ball-shaped attachments were worn at the end of a ponytail by female dancers. Balls were also a part of the Hathoric wig. Noblewomen wore small gold tubes that fit over curls of hair. They also wore small cornflowers made of gold foil. Bands of flowers, often with a lotus placed centrally over the forehead, were common hair ornaments for elite women.

Head Cloths. Men were the most likely to wear head cloths. The most famous royal head cloth was the *nemes*, which was worn only by kings. It consisted of a striped cloth that completely covered the head. Other royal head cloths were worn in the time of Amenhotep IV (Akhenaten, circa 1353–1336 B.C.E.) include the *khat* and *afnet*, which both resemble nets arranged to hold the hair.

Hairdressers. Both men and women worked as hairdressers. The army included shavers in its ranks. Shavers also worked in temples, in wealthy households, and in the king's entourage. A well-known scene of female hairdressers from the reign of Nebhepetre Mentuhotep II (circa 2008–1957 B.C.E.) shows them attaching hairpieces with pins to a princess's coiffure.

Sources:

Joanne Fletcher, "A Tale of Hair, Wigs, and Lice," *Egyptian Archaeology: Bulletin of the Egypt Exploration Society*, 5 (1994): 31–33.

Lyn Green, "Hairstyles," in *Oxford Encyclopedia of Ancient Egypt*, volume 2, edited by Donald B. Redford (Oxford & New York: Oxford University Press, 2001), pp. 73–76.

J. L. Haynes, "The Development of Women's Hairstyles in Dynasty Eighteen," *Journal of the Society for the Study of Egyptian Antiquities*, 8 (1977): 18–24.

HOUSING AND LIGHTING: THE AMARNA HOUSE AND VILLA

Amarna Houses. Though Egyptian houses changed over time, the best-understood houses were studied by German Egyptologist Herbert Ricke in the 1920s and 1930s at Tell el Amarna. Ricke described a public, private, and semiprivate section of each house. The public area was open to guests from outside the household. The semiprivate section was open to the family and special guests. The private area consisted of bedrooms and baths and would only been seen by members of the household.

Smaller Version. The smaller home was approximately two hundred square feet in size. It consisted of either three or four rooms and a forecourt, which was used to receive guests, grind grain, and feed animals. An entrance from the forecourt led to a square room called "the place of sitting." Here guests could sit on low benches that were built into the walls. From this "place of sitting" the family had access to two other private rooms that were used for sleeping or storage. One room had a staircase that led to the roof, which was often used for cooking and for sleeping during warm weather.

Lighting. Unglazed windows were located high in the walls. Most interior light would have come from small oil-burning lamps. Most likely, however, the rooms remained dark.

The Villa. The larger houses, belonging to the elite, were called villas by Ricke. They were about 430 square feet in area. Villas were located behind enclosure walls, which also protected other buildings, such as separate granaries, stables, and servants' quarters, as well as a garden.

Villa Plan. The entrance to the villa, which was square in shape, was reached by steps that led to a small entrance hall with a roof supported by a column in the middle. A room such as this one is sometimes called the "porters' lodge" because it resembles the small spaces at the entrance of modern Egyptian villas where a servant stands guard. From the entrance hall the visitor would turn ninety degrees to enter a long, narrow room that ran almost the width of the house. This front hall had a roof supported by either two or four columns. Windows sometimes pierced the exterior wall, which formed part of the facade of the structure. From the entrance hall the visitor could enter the central hall, which was the main semiprivate room of the house. The central hall was square and had a roof supported by two columns. Raised platforms, built into at least two walls, were used as chairs. There was also a platform for water jars and a place to keep a large jar full of embers to serve as a heater during cold months. Windows again were placed high in the walls and were covered by wooden screens that controlled light levels. All other rooms and a staircase to the roof could be reached from the central hall. At least one room had a central column, while another always had two supporting columns. The room with the single column was square and served for private parties. Sleeping rooms had a niche where the bed was placed. Amarna villas also had bathrooms with a

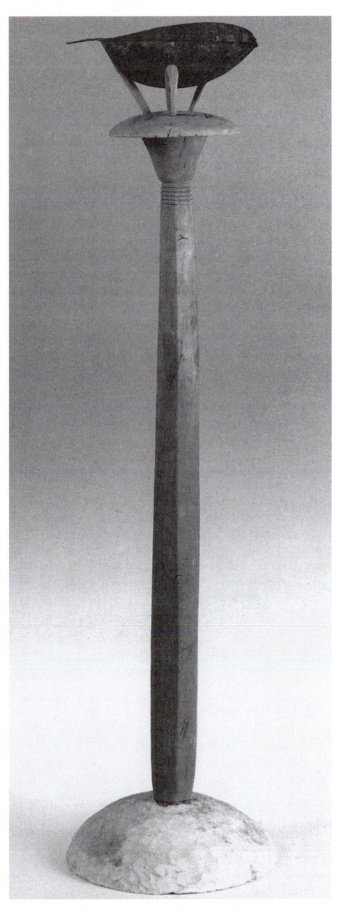

Lamp from the tomb of Kha at Deir el Medina, Dynasty 18, 1539–1295/1292 B.C.E. (from Rita Freed, *Ramses II*, 1987)

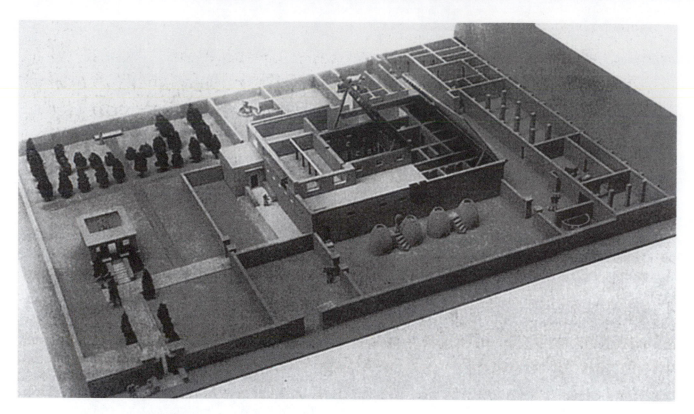

Model of a house at Tell el Amarna during the late New Kingdom, circa 1539–1075 B.C.E.
(Oriental Institute, University of Chicago)

toilet, which had a separate stone seat and a shower, which was a flat slab of stone with a hole in the middle. A servant would pour water over a kneeling person taking a shower. The staircase from the central hall led to the roof, where there was sometimes a second story with additional private rooms. Again, the roof could be used for storage and cooking. Amarna villas were decorated with paintings on plaster. Nature scenes, including flowers and marshes, were the most popular subjects.

Sources:
Felix Arnold, "Houses," in *Oxford Encyclopedia of Ancient Egypt*, volume 2, edited by Donald B. Redford (Oxford & New York: Oxford University Press, 2001), pp. 122–127.

Alexander Badawy, *Architecture in Ancient Egypt and the Near East* (Cambridge, Mass.: MIT Press, 1966).

Rosalie David, *Handbook to Life in Ancient Egypt* (New York: Facts on File, 1998), pp. 183–186.

LEISURE ACTIVITIES: NONELITE SPORTS

Combat Sports: Wrestling. Aside from running, combat sports, including wrestling and stick fighting (fencing), were practiced by commoners in ancient Egypt. Wrestling is the most-depicted sport in ancient Egyptian art. A Predynastic (circa 3100–3000 B.C.E.) palette depicts a wrestling match. The Dynasty 5 (circa 2500–2350 B.C.E.) tomb of Ptahhotep, a vizier known for his wisdom literature, shows six stages in the wrestling match between a pair of combatants. One of the wrestlers is Akhethotep, son of the tomb's owner. He is depicted wrestling a young man who is of the same age, since they both wear the side lock of hair, suggesting that there were

still quite young. They are shown naked, also a sign that they have not reached maturity. Their movements resemble modern freestyle wrestling.

RECORDS OF ATHLETIC EVENTS

Amenhotep II erected a stela at Giza that recorded many of his athletic feats.

Now when he was a lad, he [Amenhotep II] loved horses and rejoiced in them. It made him happy to work them, to learn their natures, to be skilled in training them, and to enter into their ways. When (it) was heard in the palace by his father . . . [Thutmose III] . . . the ear of his majesty was glad when he heard it, rejoicing at what was said about his eldest son. . . . Then his majesty said to those who were at his side: "Let there be given to him the very best horses in my majesty's stable which is in Memphis, and tell him: 'Take care of them, instill fear into them, make them gallop, and handle them if there be resistance to you.'" Now after it had been entrusted to the King's Son [Amenhotep II as a prince] to take care of horses of the king's stable, well then he did that which had been entrusted to him. . . . He trained horses without their equal; they would never grow tired when he took the reins, nor would they sweat even at a high gallop.

Source: William C. Hayes, "Egypt: Internal Affairs from Tuthmosis I to the Death of Amenophis III," *The Cambridge Ancient History*, second edition, volume 2, *Early History of the Middle East*, edited by I. E. S. Edwards, C. J. Gadd and N. G. L. Hammond (Cambridge & New York: Cambridge University Press, 1966), p. 334.

A stone relief of boys wrestling, from the tomb of Ptahhotep at Saqqara, Dynasty 5, circa 2500–2350 B.C.E.

Game from Thebes, Dynasty 17, circa 1630–1539 B.C.E.; the box is made of bone and ivory while the playing pieces are made of tile (from Rita Freed, *Ramses II*, 1987)

This stela is a unique record from Egypt of a long-distance race held in circa 684 B.C.E. In typical Egyptian fashion the winner is not named.

[Sixth year, third month] . . . under the majesty of . . . Taharqa . . . given eternal life.

His Majesty commanded that [a stela] be erected [at] the back of the western desert to the west of the palace and that its title be "Running Practice of the Army of the Son of the Sun Taharqa, may he live forever." His Majesty commanded that his army, raised up on his behalf, daily run [in] its five [sections].

Accordingly, His Majesty said to the men: "How lovely that is, which my Father Amon has made! No other king has done the like. He has arranged for the decapitation of the People of the Bow. The nine Peoples of the Bow are bound beneath the soles of my feet. I am served by all that is encircled by the disc of the sun. The heavens enclose no enemy of mine. There is none among my army who is not toughened for battle, no weakling who acts as a commander of mine. The king goes in person to Bia in order to inspect the good order of his army. They come like the coming of the wind, like falcons who beat the air with their wings. His body guard . . . is no better than they. The king himself is like Month [Montu the war god], a powerful one, unequaled by any in his army. A knowing one is he, skilled in every task, a second Thoth.

The king himself was in his chariot to inspire the running of his army. He ran with them at the back of the desert of Memphis in the hour 'She Has Given Satisfaction.' They reach Fayum in the hour 'Sunrise.' They return to the palace in the hour 'She Defends Her Master.' He distinguished the first among them to arrive and arranged for him to eat and drink with his bodyguard. [He] distinguished those others who were just behind him and rewarded them with all manner of things. For His Majesty loved the work of battle, for which they were selected. His God loved [him in the waters of creation]."

Source: Translated from Egyptian into German by Wolfgang Decker, *Sports and Games of Ancient Egypt*, translated by Allen Guttmann (New Haven: Yale University Press, 1992), pp. 62–63.

Wrestling in Dynasty 12. The most frequent wrestling scenes were carved in Dynasty 12 (circa 1938–1759 B.C.E.). They are found in the town of Beni Hasan in the central part of Egypt. In the wrestling scenes in the tombs of Amenemhet, Baqet I, Cheti, and Baqet III, the combatants are shown wearing belts and appear to be adults and were probably professional soldiers. Many pairs of wrestlers are depicted; the largest number, 220 pairs, appears in the tomb of Baqet III. Although the pairs are painted in different shades of red, probably to allow individuals to be recognized in the complicated holds, the rules of the sport are difficult to deduce from these scenes. The only text that mentions the sport consists of taunts called out between the wrestlers, including "I grab you by the leg," or "I make your heart weep and fill with fear!"

New Kingdom Wrestlers. Scenes of wrestling in the New Kingdom (circa 1539–1075 B.C.E.) indicate that the sport was part of a larger ceremony or ritual. Wrestling was often part of the New Year's ceremony. Scenes of wrestling from Ramesses III's (circa 1187–1156 B.C.E.) temple at Medinet Habu depicts Egyptians wrestling with foreigners—each man has either an African, Libyan, or Semitic opponent. Of course, Egyptian wrestlers are all shown triumphing. These scenes thus are part of the royal ideology, where sport is used to convey the triumph of Egypt in all parts of the world.

Egyptian Fencing. Ancient Egyptian stick fighting resembled fencing or the modern Egyptian sport called *nabbut*. Two men faced their opponent, each holding short sticks that were approximately three feet long. Leather face guards and straw arm guards were sometimes worn. The sequence of a match can be reconstructed from scenes found in the tomb of Kheruef and from Medinet Habu. The fighters, wearing kilts similar to soldiers' uniforms, first bowed to the public. At the start of the match the contestants crossed sticks, and most of the action consisted of hacking away at one another. Most scholars believe that the fencers were soldiers involved in a ceremony. Certainly the fighters depicted in the tomb of Kheruef are present at a Sed festival. The fighters at Medinet Habu are shown participating in the New Year's ceremony.

Festivals. The remaining evidence for sports in ancient Egypt associates all wrestling and stick-fighting matches with festivals. The Sed festival, celebrating the king's thirtieth year, included running, wrestling, and stick fighting. The New Year's festival also included sporting events. There is, however, no clear evidence for anything resembling the Greek Olympiad in Egypt.

Sources:
Wolfgang Decker, *Sports and Games of Ancient Egypt,* translated by Allen Guttmann (New Haven: Yale University Press, 1992), pp. 60–66.

Carl E. De Vries, "Attitudes of the Ancient Egyptians Toward Physical-Recreative Activities," dissertation, University of Chicago, 1960.

Zaki El Habashi, *Tutankhamun and the Sporting Tradition* (New York: Peter Lang, 1992).

MEAT CONSUMPTION

Beef. The highest status food in ancient Egypt was the foreleg of an ox, called the *khepesh*, which was offered to the gods and to the deceased in their tombs. Oxen were economical to raise. Though the foreleg was considered the best-tasting part of the ox, nearly all of the animal was eaten, including its internal organs.

Other Meats. Sheep and goats were the second-most-important meats eaten in ancient Egypt. Not only was the

Two butchers cutting up an ox; painted limestone relief from the tomb of the princess Idut at Saqqara, circa 2350 B.C.E.

flesh eaten, but the fat of the sheep was used in cooking, medicine, and perfume. Many peasants could afford to purchase sheep and goats, although an ox would have been beyond their means.

Prohibitions on Pork. Egyptians ate pork more often than historians have expected. Herodotus, the fifth-century B.C.E. Greek historian who wrote about Egypt, reported that Egyptians considered pork to be taboo. He also claimed that merely touching a pig was reason for a purification ceremony and that swineherds were shunned. Pigs are not depicted in tomb paintings, though most other Egyptian animals have a place in them. In the Book of the Dead and the story "Horus and Seth," pigs were associated with the evil god Seth. The fact that Islam and Judaism ban eating pork added weight to Herodotus's claims for modern Egyptologists. Yet, further investigation suggests that pork was a regular part of the Egyptian diet.

Textual Evidence. Scattered reference to pigs in Egyptian texts indicate that the attitude toward this animal was not always negative. The autobiography of the Dynasty 3 (circa 2675–2625 B.C.E.) nobleman Metjen mentions pigs. During the time of Senwosret (or Sesostris) I (circa 1919–1875 B.C.E.) the title Overseer of Swineherds existed. In the New Kingdom Amenhotep III (circa 1390–1353 B.C.E.) and Ramesses III (circa 1187–1156 B.C.E.) offered pigs to the gods. Swineherds at the temple of Sety (or Sethos) I (circa 1290–1279 B.C.E.) at Abydos also bred pigs.

Eating Pork. Archaeological evidence proves that pigs were commonly eaten by ordinary people. In sites dating to Dynasties 1 (circa 3000–2800 B.C.E.) and 2 (circa 2800–2675 B.C.E.), pig bones outnumber cattle, sheep, or goat remains at many domestic sites. Archaeologists have recovered pig bones from the New Kingdom sites of Armant, Tukh, Abydos, and Malqata. At Tell el Amarna pig bones found in garbage dumps near houses had clear butcher marks. Houses also had pigpens and areas for butchering pigs.

HERODOTUS ON PORK

Herodotus's story that Egyptians shunned pork is probably untrue.

The Egyptians think the pig an unclean animal. If any one of the Egyptians, but passing by, touch a pig, he goes to the river and dips himself therein, garments and all. Furthermore, such native-born Egyptian as are swineherds, alone of all people durst not enter any Egyptian shrine; nor is anyone willing to give his daughter in marriage to one of a family of swineherds or to marry one himself from such a family, and so the swineherds marry and are given in marriage only among their own folk. The Egyptians do not think fit to sacrifice the pig to any god except the Moon and Dionysus, and to these they sacrifice at the same time, the very full moon; it is then they sacrifice pigs and taste of their flesh. Why it is that they utterly reject the pig at other festivals and sacrifice it at this one—as to this, there is a story told about the matter by the Egyptians; I know it, but it is not quite suitable to be declared.

Source: Herodotus, *The History*, translated by David Grene (Chicago: University of Chicago Press, 1987), pp. 151–152.

Painted wood and plaster model of a man fanning a fire as he prepares to roast a duck, late First Intermediate Period, circa 2130–1980 B.C.E. (Museo Egypt, Turin)

Conclusion. The archaeological and textual evidence suggests that pigs were mostly a low-status food. Their bones are mostly associated with poorer houses. Though the gods required pigs in some New Kingdom ceremonies, they were apparently excluded from banquets and tomb offerings.

Poultry. The chicken originated in Southeast Asia. There is no evidence that the Egyptians knew of chickens before the fifth century B.C.E. No chicken bones are found in any Egyptian archeological site dated prior to 332 B.C.E. and the arrival of the Greeks.

Other Animals. The Egyptians ate other small animals such as mice and hedgehogs. Mouse bones have been found in the stomachs of mummies, and oil of mouse was added to foods. Possibly the Egyptians fed nuts and raisins to mice before eating them, as did the ancient Romans. Hedgehogs were prepared by being coated with clay and baked in a fire. When the clay was removed, the spines of the hedgehog were stripped away, leaving only the meat.

Sources:

William J. Darby, Paul Ghalioungui, and Louis Grivetti, *Food: The Gift of Osiris,* two volumes (London & New York: Academic Press, 1977).

Salima Ikram, *Choice Cuts: Meat Production in Ancient Egypt* (Leuven: Departement Oosterse Studies, 1995).

Ikram, "Diet," in *Oxford Encyclopedia of Ancient Egypt,* edited by Donald B. Redford (Oxford & New York: Oxford University Press, 2001), pp. 390–391.

Hilary Wilson, *Egyptian Food and Drink* (Aylesbury, U.K.: Shire, 1988).

SIGNIFICANT PEOPLE

AMENHOTEP II

CIRCA 1426–1400 B.C.E.
KING, DYNASTY 18

Life. Amenhotep II was the son of Thutmose III (circa 1479–1425 B.C.E.) and Great Royal Wife Meryetre-Hatshepsut. He married Queen Tiye, who was the mother of the next king, Thutmose IV (circa 1400–1390 B.C.E.). He ruled for twenty-six years, during which Egypt was prosperous and mostly at peace.

Sports and the King. Egyptian kings of Dynasty 18 (circa 1539–1295/1292 B.C.E.) had always presented themselves as warriors. During Thutmose III's reign, the beginnings of a tradition of sportsmanship were also presented to the public. The greatest sportsman king, however, was Amenhotep II, who stressed his athletic ability in political propaganda.

Horseman. As a child, Amenhotep II showed a natural aptitude for horsemanship. His father entrusted the royal stable in Memphis to him at a young age. Amenhotep II learned to exercise, train, and understand horses—according to information placed on a stela he erected in Giza.

Archer. Archery was important to kings in war, but Amenhotep II also established public demonstrations of his skill. In one spectacular performance, the king rode his chariot at top speed while shooting at targets spaced about thirty-five feet apart. The king pierced each of four copper targets with arrows that passed completely through them. On another occasion he shot arrows at a copper ingot so that they protruded from the other side. In another demonstration of his strength, Amenhotep shot three hundred bows consecutively, using this same occasion to teach the army the difference between a good bow and a bad bow. The same inscription claims that no one but the king was strong enough to draw his own bow.

Sailor. Finally, Amenhotep II claimed great skill in sailing. On one occasion he claimed to have outlasted two hundred men in rowing his own riverboat. His oar was also oversized, reaching thirty-four feet in length.

Exaggerations? It is impossible to evaluate the truth of Amenhotep II's claims to have been the greatest sportsman of all time. Certainly no one would have been able to contradict him when these claims were recorded in stone. Yet, it is striking that he insisted so often on his athletic ability as proof of his legitimacy as king. Perhaps this boast was his reaction to following his father, Thutmose III, who was without question the greatest warrior king in Egyptian history up to that time. Since Amenhotep II was trained as a warrior, but there was no need for war, he demonstrated his readiness to protect Egypt through his athletic feats.

Sources:

William C. Hayes, "Egypt: Internal Affairs from Tuthmosis I to the Death of Amenophis III," *The Cambridge Ancient History,* second edition, volume 2, *Early History of the Middle East,* edited by I. E. S. Edwards, C. J. Gadd and N. G. L. Hammond (Cambridge & New York: Cambridge University Press, 1966), pp. 333–338.

Peter der Manuelian, *Studies in the Reign of Amenophis II* (Hildesheim: Gerstenberg, 1987).

TAHARQA

CIRCA 690–664 B.C.E.
KING, DYNASTY 25

A Warrior's Life. Taharqa was the son of King Piye (or Piankhy) (circa 747–716 B.C.E.) and younger brother of King Shabaka (circa 716–702 B.C.E.). He grew up in Napata and came to Egypt when he was approximately twenty years old. He became king in circa 690 B.C.E., lived in Memphis, and built extensively throughout Egypt. Taharqa's aggressive foreign policy toward the Assyrians required a strong army. Eventually he was driven back to Napata by the Assyrians. He died there in circa 664 B.C.E.

Conditioning Plan. Taharqa encouraged running as a sport for his soldiers. He left a record on a stela of roughly a 100-kilometer (around 62 miles) race run in circa 684 B.C.E. by an elite unit of his army. In this description he talks of taking daily runs to prepare for war. A memory of this practice was perhaps preserved by the Greek historian Diodorus Siculus (flourished circa 60–56 B.C.E.), who wrote that the Egyptian army ran 30 kilometers (about 18.6 miles) daily before breakfast. This distance seems unrealistic and is a reflection of Diodorus's great admiration for the Egyptians.

Great Race of 684 B.C.E. Taharqa's *Running Stela* describes the king's decision that the army run daily for training. The inscription continues with a description of a race from Memphis to Faiyum and back, a distance of 62 miles. The king followed them in his chariot but seems to have run part of the race with his men. The race began at night, undoubtedly to take advantage of cooler temperatures; after a two-hour rest in the Faiyum, the runners returned to Memphis. The race lasted nine hours, and the winner was awarded a banquet with the royal bodyguards. All finishers also received an unspecified prize. Typically for ancient Egypt, the only individual named in this stela is the king—the name of the winner was not mentioned at all.

Comparison with Modern Runners. The sports historian Wolfgang Decker has compared the numbers in this stela with modern runner's records. On 7 June 1980 British long-distance runner Jeff Norman ran a 50-kilometer race (roughly half the distance of Taharqa's race) in two hours, forty-eight minutes, and six seconds. The record for a 100-kilometer race, about the distance of Taharqa's race, was established on 28 October 1978 by British runner Don Ritchie. He covered this distance in six hours, ten minutes, and thirty seconds. Nineteenth-century British records also suggest that the numbers in Taharqa's *Running Stela* are possible. In 1879 the record for a 32-mile race was three hours and forty minutes. In 1884 the record for a 101-kilometer race, close in distance to Taharqa's race, was eight hours. Thus, Taharqa's numbers seem perfectly reasonable.

Source:

Wolfgang Decker, *Sports and Games of Ancient Egypt,* translated by Allen Guttmann (New Haven: Yale University Press, 1992), pp. 60–66.

DOCUMENTARY SOURCES

Anonymous, *Ebers Medical Papyrus* (circa 1630–539 B.C.E.)—A treatise on internal disease that also provides recipes for several wrinkle removers.

Anonymous, *Edwin Smith Surgical Papyrus* (circa 1630–1539 B.C.E.)—Copy of an Old Kingdom text written in the Hyksos period, which, along with descriptions of cases of trauma and treatments, contains information on hygiene, such as providing a recipe for soap.

Anonymous, *Turin Erotic Papyrus* (circa 1190–1075 B.C.E.)—Among the erotic illustrations are scenes of women putting on makeup, including lipstick and rouge.

Painting of a garden with a well-stocked pool; from an unidentified Theban tomb, Dynasty 18, 1539–1295/1292 B.C.E.
(British Museum, London)

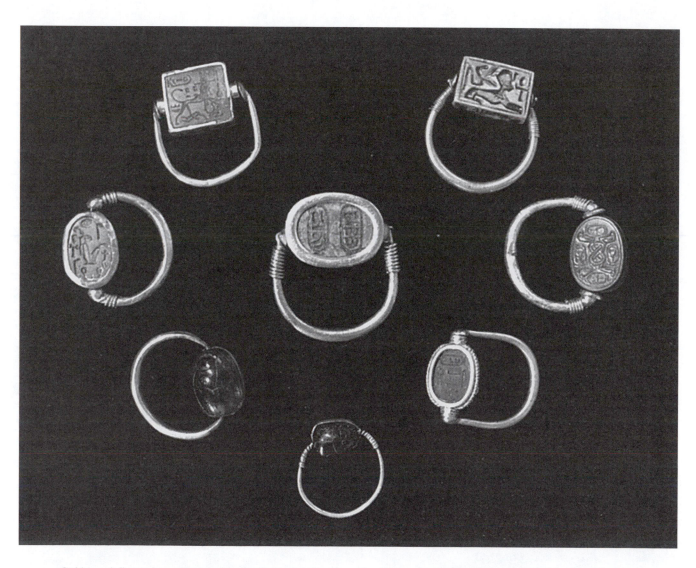

Gold scarab finger rings with swiveling heads from various dynastic periods, circa 1820–924 B.C.E. (British Museum, London)

THE FAMILY AND SOCIAL TRENDS

by EDWARD BLEIBERG

CONTENTS

Sidebars and tables are listed in italics.

2615* B.C.E.

- Only women work as musicians and weavers, unlike during the New Kingdom when men also performed these tasks.

- Scribal education is available only to the elite.

2350-2170* B.C.E.

- The tomb of Ankhmahor, a ka-priest, is carved with scenes of a circumcision rite.

- The term *abut* is used to describe the extended family of a man—his relatives on both his parents' sides, his children and servants, but not his wife nor her family—which is important for showing who will inherit two-thirds of his estate after his wife takes her one-third share.

- The dwarf Seneb, a valet and tutor, reaches high office in the royal court.

1938-1759* B.C.E.

- Papyri, which are later discovered at Kahun, describing gynecological information on cures for infertility, methods of contraception, pregnancy tests, and ways to care for pregnant women.

- Wands, inscribed with images of the dwarf-god Bes and the hippopotamus-goddess Taweret, are used to protect pregnant women and newborn children.

- Scribal education becomes available to some individuals from the lower classes.

- The sage Ptahhotep is quoted concerning the importance of rhetoric "good speech" in education.

1630-1523* B.C.E.

- The *Papyrus Westcar* is recopied; it describes labor and the delivery of human triplets.

1539-1295/ 1992 B.C.E.

- The custom that lovers call each other "brother" and "sister," a practice that led to the disproved theory that brother–sister marriage was common in ancient Egypt, begins.

- The sage Any writes on marriage, sexuality, and respect for mothers.

- Chapter 125 of the *Book of the Dead* is composed, revealing the ban on certain forms of sexuality.

- Some high officials speak in their autobiographies of the education of princes in the institution called the *Kap*.

- Musicians and weavers are both male and female, unlike in the Old Kingdom when only women played these roles.

1479-1425* B.C.E.

- Thutmose III uses scribal education as a means of "Egyptianizing" foreign rulers by taking their sons to court and training them as scribes.

* DENOTES CIRCA DATE

1292-1075*
B.C.E.

- Evidence found at Deir el Medina shows that grandfathers taught their grandchildren to read.

- Many student copies of Egyptian literature are written, including a text with a verb conjugation, which reveals that students learned grammar; many copies of these texts will survive to modern times.

- The "Satirical Letter" indicates the importance of geography in the curriculum.

1204-1193*
B.C.E.

- During the reigns of Sety II (circa 1204–1198 B.C.E.), Amenmesse (circa 1203–1200 B.C.E.), and Siptah (circa 1198–1193 B.C.E.), the foreman Paneb is accused of adultery and other crimes at Deir el Medina.

1190-1075*
B.C.E.

- During Dynasty 20, Naunakhte disinherits four of her eight children because they neglect her in her old age.

1150* B.C.E.

- The *Turin Erotic Papyrus*, depicting couples in a variety of sexual positions, is drawn, probably in Deir el Medina.

1104-1075*
B.C.E.

- The Musician of Seth, Nanefer (Rennefer), is adopted by her husband to allow her to inherit a larger share than the usual one-third of his estate. She also adopts children born to her slave girl.

1075-945*
B.C.E.

- The lieutenant and scribe of the Temple of Khonsu, Shed-su-khonsu, writes a letter to Pay-neb-andjed that illustrates the letter-writing formulae.

664-525
B.C.E.

- Marriage celebrations are described in the *Story of Setne Khaemwas.*

- Egyptians describe the source of human semen as originating in the father's bones and the origin of skin and flesh as coming from mother's milk. They believe the heart (character) comes from the mother.

332-323
B.C.E

- A period of common brother–sister marriage in the royal family begins.

* DENOTES CIRCA DATE

OVERVIEW

Wedlock. Marriage in Egypt was a private matter of little interest to the state. Ceremonies were private celebrations that might have included banquets. Love poetry suggests that parents arranged marriages for their children. Texts describing ideal marriages suggest that younger women were considered more compatible with older men, though men were urged to marry as young as possible. Evidence shows that teenage girls married, but men waited to wed until their late twenties or early thirties. The age difference resulted from the idea that men were expected to pay for maintenance of the household. Thus, men waited to marry until their careers were well established.

Marriage Contracts. Marriage contracts were written to deal with property issues, especially after the birth of children. Many ancient marriage contracts dealt with the rights of inheritance, for both the wife and the future children, and also set the terms for disposal of property in the event of divorce. Women retained considerable property rights in Egypt compared to other ancient cultures, such as in Greece, where a husband had complete control over his wife's property. In Egypt a woman's property would revert to her children, or to her parents, in the event of her death. A woman normally inherited one-third of her husband's property, while children inherited the remaining two-thirds. A woman also received back any property brought to the marriage in the event of her husband's death or a divorce.

Multiple Marriages. Most Egyptians practiced serial monogamy. Death and divorce often were followed by a new union. Marriages could be ended because of incompatibility, infertility, and adultery. No stigma was attached to divorce or remarriage. Polygamy, however, seems to be limited to the king. It was probably too expensive for ordinary men to support multiple wives and the many children that might result from polygamy. Men might have sexual contact with slaves, especially in cases where a wife was infertile, but the offspring of these unions could not inherit his property unless they were adopted. The female slave who bore these children would not have inheritance rights, in contrast to a wife.

Sexuality. Evidence for sexuality in ancient Egypt is difficult to interpret. The small amount of surviving textual remains uses rare terms that are difficult to translate. At the same time, the obviously sexual scenes—found in tombs, on papyrus, and on *ostraca*—often elicit subjective judgments from modern scholars who try to explain them. The *Turin Erotic Papyrus* (Papyrus Turin 55001), dating to circa 1150 B.C.E., depicts sketches of copulation in a great variety of positions and combinations. Some scholars have suggested that the papyrus represents prostitutes or a brothel. Yet, there is no direct evidence of any context for the actions depicted; other scholars believe that the drawings are a parody of religious scenes.

Taboo Sexuality. Spell 125 of the *Book of the Dead*, sometimes called "The Negative Confessions," is a list of actions that the deceased claims he or she did not perform while alive, since these activities would bar him or her from the next world. This list contains some sexual taboos, such as sexual conduct inside a temple, adultery, and perhaps pederasty—sexual contact with a male child. There seems to be no similar taboo on same-sex contact between adults.

Childhood. Children are depicted in art with shaved heads and a remaining sidelock of hair. When in the company of other children, they are shown playing games. With their parents, children are depicted either kneeling or standing at their father's side. Though wisdom texts, such as the *Instruction of Any*, advise a man to respect his mother since she breast-fed him, little is really known of the relationships between parents and children in Egypt.

Puberty. Men, and perhaps women, underwent circumcision at puberty. A scene in the Dynasty 6 (circa 2350–2170 B.C.E.) tomb of the religious official Ankhmahor shows a priest assuring a young man that the operation will not hurt. Male circumcision was necessary to allow a man to take up the duties of a priest. It was a part of ritual purity. Although female circumcision has not been definitively recognized in mummies, it is, however, commonly practiced in modern Egyptian villages.

Training for Professions. Education in Egypt was related to obtaining a profession. Ideally, a son followed his father in his job. Thus, it is likely that a father began to teach his profession to his son from an early age. There is some evidence at Deir el Medina that grandfathers taught their grandchildren to read. A royal institution, called the *kap*, was perhaps the training school for princes and some other children of the elite. In New Kingdom (circa 1539–1075 B.C.E.) autobiographies some high officials relate that they were educated in the *kap*.

Accepted Roles. Gender roles in Egypt corresponded to the biological sexes, and some roles were only possible for males or for females. Thus, kingship was considered a male role, even when the throne was filled by a woman such as Hatshepsut (circa 1478/1472–1458 B.C.E.). She became a female king, rather than a ruling queen. Similar to royal control, the government bureaucracy was also completely male. The few administrative titles held by women refer to domestic positions in a household. Nonelite women and men also had distinctive roles. Though both men and women could be servants, women ground grain and baked bread. Men brewed beer and butchered and cooked meat. Musicians and dancers in the Old Kingdom (circa 2675–2130 B.C.E.) were female, but in the New Kingdom both men and women were employed as musicians. Among skilled workers, women wove cloth in the Old Kingdom and Middle Kingdom (circa 1980–1630 B.C.E.). Men could weave, beginning in the New Kingdom, but were also sculptors, jewelers, and carpenters. Agricultural workers were mostly male, but during the harvest women were often called to help. Among temple professionals all cults, except Hathor's, were run by men. Hathor's cult was run exclusively by women.

TOPICS IN THE FAMILY AND SOCIAL TRENDS

BIRTH

Etiology. In the ancient Egyptian language, *mesi* is the basic word for birth. It is a component in many names, often combined with a god's name, such as in Ramesses (Re is born) and Thutmose (Thoth is born), which contain different grammatical forms of the verb "to be born." Other phrases with a similar meaning were *pery her ta* (come down to the ground), *pery em khet* (come forth from the womb), and *hay em khet* (descend from the womb).

Conception. The Egyptians understood the basic cause of conception from earliest times. In the fifth century B.C.E. they thought that the father produced semen from his bones, but that it was then stored in the testicles. They understood that the penis was used to transfer semen to the womb. Mother's milk, however, was thought to be the source of the new flesh and skin of a baby. The mother also provided the heart, considered to be the seat of thought and mind, for the newborn. Not only did this belief mean that the mother provided the physical organ but also the child's character.

Infertility. The Egyptians also understood that infertility could be caused by the mother or father. Cures were tried for both potential parents and included prayers, letters to the dead requesting assistance, and prescriptions. These formulas do not have any known medical value.

Avoiding Pregnancy. Contraception consisted of both chemical and mechanical means. A compound similar to

Stone fertility figurine, Middle Kingdom, circa 1980–1630 B.C.E. (Agyptisches Museum, Berlin)

The only description of human labor and delivery in Egypt comes from the story of the magical birth of three kings of Dynasty 5 (circa 2500–2350 B.C.E.), found in the *Papyrus Westcar*, which was written in the Middle Kingdom (circa 1980–1630 B.C.E.). It describes how the gods and goddesses assisted at the birth. This document provides the only reference to triplets in ancient Egyptian literature.

Once upon a time Rud-dedet suffered the pain of childbirth. Then the Majesty of Re, Lord of Sakhbu said to Isis and Nepthys, Meskhenet, Heket, and Khnum, "Would that you might travel, that you might deliver Rud-dedet of the three children who are in her womb who will perform this potent office in this entire land, that they might build our temples, and they might supply your altars, that they might provide richly for your offering tables, and that they might enlarge your offerings."

Then these gods traveled after they had made their appearances like musicians. Khnum was with them bearing a bundle. They reached the house of Reuser [the father]. They found him standing with his clothing disordered. They offered to him their necklaces and sistra. Then he said to them, "My Ladies. Look! It is the woman who is suffering the pain of childbirth." Then they said, "Let us see her. Look! We know about delivery." Then he said to them, "Get along!" They entered before Rud-dedet.

Then they sealed the room on account of it with her. Then Isis placed herself in front of her. Nephthys was behind her head. Heket hastened the birth. Then Isis said, "May you not be strong in her belly in this your name of 'Strength Against It' [pun on the name Userkaf]." Then this child rushed forth onto her arms, a child of one cubit, firm of bone and strong. His limbs were gold, his royal head cloth was true lapis lazuli. Then they washed him while cutting his umbilical cord. They placed him on a couch made of a brick. Then Meskenet [whose name means "birthing brick"] went to him. Then she said, "A king who will perform the office of kingship in the entire land." Khnum made his body healthy.

Then Isis placed herself before her [Rud-dedet]. Nephthys was behind her head. Heket hastened the birth. Then Isis said, "Do not tread on her belly in this your name of 'May Re tread on the earth' [pun on the name Sahure]." Then this child rushed forth onto her arms, a child of one cubit, firm of bone and strong. His limbs were gold, his royal head cloth was true lapis lazuli. Then they washed him while cutting his umbilical cord. They placed him on a couch made of a brick. Then Meskenet [whose name means "birthing brick"] went to him. Then she said, "A king who will perform the office of kingship in the entire land." Khnum made his body healthy.

Then Isis placed herself before her [Rud-dedet]. Nephthys was behind her head. Heket hastened the birth. Then Isis said, "Do not be dark in her womb in this your name of 'Darkness' [pun on the name Neferirkare Kakai]." Then this child rushed forth onto her arms, a child of one cubit, firm of bone and strong. His limbs were gold, his royal head cloth was true lapis lazuli. Then they washed him while cutting his umbilical cord. They placed him on a couch made of a brick. Then Meskenet [whose name means "birthing brick"] went to him. Then she said, "A king who will perform the office of kingship in the entire land." Khnum made his body healthy.

Then these gods went forth after they delivered Rud-dedet of these three children. Then they said, "May you be happy, Reuser! Look! Three children are born to you." Then he said, "My Ladies. What can I do for you? Give this grain to your palanquin bearer. Take if for yourselves in exchange for beer." Then Khnum loaded the grain. Then they went to the place where they had started.

Source: Translated from Egyptian by Edward Bleiberg. In *Egyptian Readingbook: Exercises and Middle Egytptian Texts*, second edition, edited by A. de Buck (Leiden: Netherlandsh Instituut voor het Nabije Oosten, 1963), pp. 79–88.

acidic contraceptive jelly was used, along with male prophylactics made from animal skins.

Pregnancy Tests. The Egyptians were aware of the physical changes in a woman's body during pregnancy. They observed that a pause in menses, swollen breasts, nausea, changes in the face and eyes, and sensitivity to strong smells were among the signs that a woman had conceived. They also used a remarkable test to confirm pregnancy. The woman urinated on barley and emmer seed. If the seeds germinated, the test was positive. If no plant came from the seeds, the test was negative. In fact, the chemical changes in a pregnant woman's urine will allow a seed to germinate, while ordinary urine is too acidic for the plant to grow. On the other hand, the Egyptians believed that if barley grew first, the child was a boy. If emmer sprouted, the child was a girl. This theory was based on the fact that the word barley is grammatically masculine in Egyptian and emmer is feminine. This test is not reliable.

Care of Pregnant Women. In ancient Egypt pregnant women massaged their bellies with oils. They believed that these lotions could prevent stretch marks and ease delivery. They were kept in calcite containers carved in the shape of a pregnant woman rubbing her abdomen. One such container showed a tampon in the shape of the Isis knot—a well-known amulet that associated pregnant woman with the goddess Isis when she carried her son, Horus—that allegedly eased the pregnancy. In an effort to prevent possible miscarriages, prescriptions were poured directly into the vagina.

Labor and Delivery. The Egyptians described human gestation as being nine months long. Actual labor and birth was assisted by a midwife, probably with other women

Stela of the royal family of Akhenaten showing the pharaoh, his wife Nefertiti, and some of their children, circa 1353–1336 B.C.E. (Agyptisches Museum, Berlin)

present. These women might have been associated with the goddesses Isis, her sister Nephthys, and Heket, the goddess of birth. During labor the attendants assisted by applying natron, a sodium nitrate, and poultices; casting magical spells; and offering intoxicating drinks. They also performed fumigations that they believed made the labor go faster. The birthing mother either squatted on bricks or sat in a specially built chair to deliver the child; they stayed in their homes, in a special hut located in the garden, or on the roof. A midwife cut the umbilical cord, placed the child on a brick, and pronounced the child's name. In at least one case the new mother then observed a fourteen-day period of purification. Some scholars believe that the placenta was saved so it could later be buried in the child's tomb.

Naming and Fate. In the only account of a birth preserved from ancient Egypt, found in the *Papyrus Westcar*, which was written during the Middle Kingdom (circa 1980–1630 B.C.E.), the midwife pronounced the name of the new child. Scholars believe the mother, with input from the father, chose this name. The Egyptians also believed that the child's fate was determined in the womb by the goddesses called the Seven Hathors, who were assisted by Renenutet, the goddess of the birthing bricks.

Death during Childbirth. A woman's life expectancy was two to four years shorter than a man's because of the high incidence of death in childbirth. To prevent such deaths the Egyptians used magic spells and amulets. The dwarf-god Bes and the hippopotamus-goddess Taweret were both believed to protect pregnant women and unborn children. Special wands inscribed with images of these deities, for instance, were used to draw magic circles around a pregnant woman's bed.

Neonatal Death. Newborns were also in danger. The Egyptians tested the strength of these infants by feeding them a portion of the placenta. If the child swallowed the offering, it was believed that it would live. The quality of a child's cry could also predict its chances for survival.

Sources:

Erika Feucht, "Birth," in *Oxford Encyclopedia of Ancient Egypt*, volume 1, edited by Donald B. Redford (Oxford & New York: Oxford University Press, 2001), pp. 192–193.

Eugen Strouhal, *Life in Ancient Egypt*, translated by Deryck Viney (Cambridge: Cambridge University Press, 1992).

CHILDREN

Words for Childhood. At least six different words are used in Egyptian to mean *child*. In English, different words—such as infant, toddler, boy or girl, and adolescent—refer to stages of childhood. In Egyptian the variety of words used do not seem to have such specific meanings. For example, scholars Rosalind and Jacobus Janssen observe that *khenu*, meaning child, derives from the root that means "to wean." Yet, this word is not limited in use to children who have recently been weaned. The High Priest Bekenkhons, who lived in the reign of Ramesses II (circa 1279–1213 B.C.E.), used this word to describe his entire childhood. Thus, it seems unlikely that the Egyptians recognized the stages of childhood as distinct. All of childhood was a period of preparation for taking on adult responsibilities.

Nurture and Nature. Few differences of opinion are voiced in Egyptian texts. Modern scholars often have the impression of an unnatural unanimity on most issues. Yet, remarkably, the instructions of the sage Any, in *The Wisdom of Any* (circa 1539–1292 B.C.E.), preserves a debate in the epilogue over whether a child can be taught virtue, as well as whether a child's nature is either virtuous or not.

Any and Khonshotep. At the end of Any's instructions, his son, Khonshotep, has the opportunity to reply to his father's advice. At first he expresses both his admiration for his father's ideas and the difficulty for a child to follow them, even when he is able to recite them. It is in the nature of a child to ignore words that are too hard to understand. Any replies with a series of images describing tamed animals that can change with

Stone relief of a woman breast-feeding her child, from the tomb of Niankh-Khunum and Khnum-hotep at Saqqara, Dynasty 6, circa 2350–2170 B.C.E.

training, and argues that children can also be molded in a similar fashion. Any suggests that foreigners, such as Nubians and Syrians, can also be changed through

Stone relief from the tomb of Mereuke at Saqqara showing girls and boys forming a "living roundabout," a game played while they were pressing grapes, Old Kingdom, circa 2675–2130 B.C.E.

The New Kingdom (circa 1539–1075 B.C.E.) scribe Any had many words of wisdom to impart to younger generations.

The scribe Khonshotep answered his father, the scribe Any:

I wish I were like (you)!
As learned as you!
Then I would carry out your teachings,
And the son would be brought to the father's place.
Each man is led by his nature,
You are a man who is a master,
Whose strivings are exalted,
Whose every word is chosen.
The son, he understands little
When he recites the words in the books.
But when your words please the heart,
The heart tends to accept them with joy.
Don't make your virtues too numerous,
That one may raise one's thoughts to you;
A boy does not follow the moral instructions,
Though the writings are on his tongue!
The scribe Any answered his son, the scribe Khonshotep:
Do not rely on such worthless thoughts,
Beware of what you do to yourself!
I judge your complaints to be wrong,
I shall set you right about them.
There's nothing [superfluous in] our words,
Which you say you wished were reduced.
The fighting bull who kills in the stable,
He forgets and abandons the arena;
He conquers his nature,
Remembers what he's learned,
And becomes the like of a fattened ox.
The savage lion abandons his wrath,
And comes to resemble the timid donkey.
The horse slips into its harness,
Obedient it goes outdoors.
The dog obeys the word,
And walks behind its master.
The monkey carries the stick,
Though its mother did not carry it.
The goose returns from the pond,
When one comes to shut it in the yard.
One teaches the Nubian to speak Egyptian,
The Syrian and other strangers too.
Say: "I shall do like all the beasts,"
Listen and learn what they do.

The scribe Khonshotep answered his father, the scribe Any:

Do not proclaim your powers,
So as to force me to your ways;
Does it not happen to a man to slacken his hand
So as to hear an answer in its place?
Man resembles the god in his way
If he listens to a man's answer.
One man cannot know his fellow,
If the masses are beasts;
One man cannot know his teachings,
And alone posses a mind,
If the multitudes are foolish.
All your sayings are excellent,
But doing them requires virtues;
Tell the god who gave you wisdom:
"Set them on your path!"
The scribe Any answered his son, the scribe Khonshotep:
Turn your back to these many words,
That are not worth being heard.
The crooked stick left on the ground,
With sun and shade attacking it,
If the carpenter takes it, he straightens it,
Makes of it a noble's staff,
And a straight stick makes a collar.
You foolish heart,
Do you wish us to teach,
Or have you been corrupted?
"Look," said he, "you, my father,
You who are wise and strong of hand:
The infant in his mother's arms,
His wish is for what nurses him."
"Look," said he, "when he finds his speech,
He says: "Give me bread.""

Source: Miriam Lichtheim, *Ancient Egyptian Literature*, volume 2 (Berkeley: University of California Press, 1976), pp. 144–145.

proper instruction. Khonshotep replies that the gods make a person with a particular nature and that only a god can alter that nature. Any then relates his belief that people can change; he uses an image of a crooked stick—even this wood can be properly shaped by a carpenter. Finally, both Khonshotep and Any use images that describe the satisfaction of consuming food. While Khonshotep refers to the infant who nurses without knowledge of anything else, Any believes that when the child learns to talk he will understand how to ask for more than mere sustenance. This comparison ends the discussion and probably reflects the official view that training is more important than nature in a child's future.

Pride in Children. Egyptians made no secret of their pride in their children and the love they felt for them. The usual caption accompanying the image of a child in a parent's tomb is "his beloved son" or "his beloved daughter." The Priest of Amun, Bekenkhons, who lived in Dynasty 22 (circa 945–712 B.C.E.) and was a descendant of the Bekenkhons who lived in Ramesses II's reign, proclaimed his love of his son on a statue he erected in the Karnak temple. He said, "I already loved him when he was still a small boy; I acknowledged him as a proper gentleman. As a child I found him already mature. His breeding was not in accordance with his (young) age. His speech was well-chosen. There was nothing uncouth in his words." (Translated by Rosalind and Jacobus Janssen)

Sources:

Rosalie David, *Handbook to Life in Ancient Egypt* (New York: Facts on File, 1998).

Rosalind M. and Jac. J. Janssen, *Growing Up in Ancient Egypt* (London: Rubicon Press, 1990).

Joyce Tyldesley, "Marriage and Motherhood in Ancient Egypt," *History Today*, 44 (April 1994): 20–27.

HOMOSEXUALITY

Textual References. Same sex intercourse was certainly known to the Egyptians. Chapter 125 of the *Book of the Dead* includes pederasty as one of the acts that can exclude a person from the land of the Blessed Dead. Yet, it is more difficult to determine the attitudes held toward sexual contact between adult men. The *Tale of Neferkare and General Sasenet* was a popular story composed in Dynasty 12 (circa 1938–1759 B.C.E.) It survives in fragmentary copies dating to Dynasty 18 (circa 1539–1295/1292 B.C.E.), Dynasty 20 (circa 1190–1075 B.C.E.), and Dynasty 25 (circa 760–656 B.C.E.). The fragments recount different parts of the story. The first fragment sets the story in the reign of King Neferkare, probably meaning Pepy II (circa 2288–2224/2194 B.C.E.). It mentions the king's desire for General Sasenet. The second fragment tells of a man trying to denounce the general to the court, which, however, ignores him. In the third fragment a man named Teti follows the king when he leaves the palace at night to meet Sasenet at the general's house. The end of the story is not preserved. Clearly the king was meeting secretly with Sasenet. The true meaning of this secrecy cannot be determined.

Active and Passive Roles. A passage from the *Story of Horus and Seth* suggests that real condemnation of homosexual activity was reserved for the passive participant. In general the story is concerned with whether Horus or Seth is the rightful heir of Osiris to the throne of Egypt. There are several episodes where first Horus, then Seth, is judged the rightful heir. In this segment of the story, Seth suggests that Horus spend the evening with him. During the night Seth thinks he is ejaculating into Horus's thighs. Horus, however, collects Seth's semen in his hand. The next day, with his mother Isis's help, they trick Seth into eating Horus's semen, which Isis had spread on a lettuce leaf. Then, in front of the court composed of other gods, Seth is humiliated for having eaten Horus's semen. The court then rules that Horus is the rightful heir of Osiris. However, Seth successfully insists that there should be other tests before a final decision is made. It is difficult to know whether this is satire, humor, or condemnation. Again, modern subjectivity interferes with our understanding of the text.

Ostraca. Some *ostraca* found at Deir el Medina might well portray sex between adult men. The sketches are so cursory that it is not always possible to tell whether men or women are intended.

THE STORY OF HORUS AND SETH

Then Seth said to Horus, "Let us celebrate in my house." Then Horus said to him, "Yes, with great pleasure." Now when evening came, a bed was prepared for them. They spent the night together. At night, Seth made his phallus strong. He placed his phallus between Horus' thighs. Then Horus put his hand between his thighs. He received the semen of Seth. Then Horus went to say to his mother Isis, "Come to me Isis, my mother, that you might see that which Seth did to me." He opened his hand. He caused her to see the semen of Seth. She cried out. She seized her knife. She cut off his hand. She threw it in the water. She gave him a similar hand. Then she brought a little sweet ointment. She put it on the phallus of Horus. She caused it to be strong. She placed it in a pot. He caused his semen to go down into it. Then Isis went, carrying the semen of Horus in the morning to the garden of Seth. She said to the gardener, "What are the plants that Seth eats here with you?" Then the gardener said to her, "He does not eat any plant here with me except for lettuce." Then Isis placed the semen of Horus on them. Then Seth came, as was his daily custom. Then he ate the lettuce. . . . Then he stood up, pregnant from the semen of Horus. Then Seth went to Horus to say, "Come, let us go that I might contend with you in the court." Then Horus said, "I certainly will." Then they went to court together. They stood before the Great Ennead [the great gods]. Then One said, "Speak!" Then Seth said, "Come! Give to me the office of ruler because Horus, who stands here, I have done manly work on him." Then the Great Ennead cried a great cry. Then they spit on Horus. Then Horus laughed at them. Then Horus took an oath to god saying, "The statement of Seth is false. Let one call the semen of Seth that we might see that which answers and then call my own and see which answers." Then Thoth, Lord of Hieroglyphs, true scribe of the Ennead laid his hand on Horus' shoulder, saying, "Come out, oh semen of Seth." It answered him from the water. Then Thoth laid his hand on Seth's shoulder. He said, "Come out, oh semen of Horus." Then it said to him, "Where should I come out from?" Then Thoth said to it, "Come out from his ear." Then it said to him, "Should I, divine semen, come out from his ear?" Then Thoth said to it, "Come out from the horns [of his head]." Then it came forth as a sun disk of gold on Seth's head. Then Seth became very angry. He reached out his hand to the golden sun disk. Then Thoth seized it from him. . . . Then the Ennead said, "Horus is right, Seth is wrong."

Source: Translated by Edward Bleiberg, from Alan H. Gardiner, *Late Egyptian Stories* (Brussels: Fondation égyptologique reine Élizabeth, 1932), pp. 51–54. Published translation in Lise Manniche, *Sexual Life in Ancient Egypt* (New York: Methuen, 1987), pp. 56–57.

Then he noticed . . . Neferkare going out at night, all alone, with nobody with him. Then he removed himself from him, without letting him see. Hent's son Tjeti stood, thinking, "So this is it! What was said is true—he goes out at night." Hent's son Tjeti went just behind this god [the king] without letting his heart misgive him—to see all that he did. He (Neferkare) arrived at the house of General Sasenet. Then he threw a brick and kicked (the wall), so that a [ladder] was let down for him. Then he ascended while Hent's son Tjeti waited until [Neferkare] returned. Now after [Neferkare] had done what he desired with him, he returned to his palace, and Tjeti went behind him. . . . Now [Neferkare] went to the house of General Sasenet when four hours had passed of the night, he had spent another four hours in the house of General Sasenet and he entered the palace when there were four hours to dawn.

Source: R. B. Parkinson, *Voices from Ancient Egypt* (Norman: University of Oklahoma Press, 1991), p. 56.

Lesbianism. Female homosexuality is even more difficult to identify in the records from ancient Egypt. One *Book of the Dead* belonging to a woman includes the declaration, "I have not had intercourse with any woman in the sacred places of my city god." However, this phrase, found in *Books of the Dead* made for men, might have been an error in copying and adapting the text for a woman. Otherwise, no textual references to lesbians are known.

Sources:

Lise Manniche, *Sexual Life in Ancient Egypt* (New York: Methuen, 1987), pp. 22–27.

R. B. Parkinson, *Voices from Ancient Egypt* (Norman: University of Oklahoma Press, 1991), pp. 54–56.

B. G. Trigger, and others, *Ancient Egypt: A Social History* (Cambridge & New York: Cambridge University Press, 1983).

KINSHIP

Kinship Systems. Scholars have speculated, from the earliest attempts to read hieroglyphs, on the Egyptian kinship system. Much has been written about the importance of matriarchy in ancient Egypt, which modern Egyptologists no longer believe to be true. In fact, recent research has shown that the Egyptian kinship system was not vastly different from later European and American kinship systems. The basic relationships between mother, father, and child are the same in ancient as in modern times. The real difference that led earlier scholars astray was the way kinship terms, such as brother or sister, were used affectionately between lovers or spouses. This use suggested to earlier Egyptologists that incestuous marriages were common.

Terms. Basic kinship terms in ancient Egyptian are *mut* (mother), *jetey* (father), *sa* (son), *sat* (daughter), *sen* (brother), and *senet* (sister). German scholar Detlef Franke points out that these terms really represent four different root words. *Sa* and *sat* are merely the masculine and feminine grammatical forms of the same word; the same is true for *sen* and *senet*. Thus, the four basic relationships are among the mother, father, male or female child, and male or female sibling. All kinship relations were described using these four words. For example, they can be combined in the form *sa senetef* (son of his sister) to yield the meaning "his nephew." Other combinations are known that would be equivalent of niece, cousin, grandmother, and grandfather.

Extended Use of Kinship Terms. Real confusion for modern readers begins with the extended meanings of these terms to other familial generations. *Mut* can be used, along with its base meaning of mother, for grandmother, great-grandmother, or mother-in-law. The same sequence of father, grandfather, and father-in-law are possible translations for *jetey*. *Sa* can refer to grandson, great grandson, or son-in-law and *sat* can refer to granddaughter, great granddaughter or daughter-in-law. *Sen* can be an abbreviation for an uncle (father's/mother's brother), male cousin (father's/mother's brother's son), nephew (brother's/sister's son) or brother-in-law. *Senet* has a basic meaning, sis-

Statue of Meryetamun, daughter and wife of Ramesses II, circa 1279–1213 B.C.E., found northwest of the Ramesseum, Thebes (from Rita Freed, *Ramses II, 1987*)

This papyrus records two different legal actions. First, Nanefer/Rennefer is adopted by her husband, to increase her share of her inheritance of his estate. The second action allows Nanefer to adopt the children of a slave, as well as her own brother, to act as support in her old age.

Year 1, 3rd month of Summer, day 20 under the Majesty of the King of Upper and Lower Egypt, Ramesses (IX). . . . On this day, proclamation to Amun of the shining forth of this noble god, he arising and shining forth and making offering to Amun. Thereupon Nebnefer, my husband, made a writing for me, the musician of Seth, Nannefer, and made me a daughter of his, and wrote down for me all he possessed, having no son or daughter apart from myself. [The husband, Nebnefer, speaks] "All profit that I have made with her, I will bequeath it to Nanefer my wife, and if <any of> my own brothers or sisters arise to confront her at my death tomorrow or thereafter and say "Let my brother's share be given (to me)—" "Behold, I have made the bequest to Rennefer, my wife, this day before Hu-irymu, my sister."

Year 18, 1st month of Inundation, day 10, under the Majesty of the King of Upper and Lower Egypt, Ramesses (XI). . . . On this day, declaration made by the stable master Nebnefer and his wife the musician of Seth of Spermeru Rennefer, to wit:

"We purchased the female slave Dini-huriry and she gave birth to these three children, one male and two female, in all three. And I took them and nourished them and brought them up, and I have reached this day with them without their doing evil towards me, but they dealt well with me, I having no son or daughter except them. And the

stable master Padiu entered my house and took Taamon-niu their elder sister to wife, he being related to me and being my younger brother. And I accepted him for her and he is with her at this day. Now behold, I have made her a free woman of the land of Pharaoh, and if she bears either son or daughter, they shall be freemen of the land of Pharaoh in exactly the same way, they being with the stable master Padiu, this younger brother of mine. And the children shall be with their elder sister in the house of Padiu, this stable master, this younger brother of mine, and today I make him a son of mine exactly like them."

And she said:

"As Amun endures, and the Ruler endures, I hereby make the people whom I have put on record freemen of the land of Pharaoh, and if any son, daughter, brother, or sister of their mother and their father should contest their rights, except Padiu, this son of mine—for they are indeed no longer with him as servants, but are with him as younger siblings, being freemen of the land of Pharaoh—may a donkey copulate with him and a donkey with his wife, whoever it be that shall call any of them a servant. And if I have fields in the country, or if I have any property in the world, or if I have merchants (?), these shall be divided among my four children, Padiu being one of them. And as for these matters of which I have spoken, they are entrusted in their entirety to Padiu, this son of mine who dealt well with me when I was a widow and when my husband had died."

Before many and numerous witnesses. . . .

Source: *The Adoption Papyrus* (Papyrus Ashmolean Museum 1945.96), translated by Janet H. Johnson, in *Mistress of the House Mistress of Heaven: Women in Ancient Egypt,* edited by Anne K. Capel and Glenn E. Markoe (New York: Hudson Hills Press, 1996), p. 183.

ter, but also can mean aunt (father's/mother's sister), niece (brother's/sister's daughter), or sister-in-law. This pattern allows the whole generation of person's parents to be called brother or sister, and the whole generation of a person's children to be called son or daughter. But there is no real merging of the kinship relations. The difference between a father and a father's brother is maintained in inheritance issues. Egyptians also felt definite obligations both to relatives on the mother's and father's side of the family.

Matriarchy/Patriarchy. Textual evidence of the kinship system extends to the beginning of Egyptian history. There is no believable evidence of matriarchy (rule by women or through the woman's line) in Egyptian texts. On the other hand, there is evidence of patriarchy in all periods. Children could, however, inherit property both from their father and mother.

Larger Groups. The Egyptians also had five terms that have sometimes been understood to refer to extended family. Franke's dissertation describes the way the Egyptians used the terms *abut* (extended family), *weheyet* (village community), *henu* (coresidents), *wedjut* (coworkers), and

khet (group, corporation). The *abut* included a man and his relatives on both his mother's and father's side, his children, and his servants. It did not include his wife's family. This term went out of use at the end of Dynasty 6 (circa 2350–2170 B.C.E.). The *weheyet* was a group of families that all lived in the same place; the *henu* included everyone who lived in a household, whether or not they were blood relatives. This term replaced *abut* beginning in Dynasty 12 (circa 1938–1759 B.C.E.). The *wedjut* were people who worked at the same place. For example, all the workers in the Temple of Osiris were a *wedjut*. Finally, the *khet* was similar to the *wedjut,* though the former term is much older. *Khet* was used in Dynasty 2 (circa 2800–2675 B.C.E.) to indicate all the gods. Thus, Egyptians were involved in multiple, important relations based on kinship, hometown, and workplace that all included many mutual obligations.

Spousal Kinship. Husband and wife did not belong to each other's kinship group. They were both included, however, in the kinship group of each of their children. Husbands and wives had no control over the property owned by their spouse's family.

Stone relief from the tomb of Queen Meresankh showing a group of ten women from her extended family, Dynasty 4, circa 2625–2500 B.C.E.

THE DECLARATION OF NAUNAKHTE

The *Declaration of Naunakhte*, a Lady of the House in Deir el Medina during Dynasty 20 (circa 1190–1075 B.C.E.), was preserved on papyrus. In it Naunakhte explains that only some of her eight children will share in her estate after her death. Naunakhte felt that some of her children had neglected her during the period of her widowhood.

Year 3, fourth month of inundation, day 5 in the reign of . . . (Ramesses V), given life for ever and eternity.

This day the lady Naunakhte made a record of her property before the following court:

The chief workman Nakhte-em-Mut

The chief workman In-her-kau

(Other names)

She said: "As for me, I am a free woman of the land of Pharaoh. I raised these eight servants of yours, and I outfitted them with every thing that is usual for people of their character. Now look, I have become old, and look, they do not care for me. As for those who put their hands in my hand, to them I will give my property; (but) as for those who gave me nothing, to them I will not give of my property."

List of the men and women to whom she gave:

The workman Ma'a-nakhte-ef

The workman Qen her khepesh-ef, She said: "I will give him a bronze washing-bowl as a bonus over and above his fellows (worth) 10 sacks of emmer."

The workman Amen-nakhte

The lady Waset-nakhte

The lady Menet-nakhte.

As for the lady Menet-nakhte, she said regarding her, 'She will share in the division of all my property, except for the oipe of emmer that my three male children and the lady Waset-nakhte gave me or my hin of oil that they gave to me in the same fashion.'

List of her children of whom she said, 'They will not share in the division of my one-third, but only in the two-thirds (share) of their father.'

The workman Nefer-hotep

The lady Menet-nakhte

The lady Henut-senu

The lady Kha-ta-nebu

As for these four children of mine, they will not share in the division of all my property.

Now as for all the property of the scribe Qen-her-khepesh-ef, my (first) husband, and also his immovable property and the storehouse of my father, and also this oipe of emmer that I collected with my husband, they will not share in them.

But these eight children of mine will share in the division of the property of their father on equal terms.

Source: A. G. MacDowell, *Village Life in Ancient Egypt: Laundry Lists and Love Songs* (New York: Oxford University Press, 1999), pp. 38–40.

Social Status. During the Old, Middle, and New Kingdoms (circa 2675–1075 B.C.E.), social status was determined by rank at court. Kinship played a less-important role for Egyptians than rank and title.

Source:

Delef Franke, "Kinship," in *Oxford Encyclopedia of Ancient Egypt*, volume 1, edited by Donald B. Redford (Oxford & New York: Oxford University Press, 2001), pp. 245–248.

Sheila Whale, *The Family in the Eighteenth Dynasty of Egypt: A Study of Representations of the Family in Private Tombs* (Sydney: Australian Center for Egyptology Studies, 1989).

MARRIAGE: ANNUITY CONTRACTS

True Nature of Contracts. The documents that Egyptologists call marriage contracts in reality were not made to legitimate a marriage or the children born of a union. These contracts listed the husband's and wife's economic responsibilities to each other and their future children at the beginning of the relationship, during the marriage, and in the event of the marriage ending either by divorce or the death of one of the parties. Egyptologist Janet H. Johnson has suggested they ought really to be called annuity contracts.

Bride and Groom Make the Contract. Though these marriage or annuity agreements might have originally been negotiated between the bride's father and the groom, the preserved examples were all made between the bride and groom. This fact is remarkable when compared to the legal status of women in other parts of the contemporary world. In Greece, and in the ancient Near East, women in general had many fewer legal rights than women in Egypt, where women were considered competent to represent themselves in court and owned property without reference to fathers, brothers, or husbands. Thus, they also negotiated and signed their own marriage or annuity contracts.

Contents of Contracts. Typically in marriage or annuity contracts the groom and bride address each other in the first person. The groom recounts the property that the woman brought to the marriage. He also tells her that he will give her a gift at the start of the

Column 5 of the will of Naunakhte in which she disinherits four of her children, with a postscript confirming her second husband's agreement to the document, circa 1187–1156 B.C.E. (Ashmolean Museum, Oxford)

This contract, made in 198 B.C.E., reflects the practices of the preceding period but it is a complete example. It includes the date, interested parties, declaration that they are man and wife, marriage gift to the woman, children's rights of inheritance, pre-agreed divorce settlement from the husband, a list of property the woman brought to the marriage, and a pledge to return all the woman's property in the event of divorce.

Date: Year 8 . . . of Ptolemy Soter and Pharaoh Ptolemy, the god Epiphanes.

Parties: Said the man of Afonti Petosiri son of Patseo and Takhnum, his mother to the lady Tshenese daughter of Petipanebtaoui and Tamerihet, her mother:

Declaration: I made you as wife.

Bride Gift: I gave to you money, 3 deben, makes 15 stators, makes money, 3 deben again as your woman's gift.

Inheritance: The children whom you will bear to me and Petihorouer, my eldest son, together with the lady Taioui, his sister, my children whom you bore to me, are the owners of all and everything which is mine, together with that which I will acquire, together with the goods of father and mother in field, temple, and the town.

Divorce: If I leave you as wife and I prefer another woman to you as wife, I will give to you money 5 deben, makes 25 stators, makes money 5 deben again, in addition to the money 3 deben, which is above and which I gave to you as your woman's gift which amounts to money 8 deben, makes 40 stators, makes money 8 deben again.

Possessions of Wife: Here is the inventory of the woman's possession which you brought to my house with you:

One Necklace	Makes money, 3 deben in the name of your woman's gift which is above;
Two pairs of gold?	Makes gold by weight 5¼ kite
One ? ring	Makes gold by weight 2¼ kite
One pair of ? rings	Makes gold by weight 2 kite
One ?	Makes gold by weight ½ kite
Makes gold by weight 1 deben makes 5 stators makes gold by weight 1 deben again	
One ? cloak	Makes money 30 deben
One garment	Makes money, 20 deben
One shawl	Makes money 5 deben
One ? garment	Makes money, 10 deben
One ?	Makes money 2 deben, 8 kite
One . . .	Makes money 10 deben
One ladle	Makes money 1 deben
One ? which is inscribed	Makes gold by weight 1½ kite
Money as money, 1 deben	Makes 5 stators, makes money, 1 deben again
Worked copper one large container	Makes by weight 10 deben
One small container	Makes by weight 2 deben
One mirror	Makes by weight 10 deben
One brazier	Makes by weight 30 deben
One ? vessel	Makes by weight 1 deben 5
Total value of the possessions which are above.	
Gold by weight	1 deben, 1½ kite makes 5 [plus] 1½ [plus] ¼ stators makes gold by weight 1 deben 1½ kite again
Money 1 deben; copper 86 deben, 8 kite	Total of money as money and copper: 87 deben, 8 kite, makes 439 stators, makes money, 87 deben, 8 kite again
Worked copper by weight	53 deben 5 kite

Total of the woman's possessions which you brought to my house with you.
I received them from you; they are complete without any remainder; my heart is satisfied with them.

Divorce: If you go away, I will give them to you. If I leave you as wife, I will also give them to you compulsorily, without delay. Yours are the _____ of all and everything which will come into being between me and you from today henceforth.

Any man in the world who will throw you out of my house and remove my possessions from your presence he will do for you the law of this document of wife which is above,

which I made for you compulsorily without delay without any blow.

Wrote Petosiri son of Patseo himself, I will act in accordance with everything which is above.

Source: Papyrus Berlin 13593, translated by Cary J. Martin, in *The Elephantine Papyri in English: Three Millennia of Cross-Cultural Continuity and Change,* edited by Bezalel Porten (Leiden & New York: E. J. Brill, 1996), pp. 366–370.

union and sets an exact monetary value. He also tells her that the property he owned prior to the marriage would be her security in the event that she wants her own property back, and that no matter who initiates a divorce, she will receive the equivalent of her property back. He also states that he will continue to support her until he is able to actually give her the property. The nature of this support is also detailed, giving the amount of clothing and food she will receive monthly until she recovers her property back in full. These contracts also mention the penalties if a man defaults on making his monthly payments. Finally, the woman will return the contract to the man when she receives her property back.

Sources:

Janet H. Johnson, "The Legal Status of Women in Ancient Egypt," in *Mistress of the House Mistress of Heaven: Women in Ancient Egypt*, edited by Anne K. Capel and Glenn E. Markoe (New York: Hudson Hills Press, 1996), pp. 175–186.

P. W. Pestman, *Marriage and Matrimonial Property in Ancient Egypt: A Contribution to Establishing the Legal Position of the Woman* (Leiden: E. J. Brill, 1961).

Joyce Tyldesley, *Daughters of Isis: Women of Ancient Egypt* (London & New York: Viking, 1994).

MARRIAGE: BROTHER AND SISTER

Kings. Brother-sister marriage was limited to the royal family in most periods of ancient Egyptian history. The king thus imitated the god Osiris, who married his sisters Isis and Nephthys. An explanation provided by early scholars of this practice, that kingship passed through the female line, has been disproved by the Egyptologist Gay Robins. Betsy M. Bryan has sug-

---

THE STORY OF SETNE KHAEMWAS

[When the steward of the palace came] Pharaoh [said to him]: "Steward, let Ahwere be taken to the house of Nanneferkaptah tonight, and let all sorts of beautiful things be taken with her."

I was taken as a wife to the house of Naneferkaptah [that night, and Pharaoh] sent me a present of silver and gold, and all Pharaoh's household sent me presents. Naneferkaptah made holiday with me, and he entertained all Pharaoh's household. He slept with me that night and found me [pleasing. He slept with] me again and again, and we lived with each other.

When my time of purification came I made no more purification. [meaning she was pregnant] It was reported to Pharaoh, and his heart was very happy. Pharaoh had many things taken [out of the treasury] and sent me presents of silver, gold, and royal linen, all very beautiful. When my time of bearing came, I bore this boy who is before you, who was named Merib.

Source: Miriam Lichtheim, "Setne Khaemwas and Naneferkaptah," in *Ancient Egyptian Literature*, volume 3, edited by Lichtheim (Berkeley: University of California Press, 1980), p. 128.

ADVICE ON SEXUALITY

The wisdom of the sage Any, Dynasty 18 (circa 1539–1295/1292 B.C.E.), represents widely held views in ancient Egypt.

Beware of a woman who is a stranger,

One not known in her town;

Don't stare at her when she goes by,

Do not know her carnally.

A deep water whose course is unknown,

Such is a woman away from her husband.

"I am pretty," she tells you daily,

When she has no witnesses;

She is ready to ensnare you,

A great deadly crime when it is heard.

Source: "The Instructions of Any," translated by Miriam Lichtheim, in *Ancient Egyptian Literature*, edited by Lichtheim (Berkeley: University of California Press, 1973), p. 137.

---

gested that incestuous marriage had the practical value of keeping property within the royal family. The best-known examples of brother-sister marriage were practiced by the Ptolemaic kings. Because these rulers were actually Greek, perhaps they emphasized the imitation of Osiris's marriages to validate their claims to the Egyptian throne.

NonRoyal Intrafamily Marriage. Though elite members of Egyptian society often married cousins, or their father's or mother's siblings, brother-sister marriage was not commonly practiced. Egyptologist Jaroslav Cerný has demonstrated that some of the confusion on this issue stems from terms of endearment used during the New Kingdom (circa 1539–1075 B.C.E.), when lovers sometimes referred to each other as *brother* or *sister*. This custom is found even on stelae. Cerný has shown, however, that this practice never occurs in legal documents before the Roman Period (circa 30 B.C.E. and after). Remarkably, Roman census records from the town of Arsinoe in the Faiyum reveal up to 25 percent of marriages were between full brothers and sisters. This rate was not repeated in any other census records from the Roman Period. The reasons for this unusual practice are not understood.

Sources:

Betsy M. Bryan, "The 18th Dynasty before the Amarna Period," in *The Oxford History of Ancient Egypt*, edited by Ian Shaw (Oxford & New York: Oxford University Press, 2000), pp. 218–271.

Jaroslav Cerný, "Consanguineous Marriages in Pharaonic Egypt," *Journal of Egyptian Archaeology*, 40 (December 1954): 23–29.

Gay Robins, *Women in Ancient Egypt* (Cambridge, Mass.: Harvard University Press, 1993; London: British Museum Press, 1993).

Relief of Kai and his wife, from the Tomb of Kai at
Giza, Old Kingdom, circa 2675–2130 B.C.E.

MARRIAGE: CELEBRATIONS

Family Celebrations. Though there was no official
state marriage license and religious ceremony, the
ancient Egyptians celebrated the beginning of a marriage. The Late Period (664–332 B.C.E.) text called *The
Story of Setne Khaemwast* narrates the marriage of
Ahwere, a daughter of Ramesses II (circa 1279–1213
B.C.E.), and Naneferkaptah, her brother. The story was
written long after the actual lifetime of Ramesses II and
his children, and probably reflects elite marriage customs of the period after 664 B.C.E., as well as the
belief—even among Egyptians—that brothers and sisters married in earlier times.

Marriage in the Story. Ahwere and Naneferkaptah
fell in love and their parents, in this case Pharaoh,
arranged the marriage. The bride went to the groom's
house, where she received presents. Her own father
gave the largest present. The couple had a party, retired
to consummate the marriage, and lived together after
that. The marriage meant that they would live together
and establish a household.

Sources:
Gay Robins, *Women in Ancient Egypt* (Cambridge, Mass.: Harvard University Press, 1993; London: British Museum Press, 1993).

Miriam Stead, *Egyptian Life* (Cambridge, Mass.: Harvard University
Press, 1986).

Barbara Watterson, *Women in Ancient Egypt* (New York: St. Martin's
Press, 1991).

ADVICE ON MARRIAGE

The sage Any, Dynasty 18 (circa 1539–1295/1292
B.C.E.), counseled prospective grooms:

Take a wife while you're young,

That she might make a son for you;

She should bear for you while you're youthful,

It is proper to make people.

Happy the man whose people are many,

He is saluted on account of his progeny.

Source: "The Instructions of Any," translated by Miriam Lichtheim, in
Ancient Egyptian Literature, edited by Lichtheim (Berkeley: University of
California Press, 1973), p. 136.

OLD AGE

Modern and Ancient Definitions. Old age in American society, especially the modern view of when the
period starts, has shifted dramatically in the last century. At the beginning of the twentieth century, life
expectancy was approximately forty-four years, but at
the start of the following century, it had lengthened to
roughly seventy-two years. The useful definitions of old
age are not expressed in years but rather in changes of
function in society and the onset of biological decline.
The Egyptians defined old age as the time when a person could no longer perform the functions of an active
adult and when they experienced physical infirmity.
Life expectancy at birth was roughly thirty-five years,
but for those living beyond five years, life expectancy
was higher. At age forty a person usually was considered
quite old.

Infirmities. Egyptian texts deal specifically with the
kinds of infirmities associated with old age. Ptahhotep,
the Dynasty 5 (circa 2500–2350 B.C.E.) vizier who is
credited with writing a wisdom text, described the old
as feeble, tired, silent, and achy. He says the old are
unable to remember the past, cannot taste their food,
and have pain whether standing or sitting. The Egyptologists Rosalind and Jacobus Janssen have observed
that the Egyptians emphasized the disadvantages of old
age rather than noting the valuable wisdom acquired by
the old, as is true in other traditional societies.

Terms for Old Age. The Egyptians used three different words—*yau, teni,* and *kehkeh*—for old age, but
the nuances of these different terms are not clear. The
determinatives used as the last hieroglyphic sign in
these words are both a man leaning over supported by a
stick and the pustule, which was also used as the determinative for the word for disease. These determinatives,
meant to place the words into a general class of ideas,
also reflect the idea that the Egyptians thought of old
age in terms of physical decline.

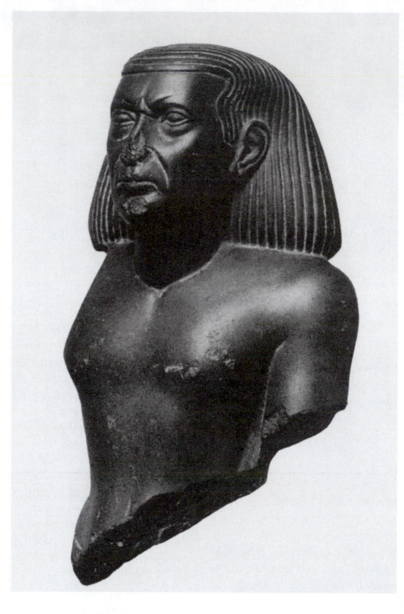

Bust of an unknown elderly Egyptian man, Dynasty 26, 664–525 B.C.E. (Walters Art Gallery, Baltimore)

Reliefs and Paintings. Depictions of the elite in old age are rare, while old workmen are more often portrayed in reliefs and paintings. Egyptian tombs, the source of most relief sculptures and paintings depicting people, were intended to rejuvenate the deceased for rebirth into the next world. It is unlikely that the deceased would want to be represented as old. The Janssens have suggested that representations of portly men in their tombs might be old people. Certainly such representations portray elite men at the height of their successful careers. In that sense they might be considered old. A rare New Kingdom (circa 1539–1075 B.C.E.) representation of an old nobleman, located now in the Brooklyn Museum, shows a man with a wrinkled forehead, deep wrinkles around the nose and mouth, a double chin, prominent collarbone, and a thin arm and wrist stretched out in greeting. Old servants or workers are

DECREE OF THUTMOSE IV

My Majesty has ordered the receiving of a goodly old age in the favor of the king, while care is taken of the standard bearer Nebamun of the royal vessel Meryamun. He has reached old age while following Pharaoh in steadfastness, and being better today than yesterday, in performing what was put in his charge, without being reproached.

I have not found any fault in him, although he was accused as an offender. Now my Majesty has ordered to appoint him to be police chief on the West of the City (of Thebes), in the places Tembu and Obau, until he will reach the blessed state of the dead.

Source: Rosalind M. and Jac. J. Janssen, *Growing Up in Ancient Egypt* (London: Rubicon Press, 1990), p. 103.

Stone relief of an old woman, from the tomb of Ti, Saqqara, Old Kingdom, circa 2675–2130 B.C.E.

often shown as bald, portly, and naked. Sometimes the legs appear to be misshapen.

Statuary. The statuary of kings and other noblemen sometimes portrayed the subjects as aged. The most famous examples come from the reign of Senwosret III (circa 1836–1818 B.C.E.). Senwosret's face is wrinkled and careworn, yet his body in the same statues is regularly shown as young, slim, and muscular. This same style was revived in late Dynasty 25 (circa 760–656 B.C.E.) and early Dynasty 26 (664–525 B.C.E.) for portraits of the Mayor of Thebes, Montuemhet.

Living With Family. Texts from Dynasty 12 (circa 1938–1759 B.C.E.) suggest that elderly mothers sometimes lived in the same household with their eldest sons after the death of their husbands. A census from the town of Kahun in Lower (northern) Egypt traces the changes in the household of a soldier named Hori. In the first census, Hori, his wife Shepset, and their infant son Sneferu, are living alone. In the next census, which occurred an unknown number of years later, significant changes had occurred. Now Hori's mother, along with her five daughters, had joined Hori's household. Probably this move occurred after the death of Hori's father. In the next census, Sneferu is now the head

of the household that consists of his widowed mother, his grandmother, and two of his aunts. The second text is a letter from a man named Heqanakht to his family. The household consists of his mother; his aunt; his married son, whose children also live with him; four younger, unmarried

---

PTAHHOTEP ON OLD AGE

Old age is here, high age has arrived,
Feebleness comes, weakness grows,
Childlike one sleeps all day.
Eyes are dim, ears are deaf,
Strength is waning, one is weary,
The mouth is silenced, speaks not,
The heart, void, recalls not the past.
The bones ache throughout.
Good has become evil, all taste is gone.
What age does to people is bad in every respect.
The nose, clogged, cannot breath,
Painful are standing and sitting.

Source: Rosalind M. and Jac. J. Janssen, *Growing Up in Ancient Egypt* (London: Rubicon Press, 1990), p. 5.

First census:

"The soldier, Dhuti's son Hori;

his wife, Satsopudu's daughter Shepset;

their son Sneferu."

Second census:

"The soldier Dhuti's son Hori;

his wife, Satsopudu's daughter Shepset;

Hori's mother Harekhni;

Her daughters Qatsennut, Mekten, Ese, Rudet, and Satsnefru."

Third Census

"The soldier, Hori's son, Sneferu.

His mother, Satsopudu's daughter Shepset;

His father's mother Harekhni;

His father's sisters Ese and Satsnefru."

Source: Rosalind M. and Jac. J. Janssen, *Growing Up in Ancient Egypt* (London: Rubicon Press, 1990), p. 38.

---

sons; a second wife; and several servants. Both Hori and Heqanakht belonged to nonelite families. Clearly, for the majority of people, aged or widowed parents lived together with them.

Ideal Old Age. Many texts from ancient Egypt refer to reaching the ideal age one hundred and ten years. Often such an age is described as "beautiful," probably meaning "whole" or "healthy." No Egyptians are known to have reached such a great age, though a few historical figures such as Amenhotep son of Hapu, builder for Amenhotep III (circa 1390–1353 B.C.E.), lived into his nineties. Nefer-kare Pepy II is thought to have reigned ninety-four years (circa 2288–2224/2194 B.C.E.) and perhaps lived until his one hundredth birthday.

Staff of Old Age. The expression "staff of old age" referred to the son of a retired man. Upper-class Egyptians hoped that their sons would follow them in office. When a man reached the point that he could no longer perform all the functions of an office, he could request that his son be appointed a "staff of old age." The son could then perform many of the functions of the office while the father still retained the title and presumably controlled the income from an office. The image, of course, is related to the tall sticks used by the elderly in Egypt to help support themselves. This title is attested in Dynasty 12 and Dynasty 18 (circa 1539–1295/1292 B.C.E.).

Pensions. Pensions took many forms in Egypt, none of which exactly correlate with modern ideals. Older laborers at Deir el Medina who could no longer work received a

reduced ration. They probably were supported by a son who had become a member of the work crew. Soldiers in the reign of Ramesses II (circa 1279–1213 B.C.E.) received grants of land at the close of their service. This land, which they were required to work themselves, provided an income in old age. Higher officials received a kind of pension in the form of rations paid to their tombs. These rations might not have actually supported the family of the deceased though they did support the cult of a high official. Other high army officials became priests. A priestly position probably was less physically demanding than army life and the income could support an older person. In another unusual case, a standard bearer on a navy ship was appointed police chief by Thutmose IV (circa 1400–1390 B.C.E.) in order to provide for his old age.

Sources:

Rosalind M. and Jac. J. Janssen, *Getting Old in Ancient Egypt* (London: Rubicon Press, 1996).

Janssen and Janssen, *Growing Up in Ancient Egypt* (London: Rubicon Press, 1990).

B. G. Trigger, and others, *Ancient Egypt: A Social History* (Cambridge & New York: Cambridge University Press, 1983).

PROSTITUTION

Sources. The only explicit references to woman accepting money in return for sex in ancient Egypt date after 450 B.C.E. Other references to "temple prostitutes" are either ambiguous or depend on the Greek understanding of Egyptian customs. These sources may be reliable or may reflect a projection of Greek customs onto Egyptian culture.

Priestesses. Two titles of priestesses might refer to women who had sexual intercourse with the priest who imitated the god in rituals. The "God's Wife" might have played the sexual role of a spouse during the "Sacred Marriage" between the god Amun and his wife. It is difficult to know how literally the title should be taken. The title "God's Hand" refers to the priestess who either literally or ritually re-enacted the creation of the world with a priest who represented the god Atum, who had created the world through masturbation. In any case, this was not truly a case of prostitution where money changed hands for male pleasure. Herodotus, who wrote circa 450 B.C.E., specifically said that only virgins served in the temple. Strabo, on the other hand, reports in 25 B.C.E. that the "most beautiful girls" were temple prostitutes, until the onset of menstruation, when they would marry. Strabo almost surely reflects here negative Roman feelings toward Egyptian religion.

Prostitutes at Deir el Medina? The Egyptologist Lise Manniche believes that there is archaeological and textual evidence for prostitutes at Deir el Medina. She believes that since wives were buried with their husbands and children, the tombs belonging to women who were buried only with their children represented those of prostitutes. Rosalind and Jacobus Janssen believe that the *Turin Erotic Papyrus,* which probably originated in Deir el Medina, depicts a visit to a brothel. This papyrus contains twelve drawings that show a man, with an over-

Setne was strolling in the forecourt of the temple of Ptah. Then he saw [a woman] who was very beautiful, there being no other woman like her in appearance. She was beautiful and wore many golden jewels, and maid servants walked behind her. . . . Setne saw her and he did not know where on earth he was. He called his man servant, saying "Hasten to the place where this woman is, and find out what her position is." The man servant hastened to the place where the woman was. He called to the maid servant who was following her . . . saying . . . "What woman is this?" She told him, "It is Tabubu, the daughter of the prophet of Bastet. . . . She has come here to worship Ptah, the great god."

The servant returned to Setne. . . . Setne said to the servant: "Go, say to the maid, 'It is Setne . . . who has sent me to say. . . 'I will give you ten pieces of gold—spend an hour with me. . . . '"

Then the servant returned to the place where Tabubu was. He called her maid and told her. She cried out as if what he said was an insult. Tabubu said to the servant: "Stop talking to this foolish maid; come and speak with me." [Setne's servant repeats the offer directly to Tabubu.]

Tabubu said: "Go tell Setne, 'I am of priestly rank, I am not a low person. If you desire to do what you wish with me, you must come to Bubastis, to my house . . . and you shall do what you wish with me . . . without my acting like a low woman of the street."

Then the servant returned to Setne and told him everything she had said to him. He said, "That suits me."

[Setne travels to Bubastis and finds her house.] Setne walked up the stairs of the house with Tabubu. He found the upper story of the house swept and adorned . . . Many couches were in it spread with royal linen. . . . A golden cup was put in his hand.

Setne said to Tabubu: "Let us accomplish what we have come here for." [She answers,] "If you desire to do what you wish with me, you must make for me a deed of maintenance and of compensation in money for everything, all goods belonging to you."

[After doing what she asks, she demands that his children agree. Setne has his children brought and has them sign the deed. Then he says] "Let me accomplish what I have come for." . . . [Then she says,] "If you desire to do what you wish with me, you must have your children killed. . . . ' [Setne answers] "Let the abomination that came into your head be done to them." She had his children killed before him. She had them thrown down from the window to the dogs and cats. They ate their flesh, and he heard them as he drank with Tabubu. . . .

He lay down on a couch . . . his wish about to be fulfilled. Tabubu lay down beside Setne. He stretched out his hands to touch her . . . [and] Setne awoke in a state of great heat . . . there were no clothes on him.

Source: Miriam Lichtheim, *Ancient Egyptian Literature*, volume 3 (Berkeley: University of California Press, 1976), pp. 133–136.

---

sized phallus, depicted in various positions with a woman. Many commentators believe the scenes are satirical or perhaps a commentary on religious practices. For example, in one scene the woman could be imitating the goddess Nut as she arches her body over the man in imitation of the scenes found on the lids of coffins and tomb paintings. But the papyrus also depicts intercourse carried out between a man and a woman in a chariot, while two other nude women pull it. The final scene shows the man exhausted, resting under a bed, as the woman continues to coax him. The scenes might represent more than one man and woman. The man's facial features are not always exactly the same from scene to scene, though if it is more than one man, they are all bald and have stubble beards. The Janssens believe the intention is to satirize an elderly man's desire. It is equally possible that these scenes represent an erotic fantasy, similar to those that Deir el Medina artists drew on *ostraca* depicting men and women together, sometimes in the presence of other adults and even children. The meaning of these scenes cannot be determined without considerable subjectivity. The only sure thing that can be said is that vivid erotic imaginations have existed throughout history.

Late Period Prostitutes. The story known as *Setne and Tabubu*, written in Demotic during the Ptolemaic Period (332–30 B.C.E.), portrays clear evidence that prostitution was known at the end of ancient Egyptian history. In the story, Setne is infatuated with a woman named Tabubu, whom he saw in the forecourt of Ptah's temple. He initially offers her ten pieces of gold for one hour of her sexual favors. Tabubu replies, "I am of priestly rank, I am not a low person. If you desire to do what you wish with me, you must come. . . to my house. . . without my acting like a low woman of the street." Here Tabubu seems to distinguish between expensive courtesans and streetwalkers. The story further illustrates the dangers of such a liaison as Tabubu's demands increase—from money, to Setne's house, to disinheriting his children in her favor, and finally to murdering his children so they can not contest their disinheritance. Luckily for Setne, he wakes at the end of the story to find it was only a bad dream.

Sources:

Anne K. Capel and Glenn E. Markoe, eds., *Mistress of the House, Mistress of Heaven: Women in Ancient Egypt* (New York: Hudson Hills, 1996).

Lise Manniche, *Sexual Life in Ancient Egypt* (New York: Methuen, 1987), pp. 12–19.

George Ryley Scott, *A History of Prostitution from Antiquity to the Present Day*, revised edition (London: Torchstream Books, 1954).

SCRIBAL EDUCATION

Purpose. Scribal education was designed to train supervisors for overseeing work in administration, construction, and temples. In most periods scribal education was available only to male children of the elite. The only exception was during the Middle Kingdom (circa 1980–1630 B.C.E.) when a shortage of scribes led to the possibility of upward mobility. Some sort of scribal education was also available to artisans at Deir el Medina. Egyptian education was available to the sons of foreign rulers during Dynasty 18 (circa 1539–1295/ 1292 B.C.E.). Thutmose III (circa 1479–1425 B.C.E.) used scribal education as a means to "Egyptianize" conquered foreign rulers. In all periods, scribal education was the key to success in Egyptian society.

How Many Scribes? Though some scholars have estimated that only 1 percent of the Egyptian population was literate, this number probably applies only to the percentage of Egyptians who were fully educated. A larger number of craftsmen and artisans most likely could write their names, or recognize the names of kings in hieroglyphs, without being fully literate. Other people paid village scribes to write letters and help them with other sorts of business that required writing.

Teaching Methods. Students first learned cursive hieroglyphs, which are a simplified writing of the elaborate signs seen on temple and tomb walls. They then progressed to hieratic, the equivalent of handwriting in English. Hieratic writing bases its signs on hieroglyphs but omits all detail and often joins one sign to another. The ordinary scribe had little need to learn to write the

Limestone ostracon with the "Instruction of Amennakht," twelve lines of hieratic written by an apprentice scribe Dynasty 20, circa 1190–1075 B.C.E. (British Museum, London)

elaborate hieroglyphs found on temple and tomb walls, a task limited to artists, but surely they could read these wall texts.

Memorization. Student scribes first learned to write, and at the same time memorize, the great classics of Egyptian literature. The average scribe was expected to learn and recite texts such as the epic *Story of Sinuhe* and religious texts. The only word meaning "to read" in Egyptian is the same as the one used for "to recite aloud."

Materials. Students learned to write on limestone flakes called *ostraca*, which were abundant near the edge of the desert. They made a good, flat writing surface. After a student had reached mastery, he was permitted to write on the more-expensive papyrus. *Ostraca* that have survived display handwriting that is much more difficult to read than that found on papyrus and also have more mistakes in spelling and grammar. Yet, *ostraca* were sometimes used by poorer people for writing legal documents.

School Subjects. Though learning to write was the most important skill for scribes, other subjects formed part of their education, including letter-writing formulae (epistolography), grammar, orthography (spelling), rhetoric, foreign languages, onomastics (lists), geography, arithmetic, and geometry.

ADVICE ON EDUCATION

The sage Any, during Dynasty 18 (circa 1539–1295/ 1292 B.C.E.), advised students that:

One will do all you say

If you are versed in writings;

Study all the writings, put them in your heart,

Then all your words will be effective.

Whatever office a scribe is given,

He should consult the writings;

The head of the treasury has not a son,

The master of the seal has no heir.

The scribe is chosen for his hand,

His office has no children;

His pronouncements are his freemen,

His functions are his masters.

Source: "The Instructions of Any," translated by Miriam Lichtheim, *Ancient Egyptian Literature*, edited by Lichtheim (Berkeley: University of California Press, 1973), p. 140.

Letter-Writing Formulae. Letters followed a standard format with three parts. The introduction was a greeting that recommended the receiver to the gods. The content of the letter followed and could concern personal matters or business. The letter closed with an address.

Grammar. Egyptian students were taught the elements of proper grammar. One exercise from Dynasties 19 (circa 1292–1190 B.C.E.) or 20 (circa 1190–1075 B.C.E.) reveals a student's attempt to conjugate verbs. Unlike English, the order of conjugation is "I, he, you (singular), we, they, you (plural)."

Orthography. Spelling mistakes made by school boys suggest that they were taught to write whole words rather than individual hieroglyphic or hieratic signs. Perhaps there is some confirmation of this theory in the way the Egyptians spoke of hieroglyphs, which they called god's words (*medu netjer*), rather than god's signs.

Rhetoric. Attention to "proper speech" was an intense concern in the advice given to students. Though the exact definition of proper speech was never described, known examples are extremely involved couplets and triplets that repeat the same thought more than once. The writers who discuss proper speech sometimes claim that it was not limited to the educated elite. Ptahhotep, a sage who perhaps lived in the Old Kingdom (circa 2675–2130 B.C.E.), believed that "Proper speech is more hidden than green stone, yet may be found among maids at the grindstones." The farmer who is the hero of the text called "The Eloquent Peasant" spoke so impressively that the king himself wrote down his words.

Foreign Languages. Reading, writing, and speaking foreign languages must have been an important skill for some scribes. The Amarna Letters, dating to the reigns of Amenhotep III (circa 1390–1353 B.C.E.) and Amenhotep IV (Akhenaten, circa 1353–1336 B.C.E.), were written in Akkadian, the language of Mesopotamia. Egyptians surely could both read the letters and compose answers. Some of the scribes of these letters clearly have Egyptian names. A writing board from Dynasty 18 is headed, "To make the names of Keftiu," an apparent attempt to write in the language, called Linear A, of Crete. The Egyptians traded extensively with the Minoans of Crete and must have learned their language. The exact means of learning foreign languages is unknown.

Making Lists. Onomastics are lists that categorize important information. This system of categorizing information perhaps began in Babylonia, but it was widely used by the Egyptians. Scribes memorized lists of town names, classes of people, professions, titles in the administration, and names of animals.

Geography. Written in the form of lists, which compiled the names of towns located along roads or rivers, geography was an important area of knowledge for

Scribal palette with a slot for storing reed pens and two inkwells, circa 1479–1425 B.C.E. (University of California, Berkeley)

A LETTER FROM ANCIENT EGYPT CONCERNING LAND USE

This letter, written in Dynasty 21 (circa 1075–945 B.C.E.), demonstrates the three basic divisions of a standard letter in ancient Egypt. The proper form for such letters would be a major subject for scribal education.

Greeting

The lieutenant and scribe of the Temple of Khonsu, Shed-su-khonsu, to the Kushite youth, Pay-neb-andjed. I greet you in life, prosperity, and health and in the favor of Amun-Re, King of the Gods, your good lord. May he give you life, prosperity, and health.

Content

Now then: I went to Thebes after I had said to you, "I will not let you plough anymore." Now look, my wife, the Mistress of my house said to me, "Do no take away this field from Pay-neb-andjed." Then I said, "Assign it to him! Let him plough it." When my letter reaches you, you give your attention to this field and you will not be lax concerning it. And you will remove its weeds and you will plough it. And you will make one aroura of the land vegetables near its plot of land. Now if anyone argues with you [about the land] you will go to Wer-djehouty, the Scribe of the Reckoning in the House of Osiris. You will take this letter with you. Indeed I have provided you my field of fresh land and my field of muddy ground also. And guard my letter in order that it may serve for you as an authorization.

Address

To the Youth of Kush, Pay-neb-andjed

Source: *Papyrus Berlin 8523*, translated by Edward Bleiberg. For other ancient Egyptian letters see Edward S. Wente, *Letters from Ancient Egypt* (Atlanta: Society for Biblical Literature, 1990).

---

scribes. The author of the "Satirical Letter," a text that dates to the Ramesside Period (circa 1292–1075 B.C.E.), accused his reader of not knowing this basic information.

Arithmetic and Geometry. Scribes kept accounts for institutions and were familiar with addition, subtraction, multiplication, and division. Geometry problems were also studied, often from texts written in such a manner that general principles could be deduced.

Educational Institutions. Schools existed in some periods, but they were not the only means of obtaining an education. The text called the *Instructions of Dua-Khety* begins with a father taking his son to school in the Dynasty 12 (circa 1938–1759 B.C.E.) capital of Itjet-Tawy near Memphis. The *kap*, an institution attached to the woman's quarters in the royal palace, was a place where elite children studied alongside the princes. Many of the children at Deir el Medina, however, were taught by their fathers or grandfathers. They may have been tutored part-time, then learned further skills on the job. During this period of apprenticeship, in which they acted as assistants, students were described as "under the hand of the scribe."

Sources:
Raffaella Cribiore, *Writing, Teachers, and Students in Graeco-Roman Egypt* (Atlanta: Scholars Press, 1996).

Hans-W. Fischer-Elfert, "Education," in *Oxford Encyclopedia of Ancient Egypt*, volume 1, edited by Donald B. Redford (Oxford & New York: Oxford University Press, 2001), pp. 438–442.

Ronald J. Williams, "Scribal Training in Ancient Egypt," *Journal of the American Oriental Society*, 92 (1972): 214–221.

SIGNIFICANT PEOPLE

NANEFER (RENNEFER)

FLOURISHED CIRCA 1104-1075 B.C.E.
MUSICIAN OF SETH

Adopted By Her Husband. During the reign of Ramesses XI, Nanefer, who was also known as Rennefer, was married to a stable master named Nebnefer. Their relationship must have been unusually close. Because they had no children, Nebnefer legally adopted his wife as his daughter. This legal procedure allowed Nanefer to inherit more than the usual one-third of her husband's estate. In fact, Nebnefer specifically disinherited his brothers and sisters, who would normally have received a share of his estate since he had no children. Nanefer now could receive the entire estate upon her husband's death.

Adopting Slave Children. Eighteen years passed. During this time Nanefer and Nebnefer purchased a slave girl, who gave birth to three children, a boy and two girls. Nanefer raised the children as if they were her own. At the same time, the children behaved toward her as if she were their mother. When the elder girl, Taamon-niu, reached marriageable age, Nanefer decided that she should marry. Nanefer chose her own brother, Padiu, to become Taamun-niu's husband. At the same time, Nanefer freed all three of her adopted children from slavery and adopted her brother, all of whom could then inherit her estate upon her death. In the meantime, they supported her in her widowhood.

Unusual Document. All of these circumstances were recorded in an unusual document called *The Adoption Papyrus* (Papyrus Ashmolean Museum 1945.96). The papyrus, written at one time, summarizes two legal processes that took place eighteen years apart—a husband adopting his wife, and then the wife adopting her brother and the offspring of her slave. The purpose of the two original legal actions must have been to protect Nanefer's economic position. First, she was able to claim a larger share of her husband's estate, taking a child's share rather than one dictated for a wife. Then, after her husband died, she could count on her adopted children to continue to support her from the proceeds of her land and other property. She would therefore have help from trusted managers who were related to her.

Sources:
The Adoption Papyrus (Papyrus Ashmolean Museum 1945.96), translated by Janet H. Johnson, in *Mistress of the House, Mistress of Heaven: Women in Ancient Egypt*, edited by Anne K. Capel and Glenn E. Markoe (New York: Hudson Hills Press, 1996), p. 183.

E. Cruz-Uribe, "A New Look at the Adoption Papyrus," *Journal of Egyptian Archaeology*, 74 (1988): 220–223.

C. J. Eyre, "The Adoption Papyrus in Social Context," *Journal of Egyptian Archaeology*, 78 (1992): 207–221.

NAUNAKHTE

FLOURISHED CIRCA 1190-1075 B.C.E.
LADY OF THE HOUSE IN DEIR EL MEDINA

Two Marriages. The Lady of the House, Naunakhte, was typical of many women in Deir el Medina. In the course of her life she married twice. Her first husband was the scribe Qen-her-khepesh-ef, a man who was probably older than she was. There is no record that they had children together. At his death, she inherited one-third of his property. This inheritance, made when she was still of childbearing age, made Naunakhte an eligible woman. Her second husband was a workman named Kha-em-nun. Perhaps her second marriage was a love match since Kha-em-nun's status was certainly lower than her first husband's had been as a scribe. With her inheritance she was able to act as she pleased. Together Kha-em-nun and Naunakhte had eight children, four boys and four girls, who grew up in the village at Deir el Medina.

Widowhood. After Kha-em-nun died, four of Naunakhte's children participated in supporting her. The other children did not live up to her expectations and were disinherited in a declaration made to the Deir el Medina court of magistrates, which is preserved in a papyrus now located in the Ashmolean Museum in

Oxford, England. This declaration is fascinating because it clearly demonstrates the usual expectations a widow had concerning inheritance. Naunakhte knew she could expect one-third of each husband's property, which she then would control. The other two-thirds went to the children or to her deceased husband's relatives. In her declaration Naunakhte acknowledged that she could not stop her neglectful children from inheriting their share from their father.

A Contradiction. One difficulty in understanding Naunakhte's declaration is the position of her daughter Menet-nakhte, who is listed both among the children who will inherit from Naunakhte and among those disinherited. Though occasionally in an Egyptian family two children have the same name, this situation cannot be the case in Naunakhte's family. At the beginning of the declaration, Naunakhte states that she has eight children. In the list of those who will inherit, Naunakhte names five children. In the list of those who will not inherit, she names four children, repeating the name of Menet-nakhte. There is also an additional paragraph that puts limitations on Menet-nakhte's inheritance compared to the four children who supplied an extra stipend to Naunakhte during her widowhood. Naunakhte distinguished also between the one-third she received from her first husband, her share from her father, and the one-third she received from her second husband. Menet-nakhte perhaps is included in the list that will share in one estate but not in the list that shared in the second estate. The reasons for this distinction are unknown and hard to explain.

Sources:

Jaroslav Cerný, "The Will of Naunakhte and the Related Documents," *Journal of Egyptian Archaeology*, 31 (1945): 29–53.

A. G. MacDowell, *Village Life in Ancient Egypt: Laundry Lists and Love Songs* (New York: Oxford University Press, 1999), p. 38.

Joyce Tyldesley, *Daughters of Isis: Women of Ancient Egypt* (London & New York: Viking, 1994).

PANEB

FLOURISHED CIRCA 1204-1193 B.C.E.
FOREMAN AT DEIR EL MEDINA

Prejudiced Sources. Paneb is known from his tomb at Deir el Medina, which preserves little information about his life. Unfortunately for Paneb, his historical reputation is entirely based on information supplied in a text written by his sworn enemy, Amen-nakhte, in *Papyrus Salt 124*. Amen-nakhte believed that Paneb had become foreman through a bribe paid to the vizier, a job that Amen-nakhte believed was rightfully his in the absence of any bribery.

List of Crimes. Amen-nakhte prepared a list of the reasons that Paneb was unworthy to be foreman. Among the reasons were Paneb's violent temper. But more importantly, Paneb was accused of adultery, bribery, misappropriation, theft, and assault. It is unclear whether Amen-nakhte ever delivered his list of charges to the vizier. The copy that is known to scholars was probably discovered at Deir el Medina, rather than at the vizier's residence across the river. However, *Ostraca Turin 57556*, written somewhat later, referred to Paneb's punishment for theft. This text is the only confirmation that he committed any crime.

Unfaithfulness. Adultery was not a criminal matter in ancient Egypt. It could be used, however, as evidence of wickedness or abuse of power when a supervisor seduced the wife of an employee. Some texts suggest that a wronged husband might murder his wife's seducer, a situation that would lead to general disorder in a village. Certainly the charges against Paneb, if true, would have interfered with the work on the king's tomb. Amen-nakhte charged that Paneb slept with the wives of two different workmen. He claimed that "Paneb slept with the lady Tuy when she was the wife of the workman Qenna; he slept with the lady Hel when she was with Pen-dua. He slept with the lady Hel when she was with Hesy-su-neb-ef," according to his son. In the case of the second woman, Paneb allegedly also slept with her daughter and procured the daughter for his own son—"And when he had slept with Hel, he slept with Webkhet, her daugher. And A'opekhty, his son, slept with Webkhet himself."

Bribery. Amen-nakhte charged that Paneb became foreman by bribing the vizier Pre-em-hab by giving him five slaves who had previously belonged to the father of the recently deceased foreman, Neferhotep. Amen-nakhte must also have had a stake in the ownership of these slaves since he was Neferhotep's brother.

Misappropriation. Paneb allegedly misappropriated the time of sixteen workmen to work on his private tomb rather than continue their work on the king's tomb. He also had the workmen use their official-issue chisels and pickaxes and reportedly even broke a tool in the construction of his tomb. These tools were provided to the workmen for labor they did "for Pharaoh." This misuse of these men's time and tools was a constant and persistent problem for the central government, an abuse directly addressed in a decree made by King Sety I (circa 1290–1279 B.C.E.) three generations earlier.

Theft. At the same time, Paneb reportedly had the men steal stone from the tomb of King Merneptah (circa 1213–1204 B.C.E.). He allegedly had them carve four columns from this stone, which they then erected in Paneb's tomb. Amen-nakhte claimed that "while the stone cutters were standing and working on top of the work of Pharaoh, the people passing by in the desert saw them and heard their voices. And he took the chisels of Pharaoh, (may he live, may he prosper, may he be healthy), and the pickax to work in his tomb."

Assault. Amen-nakhte also charged that Paneb chased Neferhotep through the village, threatening him that he would "kill him in the night!" Neferhotep was forced to lock himself in his own house and set a guard. Paneb attacked the house with stones and broke down the door. He also beat nine men that night.

Retribution. Neferhotep reported Paneb to the vizier, Amen-mose, who punished Paneb for the assaults. However, Amen-nakhte believed that Paneb was able to force the dismissal of Amen-mose on account of his punishment. Amen-nakhte complained "Now, (he) is not worthy of this office. Indeed he is behaving like the *wadjet* eye [playing Providence] (although) he is like a madman. He killed these men so that they would not be able to make a report to Pharaoh, (may he live, may he prosper, may he be healthy). Look, I have let the vizier know his behavior."

Implications. The charges against Paneb, true or not, paint a picture of life at Deir el Medina that is at odds with Egyptian ideals. They demonstrate the kinds of social problems that were possible in a small village that are usually hidden from historical view.

Sources:

Leonard Lesko, ed., *Pharaoh's Workers: The Villagers of Deir el-Medina* (Ithaca, N.Y.: Cornell University Press, 1994).

A. G. MacDowell, *Village Life in Ancient Egypt: Laundry Lists and Love Songs* (New York: Oxford University Press, 1999), pp. 46–47, 190–193.

SENEB

FLOURISHED CIRCA 2625–2170 B.C.E.
CHIEF VALET AND ROYAL TUTOR

Family. In spite of his dwarfism, Seneb married a healthy woman from the royal family. They had two children, a son and a daughter. Seneb was an important official who directed the royal textile works and instructed royal children.

Disability. Seneb was a chondro-dystrophic dwarf, a condition that was not uncommon in Egypt. In this disease, the face, pelvis, and extremities are ossified. The extremities are short, broad, and deformed. The trunk and cranium, however, are normal in size. Adult male dwarfs can reach a height of 47 to 51 inches. According to Egyptologist Zahi Hawass, Seneb may have been the son of Pernyankhu, who appears also to have achieved royal favor. Dasen has discovered 207 examples of such dwarfism in ancient Egyptian records.

Careers. Chondrodystrophy was not an obstacle to a successful career in Egypt. Seneb achieved high office, a family, and a prime tomb in Giza. Other dwarfs worked as jewelers, servants, and performers.

Sources:

Véronique Dasen, *Dwarfs in Ancient Egypt and Greece* (Oxford: Clarendon Press, 1993; New York: Oxford University Press, 1993).

Joyce Filer, *Disease* (London: British Museum Press, 1995).

Zahi Hawass, "The Peak and Splendour of the Old Kingdom from the Fourth Dynasty to the End of the Sixth Dynasty," *The Plateau*, <http://www.guardians.net/hawass/oldkingdom.htm>.

DOCUMENTARY SOURCES

Amen-nakhte, *Papyrus Salt 124* (circa 1204–1193 B.C.E.)—Describes the adultery and other crimes committed by Paneb, foreman in Deir el Medina.

Anonymous, *Book of the Dead* (circa 1539–1292 B.C.E.)—Chapter 125 of this Dynasty 18 text contains information on sexual taboos, as well as other actions that can keep a person from entering the land of the dead.

Anonymous, *Kahun Medical Papyrus,* (1938–1759 B.C.E.)—This Dynasty 12 papyrus is the earliest medical text from ancient Egypt and shows that medical treatment for females was separated early from that provided males. It contains prescriptions for infertility, contraception, and a pregnancy test.

Anonymous, *Ostracon Petrie 28* (1292–1075 B.C.E.)—Written by a student in Dynasty 19 or Dynasty 20, this shard shows that scribes learned to conjugate verbs as part of learning grammar.

Anonymous, *Papyrus Ashmolean Museum 1945.96* (circa 1104–1075 B.C.E.)—Compiled during the reign of Ramesses XI, it details adoption procedures.

Anonymous, *Story of Setne Khaemwas* (332 B.C.E.–33 C.E.)—This Ptolemaic text describes a marriage celebration.

Anonymous, *Turin Erotic Papyrus* (circa 1150 B.C.E.)—This papyrus contains drawings of many couples engaged in a variety of sexual positions.

Any, *The Wisdom of Any* (circa 1539–1292 B.C.E.)—This Dynasty 18 sages comments on education, sexuality, and marriage.

Dua-Khety, *The Instructions of Dua-Khety* (1938–1759 B.C.E.)—A Dynasty 12 text revealing that nonelite children could sometimes attend school in the capital city.

Naunakhte, *Declaration of Naunakhte* (circa 1190–1075 B.C.E.)—Written during Dynasty 20, it shows that inheritance and disinheritance was based on the proper upkeep of aged parents.

Ptahhotep, *Sayings of Ptahhotep* (1938–1759 B.C.E.)—A Dynasty 12 text that urges the importance of rhetoric "good speech" and says it is not limited to educated people.

Shed-su-Khonsu, *Papyrus Berlin 8523* (1075–945 B.C.E.)—A Dynasty 21 letter that illustrates the letter-writing formulae.

RELIGION AND PHILOSOPHY

by STEPHEN THOMPSON

CONTENTS

Sidebars and tables are listed in italics.

2585* B.C.E.

- King Sneferu finishes building the first true pyramid in ancient Egypt.

2585-2560* B.C.E.

- King Khufu builds the Great Pyramid on the Giza plateau.

2560-2555* B.C.E.

- King Redjedef becomes the first king to add the title *Son of Re* to his titulary.

2555-2532* B.C.E.

- King Khafre builds his pyramid on the Giza plateau, along with the Great Sphinx, a huge guardian statue of a human-headed lion. The Sphinx is not worshiped in its own right until Dynasty 18 (circa 1539–1295/1292 B.C.E.), when it is regarded as the image of the local form of Horus, the god of the sky.

2500-2350* B.C.E.

- The worship of the sun god Re gains new importance. Kings build sun temples in addition to their own pyramid complexes.

2371-2350* B.C.E.

- The god Osiris ("Mighty One") is first attested in Egyptian texts.
- Unas, the last king of Dynasty 5 (circa 2500–2350 B.C.E.), builds his pyramid at Saqqara. He is the first to have *Pyramid Texts* carved on the walls of his pyramid. These funerary and religious texts are meant to guide the dead in their journey to the afterlife. This practice becomes standard throughout Dynasty 6 (circa 2350–2170 B.C.E.).

2170* B.C.E.

- *Coffin Texts* are first attested in the necropolis of Balat in the Kharga Oasis. Similar to *Pyramid Texts,* they are written in ink on the sides of wooden coffins.

2130-1980* B.C.E.

- The serpent-demon Apophis is first attested during this period.

1938-1759* B.C.E.

- The use of *Coffin Texts* becomes widespread. Meanwhile, the idea of a chthonic afterlife with Osiris gains importance.
- A rise in the significance of the Theban god Amun ("Hidden One," or god of the air) occurs.
- Senwosret I builds the White Chapel at Karnak.
- Amenemhet III and Amenemhet IV build a temple to the gods Sobek, Horus, and Ernutet at Medinet Habu.

*DENOTES CIRCA DATE

1630-1539* B.C.E.

- The first attestation of the *Book of Going Forth by Day* or *Book of the Dead* occurs. It is a guidebook for the dead.

1493-1479* B.C.E.

- Thutmose I reigns in Egypt. His tomb preserves fragments of what may be the first attestation of the *Amduat*, a funerary text. Thutmose I is also the first king to be buried in the Valley of the Kings.

1479-1425* B.C.E.

- The earliest complete copy of the *Amduat* comes from the tomb of Thutmose III.

1478-1458* B.C.E.

- The first certain attestation of oracles in ancient Egypt occurs.
- Hatshepsut has scenes representing her divine birth carved on the walls of her temple at Deir el Bahri.
- The "age of personal piety," when the gods are thought of as taking a direct interest in the lives of their worshipers, begins.
- Sphinxes are used to line the "gods' roads" at various temples.

1390-1353* B.C.E.

- The first burials of sacred Apis bulls takes place in the Serapeum, a mausoleum at Saqqara.
- Amenhotep III disassembles the White Chapel at Karnak and uses it as fill in the third pylon at Karnak. Archaeologists discover the blocks and reassemble the structure in the twentieth century C.E.

1353-1336* B.C.E.

- Amenhotep IV (Akhenaten) closes the temples of Egypt and promotes the worship of the Aten (the Sun).

1332-1322* B.C.E.

- Tutankhamun abandons the city of Akhetaten for Memphis and restores the temples to the gods throughout Egypt. The *Book of the Heavenly Cow*, a funerary text, is first attested on one of the gilded shrines from Tutankhamun's tomb.

1319-1322* B.C.E.

- The first attestation of the funerary composition known as the *Book of Gates* appears.

1292-1075* B.C.E.

- Private religious practices such as praying and making offerings at special temple chapels and gates increase following the spiritual upheaval of Akhenaten's rule.

*DENOTES CIRCA DATE

1075-656* B.C.E.

- During this period of fragmented government, the Priests of Amun at Thebes control much of Southern and Middle Egypt.

1075-945* B.C.E.

- The Priests of Amun at Thebes become the first private individuals to be buried with papyrus copies of the *Amduat*.

716-702* B.C.E.

- The only preserved copy of the Memphite Theology is made. This cosmogony tells the story of Ptah, the father of all the gods.

664-525 B.C.E.

- The *Book of the Dead*, which had gone out of use after Dynasty 22 (circa 945–712 B.C.E.), reappears. New spells are included, and the order of the texts becomes standardized. This version of the *Book of the Dead* is known as the *Saite Recension*.

- During this period, the veneration of animals reaches new heights, and millions of animal mummies are interred throughout Egypt.

- Formal "cult guilds," individual organizations for the worship of a deity, are founded.

525-404 B.C.E.

- The Persians conquer Egypt for the first time. They construct the only substantial religious monument from this period, the Hibis temple at Kharga Oasis.

* DENOTES CIRCA DATE

Sacred lake at Karnak

OVERVIEW

Definition. The ancient Egyptians had no word for "religion." For them, religion was not a separate category of thought requiring an approach different from that used when discussing philosophy, science, or any other topic. In order to study Egyptian religion, one must first decide what religion is and then examine the Egyptian record for data relating to this definition. Attempts to define religion as a phenomenon are plentiful, and no universal definition has been decided. The definition used here will follow that of Melford Spiro, who suggested that religion is an "institution consisting of culturally patterned interaction with culturally postulated superhuman beings."

Components. This definition consists of several main components. Religion is first an institution, or something practiced by social groups. In other words, a person cannot have a religion of one. An individual can have his or her own beliefs, but for those beliefs to be called a religion a wider group must practice them. Egyptian religion could be practiced in the formal setting of the massive state temples, with their extensive holdings of land, buildings, and personnel, or in the privacy of an Egyptian home. Religion also assumes the existence of "culturally postulated superhuman beings," beings one may call gods, demons, or spirits. These beings were thought to be able to influence the lives of human beings, either for good or bad. The ancient Egyptian term for these beings was *netjer*. Finally, there is the interaction between people and these superhuman beings. These interactions can take two forms. First are those activities that people engage in because they think such actions please the superhuman beings, such as behaving morally and ethically, carrying out prescribed rituals, and participating in festivals. Second are activities such as prayers, sacrifices, or votive offerings that people engage in for the purpose of influencing the superhuman beings to act on behalf of (or cease acting against) a particular individual or group of individuals.

Characteristics. Ancient Egyptian religion has certain characteristics, and it differs from what most western observers would call religion in several ways. Unlike Judaism, Christianity, and Islam, the Egyptian religion was not a founded religion; in other words, there is no single individual (other than the Amarna interlude with Akhenaten) who is credited with establishing it. Because there is no set

of writings thought to be revealed by the gods to mankind explicating the tenets, it is not considered "scriptural." This statement does not mean that the Egyptians did not have religious texts; they did. Yet, these writings never achieved the status of a canon against which all else could be judged. There were no doctrines for people to believe and no creeds to which people had to agree. Egyptian religion was greatly influenced by the natural world. The Egyptians did not worship nature, but it was through nature that they gained their knowledge of the gods. The landscape, plants, and animals could all have religious significance. The Nile River and the scorching Egyptian sun played prominent roles in Egyptian theology.

Multiplicity of Approaches. One of the most striking characteristics of Egyptian religion to the modern student is what has been termed the "multiplicity of approaches." The Egyptians did not seek a single explanation for phenomena or events. Rather, one phenomenon could have several different, and to modern people mutually exclusive, explanations. The creation of the world was ascribed to various gods, and that phenomenon could be described through several different symbols. For example, the Egyptians imagined the sky as a cow with stars adorning her belly, as a body of water on which the sun-god sailed in his boat, as a woman's body stretched out over the earth, and as a roof or canopy, all at the same time.

Spoken Words and Names. Another feature of Egyptian religion was the importance of the spoken word and names. Words were not simply vibrations of sounds or collections of letters; they possessed power. Similarities in sound between words were not thought to be coincidental but were thought to reveal essential information about the relationship between the entities. Just as individuals such as the king or vizier could accomplish things by giving verbal orders, the speaking of words was thought to bring about concrete events. Reading the offering formula on behalf of a deceased relative was thought to provide him with the commodities needed in the afterlife. Names were thought to refer to the essence of a person or deity, and manipulation of an entity's name was thought to grant control over the entity. In order to bring about the destruction of an enemy, his name could be written on an object of clay, either a bowl or anthropomorphic figurine, and the figurine would then be smashed. Knowing the true name of a god granted one power over the god. The names of gods became the building blocks for expanding knowledge of the deities, and the more names a god had the more aspects to his being he possessed.

Evidence. When studying Egyptian religion, modern students must always keep in mind that they are basing their interpretations on evidence spread out over more than three thousand years of history. The main source of information about Egyptian religion is the abundant written material that has been preserved. The first written evidence for Egyptian religion comes from the period of Dynasty 0 (circa 3100–3000 B.C.E.) and the Early Dynastic Period (circa 3000–2675 B.C.E.). This evidence is in the form of names of individuals that include a god's name as an element. Names such as *he whom Khnum has saved, he whom Anubis has created,* or *she whom Neith loves* indicate which gods were being worshiped and the types of actions and relationships people expected from their gods. Labels and clay seals used to close jars also preserve brief texts that give evidence for temples in ancient Egypt. The texts occasionally indicate that the commodities in the containers were destined for, or came from, a particular temple.

Texts. The texts that the Egyptians buried with their dead to aid them in making a successful transition to the afterlife are an extremely important source of information on the Egyptian gods and their doings. The earliest of these texts and, in fact, the oldest religious texts known anywhere in the world, are found on the walls of the pyramids of the last king of Dynasty 5 (circa 2500–2350 B.C.E.), Unas, and in the pyramids of the Dynasty 6 (circa 2350–2170 B.C.E.) kings and even some of their queens. Because of their location they are called by Egyptologists *Pyramid Texts.* These texts were initially the exclusive prerogative of royalty. Toward the end of the Old Kingdom (circa 2675–2130 B.C.E.) a new type of funerary text appeared among the high officials of the bureaucracy. These texts, which became frequent during the Middle Kingdom (circa 1980–1630 B.C.E.), are found mainly on the walls of wooden coffins and therefore are called *Coffin Texts.* At the end of the Middle Kingdom, the *Coffin Texts* were replaced by funerary spells written on papyri (or painted on tomb walls) buried with the deceased. The Egyptian title of these spells was *The Book of Going Forth by Day.* Once introduced, these texts continued in use until the end of the Roman period of Egyptian history. In 1842 Karl Richard Lepsius published a Ptolemaic period papyrus of this text and coined the name *Totenbuch,* which in English is *Book of the Dead,* and that is how these texts have been known ever since.

New Kingdom. In addition to the *Book of the Dead,* the New Kingdom (circa 1539–1075 B.C.E.) pharaohs included in their tombs a new type of funerary text, which is called by scholars *Underworld Books.* These books described the nightly journey of the sun through the Underworld, and it was a goal of the dead pharaoh to join the sun god on this voyage. There are several different compositions classified as *Underworld Books,* the most important being the *Amduat,* the *Book of Gates,* the *Book of Caverns,* and the *Book of the Earth.* A similar category of text, called *Books of the Sky,* is found in tombs after the Amarna period. These texts represent the sun's voyage as a passage along the body of the sky-goddess Nut. During the day the sun passes along her body, and at night it is swallowed by Nut and passes through her internally until dawn, when the sun is reborn between her thighs. The compositions, known as the *Book of Nut, Book of Day,* and *Book of Night,* belong to this genre of text.

Literature. Funerary texts are not the only source of knowledge on Egyptian religion. Egyptian literature is replete with references to the gods and to people's interactions with them. Hymns and prayers are commonly found carved on tomb walls and on stelae set up as monuments to the king, memorials to the deceased, or as votive offerings to the gods. Private letters, contracts, royal decrees, and medical texts, while not "religious" in purpose, all contain references to the gods, as well as preserve important information on Egyptian religion. Instruction texts, used to train scribes, contain advice on how to live a life pleasing to the gods. Magical spells are an important source for some of the myths of the gods. Fortunately for scholars, the ancient Egyptians covered the walls of their temples with texts and scenes relating to the activities that went on inside these massive buildings. The best-preserved temples are also the latest (Ptolemaic and Roman periods), and caution must be exercised when using these late sources to throw light on earlier religious practices.

Artifacts. The practice of burying goods with the deceased has preserved important artifacts relating to Egyptian religion. Some of the earliest evidence for Egyptian religion comes from the burials of people and animals during the Predynastic Period (circa 3100–3000 B.C.E.). The fact that people at this early stage were buried with grave goods and foodstuffs indicates a belief in some sort of life after death. Human figurines of clay and ivory included in some of the burials may represent deities, but this fact is uncertain. The number of animal burials attested for this period may indicate that divine powers were being worshiped in animal form. Excavations at the New Kingdom town sites of Amarna and Deir el Medina have revealed important information about the personal religious practices of their inhabitants and about the types of shrines at which these practices were carried out.

TOPICS IN RELIGION AND PHILOSOPHY

THE AFTERLIFE

Ascending to the Sky. Information concerning the Egyptian ideas of the hereafter comes from the texts buried with the dead and the illustrations found on tomb walls. As with so much in Egyptian religion, there was no single destination but a multiplicity of destinations, all of which an Egyptian wished to reach after death. The earliest postmortal destination was celestial, and in the *Pyramid Texts* it was a goal of the deceased king to ascend to the sky to live as a star among the circumpolar stars that never set. In Spells 1455 and 1456 the king states, "I am a star which illuminates the sky; I mount up to the god that I may be protected, for the sky will not be devoid of me and this earth will not be devoid of me for ever. I live beside you, you gods of the Lower Sky, the Imperishable Stars. . . ."

Re. In addition to ascending to the sky as a star, an Old Kingdom (circa 2675–2130 B.C.E.) king also wished to ascend to the sky to assume a seat in the boat of the sun god Re. Re was thought to travel throughout the sky in his solar bark by day and through the underworld at night. By taking a seat in the solar bark, the deceased king was allowed to participate in the eternal, rejuvenating voyage of the sun.

Underworld. Yet another destination for the deceased king was the underworld kingdom of Osiris. Osiris, after his death at the hands of his brother Seth, became the ruler of the Egyptian Underworld. As a result of undergoing the ritual of mummification and burial, the dead king becomes identified with Osiris and, as such, became the ruler of the Underworld.

Scene from the *Book of the Dead of Ani* showing, at left, the deceased enjoying the pleaures of the Field of Reeds and, at right, greeting the sun god, circa 1539–1190 B.C.E. (British Museum, London)

Pyramid Texts (wall inscriptions) in the tomb chamber of Unas, Saqqara, Dynasty 5, circa 2500–2350 B.C.E.

Private Individuals. These destinations describe the fate of the deceased king. After death the private Egyptian expected to continue to enjoy a life similar to that which he had experienced on earth, judging from the types of burial goods included in the tombs and the scenes found on tomb walls. Toward the end of the Old Kingdom, however, the formerly exclusively royal prerogatives of the afterlife became available to private individuals as well. During the First Intermediate Period (circa 2130–1980 B.C.E.) and Middle Kingdom (circa 1980–1630 B.C.E.) the idea of a postmortal life in the underworld realm of Osiris became more prominent but was not the exclusive goal of the deceased. The New Kingdom (circa 1539–1075 B.C.E.) *Book of the Dead* placed even more emphasis on the Osirian hereafter.

Dangerous Journey. The journey to the realm of Osiris was fraught with danger. The paths of the underworld were guarded by knife-wielding demons who lay in wait for the unprepared dead. At times these demons guarded gates through which the deceased had to pass. In addition, these gates could be guarded by encircling walls of flame. During the New Kingdom the number of gates through which the dead had to pass was variously given as seven (*Book of the Dead,* Spell 147) or twenty-one (*Book of the Dead,* Spells 145 and 146). The key to safely negotiating these dangers was a knowledge of the names of the demons and obstacles that one was likely to encounter. Knowing their names rendered them unable to harm the deceased. Such knowledge was available in the texts buried with the deceased.

Field of Reeds. After finally reaching the Hall of Osiris, the deceased had to undergo the final judgment and the weighing of his heart against the feather of *Maat* in the presence of Osiris and the forty-two judges of the afterlife. If the applicant passed successfully, he was admitted to the paradise of Osiris, referred to as the "Field of Reeds" or "Field of Offerings." This realm was modeled on Egypt itself. The land was crisscrossed by irrigation canals, and the deceased was responsible for such agricultural tasks as plowing, sowing, and reaping. Since this realm was paradise, the fruits of such labor were much greater than they were on earth. Wheat was said to grow to a height of five cubits, with ears two cubits in length. Barley grew seven cubits high, with ears of three cubits (a cubit was roughly half a meter). In order to avoid performing such backbreaking labor personally, the well-prepared Egyptian was buried with several *shawabti*-figurines, which responded when the deceased was called on to do manual labor in the afterlife.

Beginning a New Day. Although the idea of spending the afterlife in the company of Osiris was prominent in the *Book of the Dead*, the idea of spending eternity in the solar bark with Re had not disappeared. Beginning with the Dynasty 18 (circa 1539–1295/1292 B.C.E.) tomb of Thutmose I, a new type of funerary text made its appearance, the so-called *Underworld Books*. Included in this category are such works as the *Amduat* ["That Which Is in the Underworld"], the *Book of Gates,* the *Book of Caverns,* and the *Book of the Earth*. These works describe the sun's journey through the underworld, which begins at sunset, and concludes with the sun's rise from the waters of Nun, rejuvenated and ready to begin a new day. The Underworld is described as divided into twelve sections, corresponding to the twelve hours of the night. During this time Re, as the sun, bestows his life-giving rays on the dead who inhabit the underworld. Re is shown traveling through the underworld in his bark, which sails on the waters of Nun, the primeval ocean. At times, hostile creatures try to stop the bark, but because of the efforts of Re's entourage, they fail. At sunrise Re has successfully completed his journey through the underworld, bringing life and light to its inhabitants (including Osiris), and begins the new day rejuvenated.

The Damned. Not all the dead, however, were allowed to share in the life-giving rays of the sun during the night. The lowest level of the Underworld was reserved for the damned, those who had not successfully passed the final judgment. These unfortunate individuals became identified with the enemies of Osiris and Re and were consigned to *Hetemit* (the "Place of Destruction"). There they suffer decapitation and dismemberment (including removal of the genitals and heart). They are shown suspended upside down, with their severed heads between their feet. Other scenes show them being boiled in cauldrons heated by fire-breathing snakes or being incinerated directly by such serpents. They are doomed to spend eternity submerged in the "Lake of Fire." Perhaps worst of all, not only their bodies are subject to torture and destruction, but so are their *ba*s. Scenes from the Underworld depict the *ba*s of the condemned dead, represented by the *ba*-bird hieroglyph, being boiled in cauldrons. Through these means these unfortunate Egyptians, whose crimes we are not informed of, were consigned to oblivion.

Sources:

Werner Forman and Stephen Quirke, *Hieroglyphs and the Afterlife in Ancient Egypt* (Norman: University of Oklahoma Press, 1996).

Erik Hornung, "Black Holes Viewed from Within: Hell in Ancient Egyptian Thought," *Diogenes,* 42 (1994): 133–156.

Hornung, *The Valley of the Kings Horizon of Eternity,* translated by David Warburton (New York: Timken, 1990).

AMUN

The Hidden One. Amun, whose name means "the hidden one," was originally associated with the area of Thebes. When Theban families rose to prominence and became the rulers of all Egypt, first in Dynasty 12 (circa 1938–1759 B.C.E.), and again in Dynasty 18 (circa 1539–1295/1292 B.C.E.), Amun's power and influence also increased. As the Dynasty 18 kings expanded Egypt's empire into Asia, they attributed their successes to Amun's blessings and rewarded his priesthood accordingly. Eventually, Amun joined with Re and rose to become the state god of Egypt, known as Amun-Re, king of the gods, lord of the thrones of the two lands. During the Third Intermediate Period (circa 1075–656 B.C.E.) the priesthood of Amun at Thebes became the

Statue of the Ram of Amun protecting an image of Ramesses II at Karnak, circa 1279–1213 B.C.E.

Gold statuette of the god Amun, circa 900 B.C.E.
(Metropolitan Museum of Art, New York)

virtual rulers of southern Egypt, and one of the most important priestly offices was that of God's Wife of Amun.

Wind and Air. Amun was usually depicted as a human wearing a cap adorned with two tall, multicolored feathers. His skin is blue, perhaps related to Amun's association with the wind and air. His principal cult center was at Karnak, where he was worshiped in conjunction with his consort Mut (goddess representing motherhood) and their son Khonsu (the wanderer, representing the Moon). He was associated with the ram and the goose.

Progenitor. In the Hermopolitan cosmogony (so-called because it is thought to have originated in Hermopolis, before being transferred to Thebes) Amun is one of the sixteen gods representing the state of the world before creation. These gods make up an *ogdoad,* or group of eight pairs of deities. This group includes Nu(n) and Naunet (representing the primeval water and formlessness), Huh and Huhet (spaciousness), Kek and Keket (darkness), and Amun and Amaunet (hiddenness). Another tradition describes how Amun, in his form of Kematef (a serpent deity), fathers the *ogdoad.* This idea of Amun being his own progenitor and therefore having no creator is also encountered in the form of Amun Kamutef, "Amun, bull of his mother," that is to say, Amun was his own father.

Kingship. Amun was closely associated with kingship. Reliefs from New Kingdom (circa 1539–1075 B.C.E.) temples describe the divine birth of the king. Amun was said to have fallen in love with the queen of Egypt. He visited her in the guise of her current husband, the reigning king, and fathered the next king of Egypt. When the child was born, Amun acknowledged his paternity and presented the child to the gods as the future king of Egypt.

Sources:

Jan Assmann, *Egyptian Solar Religion in the New Kingdom: Re, Amun and the Crisis of Polytheism,* translated by Anthony Alcock (London & New York: Kegan Paul International, 1995).

Assmann, *The Search for God in Ancient Egypt* (Ithaca, N.Y.: Cornell University Press, 2001).

Eberhard Otto, *Egyptian Art and the Cults of Osiris and Amon,* translated by Kate Bosse Griffiths (London: Thames & Hudson, 1968).

ANIMALS

Significance. Animals played an important role in Egyptian religion. Most of the Egyptian gods could at times be depicted either as an animal or an animal-headed human. Since the Egyptians apprehended their gods through the natural world, it is not surprising to find that animals were viewed as manifestations of the divine. Several theories have been suggested as to why this view was the case. Henri Frankfort has suggested that it was the apparently unchanging nature of the animals that impressed the Egyptians. From generation to generation, humans exhibit changes in appearance, while animals appear the same. An important element in Egyptian theology was that the perfect pattern of existence had been established by the gods at the time of creation, called the *sep-tepy,* the first time, and it was important that this pattern be maintained. Animals would seem to have been more successful than man at maintaining their form established at the first time. Another suggestion, by Hellmut Brunner, is that it was the animals' possession of superhuman powers, such as flight, speed, stealth, heightened senses, and strength that made the Egyptians perceive them as beings through whom the gods were manifest. One thing is certain: the Egyptians did not see a wide gulf separating gods and humans from the animals. The creative powers of the mind and tongue were thought to be operative in the gods, mankind, and animals equally. A hymn to Amun states that he cares even for worms, fleas, mice in their holes, and insects. The First Intermediate Period (circa 2130–1980 B.C.E.) nomarch (provincial governor) Henqu states that not only did he give bread to the hungry and clothing to the naked in his nome, but he also provided the jackals of the mountains and the birds of the sky with food, putting good deeds toward humans and animals on the same level. Given the close association between animals and the gods, it is not surprising that animals could be worshiped not as gods but as the means through which the gods manifested themselves, much as a statue was worshiped as a vehicle through which the god was manifest. This distinction was lost on the Greeks, who, when they encountered Egyptian religion, thought the Egyptians were worshiping the animals *as* their gods, as the following quotation from *Clemens Alexandrinus* makes clear:

> The temples [of the Egyptians] sparkle with gold, silver and mat gold and flash with colored stones from India and Ethiopia. The sanctuaries are overshadowed by cloths studded with gold. If, however, you enter the interior of the enclosure, hastening towards the sight of the almighty and look for the statue residing in the temple, and if a [priest] or another celebrant, after having solemnly looked round the sanctuary, singing a song in the language of the Egyptians draws back the curtain a little to show the god, he will make us laugh about the object of worship. For we shall not find the god for whom we have been looking inside, the god towards whom we have hastened, but a cat or a crocodile, or a native snake or a similar animal, which should not be in a temple, but in a cleft or a den or on a dung heap. The god of the Egyptians appears on a purple couch as a wallowing animal. *Translation by K. A. D. Smelik*

Sacredness. Evidence for the veneration of animals dates back to the fourth millennium B.C.E. Predynastic burials of gazelles, dogs, cattle, monkeys, and rams have been found at Badari, Naqada, Maadi, and Heliopolis. The care taken in the burial of these animals and the fact that they were buried with grave goods is considered to be evidence for a cult of sacred animals in Egypt at this early date. The earliest mention of a particular sacred animal, the Apis bull, dates to the reign of King Aha of Dynasty 1 (circa 3000–2800 B.C.E.). During Dynasty 26 (664–525 B.C.E.) the cult of sacred animals received renewed emphasis, perhaps as a resurgence of Egyptian nationalism, and

Bronze figure of a cat, the sacred representation of the goddess Bastet, Late Period, 664–332 B.C.E. (British Museum, London)

reached their acme during the Late (664–332 B.C.E.) and Ptolemaic (332–330 B.C.E.) periods. Most of the large animal necropolises date to the latter period.

Temple Animal. There were three types of sacred animals in ancient Egypt. One type is the temple animal. These animals performed the same function as cult statues and were considered vessels through which the gods could make their wills manifest. These animals lived in or near a temple and were distinguished by special markings. For example, the Apis bull, which lived at Memphis, was a bull with a white triangle on its forehead, a crescent moon on its chest and another on its flanks, and double hairs (black and white) in its tail. The Apis bull was thought to be the *ba*, or manifestation, of the god Ptah. At certain times of day the bull was released into a courtyard where worshipers would gather to see him and receive oracles. People could put a yes-or-no question to the bull, and the answer was received when the bull entered one of two stables. When the bull died, there was a time of widespread mourning, and an elaborate embalming and burial ceremony was carried out. The Apis bull was buried in a stone sarcophagus in a mausoleum known as the Serapeum at Saqqara. The search for the new Apis bull then began. Other examples of such temple animals include the Mnevis bull at Heliopolis (Atum-Re), the Buchis bull of Hermonthis (Montu), the

Cow of Hathor from the temple of Hatshepsut at Deir
el Hahari, circa 1478/1472–1458 B.C.E.

ram of Mendes (Osiris-Re), and the ram of Elephantine
(Khnum).

Same Species. Those animals that belong to the same
species as the temple animal represent the second type.
These animals were not thought to be special manifestations of particular gods, but because the god or goddess
could appear in the guise of one of these animals, others of
the same species were considered dear to the god. Large
numbers of these animals could be kept near a temple. At
Saqqara there was an extensive complex of buildings dedicated to the care of flocks of ibises (associated with Thoth),
falcons (associated with Horus), and cats (associated with
Bastet). Such large collections of animals served as the
source of the enormous number of animal mummies that
have been preserved. Sacred animal necropolises throughout Egypt contain literally millions of mummified animal
burials. In addition to the ibis necropolis at Saqqara, there
are necropolises for cats at Bubastis, rams at Elephantine,
crocodiles, snakes, falcons, and ibises at Kom Ombo, and
ibises and falcons at Abydos. Other animals that were buried include sheep, dogs, baboons, jackals, fish of several
species, shrews, scorpions, and scarab beetles. The main

differences that separate this category of sacred animal
from the first is that there was only one temple animal at a
time; the temple animal received a cult, while these animals
did not, and the mortuary services for the temple animals
were much more elaborate.

Votive Offerings. The reason for the mummification
and burial of such enormous numbers of animals in ancient
Egypt is related to their association with the gods. People
who visited the various temples during festival periods were
anxious to make an offering to the god in an attempt to
earn his blessing. One acceptable votive offering was the
mummified remains of an animal associated with the god.
A prayer inscribed on a jar containing an ibis mummy
asked Thoth to be benevolent toward the woman who had
embalmed his sacred animal. Most such offerings took
place during festivals. In order to ensure a plentiful supply
of animals for pilgrims, the priests were not adverse to has-
tening the death of an animal. At this point, the extent of
this practice is uncertain. The one population of animal
mummy that has been systematically studied is cats. An
examination of their mummies at the British Museum
reveals that the majority of them died either at two or four
months old, or between nine and twelve months, although
the average life span of a cat should have been around
twelve years. In addition, a common cause of death among
the cats was a dislocation of the cervical vertebrae, which
could be the result of violently twisting the head of an animal until its neck broke. Other cat mummies show evidence of having been bashed over the head. Apparently the
sacredness of these animals to the gods did not prevent the
priests from doing what was necessary to supply a pilgrim
with a mummified animal.

Private Homes. The third type of sacred animal
includes members of the same species as the temple animals that were kept in private homes as representatives of
the gods. For example, snakes, cats, or dogs were often kept
in homes and buried at their deaths. This practice is analo-
gous to the construction of household shrines to allow for
domestic worship.

Sources:
Ann Rosalie David, *The Ancient Egyptians: Religious Beliefs and Practices*
(London & Boston: Routledge & Kegan Paul, 1982).

Jaromir Malek, *The Cat in Ancient Egypt* (Philadelphia: University of
Pennsylvania Press, 1993).

H. te Velde, "A Few Remarks upon the Religious Significance of Animals
in Ancient Egypt," *Numen*, 27 (1980): 76–82.

ETHICS

Firm Basis. For the ancient Egyptians the matter of
ethics was firmly grounded in their religious worldview, so
much so that one scholar has written that "in the Egyptian's terms, morality and religion can hardly be separated."
At the basis of all moral and ethical behavior in ancient
Egypt was the concept of *Maat*. It was every Egyptian's
duty to conduct his or her life in accordance with *Maat*,
and to avoid committing deeds considered the opposite of
Maat, *Isfet* (wrongdoing) or *Gereget* (falsehood). In this way
the continued existence and prosperity of Egypt was

Chapter 125, the last section of the *Book of the Dead*, is a recitation of all the evil deeds the deceased did not commit during life. It forms an excellent collection of Egyptian beliefs about right and wrong behavior.

To be said on reaching the Hall of the Two Truths so as to purge N [name of the deceased] of any sins committed and to see the face of every god:

Hail to you, great God, Lord of the Two Truths!
I have come to you, my Lord,
I was brought to see your beauty.
I know you, I know the names of the forty-two gods,
Who are with you in the Hall of the Two truths,
Who live by warding off evildoers,
Who drink of their blood,
On that day of judging characters before Wennofer.
Lo, your name is "He-of-Two-Daughters,"
And "He-of-Maat's-Two-Eyes."
Lo, I come before you,
Bringing Maat to you,
Having repelled evil for you.
I have not done crimes against people,
I have not mistreated cattle,
I have not sinned in the Place of Truth.
I have not known what should not be known.
I have not done any harm.
I did not begin a day by exacting more than my due,
My name did not reach the bark of the mighty ruler.
I have not blasphemed a god,
I have not robbed the oor.
I have not done what the god abhors,
I have not maligned a servant to his master.
I have not caused pain,
I have not caused tears.
I have not killed,
I have not ordered to kill,
I have not made anyone suffer.
I have not damaged the offerings in the temples,
I have not depleted the loaves of the gods,
I have not stolen the cakes of the dead.
I have not copulated or defiled myself.
I have not increased or reduced the measure,
I have not diminished the arura,
I have not cheated in the fields.
I have not added to the weight of the balance.
I have not falsified the plummet of the scales.
I have not taken milk from the mouth of children,
I have not deprived cattle of their pasture.
I have not snared birds in the reeds of the gods,
I have not caught fish in their ponds.
I have not held back water in its season,
I have not dammed a flowing stream,
I have not quenched a needed fire.
I have not neglected the days of meat offerings,
I have not detained cattle belonging to the god,
I have not stopped a god in his procession.
I am pure, I am pure, I am pure, I am pure!
I am pure as is pure that great heron in Hnes.
I am truly the nose of the Lord of Breath,
Who sustains all people,
On the day of completing the Eye in On [Heliopolis].
In the second month of winter, last day,
In the presence of the lord of this land.
I have seen the completion of the Eye in On!
No evil shall befall me in this land,

In this Hall of the Two Truths;
For I know the names of the gods in it,
The followers of the great God!
O Wide-of-stride who comes from On: I have not done evil.
O Flame-grasper who comes from Kheraha: I have not robbed.
O Long-nosed who comes from Khmun: I have not coveted.
O Shadow-eater who comes from the cave: I have not stolen.
O Savage-faced who comes from Rostau: I have not killed people.
O Lion-Twins who come from heaven: I have not trimmed the measure.
O Flint-eyed who comes from Khem: I have not cheated.
O Fiery-one who comes backward: I have not stolen a god's property.
O Bone-smasher who comes from Hnes: I have not told lies.
O Flame-thrower who comes from Memphis: I have not seized food.
O Cave-dweller who comes from the west: I have not sulked.
O White-toothed who comes from Lakeland: I have not trespassed.
O Blood-eater who comes from slaughterplace: I have not slain sacred cattle.
O Entrail-eater who comes from the tribunal: I have not extorted.
O Lord of Maat who comes from Maaty: I have not stolen bread rations.
O Wanderer who comes from Bubastis: I have not spied.
O Pale-one who comes from On: I have not prattled.
O Villain who comes from Andjty: I have contended only for my goods.
O Fiend who comes from slaughterhouse: I have not committed adultery.
O Examiner who comes from Min's temple: I have not defiled myself.
O Chief of the nobles who comes from Imu: I have not caused fear.
O Wrecker who comes from Huy: I have not trespassed.
O Disturber who comes from the sanctuary: I have not been violent.
O Child who comes from the nome of On: I have not been deaf to Maat.
O Foreteller who comes from Wensi: I have not quarreled.
O Bastet who comes from the shrine: I have not winked.
O Backward-faced who comes from the pit: I have not copulated with a boy.
O Flame-footed who comes from the dusk: I have not been false.
O Dark-one who comes from darkness: I have not reviled.
O Peace-bringer who comes from Sais: I have not been aggressive.
O Many-faced who comes from Djefet: I have not had a hasty heart.
O Accuser who comes from Utjen: I have not attacked and reviled a god.
O Horned-one who comes from Siut: I have not made many words.
O Nefertum who comes from Memphis: I have not sinned, I have not done wrong.
O Timeless-one who comes from Djedu: I have not made trouble.
O Willful-one who comes from Tjebu: I have not waded in water.
O Flowing-one who comes from Nun: I have not raised my voice.
O Commander of people who comes from his shrine: I have not cursed a god.
O Benefactor who comes from Huy: I have not been boastful.
O Nehebkau who comes from the city: I have not been haughty.
O High-of-head who comes from the graveyard: I have not cursed god in my town.

Source: "Chapter 125, Book of the Dead," in *Ancient Egyptian Literature: A Book of Readings*, volume II, compiled by Miriam Lichtheim (Berkeley: University of California Press, 1976), pp. 124–127.

assured. The main source of knowledge concerning what behavior was in accordance with *Maat* is the instruction literature from ancient Egypt. These texts, similar to the biblical Book of Proverbs, date from the Old Kingdom (circa 2675–2130 B.C.E.) to the Greco-Roman period (circa 332 B.C.E.–395 C.E.), and were used as exercises for student scribes. They are portrayed as books of practical wisdom written by famous sages, in which they distilled their lifetime of experience concerning which actions were and were not in accordance with *Maat*. Living a life in accordance with the principles of *Maat* was not only good for Egypt but also good for the individual, and the instruction texts assured the individual that living a life based on *Maat* was the path to success.

Texts. *Maat* was not only good for the living but was also beneficial to a person after death. In the *Story of the Eloquent Peasant* the peasant exhorts his audience (and the reader) to "speak *Maat*, do *Maat*, for it is great; it is important; it is everlasting; its usefulness will be discovered; it will lead (a person) to a blessed state (after death)." The ancient Egyptians believed in a postmortem judgment of the individual, symbolized as the weighing of his or her heart against the feather representing *Maat*. The earliest hints of such a judgment appear in the Old Kingdom *Pyramid Texts,* but the first certain reference of a postmortal ethical judgment is found in the First Intermediate Period (circa 2130–1980 B.C.E.) text known as the *Instructions for Merikare*, where one reads "a man survives after death, and his deeds are laid before him in a heap." In the *Coffin Texts* it is the balance of Re that weighs the individual against *Maat*. The idea of postmortal judgment reaches its peak in the New Kingdom (circa 1539–1075 B.C.E.) *Book of the Dead,* Spell 125. This spell is accompanied by an elaborate scene showing Osiris presiding over the weighing of the heart of the deceased against the feather of *Maat,* while the forty-two judges look on. The god Thoth is present to assure the accuracy of the balance and to record the results. Standing nearby is the demon Amemet, the swallower of the dead, who gobbles up the heart that fails to measure up to *Maat*, assuring the eternal destruction of the sinner.

Negative Confession. In order to prevent the deceased from suffering this fate, the scene was accompanied by a text that scholars call the "Negative Confession." This spell consists of two long lists of denials of wrongdoing by the deceased. One list is spoken before Osiris, the other before the forty-two assessor demons/judges. A study of the lists reveals the types of activities the Egyptians believed were contrary to *Maat*. Deeds found in the lists include blasphemy, thievery, murder, damaging offerings to the temples, being dishonest in weights and measures, and stealing cattle from the temple herds. Sexual sins such as adultery, pederasty, ejaculation, and copulation (when in violation of purity regulations) also turn up. Less physical offenses include coveting, lying, sulking, "prattling," and boasting.

Heavy Burden. The negative confession placed a heavy burden on an Egyptian wishing to live a life in accordance with *Maat*. The question has been raised as to what extent

---

HOMAGE TO THEE

Hymn To Osiris

Homage to thee, Osiris, Lord of eternity, King of the Gods, whose names are manifold, whose forms are holy, thou being of hidden form in the temples, whose Ka is holy. Thou art the governor of Tattu (Busiris), and also the mighty one in Sekhem (Letopolis). Thou art the Lord to whom praises are ascribed in the nome of Ati, thou art the Prince of divine food in Anu. Thou art the Lord who is commemorated in Maati, the Hidden Soul, the Lord of Qerrt (Elephantine), the Ruler supreme in White Wall (Memphis). Thou art the Soul of Ra, his own body, and hast thy place of rest in Henensu (Herakleopolis). Thou art the beneficent one, and art praised in Nart. Thou makest thy soul to be raised up. Thou art the Lord of the Great House in Khemenu (Hermopolis). Thou art the mighty one of victories in Shas-hetep, the Lord of eternity, the Governor of Abydos. The path of his throne is in Ta-tcheser (a part of Abydos). Thy name is established in the mouths of men. Thou art the substance of Two Lands (Egypt). Thou art Tem, the feeder of Kau (Doubles), the Governor of the Companies of the gods. Thou art the beneficent Spirit among the spirits. The god of the Celestial Ocean (Nu) draweth from thee his waters. Thou sendest forth the north wind at eventide, and breath from thy nostrils to the satisfaction of thy heart. Thy heart reneweth its youth, thou producest the. . . . The stars in the celestial heights are obedient unto thee, and the great doors of the sky open themselves before thee. Thou art he to whom praises are ascribed in the southern heaven, and thanks are given for thee in the northern heaven. The imperishable stars are under thy supervision, and the stars which never set are thy thrones. Offerings appear before thee at the decree of Keb. The Companies of the Gods praise thee, and the gods of the Tuat (Other World) smell the earth in paying homage to thee. The uttermost parts of the earth bow before thee, and the limits of the skies entreat thee with supplications when they see thee. The holy ones are overcome before thee, and all Egypt offereth thanksgiving unto thee when it meeteth Thy Majesty. Thou art a shining Spirit-Body, the governor of Spirit-Bodies; permanent is thy rank, established is thy rule. Thou art the well-doing Sekhem (Power) of the Company of the Gods, gracious is thy face, and beloved by him that seeth it. Thy fear is set in all the lands by reason of thy perfect love, and they cry out to thy name making it the first of names, and all people make offerings to thee. Thou art the lord who art commemorated in heaven and upon earth. Many are the cries which are made to thee at the Uak festival, and with one heart and voice Egypt raiseth cries of joy to thee.

Source: *The Papayrus of Ani* (1240 B.C.E.), *Egypt: Egyptian Book of the Dead,* Internet website, http://www.touregypt.net/bod1.htm.

Painting from the *Book of the Dead of Ani*, showing Ani's *ba* leaving his body, circa 1539–1190 B.C.E. (British Museum, London)

boxlike constructions called *mastabas,* and tombs cut deep into the rock, known most famously from the Valley of the Kings. The construction of the tomb was to begin as soon as a man had the means to do so. The *Instruction of Prince Hardjedef* gives this advice: "When you prosper, found your household, take a hearty wife, a son will be born to you. . . . Make good your dwelling in the graveyard, make worthy your station in the West (another euphemism for the land of the dead)" [translation by Miriam Lichtheim]. Whatever its form, the tomb had two main purposes, to house the body and to provide a place where the cult of the deceased could be carried out. This cult took the form of regular offerings and special rituals carried out during particular festivals. The two main parts of the tomb correspond to these two functions. The burial chamber, usually located belowground, housed and protected the body. Aboveground could be found the superstructure: the chapel, which served as the public part of the tomb, accessible to priests and visitors.

Burial Chamber. The burial chamber frequently contained the equipment necessary for a proper burial and a pleasant afterlife. Inside the burial chamber were found the coffin, four canopic jars (containing the liver, lungs, stomach, and intestines, which were removed at mummification), *shawabti*-figures (which were figurines designed to act as stand-ins whenever the deceased was called upon to do any work in the afterlife), amulets, and texts. Objects of daily life that were thought necessary for the comfort of the

deceased were also included in the burial chamber. These objects included food containers, furniture, tools, games, clothing, and any other object the deceased could have used. The walls of the burial chamber could be left plain or could be decorated with scenes from daily life, offering scenes, or scenes of the deceased in the afterlife.

False Door. The chapel could also take different forms. It could be as simple as a stele erected above the burial. Wealthier individuals could have a chapel of many rooms, usually, but not necessarily, above the burial chamber. The focal point of the chapel was a stele called by Egyptologists a "false door," since it represented a door carved in stone. This door, usually located directly above the burial chamber, was thought to be the place where the *ba* of the deceased could leave and enter the burial chamber. In front of the door could be found a stone table on which offerings could be left. The sides of the door were frequently engraved with the text of the offering formula, and it was thought that if any passersby would stop and recite the formula on behalf of the deceased, he would be magically provided with nourishment.

Scenes of Daily Life. The walls of the chapel could be decorated with many types of scenes. Some scenes depicted activities associated with agriculture, such as plowing, planting, and harvesting of crops, and the herding of animals. Scenes showing the processing of foodstuffs include those of brewing beer and making bread. Scenes of daily life include such activities as fishing and fowling, boating

Food offerings for the sustenance of the dead, including bread and fowl on a stand of reeds, circa 1450 B.C.E. (British Museum, London)

and boat-jousting matches, and the manufacturing of goods such as jewelry, chairs, beds, coffins, pottery, or cloth. During the First Intermediate Period (circa 2130–1980 B.C.E.) chapel walls were rarely decorated with such scenes. Rather, small wooden models depicting the same types of activities were included in the burials. The purpose of the scenes and models was the same, to ensure the deceased a steady supply of those goods he would need in the afterlife.

West of the Nile. The funeral began when the coffin of the deceased left his house. It could be carried by pallbearers or drawn on a sledge. The family of the deceased accompanied the procession, and they were said to be in a state of mourning. Tomb scenes show these individuals pulling at their hair, throwing dust on their heads, and collapsing from grief. Apparently men and women mourned separately, men outside, and women inside the home. Two women fulfilled the roles of the goddesses Isis and Nephthys, who mourned for Osiris (the wife of the deceased usually took the part of Isis). Also present were the embalmer, the lector priest, and the *Sem*-priest. Since most Egyptians lived on the East Bank of the Nile, and most cemeteries were located on the West Bank (west being the direction of the land of the dead, since the sun set in the west), a trip to the necropolis required travel by water. When the procession reached the river, the coffin was placed on a barge and towed to the *wabet*, the "place of purification" on the west bank of the Nile. In the *wabet*

various rituals of purification were carried out. From there the coffin was again placed on a sledge that was drawn by oxen to the tomb. Here the deceased was purified by the *Sem*-priest, and the Opening of the Mouth ritual was performed by the lector priest. The Opening of the Mouth ritual restored the vital faculties that the deceased had lost and allowed him to make use of the funerary offerings. This ritual derived from the statue workshops of Memphis and was originally used to animate statues of the gods after they were completed. Through a series of ritual passes made with an adze, the eyes, ears, nostrils, and mouth of the deceased were opened, restoring his senses and faculties. Glorification spells were recited in order to help the deceased transform into a glorified *akh*. The offering ritual involved the presentation of food, drink, incense, and many other goods before the false door of the tomb. The text stresses that the deceased had his own heart. This fact was essential, since in the final judgment before Osiris, it was the deceased's heart that was weighed in the balance against the feather of *Maat*. If the heart failed to measure up to *Maat*, it (and the deceased) would be devoured by the demon Amemet. As a result the heart was often carefully wrapped and replaced in the chest cavity of the mummy. The heart scarab frequently placed inside the chest was engraved with a spell to prevent the heart from opposing the deceased in the tribunal before Osiris. Completion of the rites of mummification and burial are what allowed the deceased to acquire the status of *netjer*.

Beloved Son. At burial the deceased was the recipient of offerings of food and drink. The need for such sustenance lasted far beyond the funeral, however. In order to ensure that he would have a steady supply of offerings to support him in the afterlife, an Egyptian would endow a foundation with land or with the income from a priestly office that he held. Usually, this endowment went to the eldest son of the deceased, called his "beloved son," on the condition that some of the income from the endowment went to provide offerings for the deceased. Such individuals functioned as "*ka* priests" for the deceased. They could be bequeathed to descendants of the *ka* priest for generations. During the New Kingdom (circa 1539–1075 B.C.E.) an individual who had royal permission could set up a statue of himself in the temple precincts and, through the intermediary of this statue, share in the prayers and offerings that went on in the temple.

Influence Beyond the Grave. Although the dead were buried in the necropolis, they did not cease to form part of the Egyptian family. During certain religious festivals, the dead were the recipients of special offerings. During the New Kingdom, at the "Feast of the Valley" families would cross over to the West Bank of the Nile to visit the tombs of their relatives and hold picnics within their chapels. Within the home, busts of deceased relatives as "effective spirits" could be set up to be the focal point of prayers and offerings. The deceased were still thought to be able to influence the lives of the living, hence the necessity to make sure that their needs were addressed.

Sources:

Sue d'Auria and others, *Mummies & Magic: The Funerary Arts of Ancient Egypt* (Boston: Museum of Fine Arts, 1988).

Salima Ikram and Aidan Dodson, *The Mummy in Ancient Egypt: Equipping the Dead for Eternity* (London: Thames & Hudson, 1998).

A. J. Spencer, *Death in Ancient Egypt* (Harmondsworth, U.K. & New York: Penguin, 1982).

THE GODS

Birth and Death. For the Egyptians, those gods that came into existence possessing the status of *netjer* represented the powers of nature conceived as personalized beings. They helped to explain the world, how it came into existence, why it continued to exist, and why events occurred as they did. The Egyptian gods had many characteristics that distinguish them from the Western conception of God. Egyptian gods had a beginning; they did not always exist. Egyptian texts speak of a time when the gods did not yet exist. The creator god (of whom there are several) is unique in that he (or she, in one instance) creates himself; the other gods were born to mothers and fathers. This situation brings up another characteristic of Egyptian gods; they have gender, male and female. Some are said to go through a childhood and grow to maturity. Not only did the Egyptian gods grow up, they grew old, and even died. An Egyptian deity could be killed, as when Seth killed his brother Osiris, or they could simply grow old and die. Every day, the setting sun was visualized as an old man near death. The ibis-headed god

Thoth was said to determine the life spans of both men and the gods. Egyptian texts even make references to the tombs of the gods, and one late text even mentions an entire graveyard of gods.

Other Limitations. Egyptian gods had other limitations as well. They were not considered to be omnipotent. Most gods and goddesses were thought to have power only within certain closely defined areas, such as a particular town, nome, or region of the world. Egyptians had a term that meant "local gods," meaning the deities of any particular locality. When an Egyptian traveler was in another part of Egypt or in another country, such as Nubia, he would pray to the local gods to protect him. Egyptian gods were not considered omniscient; they did not know everything. The story of Isis and Re, in which Isis concocts a plan to learn Re's secret name, and therefore gain power over him, shows that Isis was ignorant of Re's name and that Re was ignorant of Isis's plan, because he falls into her trap.

Names. The Egyptian gods did not have well-defined personalities. There are a few stories that give some insight into the character of Osiris, Isis, Seth, Horus, Re, Hathor, and a few other deities, but most of what is known of the gods comes from what one learns from their names and iconography. An Egyptian god could have more than one name, and the more powerful the god, the more names he could have. A name was not merely a label but was part of the personality of the god, revealing something about him. Almost all of the gods' names can be translated, and the translations generally denote a characteristic feature or function of the god. Examples include Amun (the Hidden One), the invisible god of the air; Khonsu (The Traveler), the moon god; and Wepwawet (Opener of the Ways), the jackal guide of the deceased. Some names reveal the god's origin, such as the snake goddess Nekhbet, whose name means "she of Nekheb," (present-day el-Kab, a town in southern Upper Egypt).

Groupings. The Egyptians grouped their deities together using several different numerical schemas. The simplest grouping was in pairs, usually of a god and goddess, although pairs of the same sex did exist (examples are Isis and Nephthys; Horus and Seth). The most common method of organizing deities was based on the triad, usually consisting of a god, a goddess, and their offspring. There are many examples of such triads in Egyptian religion: Osiris, Isis, and Horus; Amun, Mut, and Khonsu; and Ptah, Sekhmet, and Nefertem. Triads could consist of a god and two goddesses, for example, Osiris, Isis, and Nephthys or Khnum, Satis, and Anukis. The all-male triad of Ptah, Sokar, and Osiris was worshipped at Memphis. There was also an all-female triad consisting of Qadesh, Astarte, and Anat (all foreign deities introduced into Egypt). In the grouping Qadesh, Reshep, and Min one finds a goddess paired with two gods. These numerical groupings could grow larger, as with the *ogdoad* (grouping of eight pairs of gods) and the *ennead* (grouping of nine gods). An *ennead* could simply refer to the genealogical

The Gods

Drawings of various Egyptian deities (from Paul Johnson, *The Civilization of Ancient Egypt*, 1978)

classification of gods and was not limited to only nine members; some *ennead*s had as few as seven members, while others could have as many as fifteen.

Syncretism. There was an additional method of associating deities that is difficult for modern students of Egyptian religion to comprehend. The Egyptians could combine two or more gods into a single god. This phenomenon has been called syncretism by scholars and gives rise to the compound names such as Amun-Re. What has occurred with the god Amun-Re is that Amun and Re have merged to form a new god, Amun-Re. The gods Amun and Re continue to have a separate existence, however; where there were once two gods, Amun and Re, there are now three, Amun, Re, and Amun-Re. Generally, the second name in the pairing is the older god. Syncretism is a way for one deity to extend his sphere of action and influence. In a compound deity consisting of two components, the first name is the individual, while the second indicates the role that the deity is fulfilling. For example, Khnum-Re means Khnum in his role as life-giver and sustainer, powers associated with Re. The number of such combinations a deity can enter into is not limited; in addition to Amun-Re we find Sobek-Re, and from the *Pyramid Texts,* Re-Atum. Syncretism is not limited to two deities; examples of combinations of three (Ptah-Sokar-Osiris) and even four (Harmakis-Kheper-Re-Amun) occur. In each instance a new deity possessing all the powers and attributes of the individual constituents is formed, while each individual deity retains its own unique existence and influence. A striking example of this situation is found at the Great Temple of Ramesses II at Abu Simbel, where one finds sanctuaries dedicated to the gods Amun-Re, Re-Horakhty, and Ptah. Re occurs simultaneously in two different syncretistic combinations.

Sources:

Erik Hornung, *Conceptions of God in Ancient Egypt: The One and the Many,* translated by John Baines (London: Routledge & Kegan Paul, 1982).

Dimitri Meeks and Christine Favard-Meeks, *Daily Life of the Egyptian Gods,* translated by G. M. Goshgarian (Ithaca, N.Y.: Cornell University Press, 1996).

David Silverman, "Divinity and Deities in Ancient Egypt," in *Religion in Ancient Egypt: Gods, Myths, and Personal Practice,* edited by Byron E. Shafer (Ithaca, N.Y.: Cornell University Press, 1991), pp. 7–87.

HORUS

Sky God. Horus, in the form of a falcon, or falcon-headed human, is one of the oldest gods of the Egyptian pantheon. He was the god of the sky, whose right eye was associated with the sun, and whose left eye was the moon. A Dynasty 1 (circa 3000–2800 B.C.E.) comb shows the sky as the two wings of a bird, probably Horus. He was also associated with the king, and from Dynasty 1 onward one of the king's names was preceded by the Horus falcon, making the king the earthly embodiment of the cosmic Horus.

Battle with Seth. In the earliest version of the myths surrounding Horus, he was involved in a struggle with his brother, Seth, for the rulership of Egypt. This conflict is apparently a reflection of the political situation in which the city of Hierakonpolis (a major cult center for Horus) gradu-

Pectoral of Horus from Tutankhamun's tomb, Valley of the Kings, Thebes, circa 1322 B.C.E. (Egyptian Museum, Cairo)

ally expanded and engulfed Nagada (Ombos), a center of Seth-worship. This version of the myth must be reconstructed from allusions in the *Pyramid Texts.* For unstated reasons, Seth attacks Horus, and a violent struggle ensues. Horus loses an eye, and Seth loses his testicles. Eventually, the missing pieces are restored to their rightful owners, and the two gods go before a tribunal of the gods of the Heliopolitan *ennead,* with either Geb or Atum presiding. The verdict of this tribunal is that Horus is the rightful ruler of Egypt because he is the older of the two.

Son of Osiris. With the entrance of the god Osiris into the Egyptian pantheon, the protagonists in the myth shift roles. When Osiris becomes equated with the dead king, the living king, Horus, comes to be thought of as the son of Osiris, since the dead king was usually the father of the living ruler. The conflict between Horus and Seth then shifts to become a conflict between Osiris and Seth and serves to explain why Osiris is dead (he was killed by his brother Seth). Horus then assumes the role of a son avenging the wrong done to his father and fighting for his rightful inheritance, which in this instance is the throne of Egypt. Horus also takes on two aspects, Horus the Elder, ruler of Egypt, and Horus the Child (Greek Harpocrates), the son of Osiris and Isis. The trial before the gods becomes one of punishing Seth for the murder of Osiris and awarding Horus his inheritance.

Seth's Banishment. The New Kingdom (circa 1539–1075 B.C.E.) story of *The Contendings of Horus and Seth* is a narrative detailing the events that take place during the trial of Horus and Seth before Atum and the gods of the *ennead.* Each god has his supporters, and the tribunal sways first one way and then the other. The gods are depicted as petty, petulant bickerers who cannot make up their minds. Finally, Seth suggests a contest between the two. They are to transform themselves into hippopotamuses to see who can stay submerged longer. Because of Isis's interference, first on one side and then the other, the contest is indecisive. Seth then commits a sexual assault against Horus, intending to call forth his semen from Horus's body in the presence of the judges, thereby demonstrating his superiority over Horus. Again, Seth's efforts are thwarted by Isis, who rids Horus of Seth's semen, and tricks Seth into unwittingly ingesting Horus's semen. In desperation, Seth suggests the two gods build and race boats of stone, with the winner being declared the rightful heir. Seth proceeds to build a boat of stone, while Horus builds his boat of pine wood plastered over with gypsum, to give it the appearance of stone. When the race begins, Seth's boat sinks while Horus's continues on the course. Seth transforms himself into a hippopotamus and scuttles Horus's boat. Again, there is no clear winner. Finally, the judges decide to write a letter to Osiris and ask him who he would have as his heir. Osiris chooses Horus, who becomes the ruler of all Egypt. As a consolation prize, Seth is sent to live in the sky with Re, where he becomes the god of storms and thunder.

Poisoned Child. Another series of stories relate the events of Horus's childhood. After Isis finds herself pregnant by Osiris, Re-Atum suggests she hide this fact from Seth, lest he try to destroy the infant Horus. When Horus is born, Isis hides him in the marsh at Khemmis. Isis leaves the infant alone while she goes in search of food. When she returns, she finds the baby weak and unable to suckle. A local wise woman diagnoses the child as suffering from a poisonous sting, either of a scorpion or snake. Isis cries out for help, and the sound of her anguish brings even Re in his solar bark to a stop. The god Thoth arrives to aid Isis and recites spells that remove the poison from the child. Texts describing such events in the life of the infant Horus were carved on stone stelae known as *cippi*. These stelae depicted the infant Horus standing on the backs of crocodiles, grasping snakes, scorpions, and other dangerous animals by the tails. Water poured over the stelae was thought to absorb the power of the spells and was drunk by those seeking a cure for snake bite or scorpion sting.

Sources:

J. F. Borghouts, *Ancient Egyptian Magical Texts* (Leiden, Netherlands: E. J. Brill, 1978).

John Gwyn Griffiths, *The Conflict of Horus and Seth from Egyptian and Classical Sources: A Study in Ancient Mythology* (Liverpool: Liverpool University Press, 1960).

Geraldine Pinch, *Magic in Ancient Egypt* (Austin: University of Texas Press, 1994).

ICONOGRAPHY OF THE GODS

Various Depictions. Just as a god could have many different names, each revealing something about the nature of the deity, so could a god be depicted in many different ways. Egyptian gods could be shown as fully human, fully animal, or perhaps most familiar to even the most casual student of

Bronze figure of Wadjyt as a lion-goddess, Late Period, 664–332 B.C.E. (John Kluge Collection, Virginia)

ancient Egypt, in a hybrid form combining both human and animal elements. When creating images of a god, the Egyptians were not attempting to depict the god as he really was, but rather their goal was to communicate something essential about the god's nature.

Animal Form. The earliest evidence for the depiction of Egyptian gods seems to indicate that in the prehistoric period the Egyptians worshiped divine powers in animal form. Around the beginning of the Early Dynastic Period (circa 3000–2675 B.C.E.), powers that had been worshiped as deities came to be represented in human form. Toward the end of Dynasty 2 (circa 2800–2675 B.C.E.) the method of depicting Egyptian deities that was to become so commonplace is first used. On cylinder seal impressions from King Peribsen one finds gods in human form with animal heads, in this case the Seth animal and the hawk. Once these different methods of representing the deities make their appearance, they continue to coexist with the others; one form does not replace another. The same god could be represented using all three methods of purely human, purely animal, or animal-human hybrid. The goddess Hathor could be shown as a woman, as a cow's head on a woman's body, or simply as a cow.

Shades of Meaning. If the same deity could be represented in several different forms, it is obvious that not all of these depictions could represent the actual appearance of the deity. In fact, none of these depictions represented the "true" form of the deity; this form was forever hidden to man, just as the true name of the deity was a closely guarded secret. The task for the modern student of ancient Egyptian religion is to attempt to discern what meanings were intended by the different methods of representation of the Egyptian deities. An animal head on a human body revealed certain characteristics or attributes of the deity. The symbolism intended by the use of particular animals is not clearly understood. A human head combined with an animal's body seems to indicate the acquisition or possession of divine aspects by humans. For example, the human-headed *ba*-bird represents the ability of a deceased individual to freely move about and transform himself into different forms. That classic Egyptian symbol, the Sphinx, which places a human head on a lion's body, represents the royal power of the individual. A sphinx was not solely human-headed; it could take the head of several different animals, each representing a particular deity. A ram-headed sphinx represented the royal power of the god Amun-Re. A falcon-headed sphinx indicated the royal power of the god Horus, while a sphinx with the head of the Seth-animal represented the same for Seth. Each mixed figure, whether it be human head with animal body, or animal head with human body, represented a theological statement in iconographic form about the Egyptian god. These statements are not always clear to modern students of Egyptian religion.

Crowns and Other Symbols. The items the gods and goddesses were shown wearing or carrying also contribute information regarding their characteristics. The double crown of kingship was worn by several deities, including Atum, Horus, and even Seth. The Hathor-crown, consisting of cow horns with a sun-disk in the middle, was worn by goddesses known for their motherly nature, such as Hathor, Isis, and Renenutet. A deity shown wearing a crown with a sun-disk incorporated into it was thought to have some sort of relationship to the sun god. Deities could also be shown wearing an identifying hieroglyph as a headdress. Deities could be shown carrying the *ankh*-symbol, representing their power to bestow life. Gods could be shown carrying a *was*-scepter, indicating their dominion and control, while goddesses carried the *wadj*-staff, representing fertility and renewal in nature. The goddess Taweret, the protector of women in childbirth, was shown carrying a large *sa*-amulet, representing protection. Even the color associated with the gods was significant. Amun, the king of the gods during the New Kingdom (circa 1539–1075 B.C.E.), was shown with a blue skin, possibly representing the color of the sky. Osiris, Anubis, Isis, and various demons could be shown as black, indicating their association with the underworld and the afterlife. Osiris could also be depicted with a green face, an allusion to his powers of revival associated with fertility. The aggressive and hostile Seth was shown as red, the color of the rising and setting sun.

Sources:

Ann Rosalie David, *The Ancient Egyptians: Religious Beliefs and Practices* (London & Boston: Routledge & Kegan Paul, 1982).

Henri Frankfort, *Ancient Egyptian Religion: An Interpretation* (New York: Harper, 1961).

Erik Hornung, "Ancient Egyptian Religious Iconography," in *Civilizations of the Ancient Near East*, volume 3, edited by Jack M. Sasson (New York: Scribners, 1995), pp. 1711–1730.

THE KING

Divine Status. The king of Egypt was the only living person who possessed the status of *netjer*. He could be called "the good god," the "great god," or simply "god." Because of the king's special status, he could serve as the link between the worlds of the gods and of men. The king was the only mortal who could directly approach the gods. The temples throughout Egypt show only the king performing the rituals. This image was a polite fiction, because in reality the king commissioned the priests to act in his stead. The king's "divinity," however, is different from that of the gods. The king's divinity is an acquired status, bestowed when he ascends the throne. Beginning with his coronation, and extending throughout his reign, the king participates in rituals whose purpose is to reinforce and strengthen his divine status.

Descriptions. The Egyptians had many ways of describing the king's unique nature. He could be called a god, the son of a god, the image of a god, or he was described as like a god. For example, Merneptah was described as "the good god that lives on Maat . . . son of Kheperi [a form of the sun], descendant of the Bull of Heliopolis [probably a reference to Amun, Re, or Atum], . . . born of Isis." Redjedef, the third king of Dynasty 4 (circa 2625–2500 B.C.E.), and the successor of Khufu, was the first king to be called the Son of Re. From this point on, every king has a "Son of Re" name, usually his birth name, which was one of the king's two names enclosed in a cartouche. This king's status as the son of a god is elaborated on in the *Westcar Papyrus*, where scholars found the first allusion to the myth of the king's divine birth. There one reads about Ruddedet, the wife of a priest of Re, who was impregnated by Re himself. She gave birth to triplets, who grew up to be the first three kings of Dynasty 5 (circa 2500–2350 B.C.E.). Later, in Dynasty 18 (circa 1539–1295/1292 B.C.E.), Hatshepsut has a set of reliefs carved in her temple at Deir el Bahri depicting the myth of her divine birth. The god Amun, in the guise of her father Thutmose I, visits her mother one night. As a result of their union, Hatshepsut is conceived. The myth of the divine birth of the king was not confined to only Re and Amun. An inscription from the time of Ramesses II mentions that Ptah engendered the king in his form of Banebdjed.

Horus. The king could be equated with any number of deities when he was said to be fulfilling the functions of those gods. From the earliest periods of Egyptian history, the king was thought to be the embodiment of the ancient sky god Horus. Amenemhet I is described as "driving out evil (*isfet*, the opposite of Maat) when he appears like Atum." Senwosret III was described as Sekhmet, a fierce lion goddess representing the fiery heat of the sun, when attacking the enemies who trespassed on the borders of Egypt. The Loyalist Inscription (Sehetepibre stele) describes King Amenemhet III as Sia (goddess of perception), Re, Khnum, Bastet, Hapi, Montu, and Sakhmet. Here, the king was not the incarnation of these deities, but equating the king with these gods was descriptive of his roles, as warrior (Montu), nourisher (Hapi), protector (Sakhmet), and father figure (Khnum).

Four Purposes. According to an Egyptian text referred to by scholars as *The King as Sun Priest*, Re established kingship in Egypt for four purposes: "judging men, for making gods content, for creating Truth (*Maat*), and for destroying evil (*Isfet*)." The first of these duties, judging men, refers to the king's civil duties as the source of law and justice. The second, making the gods content, refers to the king's responsibility to see to it that temples to the gods are built and maintained throughout Egypt, and that in them the gods receive the necessary offerings and the required rituals are performed. The third and fourth duties, creating *Maat* and destroying *Isfet*, go together. *Maat* has been translated as truth, order, justice, or righteousness. It refers to the order established by the gods at creation, when a space was established in the chaos of Nun for life to take place. It refers to the natural order as well as to the social order, and embraces the concepts of duty, responsibility, social justice, and ethical behavior. It was

Grey granite sphinx, circa 1818–1772 B.C.E., originally sculpted as a representation of Amenemhet III and later usurped by a Hyksos ruler (Egyptian Museum, Cairo)

Wooden sculpture from Dahshur of King Auyibre Hor, showing on the king's head two raised hands, the hieroglyph for *ka* (life force), Dynasty 13, circa 1759–1630 B.C.E. (Egyptian Museum, Cairo)

the way the Egyptians thought things ought to be. It was the king's responsibility to ensure that *Maat* was preserved and that its opposite, *Isfet* (evil, disorder, injustice) was overcome. One of the most important duties of the king was to present *Maat*, represented as a small figure of the kneeling goddess, to the gods in their temples daily. In this way, the king reaffirmed that he was fulfilling his duty of preserving *Maat*.

Sources:

Henri Frankfort, *Kingship and the Gods: A Study of Ancient Near Eastern Religion as the Integration of Society and Nature* (Chicago: University of Chicago Press, 1978).

David O'Connor and David P. Silverman, eds., *Ancient Egyptian Kingship* (Leiden, Netherlands & New York: E. J. Brill, 1995).

Silverman, *Ancient Egypt* (New York: Oxford University Press, 1997).

KINGSHIP RITUALS

Formal Titulary. The king acquired and maintained his divinity through a series of rituals. The first such ritual the king participated in was his coronation, called in Egyptian *khai*, which means "to arise," and was also used to describe the sun's rising. At this time, the five elements of the king's formal titulary were announced: a Horus name, representing the king as the earthly embodiment of the sky god Horus; a "Two Ladies" name, the two ladies being the goddesses Nekhbet and Uadjit, the two protective goddesses of Upper and Lower Egypt; the Golden Horus (or simply the Gold) name, whose exact significance is uncertain; his throne name, assumed at accession, was preceded by the title "King of Upper and Lower Egypt"; and the birth name, which beginning in Dynasty 4 (circa 2625–2500 B.C.E.) was compounded with the title "son of Re." It is the throne name and birth name that were surrounded by a cartouche (an oval or oblong figure on a monument).

Opet **Festival.** Once being inducted into the office of kingship, the king participated in rituals designed to maintain and renew his divine status. Once a year the king traveled to Thebes to participate in the *Opet* festival at the temple of Luxor. During this festival, which began on the fifteenth or nineteenth day of the second month of the first season, *Akhet* (Inundation), the king participated in a procession from Karnak to the Luxor temple, where some of the rituals of the coronation were reenacted. The purpose of these rituals was to renew or restore the king's royal *ka* and reconfirm his right to rule. Each Egyptian was thought to possess a *ka*, which can roughly be translated "life force." It was a separate entity that was thought to inhabit the body. The *ka* was transmitted from parent to child and embodied the procreative power. The *ka* represented a bridge between the physical world and the world of the spirit. At his coronation, the king had received the royal *ka*, the same *ka* possessed by all the previous kings of Egypt. It was possession of this *ka* that rendered the king divine. As the vessel of the royal *ka*, some kings had temples dedicated to their worship built during their lifetimes. Amenhotep III erected temples to himself at Soleb, Sedeinga, and Sesebi; Tutankhamun built at Kawa and Faras; and Ramesses II at Gerf Hussein, es-Sebua, ed-Derr and most

This hymn was carved on the west wall of the Tomb of Ay, a courtier at Amarna who became king after Tutankhamun. It contains the most complete statement of Akhenaten's new theology. Many scholars have compared it to Psalm 104.

Adoration of Re-Harakhti-who-rejoices-in-lightland. In his name Shu-who-is-Aten, living forever; the great living Aten who is in jubilee, the lord of all that the Disk encircles, lord of sky, lord of earth, lord of the house-of-Aten in Akhet-Aten; and of the King of Upper and Lower Egypt, who lives by Maat, the Lord of the Two Lands, Neferkheprurue, Sole-one-of-Re; the Son of Re who lives by Maat, the Lord of Crowns, Akhenaten, great in his lifetime; and his beloved great Queen, the Lady of the Two Lands, Nefer-neferu-Aten Nefertiti, who lives in health and youth forever. The Vizier, the Fanbearer on the right of the King, . . . [Ay]; he says:

Splendid you rise in heaven's lightland,
O living Aten, creator of life!
When you have dawned in eastern lightland,
You fill every land with your beauty.
You are beauteous, great, radiant,
High over every land;
Your rays embrace the lands,
To the limit of all that you made.
Being Re, you reach their limits,
You bend them for the son whom you love;
Though you are far, your rays are on earth,
Though one sees you, your strides are unseen.
When you set in western lightland,
Earth is in darkness as if in death;
One sleeps in chambers, heads covered,
One eye does not see another.
Were they robbed of their goods,
That are under their heads,
People would not remark on it.
Every lion comes from its den,
All the serpents bite;
Darkness hovers, earth is silent,
As their maker rests in lightland.
Earth brightens when you dawn in lightland,
When you shine as Aten of daytime;
As you dispel the dark,
As you cast your rays,
The Tow lands are in festivity.
Awake they stand on their feet,
You have roused them;
Bodies cleansed, clothed,
Their arms adore your appearance.
The entire land sets out to work,
All beasts browse on their herbs;
Trees, herbs are sprouting,
Birds fly from their nests,
Their wings greeting your ka.
All flocks frisk on their feet,
All that fly up and alight,
They live when you dawn for them.
Ships fare north, fare south as well,
Roads lie open when you rise;
The fish in the river dart before you,
Your rays are in the midst of the sea.
Who makes seed grow in women,
Who creates people from sperm;
Who feeds the son in his mother's womb,
Who soothes him to still his tears.
Nurse in the womb,
Giver of breath,
To nourish all that he made.
When he comes from the womb to breath,

On the day of his birth,
You open wide his mouth,
You supply his needs.
When the chick in the egg speaks in the shell,
You give him breath within to sustain him;
When you have made him complete,
To break out from the egg,
He comes out from the egg,
To announce his completion,
Walking on his legs he comes from it.
How many are your deeds,
Though hidden from sight,
O Sole God beside whom there is none!
You made the earth as you wished, you alone,
All peoples, herds, and flocks;
All upon earth that walk on legs,
All on high that fly on wings,
The land of Khor and Kush,
The land of Egypt.
You set every man in his place,
You supply their needs;
Everyone has his food,
His lifetime is counted.
Their tongues differ in speech,
Their characters likewise;
Their skins are distinct,
For you distinguished the peoples.
You made Hapy in *dat* [the netherworld],
You bring him when you will,
To nourish the people,
For you made them for yourself.
Lord of all who toils for them,
Lord of all lands who shines for them,
Aten of daytime, great in glory!
All distant lands, you make them live,
You made a heavenly Hapy descend for them;
He makes waves on the mountains like the sea,
To drench their fields and their towns.
How excellent are your ways, O Lord of eternity!
A Hapy from heaven for foreign peoples [rain],
And all lands' creatures that walk on legs,
For Egypt the Hapy who comes from *dat* [the Nile].
Your rays nurse all fields,
When you shine they live, they grow for you;
You made the seasons to foster all that you made,
Winter to cool them, heat that they taste you.
You made the far sky to shine therein,
To behold all that you made;
You alone, shining in your form from yourself alone,
Towns, villages, fields, the river's course;
All eyes observe you upon them,
For you are the Aten of daytime on high.
You are in my heart,
There is no other who knows you,
Only your son Neferkheprure, Sole-one-of-Re,
Whom you have taught your ways and your might.
(Those on) earth come from your hand as you made them,
When you have dawned they live,
When you set they die;
You yourself are lifetime, one lives by you.
All eyes are on your beauty until you set,
All labor ceases when you rest in the west;
When you rise you stir everyone for the King,
Every leg is on the move since you founded the earth.
You rouse them for your son who came from your body,
The King who lives by Maat, the Lord of the Two Lands,
Neferkheprure, Sole-one-of-Re,
The Son of Re who lives by Maat, the Lord of crowns,
Akhenaten, great in his lifetime;
And the great Queen whom he loves, the Lady of the Two Lands,
Nefer-neferu-Aten Nefertiti, living forever.

Source: "Great Hymn to the Aten," in *Ancient Egyptian Literature: A Book of Readings,* volume II, compiled by Miriam Lichtheim (Berkeley: University of California Press, 1976), pp. 96–99.

Stone relief of Nectanebo I offering a statuette of the the goddess Maat to Thoth (in the form of a baboon), circa 381–362 B.C.E. (Egyptian Museum, Cairo)

famously, Abu Simbel. In these temples the king could even be shown worshiping himself. The king really was not worshiping himself, but the royal *ka*, of which he was only the vessel.

Sed **Festival.** After about thirty years on the throne, the king participated in a festival designed to restore his flagging powers. This event, called the *Sed* festival (named for an ancient jackal god Sed), could be held wherever the king chose. Generally, the festival would be held near the capital. Amenhotep I and Amenhotep III of Dynasty 18 (circa 1539–1295/1292 B.C.E.) held their *Sed* festivals at Karnak; Ramesses II celebrated a *Sed* festival at the city of Pi-Rameses in the Delta. The exact elements of the *Sed* festival are uncertain, and the available evidence indicates that the rituals underwent changes over the course of Egyptian history. The two major aspects of the *Sed* festival remained fairly constant. The king would sit on two thrones in succession, first wearing the crown of Upper Egypt, and then the crown of Lower Egypt. He would then pay a visit to each of the provincial gods in their shrines, which had been built for this occasion. Next he ascended the throne to receive visits from these same gods. Secondly, the king performed a ritual race or dance in which he strode across a field, crossing it along the two axes formed by the cardinal points. This activity took place between two territorial cairns, designated respectively as

the southern and northern boundary markers. During this circuit, the king wore alternately the two crowns of Egypt, a *shendyt* kilt, and carried a flail (a symbol of rulership) and a document container containing the deed to Egypt. The ritual of crossing the field was intended to symbolize the king's taking possession of Egypt.

Rejuvenation. The result of completing the *Sed* festival was the rejuvenation of the king. An inscription from the temple of Seti I at Abydos stated of the king that "you experience renewal again, you begin to flourish . . . as a young infant. You become young again year after year. . . . You are born again by renewing *Sed* festivals. All life comes to your nostrils. You are sovereign of the whole land forever." After completing his first *Sed* festival, the king could celebrate subsequent festivals at intervals of two to three years. Amenhotep III celebrated three such festivals, while Ramesses II held fourteen.

New Year. The third major festival associated with the king was the New Year's festival. This festival began on the last five days of the year, called *epagomenal* days, because they were added by the Egyptians to their 360-day calendar to bring the year up to 365 days. The festival lasted until about the ninth day of the first month. The festival had three main purposes: protect the king from the ills and dangers that were thought to threaten creation during the five *epagomenal* days; renew royal power for the coming year; and purify the king and Egypt from the miasmal effects of the end of the year and of their misdeeds of the past year. There were two main parts to the festival: the Ceremony of the Great Throne and the Rites of the Adoration of Horus Who Bestows the Heritage.

Ceremony of the Great Throne. During the Ceremony of the Great Throne the king was purified, dressed in new garments, provided with amulets of protection such as the *ankh*-sign (for life), and anointed nine times as a means of protection. After the last anointing, "Pharaoh is a god among gods, he is come into being at the head of the *ennead*, he has become great in the heaven and eminent in the horizon. Pharaoh is one of the victors who causes Re to triumph over Apophis; he is without wrongdoing, and his obstacles are dispelled." This last line is a quotation from *Book of the Dead* Spell 125, called the "negative confession" in which the deceased denies any wrongdoing. In a hymn to Isis from the temple at Philae (built in the third century B.C.E.) one reads: "The evils of the past year that had adhered to [the king] have been repelled. His evils of this year are destroyed. His back is turned to them. . . . He has not done anything abominable toward the god of his town. He has not committed any evil. Nothing will be counted against him among the assessors and the scribes of the Two Lands." Here the king is essentially performing two functions; he is making amends for his past wrongdoings and, by extension, the people of Egypt, and as a result, the king can claim ritual purity and sinlessness. The king can claim that he has fulfilled the divine commission to uphold *Maat* and destroy *Isfet* (wrongdoing), and, as a result, he and the

Wall scene from the Temple of Sethos I at Abydos showing a purification rite in which the gods pour sacred water over the king, Dynasty 19, circa 1292–1190 B.C.E.

people of Egypt are entitled to the blessings and favors of the gods.

Rites of the Adoration of Horus. In the Rites of the Adoration of Horus the king participated in a series of events that renewed his powers through recalling the coronation. The king spent a night in a chapel in the temple (which temple was not significant) during which he received a scepter and had four seals placed on his head, two with the name of Geb, one with Neith, and the other with *Maat*. The next morning, when the king appeared from the chapel, two birds were sent out as messengers to proclaim the king's dominion. The king then engaged in the symbolic massacre of Egypt's enemies by cutting off the tops of seven papyrus stalks. Next the king made offerings to all the deceased former kings of Egypt. This last act was related to the concept of the royal *ka* that we encountered in the *Opet* festival. Each king, by virtue of the fact that he was endowed with the royal *ka* at his coronation, was thought to be a direct descendant of all the previous kings of Egypt. One responsibility of possessing this *ka* was that of providing for the king's deceased predecessors. In ancient Egypt one way for the eldest son to ensure his right to the primacy of inheritance was to provide for the burial and continued funerary offerings of his father. By providing his deceased predecessors with the necessary offerings, the king is confirming his right to inherit the throne.

Importance. As can be seen from this brief description of the coronation, *Opet* festival, *Sed* festival, and the New Year festival, the maintenance of the king's divine status was of great importance in the royal ideology of Egypt.

An acquired status can be lost. In order to prevent this from happening, the king participated in several rituals intended to reinforce his divinity and relationship to the royal *ka*. This process was essential to the well-being of the country, because without his status of *netjer*, the king could neither meet the needs of the gods nor successfully intercede with the gods on behalf of the Egyptian people. If this happened, all sorts of calamities could be expected. After the period of the Amarna interlude, during which the gods and their temples were neglected, we are told that "the land was topsy-turvy, and the gods turned their backs upon this land." So it was vitally important to the well-being of Egypt that the king's status as *netjer* be constantly maintained.

Sources:
Lanny Bell, "Luxor Temple and the Cult of the Royal *Ka*," *Journal of Near Eastern Studies*, 44 (1985): 251–294.

H. W. Fairman, "The Kingship Rituals of Egypt," in *Myth, Ritual, and Kingship: Essays on the Theory and Practice of Kingship in the Ancient Near East and in Israel*, edited by S. H. Hooke (Oxford: Clarendon Press, 1958), pp. 74–104.

Eric Uphill, "The Egyptian Sed Festival Rites," *Journal of Near Eastern Studies*, 24 (1965): 365–383.

MYTHS: CREATION STORIES

Scarcity. Myths are stories that have a beginning, middle, and end, and which describe the activities of superhuman beings. Prior to the New Kingdom (circa 1539–1075 B.C.E.), myths are scarce in Egyptian texts, but allusions to them are plentiful. The reasons for this situation are uncertain, but it is probably related to the types of text that have survived. Allusions to the activities of the gods are found in

The *Shabaka Stone,* the principal surviving source of the Memphite account of creation, circa 716–702 B.C.E. (British Museum, London)

texts whose purpose is to provide for the successful transition of the dead into the afterlife or texts that accompany ritual activities. For these purposes, references to the doings of the gods are sufficient. Prior to the New Kingdom, Egyptian myths may have been transmitted orally.

Continuous Creation. While mythic narratives do not appear in the Egyptian records until the New Kingdom, the frequent allusions to the activities of the gods found in the *Pyramid Texts* and *Coffin Texts* allow scholars to reconstruct a fairly comprehensive and consistent view of the earliest Egyptian stories about the gods. One of the most important categories of myth for the Egyptians was that of creation stories. The Egyptians believed that for existence to continue, it had to be continually re-created at each dawn, at each full moon, or at each New Year. One part of the process of this re-creation was to recall the first time of creation. Characteristic of the Egyptians, they did not have only one creation account, but the creation of the universe was ascribed to several gods, and even a goddess. These creation accounts are named after the location where the creator-god or goddess had a major temple.

Atum. The earliest of all creation accounts is that associated with the god Atum at Heliopolis (Iunu in Egyptian or On in the Bible), and called by scholars the Heliopolitan Cosmogony (a cosmogony is a story of how the world came to be). In this version of creation the universe is originally an infinite, dark, watery expanse called Nun, or Nuu. Within this watery expanse, the god Atum essentially created himself and looked about for a place to stand. One tradition states that Atum stood on Mehet-weret, a goddess in the form of a cow representing a solid emerging from the waters. According to another tradition Atum stood on the primeval hill (located at Heliopolis), an image deriving from the emergence of land after the annual Nile flood recedes. After finding a place to stand, Atum masturbates with his hand (personified as the goddess Iusaas, "she who comes and grows"), and from his semen are produced the first god and goddess, Shu (male) and Tefnut (female). The name Shu means void, or emptiness. The meaning of Tefnut is uncertain; one tradition may associate her with moisture.

Birth of Mankind. After being emitted by Atum, Shu and Tefnut become separated from him in the dark expanse of Nun. Atum, finding himself alone again, sends out his eye to find his missing children. While his eye is away, Atum creates another eye to take its place. When the first eye returns with Shu and Tefnut, it becomes angry at being replaced. Atum then puts the eye on his forehead, where it becomes the protective, fire-spitting uraeus snake found on the headdress of the Egyptian kings and gods. A late tradition connects this event with the creation of mankind. When the eye returned with Shu and Tefnut, Atum became so happy he wept, and from his *remut* (tears) mankind (*remech*) came into being.

Father Earth. Shu and Tefnut mate and give birth to the god Geb and the goddess Nut. Geb represents dry land, while his sister-wife Nut is the sky. Originally, Geb and Nut are locked in an embrace, and Geb impregnates Nut. A significant event in the creative process occurs when Shu separates Geb from Nut, thereby creating a space in which

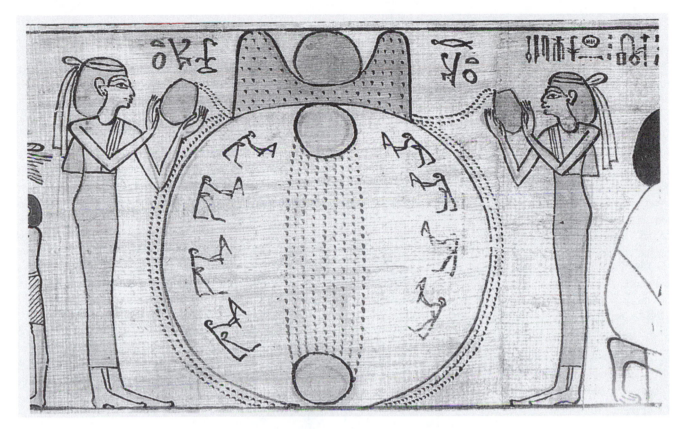

Drawing from the *Book of the Dead of Khensumose* depicting the first day of creation, Dynasty 21, circa 1075–945 B.C.E. (Akademie der Bildenden Kuenste, Vienna)

life can take place, a bubble in the expanse of Nun. This act is represented as Shu standing on a prone Geb while lifting the arching body of Nut high overhead. Shu represents the air and light separating the earth from the sky. A late text explains why Shu separated Geb and Nut; apparently they were quarreling because Nut kept swallowing her own children (that is, every morning the stars disappeared). Shu stepped in to stop the quarreling. One important aspect of this myth is the gender of the earth and sky. In most societies the earth was thought of as female (mother earth) and the sky as male. In Egypt this imagery is reversed. This situation is probably owing to the fact that in Egypt, the fertility of the land did not depend on rainfall (seen as the semen of the sky god), which was scarce in Egypt but rather on the rising floodwaters of the Nile. Since the earth was considered to be the source of these waters, it would follow that the earth was male.

Apophis. Another important aspect to this myth is the precariousness of the continued existence of the world. All life as the Egyptians knew it took place within the bubble created by the bodies of Geb and Nut separated by Shu. This bubble existed within the vast realm of chaos, Nun. At any point, the sky could come crashing down on the earth, obliterating all life and returning everything to Nun. Magical spells threatened to cause this development to come about if the practitioner did not gain what he desired. Rituals were carried out in Egyptian temples in order to prevent this watery chaos, represented by the serpent Apophis, from overcoming Re, the sun god. In one

passage in the *Book of the Dead*, Atum, in dialogue with Osiris, says that one day "this land will return to Nun, to the flood, like it was before."

Heliopolitan Ennead. Geb and Nut eventually give birth to two gods, Osiris and Seth, and two goddesses, Isis and Nephthys. Osiris and Isis give birth to the god Horus. The birth of these gods completes the Heliopolitan *ennead*, Atum, Shu, Tefnut, Geb, Nut, Osiris, Isis, Seth, and Nephthys. Horus, the tenth member of the *ennead*, is a later addition.

Hermopolis. A different version of the creation story is associated with the town of Hermopolis (Ashmounein) in Middle Egypt. This account centers around the Hermopolitan *ogdoad*, or group of eight gods. These deities were grouped in pairs of male-female gods: Nun and Naunet (primeval water and formlessness), Heh and Hehet (spaciousness), and Kek and Keket (darkness). These three pairs of gods are constant; the identity of the fourth pair varies. At times it is Tenem and Tenemet (confusion and gloom). It can also be Gereh and Gerehet (completion) or Niu and Niut (void). Eventually, the god Amun and his female counterpart Amaunet, representing hiddenness, become the customary fourth pair in the *ogdoad*. The gods of the *ogdoad* all represent characteristics of the chaos that existed before creation. A late tradition associates the origin of these gods with the main city of Amun, which is Thebes. The serpent god Kematef, "he who accomplishes his time," had a son, another snake god Irta, "he who makes the land." Irta was said to have traveled from Thebes to Hermopolis, where he created the *ogdoad*. Another late tradition describes Thoth as the creator of the *ogdoad*. The gods of the *ogdoad* were depicted as frog-headed (male) and snake-headed (female) humans.

Great Cackler. When the primeval hill, called the *iu neserer* (island of flame), arises out of chaos the *ogdoad* comes together and creates the sun on this hill. Building inscriptions reveal that there was once a shrine called the "island of flame" at Hermopolis, but its location has yet to be found. The *ogdoad* was said to create the sun in two ways. One tradition says that the *ogdoad* came together and created an egg on the primeval hill. The goose that laid this egg, called the Great Cackler, came to be associated with Amun. This deity can occasionally be found depicted on stelae from Deir el Medina as a goose, at times accompanied by eggs. An inscription from the tomb of Petosiris, dated to the fourth century B.C.E., claims that the shell of this egg was buried at Hermopolis.

Lake of Origin. During the Ptolemaic Period (332–330 B.C.E.) another version of the creation of the sun arose. In this account the sun emerges from the opening blossom of a lotus. The male members of the *ogdoad* were said to have placed their semen in the waters of Nun. This semen traveled to a vegetable ovary called *benen* (which was also the name of the temple to Khonsu at Thebes). In the hieroglyphic script, *benen* is represented as an egg. This egg is the contribution of the female members of the *ogdoad*. The place where the egg was fertilized was called the "lake of origin." From the *benen* a lotus sprouts and takes root on the island of flame. When the lotus blossom opens, the sun rises, depicted as a child sitting inside the flower. The association of the lotus blossom and the sun arises from the fact that the Egyptian blue lotus sinks underwater at night, and rises and opens at daylight.

Death at Thebes. The remainder of the cosmogony is not detailed. The sun-god created the gods from his mouth, mankind from his tears, and cattle from his limbs. After the *ogdoad* completed their work of creation (either by creating the egg or lotus blossom), they are said to have traveled to Thebes, where they died. They were supposedly buried at Medinet Habu, Edfu, and Esna. At these locations they were the recipients of a funerary cult.

Memphite Theology. Another cosmogony, called the Memphite Theology, is preserved in only one text, known as the *Shabaka Stone*, after the Dynasty 25 (circa 760–656 B.C.E.) king who had it carved. Because of the archaic nature of the writing and language, it was originally thought that this text originated in the early Old Kingdom (circa 2675–2130 B.C.E.). Subsequent studies have shown that the text cannot be earlier than the New Kingdom, perhaps dating to the reign of Ramesses II. One scholar has even suggested that the text should be dated to the time of the copy, that is, to Dynasty 25. Such a discrepancy in assigning a date to the text arises from the fact that Egyptian scribes would copy and recopy religious texts for hundreds, and in some cases, thousands of years, and if scholars have only one copy of a text it is difficult to be cer-

tain when the text originated. For example, some Ptolemaic funerary papyri contain examples of *Pyramid Texts*, and if Egyptologists did not have copies from the Old Kingdom pyramids they would never have known how old these texts really were. Another problem in dating texts is that the Egyptians would deliberately write in an archaic style and attribute a text to an ancient pseudepigraphic author to lend the text an aura of antiquity, and therefore enhance its authority.

Ptah. The main actor in the Memphite Theology was the god Ptah. He was originally a patron god of craftsmen and artisans. By the New Kingdom he has risen to become a universal creator god. Hymns call him the father of the fathers of all the gods (possibly a reference to the Hermopolitan *ogdoad*, who were called the fathers of the gods), and describe him as the one who carries Nut and lifts up Geb (equating him with Shu). Ptah is said to have brought about creation by first planning it in his mind (literally heart), and then by speaking the name of everything and calling it into existence. The Memphite Theology has received considerable attention because it reminds scholars brought up in the Judeo-Christian tradition of a god who creates through speaking ("God said. . . . And it was so."), rather than by the physical methods of creation employed by the other Egyptian creator gods.

Esna Cosmogony. The final cosmogony to be discussed merits mention because, unlike the other creation accounts examined so far, the creator in the Esna Cosmogony is not a god but the goddess Neith. This cosmogony is found on the walls of the Temple of Khnum at Esna, and dates to the period of the Roman emperor Trajan in the first century C.E. This creation story borrows significantly from earlier accounts. Neith is said to have been the first being to emerge from Nun. She changes herself into a cow, and then a *lates*-fish. These images derive from the cult of Neith. She was worshiped in the form of a cow and *lates*-fish at Esna. Neith creates a place for herself to stand and then turns herself back into a cow. She pronounces thirty names, which become thirty gods to help her in the process of creation. These gods are said to be *khem* (ignorant), and they then transform themselves into the *khemenu* (Hermopolitan *ogdoad*). Neith then creates the sun god through producing an excrescence from her body and placing it in an egg, which hatches as Re, the sun, who promptly takes the name of Amun. He then continues the act of creation through emanations from his body, creating the *netjeru* (gods) from his saliva, which is *nety* (spat out), and mankind from his tears.

Sources:

James P. Allen, *Genesis in Egypt: The Philosophy of Ancient Egyptian Creation Accounts* (New Haven: Yale Egyptological Seminar, 1988).

Rudolf Anthes, "Mythology in Ancient Egypt," in *Mythologies of the Ancient World*, edited by Samuel Noah Kramer (Garden City, N.Y.: Doubleday, 1961), pp. 16–92.

Leonard Lesko, "Ancient Egyptian Cosmogonies and Cosmology," in *Religion in Ancient Egypt: Gods, Myths, and Personal Practice*, edited by Byron E. Shafer (Ithaca, N.Y.: Cornell University Press, 1991), pp. 88–122.

John Wilson, "Egypt," in *The Intellectual Adventure of Ancient Man* (Chicago: University of Chicago Press, 1946), pp. 31–61.

Painting of Osiris holding the crook and flail of rulership, from the tomb Sennedjem at Deir el Medina, circa 1279–1213 B.C.E.

OSIRIS

Mighty One. Osiris played an important role in Egyptian mythology as the god of the underworld and judge of the dead. As a chthonic deity, he also became associated with the fertility of the earth. Osiris first appears in Egyptian texts at the end of Dynasty 5 (circa 2500–2350 B.C.E.), when he is mentioned in both inscriptions in private *mastabas* (boxlike tombs) and in the *Pyramid Texts* found in Unas's pyramid. His name was written with the hieroglyph of an eye surmounting a throne, and this combination has given rise to much speculation as to the origin and meaning of the name Osiris. At this point, there is no agreement about the significance of the name or its spelling. The simplest etymology would connect his name to the word *wsr*, meaning "mighty," making Osiris the "mighty one."

Fertility and the Underworld. Apparently, Osiris was not originally viewed in a positive light. He may have been the god of the unsuccessful dead, that is, those who did not ascend to the sky to become a star or gain a spot in Re's bark. Osiris seems to have originally been thought of in the form of a dog, based on a *Pyramid Text* passage, which says that the king has the face of a jackal, like Osiris. He quickly lost this form, however, and his earliest depictions show him as a mummiform human with his hands protruding from the mummy bandages and gripping the symbols of kingship, the crook and flail. He is frequently shown wearing the white crown of Upper Egypt, or the *atef*-crown. His face and hands are often painted green, representing his association with fertility, or black, a color associated with the underworld.

Dead Kings. Whatever Osiris's origin, the *Pyramid Texts* show that by the end of Dynasty 5, the dead king has come to be identified with Osiris. These texts frequently refer to the dead king as the *Osiris N* (representing the name of the dead king). As such, the king has gone from being the king of Egypt to being the king of the underworld. In these texts scholars find the first allusions to the myth of Osiris, which is not recorded in narrative form until the first century C.E., when the Greek writer Plutarch recorded the myth. In this version Osiris was a king of Egypt who was murdered by his jealous brother Seth. How this takes place is uncertain. Some texts refer to Osiris as being "thrown down" in Nedyet in the land of Gehesty, while others refer to Osiris being drowned in the water of Djat. There may also be references to the dismemberment of Osiris. In the Greek version, Seth hosts a banquet and offers an exquisitely carved chest to whomever can fit inside it. When Osiris climbs into the chest, Seth slams it shut, seals it with molten lead, and throws it into the Nile. From there, it makes its way along the currents to the shores of Lebanon, where it becomes enfolded in the trunk of a tree, which is used as a column of a temple by the king of Lebanon.

First Mummy. All versions of the myth include the search and discovery of Osiris's body. There are some indications in the *Pyramid Texts* that his father Geb found Osiris's body. Most commonly, however, his sister-wife Isis and sister Nephthys are the ones who discover the body of Osiris. They are able to restore the body to life just long enough to allow Osiris to impregnate Isis with his son and heir, Horus. In later versions of the myth the god Anubis transforms the corpse of Osiris into the first mummy, which serves as the prototype of the treatment all deceased Egyptians wished to receive. According to the Greek version of the story, Isis leaves the chest containing the body of Osiris in Buto, while she attends to her newborn child. Seth discovers the chest, becomes enraged, and dismembers the body of Osiris, scattering the pieces throughout Egypt. Isis finds each part and buries it. This action provides an explanation for the various tombs of Osiris found up and down the Nile. Osiris then assumes his permanent position as ruler of the underworld.

Cult. The major cult center of Osiris was Abydos. Originally, this city was the cult center of the jackal god of the dead Khentiamentiu, "foremost of the Westerners (that is, the dead)." During Dynasties 5 (circa 2500–2350 B.C.E.) and 6 (circa 2350–2170 B.C.E.), however, Khentiamentiu became assimilated with Osiris. Beginning in Dynasty 12 (circa 1938–1759 B.C.E.), his temple at Kom el-Sultan was taken over by Osiris. Also in Dynasty 12, the Dynasty 1 (circa 3000–2800 B.C.E.) *mastaba* of King Djet was mistaken as the tomb of Osiris. Every year, Abydos was witness to a huge festival during which a dramatic presentation of the myth of Osiris took place. In order to participate vicariously in this festival, kings would build cenotaphs (false tombs) for themselves at Abydos. Along the festival route, private individuals erected small chapels for themselves. These chapels, called *mahat*, could contain a small stele or statue of the owner. This object would become the conduit through which the individual could magically share in the bounty of the festival.

Sources:

Jan Assmann, *The Search for God in Ancient Egypt* (Ithaca, N.Y.: Cornell University Press, 2001).

John Gwyn Griffiths, *The Origin of Osiris and His Cult* (Leiden, Netherlands: E. J. Brill, 1980).

Eberhard Otto, *Egyptian Art and the Cults of Osiris and Amon*, translated by Kate Bosse Griffiths (London: Thames & Hudson, 1968).

PERSONAL RELIGION

Evidence. Personal piety is not uniformly attested throughout Egyptian history. Before the New Kingdom (circa 1539–1075 B.C.E.) it is rare to find a private person depicted on a stele worshiping a deity. Old Kingdom (circa 2675–2130 B.C.E.) tomb biographies tended to stress the service the tomb owner had performed for the king, and any mention of his deeds for the gods is largely absent. During the First Intermediate Period (circa 2130–1980 B.C.E.) scholars find the first indications of the belief in divinities who would intervene in the lives of individuals. Such references are few, however, and seem to be outside the norm of general religious experience. Beginning in the New Kingdom, however, the evidence indicates a much-greater emphasis on an individual's personal relationship with the gods, and the gods' actions on behalf of the individual. Evidence for such personal piety becomes abundant during the Ramesside Period (circa 1295–1069 B.C.E.), and it has been suggested that this is a

Private votive stele recording an incident when the god Wepwawet saved a priest of Amun from a crocodile, circa 1295–1069 B.C.E. (British Museum, London)

reaction to the religious upheaval that took place in Egypt during the Amarna Period.

Encountering the Gods. A primary locus for the individual's encounter with the gods was the temple. While most of the temple activities were closed to the public, there were occasions when the gods appeared publicly. During festivals, when the gods left their temples in processions, people had the opportunity to present the gods with questions and receive oracular responses. In addition, there were places set aside within the temple complex where people could approach the gods with their prayers. At the rear of some temples, directly behind the sanctuary of the temple, could be found a chapel of the "hearing ear." This structure could vary between an elaborate chapel to a simple niche with a statue of the main god of a temple, or even only a pair of carved ears, representing the god's ability to hear prayers. There were also places in the gates of the *temenos* wall where people could make prayers and offerings to the gods. The south gate of the temenos wall at Edfu was described as "the standing place of those who have and those who have not, in order to pray for life from the lord of life." Even the relief images of the gods in the accessible parts of the temple could become the focus of prayers and offerings. Some of these figures show evidence that at one time structures were built around some relief sculptures, forming small shrines, with a shelf for offerings and at times a curtain to conceal the relief.

Purposes. People would visit a temple for three main purposes: to pray, to make sacrifice, and to dedicate votive offerings. Prayers were generally delivered orally and began with a low bow, called "kissing the ground." The petitioner would then kneel or stand, with arms raised, to praise the deity and make his or her requests. Fortunately, visitors sometimes carved their prayers into the temple as graffiti, which preserve for scholars evidence of the types of things people prayed for. People could pray to receive the favor of the gods, or to be loved by their gods. Other requests included the opportunity to go on pilgrimages, to avoid evildoing, or to receive the material necessities of life, good health, and a long lifetime of the ideal 110 years. One man left a prayer for potency and a good wife as a companion. Another left a request that he gain favor in the eyes of a certain chantress in the temple of Amun. Letters written by officials of the Ramesside period who were away on business to their family members back in Egypt made requests for prayers to be offered on their behalf. One such official, Dhutmose, instructed his family and servants to "please call upon Amun to bring me back, for I have been ill since I arrived north and am not in my normal state. Don't set your minds to anything else. As soon as my letter reaches you, you shall go to the fore-court of Amun Lord of the Thrones of the Two Lands, taking the little children along with you and coax him and tell him to keep me safe."

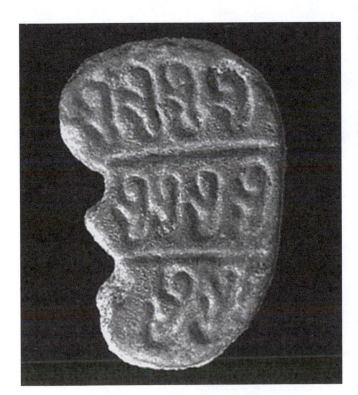

Votive ear stele from the reign of Akhenaten, circa 1353–1336 B.C.E. It represents the ear of a god, into which a person could recite his prayers directly (Petrie Museum of Egyptian Archaeology, University College, London).

DREAM BOOK

To the Egyptians, sleep allowed a person to communicate with the gods and the dead. The information that those in the afterlife could impart to the living was considered to be invaluable. The following list is from a Middle Kingdom (circa 1980–1630 B.C.E.) dream book:

Auspicious Dreams:	Meaning:
Sitting in a Garden in the Sun	Pleasure
Eating Excrement	Consuming One's Property
Mating with a Cow	Happy Day at Home
Eating Crocodile Meat	Becoming an Official
Offering Water	Prosperity
Drowning in a River	Purification from Every Evil
Seeing the Moon Shining	Pardon from a God
Veiling Oneself	Enemies are Fleeing
Sawing Wood	Enemies are Dead
Cultivating Vegetables	Finding Victuals

Inauspicious Dreams:	Meaning:
Being Seized by One's Lower Leg	The Dead are Reporting on You
Seeing Oneself in a Mirror	Another Wife
Eating Hot Meat	Not Being Found Innocent
Shod with White Sandals	Roaming the Earth
Copulating with a Woman	Mourning
Dog Bite	Magic Spell
Measuring Barley	Words Arising against You
Writing on Papyrus	A God is Reckoning Your Wrongs
Stirring up One's House	Illness
Bed Catching Fire	Driving Away One's Wife

Source: A. G. McDowell, *Village Life in Ancient Egypt: Laundry Lists and Love Songs* (Oxford & New York: Oxford University Press, 1999), pp. 110–113.

Offerings. Worshipers did not approach their gods empty-handed. When they visited the temples to offer prayers, they frequently brought sacrifices along as an inducement to the god to grant their requests. Common sacrifices included libations of wine, beer, milk, or water. The presentation of bread, fruit, or flowers, or the burning of incense or foodstuffs was also common. Most temple visitors brought their offerings with them, but they could also be acquired at the temple. A more permanent type of offering was the votive offering, a permanent memorial of a prayer to a deity. Votives could include stelae, showing the petitioner praising the god, model ears, or stelae with images of ears, intended to induce the deity to hear the petitioner's prayers. Other types of offerings included model phalluses, intended to gain fertility for the offerer, or small images of deities or cult objects used in the temples.

Sources:

John Baines, "Society, Morality, and Religious Practice," in *Religion in Ancient Egypt: Gods, Myths, and Personal Practice,* edited by Byron E. Shafer (Ithaca, N.Y.: Cornell University Press, 1991), pp. 123–200.

Florence Friedman, "Aspects of Domestic Life and Religion," in *Pharaoh's Workers: The Villagers of Deir el Medina,* edited by Leonard H. Lesko (Ithaca, N.Y.: Cornell University Press, 1994), pp. 95–115.

Geraldine Pinch, *Votive Offerings to Hathor* (Oxford: Griffith Institute, 1993).

PUBLIC CHAPELS AND PRIVATE SHRINES

Deir el Medina. Temples were not the only location at which the worship of the gods occurred. The site of Deir el Medina has preserved the remains of public chapels dedicated to the gods. These chapels show a fairly consistent design. They consisted of an open forecourt leading to a roofed hall, often with one or two pillars, with benches along each side wall. On the benches were seats, seven along one side of the hall, five along the other. Some seats from these chapels were inscribed with the names of individuals, which may indicate that participation in worship in the chapel was by subscription. There is evidence later in Egypt of the existence of "cult guilds," in which individuals would enter into a legal contract to band together in the worship of a particular deity. Such evidence does not appear until Dynasty 26 (664–525 B.C.E.), and as yet no written evidence of such societies has turned up for New Kingdom (circa 1539–1075 B.C.E.) Egypt. The open forecourt gave way to a small room, called the *pronaos,* which led to a series of one to three sanctuaries for cult statues, or more probably, stelae, to the gods of the shrine. Around the sides of these rooms were subsidiary service rooms or rooms in which the guardian of the chapel could live. The priests who served these chapels were the workmen who

Domestic shrine, from Thebes, with a prayer to Amen and Thutmose III, circa 1539–1295/1292 B.C.E.
(Cleveland Museum of Art)

lived at Deir el Medina and served part-time in the chapel. The chapels were places where worshipers could go to make prayers, offerings, and to receive oracles.

Domestic Shrines. Houses at Amarna have preserved evidence of domestic shrines. These shrines were located in the garden, surrounded by trees and separated from the rest of the garden by a wall. They consisted of a sloping flight of stairs leading up to a platform, on which was a walled room containing an altar of brick or limestone. Found within these shrines were statues of Akenaten and his family, or stelae showing the royal family worshiping the Aten. Again, at Deir el Medina, the hills around the town are dotted with more than fifty tiny shrines arranged in rough rows. These shrines consisted of a few rough stones each, arranged to form a back, floor, two sides and a roof. Sometimes stones marked off a miniature forecourt. Inside each shrine was originally a small stele, commemorating its donor's dedication to his gods. Finally, there were places set aside within the house itself where people could worship their gods. The walls of a house could contain niches in which could be placed a stele of a god. Such niches could be fitted with a wooden door and could be found in any room of the house. Deities particularly popular in such house shrines were Meretseger (protective goddess of the Theban necropolis), Renenutet (goddess of harvest), Sobek (crocodile god), Amun, Taweret (goddess who protected women during childbirth), and Hathor (mother goddess). In addition to the gods, stelae depicting deceased relatives or anthropoid busts of such relatives were erected and served as the recipients of offerings. Deceased relatives were worshipped as *akh aper*, effective spirits, and were thought to be able to influence the lives of their living relatives.

Unknown Cult. The nature of the cult carried on in these private venues is not well known. From the images on the stelae, it seems that offerings of incense, food, and libations were made to the gods. The ritual involved in these offerings, or their frequency, is unknown. One suggestion is that a smaller, less-elaborate version of the daily temple ritual may have been celebrated, but this is just conjecture.

Sources:

Ann Rosalie David, *The Ancient Egyptians: Religious Beliefs and Practices* (London & Boston: Routledge & Kegan Paul, 1982).

Henri Frankfort, *Ancient Egyptian Religion: An Interpretation* (New York: Harper, 1961).

Ashraf I. Sadek, *Popular Religion in Egypt during the New Kingdom* (Hildesheim: Hildesheimer Ägyptologische Beiträge, 1987).

RE

Sun God. Re was the Egyptian god of the sun par excellence. His primary cult center was the city of Iunu (Biblical On), called Heliopolis by the Greeks. Re was worshipped as a falcon, or as a human with a falcon head, or simply as a human. Re was most often shown with a sun-disk on his head, surrounded by a protective uraeus serpent. At night, while in the underworld, Re is shown as a ram-headed human.

Royal Title. Re first rose to prominence in Dynasty 4 (circa 2625–2500 B.C.E.), when Redjedef became the first king to add the title "son of Re" to his titulary. From this time on, every king of Egypt took a name that symbolized his descent from Re. The Middle Kingdom (circa 1980–1630 B.C.E.) tale of King Khufu and the Magicians relates how the first three kings of Dynasty 5 (circa 2500–2350 B.C.E.), Userkaf, Sahure, and Neferirkare Kakai, were the sons of Re and the wife of one of his priests.

Temples. Some of the greatest architectural remains of ancient Egypt are related to Re. The pyramid was a solar symbol. It was a physical representation of the sun's rays, as seen streaming down through the clouds. As such, these rays were thought to form a path on which the deceased king could ascend to the sky to join Re in his voyage across the sky. In addition to building their own pyramids, the Dynasty 5 kings constructed temples specifically for the worship of Re. These structures, called sun temples, consisted of an open-air altar for sacrifices, a huge stone whose top was shaped like a small pyramid (the precursor of the obelisk), called a *benben*, and a large, brick model of the solar boat. The *benben* represented the first hill to emerge

Faience plaque of Bes, a good luck charm for the protection of newborns and the continued prosperity of the family, circa 1075–656 B.C.E. (University of Pennsylvania Museum of Archaeology and Anthropology)

Stone carving from a Dynasty 30 (381–343 B.C.E.) sarcophagus depicting the daily birth of the sun with the primeval forces of nothingness on either side (Egyptian Museum, Cairo)

from the waters of Nun at the time of creation. This *benben*-stone served as a model for the later obelisks erected by Egyptian kings.

Regeneration. Re was considered to be the creator and sustainer of the universe. Every morning, Re was reborn from the waters of Nun and began his voyage through the sky. He was thought of as sailing across the sky in his solar bark, called Mandjet. Re assumed a different form at various periods of the day. At dawn, the newly born Re was thought of as the scarab-form god Kheperi. Kheperi took the form of a dung beetle. His name meant "he who has come into being." The dung beetle rolling his ball of dung across the desert floor served as a symbol of the sun crossing the sky. The fact that the ball of dung served as an incubator for the beetle larva, and that out of the ball emerged new beetles, demonstrated to the Egyptians that the beetle was a symbol of regeneration. As such, Kheperi represented the powers of creation, which kept the cosmos functioning.

Apophis. At midday the sun god took the form of Re, a man in his prime. As such, Re was the ruler of the universe, the provider of justice for all his creation. In this form he was closely associated with the Egyptian king. At midday the sun was thought to come to a brief standstill (the Egyptian word for midday means standstill), brought on by the serpent Apophis. Apophis was the enemy of Re and of all creation. He represented the power of chaos to overcome creation. He makes his first appearance in Egyptian texts during the instability of the First Intermediate Period. At noon he was thought to swallow up the waters of the celestial river, grounding Re's bark on the "sandbank of Apophis." Seth forces Apophis to regurgitate the water by stabbing him with his spear, thereby allowing Re to continue on his journey. At times Isis is said to use her magic to defeat Apophis. In order to insure that the sun continued on its daily journey and to aid in the overthrowing of chaos, in temples throughout Egypt, priests would perform hymns hourly during the day and night to keep the sun moving.

Nocturnal Voyage. At sunset the sun was visualized as Atum, an old man, symbolizing the potential of regeneration, because at night the sun descended into the underworld, where he was regenerated by the waters of Nun, to be reborn again the next day as Kheperi. This nightly, rejuvenating journey of the sun became a symbol of the regeneration of the dead. The New Kingdom (circa 1539–1075 B.C.E.) underworld books depict in graphic detail the dangers and denizens the sun faced during his nocturnal voyage, which took place in the Meskett bark. This journey could also be thought of as taking place within the body of Nut, the goddess representing the sky. At night, Nut swallowed Re and he passed through her body, to be reborn from between her thighs at dawn. This journey took twelve hours, and at midnight Re was thought to join with Osiris in the depths of the under-world, bringing about his regeneration.

Negative View. Not all descriptions of Re cast him in a positive light. In a magical spell designed to provide relief from the pain of a scorpion's sting, Re is described as an old man whose limbs trembled and who drooled. Isis took some of Re's saliva that had fallen to the ground and mixed it with clay to form a serpent. She then hid the snake near the path frequented by Re daily, and when Re passed by, it bit him. When he asked Isis to help relieve his suffering, she replied that she could only aid him if he told her his true name. Re hedged, revealing many of his names and epithets, but not his true name. To do so would grant Isis power over him. Finally, when the pain became unbear-able, he revealed his true name to Isis, and she healed him of his affliction. In the *Book of the Heavenly Cow* Re is described as an old man against whom his subjects, mean-ing mankind, plot. When he learns of their treachery, Re sends his fiery eye, as Hathor, down to destroy them. In this instance the eye represents the searing heat of the sun. After many have died, Re relents, and in order to save mankind he tricks Hathor into getting drunk and falling asleep, thereby ending her rampage.

Sources:
Jan Assmann, *Egyptian Solar Religion in the New Kingdom: Re, Amun and the Crisis of Polytheism,* translated by Anthony Alcock (London & New York: Kegan Paul International, 1995).

J. F. Borghouts, *Ancient Egyptian Magical Texts* (Leiden, Netherlands: E. J. Brill, 1978).

Manfred Lurker, *The Gods and Symbols of Ancient Egypt* (New York: Thames & Hudson, 1980).

TEMPLE ARCHITECTURE AND SYMBOLISM

God's House. One of the king's duties was to build and maintain temples throughout Egypt. The Egyptian word for temple meant "god's house," and temples were designed to be the earthly dwellings of the gods. As such, they included all the elements necessary to provide for the care and feeding of the gods. To meet the needs of the gods, a temple needed to control an extensive network of land, livestock, and personnel. All of the elements necessary to conduct the business of the temple were referred to as the *r-pr,* or temple estate. There were two main classes of tem-ples in ancient Egypt, the cult temple and the mortuary temple, called by the Egyptians the "House of Millions of Years." The cult temple had as its main purpose to carry out the worship of a particular deity or deities. The mortuary temple was built by the reigning king in order to carry out his cult while living and to provide for his mortuary cult after he died. Since much that went on in cult temples had to do with the king, and the "houses of millions of years" could have areas dedicated to the cults of the gods, it has been suggested that the difference between the two was a matter of focus: the cult temple having as its primary focus the carrying out of the cult of a god, and a mortuary temple having as its primary focus the carrying out of the cult of the divine king, but not to the exclusion of the cults of other gods.

VALLEY OF THE KINGS

Wadi al-Muluk (Valley of the Kings) is located in Upper Egypt where the ancient city of Thebes once stood. It was the burial site of nearly all of the kings of Dynasties 18 (circa 1539–1295/1292 B.C.E.), 19 (circa 1292–1190 B.C.E.), and 20 (circa 1190–1075 B.C.E.). There are sixty-two known tombs, and aside from monarchs ranging from Thutmose I to Ramesses X, two queens, some children of Ramesses II, and several high government officials also are interred there.

Fearing for the security of their funerary treasures, the kings of the New Kingdom (circa 1539–1075 B.C.E.) chose this valley in the western hills near Deir al Bahri because of its isolation. Each tomb is set deep into the mountainside and has a descending corridor with intermittent shafts to confuse poten-tial thieves. At the end of the corridor is the burial chamber with a stone sarcophagus containing the royal mummy. Special rooms filled with clothes, furniture, gold, statuary, weapons, and other items surround the burial chamber and the contents were meant for the king's use in the afterlife.

Practically all of the tombs in the Valley of the Kings were pillaged in antiquity; as early as the first century B.C.E. the Greek geographer Strabo men-tions that travelers could tour about forty of them. Only one tomb, that of Tutankhamun's, has been found intact by modern archaeologists. (Located on the valley floor, it was covered over by rocks dumped down the mountainside during the digging of a later tomb). The longest sepulchre belongs to Queen Hatshepsut and measures seven hundred feet in length, while the most complex one belongs to Ramesses II and was built to house the remains of his fifty-two sons.

Wadi al-Harim (Valley of the Queens) also exists near the location dedicated to the kings. It served as the necropolis for the queens and some royal children of Dynasties 19 and 20. There are more than ninety known tombs and the queens interred there include Sitre (wife of Ramesses I) and Nefertari (wife of Ramesses II).

Sources: Carl N. Reeves, *Valley of the Kings: The Decline of a Royal Necropolis* (London & New York: Kegan Paul International, 1990).

Nicholas Reeves and Richard Wilkinson, *The Complete Valley of the Kings: Tombs and Treasures of Egypt's Greatest Pharaohs* (London: Thames & Hudson, 1996).

John Romer, *Valley of the Kings* (New York: Morrow, 1981).

Pylon of Ramesses II's temple, circa 1213 B.C.E.

Building Materials. For information on the layout of Egyptian temples scholars depend primarily on the large stone temples dating from the New Kingdom (circa 1539–1075 B.C.E.) until the Roman Period (30 B.C.E.–395 C.E.). The earliest temples in Egypt were built of perishable materials such as mud brick or reeds. For information on these early structures, Egyptologists rely on archaeological evidence combined with images found on labels, pottery, and other materials. The earliest religious structures built of stone were those intended for King Djoser's cult at Saqqara. The use of stone in cult temples did not begin until the Middle Kingdom (circa 1980–1630 B.C.E.), and the only surviving nonroyal cultic structures from the Middle Kingdom are the White Chapel of Senwosret I at Karnak and the small temple dedicated to Sobek, Horus, and Ernutet built by Amenemhet III and IV at Medinet Maadi. The White Chapel was dedicated to Amun at Karnak and served as a place for the priests to rest the bark of Amun when the god was out in procession. The only reason the White Chapel stands is because it was disassembled and used as fill in the Third Pylon of Amenhotep III at Karnak. When archaeologists discovered the blocks, they carefully reassembled them.

Temple Complex. The main elements of a temple complex were fairly standard throughout Egypt. The temple area was segregated from profane space by a large brick wall, called a temenos. Entrance into the complex was gained through a gateway called a pylon. The pylon was a pair of high trapezoidal towers flanking a doorway, one on each side of the road leading up to the temple. The only limit on the number of pylons a temple could have was the space available and the resources that the king wanted to expend. Some temple complexes, such as the temple of Amun at Karnak, had ten pylons. For hundreds of years, successive kings would add a pylon to the temple. In front of pylons, tall poles with pennants were raised. Generally, four such poles were in front of each pylon, although Karnak had eight. Colossal statues of the king or obelisks could also be set up in front of the pylon. These colossal statues could serve as focal points for the worship of the king. Obelisks were tapering shafts topped with a pyramid-shaped stone called a pyramidion. They were usually made of pink granite, and the pyramidion could be plated in gold. As such, they served as solar symbols, and the pyramidion was perhaps the first and last part of the temple to receive the sun's rays.

God's Road. The road to the temple, leading through the pylon, was called the "god's road." It was the path the god took when he left his temple in procession during festivals. Beginning with the reign of Hatshepsut, this path could be lined with small sphinxes. Smaller gateways, called propylons, could also be built along this pathway. As one passed through the last pylon, one entered the forecourt of the temple, called the "court of the multitude." This open courtyard was as far as the general public could go. Here devotees could gather to participate in the public aspects of temple festivals. Individuals who received the permission of the king could erect statues of themselves within this courtyard. These statues, serving as proxy for the deceased donor, allowed the donor to continually enjoy the god's presence and to participate in the offerings donated to the temple.

Interior Design. Passing through the forecourt, one entered the hypostyle hall, called the "fore-hall" or the "great court." This room was filled with gigantic columns spaced close together. The columns took the form of plants such as palm trees, bundles of papyrus, or lotus stalks, with capitals of papyrus umbels or lotus blossoms (open or closed). The hypostyle hall gave way to the offering chamber, a room containing many small tables and stands set up to receive the offerings for the gods. Next was the bark shrine, a room that included a large platform intended to support the god's boat when not in use. Egyptian gods generally traveled by boat when they left their temples. These boats were carried on the backs of priests and contained a small shrine to house the portable image of the god. Leaving the bark shrine, one enters the inner shrine of the temple, the room that housed the god's image. As the visitor proceeded from the hypostyle deeper into the temple, the ceiling became progressively lower, and the floor rose slightly. As a result, the main sanctuary of the temple was the highest point on the ground floor. This room had a low roof and was usually totally dark. It contained a small shrine, called a *naos*, which contained the image of the god. The image could be made of wood, stone, or gold, and has been estimated to be approximately twenty inches high; it was the focus of the daily temple ritual. Since more than one deity could be worshipped in a temple, there was usually more than one sanctuary.

Subsidiary Rooms. The subsidiary rooms lay along the main axis of the temple, usually oriented east to west. In addition, a temple had subsidiary rooms used for the various functions necessary to the cult. There could be a laboratory, where incense and ointments were prepared; a treasury where sacred vessels were kept; and a room through which libations entered the temple, sometimes called a Nile room.

House of Life. The temple proper was often surrounded by auxiliary buildings such as storehouses, granaries, kitchens, administrative offices, workshops, studios for the manufacture and repair of statues and furniture used in the temple, and dwellings for the priests. One such building was called the "House of Life." This structure served as the place where texts were studied, copied, and assembled. Priests in the House of Life prepared the texts that the lector priests read during the daily temple ceremony. Papyri containing spells for protection for the living and for the dead (*Book of the Dead*) were also composed there. Medical textbooks and astronomical information were also compiled and copied in the House of Life. Temples of the Greco-Roman period could include a building called by the nineteenth-century French archaeologist Jacques-Joseph Champollion *mammisi*, meaning birth house, and a sanatorium. A *mammisi* depicted the events surrounding the con-

Osiris pillars in the hypostyle hall leading to the sanctuary of Ramesses II at Abu Simbel, circa 1213 B.C.E.

ception and birth of a god's offspring, such as Ihy, son of Horus and Hathor (found at Dendera). A sanatorium was a building to which the sick could be brought to seek healing from the gods or medical treatment from the priests. Here pilgrims could practice incubation, in which they would spend the night in hopes of receiving a dream detailing the cure for their illness or the answer to their problem. A central courtyard of the sanatorium could contain statues covered with magical healing texts; water poured over these texts was thought to become charged with their power and was used for drinking or bathing.

Sacred Waters. Within the temenos of each temple was a sacred lake, usually rectangular, filled with groundwater. This water was thought to originate in Nun, the cosmic water of creation, and as such it served several purposes. The king and priests would purify themselves in the sacred lake before performing rituals in the temple. This water also served to purify the sacred vessels used in the ceremonies, and was a source of water for libations poured out before the gods. Even the fish in the lake were considered important, and one of the sins the king denied when making his denial of guilt at the New Year's festival was that he had not poached fish from the sacred lakes.

Model of the Cosmos. The architectural design of the temple was intended to represent a scale model of the cosmos, the created world. The bricks of the temenos wall were not laid in straight lines, but in undulating rows, giving the effect of a wave. This wall represented Nun, the primordial water surrounding the created universe. The temple itself could be called an *akhet,* or horizon, and represented the place where this world and the world of the gods and the deceased came together. The pylons could also be called *akhet,* and represented the mountains between which the sun was thought to rise and set. The two portions of the pylon could also be called Isis and Nephthys or the two Meret goddesses, who were thought to lift the sun out of Nun daily. The pylons could be decorated with scenes of the king smiting his enemies in battle, or engaging in hunting expeditions, all activities that the Egyptians associated with the role of the king as the repulser of chaos and guarantor of order. Similar scenes could be carved on the outer walls of the temple and served to protect the temple from the evil forces of chaos. The floor of the temple was also associated with Nun's waters, and the large papyriform columns of the hypostyle hall seemed to grow out of this water. The bases of these columns and interior walls of the temple were frequently decorated with scenes of aquatic plants, papyrus plants and lilies, as if they were growing out of the floor of the temple. The ceiling of the temple could be decorated with stars or astronomical texts, or with winged sun-disks, all elements belonging to the sky. The sanctuary containing the god's image was thought of as both the *akhet,* the place from which the sun god appeared, and as the sky. The priest opening the shrine each morning was said to "open the doors of heaven." The steadily rising floor had

the effect of rendering the sanctuary the highest point within the temple. As such, it represented the primeval hill, the first land to emerge from the waters of Nun on which creation began.

Sources:

Ann Rosalie David, *The Ancient Egyptians: Religious Beliefs and Practices* (London & Boston: Routledge & Kegan Paul, 1982).

Stephen Quirke, ed., *The Temple in Ancient Egypt* (London: British Museum Press, 1997).

Byron E. Shafer, ed., *Temples of Ancient Egypt* (Ithaca, N.Y.: Cornell University Press, 1997).

Richard H. Wilkinson, *The Complete Temples of Ancient Egypt* (New York: Thames & Hudson, 2000).

TEMPLE PERSONNEL

Staff. In view of the various activities that went on daily in an Egyptian temple, it should come as no surprise that a large staff of priests, priestesses, and other support staff was necessary for the efficient functioning of the temple. For example, the temple of Amun-Re at Karnak employed 81,322 men, while the temple at Heliopolis employed 12,963, and the temple at Memphis a paltry 3,079. Technically, only the king could officiate in the cult before the gods. He was considered to be the high priest of all the gods and goddesses of Egypt. In actual practice the king delegated this responsibility to the priesthoods of the various gods throughout Egypt. Many priestly appointments came directly from the king. Some priestly appointments could be made by local administrators. Frequently, priestly offices could be inherited.

Priestly Functions. There were two main classes of priests. The higher class of priest was the *hem-netjer,* "god's servant." These priests functioned in the cult before the god's statue. The Greeks translated *hem-netjer* as "prophet," an equation that derived from the priests' role in interpreting oracles. The lower class of priests was the *wabu,* or "pure ones." They served as the carriers of the god's bark, as the pourers of water for the various libations required during the temple service, as overseers of craftsmen, artisans, or scribes, or as craftsmen themselves, making such sacred objects as the god's sandals. In addition to these two titles, there was a third, the *it-netjer,* or "god's father." It has been suggested that the title "god's father" was given to senior *wab* priests who had reached the level of prophet but were not yet formally inducted into that office. One of his functions seems to have been to walk in front of the god's image when it was in procession and sprinkle water in order to purify the path.

Purity. Inherent in one of the Egyptian words for "priest" is the concept of purity. Priests were required to maintain a status of ritual purity while serving in their office. Such purity was attained and maintained through several means. During the Ramesside period, priests had to bathe in the sacred lake of a temple three times a day; Herodotus says that in his day priests bathed twice a day and twice during the night. Priests had to cleanse their mouths with natron dissolved in water, remove all hair

Tanefer, third prophet of Amun, pouring libation and burning incense at a table with offerings in honor of Osiris; drawing on papyrus, *Book of the the Dead of Tanefer*, Dynasty 21, circa 1075–945 B.C.E. (Egyptian Museum, Cairo)

from their bodies (Herodotus says they shaved their whole bodies every third day), and be circumcised. Before entering their service as priests, they had to abstain from sexual activity for several days and during the period of their service. While serving in the temple, they were not allowed to wear wool, and were required to wear white sandals. Priests had to observe certain food taboos, which differed from nome to nome. For example, in the Third Upper Egyptian nome, eating fish was forbidden, and in the Sixth Upper Egyptian nome, honey could not be eaten.

Gangs of the Service. Priests were divided into four groups, called "gangs of the service," to which the Greeks gave the name *phyles*. Each phyle served one lunar month in rotation, so that during the year each gang served for a total of three months, with three months off between each month of service. This free time allowed individuals to hold priesthoods in several temples. The chief priests of a temple were designated by ordinal numbers, and the high priest of the temple was called the first prophet, the next most-senior priest was the second prophet, followed by third and fourth prophets. The high priests of some gods bore special titles. The high priest of Ptah was called "he who is great at directing the crafts," the high priest of Re was "he who is great at seeing," the high priest of Thoth was called "the arbitrator between the two," and the high priest of Khnum was called

the "modeler of limbs." These titles derive from the various spheres of influence or mythological roles these gods played.

Specialists. In addition to these classes of priests, there were also priestly specialists. The *hery-heb* (he who carries the festival roll) was responsible for reading the hymns and spells that accompanied many of the rituals in the temple. The "scribe of the house of life" was responsible for copying the papyri used in temple and funerary ritual. Women also played a role in the temple priesthood. During the Old Kingdom (circa 2675–2130 B.C.E.) women of high social station could hold the office of priestess (*hemet-netjer*) of Hathor, or of Neith. Women only rarely served as priestesses in the cult of a god. Prior to the New Kingdom (circa 1539–1075 B.C.E.) the priesthood was not viewed as a full-time occupation, but with the introduction of a professional class of priests, women no longer were able to hold priestly titles. They then served mainly as musicians, singers, and dancers in the temple.

Sources:

Stephen Quirke, ed., *The Temple in Ancient Egypt* (London: British Museum Press, 1997).

Serge Sauneron and Jean-Pierre Corteggiani, *The Priests of Ancient Egypt*, translated by David Lorton (Ithaca, N.Y.: Cornell University Press, 2000).

Byron E. Shafer, ed., *Temples of Ancient Egypt* (Ithaca, N.Y.: Cornell University Press, 1997).

Richard H. Wilkinson, *The Complete Temples of Ancient Egypt* (New York: Thames & Hudson, 2000).

TEMPLE RITUAL

Ensuring Prosperity. Fortunately for the modern scholar, the Egyptians decorated the walls and ceilings of their temples with scenes and texts relating to the activities that went on in the temples. A few papyri relating to the temple rituals have also survived, and by putting the two together, scholars have been able to draw a fairly detailed picture of the rituals that went on within the temple. These rituals fall into two main categories, those that were intended to satisfy the god's needs, conducted on a daily basis, and those representing the god's function, either cosmic or political. These festivals were celebrated during particular times of the year. The Egyptians believed that the well-being of Egypt was dependent on their continued performance of temple rituals. The papyrus *Jumilhac* states that "if the gifts are poor on its [the sanctuary's] tables, then the same thing will happen in the entire country; life will be poor for the living. If the gifts are multiplied in this place, then abundance will happen throughout the entire country, and every belly will be filled with grain."

Caring for the God. The daily temple ritual had as its focus the care and feeding of the god, mediated through the divine image in the *naos*. This ritual took essentially the same form in every temple in Egypt. It derived from the ritual for the sun god Re at Heliopolis, and represented the rebirth of the sun each morning. At a later date elements of Osirian belief were incorporated into the ritual, and it also came to symbolize the restoration and revivification of the dismembered body of Osiris. For the purposes of the ritual the cult-statue was identified as both Re and Osiris. Information regarding the sequence of events of this ritual comes from two main sources: temple reliefs that show the king performing the various rituals of the ceremony, and papyri that list the rituals and the hymns that accompany them. Analysis of these various sources has allowed scholars to reconstruct the likely sequence of events of this ritual. Since all of the sources are not in agreement as to the order of events, scholarly reconstructions differ, depending on which source is taken as a guide.

Colored Cloths. Before dawn two priests would fill containers with water from the sacred well of the temple and replenish all the libation vessels of the temple. Priests would be busy in the temple kitchens preparing offerings for the gods. The main officiating priest would go to "the house of the morning" where he was ceremonially purified, dressed, given a light meal, and prepared to conduct the morning ceremony. The priest would approach the shrine containing the god's image, and as the sun rose the bolt would be drawn back and the door opened. Since only the king was able to confront the god, the officiating priest would declare that "it is the king who has sent me to see the god." Once the doors to the shrine had been opened, the priest would prostrate himself before the image, and a ritual purification of the chapel with water and incense would take place in preparation for removing the image from its shrine. At this point, the statue would be presented a small figure of the goddess Maat, which symbol-

Relief from the White Chapel of King Senwosret I at Karnak of Horus as the *ka* or sustaining spirit of kingship, circa 1919–1875 B.C.E.

ized the proper order established for the world at creation. The image was then removed from its shrine, and the clothing and ointment that had been placed on the image the previous day were removed. The image was then placed on a pile of clean sand and the shrine was purified with water and incense. Next, green and black eye paints were applied to the image and it was anointed with several oils. The god was dressed in four colored cloths: white, green, blue, and red. The white and red cloths protected the god from his enemies; the blue hid his face; and the green ensured his health. The god was presented with various objects such as his crowns, scepter, crook, flail, and collar. Next, the god's face was anointed; sand was scattered around the chapel; the cult image was replaced in the shrine; the door bolt was thrown and sealed. Finally, the priest performed the last purifications and exited the sanctuary, dragging a broom behind him to obliterate his footprints.

Breakfast. At some point during the morning ritual, the offering ritual would take place. The purpose of this ritual was to provide the god with his "breakfast." Some reconstructions of the ritual have it occurring before the final purification of the chapel in preparation for replacing the statue in the shrine, while others have the offering ritual take place before the undressing and dressing of the statue. In this ritual the offerings that had been prepared that morning by the priests were presented to the god. Although an enormous meal consisting of meat, bread, cakes, beer, milk, honey, vegetables, and fruit, was prepared for the god, only a small part of this repast was actually placed before the statue. An offering formula listing the various items of the offering was recited by the priest, and incense was burned and libations made to purify and sanctify the offerings. Since the god did not actually consume the offerings but simply partook of their essences, they could be shared with the other deities in the temple. The offerings were also used in the ritual of the royal ancestors, in which the king made offerings to all of his predecessors in office, often depicted in the form of a list of their names. After this ritual the offerings could then be made to the statues of other individuals found in the temple, and finally they became the property of the priests, who received a share based on their rank in the priestly hierarchy. This reuse of the offerings until they were finally consumed by the priests was called the "reversion of offerings" and was one way in which the priests were compensated for their work.

Threats to Existence. This morning ritual was the main ritual of the day, but less-elaborate ceremonies were also held at noon and in the evening. During these rituals, the doors of the sanctuary housing the god's statue were not opened. These rituals consisted primarily of pouring water libations and burning incense before the shrines of the gods. In addition to these offering rituals, certain apotropaic rituals were conducted in the temples throughout the day and night in order to repel the threats to existence, frequently thought of in terms of Seth, the murderer of Osiris, or Apophis, the serpent who tried to stop the daily voyage of Re and thereby bring an end to creation. Hymns were sung during the twelve hours of the day and night to protect Re from Apophis and keep the solar bark moving along on its voyage. Images of enemies were created from wax or clay then and destroyed, thereby bringing about their destruction through magic.

Festivals. In addition to their daily rituals, temples also celebrated festivals throughout the year. For example, during the reign of Thutmose III, the temple of Amun-Re at Karnak celebrated fifty-four festival days, and Ramesses III's temple at Medinet Habu celebrated sixty festival days. Festivals could last from one to twenty-seven days, and

involved large expenditures of food and drink for those participating in or observing the festival. Work records from the village of Deir el Medina indicate that workers were frequently given days off to allow them to participate in many festivals. During the festival of Sokar, 3,694 loaves of bread, 410 cakes, and 905 jars of beer were distributed. Important festivals included New Year's Day, the festival of Osiris at Abydos, during which the "mysteries" of this god were celebrated, the festival of Hathor, during which the goddess would visit the royal cult complex, as did the god Sokar during his festival, and the Festival of the Coronation of the Sacred Falcon at Edfu. The Beautiful Festival of the Valley was an important occasion during which Amun-Re traveled from Karnak to the temple at Deir el Bahri and visited the royal cult complexes on the West Bank of the Nile, particularly that of the reigning king. This was also an occasion for people to visit the tombs of their relatives, where they observed an all-night vigil and shared a feast among themselves and their deceased relatives.

Bark Shrines. The focus of one festival was the gods in their bark shrines. Egyptian gods always traveled in boats, either in real boats when traveling by water, or in bark shrines, carried over land on the shoulders of priests. Festivals could involve the procession of the god in his boat within the temple, or the god could leave the temple to visit another deity. These shrines were carried along processional avenues, often lined with sphinxes. At intervals, small altars were built that were essentially open-ended buildings that contained a station on which the priests could rest the bark. When the porters rested, priests performed fumigations and libations and sang hymns to the god in its boat.

Access to the Gods. Such festivals and processions provided most people with their greatest access to the gods, since the furthest point where most people were admitted into the temples was the open forecourt. It is usually thought that the shrine in the bark containing the god's image was closed during the procession, hiding the god's image from onlookers. It has recently been suggested that the doors of the bark shrine were open during such travels, since various texts describe the desire of people to see the image of a god during a procession. It was believed that beholding the image of a god during a procession could heal an individual from illness.

Oracles. During such festival processions people seeking an oracle could approach the gods. The first clear evidence for oracles occurs in the New Kingdom (circa 1539–1075 B.C.E.). John Baines, however, has argued that evidence for the existence of oracles occurs much earlier, perhaps as early as the First Intermediate Period (circa 2130–1980 B.C.E.). During processions people could approach the god with a yes or no question, which would be written on small flakes of limestone, or on ostraca, which would be placed before the god. Surviving examples of such questions include "Is it he who has stolen this mat?"; "Shall Seti be appointed as priest?"; and "Is this calf good so that I may accept it?" The movement of the bark shrine as it was carried on the shoulders of the priests indicated the answer, forward for affirmative, backward for negative.

Sources:

Ann Rosalie David, *The Ancient Egyptians: Religious Beliefs and Practices* (London & Boston: Routledge & Kegan Paul, 1982).

Stephen Quirke, ed., *The Temple in Ancient Egypt* (London: British Museum Press, 1997).

Byron E. Shafer, ed., *Temples of Ancient Egypt* (Ithaca, N.Y.: Cornell University Press, 1997).

Barbara Watterson, *The House of Horus at Edfu: Ritual in an Ancient Egyptian Temple* (Gloucestershire, U.K.: Tempus, 1998).

Richard H. Wilkinson, *The Complete Temples of Ancient Egypt* (New York: Thames & Hudson, 2000).

TERMINOLOGY: NETJER

Debate. The Egyptian word that is translated into English as god is *netjer*. This word is written with a hieroglyph resembling a flag (yellow in color) on a flagpole, often shown in green. It has been described as "a pole wrapped with a band of cloth, bound by a cord, the end projecting as a flap or streamer." Exactly what this image has to do with the concept of god has been the subject of much discussion. It could represent a cult flag that is seen flying from tall flagpoles found at the entrances to New Kingdom (circa 1539–1075 B.C.E.) temples. Another suggestion is that the object represented a fetish, an inanimate object believed to have supernatural power. A more recent theory is that the flag represents the pennants found hanging from poles that were surmounted by hieroglyphs representing various deities. Usually a symbol representing a particular deity was found above the pennants, and it has been suggested that the pennant without the symbol came to represent the general concept of deity.

Etymology. The etymology of the word *netjer* is uncertain. It corresponds roughly to the word *god*, because in the Ptolemaic period of Egyptian history, bilingual decrees in Greek and Egyptian translate the Egyptian *netjer* with Greek *theos* (god). A detailed examination of the Egyptian texts reveals that the word *netjer* has a far wider frame of

Restored statue of Ramesses III being crowned by the gods Horus and Seth (Egyptian Museum, Cairo)

reference than the English "god." The Egyptians used the term *netjer* to refer to beings that one would call gods, demons, and spirits. The term could also refer to the Egyptian king, certain living animals, and to dead people or animals. A close examination of the different beings that the Egyptians designated as *netjer* has led one scholar to suggest that the Egyptians used the term to refer to any being which was the object of a ritual, or received some sort of cult (meaning offerings).

Classes of Beings. When looked at in this light, there are several classes of beings that the Egyptians called "*netjer*." First are those beings one would call gods. They were created as *netjer* from the beginning and did not acquire the status at a later date. For them, ritual served to maintain and preserve their status as *netjer*, much as food allows a person to maintain the status of living being. A passage from the *Coffin Texts* states that an offering of grain "makes the gods divine." These beings were the objects of daily rituals and offerings in the temples and shrines throughout Egypt. Throughout the three thousand years of Egyptian history, approximately two thousand deities were worshiped.

Acquired Status in Life. In contrast to the gods are those beings who acquired the status of *netjer* through undergoing a ritual at some time after their birth. These entities fall into two categories, those who become *netjers* while living and those who become *netjers* after death. In the first category are the king of Egypt and certain sacred animals. The king at his accession underwent a coronation ritual and as a result acquired the status of *netjer*. The king was the only living person in Egypt who had this status. In addition to the king, specific animals were viewed as being special manifestations of particular gods, usually based on the presence of special markings or characteristics. These animals also underwent a ritual that inducted them into the category of *netjer* and made them instruments through which a particular god could make his presence manifest.

Acquired Status in Death. The last class of beings that were considered to be *netjer* are those beings that underwent a ritual, and hence became *netjer* after death. The funerary ritual had the effect of turning every deceased Egyptian for whom it was practiced into a *netjer*. The dead person would become an *akh*, a glorified spirit, and would be the recipient of offerings of food and drink from his family members. Particularly important individuals might acquire a prominent cult after their deaths and receive offerings from people in addition to family members. Finally, animals belonging to particular species that were kept at Egyptian temples would be mummified and buried at death, conferring on them the status of *netjer*.

Sources:

Erik Hornung, *Conceptions of God in Ancient Egypt: The One and the Many,* translated by John Baines (London: Routledge & Kegan Paul, 1982).

Dimitri Meeks and Christine Favard-Meeks, *Daily Life of the Egyptian Gods,* translated by G. M. Goshgarian (Ithaca, N.Y.: Cornell University Press, 1996).

David Silverman, "Divinity and Deities in Ancient Egypt," in *Religion in Ancient Egypt: Gods, Myths, and Personal Practice,* edited by Byron E. Shafer (Ithaca, N.Y.: Cornell University Press, 1991), pp. 7–87.

Wall painting from the tomb of Inerkha showing a priest wearing a mask of Anubis and performing the "Opening of the Mouth," circa 1190–1075 B.C.E. This ritual is the last funeral rite before the entombment of the mummy.

SIGNIFICANT PEOPLE

AKHENATEN

CIRCA 1353-1336 B.C.E.
KING, DYNASTY 18

Beginnings. Akhenaten was the second son of King Amenhotep III of Dynasty 18 (circa 1539–1295/1292 B.C.E.) and his wife Tiye. When his older brother Thutmose died young, he became the crown prince. It is possible that Akhenaten served for a time as co-regent (co-king) with his father, but the evidence for a co-regency is disputed. When his father died around 1353 B.C.E., he ascended to the throne as Amenhotep IV. He was married to the beautiful Nefertiti, as his Great Royal Wife. She may have been his cousin, although this is uncertain. He was also married to a woman named Kiya, who may have been a Mitannian princess. By Nefertiti, Akhenaten had six daughters, three of whom died in infancy. It is also possible that he was the father of Tutankhamun (born Tutankhaten), but, as with so much from this period of Egyptian history, the evidence is inconclusive.

Aten. In the fifth year of his reign the king signaled a new religious direction for his kingdom by changing his name to Akhenaten, "He who is effective for the Aten." *Aten* was the Egyptian word for the physical disk of the sun. In the same year the king began construction of a new capital for Egypt. At a vacant site in Middle Egypt he built the city of Akhetaten, "the horizon of the sun-disk." In the sixth year of his reign Akhenaten moved his family and administration into his new capital.

New Religion. Akhenaten introduced a new religion to Egypt. He worshiped only one god, the light that was in the sun. This light was believed to grant the world life and to keep it alive. This new god was depicted as a sun-disk emanating rays that ended in hands. These hands were frequently directed toward Akhenaten and his family and could be shown offering the breath of life, symbolized by *ankh*-signs, to their noses. In order to worship the Aten, Akhenaten had a new type of temple constructed, reminiscent of the sun temples of Dynasty 5 (circa 2500–2350 B.C.E.). These temples consisted of a series of open courts oriented toward the east, centering on an altar. Such temples were built at Thebes, Memphis, Heliopolis, and Akhetaten. In these temples even the doorways had broken lintels to allow the sun's rays to reach all parts of the temple.

Royal Family. While Akhenaten and his family worshiped the Aten, the people of Egypt, especially those living at Akhetaten, were to worship the royal family. Akhenaten was considered to be the son of the Aten, and it was through him that the Egyptians were to worship the sun. Egyptian homes at Akhetaten contained stelae showing the royal family worshiping the Aten. These stelae served as the focal point of the cult of the Aten within their homes. One official, Panehsy, praised Akhenaten as "my god, who built me, who determined good for me, who made me come into being and gave me bread" (translation by Erik Hornung).

Afterlife. Even the traditional conception of the afterlife underwent a drastic change. No longer did the dead live on in the underworld in the company of Osiris or journey through the sky in the bark of Re. Essentially, there was no longer a world of the beyond. Both the living and the *ba*-spirits of the dead continued to live here on earth, under the sun's rays. At sunrise the *ba*s of the justified dead traveled to the Great Temple of the Aten in Akhetaten to receive the sun's life-giving rays and to participate in the offerings made to Aten in his temple. Justification no longer meant being found innocent in the tribunal of Osiris but was a status reserved for those who were loyal to the king during life. Akhenaten, as Aten's sole representative on earth, was the dispenser of provisions to the dead.

Amun. Not only did Akhenaten promote the worship of a new deity, he went so far as to close down the temples to the other gods of Egypt, particularly the temples of Amun. Also in his fifth year Akhenaten sent workmen throughout Egypt to remove the names of Amun, his consort Mut, and even the plural term "gods" from the monuments of Egypt. Akhenaten referred to the Aten as a god of whom "there is no other but him." Aten had no consort, no children (other than Akhenaten), and no opponent. Akhenaten may have been the world's first monotheist.

Lack of Appeal. Although Akhenaten's new religion was popular among the royal family and the officials at Akhetaten, it never caught on among the masses. Prayers to Amun have been found even at the workmen's village at Akhetaten. Akhenaten's new religion was so closely associated with his person that it could not outlive him. When his seventeen-year reign came to an end, he was succeeded briefly by Semenkhkare, who was followed by Tutankhaten, who changed his name to Tutankhamun during his third year as king. He then abandoned Akhetaten, moving his capital to Memphis. In what has come to be called his "restoration stele," Tutankhamun records that when he became king, the temples of the gods "had become desolate" and were overgrown with weeds. Because the gods were not being worshiped, they did not bless Egypt and ceased to answer prayers. Tutankhamun described how he had new statues of the gods fashioned, using the finest of materials. He restored the property of the temples to their rightful owners. As a result, the traditional gods of Egypt were said to rejoice once again.

Sources:

Cyril Aldred, *Akhenaten, King of Egypt* (London: Thames & Hudson, 1988).

Erik Hornung, *Akhenaten and the Religion of Light,* translated by David Lorton (Ithaca, N.Y.: Cornell University Press, 1999).

Donald Redford, *Akhenaten, The Heretic King* (Princeton: Princeton University Press, 1984).

Redford, *The Akhenaten Temple Project* (Warminster, U.K.: Aris & Phillips, 1976).

Carl N. Reeves, *Akhenaten: Egypt's False Prophet* (New York: Thames & Hudson, 2001).

AMENHOTEP, SON OF HAPU

CIRCA 1479-1353 B.C.E.
ROYAL SCRIBE, PRIEST, AND OVERSEER

Special Status. Amenhotep, son of Hapu, was born during the reign of pharaoh Thutmose III (circa 1479–1425 B.C.E.) in the town of Athribis, in the Delta. Like Imhotep, the vizier of the Dynasty 3 (circa 2675–2625 B.C.E.) ruler Djoser, he attained *netjer* (god) status. His father was Hapu, and his mother was Itu. As a young man he attended the temple school and learned "the words of Thoth" (hieroglyphs). Amenhotep served as an official during the reign of King Amenhotep III (circa 1390–1353 B.C.E.) of Dynasty 18 (circa 1539–1295/1292 B.C.E.). He was first appointed as a royal scribe and priest in the temple of Horus-Khentikheti. He was later promoted to the office of "Scribe of Recruits," where he was responsible for organizing the manpower of

Egypt for the king. From there he rose to the position of "Overseer of all the works of the King." In this position he was responsible for the construction of the king's temples at Soleb and Karnak, and for the monumental statues of the king set up at Thebes. As a reward for his services, Amenhotep was allowed to erect statues of himself throughout the processional way in the temple of Karnak. There, he could serve as an intermediary between visitors to the temple and the gods worshiped therein. When he died, he was buried at Qurnet Murai, near his king's funerary temple. He was given the honor of having his own funerary temple, built near that of his sovereign. From there, the cult of Amenhotep, son of Hapu, grew in renown until he was revered as a local saint at Thebes. A Dynasty 26 (664–525 B.C.E.) statue of Amenhotep dedicated by Merit-Neith, daughter of Pharaoh Psammetichus I, asks him to heal her of an unnamed affliction of the eyes. By the Ptolemaic period Amenhotep had entered the pantheon of the gods and was revered as a god of wisdom and a healer, with major cult centers at Deir el Bahri and Deir el Medina.

Sources:

Eric Cline and David O'Connor, eds., *Amenhotep III: Perspectives on His Reign* (Ann Arbor: University of Michigan Press, 1998).

Rosalie and Antony E. David, *A Biographical Dictionary of Ancient Egypt* (London: Seaby, 1992).

Dietrich Wildung, *Egyptian Saints: Deification in Pharaonic Egypt* (New York: New York University Press, 1977).

IMHOTEP

DIED CIRCA 2600 B.C.E.
VIZIER, HIGH PRIEST, ASTROLOGER, AND ARCHITECT

Divinity. The Egyptian term for god, *netjer,* could be applied to a range of entities. In addition to gods properly speaking, the word could be applied to the king, certain animals, and the dead. Egyptians venerated their deceased ancestors as being divine. There are a few individuals in Egyptian history whose divinity grew to exceed the bounds of their own families, and who eventually came to have a place in the pantheon of Egyptian gods. One such individual was Imhotep.

Offices. Imhotep served as a vizier and architect under King Djoser of Dynasty 3 (circa 2675–2625 B.C.E.). He also held the offices of high priest of Re at Heliopolis and the chief of sculptors and makers of stone vessels. He is credited with designing the king's step pyramid complex at Saqqara, and therefore with inventing monumental construction in stone. He outlived his patron, and his name is found in a graffito on the enclosure wall of an unfinished pyramid started during the reign of Sekhemket, the successor of Djoser. Imhotep died around 2600 B.C.E.

Cult. Imhotep disappears from view until the New Kingdom (circa 1539–1075 B.C.E.). Texts from this period credit him as one of the great sages of Egypt, who authored a collection of proverbs (now lost) that were revered for their wisdom. Imhotep was considered to be a patron of scribes and intellectuals. Scribes would frequently pour out a water libation to him from their water pots before beginning to write. By Dynasty 26 (664–525 B.C.E.) Imhotep was considered to be the son of Ptah and Khereduankh, his natural mother. Later on, Imhotep was given a wife, Renpet-neferet. Eventually, a sanctuary in honor of Imhotep was built at Saqqara. Here in the area of Memphis, Imhotep was considered to be a god with special powers of healing. He was thought to be able to grant requests for wives and children. By the time of Roman domination of Egypt, the cult of Imhotep had spread throughout Egypt. In addition to being a god of healing and wisdom, Imhotep acquired a reputation as a famous astrologer and was thought to have the power to bring fertility to the earth.

Sources:
Ann Rosalie and Antony E. David, *A Biographical Dictionary of Ancient Egypt* (London: Seaby, 1992).

Nigel Strudwick, *The Administration of Egypt in the Old Kingdom: The Highest Titles and Their Holders* (London & Boston: Kegan Paul International, 1985).

Dietrich Wildung, *Egyptian Saints: Deification in Pharaonic Egypt* (New York: New York University Press, 1977).

DOCUMENTARY SOURCES

Book of Going Forth by Day (circa 1630–1539 B.C.E.)— More commonly known as *Book of the Dead*. Written on papyri and/or painted on tomb walls, this collection of about two hundred spells was meant to provide protection for the dead as well as the living. It was revised in Dynasty 26 (664–525 B.C.E.).

Book of Two Ways (circa 1980–1630 B.C.E.)—A set of instructions for safely reaching the afterlife.

Coffin Texts (circa 1980–1630 B.C.E.)—Funerary texts written on the sides of wooden coffins. Later replaced by *Book of Going Forth by Day*.

The Contendings of Horus and Seth (circa 1539–1075 B.C.E.)—A narrative account of the trial of Horus and Seth before Atum and the other gods. Seth is punished for killing Osiris, while Horus becomes ruler of all Egypt.

Dialogue between a Man Tired of Life and his "Ba" (circa 1980–1630 B.C.E.)—A philosophical treatise on suicide written during the Middle Kingdom.

Hymn to Hapy (circa 1980–1630 B.C.E.)—A religious and philosophical work of the Middle Kingdom.

Pyramid Texts (circa 2371–2350 B.C.E.)—The oldest religious texts in the world. Carved on the walls of pyramids, they were meant to guide the dead in their journey to the afterlife. Replaced in the Middle Kingdom (circa 1980–1630 B.C.E.) by *Coffin Texts*.

Shabaka Stone (circa 760–656 B.C.E.)—A cosmogony or statement on the creation of the universe. It is the only ancient Egyptian text to contain the Memphite Theology, which tells the story of Ptah, the father of all gods.

Underworld Books (circa 1539–1075 B.C.E.)—A collection of New Kingdom funerary texts describing the nightly journey of the sun through the underworld. These books include the *Amduat, Book of Gates, Book of Caverns,* and *Book of the Earth.*

Entranceway of the temple of Ramesses II at el-Sebu'a, circa 1213 B.C.E.

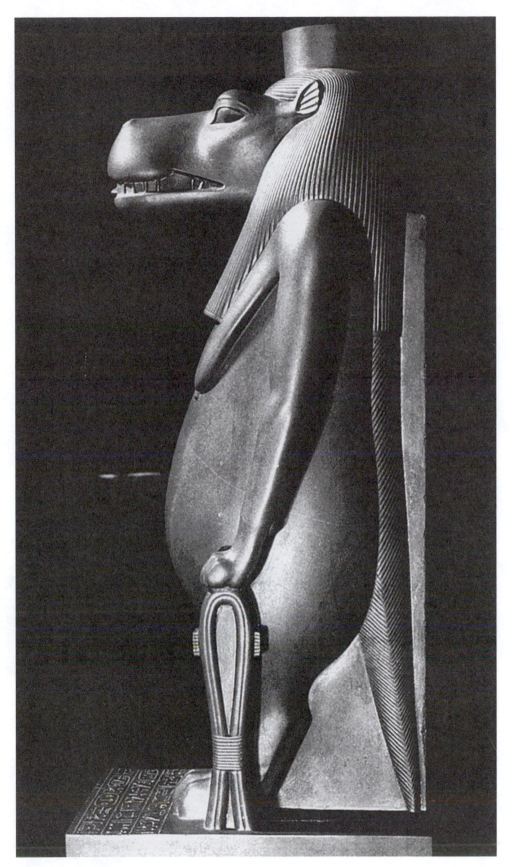

Graywacke statue of the goddess Thoeris, Dynasty 26, 664–525 B.C.E. (Egyptian Museum, Cairo)

Limestone funerary statues of Rahotep and Nofret, found in their mastaba-tomb at Meidum, early Dynasty 4, circa 2625–2500 B.C.E. (Egyptian Museum, Cairo)

SCIENCE, TECHNOLOGY, AND HEALTH

by EDWARD BLEIBERG and STEPHEN THOMPSON

CONTENTS

Sidebars and tables are listed in italics.

2585-2560*
B.C.E.

- Khufu (or Cheops) builds the Great Pyramid of Giza. It is used for astronomical observations to mark the night hours, and it is also a tomb. Trigonometry is used to calculate the slope of the pyramid.

- The first preserved mummy is made for the tomb of Queen Hetepheres, the former wife of Sneferu.

2555-2532*
B.C.E.

- Khafre (Chephren, or Rekhaef) builds the second pyramid at Giza, which is also used for astronomical observations, as well as for a tomb.

2532-2510*
B.C.E.

- Menkaure (or Mycerinus) builds the third pyramid placed at Giza.

2500-2350*
B.C.E.

- The Sun Temples, built at Abu Ghurab, are used for astronomical observations and devotions.

- Pesehet, a female physician in Egypt, flourishes.

- Relief sculptures depicting surgery for male circumcision are carved.

2371-2350*
B.C.E.

- Relief sculptures are carved that depict boats transporting granite obelisks from Aswan to Memphis, roughly a distance of 580 miles.

- Evidence that magic is used, such as swallowing liquid along with saying magic words, is attested in Pyramid Texts.

2130-1980*
B.C.E.

- The first "star clocks" are painted on coffin lids. These charts allowed priests to measure the night hours.

2081-1938*
B.C.E.

- Methods are developed to equalize the length of the night hours.

1844-1837*
B.C.E.

- The first calendar of Lucky and Unlucky Days is preserved.

1836-1818*
B.C.E.

- A tomb painting is completed depicting the transportation of the colossal statue of Djeheutyhotep, a nomarch of Bersheh.

*DENOTES CIRCA DATE

1630–1539*
B.C.E.

- The *Papyrus Ebers*—a medical text that prescribes scientific observation, combined with magical spells, potions, and ritual actions to effect cures—is copied. It is the basis of modern understanding of *wekhedu*, a waste product in human blood that was the root of the Egyptian theory of decay as a cause of disease.

- The *Edwin Smith Surgical Papyrus,* a medical text describing surgical procedures, is copied.

- The *Rhind Mathematical Papyrus,* a text describing mathematical operations, is copied.

1539–1514*
B.C.E.

- The first known water clock is used to calibrate star clocks.

- The first known shadow clocks are used to equalize daytime hours.

1479–1425*
B.C.E.

- The *Papyrus Hearst,* which includes information on magical and medical cures, is copied.

1412* B.C.E.

- Amenhotep, son of Hapu, is born and he later becomes a healing saint.

1353–1336*
B.C.E.

- Architectural plans are placed in tombs.

1279–1213*
B.C.E.

- The first love spell is recorded.

- Topographical maps of the Battle of Qadesh are carved in the Luxor and Karnak temples.

- The most complete copy of the Calendar of Lucky and Unlucky Days is finished.

- The Hittite king requests Egyptian medical help from Ramesses II.

1156–1150*
B.C.E.

- A topographical map of Wadi Hammamat, an area of valuable quarries, is created.

- A plan of the royal tomb is created.

- New twelve-hour star clocks are painted in the royal tombs.

332–323*
B.C.E.

- The first evidence occurs associating one's birthday and the position of stars in predicting the future.

*Denotes Circa Date

OVERVIEW

Science? What was science for the Egyptians? They might not have recognized the category of knowledge that is now called science, but many of their activities would fall within the realm of modern science. Ancient Egyptians observed and described the world, the heavens, and the human body. They measured and mapped the world around them, sometimes describing phenomena mathematically, but they also used religious imagery—as when they associated a star with a god.

Control. Egyptian scientists also tried to control forces in the world. Again, they sometimes used scientific methods that one would recognize as conforming to the laws of cause and effect. But they also used methods that modern people would classify as magic or religion rather than science. The Egyptians, however, would not have made the distinction between magic and religion on the one hand and science on the other. Physicians were most likely to combine natural and supernatural methods. For example, prescriptions prepared from plants, which modern science has confirmed as effective, were applied with the repetition of "magic" spells. The ancient Egyptian physician would have insisted on combining both approaches to healing. For this reason, scholars try to understand Egyptian knowledge as a whole, rather than artificially separating these components according to modern categories. Nevertheless, this combination of religion, magic, and science does not suggest that Egyptian science was illogical or mere superstition. It is rather another demonstration that learning about a foreign culture teaches us about different ways of organizing our conceptions of the world.

Scientists and Training. One connection between science, religion, and magic in Egypt was that scientists were mostly priests, and training could only be obtained at the temple. A "House of Life" was attached to most temples, which served the same purpose as a university. Young men were trained as priests here, where they first learned to read and write, and where they later specialized in a particular branch of knowledge. Specialization was achieved through a relationship with a master. The House of Life was also the place where texts on papyrus were created and copied, so it served the same function as a publishing company. Since the papyri produced in the House of Life were also stored there, it served the same function as a library.

Branches of Science. Egyptians were knowledgeable in many areas of science. Astronomy, biology, chemistry, geography, geology, mathematics, and medicine were utilized for practical purposes. Specialization was known in medicine—early texts differentiated between ophthalmologists (eye doctors) and gynecologists (specialists in treating women), in addition to the category of general practitioners.

Methods. Egyptian scientists did not use the "scientific method." They did not propose a hypothesis about a scientific idea and then test the idea through experimentation. They were less interested in general principles and pure research than in solving particular problems. Their methodological tools included analogy, approximation, comparison, definition, description, etymology, schematization, and sequences. Each of these tools required close observation and application of reason. Though Egyptians sometimes expressed their knowledge of the real world in terms of gods and myths, they were completely capable of applying reason to a problem and arriving at logical solutions. Engineering feats such as the construction of the pyramids demonstrate the Egyptians' ability to achieve logical ends with logical means.

Records. Knowledge was preserved in writing, often through long periods of time. Sometimes old texts were explained through a gloss, a further explanation of a difficult or obsolete term added to a scientific text in more contemporary language. These texts had no named author and were seen as general cultural property rather than the results of an individual working toward a solution. Thus, almost no individuals are credited with scientific discoveries. Rather, the gods received credit for inventing most solutions to scientific problems. In rare cases where individuals had clearly invented something new, as in the case of Imhotep and the engineering of the Step Pyramid in Dynasty 3 (circa 2675–2625 B.C.E.), the individual was then regarded as a god.

Conclusion. Though ancient Egyptian science did not conform to modern notions, it formed the basis for further research. Some contributions, such as the 365-day year, were passed to future generations through Roman science. Other Egyptian scientific ideas were elaborated by the Greeks and entered the Western body of knowledge that formed the base for modern science.

Topics in Science, Technology, and Health

ASTRONOMY AND TIME MEASUREMENT

Observing the Heavens. The Egyptians studied the movements of heavenly bodies for religious reasons. Cycles of astronomical phenomena were used to measure time and thus allowed the Egyptians to perform rites on the correct day and at the precise hour. By observing the movement of a particular star, especially its disappearance for a period and return to a starting point, the Egyptians could calculate when a festival for a particular god should be celebrated. Egyptian astronomers could predict the time of sunrise and the appearance of certain stars associated with deities. These observations allowed a ritual to start at exactly the correct time. The Egyptian descriptions of these observations and calculations were expressed in mythological language, and noticeable changes in their methods and descriptions can be traced through their long history.

Prehistoric Astronomy. Evidence from Nabta in the Western Desert suggests that the Egyptians tried to mark the summer solstice in circa 6000 B.C.E. A twelve-foot-wide circle of stones, purposely laid in a pattern, was constructed along the summer solstice sunrise-sunset line. Another set of upright stones marked the north-south axis. These constructions suggest that Egyptians of this period were already developing a calendar based on the movement of the sun, with a fixed point at the summer solstice.

Predynastic Astronomy. Two myths with origins in the Predynastic Period (circa 3100–3000 B.C.E.) suggest that the Egyptians knew that the point of sunrise and sunset moved along a north-south line through the year. They probably recognized that the northern end of this line was the place where the sun rose and set on the summer solstice (modern 21 June) and that the southern end of this line was the point where the sun rose and set at the winter solstice (modern 21 December). The two myths that described sunrise, sunset, and the disappearance of the sun at night are known as the Myth of Nut and the Birth of Re and the Myth of Re's Night Journey.

Nut and the Birth of Re. The Egyptians described the Milky Way as a female goddess named Nut (pronounced like "newt"). The sun was associated with the god Re. The whole of the Milky Way was visualized as a woman's body with outstretched arms and legs. Near the constellation Gemini (the twins) in the western sky, the Egyptians saw Nut's head. In the constellation Cygnus (the swan) in the eastern sky, the Egyptians saw cross shapes formed by the stars. The Egyptians re-created these shapes to mark the genital area on female figurines. The bright star in Cygnus, which the Egyptians called Deneb, was associated with the birth canal.

Movements of the Sun. The Egyptians also described the rising and setting of the sun in mythological terms. The god Re, the sun, was swallowed by Nut, whose head was in the western sky each evening at sunset. During the night, Re passed through Nut's body. In the morning, at sunrise, Re was reborn through the star they called Deneb in the eastern sky. Though this swallowing and rebirth was a daily occurrence, the "original" swallowing of the sun took place at the vernal equinox (21 March) when the constellation Gemini, Nut's head, appeared to drop below the western horizon and the "mouth" appeared to be located exactly where the sun had disappeared. The sun was born 272 days later (38.8 weeks, the average time from human conception to birth) through Deneb. The period from the swallowing, or conception, of Re to his birth is exactly the period from 21 March to 21 December. When Re was born, Deneb was thus located exactly at its southernmost point, the winter solstice. The myth of Nut and Re thus was used to describe certain astronomical phenomena and gave them a "cause." The myth accurately described the movements of the stars, yet the mythological explanation relied on religious imagery to describe what was happening.

The Myth of Re's Night Journey. The Egyptians needed to know the exact hour of sunrise so the rituals for Re could start exactly on time. They observed that twenty-four different clusters of stars, one bright and others dimmer, consistently rose on the horizon one hour before sunrise at different times of year. Each cluster's rise accurately marked the moment one hour before sunrise for a fifteen-day period each year. Thus, the Egyptians worked out a sequence of twenty-four star clusters that could be observed to "fore-

Ceiling of a sarcophagus hall for Sety I, with the list of the northern constellations and stars,
Valley of the Kings, Western Thebes, circa 1290–1279 B.C.E.

tell" the sunrise. Each cluster had a known fifteen-day period—the half month—when it accurately foretold that the sun would rise one hour later. Only twelve of these twenty-four clusters were visible at any one time of the night in any one season of the year. The twenty-four clusters came to be associated with the hours of the day and night. These observations resulted in a day and night divided into twenty-four equal units, which we call hours.

Book of Gates. The Egyptians described these observations in the *Book of Gates.* This text gives an account of the Myth of Re's Night Journey, in which Re passed through twelve doorways, one for each of the twelve hours of the night. Demons (dim stars) and a chief gatekeeper (the bright star) guarded each gate. Only knowledge of the correct magic spell would allow Re to pass through the gate. Later the myth and the *Book of Gates* were adapted for kings and others who, after death, approached the gods through the gates. When the *Book of Gates* was written down, these gates were regarded as a series of twelve nighttime hours. Since some versions of the *Book of Gates* have eight or ten hours, rather than twelve, some locations must have used longer "hours," dividing the same amount of time into fewer units.

Earliest Calendar. A calendar needs at least one fixed, astronomical point that can be used to begin the count of 365 days, until that point is reached again. The Egyptians used two different astronomical phenomena to fix the beginning of the year. The fact that they used two points rather than one has suggested to scholars that originally there were two different calendars that were later combined. The two start points seem to be the Birth of Re (21 December, the winter solstice) and the reappearance of the star Sirius (19 July, its heliacal rising) one hour before the sunrise after a seventy-day disappearance from the sky. This latter event correlated loosely with the rising of the Nile flood.

Balancing the Year. The winter solstice, the day when the sunrise occurs at its southernmost point of the year, was called the Birth of Re. The Egyptians recognized early that 365 days passed between repetitions of this phenomenon. In Heliopolis, priests at the temple of Re used a calendar of 354 days—based on 12 lunar months. These months averaged 29 or 30 days. Each month the priest announced when he had observed the new moon. Such announcements were the only way to determine when the new month had started. Because each year lacked 11 days of the needed 365 separating the annual Birth of Re, every second or third year the priests added an extra month of 22 or 33 days. This procedure kept the Birth of Re in the same month every year, if not on the same day.

Timing the Flood. The second Predynastic calendar was related to the cult of the goddess Satet at her temple on Elephantine Island on the southern border of Egypt. The calendar was fixed on a celestial event the Egyptians called the Going Forth of Sopdet (the star, Sirius). On 19 July this star reappeared just before sunrise after a 70-day disappearance from the sky. This event loosely coincided with the beginning of the annual Nile flood. The Egyptians needed to predict the flood to time the planting and harvesting of their crops. The calendar was based on a 365-day year.

Early Dynastic Period. Sometime during Dynasties 1 and 2 (3000–2675 B.C.E.) in the Early Dynastic period the two calendars were combined, probably soon after the unification of Upper and Lower Egypt. The religious explanation for this combination was that the star Sopdet represented the goddess Isis, the daughter of Re. Perhaps because both Sopdet and Deneb rose near each other on their festivals, the priest could link the stars in one myth. Egyptologists call this Early Dynastic construction the religious calendar. It regulated festivals by reference to both the Birth of Re and the Going Forth of Sopdet. A major drawback of this calendar was the need to announce the new month based on observation. It was difficult for people outside the temple to know in advance whether a particular month would have twenty-nine or thirty days. The number of days assigned to each month depended on observing the moon.

The Civil Calendar. Scholars speculate that a more widespread need to know the actual date led to regularizing the calendar. Some time rather early in Egyptian history the 12 months were standardized to have 30 days. This organization established a year that contained 360 days. The additional 5 days needed to keep the Birth of Re on the winter solstice and the Going Forth of Sopdet near the start of the flood were added between the end of one year and the beginning of the next. Four months were included in each of three seasons. This new system is known as the civil calendar, from which anyone could calculate the proper date because all the months had the same number of days.

Astronomy and Old Kingdom Architecture. The major funeral monuments of the Old Kingdom reflect the relationship between religious ritual and astronomy. Both the pyramids at Giza, built in Dynasty 4 (circa 2625–2500 B.C.E.), and the Sun Temples, built by the kings of Dynasty 5 (circa 2500–2350 B.C.E.), were constructed to allow star observation, which controlled time measurement and insured that rituals were celebrated at the proper time. The Pyramids were both tombs and symbolic staircases allowing the king's soul to climb to heaven and join with the stars. The deceased king then became one of the circumpolar stars that the Egyptians called the *ikhemu-sek,* "the ones that do not know destruction." These stars never disappeared from the sky. All three Giza pyramids have north entrances that slope down so that the circumpolar stars are visible from the interior of the structure. The orientation of the pyramids to each other thus makes sense. They are not, therefore, arranged in a straight row, because this placement would block the view of the circumpolar stars.

Predicting Sunrise. The valley temples attached to the Sun Temples of Dynasty 5 also had a close connection to astronomy. These structures were aligned so that the axis

Painted relief scene from the *Book of Gates*, found in the tomb of Sety I, Valley of the Kings, Western Thebes, circa 1290–1279 B.C.E.

of each temple was oriented to the northeastern horizon, which allowed the roof to serve as an observatory for marking the nighttime hours. Userkaf's temple (circa 2500–2485 B.C.E.) was oriented to a group of stars that included Deneb, the site of the birth of Re. All six of the known valley temples were used to predict the arrival of sunrise, although each used different groups of stars. Thus, they would have had different nighttime hours of varying lengths.

Middle Kingdom Timekeeping. Evidence from the Middle Kingdom (circa 1980–1630 B.C.E.) suggests that the Egyptians wanted to regularize the calculation of the hours. They searched for new methods of timekeeping that would use hours of equal lengths during the night and would start and end simultaneously everywhere. The evidence comes from star clocks that were inscribed on coffin lids dating to Dynasties 9 and 10 (circa 2130–1980 B.C.E.). These star clocks depicted thirty-six rising stars, called *decans*, that marked a night hour equivalent to forty minutes on a modern clock. The principal star was Sirius, already an important marker from the previous civil calendar. All the *decans* disappear from the sky for seventy days, then first return to view just before sunrise (helical rising). Each rising of a star pinpointed the start of a new ten-day week on the civil calendar. Three of these weeks formed one month. After each star reappeared, it joined the others that were now visible. At any one time there were eighteen visible stars, which were spaced in one-hour intervals across the sky. This system created a clock consisting of eighteen Middle Kingdom hours at night, which is equivalent to the modern twelve hours. Scholars have not yet identified most of the decans, with the exception of Sirius, although stars from the constellations Orion and the Big Dipper also were decans.

Synchronized Calendar. Though this system regularized the length of nighttime hours and made the hours simultaneous everywhere, a major problem remained. This system accounted for only 365 days in a year. The true astronomical year, of course, is 365.25 days. Thus, after four years the calendar of stars was one day off the true astronomical year. After 120 years, the calendar deviated a full month from the actual seasons. The Egyptians recognized this problem and attempted to reset the star clocks regularly throughout the Middle Kingdom to keep the seasons and the calendar synchronized.

New Kingdom Astronomy. A new star clock consisting of twelve night hours was recorded in royal tombs during Dynasty 20 (circa 1190–1075 B.C.E.). This clock was probably calibrated with a water clock, known to be in use by the beginning of Dynasty 18 (circa 1539 B.C.E.), about 380 years earlier. The new system of timekeeping was based on a series of twelve constellations crossing an imaginary line drawn in the sky. To make the system work, two priests observed the night sky while sitting facing each other. One priest could watch the star group "pass" the other's shoulder or ear. He then could announce that the next hour had started. This system was more accurate than previous night-hour calculations because it was calibrated to a water clock, which resembled a large vase with a small hole in the bottom. Priests filled it each night and the water gradually escaped through the hole. Water-level measurements, carved into the side of the clock, marked the hours of the night. Daytime shadow clocks, also in use in the New Kingdom, were accurate from about 8 A.M. to 4 P.M.—any earlier or later in the day and the shadows were too long to record accurately. No major advances in astronomy are known until after Alexander the Great invaded Egypt, when local astronomy was combined with Greek and Babylonian sciences to make further advances.

Sources:

R. A. Wells, "The 5th Dynasty Sun Temples at Abu Ghurab as Old Kingdom Star Clocks; Examples of Applied Ancient Egyptian Astronomy," *Beihefte zu Studien zur Altägyptischen Kultur, Akten des Vierten Internationalen Ägyptologen Kongresses München 1985*, volume 4 (1990): 95–104.

Wells, "The Mythology of Nut and the Birth of Ra," *Studien zur Altägyptischen Kultur*, 19 (Hamburg: H. Buske Verlag, 1992): 305–321.

Wells, "Origin of the Hour and the Gates of the Duat," *Studien zur Altägyptischen Kultur*, 20 (Hamburg: H. Buske Verlag, 1993): 305–326.

Wells, "Re and the Calendars," in *Revolutions in Time: Studies in Egyptian Calendrics*, edited by Anthony John Spalinger (San Antonio: Van Siclen Books, 1994), pp. 1–28.

Wells, "Sothis and the Satet Temple at Elephantine: A Direct Connection," *Studien zur Altägyptischen Kultur*, 12 (Hamburg: H. Buske Verlag, 1985): 255–302.

CARTOGRAPHY

Similarities to Art. Maps preserved from ancient Egypt attest to the ancient interest in recording and interpreting the world. Egyptian maps described topography, architecture, the mythological world, and the whole cosmos. The scholar James A. Harrell has isolated three characteristics of these maps that associate them with the conventions of

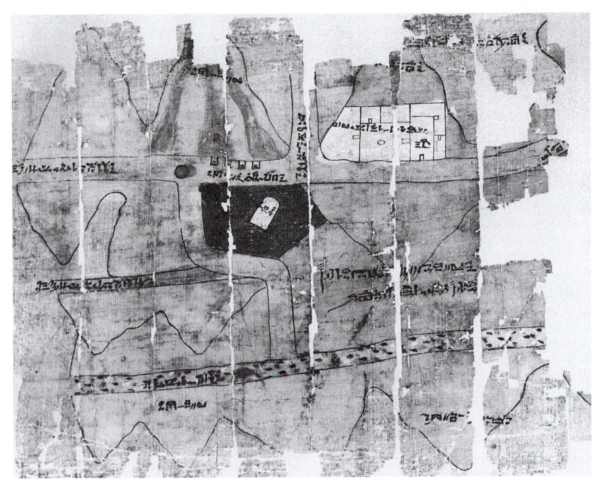

Map of gold mines showing the route between the Nile and the coast of the Red Sea, from the *Turin Papyrus,* Ramesside Period, circa 1295–1069 B.C.E. (Soprintendenza per le Antichita Egizie, Turin)

Egyptian art in general; for example, making a picture of a space rather than an actual plan. One map also can combine a bird's-eye view with profiles and plan-views simultaneously. Thus, a map resembles in concept an Egyptian rendering of a human body. It also shows multiple perspectives within one drawing, such as a whole eye within a profiled face. Finally, scale was not recorded in the drawing but rather through written annotations. A note added to the map tells the actual distance between two places. This connection between importance and size of representation was also reflected in Egyptian art.

Topographic Maps. The Egyptians represented topography as early as the Naqada I period (circa 4000–3600 B.C.E.) and continued into the New Kingdom (circa 1539–1075 B.C.E.). For example, early pots depicted rivers, mountains, and deserts. Topographical maps of battles are also known from the New Kingdom. One map detailed the terrain of Qadesh, where a battle was fought between the forces of Ramesses II (circa 1279–1213 B.C.E.) and the Hittite king Muwatallis. The maps included the Orontes River, its tributary, and the position of towns, as well as represented Egyptian and Hittite troop positions. This map was reproduced on temple walls in both Luxor and Karnak.

Quarry Guide. One known topographical map might have been used to guide an expedition through the Wadi Hammamat in the Eastern Desert. It was discovered in Deir el Medina, the workman's village near the Valley of the Kings. Amennakhte, son of Ipuy, was the scribe who made it during the reign of Ramesses IV (1156–1150 B.C.E.). The Egyptians highly prized *bekhen*-stone (greywacke) for its hardness and beauty when polished. The map depicted the location of the *bekhen*-stone quarry, its position relative to the Wadi Hammamat, and its relationship with the Wadi Atalla and Wadi Sid. Amennakhte also delineated the hills surrounding the quarry, a gold mine in the Wadi, and a settlement. Annotations identified place-names, distances between important points, and routes. The map is oriented to the south, the source of the Nile, and recorded geological features. It used different colors to represent distinct types of stone in the mountains and even various gravels found on the Wadi floor. This representation parallels modern maps in its ambitions to present a complete picture of one area. It is impossible to know whether other such maps existed in ancient times since this example is the only one known to have survived.

Architectural Plans. The Egyptians created architectural plans as early as the Old Kingdom (circa 2675–2130

B.C.E.), although some of the most impressive ones were made in the New Kingdom (circa 1539–1075 B.C.E.). Among them were elaborate carved plans on tomb walls and ink sketches on limestone chips. An architectural plan of Akhenaten's palace buildings and gardens was carved in relief in the tomb of Meryre I at Amarna (circa 1353–1336 B.C.E.). This plan combines bird's-eye views of buildings with profiles of gates and cross sections of storage facilities. Each feature was presented from the perspective most likely to make it clear. Ink-sketch plans of tombs are also known from Dynasty 20 (circa 1190–1075 B.C.E.). Amennakhte, son of Ipuy, prepared a sketch on papyrus of Ramesses IV's tomb in the Valley of the Kings. An ink sketch on limestone represented the plan of Ramesses IX's tomb. These plans resemble the map of the Wadi Hammamat in concept—drawn distances and the shapes of features are approximate, while annotations were used to convey precise distances.

Mythological and Cosmological Maps. The Egyptians represented the universe in mythological and cosmological maps. Mythological maps depicted the Land of the Dead and were drawn on coffins and papyrus. They depicted the twelve gates leading to the entrance of the Land of the Dead and also the guardian demons at each gate. Maps included in the *Book of the Two Ways* also recorded the spells that allowed the deceased to pass through the gates, as well as the rivers, canals, and fields in the idealized Land of the Dead. Cosmological maps showed the world according to Egyptian conceptions of the universe and were painted on coffins and tomb walls. They show the sky goddess Nut stretched above the air god Shu and the earth god Geb. In the central space is a ring with the names of the Egyptian *nomes* (provinces) inside it. Outside this ring are the names of foreign countries.

Sources:
James A. Harrell and V. Max Brown, "The Oldest Surviving Topographical Map from Ancient Egypt (Turin 1879, 1899 and 1969)," *Journal of the American Research Center in Egypt*, 29 (1992): 81–105.

A. F. Shore, "Egyptian Cartography," in *The History of Cartography*, volume 1, edited by J. B. Harley and D. Woodward (Chicago: University of Chicago Press, 1987), pp. 117–129.

HOROSCOPES

Predicting Futures? In popular Western thought the Egyptians are intimately connected with astrology and tarot cards, used to predict an individual's future. Yet, the evidence for these horoscopes is ambiguous. It is not clear if the average ancient Egyptian believed that the future could be foretold based on the position of the stars at the time of an individual's birth. In fact, the association between a lucky or unlucky birthday and the stars was probably made after the Greeks conquered Egypt (332 B.C.E.).

Lucky and Unlucky Days. The texts that Egyptologists call Calendars of Lucky and Unlucky Days were devoted to various activities of the gods. Good or bad luck was then attached to the day because of something the gods did on that day. Birth on a particular day was judged lucky or

---

FROM A CALENDAR OF LUCKY AND UNLUCKY DAYS

The Calendars of Lucky and Unlucky Days give specific information about a god's activities for each date and whether it is a good day or bad day. This calendar was written in the reign of Ramesses II (circa 1279–1213 B.C.E.). Such calendars were first written at least in Dynasty 12 (circa 1938–1759 B.C.E.) and continued until Dynasty 20 (circa 1190–1075 B.C.E.).

First Month of Harvest Season, Day 2: If you see anything, it will be good on this day. It is the day that the Ennead goes out before Re, their hearts being pleased by his youth, after they had killed the rebel . . . Apophis. . . .

Day 3: Anyone born on this day will die by a crocodile. It is the day of making [?] in the river by the gods of the [?].

Day 4: Do not do anything [on this day]. It is the day when Hathor goes forth together with the executioners in order to approach the riverbank. Now the gods go in a contrary wind. Do not navigate a boat on this day.

Day 5: If you see anything, it will be good on this day. The gods are peaceful in heaven, navigating the great barque.

Day 6: Anyone born on this day will die of the trampling of a bull.

Source: Abd el-Mohsen Bakir, *The Cairo Calendar No. 86637* (Cairo: General Organization for Government Printing Offices, 1966), pp. 13–14.

---

unlucky according to these calendars, which also explained how best to benefit from a lucky day or how to reduce ill fortune of a particular day through spells. Beyond the influence of a day's luck for general welfare, specific activities were likely to be more dangerous on some days than others. For example, priests warned individuals against going out of the house, consuming a specific drink, eating a specific food, traveling on the river, passing a bull, constructing a boat or house, or working at a particular occupation on specific days. Egyptologists disagree on whether these prohibitions were directed at the general public or only at priests. All of the calendars have been found in temples; thus, it is possible that only priests had to worry about these prohibitions and that they were related to ritual purity. Unlucky activities had to be avoided so that the priest could perform his rituals. Other scholars believe that the warnings were intended for everyone. Certainly, many Egyptians had small altars in their homes, and thus they performed private rituals that would have required purity. Maintaining ritual purity was a complex process for any Egyptian.

Astrology and Luck. None of these calendars associated the position of the stars with the luck of any day. After the Greeks conquered Egypt, however, new omen texts appeared that combined star observations with good and bad fortune. It is likely that Greek and Egyptian astrologers of the period after 323 B.C.E. incorporated their own traditions with Babylonian astrology. It seems that the zodiac tables known from the Ptolemaic Period (circa 332–31 B.C.E.) draw on all three national traditions.

Sources:

Jack Lindsay, *Origins of Astrology* (New York: Barnes & Noble, 1971).

A. Spalinger, "An Unexpected Source in a Festival Calendar," *Revue d'Egyptologie,* 42 (1991): 209–222.

Lana Troy, "Have a Nice Day! Some Reflections on the Calendars of Good and Bad Days," in *The Religion of the Ancient Egyptians: Cognitive Structures and Popular Expressions,* edited by Gertie Englund (Uppsala: S. Academiae Ubsaliensis, 1989), pp. 127–143.

MAGIC

Multiple Uses. The Egyptians believed that magic, called *"heka,"* was a useable and controllable force in the world, which could be accessed through performing rituals and reciting or writing spells. Magic was useful in medicine, improving agricultural production, cursing opponents, compelling love from sexual partners, and communicating with dead ancestors. For the Egyptians, magic was a neutral force like any other sort of energy in the natural order of things. Magic was studied in the "House of Life" located in the temple, much like the other sciences such as astronomy or medicine. Magic could control the natural world, other people, and dangerous animals. It was a component of medicine, included in a variety of issues such as general health maintenance, both while the subject was awake and asleep, as well as was used to prevent snake and crocodile bites.

Part Of Science. At the beginning of the twentieth century C.E., some Egyptologists argued that Egyptians in the Old Kingdom were more "scientific" than their descendants in the New Kingdom (circa 1539–1075 B.C.E.) and later. The *Ramesseum Papyri,* and the magician's kit found with them, show that magic was an integral part of Egyptian science in the Middle Kingdom. No real change occurred in the relationship between magic and other sciences over the whole period of Egyptian history. The reliance on magic did not increase over time, nor were there any changes in the way magic was used.

Mechanics. Egyptologist Robert Kriech Ritner has described the techniques of using magic as its "mechanics," which included licking and/or swallowing liquids that had had contact with magical images, manipulation of images, and recitation of spells. Another common technique was walking a circuit around a space to be protected, called circumambulating. Rituals also included tying special knots, using numerology, utilizing color symbols, and breaking, trampling, burning, burying, or spitting on objects. Egyptian magic also included intercession from the dead.

Recitation techniques. Often the speaker of magic assumed the identity of a god in a recitation. Many spells take the form, "I am the deity NN." The magician thus associated himself with a god whose story could be related to the situation at hand. The god Horus, for example, was renowned for his recovery after the god Seth attacked him. Thus, recovery from illness was associated with Horus. Many of the medical spells begin, "I am Horus." A second recitation technique was to recite patterns of sound that imitated speech but used no Egyptian words. These patterns were literally "magic words."

Priests As Magicians. Magic relied on the proper use of words as well as rituals and gestures, which were composed and copied at the House of Life, a unit of the temple. Thus magic was related to religion, as were other sciences in Egypt. The majority of magicians were priests. A specific priest called the "Prophet of Magic" and a "Chief of Secrets" were responsible for the use of magic in the temple. A "Chief Lector Priest" recited prayers for rituals and also pronounced spells for magical acts. Many lower-level lector priests were available both for official duties in the temple and private consultations that required magical intervention. Evidence from Deir el Medina also suggests that "wise women" had access to magic spells. Female magicians were especially consulted for divinations that determined the cause of events. For example, a death under suspicious circumstances could have been caused by magic. The wise woman was especially equipped to investigate such charges if there was reason to believe an event was related to magic.

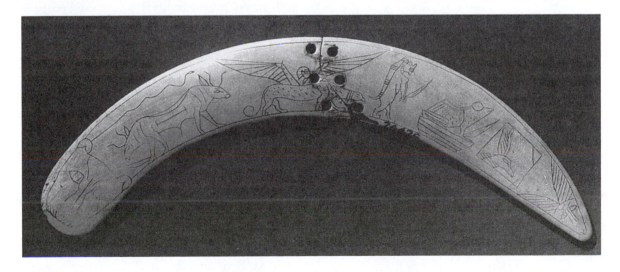

Wand made from a hippopotamus tusk and used by nurses to ward off evil, circa 1800 B.C.E. (British Museum, London)

A protective gilt and painted statue of the scorpion goddess Selqet, from the tomb of Tutankhamun, circa 1332–1322 B.C.E. (Egyptian Museum, Cairo)

Protecting Property. Magic was used to protect property. The major method used was a procession around the property, either with an image of a god or a special stick of wood. Such processions could be made around a temple as a god's house. Similar processions of this type were made by individuals to protect their residences.

Protecting People. Magic also protected people from wild animals. Using songs, spells, gestures, and rituals, a person could ward off crocodiles. The *Harris Magical Papyrus* recorded the necessary words and actions used in the Ramesside Period. An egg was made from clay and a professional magician recited the proper spell. A man then stood lookout in the prow of a boat holding the egg. He was directed to throw it at a surfacing crocodile to protect the boat.

Protection From Ghosts. Egyptians believed that people were also at risk while asleep. Ghosts were a particular worry. According to a papyrus in the Brooklyn Museum of Art, ghosts could inject poisoned fluid in a person's ear while he was asleep. A spell from Deir el Medina was used in conjunction with clay figures of snakes to prevent ghosts from entering a bedroom. Such clay figurines have been discovered in houses dating to the New Kingdom.

Protecting Fields and Animals. Fields were magically charged to make them more fertile by parading an image of the gods Amun, Mut, and Khonsu around them. Priests carried an image of the harvest goddess, Renenutet, around granaries to protect the harvest from harm. Spells were also useful to protect the fields from pests; for example, they could be used to keep birds from eating grain. A special cake was first baked and then placed over a piece of acacia wood. The spell called on the falcon-god Horus to protect the field from other birds. Many other magic remedies were used to protect the herds. Horus was again invoked to keep the herd safe from predatory animals such as lions and hyenas. Spells were also used to identify and remove infected animals from the herds. Cattle were especially at risk when they forded streams. Many scenes carved in Old Kingdom (circa 2675–2130 B.C.E.) tombs depict cattle crossing a stream while a magician supervised and recited a spell. A magician's toolbox found at the Ramesseum contained a small statue of a man with a calf on his shoulders, which probably was also used to protect cattle while they crossed streams.

Defeating Enemies. The Egyptians also believed that misfortune could be directed at their enemies. Commonly, foreign enemies of the state were portrayed as bound and defeated on buildings and furniture. Among common objects decorated with defeated enemies were door hinges, paving stones, sandal bottoms, footstools, throne bases, canes, jar handles, and oar stops. Thus, opening a door ground the enemy; walking on a path in sandals trampled them; resting one's feet, or sitting, caused them distress; pouring from a jar squeezed them; and rowing crushed them. Depictions that caused the enemy pain were used in both private and public life. Both ordinary people and government officials could use them. Figurines were sometimes decorated with the name of a foreign group or even a local individual. These figurines could be smashed or sealed inside a jar and buried. These methods brought distress to either a state or personal enemy.

Love Spells. People could also use magic to compel love from another person. The earliest example of a love spell was discovered in Deir el Medina and dates to the Ramesside Period (circa 1292–1075 B.C.E.). In the spell a man asks that a woman "run after me like a cow after grass, like a servant after her children, like a drover after his herd." Some other examples attempt to break up existing marriages and relationships through magical means.

Conclusion. Magic provided a source of control over the world for Egyptians of all social and political classes. Though professional practitioners were often consulted, the workmen at Deir el Medina, for instance, had access to magic themselves.

Magic gave Egyptians the comfort of knowing that certain dangers to themselves and their property could be confronted.

Sources:

Joris F. Borghouts, trans, *Ancient Egyptian Magical Texts* (Leiden: Brill, 1978).

Borghouts, "Magical Practices among the Villagers," *Pharaoh's Workers: The Villagers of Deir el Medina*, edited by Leonard H. Lesko (Ithaca, N.Y.: Cornell University Press, 1994), pp. 119–130.

Christian Jacq, *Egyptian Magic*, translated by Janet M. Davis (Wiltshire, U.K.: Aris & Phillips, 1985; Chicago: Bolchazy-Carducci, 1985).

Robert Kriech Ritner, *The Mechanics of Ancient Egyptian Magical Practice* (Chicago: Oriental Institute of the University of Chicago, 1993).

MATHEMATICS

Mathematical Knowledge. The Egyptians developed practical knowledge of arithmetic, algebra, geometry, and trigonometry. They applied these mathematical operations to practical problems such as figuring out the number of people needed to dig a lake of a particular size, build a ramp, transport an obelisk, erect a colossus, or provide necessities for an army. They could also compute the area of buildings and the slope of a pyramid. The most important mathematical text preserved from ancient Egypt is the *Rhind Mathematical Papyrus*, now located in the British Museum. Some fragments of the papyrus are also kept in the Brooklyn Museum of Art. A scribe named Ahmose recopied this text in the Second Intermediate Period (1630–1539/1523 B.C.E.) from a copy he claimed was made in the reign of Amenemhet III (circa 1818–1772 B.C.E.). Many commentators believe the text also draws on materials already known in the Old Kingdom (circa 2675–2130 B.C.E.). Nevertheless, this text probably does not contain all mathematical knowledge available to ancient Egyptians. Egyptian mathematics was sophisticated enough that major engineering feats, such as the Great Pyramid and other monumental buildings, could be constructed.

Arithmetic and Algebra. Arithmetic is the manipulation of numbers, including fractions. Algebra uses arithmetical operations to solve an equation for an unknown number. Modern arithmetic is taught as adding, subtracting, multiplying, and dividing numbers. These operations are also used to solve equations. The basic Egyptian method was doubling; their number system was base 10, similar to the modern system of numbers. The doubling method is best illustrated in the following solution to the problem 47 x 33:

1	47
2	94
4	188
8	376
16	752
32	1504
TOTAL: 33	1551

Here the number 47 is doubled, that sum is doubled, then that sum is doubled, until the result comes within one

Part of the *Rhind Mathematical Papyrus*, written during the Hyksos Period (circa 1630–1523 B.C.E.), containing a series of problems about calculating the volume of rectangles, triangles, and pyramids (British Museum, London)

unit of the desired answer (that is, 32 x 47). Then the one additional unit of 47 can be added to result in the answer, 33 x 47=1551. Using a set of tables reproduced in the *Rhind Mathematical Papyrus*, a similar set of operations could be performed with fractions. This table allowed the Egyptians to solve for unknowns (algebra).

Geometry. Geometry is the measurement of areas and volumes. Egyptian accomplishments in geometry include knowledge of π and of the special properties of right-angle triangles. They knew the accurate value of π to within 0.6 percent—3.16 rather than 3.1416, as used for modern calculations. This value is needed to calculate the area of a circle. It represents a ratio between the circumference of a circle and its diameter. Using π, the Egyptians could calculate both areas and volumes. The Egyptians also understood the special properties of the right-angle triangle, which include the proportions of the sides (3:4:5) and the fact that the square of the sides is equal to the square of the hypotenuse (the side opposite the ninety-degree angle). These calculations made it possible to square the corners of the pyramids.

Trigonometry. The Egyptians needed to calculate the slope of a pyramid in order to know that the four sides would meet in a point at the top. They also had to calculate the height of a pyramid given a particular length of a side and a particular slope. The slope was called the *seked*, the lateral displacement for a drop of one unit. The primary *seked* for an Old Kingdom pyramid was 5.5. The *Rhind Mathematical Papyrus* used a *seked* of 5.5 in its problems, suggesting that the text used materials dating from the Old Kingdom.

Sources:

Arnold Buffum Chace, *The* Rhind Mathematical Papyrus: *Free Translation and Commentary with Selected Photographs, Transcriptions, Transliterations, and Literal Translations* (Reston, Va.: National Council of Teachers of Mathematics, 1979).

Richard J. Gillings, *Mathematics in the Time of the Pharaohs* (Cambridge, Mass.: MIT Press, 1972).

Gay Robins and Charles Shute, *The* Rhind Mathematical Papyrus: *An Ancient Egyptian Text* (London: British Museum Publications, 1987).

MEDICINE

Famous Doctors. Egyptian records allow scholars to reconstruct a history of medicine stretching from 3000 B.C.E. to the seventh century C.E. Egyptian doctors were famous in the ancient world, attracting calls for aid from the Hittite royal court in Dynasty 19 (circa 1292–1190 B.C.E.). Egyptians were also aware of the foreign practice of medicine in Syria-Palestine and Babylonia. At the very end of ancient Egyptian history, the Greeks adopted much of Egyptian theory and practice through collaborations in Alexandria.

General State of Health. The fertility of Egypt in ancient times meant that the population enjoyed a healthy diet. One farm laborer produced enough food for twenty adults. This fruitfulness was the reason that Egypt was known for food production in the stories of the patriarchs Abraham, Isaac, and Jacob in the biblical Book of Genesis. Wealthy Egyptians regularly consumed a mixture of grains, vegetables, fruits, fish, fowl, cattle, milk, beer, and wine. Even the mass of the population ate a mixture of grains that provided an adequate diet. Life expectancy averaged thirty to thirty-six years. Documents attest that some individuals lived to be sixty years old and even older.

Medicine and Religion. All Egyptian knowledge was organized through religion, and medicine was no different. Thoth, god of writing, also supported healing. Sakhmet, goddess of disease, maintained a priesthood that performed some medical tasks. Other deities concerned with medicine were Selket, the scorpion goddess, who cured scorpion bites; Isis, goddess of magic; and Horus, the divine physician. Imhotep (who lived in Dynasty 3, circa 2675–2625 B.C.E.) and Amenhotep, son of Hapu (born in the reign of Amenhotep II, circa 1412 B.C.E. to the reign of Ay, circa 1345 B.C.E.), were humans who were later regarded as healing saints. Medical training, along with other scientific training, took place in the temple. Medical texts were prepared and stored in the House of Life, a unit of the temple.

Doctors and Titles. Egyptian bureaucratic hierarchies in medicine were well established by the Old Kingdom (circa 2675–2130 B.C.E.). The basic term for physician was *sunu*, which combined with many titles, including Overseer of Physicians, Inspector of Physicians, Chief Physician, Palace Physician, Inspector of Palace Physicians, and Chief Palace Physician. Separate titles were used to describe specialists in ophthalmology, dentistry, internal medicine, and proctology. Embalmers were medical specialists in making mummies and were also called *sunu* during the Late Period. Allied medical practitioners included pharmacists, bandage dressers, and masseurs. Priests of Sakhmet, priests of Selket, and amulet sellers were all trained in taking the

Relief of a squatting woman giving birth and being assisted by the goddesses Hathor and Taweret, from the temple of Hathor at Dendera, circa 350 B.C.E. (Egyptian Museum, Cairo)

pulse, which was early recognized as indicative of overall health. Male physicians are best represented in the record, though female practitioners existed. A woman named Peseshet was the Overseer of Female Physicians in Dynasty 5 (circa 2500–2350 B.C.E.). Her title strongly suggests there were other female physicians whom she supervised. Women also practiced as midwives and wet nurses.

Theory of Disease. The *Papyrus Ebers,* written during the Hyksos Period (circa 1630–1523 B.C.E.), recorded details of the Egyptian theory of disease. The Egyptians understood that the circulatory system carried blood, water, and air around the body. They believed that an additional substance, which they called *wekhedu,* also traveled through the circulatory system. *Wekhedu* was the name for a waste product that the Egyptians believed the body produced over time. Excess *wekhedu,* the Egyptians thought, was the cause of disease, aging, and death. It was easily recognized in the pus formed in an infected wound, and it was thought to clog the veins and arteries as the body continued to produce it over a lifetime. Egyptian medicine aimed to reduce *wekhedu* through enemas and purges. Even embalming a mummy was an attempt to remove all *wekhedu* so that the body would be preserved after death. *Wekhedu* continued to be understood as the cause of disease into the Hellenistic Period (after 332 B.C.E.), when some Greek physicians adopted this theory to

MEDICAL TEXTS

Medical treatments often included both spells and prescriptions. The following extracts from the *London Medical Papyrus* (10059) are treatments for bleeding:

Prescription to prevent bleeding from a wound: Fly excrement, red ochre. To be given for it. Words spoken as magic: The mar-demon is to be seized by the nekhet-demon and vice-versa. Yet it is the mar-demon that is to smite the nekhet-demon. This against this!

This spell, recited while applying the bandage, shows how the practitioner associates the disease with a mythological story. The spell and bandage stem bleeding thought to cause a miscarriage.

Another spell to repel bleeding: Anubis comes forth, to drive back the Nile flood from treading the sanctuary of Tait. What is in it is protected. This spell is to be spoken over linen of *rayaat* weave, made into an amuletic knot and placed into the inside of her vulva.

Source: Christian Leitz, *Magical and Medical Papyri of the New Kingdom* (London: British Museum Press for the Trustees of the British Museum, 1999), 69–70.

explain disease. The theory of *wekhedu* was the earliest known rational explanation of disease recorded in history. It provided a cause and a theory of treatment that underlay all Egyptian medicine. Though magical treatments were included in the removal of *wekhedu* from the body, the theory has impressed modern scientists with its rational progression from the hypothesis that *wekhedu* existed to proposals for treating disease by its elimination.

Known Diseases. Paleopathology is a modern science that investigates human remains to determine the extent and nature of disease in the ancient world. Paleopathologists have made great use of Egyptian mummies, an important source of data, to identify many diseases related to parasites—including bilharziasis (*schistosomiasis*), roundworm (*ascaris*), guinea worm (*dracunculus*), and tapeworm (*taenia*). Other diseases identified in ancient Egypt include malaria, tuberculosis, smallpox, and cancer.

Tooth Decay. Dental caries (cavities) were actually rarer in ancient Egypt than in the modern American population before the introduction of fluoridated water. The Egyptians had no refined sugar, the primary cause of cavities. Their diet also was abrasive, including grit and sand—especially in stone-ground grain products such as bread. This grit effectively cleaned the average person's teeth.

Medical Procedures. Surgical and other medical procedures conducted during life are often visible in mummies. The most common medical procedure was male circumcision. Not only do mummies illustrate that this procedure was widespread, but also the technique was illustrated in relief sculptures found on tomb walls. A Middle Kingdom text described circumcision as part of group initiation. The text described it as occurring in early adolescence. Other medical interventions included splints, sutures (stitches), and trephination—perforating the skull with a surgical instrument. The Egyptians used recognizable medical instruments such as scalpels, needles, tweezers, clysters (enema bags), and measuring vessels.

Texts. Medical knowledge was preserved in written descriptions of cases. Currently, seventeen different compilations of medical data on papyrus are known. In general the texts were descriptions of specific cases rather than general theory. They included carefully observed descriptions of the progress of a disease, recommendations for treatment, and whether the treatment was generally successful. Some diseases were described as incurable.

Magical Methods in Medicine. A close connection existed between doctors (*sunu*) and magicians (*hery-hebu*) in Egypt. Both kinds of specialists were trained at the House of Life in the temple and used methods that were based on cause and effect, as well as on supernatural methods. They used objects that were magically charged in their treatments, as well as incantations and ritual actions that modern people associate with magic. Even common events in medical practice, such as mixing and measuring ingredients for remedies, loosening bandages, and drinking a remedy, were accompanied by magical spells. The priest of Sakhmet, goddess of

Restored basalt statue of the chief of physicians, Psammetikseneb, Dynasty 18, circa 1539–1295/1292 B.C.E. (Museo Gregoriano Egizio, Vatican City)

plague, and the "controller of Selket," goddess of scorpions, both played medical roles in the control of disease and scorpion bite.

Gynecology. New mothers and newborn children were a special concern for medical practice and magic. The lector priest and the "magician of the nursery" used specific spells to protect mothers and newborns during delivery and in the first months of life. Objects called magical knives, actually protective wands inscribed with symbols of protection and inscriptions to repel evil, were used to draw defensive circles around the child's bed. The demigoddess Beset was represented on these knives. She was responsible for the protection of bedrooms, mothers, and children.

Spells. Another widespread magical cure consisted of carved images and spells of the god Horus on stelae. In the New Kingdom a new, standardized imagery with spells was created to prevent or counter the effects of snakebite and scorpion sting. Basically, the patient poured water over the images, recited the spell, collected the water, and drank it. This ritual was a basic healing technique known as early as the Pyramid Texts of Dynasty 5 (reign of Unas, circa 2371–2350 B.C.E.) and 6 (reign of Teti, circa 2350–2338 B.C.E., to the reign of Meryre Pepy I, circa 2338–2298 B.C.E.). The Coffin Texts of the Middle Kingdom (circa 1980–1630 B.C.E.) also contained knowledge of this process. The underlying theory assumed that liquid that came in contact with magical words or objects could transfer its power to the person who drank it. The verb "to swallow" thus became a synonym for "to know" because of this magical technique. Such stelae were distributed widely, including larger ones placed in public places for general use.

Sources:

J. Worth Estes, *The Medical Skills of Ancient Egypt* (Canton, Mass.: Science History Publications, 1989).

John F. Nunn, *Ancient Egyptian Medicine* (Norman: University of Oklahoma Press, 1996).

Cornelius Stetter, *The Secret Medicine of the Pharaohs: Ancient Egyptian Healing* (Chicago: Edition Q , 1993).

MUMMIFICATION

Preserving the Dead. Embalming, or mummification, was a basic technology important to ancient Egyptian culture. The mummy is the embalmed remains of the deceased. The word derives from the Arabic (or Persian) *mumia*, meaning pitch or bitumen, and was used to describe the embalmed remains of the Egyptians because they appeared to be covered with pitch. The practice of mummification may have arisen because of the natural desiccating property of the Egyptian sand. The earliest Egyptian burial sites, from the Predynastic Period (circa 3100–3000 B.C.E.), were simply shallow pits on the edge of the desert. The heat, combined with the desiccating property of the sand, served to dry out the tissues of the body before they could decompose, leaving a considerably lifelike appearance. With the introduction of more elaborate tombs, however, the body was no longer buried in sand and, as a result, quickly decomposed. Consequently, various attempts were made to preserve the body.

A Renewed Life. The justification for the process of mummification derives from the myth of Osiris. After

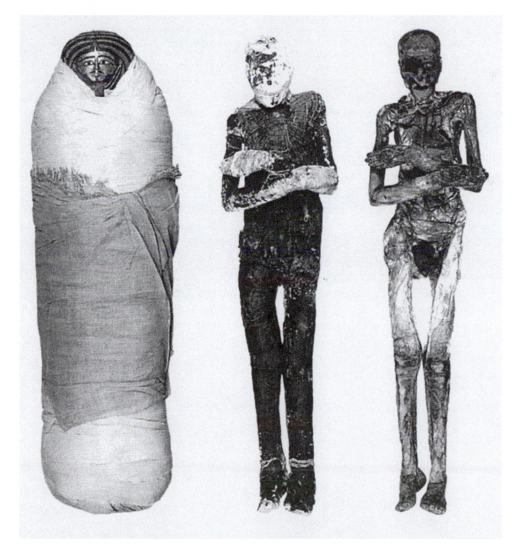

The mummy of Wah during various stages of unwrapping, from Deir el Bahri, Thebes, circa 1991–1962 B.C.E. (Metropolitan Museum of Art, New York)

SCIENCE, TECHNOLOGY, AND HEALTH

Canopic jars containing the intestines, lungs, liver, and stomach (l.–r.) of General Psametek-sineit, circa 530 B.C.E. (Musee du Louvre, Paris)

Seth had dismembered his brother Osiris, Isis traveled throughout Egypt gathering up the pieces of his body. The god of embalming, Anubis, then reassembled the pieces and rejuvenated the body of Osiris to allow him to sire a son with Isis. Each deceased Egyptian was thought to become an Osiris and, by reenacting the same mummification process, to gain renewed life. The earliest example of mummification dates to the Dynasty 4 burial of Queen Hetepheres (circa 2585–2560 B.C.E.).

Mummification Process. Throughout Egyptian history, several different methods of mummification were used, depending on what the deceased (or his or her family) could afford. An elaborate mummification could have proceeded along the following lines. First, the corpse was taken to the Per-Nefer, the House of Mummification, where it was placed on the embalming table, which was supposed to resemble the one on which Osiris had been placed. The table is frequently shown with lion's feet. Next, the brain was removed through the nose and thrown away. The Egyptians did not recognize the significance of the brain and thought it to be of no use. The embalmer, known as the *ut*-priest, made a cut in the left side of the abdomen, and the liver, lungs, stomach, and intestines were removed. They were wrapped separately and each was placed in its own jar. These canopic jars were buried in the tomb with the mummy, often in a special chest. At times, the heart was removed and carefully wrapped and returned to its place. At other times, it was simply left in place. Near the heart could be placed what is called a "heart scarab." The body cavity was packed

with linen, other stuffing material, and natron, a salty powder similar to baking soda that was used to dry out the body. This process took about forty days, after which the natron was removed, the body cavity was packed with linen bags of sawdust or myrrh soaked in resin, and the abdominal incision was sewn up. The body was rubbed with a mixture of cedar oil, wax, natron, and gum; it was then sprinkled with spices. The skin was smeared with molten resin, which, when hardened, kept moisture out of the body. The last step was the wrapping of the body with linen. This process could involve the use of hundreds of yards of linen. Beginning in Dynasty 30, texts from the *Book of the Dead* were written on some of the mummy bandages. During the wrapping process, amulets were deposited on the mummy to protect it. Throughout the whole process appropriate incantations were recited. Some of these spells have been preserved on papyri. For example, after anointing the head of the mummy with good-quality resin, the embalming priest was to recite the following:

Ho, Osiris N [N represents the name of the deceased], resin which came forth from Punt is on you in order to make your odor agreeable as the divine scent. The efflux which comes forth from Re is on you in order to make [your odor] agreeable in the broad hall of the Two Truths.

The process of making a mummy was said to take seventy days, deriving from the number of days the star Sirius was invisible. In actuality, mummification could last anywhere from thirty to more than two hundred days. Once the mummy was completed, the funeral could begin.

Sources:

Bob Brier, *Egyptian Mummies: Unraveling the Secrets of an Ancient Art* (New York: Morrow, 1996).

Rosalie David and Eddie Tapp, eds., *Evidence Embalmed: Modern Medicine and the Mummies of Ancient Egypt* (Manchester, U.K. & Dover, N.H.: Manchester University Press, 1984).

Christine El Mahdy, *Mummies, Myth, and Magic in Ancient Egypt* (New York: Thames & Hudson, 1989).

TECHNOLOGY AND ENGINEERING: BUILDING THE PYRAMIDS

Giza. The best-known monuments from ancient Egypt are the pyramids of Giza (circa 2585–2510 B.C.E.). They also serve as a good example of the way the Egyptians approached engineering and architecture. The Egyptians used extremely simple technology to accomplish sophisticated ends. Archaeological remains, relief sculpture, paintings, and experimental archaeology have all contributed to modern knowledge of Egyptian techniques for building the pyramids.

Supply and Transport of Materials. The Egyptians transported the stone used to build the pyramids by boat and sledge. Stone, quarried a long distance from the building site, was loaded onto boats. A relief sculpture carved on the causeway of the pyramid temple of Unas (circa 2371–2350 B.C.E.) depicted a boat carrying granite columns from Aswan to Memphis. The *Autobiography of Weni*, a text dating to Dynasty 6 (circa 2350–2170 B.C.E.), also described the hauling of large pieces of granite and alabaster by boat. Canals, dug directly to the site of the pyramids, allowed the Egyptians to bring the stone close to the building site by boat. The stone blocks rested on sledges, which resembled modern sleds, and their runners were designed to run on wet mud that was scattered on tracks built from a series of wooden frames filled with limestone chips and covered with plaster. Such roads have been discovered at Lisht near the Dynasty 12 pyramids of Amenemhet I (circa 1938–1909 B.C.E.) and Senwosret I (circa 1919–1875 B.C.E.). Large ropes were secured around the blocks, allowing men to haul them directly to the pyramid site. A painting from the Dynasty 12 tomb of Djeheutyhotep (circa 1842–1818 B.C.E.) the nomarch in the town of Bersheh shows 172 men hauling an approximately 58-ton statue in this manner. A man sprinkled water in front of the sledge, keeping the mud moist, as it proceeded along the track. Experimental archaeology has demonstrated that fewer men were needed to haul blocks of the size found at the Great Pyramid using these methods.

Obtaining Stone. Quarries were located near the building site of the Great Pyramids of Giza. The location of the

The pyramids of Giza viewed from the south

quarry may well have helped determine the site for the pyramids. Only the external stone covering of the pyramid traveled a long distance. The remains of the quarries at Giza supply some clues to how quarrymen worked. A man with a pick cut channels, wide and thick enough to allow wooden levers to enter, around the rectangular blocks that would be removed from the bedrock. The blocks were then pried from bedrock with levers. Though earlier reconstructions of this process suggest that wedges were used to remove the block, experimental archaeology indicates that wooden levers worked better than wedges. Modern quarrymen use iron wedges in this process. Further experiments with ancient tools made of wood, stone, and copper have demonstrated that 12 workmen can produce 8.5 stones in a day. The archaeologist Mark Lehner has calculated that a crew of 1,212 men working for twenty-three years—the Greek historian Herodotus's estimate of the time it took to build Khufu's pyramid—could have easily quarried all the stone in the Great Pyramid. These men, of course, worked in rotation.

Tools, Techniques, Operations. The Egyptians designed and used simple tools needed to build the pyramids. They used plumb bobs and square levels to ensure that corners of blocks were square and that surfaces were flat. These instruments were made of wood, twine, and lightweight stones. Stonecutters used copper drills and saws, probably using a quartz slurry to aid in the process. The slurry was a solution of water, sand, and gypsum. Remains of such slurries have been found in ancient cuts where they stain the stone green, the result of oxidation. Copper chisels were used to smooth the sides of stones. Copper is so soft that the chisels needed constant sharpening. Lehner estimated that each one hundred masons using such a chisel would require one full-time chisel sharpener. Large dolerite stones were used as pounders to excavate the channels needed to free a block from the bedrock. Finally, a mushroom-shaped stone with three grooves cut across the round section probably acted as a primitive pulley that could redirect the force on the ropes used to move blocks. All of the tools needed to perform the operations for building the pyramids have been found archaeologically.

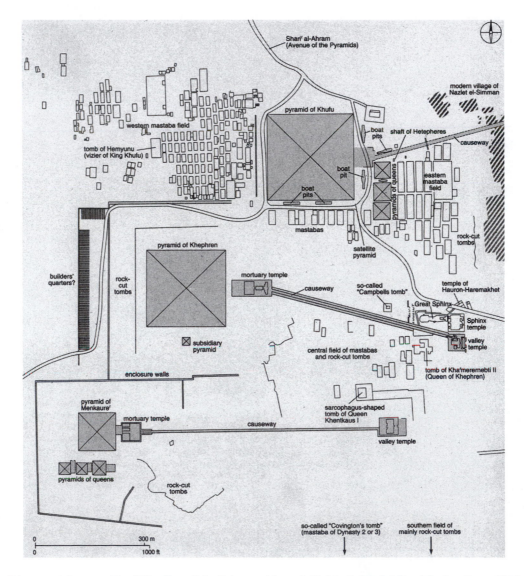

Diagram of the pyramids of Giza (from John Baines and Jaromir Malek, *Cultural Atlas of Ancient Egypt*, 2000)

Survey and Alignment. Three characteristics of the pyramids lead to questions about the Egyptians' ability to survey and align buildings. First, the sides of pyramids are aligned to the cardinal points of the compass. Second, the corners of the pyramids form perfect right angles. Finally, the foundation of the pyramid had to be perfectly level in order to support the enormous weight of the upper courses.

Using the Stars. Alignment to the cardinal points of the compass was most likely accomplished by astronomical observation. Because stars appear to move in Egypt from east to west, true north could have been established by dividing the angle of a rising and setting star by two. Or the sun could have been used to establish true north though measuring the length of a shadow of a vertical at various times of the day. Neither method can be proved, but both could have been performed given Egyptian knowledge of astronomy.

Figuring Angles. Three methods have been proposed for establishing the right angles at the corners of the pyramids. A setsquare could have been used to establish the corner. The difficulty would have been to extend the lines of the square 754 feet in two directions. The 90-degree angle of the corner also could have been established using a right triangle, also called the sacred, or Pythagorean, triangle. In this kind of triangle a side of three units, four units, and five units yields a triangle with one 90-degree angle opposite the side of five units. Using this method, the sides could have extended 48 feet before the hypotenuse of the triangle disappeared into the base of the pyramid. Finally, the Egyptians could have established the right angle by drawing two intersecting arcs with a stick and string placed at any two points on the same line. Though this method would work approximately, it would be difficult not to stretch Egyptian string, thus reducing the accuracy of the operation.

Leveling. The final survey and alignment problem was leveling the base of the pyramid. Lehner has realized that the first course itself was used to establish the level platform rather than leveling the bedrock, as previous commentators believed. This method allowed for a perfectly level base.

Ramps. The final stones raised to the top of the Great Pyramid traveled 479 feet. Scholars have long agreed that some form of ramp was used to raise the stones to the upper courses and envisioned ramps running perpendicular and parallel to the sides of the pyramids. They also hypothesized that a ramp encircled the pyramid. Archaeological evidence suggests that there were some ramps perpendicular to the face of the pyramid, and in addition, others that wrapped around the structure.

Setting the Blocks and Controlling the Slope. A variety of methods were used to ensure that the four sides of the pyramid would meet evenly at the top and form a point. In Dynasty 3 (circa 2675–2625 B.C.E.) the walls were built of vertical layers that sloped toward the center. In Dynasty 4 (circa 2625–2500 B.C.E.) the walls were built of horizontal layers that were shaped to a slope on the outside edges. In Dynasty 5 (circa 2500–2350 B.C.E.) and 6 (circa 2350–2170 B.C.E.) the pyramids had rough cores with casing stones layered on the outside. Finally, in Dynasty 12 (circa 1938–1759 B.C.E.) the pyramids had mud-brick cores and outer casings.

Sources:

Peter Hodges, *How the Pyramids Were Built*, edited by Julian Keable (Longmead, U.K.: Element Books, 1989).

Mark Lehner, *The Complete Pyramids* (New York: Thames & Hudson, 1997).

J. P. Lepre, *The Egyptian Pyramids: A Comprehensive, Illustrated Reference* (Jefferson, N.C.: McFarland, 1990).

Peter Tompkins, *Secrets of the Great Pyramid* (New York: Harper & Row, 1971).

SIGNIFICANT PEOPLE

PENTU

FLOURISHED CIRCA 1353–1322 B.C.E.

KING'S PHYSICIAN, VIZIER

Priest and Chamberlain. Little is known about Pentu's life, but by the reign of Amenhotep IV (Akhenaten) (circa 1353–1336 B.C.E.) this priest and physician had achieved the high status of Chief Servitor—the private doctor and chamberlain to the king. Despite his close proximity to the royal family, which earned him official praise from the king, as well as the placement of his picture on the walls of the temple to Aten, Pentu did not agree with the religious and social changes Akhenaten and his wife, Nefertiti, were instituting, especially the elimination of references to the god Amen and the placement of Aten in his place. Pentu appeared outwardly loyal to his king; yet, at the same time, he developed firm relationships with officials who opposed the changes.

Survivor. Pentu was one of only a few of Akenaten's officials to maintain a position of importance after the death of the king. Most likely because of his orthodox religious views and his friendship with Ay, a court official who may have actually been running the kingdom while Akhenaten concentrated on religion and who later served as pharaoh (circa 1322–1319 B.C.E.), Pentu was made the Southern Vizier during the reign of Tutankhamun (circa 1332–1322 B.C.E.). He helped overthrow the worship of Aten and return the former status of Amen. There is evidence that Pentu survived this king as well and even participated in his funerary procession. When the physician died, he was buried in a tomb that he had been granted in Amarna.

Sources:

Cyril Aldred, *Akhenaten: King of Egypt* (London: Thames & Hudson, 1988).

Ian Bolton, "Pentu: Chief Physician to the King," *Egypt: Land of Eternity*, <http://members.tripod.com/ib205/pentu.html>.

PESESHE

FLOURISHED CIRCA 2500–2350 B.C.E.

PHYSICIAN

Female Doctors. During the Old Kingdom (circa 2675–2130 B.C.E.) women occupied some specialized positions and even achieved supervisory status in a few cases. Women worked as singers, musicians, dancers, weavers, midwives, priestesses, and scribes. Hundreds of women, however, became physicians and some even attained positions of authority. This fact does not seem strange, as the patron god for physicians was Sekmet, a vengeful lioness (a woman with the head of a lion) deity who could send or remove disease and was often depicted with a mirror upon her head. Physicians were not only responsible for the physical healing, such as through surgery, but they also combined religion and magic, natural healing, and diet in their medical plan.

Supervisor. One such woman, probably from a wealthy family, was Peseshet, a physician who attained the title of "Overseer of the Doctors," supervising the activities of many female doctors. Her specific duties are lost to modern scholars, although she seems to have been responsible both for medical care and funeral rites as well as possibly training midwives. It is unclear as to who their clients were—women only or the sick of both genders.

Sources:

W.B. Harer Jr. and Z. el-Dawakhly, "Peseshet—The First Female Physician," *Obstetrics & Gynecology*, 74 (December 1989): 960–961.

Théophile Obenga, "Lady Peseshet: The First Woman Doctor in World History," *Era of Masses*, 1 (February 1997), <http://www.pond.com/~zizwe/ng/ngPeseshet.htm>.

PSAMTIK (PSAMMETICHUS) I

664–610 B.C.E.

KING, DYNASTY 26

Reunification. Psamtik I, a governor in Upper Egypt, was the son of Nekau I (672–664 B.C.E.), who ruled from Sais during a period of Assyrian influence. Egypt had experienced a period of division and weakness for more than four hundred years, and Nekau I was defeated during a Nubian invasion, forcing his son to leave Egypt. Initially using Assyrian support, Psamtik returned and gained control of the Delta; he then gradually expanded his authority as the Assyrians, who were fighting incursions in the home territories, weakened and withdrew. Psamtik used Greek mercenaries in his army, having negotiated an alliance with King Gyges of Lydia, and he gave land to them, forming a colony of Greeks in the Delta. The new king built a strong military, opened trade in the Mediterranean, reestablished a strong religion, and constructed grand buildings.

Revival and Research. He ruled during a period when Egyptians looked backward to the glory of former dynasties, often copying the artistic and architectural styles of earlier days. In addition to constructing traditional temples and art, there seems to have occurred advances in the use of metals, especially bronze. Several small lion gods made of bronze have been discovered, all revealing advanced metallurgical skills during this period.

Scientific Experiments? Psamtik I earned a reputation for research and even for changing his conclusions when the results did not agree with his prior beliefs. The Greek historian Herodotus reports that Psamtik I was interested in discovering the oldest language, which the pharaoh believed could be none other than Egyptian. He concluded that placing two newborns in the care of shepherds (possibly deaf), who had been bound not to teach them how to speak, might show what manner of language would develop spontaneously. He allegedly discovered, after the children were presented a few years later and uttered a word that the observers believed was "bread," that they spoke a form of Phrygian. This test, according to scholar Antoni Sulek, is often cited as the "first instance of using the experimental method in the study of social phenomena, and in psychology—as the prototype of research on the relative role of heredity and environment in the development." Psamtik I ruled for fifty-four years and was succeeded by his son, Necho II (610–595 B.C.E.), who continued his father's penchant for research by sending out expeditions of exploration.

Sources:

Alan B. Lloyd, "The Late Period (664–610 BC)," in *The Oxford History of Ancient Egypt*, edited by Ian Shaw (Oxford & New York: Oxford University Press, 2000), pp. 369–394.

Antoni Sulek, "The Experiment of Psammetichus: Fact, Fiction, and Model to Follow," *Journal of the History of Ideas*, 50 (October–December 1989): 645–651.

DOCUMENTARY SOURCES

Anonymous, *Ebers Medical Papyrus* (circa 1630–1539 B.C.E.)—A treatise on internal disease, copied by the same scribe as the *Edwin Smith Surgical Papyrus*. It contains the first comprehensive theory of disease that explains all disease as the accumulation of waste products in the blood (*wekhedu*). All treatments are based on removing this waste product.

Anonymous, *Edwin Smith Surgical Papyrus* (circa 1630–1539 B.C.E.)—Copy of an Old Kingdom text written in the Hyksos Period. It was made by the same scribe as the *Ebers Medical Papyrus*. It contains the descriptions of forty-eight cases of trauma and the prescribed treatments. It is organized by injuries, starting with those to the head and working down the body, and follows the standardized procedure in describing each case.

Anonymous, *Kahun Medical Papyrus* (circa 1938–1759 B.C.E.)—This papyrus is the earliest medical text from ancient Egypt. It is written in two parts. The gynecology section shows that medical treatment for females was separated early from male treatment. The second section contains the only known veterinary documents from ancient Egypt.

Anonymous, *London Medical Papyrus, BM 10059* (circa 1292–1190 B.C.E.)—An unusual medical papyrus that contains transcriptions of foreign spells from the Levant and from Crete.

Anonymous, *Ramesseum Papyri III-V* (circa 1759–after 1630 B.C.E.)—This collection of papyri was discovered in the Ramesseum, a temple built by Ramesses II (circa 1279–1213 B.C.E.), and includes information on ophthalmology, gynecology, pediatrics, and the vascular system.

Anonymous, *Rhind Mathematical Papyrus* (circa 1650 B.C.E.)—Copied by the scribe Ahmes, this scroll provides much of the information available to modern historians about ancient Egyptian knowledge of mathematical computations.

Limestone relief of a cargo boat carrying a huge block of stone, from the tomb of Ipi, Saqqara, Dynasty 6, circa 2350–2170 B.C.E. (Egyptian Museum, Cairo)

Mummy and coffin of an unnamed priestess, circa 1500 B.C.E. (British Museum, London)

GLOSSARY

A-amu: "Asiatic"; slave.

Afnet: a kind of cloth head covering.

Akh: The glorified spirit of a deceased person entitled to offerings from his family members.

Akhet: Horizon; the place where the temporal world and the world of the gods meet; used to refer to temples, sanctuaries, and pylons.

Amarna: City on the East bank of the Nile midway between Thebes and Memphis built circa 1353–1336 B.C.E. Called Akhetaten, "Horizon of the Aten," it was the capital of the Atenist religion under Amenhotep IV (Akhenaten).

Amarna Period: The reign of Amenhotep IV (Akhenaten), circa 1353–1336 B.C.E., centered at the new capital city of Amarna.

Amun: "Hidden One"; god of the air. *See* **Amun-Re.**

Amun-Re: The king of the gods; the state god of Egypt.

Ankh: A symbol for life sometimes bestowed by deities.

Anubis: God of the dead; represented by a jackal or a man with the head of a jackal.

Aten: A deity represented by the disc or orb of the sun; also the cult promoted by Amenhotep IV when he changed his name to Akhenaten, circa 1353–1336 B.C.E.

Ba: Manifestation of a spirit.

Baharawiya: Northern Egyptians.

Bak: "Worker"; slave.

Baris: An Egyptian freight boat.

Bastinato: A form of torture in which the bottoms of a prisoner's feet are beaten with a stick.

Cataracts: The six rapids in the Nile River between Aswan and Khartoum.

Chantress: A woman responsible for the music used in the rituals at major temples. She usually earned a salary independent of her husband or father.

Coptic: An Egyptian alphabetic script based on the Greek alphabet, with additional letters derived from Demotic signs.

Deben: A measure of weight used for copper as well as gold and silver. One *deben* of copper weighed 91 grams; it equaled 10 *kite.*

Deir el Medina: A New Kingdom (circa 1539–1075 B.C.E.) village in the hills of West Thebes occupied by workmen who labored on the royal tombs.

Delta: The mouth of the Nile River in Lower Egypt. In antiquity, it consisted of seven major branches and was the site of several important ports and cult centers.

Demotic: An Egyptian script developed around 650 B.C.E. that was more cursive than hieratic.

Desheret: "The Red Land"; desert.

Divine Adoratrice of Amun: *See* **God's Wife of Amun.**

Djet: "Personnel"; slaves.

Dynasty: A powerful group or family that ruled Egypt for a considerable time. Egyptian history is divided into thirty dynasties.

Electrum: A mixture of silver and gold.

Ennead: A grouping of nine gods.

Faiyum: A depression or low area in north central Egypt.

Fay: "That which is carried"; a tax.

First Intermediate Period: The era of Egyptian history from circa 2130–1980 B.C.E. when the central government collapsed and local governors ruled the various provinces.

Gereget: Falsehood.

God's Wife of Amun: Chief priestess from the New Kingdom (circa 1539–1075 B.C.E.) to the Late Period (circa 664–332 B.C.E.); later called Divine Adoratrice of Amun.

Graywacke: A hard gray sandstone, composed of quartz and feldspar, that Egyptian carvers prized for their sculptures. Also known as *bekhen*-stone.

Haset: Mountains.

Hathor: Goddess of love and music, usually represented as a cow or a cow-headed woman.

Haty-a: See **Nomarch.**

Heka-Hasut: See **Hyksos.**

Hem: "Servant"; slave.

Hemef: "His Majesty"; the king as human ruler who sees royal decrees carried out. *See Hemei.*

Hemei: "My Majesty"; the king as human ruler who sees royal decrees carried out. *See Hemef.*

Hem-nesu: "Royal servant"; slave.

Hem-netjer: "God's servant"; the highest class of priests.

Hemet-netjer: High priestess.

Henu: Everyone who lived in a household, whether or not they were blood relatives.

Hery-hebu: A magician.

Heseb: "Forced laborer"; slave.

Hetemit: "Place of Destruction"; the lowest level of the Underworld.

Hieratic: A cursive script closely based on hieroglyphic writing.

Hieroglyph: A pictorial script used by ancient Egyptians from approximately 3000 B.C.E. to 450 C.E.

Hin: A measure of volume equal to 0.48 liters. Its value is one-sixth a *senyu* or one copper *deben.*

Hittites: A people of Anatolia. Between 1400 and 1200 B.C.E. they contested Egyptian control of Syria-Palestine.

Horus: God of the sky; brother of Seth.

Hyksos: "Rulers of Foreign Lands"; the Amorites, a western Semitic people who ruled Lower Egypt during the Second Intermediate Period (circa 1630–1539/1523 B.C.E.).

Ikhemu-sek: Circumpolar stars that never disappear from the sky and are considered the manifestation of a deceased king in heaven.

Isfet: Evil, disorder, injustice, or wrongdoing. The opposite of *Maat.*

It-netjer: "God's father"; a senior *wab* priest who has yet to formally receive the title of *prophet.*

Iti: "Sovereign"; another term for king; used parallel to *nisut. See Neb* and *Nisut.*

Ka: Life force.

Kap: A school attached to the women's quarters in the royal palace, where elite children studied alongside princes.

Karnak: City on the East bank of the Nile in Upper (southern) Egypt. The northern section of ancient Thebes. The site of various temples, pylons, sphinx-lined avenues, and obelisks built by Amenhotep III, Sety I, and Ramesses II.

Kemet: "The Black Land"; inhabitable zone along the Nile River.

Kenbet: Court of magistrates.

Khai: Literally "arise"; used in reference to a king's coronation and the sun's rising.

Khar: "Sack"; a measure of the volume of grain equal to 76.88 liters; one *khar* was valued at two *deben* of copper; it was divided into four *oipe.*

Khat: A type of cloth head covering.

Khepesh: The foreleg of an ox.

Khet: A term indicating the kinship of all the gods.

Kinnarum: A type of lyre popular in the Near East and Egypt.

Kite: A measure of weight equal to one-tenth of a *deben.*

Late Period: An era of Egyptian history from 664–332 B.C.E. marked by Libyan and Persian rule.

Lower Egypt: Northern Egypt, which is lower in altitude than southern Egypt. It is also called the Delta.

Luxor: City on the East bank of the Nile in Upper (southern) Egypt. The southern section of ancient Thebes. Amenhotep III and Ramesses II built several temples and other structures here.

Maat: The concept of right conduct approved by the gods. The opposite of *Isfet.*

Mahat: A private chapel containing a small stela, or statue, of the owner.

Mastaba: Bench-shaped tombs that were commonly constructed for the elite and then were used to construct the first step pyramids.

Medjoi: A special group of Nubians used as military police during the New Kingdom (circa 1539–1075 B.C.E.); eventually the word came to mean "policeman" rather than a separate ethnic group.

Memphis: City in Lower (northern) Egypt, traditional political capital of Egypt since the beginning of Dynasty 1 (circa 3000–2800 B.C.E.). At this site are a temple to Ptah, royal palaces, and an extensive necropolis; the pyramids of Saqqara and Giza are located nearby.

Menat: A musical instrument resembling a clarinet.

Meryet: "Dependent"; slave.

Mesha: A term used to refer to the personnel of military as well as trade, mining, and quarrying expeditions. Also used to designate the expedition itself.

Middle Kingdom: The period of Egyptian history from circa 1980–1630 B.C.E. characterized by a central government located at Memphis.

Migdol: A small square tower used in fortified positions.

Naos: An inner room in a temple where the statue of the god was located.

Naukleroi: Special shipping agents; the Greek term literally meant "man in charge of a ship."

Neb: "Lord"; another term for king; used parallel to *nisut. See Iti* and *Nisut.*

Nemes: A royal headdress worn only by the king.

Nemhu: A person who paid dues directly to the state and lived independently of state support, outside of the system of government rations.

Netjer: "God"; a term used to refer to a deceased king becoming Osiris, the divine king of the dead. *See Netjer Nefer.*

Netjer Nefer: "Good God" or "Perfect, Youthful God"; a term used to describe the king as the junior partner of the Great God Amun. *See Netjer.*

New Kingdom: The period of Egyptian history from circa 1539–1075 B.C.E. characterized by territorial expansion into Syria-Palestine and Nubia.

New Year: An annual royal festival signifying renewal and purification of a king's reign.

Nile River: The longest river in the world (approximately 4,160 miles in length) flowing north through present-day Uganda, Sudan, and Egypt.

Nisut: The king as the representative of justice and the legal order; a religious concept.

Nisut-biti: "King of Upper and Lower Egypt"; the king as the embodiment of power on earth.

Nomarch: A local governor of a nome.

Nomes: Administrative provinces.

Nubia: Sudan and the southern portion of Egypt.

Ogdoad: A grouping of eight pairs of gods.

Oipe: A measure of the volume of grain equal to one-fourth of a *khar.*

Old Kingdom: The period of Egyptian history from circa 2675–2130 B.C.E. characterized by a strong centralized government and the building of massive pyramids.

Opet **Festival:** An annual event at Thebes to celebrate a king's reign.

Osiris: "Mighty One"; god of the Underworld.

Ostracon: *plural* **ostraca.** Pottery shards or limestone flakes bearing drawings, sketches, personal thoughts, letters, scribal exercises, or literary texts.

Papyrus: A material, used by Egyptians to write upon, that was made from the pressed pith of the papyrus plant.

Pat: Officials of all types below the king.

Pefsu: "Baking value"; based on the number of loaves or beer jars produced from a set measure of grain.

Pharaoh: "The Great House"; the term used to describe the rulers of ancient Egypt from the reign of Thutmose III (circa 1479–1425 B.C.E.) in Dynasty 18 onward.

Phyles: Five labor groups (Great Phyle, Eastern Phyle, Green Phyle, Little Phyle, and Perfection Phyle) organized during the Old Kingdom (circa 2675–2130 B.C.E.). A phyle's name probably referred to its protective deity. The phyles served in rotation, each working for part of the year. By the New Kingdom (circa 1539–1075 B.C.E.) they had been abolished.

Predynastic Period: Egyptian history before Dynasty 1 (circa 3000–2800 B.C.E.).

Pronaos: An antechamber to the inner room (*naos*) in a temple.

Ptah: Creator-god and maker of all things; a patron of craftsmen and sculptors.

Ptolemaic Period: The era of Egyptian history from 332–30 B.C.E. when the descendants of the Macedonian general Ptolemy ruled Egypt.

Punt: Present-day Ethiopia and Djibouti.

Pylon: Decorated tower that dominated the entrance to an Egyptian temple.

R-pr: The temple estate.

Ramesside Period: An era during the New Kingdom (circa 1539–1075 B.C.E.) when eleven powerful pharaohs (each named Ramesses) ruled Egypt, circa 1292–1075 B.C.E.

Re: God of the Sun.

Redy: "That which is given"; a tax.

Remetch: The people of Egypt, most of whom were farmers.

Remetj: See Remetch.

Roman Period: The era of Egyptian history from 30 B.C.E.–395 C.E. when Egypt was a Roman province.

Sayidi: Southern Egyptians.

Second Intermediate Period: The era of Egyptian history from circa 1630–1539/1523 B.C.E. when foreign invaders known as the Hyksos seized control of northern Egypt.

Sed **Festival:** A royal celebration that could occur anytime after a king has reigned for at least thirty years.

Seker-ankh: "Prisoner of war"; slave.

Senyu: "Piece"; a unit of weight in silver equal to one-twelfth a *deben,* or 7.6 grams. Its value was equal to five copper *deben.*

Sep-tepy: "First time"; the time of creation.

Sepat: See **Nomes.**

Serdab: An enclosed area that contained a statue of the deceased in a mastaba tomb.

Shaduf: A pot attached to a swinging pole that simplifies the irrigation of gardens.

Shedy: "That which is taken"; a tax.

Shendjet: A kilt that was worn only by kings.

Sistrum: An instrument that resembles a rattle.

Stela: An inscribed stone or pillar.

Sunu: A physician.

Ta: Nile River valley.

Ta-mehew: Lower Egypt or the Delta.

Ta-Sety: See **Nubia.**

Ta-shemayet: Upper Egypt or the Nile River valley.

Tawy: "The Two Lands"; Egypt proper, refers to Narmer's unification of Upper and Lower Egypt in circa 3000 B.C.E.

Temenos: A brick wall that surrounded a temple.

Thebes: City on the West bank of the Nile in Upper (southern) Egypt. At one time it included Luxor and Karnak on the East bank. It became the capital of Upper Egypt in Dynasty 11 (circa 2081–1938 B.C.E.) and the political center of all of Egypt during the New Kingdom (circa 1539–1075 B.C.E.).

Third Intermediate Period: An era of Egyptian history from circa 1075–656 B.C.E. when southern Egypt was ruled by kings from Thebes and northern Egypt was ruled by kings from the Delta cities of Tanis and Bubastis.

Thoth: God of scribes, writing, and wisdom. He is represented as an ibis, an ibis-headed man, or sometimes as a baboon.

Tjaty: See **Vizier.**

Upper Egypt: Southern Egypt, which is higher in altitude than northern Egypt.

Valley of the Kings: Also known as the Valley of the Tombs of the Kings. The burial site (just west of the Nile River in Upper Egypt) for the kings of the New Kingdom (circa 1539–1075 B.C.E.).

Valley of the Queens: Also known as the Valley of the Tombs of the Queens. The burial site (just west of the Nile River in Upper Egypt) for the queens and royal children of the late New Kingdom (circa 1539–1075 B.C.E.).

Vizier: A Turkish word meaning prime minister; the most senior government official below a king.

Wa'u: A common soldier in the New Kingdom (circa 1539–1075 B.C.E.) .

Wabet: "Place of purification"; the site on the West bank of the Nile where coffins were ritually purified.

Wabu: "Pure ones"; the lowest class of priests.

Wadi al-Harim: See **Valley of the Queens.**

Wadi al-Muluk: See **Valley of the Kings.**

Wadj: A staff carried by goddesses; it represented fertility and renewal in nature.

Wagh Bahari: Northern Egypt.

Wagh Gibli: Southern Egypt.

Was: A scepter carried by a god indicating his dominion and control.

Wedjut: People who worked at the same place.

Weheyet: A group of families that lived in the same place.

Wekhedu: A waste product in the blood that the Egyptians believed was a cause of disease and decay.

Yedenu: A junior government official.

Yenu: "That which is brought"; a tax.

Yesu: "The Gang"; a group of tomb laborers; also used to describe a ship's crew.

GENERAL REFERENCES

GENERAL

Roger S. Bagnall, *Egypt in Late Antiquity* (Princeton: Princeton University Press, 1993).

Kathryn A. Bard, *From Farmers to Pharaohs: Mortuary Evidence for the Rise of Complex Society in Egypt* (Sheffield, U.K.: Sheffield Academic Press, 1994).

Alan K. Bowman, *Egypt After the Pharaohs 332 BC–AD 642: From Alexander to the Arab Conquest* (Berkeley: University of California Press, 1986).

James Henry Breasted, ed., *Ancient Records of Egypt,* volume 1, *The First to the Seventeenth Dynasties* (Chicago: University of Chicago Press, 1906).

Sergio Donadoni, ed., *The Egyptians,* translated by Robert Bianchi and others (Chicago: University of Chicago Press, 1997).

Alan Henderson Gardiner, *Egypt of the Pharaohs: An Introduction* (Oxford: Clarendon Press, 1961).

Michael A. Hoffmann, *Egypt Before the Pharaohs: The Prehistoric Foundations of Egyptian Civilization* (New York: Knopf, 1979).

Amélie Kuhrt, *The Ancient Near East, c. 3000-330 BC,* volume I (London & New York: Routledge, 1995).

William J. Murnane, *The Penguin Guide to Ancient Egypt* (Harmondsworth, U.K.: Penguin, 1983).

Donald B. Redford, ed., *The Oxford Encyclopedia of Ancient Egypt,* 3 volumes (Oxford & New York: Oxford University Press, 2001).

Jack M. Sasson, ed., *Civilizations of the Ancient Near East,* 4 volumes (New York: Scribners, 1995).

Ian Shaw, ed., *The Oxford History of Ancient Egypt* (Oxford & New York: Oxford University Press, 2000).

Peter Tompkins, *Secrets of the Great Pyramid* (New York: Harper & Row, 1971).

B. G. Trigger, and others, *Ancient Egypt: A Social History* (Cambridge & New York: Cambridge University Press, 1983).

John A. Wilson, *The Culture of Ancient Egypt* (Chicago: University of Chicago Press, 1956).

THE ARTS

Cyril Aldred, *Egyptian Art, in the Days of the Pharaohs, 3100–320 BC* (New York: Oxford University Press, 1980).

Dieter Arnold, *Temples of the Last Pharaohs* (New York: Oxford University Press, 1999).

Aidan Dodson, *Egyptian Rock-cut Tombs* (Princes Risborough, U.K.: Shire, 1991).

Egyptian Art in the Age of the Pyramids (New York: Metropolitan Museum of Art, 1999).

John L. Foster, *Thought Couplets in the Tale of Sinuhe* (Frankfurt & New York: Peter Lang, 1993).

Foster, ed., *Echoes of Egyptian Voices: An Anthology of Ancient Egyptian Poetry* (Norman: University of Oklahoma Press, 1992).

Foster, ed., *Love Songs of the New Kingdom* (New York: Scribners, 1974).

Barbara Hughes Fowler, *Love Lyrics of Ancient Egypt* (Chapel Hill: University of North Carolina Press, 1994).

Sigrid Hodel-Hoenes, *Life and Death in Ancient Egypt: Scenes from Private Tombs in New Kingdom Thebes,* translated by David Warburton (Ithaca, N.Y.: Cornell University Press, 2000).

Miriam Lichtheim, *Ancient Egyptian Autobiographies Chiefly of the Middle Kingdom: A Study and an Anthology* (Freiburg & Göttingen: Vandenhoeck & Ruprecht, 1988).

Lichtheim, *Ancient Egyptian Literature: A Book of Readings,* 3 volumes (Berkeley: University of California Press, 1976–1980).

Jaromir Malek, *Egyptian Art* (London: Phaidon Press, 1999).

Samuel Mark, *From Egypt to Mesopotamia: A Study of Predynastic Trade Routes* (College Station: Texas A&M University Press, 1998; London: Chatham, 1998).

Raymond A. McCoy, *The Golden Goddess: Ancient Egyptian Love Lyrics,* translated by McCoy (Menomonie, Wis.: Enchiridion Publications, 1972).

Kazimierz Michalowski, *Great Sculpture of Ancient Egypt,* translated by Enid Kirchberger (New York: Reynal, 1978).

R. B. Parkinson, *Voices from Ancient Egypt: An Anthology of Middle Kingdom Writings* (Norman: University of Oklahoma Press, 1991).

Gay Robins, *Proportion and Style in Ancient Egyptian Art* (Austin: University of Texas Press, 1994).

Edna R. Russmann, *Egyptian Sculpture: Cairo and Luxor* (Austin: University of Texas Press, 1989).

Byron E. Shafer, ed., *Temples of Ancient Egypt* (Ithaca, N.Y.: Cornell University Press, 1997).

William Kelly Simpson, *The Literature of Ancient Egypt: An Anthology of Stories, Instructions, and Poetry,* translations by R. O. Faulkner, Edward F. Wente Jr., and Simpson (New Haven: Yale University Press, 1972).

W. Stevenson Smith, *The Art and Architecture of Ancient Egypt,* third edition (New Haven & London: Yale University Press, 1998).

Philip J. Watson, *Egyptian Pyramids and Mastaba Tombs of the Old and Middle Kingdoms* (Princes Risborough, U.K.: Shire, 1987).

Richard H. Wilkinson, *The Complete Temples of Ancient Egypt* (New York: Thames & Hudson, 2000).

COMMUNICATION, TRANSPORTATION, AND EXPLORATION

James P. Allen, *Middle Egyptian: An Introduction to the Language and Culture of Hieroglyphs* (New York: Cambridge University Press, 2000).

Carol Andrews, *The Rosetta Stone* (London: British Museum Publications, 1981).

William S. Arnett, *The Predynastic Origin of Egyptian Hieroglyphs: Evidence for the Development of Rudimentary Forms of Hieroglyphs in Upper Egypt in the Fourth Millennium B.C.* (Washington, D.C.: University Press of America, 1982).

Abd el-Mohsen Bakir, *Egyptian Epistolography from the Eighteenth to the Twenty-First Dynasty* (Cairo: Institut Français d'Archéologie Orientale, 1970).

Raymond Cohen and Raymond Westbrook, eds., *Amarna Diplomacy: The Beginnings of International Relations* (Baltimore: Johns Hopkins University Press, 2000).

Raffaella Cribiore, *Writing, Teachers, and Students in Graeco-Roman Egypt* (Atlanta: Scholars Press, 1996).

W. Vivian Davies and Louise Schofield, eds., *Egypt, the Aegean and the Levant: Interconnections in the Second Millenium B.C.* (London: British Museum Press for the Trustees of the British Museum, 1995).

Leo Depuydt, *Conjunction, Contiguity, Contingency: On Relationships Between Events in the Egyptian and Coptic Verbal Systems* (New York: Oxford University Press, 1993).

Trude Dothan and Moshe Dothan, *People of the Sea: The Search for the Philistines* (New York: Macmillan, 1992).

David Frankfurter, ed., *Pilgrimage and Holy Space in Late Antique Egypt* (Leiden & Boston: E. J. Brill, 1998).

Alan Henderson Gardiner, *Egyptian Grammar,* third edition (London: Oxford University Press, 1957).

F. Ll. Griffith, *Catalogue of the Demotic Graffiti of the Dodecaschoenus,* volume 1 (Oxford: Oxford University Press, 1937).

Björn Landström, *Ships of the Pharaohs: 4000 Years of Egyptian Shipbuilding* (Garden City, N.Y.: Doubleday, 1970; London: Allen & Unwin, 1970).

Paul Lipke, *The Royal Ship of Cheops* (Oxford: B.A.R., 1984).

M. A. Littauer and J. H. Crouwel, *Chariots and Related Equipment from the Tomb of Tut'ankhamun* (Oxford: Griffith Institute, 1985).

Antonio Loprieno, *Ancient Egyptian: A Linguistic Introduction* (Cambridge & New York: Cambridge University Press, 1995).

Leslie S. B. MacCoull, *Coptic Perspectives on Late Antiquity* (Brookfield, Vt.: Variorum, 1993).

Edmund S. Meltzer, ed., *Letters From Ancient Egypt,* translated by Edward F. Wente (Atlanta: Scholars Press, 1990).

William L. Moran, ed., *The Amarna Letters* (Baltimore: Johns Hopkins University Press, 1992).

Alessandra Nibbi, *Ancient Egypt and Some Eastern Neighbors* (Park Ridge, N.J.: Noyes Press, 1981).

Robert Partridge, *Transport in Ancient Egypt* (London: Rubicon Press, 1996).

Bezalel Porten, *Archives from Elephantine: The Life of an Ancient Jewish Military Colony* (Berkeley: University of California Press, 1968).

N. K. Sandars, *The Sea Peoples: Warriors of the Ancient Mediterranean, 1250–1150 B.C.* (London: Thames & Hudson, 1978).

Thurston Shaw, and others, *The Archaeology of Africa: Food, Metals, and Towns* (London & New York: Routledge, 1993).

Eleni Vassilika, *Ptolemaic Philae* (Leuven, Belgium: Uitgeverij Peeters, 1989).

Steve Vinson, *Egyptian Boats and Ships* (Princes Risborough, Buckinghamshire, U.K.: Shire, 1994).

Vinson, *The Nile Boatman at Work* (Mainz: von Zabern, 1998).

Shelley Wachsmann, *Aegeans in the Theban Tombs* (Leuven, Belgium: Peeters, 1987).

Cheryl A. Ward, *Sacred and Secular: Ancient Egyptian Ships and Boats* (Boston: University Museum for the Archaeological Institute of America, 1999).

William A. Ward, *Egypt and the East Mediterranean World, 2200–1900 B.C.: Studies in Egyptian Foreign Relations during the First Intermediate Period* (Beirut: American University of Beirut, 1971).

Edward F. Wente, *Late Ramesside Letters* (Chicago: University of Chicago Press, 1967).

THE FAMILY AND SOCIAL TRENDS

Anne K. Capel and Glenn E. Markoe, eds., *Mistress of the House, Mistress of Heaven: Women in Ancient Egypt* (New York: Hudson Hills, 1996).

Véronique Dasen, *Dwarfs in Ancient Egypt and Greece* (Oxford: Clarendon Press, 1993; New York: Oxford University Press, 1993).

Zahi Hawass, *Silent Images: Women in Pharaonic Egypt* (New York: Abrams, 2000).

Leonard H. Lesko, ed., *Pharaoh's Workers: The Villagers of Deir el Medina* (Ithaca, N.Y.: Cornell University Press, 1994).

A. G. MacDowell, *Village Life in Ancient Egypt: Laundry Lists and Love Songs* (New York: Oxford University Press, 1999).

P. W. Pestman, *Marriage and Matrimonial Property in Ancient Egypt: A Contribution to Establishing the Legal Position of the Woman* (Leiden: E. J. Brill, 1961).

Gay Robins, *Women in Ancient Egypt* (Cambridge, Mass.: Harvard University Press, 1993).

Eugen Strouhal, *Life in Ancient Egypt*, translated by Deryck Viney (Cambridge: Cambridge University Press, 1992).

Joyce Tyldesley, *Daughters of Isis: Women of Ancient Egypt* (London & New York: Viking, 1994).

Barbara Watterson, *Women in Ancient Egypt* (New York: St. Martin's Press, 1991).

Sheila Whale, *The Family in the Eighteenth Dynasty of Egypt: A Study of Representations of the Family in Private Tombs* (Sydney: Australian Center for Egyptology Studies, 1989).

GEOGRAPHY

O. Kimball Armayor, *Herodotus' Autopsy of the Fayoum: Lake Moeris and the Labyrinth of Egypt* (Amsterdam: J. C. Gieben, 1985).

John Baines and Jaromir Malek, *Atlas of Ancient Egypt* (Oxford: Phaidon, 1980).

Karl W. Butzer, *Early Hydraulic Civilization* (Chicago: University of Chicago Press, 1976).

Butzer, *Physical Conditions in Eastern Europe, Western Asia and Egypt Before the Period of Agricultural and Urban Settlement* (Cambridge: Cambridge University Press, 1965).

Pavel Dolukhanov, *Environment and Ethnicity in the Middle East* (Aldershot, U.K. & Brookfield, Vt.: Avebury, 1994).

Maria Rosaria Falivene, ed., *The Heracleopolite Nome: A Catalogue of the Toponyms* (Atlanta: Scholars Press, 1998).

Hermann Kees, *Ancient Egypt; A Cultural Topography*, edited by T. G. H. James, translated by Ian F. D. Morrow (Chicago: University of Chicago Press, 1961).

Barry J. Kemp, *Ancient Egypt: Anatomy of a Civilization* (London & New York: Routledge, 1991).

Neil D. MacKenzie, *Ayyubid Cairo: A Topographical Study* (Cairo: American University in Cairo Press, 1992).

Bill Manley, *The Penguin Historical Atlas of Ancient Egypt* (London & New York: Penguin, 1996).

Richard Stoneman, and others, *The Empire of Alexander, the Great* (London: Routledge, 1991).

J. M. Wagstaff, *The Evolution of Middle Eastern Landscapes: An Outline to A.D. 1840* (London: Croom Helm, 1985; Totowa, N.J.: Barnes & Noble, 1985).

LEISURE, RECREATION, AND DAILY LIFE

Denise Ammoun, *Crafts of Egypt* (Cairo: American University in Cairo Press, 1991).

Edda Bresciani, *Food and Drink: Life Resources in Ancient Egypt*, translated by Hayley Adkins (Lucca: M. Pacini Fazzi, 1997).

William J. Darby, Paul Ghalioungui, and Louis Grivetti, *Food: The Gift of Osiris*, 2 volumes (London & New York: Academic Press, 1977).

Rosalie David, *Handbook to Life in Ancient Egypt* (New York: Facts on File, 1998).

Wolfgang Decker, *Sports and Games of Ancient Egypt*, translated by Allen Guttmann (New Haven: Yale University Press, 1992).

Walter B. Emery, *A Funerary Repast in an Egyptian Tomb of the Archaic Period* (Leiden: Nederlands Instituut voor het Nabije Oosten, 1962).

Joann Fletcher, *Oils and Perfumes in Ancient Egypt* (London: British Museum Press, 1998).

Zaki el-Habashi, *Tutankhamun and the Sporting Traditions* (New York: Peter Lang, 1992).

Salima Ikram, *Choice Cuts: Meat Production in Ancient Egypt* (Leuven, Belgium: Departement Oosterse Studies, 1995).

Geoffrey Killen, *Ancient Egyptian Furniture*, volume 1, *4000–1300 B.C.* (Warminster, U.K.: Aris & Phillips, 1980.

Killen, *Egyptian Woodworking and Furniture* (Princes Risborough, U.K.: Shire, 1994).

Lise Manniche, *An Ancient Egyptian Herbal* (Austin: University of Texas Press, 1989).

Manniche, *Sacred Luxuries: Fragrance, Aromatherapy, and Cosmetics in Ancient Egypt* (New York: Cornell University Press, 1999).

A. G. McDowell, *Village Life in Ancient Egypt: Laundry Lists and Love Songs* (New York: Oxford University Press, 1999).

Barbara Mertz, *Red Land, Black Land: Daily Life in Ancient Egypt,* revised edition (New York: Peter Bedrick Books, 1998).

Lynn Meskell, *Archaeologies of Social Life* (Malden, Mass. & Oxford: Blackwell, 1999).

Edwin T. Morris, *The Scents of Time: Perfume from Ancient Egypt to the 21st Century* (Boston: Metropolitan Museum of Art: Bulfinch Press/Little, Brown, 1999).

Mu-Chou Poo, *Wine and Wine Offerings in the Religion of Ancient Egypt* (London & New York: Kegan Paul International, 1995).

Miriam Stead, *Egyptian Life* (Cambridge, Mass.: Harvard University Press, 1986).

W. J. Tait, *Game Boxes and Accessories from the Tomb of Tut'ankhamun* (Oxford: Griffith Institute, 1982).

Alix Wilkinson, *The Garden in Ancient Egypt* (London: Rubicon Press, 1998).

Hilary Wilson, *Egyptian Food and Drink* (Aylesbury, U.K.: Shire, 1988).

POLITICS, LAW, AND THE MILITARY

Trevor Bryce, *The Kingdom of the Hittites* (Oxford: Clarendon Press/New York: Oxford University Press, 1998).

John Carman and Anthony Harding, eds., *Ancient Warfare: Archaeological Perspectives* (Stroud, U.K.: Sutton, 1999).

Lionel Casson, *The Pharaohs* (Chicago: Stonehenge, 1981).

Peter A. Clayton, *Chronicle of the Pharaohs: The Reign-by-Reign Record of the Rulers and Dynasties of Ancient Egypt* (New York: Thames & Hudson, 1994).

Aidan Dodson, *Monarchs of the Nile* (London: Rubicon Press, 1995).

Christine El Mahdy, *Tutankhamen: The Life and Death of a Boy-King* (New York: St. Martin's Press, 1999).

El Mahdy, *The World of the Pharaohs* (New York: Thames & Hudson, 1987).

Adrian Gilbert, *The Encyclopedia of Warfare from Earliest Times to the Present Day* (Chicago & London: Fitzroy Dearborn, 2000).

John Hackett, ed., *Warfare in the Ancient World* (New York: Facts on File, 1989).

George Hart, *Pharaohs and Pyramids: A Guide through Old Kingdom Egypt* (London: Herbert, 1991).

Kenneth A. Kitchen, *Pharaoh Triumphant: The Life and Times of Ramesses II, King of Egypt* (Warminster, U.K.: Aris & Phillips, 1982).

Arielle Kozloff and Betsy M. Bryan, *Egypt's Dazzling Sun: Amenhotep III and His World* (Cleveland: Cleveland Museum of Art, 1992).

William MacQuitty, *Ramesses the Great: Master of the World* (New York: Crown, 1978).

Jaromir Malek, *In the Shadow of the Pyramids: Egypt During the Old Kingdom* (Norman: University of Oklahoma Press, 1986).

Charles L. Nichols, *The Library of Ramesses the Great* (Berkeley, Cal.: Peacock, 1964).

Eliezer D. Oren, ed., *The Hyksos: New Historical and Archaeological Perspectives* (Philadelphia: University Museum, University of Pennsylvania, 1997).

Donald B. Redford, *Pharaonic King-Lists, Annals and Day-Books: A Contribution to the Egyptian Sense of History* (Mississauga, Canada: Benben, 1986).

Nicholas Reeves, *The Complete Tutankhamun: The King, the Tomb, and the Royal Treasure* (London & New York: Thames & Hudson, 1990).

John Van Seters, *The Hyksos: A New Investigation* (New Haven: Yale University Press, 1966).

Kent R. Weeks, *The Lost Tomb* (New York: Morrow, 1998).

RELIGION AND PHILOSOPHY

Carol Andrews, ed., *The Ancient Egyptian Book of the Dead,* translated by R. O. Faulkner (London: British Museum Publications, 1972).

The Book of the Dead: or, Going Forth by Day, translated by Thomas George Allen, prepared for publication by Elizabeth Blaisdell Hauser (Chicago: Oriental Institute of the University of Chicago, 1974).

Jaroslav Cerný, *Ancient Egyptian Religion* (London & New York: Hutchinson University Library, 1952).

Gertie Englund, ed., *The Religion of the Ancient Egyptians: Cognitive Structures and Popular Expressions* (Uppsala, Sweden: S. Academiae Ubsaliensis, 1989).

R. O. Faulkner, ed., *The Ancient Egyptian Coffin Texts,* translated by Faulkner, 3 volumes (Warminster, U.K.: Aris & Phillips, 1973–1978).

Faulkner, trans., *The Ancient Egyptian Pyramid Texts* (Oxford: Clarendon Press, 1969).

Faulkner, trans., *The Egyptian Book of the Dead: The Book of Going Forth by Day, Being the Papyrus of Ani,* with additional translations and commentary by Ogden Goelet Jr. (San Francisco: Chronicle Books, 1994).

Henri Frankfort, *Ancient Egyptian Religion* (New York: Columbia University Press, 1948).

George Hart, *A Dictionary of Egyptian Gods and Goddesses* (London & Boston: Routledge & Kegan Paul, 1986).

Erik Hornung, *The Ancient Egyptian Books of the Afterlife,* translated by David Lorton (Ithaca, N.Y.: Cornell University Press, 1999).

Hornung, *Idea into Image: Essays on Ancient Egyptian Thought,* translated by Elizabeth Bredeck (New York: Timken Publishers, 1992).

Barbara S. Lesko, *The Great Goddesses of Egypt* (Norman: University of Oklahoma Press, 1999).

Siegfried Morenz, *Egyptian Religion,* translated by Ann E. Keep (Ithaca, N.Y.: Cornell University Press, 1973).

Geraldine Pinch, *Magic in Ancient Egypt* (Austin: University of Texas Press, 1994).

Stephen Quirke, *Ancient Egyptian Religion* (London: British Museum Press, 1992).

Quirke, *The Cult of Ra: Sun-Worship in Ancient Egypt from the Pyramids to Cleopatra* (New York: Thames & Hudson, 2001).

Serge Sauneron, *The Priests of Ancient Egypt,* translated by Ann Morissett (New York: Grove, 1960).

Barbara Watterson, *The Gods of Ancient Egypt* (New York: Facts on File, 1984).

SCIENCE, TECHNOLOGY, AND HEALTH

Abd el-Mohsen Bakir, *The Cairo Calendar No. 86637* (Cairo: General Organization for Government Printing Offices, 1966).

Joris F. Borghouts, trans., *Ancient Egyptian Magical Texts* (Leiden: E. J. Brill, 1978).

Bob Brier, *Egyptian Mummies: Unraveling the Secrets of an Ancient Art* (New York: Morrow, 1996).

Arnold Buffum Chace, *The Rhind Mathematical Papyrus: Free Translation and Commentary with Selected Photographs, Transcriptions, Transliterations, and Literal Translations* (Reston, Va.: National Council of Teachers of Mathematics, 1979).

Rosalie David and Eddie Tapp, eds., *Evidence Embalmed: Modern Medicine and the Mummies of Ancient Egypt* (Manchester, U.K. & Dover, N.H.: Manchester University Press, 1984).

Christine El Mahdy, *Mummies, Myth, and Magic in Ancient Egypt* (New York: Thames & Hudson, 1989).

J. Worth Estes, *The Medical Skills of Ancient Egypt* (Canton, Mass.: Science History Publications, 1989).

Richard J. Gillings, *Mathematics in the Time of the Pharaohs* (Cambridge, Mass.: MIT Press, 1972).

J. B. Harley and D. Woodward, eds., *The History of Cartography* (Chicago: University of Chicago Press, 1987).

Peter Hodges, *How the Pyramids Were Built,* edited by Julian Keable (Longmead, U.K.: Element Books, 1989).

Christian Jacq, *Egyptian Magic,* translated by Janet M. Davis (Wiltshire, U.K.: Aris & Phillips, 1985; Chicago: Bolchazy-Carducci, 1985).

Mark Lehner, *The Complete Pyramids* (New York: Thames & Hudson, 1997).

Christian Leitz, *Magical and Medical Papyri of the New Kingdom* (London: British Museum Press for the Trustees of the British Museum, 1999).

J. P. Lepre, *The Egyptian Pyramids: A Comprehensive, Illustrated Reference* (Jefferson, N.C.: McFarland, 1990).

Jack Lindsay, *Origins of Astrology* (New York: Barnes & Noble, 1971).

John F. Nunn, *Ancient Egyptian Medicine* (Norman: University of Oklahoma Press, 1996).

Robert Kriech Ritner, *The Mechanics of Ancient Egyptian Magical Practice* (Chicago: Oriental Institute of the University of Chicago, 1993).

Gay Robins and Charles Shute, *The Rhind Mathematical Papyrus: An Ancient Egyptian Text* (London: British Museum Publications, 1987).

Anthony John Spalinger, ed., *Revolutions in Time: Studies in Egyptian Calendrics* (San Antonio: Van Siclen Books, 1994).

Cornelius Stetter, *The Secret Medicine of the Pharaohs: Ancient Egyptian Healing* (Chicago: Edition Q, 1993).

SOCIAL CLASS SYSTEM AND THE ECONOMY

Morris Bierbrier, *The Tomb Builders of the Pharaohs* (London: British Museum, 1982).

Jaroslav Cerný, *A Community of Workmen at Thebes in the Ramesside Period* (Cairo: Institut Français d'Archéologie Orientale, 1973).

Jac Janssen, *Commodity Prices from the Ramesside Period: An Economic Study of the Village of Necropolis Workmen at Thebes* (Leiden: E. J. Brill, 1975).

Alfred Lucas, *Ancient Egyptian Materials and Industries,* fourth revised edition (London: Arnold, 1962).

Pierre Montet, *Everyday Life in Egypt in the Days of Ramesses the Great,* translated and by A. R. Maxwell-Hyslop and Margaret S. Drower (London: Arnold, 1958).

John A. Wilson, *The Culture of Ancient Egypt* (Chicago: University of Chicago Press, 1956).

Robin W. Winks, ed., *Slavery: A Comparative Perspective. Readings on Slavery from Ancient Times to the Present* (New York: New York University Press, 1972).

CONTRIBUTORS

Edward Bleiberg is Associate Curator in the Department of Egyptian, Classical, and Ancient Middle Eastern Art at the Brooklyn Museum of Art. He earned a Ph.D. in Egyptology at the University of Toronto. He is the author of *The Official Gift in Ancient Egypt* (1996), an editor of *The Oxford Encyclopedia of Ancient Egypt* (2001), and a co-editor of *Fragments of a Shattered Visage: The International Symposium on Ramesses II* (1991). He has also written scholarly articles on the ancient Egyptian economy.

Stephen E. Thompson is the chairman of the History Department at the Dora Klein Jewish Academy in Boca Raton, Florida. He earned his Ph.D. in Egyptology from Brown University. He is the author of *A Lexicographic and Iconographic Analysis of Anointing in Ancient Egypt* (1991) and collaborating editor on *A Dictionary of Late Egyptian* (1982–present).

Steve Vinson is Assistant Professor of Ancient History at the State University of New York at New Paltz. He earned his Ph.D. in Egyptology at Johns Hopkins University. He is the author of two books, *Egyptian Boats and Ships* (1994) and *The Nile Boatman at Work* (1998), as well as several articles dealing with ships and the economics of transportation.

INDEX OF PHOTOGRAPHS

INDEX

Page numbers in boldface refer to a topic upon which an essay is based.
Page numbers in italics refer to illustrations, figures, and tables.

borders, 137
climate, **25–26**
foreign descriptions, 27
knowledge of, **26–28**
learning, 205–206
natural divisions, 24
place-name lists, 26–27
political divisions, 24, 30, 128–129
topography, **32–34**
See also Cartography; Maps
Geometry, 206, 278
Ghosts, 276
Giza, Pyramids of, 283–285
Giza necropolis, *29*
Gods and goddesses, **230–244**
Amun, **219–221**, 259–260
appeasing, 226
Aten, 259–260
Atum, 240
birth and death, 230
caring for, 255–256
creation stories, **239–242**
deification of kings, 128, 146, 150, 234
drawing of various, *231*
groupings, 230, 232
Horus, *20*, **232–233**, 235
iconography of, **233–234**
individual's access to, 244–245, 256–257
judicial oracles, 134
limitations, 230
manifestation of displeasure, 226
names, 230
netjer, 257–258
Osiris, 217, 219, 232, **243–244**, 281–282
Ptah, 242
Re, 217, **247–249**, 269
Seth, *20*, 232–233
syncretism, 232
terminology, 257–258
Thoeris, statue of, *263*
Wadjyt, *233*
God's Road, 251
God's Wife, office of, 144
Gold mines, map of, *273*
Government and politics
under Amenhotep III, 145
bureaucracy, 99–100, **132**
co-regency, 139, 141
forts, **134–137**
government departments, 128
Hyksos, 136, **137–138**
officials, 128
overseers, 103, 132
overview, **127–129**
pharaohs, 139
religious influence, 138–139
viziers, 132
women in, **143–144**
See also Kings
Grain, 104
Grammar, 205
Granary, Overseer of the, 132
Great Cackler, 242
Great Hymn to the Aten, 237
Greece
contact with, **70–72**
influence on language, 76, 78–79
language, 69–70
Grid systems for visual art, **44–47**

Guardians of the Tomb, 114
Gynecology and magic, 280

H

Hairstyles, **170–172**
Harkhuf, 108, **117**
Hatshepsut, 138, **146–147**
Hatshepsut temple at Deir el Bahri, *62*
Health and medicine, **278–281**
Heliopolitan Cosmogony, 240–241
Henenu, **91–92**
Herakleion, 32
Herakleopolis, 149
Herihor, 144
Hermoplis Cosmogony, 241–242
Herodotus, 83, 84, 177
Hieroglyphics
deciphering, 90
decline of use, 70
learning, 204–205
system of, 68–69
Tjetji's autobiography, 55
Hin, 104
Hittites
Battle of Qadesh, 130–132
war with, 150
Hoe, wooden, *102*
Homosexuality, **192–193**
Horoscopes, **274–275**
Horus, *20*, **232–233**, 235
Hours, 269, 271
House of Life, 251, 253
Housing, 158, **173–174**
Hygiene, 165
Hyksos, 136, **137–138**
Hymn to Osiris, 225
Hypostyle Halls, 54

I

Iconography of the gods, **233–234**
Imhotep, **260–261**
Imports, 101, 108
Ineni, **58**
Infertility, 187
Infirmities, 199
Inflation, 105–106
Inheritance, 186, 194–195, 207–208
Inscriptions
place-names, 26
sculpture, 51
Intellectual class, 108
Interpreters and ambassadors, **79–80**
Invention, 268
Irrigation, *25,* 32–33, 169

J

Joints, furniture, 168
Jubilee festival, 141, 151
Judgment, postmortal, 225
Judicial oracles, 134

K

Ka, 227, *255*
Kahun Census, 201–202
Kai and his wife, relief of, *199*
Kamose, 138
Kamose, stela of, *137*
Karnak, sacred lake at, *214*
Karnak Temple, *54,* 137
Kawit, relief of servants attending, *172*
Kha, tomb of, 163–165
Khafre (Chephren), **58–59**
Khafre pyramid, *29*
Khonshotep, 190–191
Khonsu temple, *55*
Khufu (Cheops), **147–148**
funerary boat of, *86*
royal ship of, 84–85
stories told to, by his sons, 170
Kings, **138–141**, **234–239**
Amun's association with, 221
coronation, 236
dead kings' association with Osiris, 243
deification of, 128, 146, 150, 234
four purposes, 235–236
hairstyles, 171
king lists, 141
Kushite, 144
limits on power, 128
marriage, 198
New Kingdom, 112
purification rite, wall scene of, *239*
rejuvenation, 238
rituals, **236–239**
role of, 128
wives, 143
See also Government and politics; Pharoahs;
    Individual kings
Kinship, **193–196**
Kushite kings, 144

L

Labor
Deir el Medina, 113
organization, 99
pensions, 202
Labor and delivery, 188–189
Laborers branding cattle, tomb painting of, *103*
Lamp from tomb of Kha, *173*
Land ownership, 101, 115
Land transportation, 67–68
Language
Demotic, 69–70
development of Egyptian, 68–70
dialects, **76–77**
foreign languages, **77–79**
Greek, 69–70
literacy, 69, **80–81**, 99–100
Middle period, 69
written, 68–70, 75–76, 77, **88–90**
Late Bronze Age. *See* New Kingdom
Late Period
army, 129
class system, 100
grid system in visual art, 46–47
overview, 127–128

S

Sacred animals, 222–223
Sacred lakes, *214, 253*
Sahidic dialect, 76
Sahure, **92, 108**
Sailboats, 67
Saites, 129
Sandals, 166–167
Sarcasm, 89
Scarab finger rings, *182*
Schools, 206
Science
    astronomy, **269–272**
    magic as part of, 268, 275
    overview, **268**
    Psamtik I, **286**
    time measurement, **269–272**
Scorpion goddess Selqet, statue of, *276*
Scribal palette, *205*
Scribes, **108**
    Deir el Medina, 114
    Dhutmose, **91**
    education, **204–206**
    relief of, *122*
    statue of, *80, 109*
Sculpture
    Bek, **57–58**
    conventions for female, 49
    overview, 41
    relief sculpture grid system, **44–47**
    standing, **48–51**
    structural supports, 51
    style, 49, 51
    Tjetji's stela, **55–57**
    See also Art
Sea Peoples, 71, 150–151
Second Intermediate Period, 127, 136
Sed Festival, 141, 151, 176, 238
Sediment levels of the Nile Valley, *23*
Selqet, statue of scorpion goddess, *276*
Semitic languages, 78
Seneb, **209**
Senmut (Senenmut), **59**
Senyu, 104
Serfs. *See* Slaves and serfs
Seth, *20,* 232–233
Setne and Tabubu, 203
Sexuality, 186, **192–193,** 198
    See also Prostitution
Shabaka Stone, 240
Ships and boats
    anatomy of, *92*
    Byblos, 92
    construction, **84–85**
    as key technology, 67
    women skippers, 88
Shoes, 166–167
Shrines, private, **246–247**
Siege of Dharpur, relief of, *142*
Sinai Desert expeditions, **111–112,** 151
Sinuhe. *See Story of Sinuhe*
Sistra, 47
Sitepehu, block statue of, *106*
Skippers, women, 88
Slaves and serfs, 100, **109–111**
    adoption of slave children, 207
    Deir el Medina, 114
    legal status, 109, 111

women, 114
Sneferu, **35**
Soap, 165
Social class. *See* Class system
Social trends, **186–187**
Soldiers, **114–115**
Spearmen and archers, wooden models of, *141*
Spells, 280–281
Sphinx, *29,* 58–59, *235*
Spices, 159
Spoked wheels, 87
Spoken words, importance of, 215–216
Sports, 159, **174–176,** 179
    See also Recreation and leisure
Spousal kinship, 194
Star clocks, 272
Star lists, *270*
Statuette of woman, man and boy, *30*
Status and clothing, 158
Stool, wooden, *168*
Stories and tales, **53**
Story of Horus and Seth, 192
The Story of Setne Khaemwas, 198, 199
Story of Sinuhe, **51–53**
Stringed musical instruments, 47–48
Sumerian contact, 72–74
Sun, movement of the, 269
Sun, stone carving of daily birth of the, *248*
Sun god. *See* Re
Sun temples, 247–248
Surgery, 280
Surveying, 285
Sweets, 159
Symbolism
    in depictions of gods, 234
    temple, **249–253**
Syncretism, 232
Syria-Palestine
    contact with, **74–75**
    forts, 136–137
    map, *19*

T

Taharqa, **180**
Faiyum, 34
Tales and stories, **53**
Tanefer pouring libation and burning incense, *254*
Tattoos, 166
Taxation, 100, 102–103
Technology and engineering, 67, 84–85, **283–285**
    See also Architecture; Construction
Temenos, 54
Temple day, 116
Temples
    Amun at Karnak, *27*
    architecture and symbolism, **249–253**
    construction, 251
    cosmological design, 253
    Deir el Bahri, 146–147, 149
    festivals, 256–257
    function of, 53–54
    gardens, 169–170
    Hatshepsut temple at Deir el Bahri, *62*
    House of Life, 251, 253

individual's access to the gods, 244–245, 256–257
    interiors, 251
    Karnak, *54,* 137
    Khonsu, *55*
    New Kingdom, **53–55**
    offerings, 245–246, 247, 256
    personnel, **253–254**
    prostitutes, 202
    Ramesses II, *250, 252, 262*
    Ramesses III, 75, 151
    Re, 247–248
    rituals, **255–257**
    sacred lakes, 253
    temple animals, 222–223
    Temple of Isis at Philae, *82*
    Thutmose III, *152*
    See also Architecture; Funerary beliefs and practices; Priests
Texts
    medical, 279, 280
    religious, 216
Theater, 42
Thebes
    building program of Hatshepsut, 146–147
    relations with, 138
    roads, **86**
    Theban drawing board, *46*
    Theban relief style, 55, 57
Third Intermediate Period, 127, 137
Thoeris, statue of, *263*
Thutmose II, 146
Thutmose III, 144, 146, **151–152**
Thutmose IV, 200
Time measurement, **269–272**
Tjeker, 117
Tjetji, **55–57**
Tokens and tallies, 116
Tombs
    burial chambers, 228–229
    construction, 227–229
    decorative zones, 43–44
    false doors, 228
    funerary images from Theban tomb, *60*
    furniture, 167
    Hatnofre, 165
    Ka(i)pura, *42*
    Kha and Merit, 163–165
    Mastaba, 148
    Nefertari's tomb, *43*
    private, **42–44**
    robbery, 133–134
    Sobekhotep tomb wall painting, *72, 93*
    Tutankhamun, 152
Tools
    carpenter, *112*
    furniture-making, 168
    hairdressing, 172
    for pyramid building, 284
Tooth decay, 280
Topographic maps, 273–274
Topography, **32–34**
Torture, 129, 134
Trade
    barter, 101, 104
    expeditions, 27, 117–118
    Greece, 71–72
    international, 101
    map of trade routes, *31*